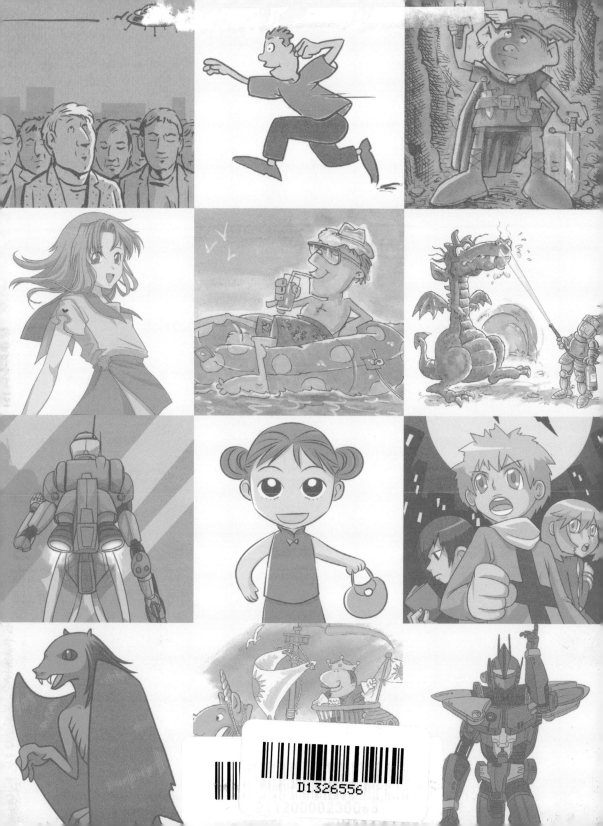

D1326556

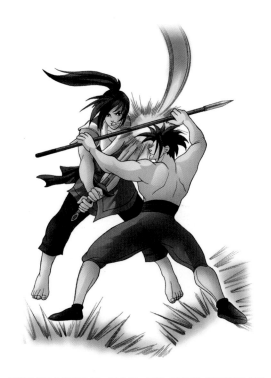

# THE PRACTICAL STEP-BY-STEP GUIDE TO
# DRAWING CARTOONS
# MANGA AND ANIME

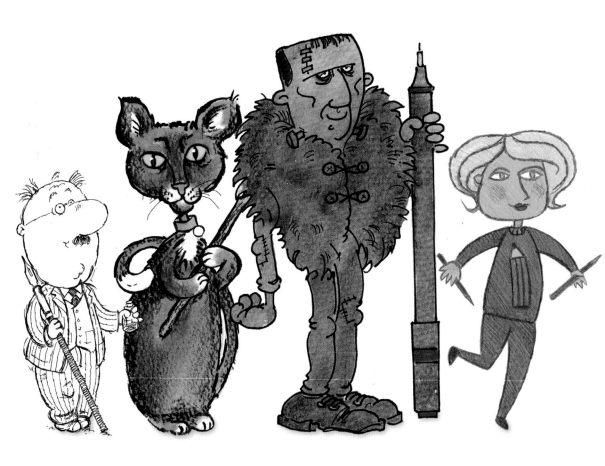

# THE PRACTICAL STEP-BY-STEP GUIDE TO
# DRAWING CARTOONS MANGA AND ANIME

## EXPERT TECHNIQUES AND PROJECTS, SHOWN IN MORE THAN 2500 ILLUSTRATIONS

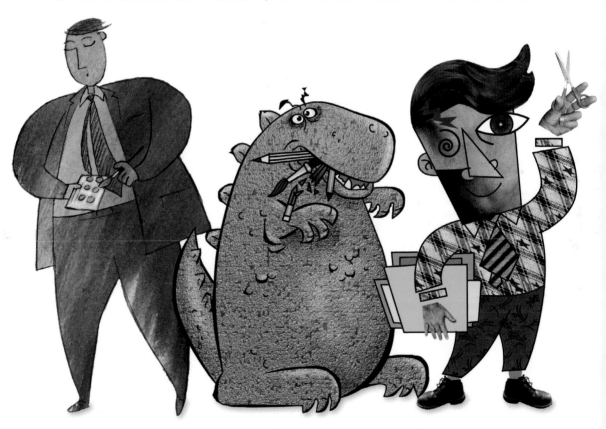

IVAN HISSEY, CURTIS TAPPENDEN, TIM SEELIG, YISHAN LI AND RIK NICOL

HERMES HOUSE

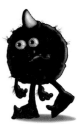

This edition is published by Hermes House,
an imprint of Anness Publishing Ltd,
Blaby Road, Wigston, Leicestershire LE18 4SE

Email: info@anness.com

Web: www.hermeshouse.com; www.annesspublishing.com

Anness Publishing has a new picture agency outlet for images for
publishing, promotions or advertising. Please visit our website
www.practicalpictures.com for more information.

© Anness Publishing Ltd 2011

Publisher: Joanna Lorenz
Editorial Director: Helen Sudell
Editor: Elizabeth Young
Cover Designer: Oil Often
Production Controller: Christine Ni

Designed and produced for Anness Publishing
by The Bridgewater Book Company Limited/Ivy Contract
Project Editors: Polita Caaveiro, Hazel Songhurst,
Sarah Doughty and Susie Behar
Designers: Glyn Bridgewater, Jan Lanaway, Kevin Knight
and Steve Knowlden
Art Director: Lisa McCormick
Artists and Contributors: Yishan Studio, Rik Nicol,
Wing Yun Man, Jacqueline Kwong and Tim Pilcher

ensures forests are managed in an environmentally sustainable and
socially responsible way. For further information about this scheme,
go to www.annesspublishing.com/trees

Previously published in two separate volumes, *The Professional
Step-by-Step Guide to Cartooning* and *Mastering the Art of Manga*

Publisher's Note
Although the advice and information in this book are believed to
be accurate and true at the time of going to press, neither the
authors nor the publisher can accept any legal responsibility or
liability for any errors or omissions that may have been made nor
for any inaccuracies nor for any loss, harm or injury that comes
about from following instructions or advice in this book.

# Contents

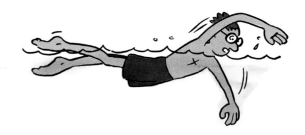

▶

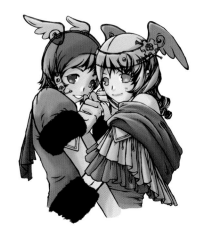

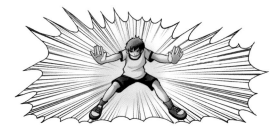

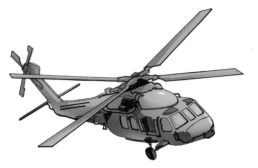

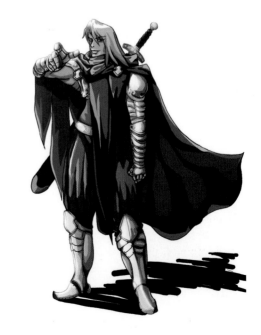

# Introduction

Drawing cartoons and manga is a popular artform. Using a selected number of drawn strokes, cartoons can not only communicate to the masses through simple sketches but can encapsulate complex information on an infinite range of topics. They can also carry a message with humour, appealing to an innate comic faculty found in each and every one of us, irrespective of language, creed or social standing. The art of drawing cartoons and manga as we know them may be relatively new forms of art, but their roots stretch back hundreds of years.

This practical volume introduces you to the exciting world of cartoons and manga styles, from anthropomorphized animals and caricatures to creating manga super-heroes, aliens and giant robots. The book begins by explaining the techniques of designing characters, from drawing the eyes, noses, mouths and hair to hands, feet, clothes and settings. A range of exercises and projects offer the opportunity to practice the disciplines your have learned, from portraying children, heroes and villains to composing a panel story, creating a sinister narrative or planning battle scenes.

## Cartooning through the ages

The cartoon has its origins in the 14th and 15th centuries, when Renaissance artists prepared full-size drawn studies for fresco wall paintings or mosaics. The actual word, *cartone*, defines the board used for these drawings. Yet it was only around 270 years ago – thanks to the rapid expansion of the printing trades and their mass production of pamphlets and journals – that humorous and sardonic drawings become known as cartoons, and the strip cartoon was born.

Cartoons can provide witty comment on the social stories of the day, such as with the satirical social cartoons of William Hogarth during the 18th century, and the small politcal gags in Punch magazine from the 1840s. From Frank Hampson's space hero, Dan Dare, in the 1950s comic, *Eagle*, through the dynasties of Marvel and DC Comics superheroes – Batman,

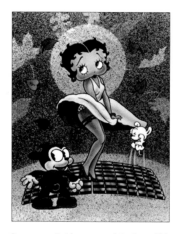

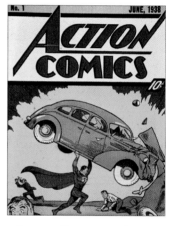

Superman, Spiderman and the Incredible Hulk – generations have enjoyed the struggle of good over evil. Today, Matt Groening's dysfunctional family, the Simpsons, currently plays an essential and humorous role as a running social commentary on American Society.

Cartoons still use many traditional formats but technology has made them 'larger than life' with sophisticated, digital animation. The pioneering work of the Dreamworks and Pixar studios have harnessed and developed cutting-edge methods. They produce stunning and innovative animation works that are much-loved as the films by animator Walt Disney in the early 20th century.

**Above left** ▲
*Betty Boop*, based on Marilyn Monroe, was among the first cartoons to be animated in the 1950s.

**Above right** ▲
Superheroes, and their endless battle against various forces of evil, remain a staple of printed comics.

**Left** ◄
Deceptively simple, the *Peanuts* comic strip by Charles Schultz revealed a insightful view of American life.

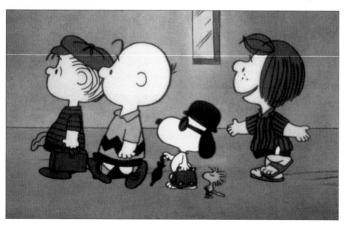

## The birth of manga

If you are a fan of manga, you will probably have read the headlines proclaiming its sweeping successes across the globe, noticed the titles creeping to the top of the bestseller charts, or seen teenagers on the bus reading the latest volume of *Naruto* or *Fruits Basket*. But what is manga, and what does 'manga' really mean? At its simplest level, it is the Japanese term for a comic book: the sequential fusion of illustrated panels and written dialogue. In practice, however, manga has come to represent a series of styles, subgenres and types of story that are recognized, and exported, all over the world.

Unlike Western comics, which have sometimes been perceived as the sole purview of young males reading about Spandex-clad superheroes, manga has been strongly embraced by girls and women.

Manga as we know it may be a relatively new form of art, but its roots stretch back to the 17th century. The genesis of manga ties most closely with a form of mass-produced woodcut print called *ukiyo-e*. These colourful prints showed scenes of urban life, from courtesans to sumo wrestlers; before long, it had expanded into rural landscapes, too. They were affordable, mass-produced and very popular. Ukiyo-e could also be found alongside text stories in picture books called 'ehon', another forerunner of modern manga.

One of the most famous and well-regarded artists of ukiyo-e, operating at the height of the Edo period (1603–1868), was a man named Hokusai. Born in 1760, he published his first prints before 1780. He was among the first to use the term 'manga' in the title of one of his bound collections.

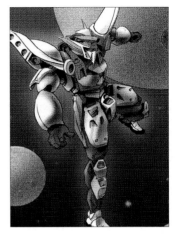

**Above** ▲
Robots or "mechanoids" are a common theme of science-fiction manga.

## Using this book

This practical encyclopedia aims to provide a comprehensive resource for the aspiring cartoonist, or those who wish to further develop their skills, both manual and digital, beyond the simple and traditional techniques. The first half, How to Draw Cartoons, provides guidance on how to create characters from how to show a range of facial expressions using different shaped heads to drawing hands, feet, shoes and clothing. It also explains the importance of viewpoint, perspective, lighting, scale and focus.

The second half, How to Draw Manga, is an illustrated guide to creating your own manga characters. It begins by explaining the rules of designing manga characters. The importance of settings and backgrounds are highlighted, and how to use them to create all kinds of fantasy or futuristic worlds that bring your characters to life. There are features on genres such as shojo and shonen, and super-deformed manga characters in both hand-drawn and digital mediums, as well as on anime – Japanese animation – which shows how to transform your drawings into live-action cartoons.

To get the most out of this book, work consistently through the spreads, take your time and try out the exercises and projects at a pace that suits you. If you need to spend longer or go back and repeat any sections, do so to gain fuller understanding and greater mastery and show you how to produce your own amazing cartoons.

**Below left** ▼
Popeye first appeared in a black-and-white comic strip in 1929, and still delights fans across the globe today.

**Below right** ▼
Manga characters are usually recognizable through their exaggerated features and abnormal hair colour.

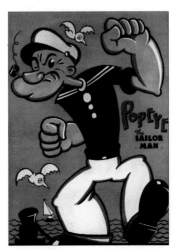

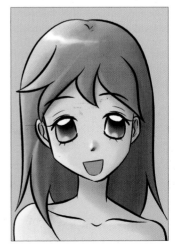

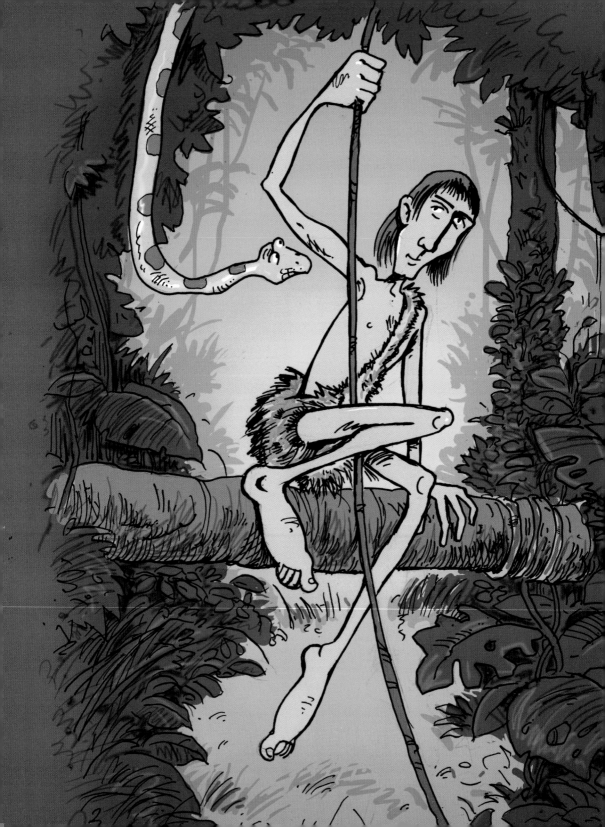

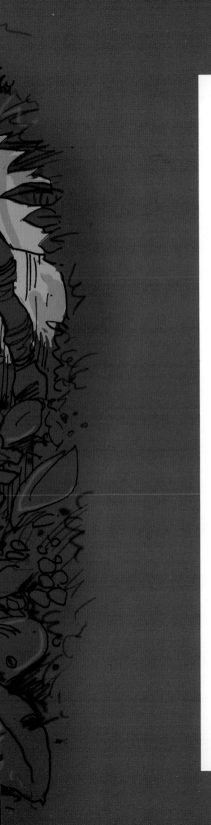

# How to Draw Cartoons

This section provides a comprehensive and practical guide to creating your own cartoons, from inanimate objects and people to animals and monsters. It begins by introducing traditional drawing and digital techniques, and features plenty of informative screen grabs and illustrations. This is followed by an extensive section on drawing characters, which describes how to create all kinds of figures and faces and give them personality, and there are helpful hints showing how to inject life into your drawings. Finally, a range of step-by-step projects focusing on drawing caricatures, strips with and without words, animal characters and portraits, offer the opportunity to practise the techniques and produce a variety of cartoon styles.

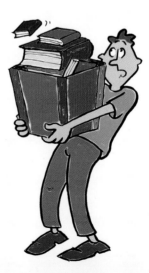

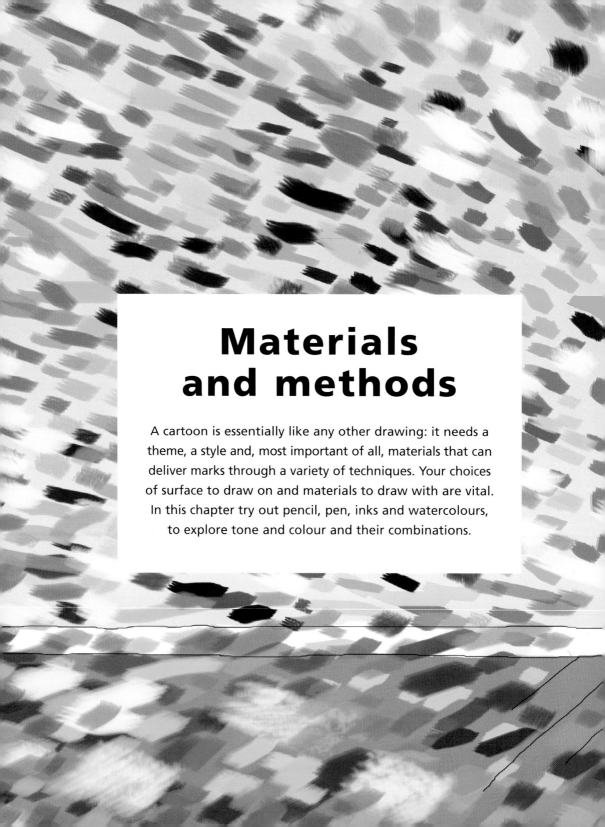

# Materials and methods

A cartoon is essentially like any other drawing: it needs a theme, a style and, most important of all, materials that can deliver marks through a variety of techniques. Your choices of surface to draw on and materials to draw with are vital. In this chapter try out pencil, pen, inks and watercolours, to explore tone and colour and their combinations.

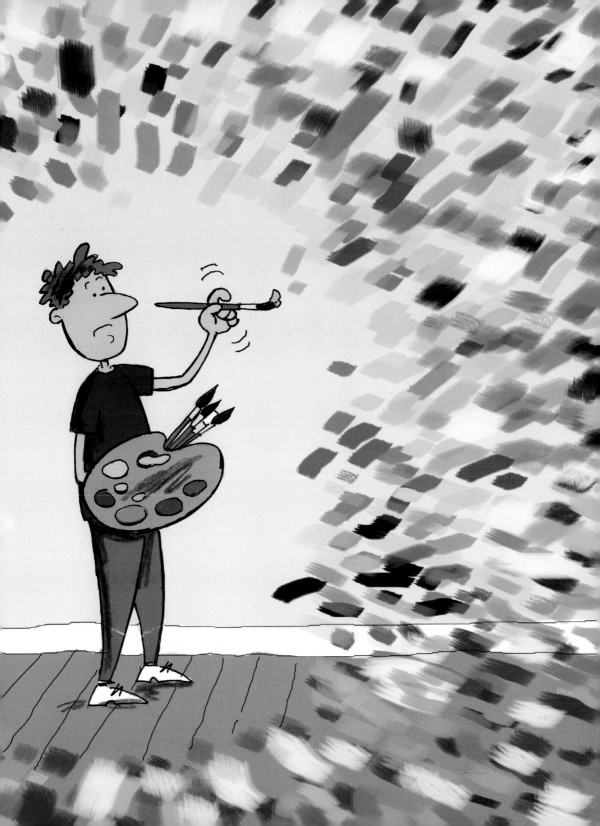

# Types of paper and card

Cartooning is rapid-fire visual communication and shouldn't require anything other than a basic surface upon which to burst into life. Like all art forms, though, there are levels of accomplishment and the presentation necessary for one image may not necessarily match that of another. For this reason it is a good idea to become acquainted with a variety of papers and boards to discover their versatility by trying them out using different media.

Of course, your choice of materials and media will be largely dictated by personal preference and individual drawing style. However, the following provides a useful guide for the beginner: a good-quality cartridge paper that allows for pencil under-drawing and takes an ink wash, a heavier type of paper for brush drawing and watercolour paper for pen drawings and watercolour washes. Watercolour papers are available in rough, smooth (hot-pressed) and 'Not' (not hot-pressed) surfaces. Any of these is suitable; your main consideration is that the pen nib won't get snagged in the surface fibres.

A firm, resilient surface, such as watercolour or heavy cartridge paper, allows you the freedom to make corrections with an eraser, whiting-out ink or paint and to collage separate elements, and can be wetted in preparation for a colour wash. Smooth boards have added chalk, which gives extra fluidity. Be aware that a tip (known as the nib) on a smooth board might break the shiny surface, causing the ink to bleed into the absorbent fibres beneath. A colour cartoon may need to be scanned, so try to make sure that you work to the maximum size of the flatbed, desktop scanner you will be using.

## Testing surfaces

The only way to know which type of surface is best for you is to try out as many different variations as possible. Many artists find a particular paper that works well for them and tend to stay with it. Below, the first skater sketch uses a 0.3mm fineliner drawing pen on standard cartridge paper. The result is a crisp black outline. The same cartoon on rough watercolour paper has a textured look.

The black ink outline is drawn directly with a medium-sized, round brush. Dryish layers of drawing ink give shading and light charcoal strokes in selected areas emphasize texture. The contrast between a textured surface and smooth Bristol board is distinct. Here, the outline is made with a fineliner pen and colour fills are in translucent ink washes. The brushed-on black strokes add extra definition.

**Types of support** ▼
Your choice of support will have a real bearing on the visual appearance of your drawings. A rough, textured paper will cause your lines to break up slightly, whereas a smooth one will deliver a continuous line. For much work a medium-grain paper is best – something that accepts a reasonably crisp line and to which a wash or two can be added.

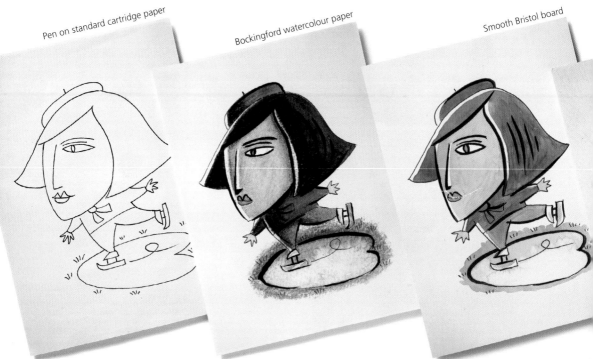

Pen on standard cartridge paper

Bockingford watercolour paper

Smooth Bristol board

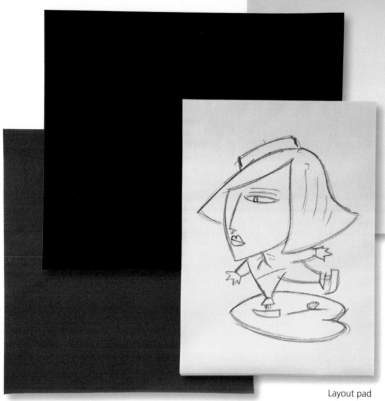

**Other useful materials** ▲
Light, tinted papers offer a softer
background; darker ones provide
a background that suits the setting,
for example dark blue or black for a
night scene. Boards are thicker and
take wet washes without cockling
(buckling). Pastel papers, such as
Ingres, are grainy. A layout pad can
be used for tracing; sketchbooks
for recording and learning.

Layout pad

Coloured paper

Soft texture weave

**Tip:** Get into the habit of keeping
sketchbooks, and record all manner
of things in them. How you maintain
an ongoing record is entirely up to
you; after all, it does need to be
personal and, most importantly, of
use to you as a practising artist.
Date all work and number your
books as it won't be long before
a library begins to emerge.

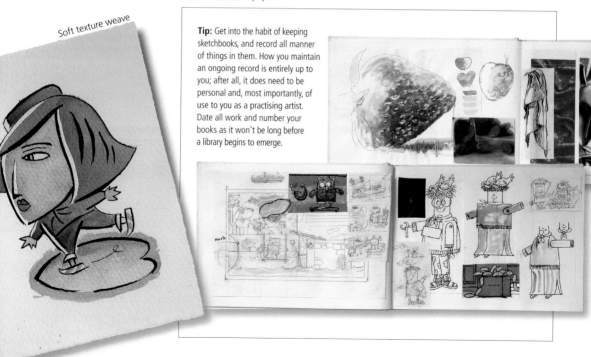

# The pencil

One of the most versatile drawing tools is the humble pencil. It is available in the H (hard) grades, which are used most commonly by designers and architects, and the softer B (black) grades preferred by artists. The 'lead' is actually graphite or a graphite and clay mix. You can choose between the classic wooden-cased style or the non-sharpening, mechanical type, which are classified by width, such as 0.5mm.

It is worth testing all the grades to find the one that you feel most comfortable using. The inexperienced artist may prefer the slighter mark of an H pencil, though note that it has a tendency to score the paper if too much pressure is used. The more confident drawer is likely to enjoy using the blacker B-grade pencils. They are ideal if a clean yet soft outline is wanted. As its name suggests, the HB pencil is a balance of hard and black:

the perfect all-round choice. The basic pencil is the ideal tool for everyday sketching and making those all-important first outlines, and it is also invaluable for shading.

Water-soluble drawing pencils have the same properties as ordinary graphite when used dry, but with added water they take on the qualities of watercolour. Dipping them in water produces a tonal range from the palest grey to the deepest black. The same effect can be achieved by washing over the pencil shading with a wet paintbrush. These pencils have a rapidity of use and are fully portable, making them ideal for quick note-taking or in the studio as a valid medium of colour and tone.

Charcoal is a highly expressive medium. Water soluble, it can be manipulated with a brush and water to create wash effects or blended directly using fingers, a soft cloth or an eraser.

## Pencil choices

By trying out the various kinds of product available, you will discover which pencil types suit you best and for what purposes. For example, a drawing made with vigour and bold expression is likely to employ a drawing pencil with soft, dark grey or black lead, bearing the coding of at least a 3B. In direct

contrast, the fine layout drawing or tracing, requiring greater accuracy, would be better executed with a 0.5mm or 0.7mm mechanical 'clutch' pencil, which features a narrow bar of graphite that is extended from the pencil barrel out to the tip by clicking through a special spring mechanism.

**A pencil plethora ▼**
An art store trip is a great way to learn how to identify pencils and their uses: graphite drawing pencils (HB–6B) for general sketching; water-soluble pencils in a wide range of colours; mechanical pencils; and chisel-edged carpenter types, which deliver a wide, blocky stroke.

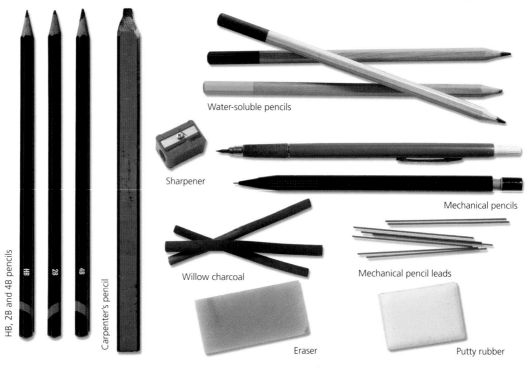

Water-soluble pencils

Sharpener

Mechanical pencils

HB, 2B and 4B pencils

HB

2B

4B

Carpenter's pencil

Willow charcoal

Mechanical pencil leads

Eraser

Putty rubber

## Matching pencils to white papers

Your choice of drawing tool and surface will always determine the outcome and should be considered carefully. It is not difficult to gauge the effects of the various grades of pencil on different textures and weights of paper. The simple swatches on this page clearly show all the necessary information: an exercise well worth doing for yourself. Try to obtain paper samples from stockists for testing purposes so that you do not purchase the wrong types.

**The swatch library** ▼
As you complete simple swatches, classify them by pencil and paper type and then glue into a sketchbook. Don't be afraid to experiment with different shading techniques.

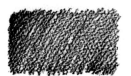

6B carpenter's pencil on rough watercolour paper

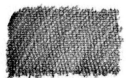

6B carpenter's pencil on artificial weave paper

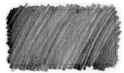

6B carpenter's pencil on very smooth paper

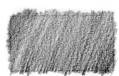

6B carpenter's pencil on medium cartridge paper

4B pencil – light shading on rough watercolour paper

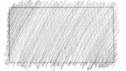

4B pencil – light shading on artificial weave paper

4B pencil – light shading on very smooth paper

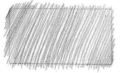

4B pencil – light shading on medium cartridge paper

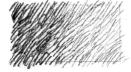

2B pencil – tonal strokes on rough watercolour paper

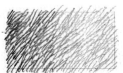

2B pencil – tonal strokes on artificial weave paper

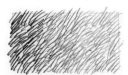

2B pencil – tonal strokes on very smooth paper

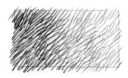

2B pencil – tonal strokes on medium cartridge paper

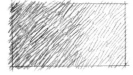

HB pencil – tonal strokes on rough watercolour paper

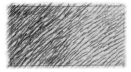

HB pencil – tonal strokes on artificial weave paper

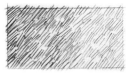

HB pencil – tonal strokes on very smooth paper

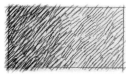

HB pencil – tonal strokes on medium cartridge paper

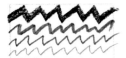

All pencils – constant zigzag lines on rough watercolour paper

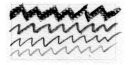

All pencils – constant zigzag lines on artificial weave paper

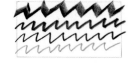

All pencils – constant zigzag lines on very smooth paper

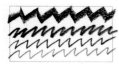

All pencils – constant zigzag lines on medium cartridge paper

## Pencil variations on coloured papers

Pencil marks against coloured paper instead of white can appear startlingly different. Tonal papers ease the brightness on the eye and are useful in setting the mood too. Test a range of smooth and rough textured papers. A pastel paper, such as Ingres, has a consistent linear weave running through it, which gives a slightly crumbling graphite line.

**Coloured-paper moods** ▼
Try out a range of strokes and marks using a variety of pencils on different colour tones of paper and compare the results to find the most appropriate.

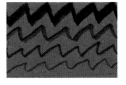

6B, 4B, 2B, B pencil zigzags on smooth blue paper

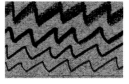

6B, 4B, 2B, B pencil zigzags on brown Ingres paper

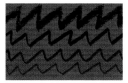

6B, 4B, 2B, B pencil zigzags on buff smooth paper

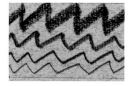

6B, 4B, 2B, B pencil zigzags on yellow Ingres paper

## Pencil shading

Much of cartooning involves creating detailed 3-D figures and settings. Shading – a crucial technique to learn – is used to make shapes appear solid. The distinction between the different planes of a solid structure, such as a cube, is made using light, medium and dark shading. The first uses a gradual build-up of cross-hatch tone; the second, gentle shading, and the third stronger shading. The cubes below all use a different type of pencil shading. How you shade can have a radical impact on the style of the drawing, which affects the mood of the cartoon: the heavier your shading, the heavier the mood.

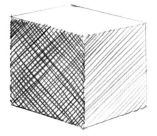

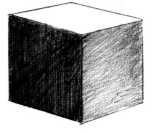

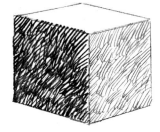

**Cross-hatch** ▲
Draw lines at a 45-degree angle across a paper surface to cover the blank, white paper. On the surface you wish to be in darker shadow, so sketch diagonal lines in the opposite direction. To darken further, add vertical lines at 90 degrees.

**Smooth tone** ▲
Sketch with control across the sides of the cube. Move the pencil along extended directional strokes – vertical, horizontal or diagonal – and try to exert even pressure throughout. Add consecutive layers to deepen the tone.

**Hatching** ▲
A more haphazard approach to shading can be practised using short covering strokes known as hatching. They have a rough-textured appearance, but when viewed from a distance they become unified with an even tonal balance.

**Tonal scale** ◄
It is important to practise rendering tonal scales as often as you can. Work a line of shaded blocks from the very darkest to the very lightest, and test your response to a range of mark-makers. It is best to begin with pencil as it is the easiest to control. Move consistently along a scale, altering the pressure as you go. The principle is simple: the greater the pressure, the heavier the mark.

## Pencil effects

Ideas need to be adjusted frequently during the drawing process. Elements are changed, moved or removed, and a pencil is the perfect tool for versatility.

Most cartoons are inked over the top of an original, lighter first drawing. The pencil lines need to be light and crisp so that they can be rubbed out. Where ink

is not used, water-soluble pencils can give greater weighting (density) to a drawing, while charcoal softened with water will add extra depth.

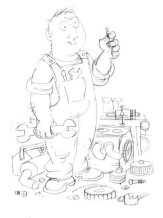

**Pencil** ▲
Keep the pencil tip sharpened for a detailed subject, such as this garage mechanic. Use an HB pencil and alter the pressure to give life to the line.

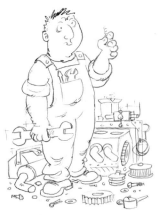

**Water-soluble pencil** ▲
The same sketch made here using water-soluble pencil is heavier and more apt as the line for the final artwork. The tip is dipped in water to darken the line.

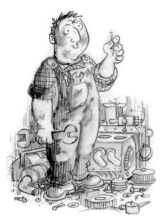

**Water-soluble pencil and charcoal** ▲
This final composition is outlined using water-soluble pencil. The line and additional charcoal shading is gently softened with a damp brush.

## Pencil and paper combinations

The choice of pencil and paper has a strong bearing on the end result: the way that you handle materials always affects the resultant drawing.

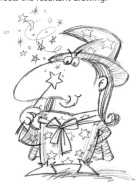

**Mechanical pencil drawing** ▲
As this sketch shows, mechanical pencils are able to deliver a broad range of creative marks, building lines and tones in much the same way as any other pencil.

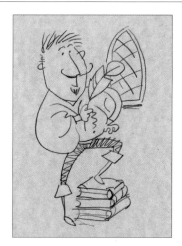

**Pencil on coloured paper** ▲
This simple line drawing is assisted by the soft shade of paper it has been created on. Coloured papers can save you laying a basic tonal wash at the start of a job.

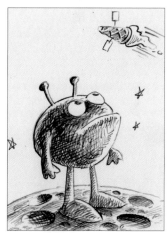

**Pencil alien** ▲
On smooth, cream paper, lightly draw the alien composition with a 2B pencil. Hatch loosely over the alien and planet surface, making the shadow areas deeper in tone.

# Pen and brush

Ask any cartoonist to name the traditional tool of the trade and most will tell you it is the dip pen. Dipping the nib into a bottle of Indian ink demands confidence. There is no going back once the nib touches the paper and the pen reservoir releases its fluid line. It takes practice to use the nib proficiently, but it is worth it: no other ink drawing tool offers such a wide range of pressure-led lines. Ensure the pen holder is comfortable to grip and buy a range of nibs. A good nib is flexible and consistent in flow.

The neater fountain pen is a worthy alternative. It requires none of the constant refilling, but its drawback is that it can become clogged with waterproof ink, making it useless for crisp line and wash work. Technical pens, including fineliners, range in nib size from 0.1mm up to 2mm and are designed to deliver a perfect mechanical line. They are excellent for dot stippling (dabbing the tip of the pen on to the paper to create a dotted effect) and regular cross-hatching, but the even flow makes them unsuitable for more expressive drawing styles.

Brushes are a bold alternative to pens, though they take more practice to control. Ranging in size from the ultra-fine 000 to the thick 12, brushes must be thoroughly cleaned with soapy water after use, since ink rots the hairs. Round brushes are the most common and available in synthetic nylon, nylon mixed fibres or, the most natural but expensive, sable. A good brush should be springy, with hairs that easily reform, tapering to a fine point. Round brushes are commonly used for drawing and adding tone; flat brushes offer slabby strokes.

## Pen and brush choices

Pens and brushes are essential to all artists, especially the cartoonist. The fountain pen delivers a flowing ink line with consistency, its beauty being that line weights alter according to pressure applied to the nib. A dip pen has a small reservoir at the tip to collect ink as it is dipped into an ink pot. The lines produced can range from blobby or scratchy, to thick or thin. Nibs are available in a range of sizes and shapes, for example the italic nib offering a definite, flat broad line. Technical pens are highly specialized for detailed drawing and are filled with cartridges. Their lines are crisp and definite, so are best on smooth papers. The beauty of fineliner pens is that they are disposable and don't need refilling.

**Pens and brushes ▼**

Here is a sample taster of what is on offer in most art stores and selected stationers. When choosing pens and brushes, you can only determine what is best for you through trial and error. Try as many varieties as you can and keep swatches of the effects in a scrap or note book as a reminder of their performance.

**Tip:** Any mistakes that may occur can be corrected by a number of means. You can scratch a small spill of ink or watercolour from the paper surface with a sharp craft knife. Use process white, white gouache or the heavier, spirit-based correction fluids to hide other unwanted drawn marks. Try them out first on scrap paper.

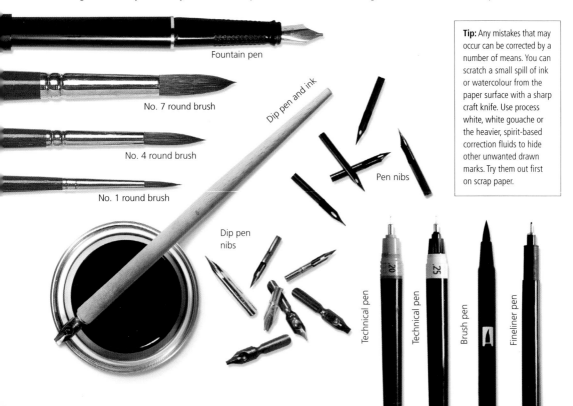

Fountain pen

No. 7 round brush

Dip pen and ink

No. 4 round brush

Pen nibs

No. 1 round brush

Dip pen nibs

Technical pen

Technical pen

Brush pen

Fineliner pen

## Practising the pen line

To begin with, try out as many different brushes and pens as you can on a variety of papers. This will help you to understand the properties of the various drawing tools in relation to the surfaces and enable you to select those that you feel most comfortable handling. For example, when using a dip pen, the choice of paper or board is critical.

Remember that practice makes perfect and the simplest lines can be improved with dedication. The more frequently you handle a pen or brush, the more confident your line work will become. Those cartoonists with a very definite style of pen line have developed their own personal language of strokes through extensive experience.

**Pen and brush line swatches** ▼
The swatches below have been created using a range of pens and brushes on smooth- and rough-surfaced paper. Start your own pen and brush swatch library with as many variations as you can. Keep adding to it so that it builds up into a valuable resource over time. Make sure that you note the variety and nib size too.

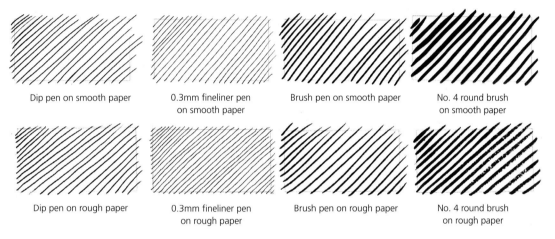

Dip pen on smooth paper

0.3mm fineliner pen on smooth paper

Brush pen on smooth paper

No. 4 round brush on smooth paper

Dip pen on rough paper

0.3mm fineliner pen on rough paper

Brush pen on rough paper

No. 4 round brush on rough paper

## Cross-hatching with a brush pen

A fineliner pen is not the only drawing tool that delivers exquisite and controlled cross-hatching. A fine brush pen can match it with some practice.

Decide where you wish the line to travel and then draw the brush along in one consistent stroke. Where your line ends, you may notice a slight taper as

the fine hairs of the point are lifted up from the paper's surface. This subtlety is what makes all the difference. Compare it to a fineliner pen. The most remarkable characteristic of the brush pen is the economy of marks that it encourages. When you draw, so few marks are needed to say so much.

**Cross-hatch variations** ▼
Fine brush pen strokes can differ widely. The combination of softness and rigidity allows lines to be freely curving or to be drawn using a range of pressures with a direct, controlled straightness. Experiment with pen combinations to develop your own personal cross-hatching notation.

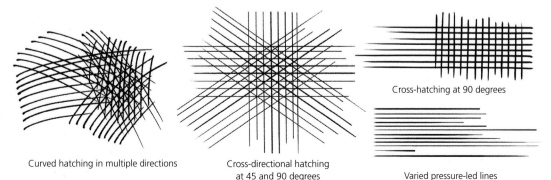

Curved hatching in multiple directions

Cross-directional hatching at 45 and 90 degrees

Cross-hatching at 90 degrees

Varied pressure-led lines

## Pen hatching to create a solid

A cube is the perfect shape on which to practise using cross-hatched tone to create a 3-D illusion. Hatch two of the surfaces, using more crossed strokes on one. It is easy to see that the closer the cross-hatching, the deeper the tone becomes.

Compare the results of a fineliner pen with those of a dip pen. Alter the length of the hatched strokes and see how tone can be given texture. Do not worry about getting your lines absolutely straight. The overall effect is what is most important.

**Comparing hatched boxes** ▼
The differences here are subtle. It is a good lesson to learn when to use one hatching technique rather than another. A blend can keep the drawing alive and prevent an overall deadness of tone.

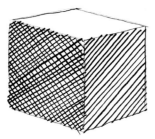

Cross-hatching on one surface with 0.3mm fineliner pen

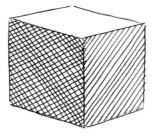

Cross-hatching on one surface with a dip pen

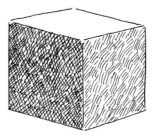

Hatching with 0.3mm fineliner pen

## Further pen techniques

The more extensive your repertoire of pen marks, the more interesting your cartoons will become. Don't be afraid to part with tradition and bring less conventional techniques into the mix.

Experimentation will keep your work fresh. In your explorations, practise the tonal scale from black to white so that you are able to gauge the response of the technique with your mark-makers.

**Further tonal swatches** ▼
Only when you put pen techniques up against one another can you really get the measure of their potential for major tonal description or background.

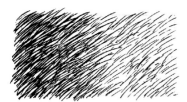

**Directional hatching** ▲
This kind of shading offers powerful movement and a rhythm that carries the eye across a drawing.

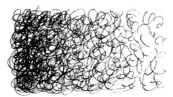

**Curly line** ▲
This is a softer, less forceful technique and is very useful for creating airy, nondescript backgrounds.

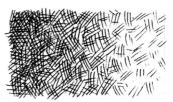

**Small hatching** ▲
An approach that offers straightforward tonal backgrounds with a good deal of freedom, yet is also controlled.

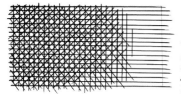

**Ruled hatching** ▲
This form of hatching offers a regular, mechanical alternative, which sets up a rigid, even tonal scale to use.

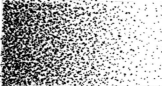

**Stipple** ▲
In this technique, each spot of ink represents a tiny area of tone, so it achieves the smoothest tonal transition.

**Smudge** ▲
This delivers true halftone qualities. You must be in full control and be careful not to use it too heavily.

## Practise doodling

A good cartoonist is not only curious, but also able to keep an audience's interest. Practise fun exercises between finished pieces to see how different pens perform. Indulge in simple doodling on a daily basis. Everything you learn can be used whenever the right time arises.

**Variety of media styles** ▶
Comparing different strokes delivered from a variety of media and placing them side by side is the best way to choose the most suitable. The hairy body of the troll enables you to explore texture with a range of thick and thin strokes.

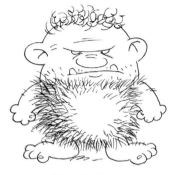

0.3mm fineliner pen

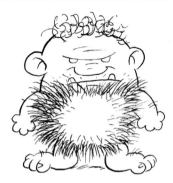

Dip pen

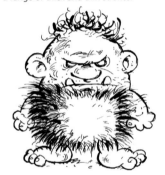

Dip pen and brush

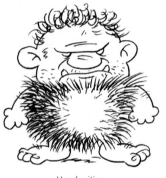

Handwriting
felt-tip pen

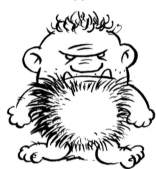

No. 4 round brush

## Texture and personality

Using different textures can alter the personality of a cartoon character. Here, three alternative hatching styles have been used to create the cat's fur. The slightly spiky directional hatching implies a suspicious nature, while the curly lines offer greater tonal range, suggesting softness and warmth. The use of the smudging technique is more ad hoc and suggests an unkempt alley cat.

**Character-building strategies** ▼
Understanding and being capable of accessing these various techniques are essential if you want to be able to display a range of personalities.

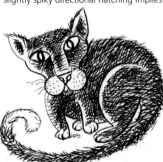

Directional hatching

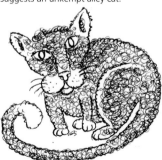

Curly line

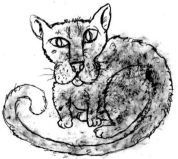

Smudging

## Further pen and brush effects

The drawings on these pages exploit the range of marks that can be made with pens and brushes. Copy these examples or create your own, but don't expect perfection. Have patience from the outset and relax into your drawings. Be prepared for every stroke to bring new possibilities, as well as the unpredictable, especially if you encounter a moppy brush or scratchy nib.

   The key to effective pen and brush work is to retain liveliness in the line. Adjust the pressure that you apply to your tools to vary the line weights at every twist and turn. This contrast in weighting will provoke an animated response in the drawing.

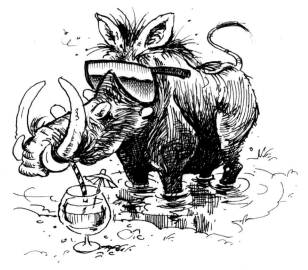

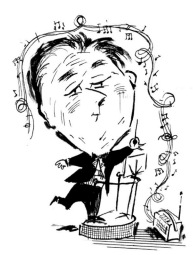

**Direct line with brush fills** ◀
The flow of the musical notes is matched by that of the pen nib and fluid brushstrokes. Dense, black patches intersperse the flowing rhythms and dry-brush greys soften the contrast.

**Bold line** ▶
Textured Ingres pastel paper is perfect for both dip pen and brush. The stark whiteness of the background is eliminated without effort.

**Dip-pen hatching** ▲
A medium-weight sheet of cartridge paper and a dip pen create this lively warthog sketch. Loose cross-hatching follows the curvy directions of the beast's rotund body, becoming denser beneath the belly. A 0.3mm fineliner pen gives a delicate contrast in the sunglasses reflection.

**Small hatching** ▶
The candle flame exudes a flickering, soft aura of light around its centre and the rising smoke above. Small hatching is perfect for this since it has movement, yet at the same time subtlety, and delivers a fluctuating overall background with good tonal range. It is most important that you initially leave the white areas with no lines. Extraneous marks can ruin the lighting effect.

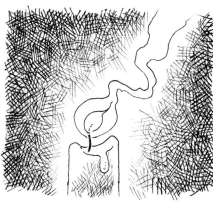

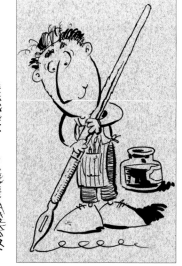

**Dip pen and gouache ▶**
To capture the bright *joie de vivre* of the Parisian café, use a dip pen sensitively and confidently, keeping your pen lines as crisp and direct as possible. Only put necessary detail into the picture to maintain focus. Ink the hat and waistcoat as solid elements, shade the background with stippling and add bands of blue and red gouache for the French tricolour flag. Allow your eye to gaze over the whole composition when you've finished to check that the lines all have enough weight. If any seem overshadowed, reinforce them carefully.

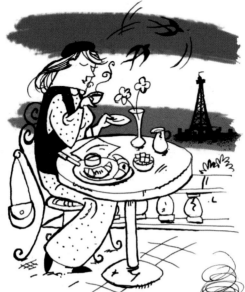

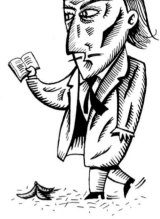

**Fake engraving ▲**
This simulated engraving or woodcut effect uses a combination of pen line weights. The key is to give equal weight to whites, hatched 'greys' and solid blacks. Spot colour is added to the banana skin to highlight its danger. Try various widths of grain-heavier line weights, or light lines placed close together. Find other wood engraving examples in books and catalogues and study the reproduced line carefully before emulating the style.

**Heavier blended marks ▼**
Filling larger areas of tone can be undertaken with a blend of heavier techniques. Smudging charcoal initially removes the whiteness of the paper, then a rag with drying ink can be rubbed over the dark, background areas. Brush and ink redefine the main detailed areas.

**Scratching and blobbing ▶**
Using a dip pen, scratching an outline directly determines the way forward. The spin of the hair is delivered with a fully loaded pen and a continual upward spiralling of hand. The eye blobs are added with a brush and larger blobs dropped in the spaces around, blown from the centre outwards through a straw.

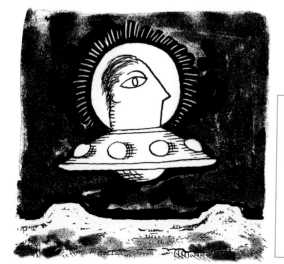

Tip: Experimentation can significantly aid your progress and help you to establish a valuable repertoire of drawing marks with a variety of wet and dry media. Once you have explored a handful of different techniques, set yourself a simple cartoon challenge in order to exploit these newly developed skills.

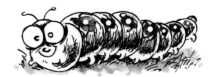

# Tonal control

The most forthright cartoons are those in which the contrast between black and white is stark, lending them enormous power and dynamism. Strong contrast and the variation of composition using black, white and some halftone (usually line-based) is essential in cartoon strips and graphic novels.

Lighting plays a key part in the process of balancing a black-and-white composition. A basic knowledge of how to display directional lighting in drawing is therefore a very useful skill to acquire at an early stage.

Start by looking around you. Observe the direction of light falling on objects and the shadows they cast. A strongly lit day will produce near-black, solid shadows, while a hazy, muted light will cause them to extend softly. The complex surface and

form of an object, or a character, can be simplified by using the fall of light and the resulting shadows to describe it. If you want to create a darkly humorous atmosphere or a heightened mood, you can do no worse than to borrow a technique from the great master artists of the Renaissance. Technically known as *chiaroscuro*, this manipulation of light and dark areas adds depth and can totally transform the mood of an image. If it worked for Caravaggio, then it can work for you!

The only way to learn how to use black and white in an effective way is to practise with simple compositions and move on to more complex themes as your understanding and skills develop. Time taken to master tonal scales all depends on practice: remember that cartoonists draw every day.

## Lighting spheres

The same sphere, with lighting falling on it from the right-hand side of the composition, can look very different depending on the treatment of the background and fall of the shadow. Because the horizon line is placed directly behind the spheres, each one appears to be resting. Where a grey tint

forms the complete background, the sphere becomes the major focus and gains natural prominence. This is then exaggerated with the inclusion of a base shadow. The partial blacking out of the background succeeds in balancing the composition, allowing the eye to 'read' the drawing more evenly.

**Spherical swatches** ▼
Use cross-hatch, stipple and opaque white hatched highlights to experiment with the compositional balance of black and white. Note the effectiveness of the halo around the rim in the bottom row of spheres, caused by light reflecting upwards from the white base.

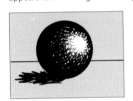
Cross-hatch on grey

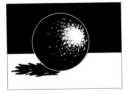
Cross-hatch on black and white

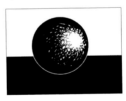
Cross-hatch on white and black

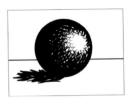
Cross-hatch on white

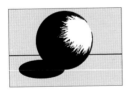
Cross-hatch highlights in white on grey

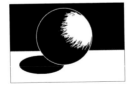
Cross-hatch highlights in white with black and white

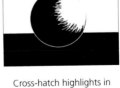
Cross-hatch highlights in white with white and black

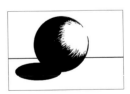
Cross-hatch highlights in white on white

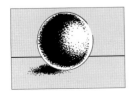
Stipple on grey

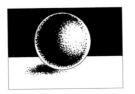
Stipple on black and white

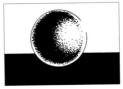
Stipple on white and black

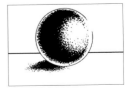
Stipple on white

## Simple drama

The cartoon spider's strong silhouette form is perfect for demonstrating lighting and shadows. The four identical black spiders reveal how a light source shining from a different direction can alter the mood of the scene and create a dramatic effect. Darkness entering from above creates oppression, while from beneath it underlines the importance of the spider as the main character. From the side there is the anticipation that something may be about to occur from the unknown dark spaces to the right, encouraging the imagination to conjur a dramatic mood.

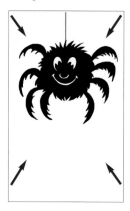

**Overall lighting ▲**
The spider hangs from its thread. The overall lighting has no prominent direction and sets a stark contrast as a flat, graphic image.

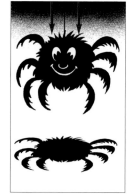

**Lit from above ▲**
The light source is at a level with the top of the spider. The stippled fade offers the picture a top and the base is provided by the shadow.

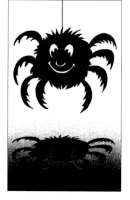

**Lit from below ▲**
Just below the spider and tilted upwards and back, the light produces a shadow that melts into the stipple, providing a stagey entrance for the spider.

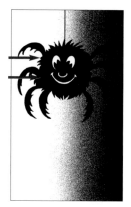

**Lit from the left ▲**
This composition carries a sense of discovery, as if a torch has just encountered the eight-legged fiend. Even tonal stippling sets a mood.

## Practice exercise: Opposing black and white

This uncomplicated scene exemplifies what you have discovered about using black and white in a composition. The torch is a common device because its beam leads the reader's eye into the next frame and a new focus in the narrative.

Once you have planned where your blacks and whites will go, define them clearly using solid, even fineliner pen lines and shapes. If you are unsure, mark them out first in pencil, but try not to become too reliant on the security of a pre-pencil mark.

### Materials
- *cartridge paper*
- *pencil*
- *1mm fineliner pen*
- *black Indian ink*
- *No. 3 round brush*

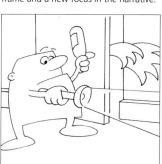

**1** Sketch the basic outlines of character and setting in pencil. Use a fineliner pen to go over for crisp, unfaltering lines.

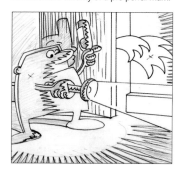

**2** Steadily define clear outline shapes that you will paint in black using Indian ink and a brush.

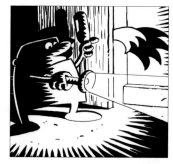

**3** Paint the outline shapes. Lessen the pressure on the brush where the lines disperse the light into jaggedness.

# Colour overlays

Colour can be applied to cartoons using a variety of methods and media. Here are some of the most popular choices on offer.

Watercolour paints are available in a vast array of colours either as moist cakes (pans) or in tubes. They are water-soluble and contain a gummy binder, which gives them body. A box of 12 artist-quality watercolours that includes the primary colours (red, yellow and blue) is a good choice.

Dyes and inks are fine, translucent liquid colours that stain the paper. Inks are waterproof and cannot be removed once dry. They are available in strong colours, making them ideal for printing, but exposure to strong natural light will fade them. Dyes are a concentrated strain of ink, extracted from plants or minerals or chemically created. Their brightness of colour means

that they are not particularly lightfast and should be avoided for any work where there is an expectation of permanence.

Gouache and poster paints contain chalk, which makes them very opaque, although they can be thinned in water to produce watercolour effects. They are excellent for laying down areas of flat colour, which dry without streakiness.

Acrylic paints deliver a highly versatile catalogue of marks, from thick to thin. These plastic-based paints can be thinned in water and are particularly useful for creating highlights.

Pastels offer smooth blending or solid colour used dry. They mix well with other media, wet and dry, and add texture.

Marker and felt-tip pens are available in two different types: water- or spirit-based (permanent) and in a variety of nib sizes.

## Your colour kit

Initially, it is not advisable to go out and buy every colour medium you have ever heard of. Much is of a highly specialized nature and within a genre of materials there is often a large range on offer, from student quality to artist quality. If you know what sort of effect you are aiming to produce and have followed

advice from this or another text, then you should begin researching. Test products in the shop where possible, and only buy what you need and can afford. As a general guide, the most expensive is the best, but if you are simply tinting a small area of a cartoon, the middle range will be fine.

**Basic colour materials ▼**
For the basic kit: buy some watercolour paints either as pans or in tubes, fluid inks in primary colours, small tubes of acrylic paint, including blue, red, yellow and green, gouache tubes in similar colours, plus white as a mixer, and a mixing palette for creating the right hues.

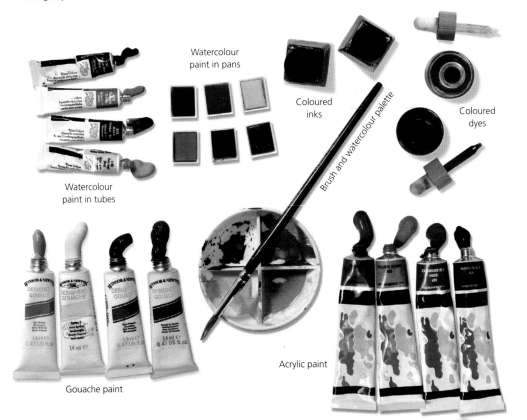

Watercolour paint in pans

Coloured inks

Brush and watercolour palette

Coloured dyes

Watercolour paint in tubes

Acrylic paint

Gouache paint

**Dry painting media ▶**
Pastels can be made of chalk or oil, and they are available in colours as well as in black and white. There is a huge range of felt-tip pens on the market; the densities and colours of their pigments often vary greatly, but they are certainly convenient.

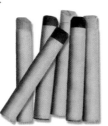
Oil pastels

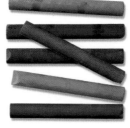
Chalk pastels

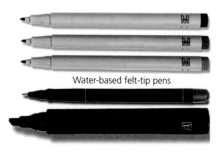
Water-based felt-tip pens

Spirit-based felt-tip pens

## Overlaying watercolour

A strong line cartoon often requires overlaying with a simple wash of colour. If you are using more than one colour in this way, always allow the first colour to overlap the next so that they blend, and make sure that this is done before the colour washes have dried.

**Tip:** If you lay a wet colour on top of another wet colour, they will merge. Allowing the first colour to dry before applying the second will produce a new combination of the two hues.

**Watercolour swatches ▼**
Explore colour blends by making experimental swatches. Be sure to test watercolour markers as well as paints and inks, using pressure to control the colour flow; certain pigments will not cover the paper as easily or as smoothly.

Watercolour, wet into wet blend

Watercolour, wet on damp; soft edge

Watercolour, dry on dry; hard edge

Dyes, vivid, permanent colours

Dyes, strong, hard-edged overlaps

Dyes, dry on dry; hard edge

Watercolour markers, controlled, softer blends

Watercolour markers, blended after drying

Watercolour markers, blending strong colours

## Practice exercise: Wet-into-wet blending

Take time to explore the effectiveness of wet-into-wet watercolour techniques on a drawing and compare the effects of the different media. Use a round brush to lay fluid trails of colour on each drawing and, while the colour is still wet, move the colour to the edges of the paper with the brush.

All three peacocks are drawn on to smooth cartridge paper with a black dip pen. The watercolour bleeds well, unlike the markers, which have greater vibrancy. The dyes are the most vivid of all and react well to the technique.

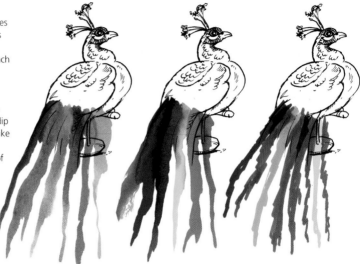

### Materials
- *cartridge paper*
- *dip pen*
- *waterproof Indian ink*
- *No. 6 round brush*
- *watercolour paints*
- *watercolour dyes*
- *watercolour felt-tip pens*

Watercolour paints     Watercolour dyes     Watercolour felt-tip pens

## Smooth and rough surface effects

Different surfaces produce a variety of results, affecting the appearance of your drawings. A rough watercolour paper allows only some paint to rest in its surface hollows, which can cause a mottled effect. In contrast, a smooth paper will give greater fluidity and transparency of colour. Concentrated dyes produce brilliant hues on paper, but cannot be blended once dry.

**Rough versus smooth surfaces ▼**
The watercolour paper allows the same soft blending for the various media. On smooth paper, there is a stained-glass effect where the hard edges overlap.

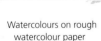

Watercolours on rough watercolour paper

Dyes on rough watercolour paper

Watercolour markers on rough watercolour paper

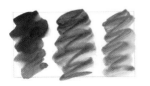

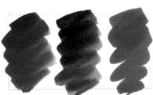

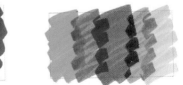

Watercolours on smooth paper

Dyes on smooth paper

Watercolour markers on smooth paper

## Overlaying gouache and acrylic

The best method of understanding the properties of gouache and acrylic paints is to create colour swatches. Place colours beside and on top of each other. This way you can discover how the paint handles and see how the colours combine. The primary colours make the strongest combinations, while the secondary colours are less reactionary when placed alongside each other.

**Colour combining ▼**
Add the spot colour when the main colour patch has dried. Note that the lower row of swatches features both liquid and tube acrylic paint.

Red and yellow gouache

Brilliant and viridian green gouache

Ultramarine and cadmium orange gouache

Cadmium red and phthalo blue liquid acrylic

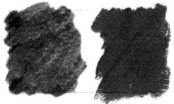

Ultramarine blue and cadmium red liquid acrylic

Cadmium orange and cadmium yellow tube acrylic

## Practice exercise: Layering gouache

Building a gouache drawing in layers allows plenty of room to manoeuvre. You can choose to paint from dark to light if you wish, whereas with transparent watercolour the lighest tone must be established first. Here, as each new layer is added, the picture becomes darker and more opaque, giving it a strong sense of structure and solidity.

**Materials**
- *cartridge paper*
- *fineliner pen*
- *No. 2 and No. 4 round brushes*
- *watercolour paints*
- *gouache paints*

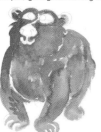

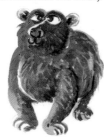

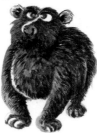

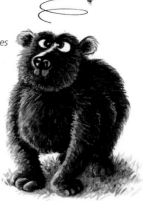

**1** Paint a light, fluid bear with yellow ochre watercolour. Don't worry about the patchy look of this layer.

**2** Use the same brush to paint on brown directional strokes in gouache. Add the facial features in a sepia tint.

**3** Add another layer of individual fur strokes using a smaller brush and a deeper burnt umber colour.

**4** Define the facial details and add fine highlights in yellow ochre gouache to the coat. Use the same layering techniques to create the grass base and sketch the wasp using a fineliner pen.

## Overlaying colour with line

It is important to be able to gauge how a colour overlay will affect the visibility of drawn lines. The examples here show a range of colour depths over various weights of fineliner pen lines. You can easily see how darker tints can obscure the lines beneath. For your future reference, it is worth creating your own swatch library of pen and brush line overlaid by colour. A small brush 'dip' of water should dilute your colour by ten per cent each time.

**Line and colour overlays ▼**
These pen lines were drawn using 0.25mm, 0.5mm, 0.75mm, 1mm, 1.5mm and 2mm pens. The colour overlay is ultramarine blue gouache in percentage tints of 10–100 per cent.

| 100% | 90% | 80% | 70% | 60% |
| --- | --- | --- | --- | --- |

| 50% | 40% | 30% | 20% | 10% |
| --- | --- | --- | --- | --- |

## Practice exercise: Using a simple palette

This cartoon demonstrates colour harmony over a single line. It uses just two hues – blue and red. Reducing the required palette allows you to focus more closely on the relationship between structural line work and simple tonal variations of colour wash. Using too many colours or those that are over-heavy will suppress the line.

### Materials
• cartridge paper
• pencil
• 0.1mm waterproof fineliner pen
• No. 4 round brush
• coloured inks

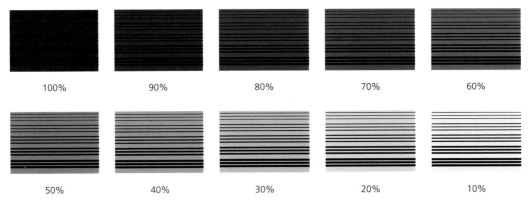

**1** Use a soft pencil to plan your composition, sketching the basic outlines of character and setting.

**2** Take your time to draw over your initial pencil sketch with a waterproof ink fineliner pen, using strong, even lines.

**3** Lay a pale, diluted wash of blue over the background sky. Colour the hat, chaps and landscape in pale red. Next, add a stronger wash of blue to the horse, waistcoat, sideburns and cuffs. Use a little yellow ochre and red mixed for the face. Finally, add some opaque white highlights to the horse and rider, as well as cloud details to the sky.

## Collage backgrounds

All kinds of coloured and textured paper and card can be used for ready-made backgrounds. Gather together samples or offcuts and look for harmonious or contrasting combinations. Try to be imaginative in your choice of materials and consider surface pattern as well as colour and texture. An unusual backdrop is capable of adding a new, surprising dimension to your artwork.

**Gathering papers ▼**
Collect paper samples that might be handy as backgrounds or textures for your drawings. Label your finds for future reference.

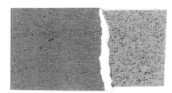

Handmade textured papers

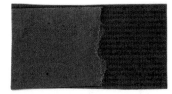

Sugar paper and brown parcel paper

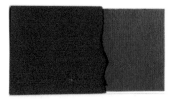

Matt-surfaced papers

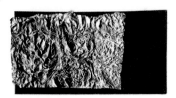

Foils and black handmade paper

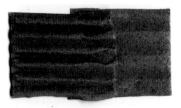

Wide and narrow corrugated card

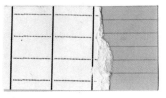

Ruled papers: old office document and filing card

## Opaque media

The light, delicate touch does not work for every cartoon subject. Political subjects or images designed to pack a punch require media with just as much impact. The opaque colours of gouache or acrylic paints, dense inks, cut paper or a combination of these is ideal. Their ability to produce flat, uniform colour over large areas makes them perfect for backgrounds and for producing works of graphic simplicity.

**Graffiti wall ▼**
The brick wall is painted in liquid acrylic and the graffiti lettering overpainted using tube acrylic. The ink line drawing of the aerosol is tinted in a red watercolour wash, and then made more opaque with a combination of red and yellow ink washes. The sky is a torn piece of blue sugar paper defined with a white gouache cloud.

**Collage ▶**
This War Of The Worlds artwork practises collage elements. The alien is drawn with a dip pen and coloured papers provide the gun's ray and background. The frayed edge of paper contrasts against the cut edge of the ray. With a layer of gouache on top, the drawing develops a simple, yet effective finish.

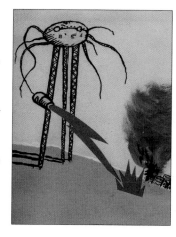

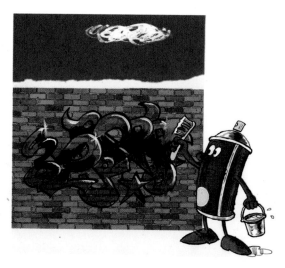

## Colour washes

Achieving a perfect colour wash takes practice. You can lay one-, two- and three-colour washes on smooth- or hard-pressed papers, or on rougher watercolour paper textures. Washes are an essential skill for the cartoonist to learn because they can provide a wide, blanket background on which the characters and settings can be placed. It is a great device for simple cartoons too.

**Comparing wash swatches** ▼
Note how banding occurs on the harder, hot-pressed smooth papers, and granulation (the grittiness of pigment resting) on the rough watercolour sheets.

Orange and yellow mix on smooth

Red and yellow mix on smooth

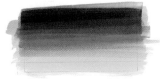

Red and blue mix on smooth

Orange and yellow mix on rough

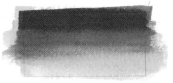

Red and yellow mix on rough

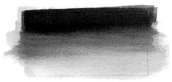

Red and blue mix on rough

## Practice exercise: Colour harmonies

Colour combinations are crucial in visual storytelling. Warm colours can denote danger or importance. Cool colours can slow the pace or support the focal characters. Spot colour is the use of a specific colour to focus attention. A spot colour in the same colour range as the background blends harmoniously. Spot colour works best when there are only a couple of contrasting colours used.

## Materials
- 'Not' watercolour paper and pencil
- dip pen and black Indian waterproof ink
- watercolour paints or dyes
- No. 12 broad brush

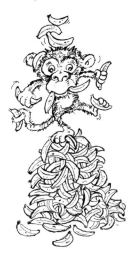

1 Outline your sketch in pencil and draw over it using the dip pen and black waterproof ink.

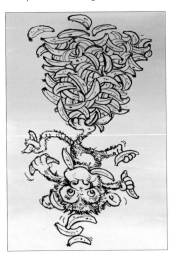

2 Turn the drawing upside down and paint a yellow watercolour or dye wash from top to bottom.

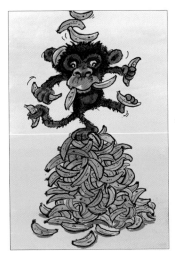

3 When dry, select harmonious colours for the details: dark yellow bananas and reddish-brown monkey.

## Contrasting spot colour

Where you need focus on a main part of an activity within a cartoon, colour can be successfully used to direct the viewer's attention. The most effective approach is to use limited colour in most of the frame, ideally monochrome tones. Then take a

contrasting colour – for example red is in powerful opposition to blue – and paint your significant subject with just a little of the contrasting hue. The result will be to strongly shift the emphasis to this distinctive area of 'spot' colour.

**Cool against warm colours ▼**
In this three-part animated explosion sequence, cool blue and warm red and yellow colours are used in a limited way to express the drama. The contrast between tints produces intensity.

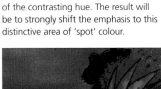 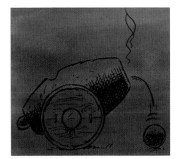

## Overlaying ink washes

Inks create new hues where colours overlap. Outline a frog using a pen nib and Indian ink, colour it in yellow ink, leaving the eyes white. Leave to dry and overlay with a red ink wash; the frog will change to warm red. Repeat the exercise, overlaying green and blue on yellow. Now start with a red frog and add yellow, then green and finally blue.

The frog will change from red to brown to deep purple. Note that the ink allows the black line to show through. When using ink as with watercolour, you can only lay a maximum of three washes on top of each other before the reflected light dulls and the colours turn muddy. Consider which hues you intend to use and make a rough paper tester swatch.

## Extra drama

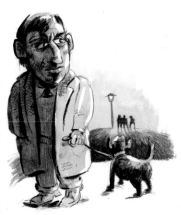

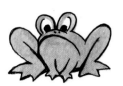

Yellow frog

Yellow frog with
red overlay

Yellow frog with
green overlay

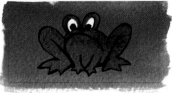

Yellow frog with
blue overlay

Two pale watercolour washes are dropped on to the loose pencil drawing, preserving the graphite tones. White gouache highlights enhance this dramatic, streetlamp-lit scene.

**Tip:** Think of simple cartoon subjects and narratives where overlays of ink wash can help to set the scene and produce a leading focus for the main element, as in the example of the cannon and explosion above. When drawn, use just two washes to tint them and evaluate their success.

# Mixed media

Unconventional combinations can be eye-catching. Media such as paint, ink and collage have their own unique properties and combining them in a cartoon can be highly effective.

It is not always necessary to draw everything in a composition and using a real object increases the impact. For example, when photos are collaged, an intriguing collision of real and unreal worlds occurs. Collaging allows you to rearrange your composition until it is right. This highly hands-on approach is

excellent for learning how to place elements successfully in a composition. When using PVA (white) glue, try not to let it drip or smear on the paper, since it will invariably leave a shiny patch that can look messy. Collage methods demand an orderly mind, which in turn requires a methodical workspace.

Make sure that you store any overmatter, collage papers and found ephemera in a small box in case the need arises to create a cut-paper cartoon.

## Practice exercise: Composite collage

Envelopes, sticky tape, bubble wrap and wrapping paper all have their uses. Closer scrutiny of your 'rubbish' will reveal an inspiring source of colour and texture combinations for new creations.

### Materials
- *brown wrapping paper*
- *scissors and PVA (white) glue*
- *paperclip*
- *red felt scrap*
- *thin white card*
- *1mm fineliner pen*
- *magazine photos*
- *card scraps*

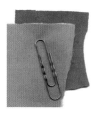

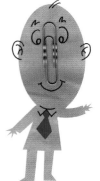

**1** Cut out an office worker from brown wrapping paper. Glue on a red felt tie and a paperclip for a nose. Lightly glue the figure on to the thin white card.

**2** Pen in the facial features and ears. Cut and glue the red felt carpet in place. Crudely cut out and glue on the filing cabinet photos. Glue on the card scraps for the files.

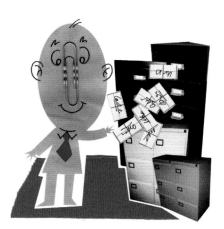

## Combining domestic materials

Before discarding household materials, consider whether they might have a use as a part of a collaged cartoon. Some packaging matter looks like something else that we recognize in the world about us. A link between material and subject can be formed, such as bubble wrap and the suckers on an octopus's tentacles. Where you can make these connections, utilize them in your images.

**Bubble wrap ▼**
Draw the shape of the tentacles with a coloured felt-tip pen directly on to the bubble wrap, then photocopy and stick down the flat representation.

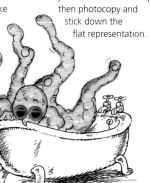

**Fabric ▶**
Collage items used sparingly can add great impact to a drawing. The key focus of this composition is a cut-out section of an old leather glove. The stitching adds a convincing touch of realism to the punchball.

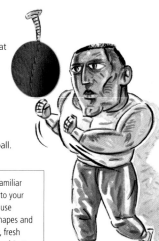

> **Tip:** As well as using familiar objects in relative size to your subject, see if you can use unintentional, found shapes and materials to bring new, fresh interpretations to your subjects.

## Practice exercise: Simple collage

Drawing every single item in a cartoon is sometimes unnecessary and can make a composition appear stilted. Virtually any 2- or 3-D material can be scanned and reproduced; the name of the game is experimentation. The interest in a book or graphic novel can be hugely increased with the surprise element of unorthodox materials incorporated into single pages, double-page spreads and cartoon sequences. Children's books are a great example of this creative approach and allow the author freedom to think directly on to emerging designs.

### Materials
- *smooth coated paper*
- *pencil and 0.3mm fineliner pen*
- *No. 3 round brush*
- *watercolour paints*
- *fern leaf*
- *PVA (white) glue*

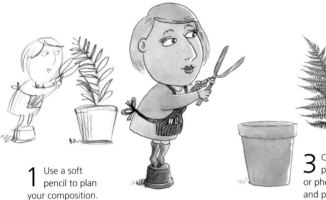

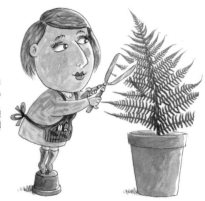

**1** Use a soft pencil to plan your composition. Outline your final drawing with a fineliner pen.

**2** Colour with light washes of red, green and yellow ochre. Leave a clear space for the fern.

**3** Colour photocopy or photograph and print out the fern sprig against a white background.

**4** Cut carefully around it and glue it into position. Darken areas of the gardener and pot to add tone.

## Further combinations

Mixed-media combinations have become very popular in the age of digital technology, and with the reproduction revolution, virtually anything can now be photographed or scanned and combined with traditional hand-drawing skills.

Trying out contrasting materials and media can be a great deal of fun and provide sparky solutions for drawn gags. Altering the natural sizes of objects that you have scanned can often lead them into a transformative stage. Suddenly they resemble other things, often by colour, shape or textural association.

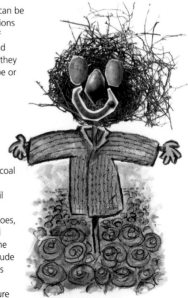

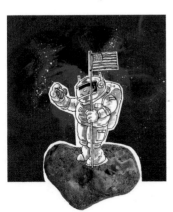

**Spaceman ◄**
Black sparkling paper is drawn upon with blue oil pastel and smudged with turpentine. A line and wash combination spaceman is created on smooth Bristol board, cut out and glued to a photocopied pebble. A spattering of white acrylic paint denotes stars. Add other moons, craft and planets to this spacescape to play with aspects of scale.

**Scarecrow ►**
A photocopy of a bird's nest is pasted on to a scarecrow body, drawn with charcoal and coloured in with smudged oil pastel. Cut-out pictures of potatoes, onion and broad beans serve as the features: their crude cutting reinforces the roughly constructed nature of the scarecrow.

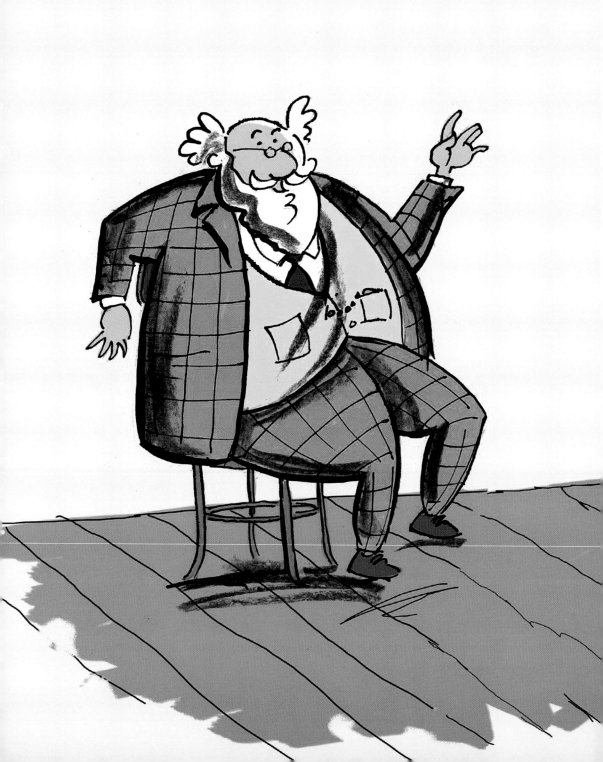

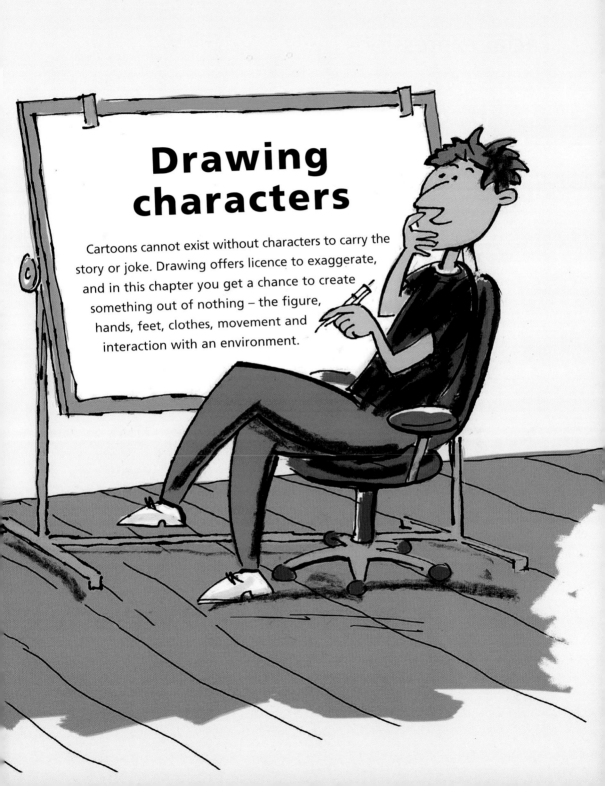

# Drawing characters

Cartoons cannot exist without characters to carry the story or joke. Drawing offers licence to exaggerate, and in this chapter you get a chance to create something out of nothing – the figure, hands, feet, clothes, movement and interaction with an environment.

# Facial expressions

Who could imagine a world devoid of expression? No smiles, smirks or looks of surprise; no frowns, screams or laughter – it would be enough to make you cry! Expression is an essential means of human communication and the most crucial feature that a cartoonist must capture. From happiness to fear, the art is to express every emotion in a few simple lines. Mastering this is the really fun part and it will enable you to convey storylines efficiently and effectively.

Before creating a range of expressions for a certain character, it is important to understand the rules for establishing the main frame: the size and shape of the head and the distinguishing features. The key to getting a character right will lie in your ability to reproduce a basic template and then position the

major facial elements correctly so that the expression springs to life through the sum of its parts. The techniques on these pages will help you to establish and develop facial expressions and to move on from basic ovoid (egg) face shapes to more characterful square, circular and triangular forms.

One great thing about cartooning lies in the simplification of detail, especially where facial expressions are concerned. While an accurate portrait requires deep and detailed understanding of the muscular structure and form to bring about a convincing result, the opposite is true of a cartoon. At its simplest, lines and dots do the job, but there is a whole tradition of different eye, nose and mouth shapes to choose from, and as you have a try, you are bound to develop personal interpretations too.

## The egg template

A perfect starting point for practising basic expressions is the egg template. It is quick and easy to sketch and uses limited media. To start, lightly sketch an ovoid (egg) shape in a single flowing

sweep with an HB pencil. Next, fill the shape with a flesh tint watercolour wash. When it is dry, quickly draw the expression using simple strokes and dots. Light symmetry lines added to the blank

shape will help you to fix the position of the eyes, nose and mouth. Don't be afraid to have a go: if a sketch doesn't work, you can simply try again. In an eggshell, that's it!

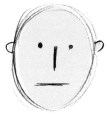

**Blank ▲**
Dot two eyes an equal distance apart, then add a central vertical nose line and an expressionless, straight horizontal mouth.

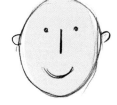

**Smile ▲**
By simply curving the horizontal mouth line, you will change the expression completely from blank look to brightly smiling.

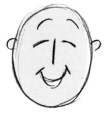

**Contented laugh ▲**
Below arching eyebrows, stretch the eyes into slits downturned at a shallower angle. Create a crescent smile from the cheeks.

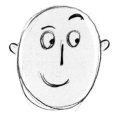

**Looking askance ▲**
The eyes are wide, defined by pupil dots glancing sideways from larger eye shapes. One raised eyebrow is offset by a lopsided smile.

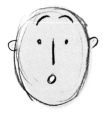

**Concern ▲**
First, raise the eyebrows high to the top of the ovoid, then dot in the eyes. Draw the vertical nose line and the elastic open-mouth circle.

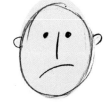

**Fed up ▲**
Tilt the curve of the mouth down and across the face to capture this mood. Increasing the pressure on the eye dots intensifies the stare.

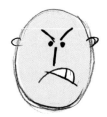

**Anger ▲**
Inverted brows slope down sharply and the eye dots are close together. An arching mouth stroke intersects the lip and bares the teeth.

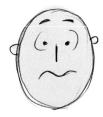

**Perplexed ▲**
Mark the short eyebrow strokes, eye dots, vertical nose and wavy mouth. The brackets enclosing the eyes set the expression.

## Modelling form with expression

Cartoon characters rarely hold the full-face pose for long. They constantly twist, turn and move within the frame. Head movements can be as important in conveying moods as facial expressions, so learning to build a head as a 3-D structure is vital. Use light symmetry lines to help maintain a visual balance in the features. Bear in mind that symmetry here means reflection. If you were to draw a line through a shape to represent a mirror, the shape could be folded along that line and each side would be a reflection of the other. Establish your repertoire of expressive marks, take the time to understand the rules of symmetry and the rest should follow. A vital clue: always have in mind that the ovoid is solid.

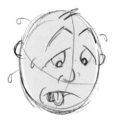 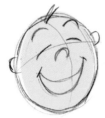 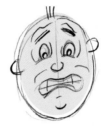 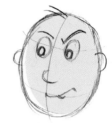

**Exhausted ▲**
Tilt the head downwards. Accentuate the arch of the eyebrows and stroke the upper eyelids parallel to them. Pull the mouth to one side and flop out the tongue.

**Laughing ▲**
The head tilts upwards. Deft strokes locate the raised eyebrows. Closed eyes, uptilted nose and beaming crescent mouth stretched across the face say it all.

**Frightened ▲**
Fear is held in the eyes: large ovoid whites with diminished pupils create a rigid stare. The head is set straight ahead, while the elastic mouth exposes rows of teeth.

**Mischievous ▲**
Keep the eye shapes open and control the expression by offsetting the line of the mouth and by deviating the eyebrow on this side of the face sharply downwards.

## Practice exercise: Inking the egg

With the basics firmly in place, start to explore the idea of the egg template using combinations of media beyond the pencil. The template sketch will quickly disappear beneath washes of black Indian ink, flat layers of gouache and added tones of dry mark-makers, such as charcoal or pastel. The egg tapers at the top, allowing for the evolution of natural comedy: features become pinched and elongated into a limited space.

### Materials
- cartridge paper
- fineliner pen
- dip pen
- black Indian ink
- No. 3 round brush
- gouache paints

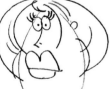 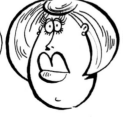 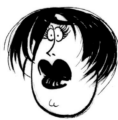  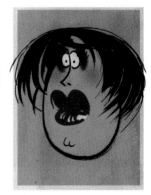

**1** Sketch the shape of the egg with a fineliner pen. Add the broad, over-arching hairstyle, surprised eyes, small delicate nose and big luscious lips. Adjust any elements that you are unhappy with.

**2** Draw over the fineliner outline using a dip pen and black Indian ink. Be confident and exploit the pressure sensitivity of the dip pen with an even balance of weighted strokes.

**3** Make a copy of the drawing using a small, round brush to make all the strokes, then flatly ink in the most prominent features of hair and lips. Do not be tempted to overdo the ink.

**Adding colour ▲**
A colour version uses flat layers of gouache. First, paint the background lilac, then use yellow ochre and red for the flesh tone, red for the lips and finally add the black ink line.

## Shaping the face

A more stylistic approach to expression can be achieved by constructing basic geometric shapes with the existing egg template. Where your subject has a specific expression aided by particular physical features, for example a square jaw or an elongated face, start with the shape that will best represent the expression. Historically, this method has served as a popular standard for many strip and animated cartoons since it creates a successful template from which characters can be formed in a recognizable style.

The logic of manipulating basic shapes through three dimensions simplifies the complexities of human or animal forms. The structure of skull and jawbone, cheeks and neck can be developed creatively from the configuration of square, triangle, oval and cube.

Once the head frame has been formed, the details can be sketched in to add life and personality. When you have mastered the head, extend the same process to the body and limbs by changing the scale and angle of the shapes.

**Circle and oval** ▶
This haughty-faced lady's expression is enhanced by the overlap of a small circle on to a larger oval. The character's details are added once the basics have been established.

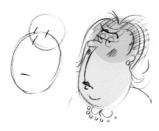

**Square and triangle** ▶
The triangle jutting from the square profile indicates from the outset that the jaw is strong and over-shot. This frame was often used in cartoons such as Hanna-Barbera's *The Flintstones*.

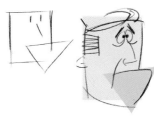

**Circle on oval: condensed** ▶
Positioning a circle on top of the oval extends the head height, allowing more to be made of the forehead expression.

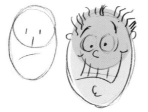

**Oval and square** ▶
The oval protruding from the square enables the thick-set neck to be drawn. This is the major characteristic of this particular composition.

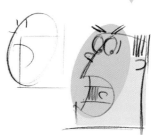

## Practice exercise: Triangular head

Create a cartoon using the shape method described above. First, locate the main features, adjusting their position until correct. Next, focus on the style and placement of the details to create the desired expression. When you are happy with your pencil sketch, develop the image further by adding gouache, pen, crayons and charcoal.

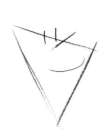

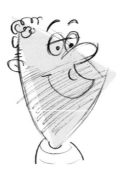

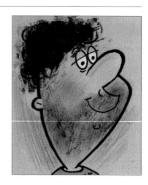

### Materials

- *cartridge paper*
- *pencil and dip pen*
- *black Indian ink*
- *gouache paints*
- *wax crayons*
- *charcoal*

**1** Lightly sketch a triangle, tilted so that one corner juts upwards to form the mouth and chin. Deftly mark the pencil strokes – the eyes, nose and mouth – within the triangle, as shown.

**2** Relax the straight edges so that they take on the rounder surfaces of the face. Form the caricatured features, adjusting as necessary and using the locator strokes as position guides.

**3** Redraw the sketch using a dip pen and ink. Apply yellow ochre and red gouache for the flesh tint to the face, pale blue to the background and burnt sienna to the hair. Add tone and texture with wax crayons and stubble with crumbled charcoal.

# Developing facial character

The principle of structural templates recurs constantly in the cartooning world and the development of stylistic drawing marks often evolves from these underlying forms. For example, features that pinch around the region of the forehead are an indication of an underlying egg template and basic geometric shapes usually provide the framework for a strong, square jawline. When you have become proficient at using these guides to produce faces, try varying the structures with inventive combinations and matching certain types of character to them.

Keep experimenting: if you are able to maintain a sense of inquisitiveness, this will drive forward the evolution of your own unique cartoon and caricature style.

**Tip:** Cut out faces from magazines and study the features closely to determine character traits, then use these references to build their structural templates. Document these experiments in your sketchbook, and be sure to stick the cut-out magazine pictures next to your drawings.

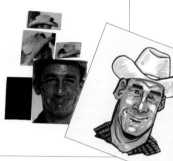

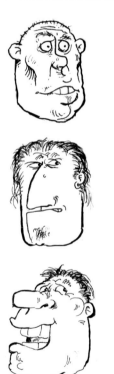

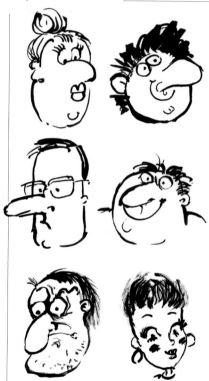

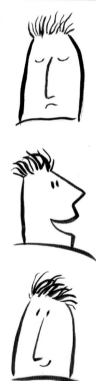

**Dip-pen detailing ▲**
Controlling the dip pen is crucial when detailing facial expressions. Keep your lines and hatching simple and let them follow the form of the face with direct strokes of the nib. It is easy to build too much hatching that describes nothing clearly. Use short strokes for wrinkles and blemishes.

**Edited line with brush ▲**
Sketch characters directly using the tip of a small, round No. 3 brush in order to enhance their quirkiness and offer a greater sense of animation. This 'scratchy' style allows you to deliver slightly less finished brushstrokes. Despite their sparse nature, such cartoons carry an endearing quality and their erratic heavier lines display a comical madness and eccentricity.

**Brush-line simplification ▲**
The simple sweeps of a dry, Indian ink-loaded brush can produce charming drawings that say a great deal in a few strokes. It is possible to become prolific quickly using this technique, but getting it right takes practice; take time to think carefully before making any marks.

## Developing characterization

By combining shapes, textures, line and colour, you can assume the limitless role of the creator of a cartoon population with as many different characters as there are in the real world. The faces below amply demonstrate that varying the combination of materials and marks you use is important: it keeps your cartoon characters lively and fresh, and prevents them from sinking into ordinariness. Cartooning as a genre must keep moving forwards; good cartoonists always leave their options open and never say never to new approaches.

**Tip:** Occasionally, work energetically and without planning. Free drawing is a good exercise to unlock creativity and release your imagination. This scribble man sprang up from an initial doodle of three squares in a row (the teeth).

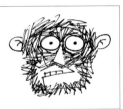

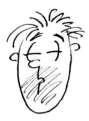

Pen line and scribble

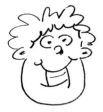

Pen direct line

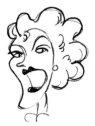

Pencil line

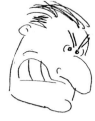

Pen broken line

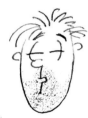

Pencil line and splatter

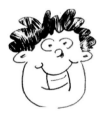

Pencil line with scraped ink
(dragged cardboard)

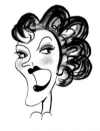

Pen line with added charcoal

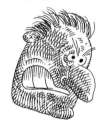

Pen cross-hatch

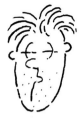

Pen broken line

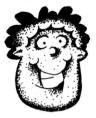

Brush ink line and
pen dot stipple

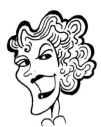

Ink line with heavier brush

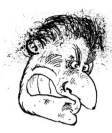

Pen cross-hatch,
line and splatter

**Doodling the line** ▲
The doodling pen or pencil moves quickly over the paper surface and rarely returns to the same place. One hit of the line is enough to communicate the mood of the character with economy.

**Adding texture** ▲
Texture in selected areas can bring a drawing to life. Try an unusual technique, such as scraping cardboard through ink to produce a stranded effect, or build tones with line and stipple.

**Stylizing** ▲
The complexity of definite shapes or textures can be reduced to simplified patterns. The hairstyle is drawn as 'bubbles' of ink and charcoal, and then joined as a maze of varied lines.

**Vigorous line** ▲
The active expression of anger requires vigorous attention. The broken line of the dip pen can lead to selective hatching, lending angry 'colour', or the furious spatter of the nib.

## Practice exercises: Reducing the template

Templating is an important method of character construction. A solid block is enough for some facial types, whereas others need an amalgamation of shapes to form strong, structural characteristics. The principles of template construction can also work in reverse: instead of adding new shapes, you can remove from the larger ones to create interesting faces. Having a template to work from is useful when you need to create a whole family of similar or related subjects. Once familiar, the lines of construction can easily be dropped.

### Materials
- *HB or pale blue pencil*
- *dip pen*
- *black Indian waterproof ink*
- *chalk pastels*
- *No. 4 round brush*
- *watercolour paints*

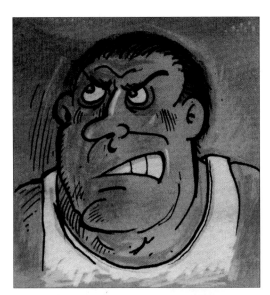

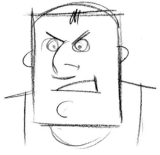

**1** The key shape here is the solid oblong that forms a square jaw and flat profile. Sketch this using an HB or a pale blue pencil.

**2** Sketch the final outline in pencil and draw over it in pen and ink. When dry, fill the background with an ochre tone of chalk pastel. Add red to the face, blue to the hair and white to the vest. Refine the face by rounding the features and hatch in some tone.

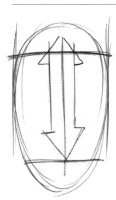

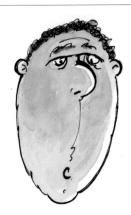

**1** The key shape in this case includes a double-ended arrow. It is a guide to positioning the facial features; a reminder of the long drop of the face from a sharp, slanting brow.

**2** The expression widening from pointed brow line to puzzled mouth shape follows the pattern and movement of the double-ended arrow. A watercolour flesh tone mixed from yellow ochre and red fills the face and the features are detailed in pen and ink.

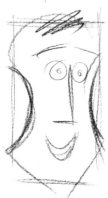

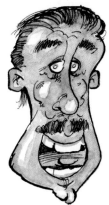

**1** Sketch in the main features, but take 'apple' bites out of each side. Reducing the oblong template by removing parts of it can lead you to create a face outside your usual style.

**2** Use the initial pencil marks as a template to help you complete the slender-faced gent. Solidify the outline using dip pen and black Indian ink along with pale washes of yellow, ochre and red watercolour. Leave areas of white paper as highlights.

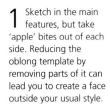

# Character faces

There are countless different ways to draw a face, but very few that are appropriate for a particular purpose. For example, a simple approach using uncomplicated shapes, dots and lines for facial features and bold, flat colours instead of tonal gradations would suit a children's picture strip. The 15 character studies shown on these pages employ a variety of techniques and require a range of skill levels to draw them.

They represent all the issues of mood, expression, stereotype and suitability for the various cartoon genres. Setting small targets of achievement in the form of fun projects is a great way of gauging how you are progressing. Testing your knowledge and abilities will also highlight any techniques that need further practice. Where better to start your learning than in a sketchbook, copying the faces of friends and family.

## Fifteen face styles

Be open to the range of techniques you have practised so far and consider each face you draw in its own context. Ask yourself who it is aimed at and what information it must convey. Think carefully about how you can communicate these points effectively in terms of facial structure and surface colour, decoration or technique. For reference and inspiration, check out cartoon styles from the many comics, graphic novels and animations that exist in the public domain. A specialist comic shop is a good primary source and the Internet may offer other resources.

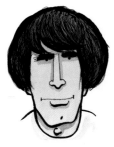

**Retro moptop** ▲
Hairstyle and shape is important to this face, setting it in a definite time and so triggering other associations. Line and wash creates the 'big' hair in contrast to the limited line used elsewhere.

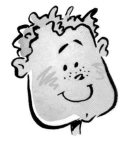

**Lively and child-friendly** ▲
Simple, clean images can dance from a brush or felt-tip pen, as this sketch shows. Felt-tip pens are associated with children; using them to add squiggles enhances the appeal.

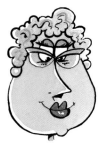

**Purple-rinse washes** ▲
Old-fashioned spectacle frames, clip-on earrings, gaudy make-up and purple-rinsed hair set this stereotype. The small, pear-shaped head will complement a large, pear-shaped body.

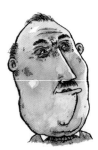

**Time-worn face** ▲
Weathered, lived-in faces can be quite a challenge to draw. In this instance, media and technique have been used to good effect. The fine cross-hatching is given extra tonal weight with rougher, blotchy watercolour washes.

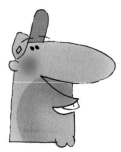

**Exaggeration and simplicity** ▲
The car mechanic, denoted only by his hat, is conspicuous for other reasons. The face is grossly over-exaggerated, placing him firmly in an unreal world. The line is broken, but the washes are very smooth on the watercolour paper.

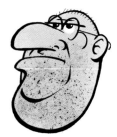

**Unshaven look** ▲
A stubbly appearance is easily created using an old toothbrush dipped in ink. Once the line work is in place, mask out any areas that you do not want spattered and then gently flick the toothbrush hairs over the sketch.

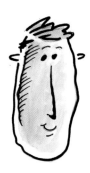

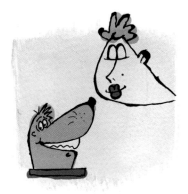

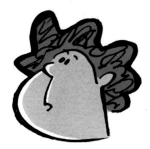

### Felt-tip head ▲
Easy-to-use felt-tip pens offer a good ink flow, and although their line is not as variable as other ink media, such a limitation often forces greater economy of thought and delivery. Simple strokes build up a simple face.

### Character interactions ▲
More than one character encourages an unfussy scene. Reducing the colour can unite the elements in a composition. The dip-pen line is accompanied by pale browns and flesh-tone colours, and the red collar matches the red lips.

### Loose-brush head ▲
Keeping the line loose and free will help keep a cartoon moving. This technique is especially good where a strip needs to be animated and lively. The squiggly pen-doodled hair is an effective way of adding tone.

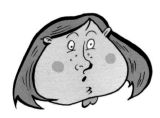

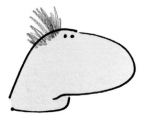

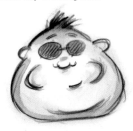

### Detailed, but child-friendly ▲
Extra detail can still be kept clean, sharp and to the point. The strokes indicating the direction of the hair, the freckle dots and the symmetrical features sum up the face in economical terms.

### Simple man ▲
One consistent line chugging across the page delivers broad curves. Two dots and the pressure-led softness of crayon complete what has to be the simplest way of creating a lovable character.

### Charcoal and smudge face ▲
The fullness is achieved by using smudged charcoal to create the soft, fleshy form. Leaving the face white and blending tone only into the corners and around the edge accentuates this.

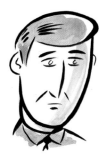

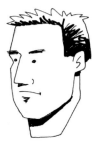

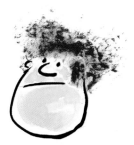

### Graphic novel ▲
Once it is mastered, brush drawing breeds confidence and quickens drawing time. A medium brush with a fine tip delivers pressure-weighted strokes. Add soft washes to tint. This is a popular technique for graphic novels.

### Continuous-line man ▲
Test your control by drawing the character with a continuous line that follows the contours of the profile. A fineliner pen will allow you to stop momentarily before changing direction. Use felt-tip to fill the shadows and hair.

### Splattered red head ▲
The humour is in the hair. A shock of apparently uncontrolled splattered ink is the starting point for this simplistic depiction. The slight awkwardness adds to the charm and the crude pen line equally complements and contrasts.

# Detailed faces

With a gamut of techniques at your disposal, detailing faces will put your abilities to the test and also provide excellent practice for your tonal rendering skills. The key to effective detailing is actually to draw on a bigger scale, allowing enough space to relax into the strokes and marks. The slick finish of a cartoon face often masks the difficulty of its execution. The end result is significantly affected by variations of paper, line markers and colour media, and it is worth experimenting with as wide a range as possible. Although cartoons are most commonly drawn on a relatively smooth surface, textured paper can add interest by interrupting the flow of the line or the wash. Adding a textured object can also serve to enhance the life of your creations and to move them away from the norms of stylistic cartooning.

## Practice exercise: Indian ink and wash

For this sparkling character, keep the rendering clean and bright. Match his zinging personality by using a crisp, Indian-ink line, which can be filled with light, translucent washes of watercolour. Remember, freshness of application is key and avoid oversaturating the washes with colour that is too heavy. The retention of the highlighted areas maintains the three-dimensional facial structure and illuminates the fresh quality of this illustration.

### Materials
- *rough watercolour paper*
- *dip pen*
- *black Indian ink*
- *watercolour paints*
- *No. 4 round brush*

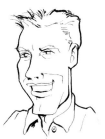

1 Outline your sketch using a pressure-led ink line over the surface of the sheet of watercolour paper. Leave it to dry.

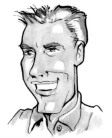

2 Add a first wash of diluted yellow ochre to the face, blue to the shirt and brown to the hair leaving white-paper areas as highlights.

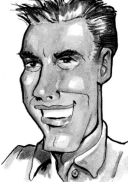

3 Add the second wash of each tint, 'reserving' the white areas. Mix a little red with the skin tone for warmth. Blend it softly into the yellow ochre to avoid streaking in the paint.

## Practice exercise: Exaggerating a feature

Once you are able to detail a face using regular proportions, consider exaggerating certain characteristics in order to elicit a humorous response. Knowing what to enlarge, stretch, pinch or squash is vital if recognition is not to be lost.

### Materials
- *cartridge paper*
- *pencil and dip pen*
- *black Indian ink*
- *watercolour paints*
- *No. 4 round brush*

1 Draw initially in pencil on smooth paper to develop the character of the pirate. Establish detail on the face and hair, even at this early stage, to keep your intentions clear.

2 Draw over the pencil with dip pen, reinforcing your original marks. Individual strands of hair significantly increase the level of finish on this drawing, and they are easier to draw on this paper. Tint your pirate with soft washes of watercolour, which will not obliterate the crisp outline.

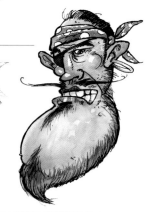

**Tip:** Get into the habit of exaggerating features: big noses, ears and chins increase the humour of a cartoon and are an ideal main focus.

## Practice exercise: Animated line

Match a bubbly character with light, 'fizzy' lines. The stray locks are playful and add more energy to this lively individual. The 'jogging' line of the dip pen nib animates the face giving it spontaneity. Note how this is under control with no stray lines.

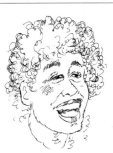 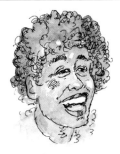 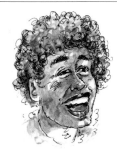

### Materials
- *cartridge paper*
- *dip pen*
- *black Indian ink*
- *watercolour paints*
- *No. 2 large, soft brush*

**1** Lightly sketch the face. Go over it in pen using a loose grip close to the nib to make the hair curls.

**2** Drop a pallid red wash over the drawing. Float a pale blue wash on top. Reserve the white highlights.

**3** Increase contrast and tonal depth with strokes of blue paint. Add bouncy brush curls to the inked ones.

## Practice exercise: Cross-hatch

Cross-hatching is an essential technique that is ideal for the crisply modelled, 3-D face. The idea is to create levels of grey shading with parallel and crossing pen lines. Increasing the number of lines makes the tone blacker.

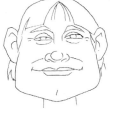 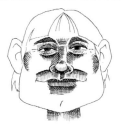 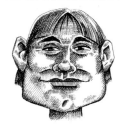

### Materials
- *cartridge paper*
- *HB or pale blue pencil*
- *fineliner pen*

**1** Sketch a sharp, regular outline. Widening the facial features will give you a broader 'canvas' so that you fully fill the drawing area.

**2** Locate a central focus and create small sections of criss-cross pen lines. Work from dark to light and leave white highlights.

**3** The mid-tones are the hardest to establish. Add these only when you have built up your darkest and lightest areas.

## Practice exercise: Shadow and colour

A single light source can heighten the drama of a face. Shadows across one side will make it recede because they draw the eye into the background. Colour will vary the mood and counteract this, focusing the eye to the foreground.

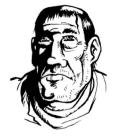 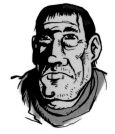 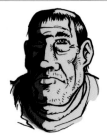

### Materials
- *cartridge paper*
- *No. 4 round brush*
- *black Indian ink*
- *watercolour paints*

**1** Create the basic structure of the face using brush and ink and then fill in the shadow sections. Observe this from life, photographs or comics.

**2** Mix yellow ochre and red for the flesh tint. Drop this evenly around the dry, inked line. It warms the character considerably and gives depth to your established modelling.

**3** Stain two-thirds of the face yellow. Note how this hue adds suspense. The blue abutting the black shadow heightens the contrast intensely.

# The figure

In a cartoon it is the figure that takes precedence. We notice the human character over everything else because it is the element that tends to carry the narrative. Even when an animal or bird is the main character, it is most likely to embody a mixture of features and move with human mannerisms. This is why it is so important to observe people as they engage in their everyday lives.

To draw cartoons well requires a good working knowledge of the human figure: how it is constructed and how it moves. It helps to look at the body as a set of geometric shapes, interlinked and jointed in strategic places, namely the elbows, knees, wrists and ankles. Accuracy is vital, so do not hesitate to redraw figures until they are proportionally correct. When

you have mastered the body proportions and understood fully the way in which the anatomy connects, you will be able to distort your figures with ease.

Getting into the habit of keeping a sketchbook will allow you to record humorous incidents, interesting faces and character likenesses. Visit public spaces, such as parks, railway stations and busy shopping areas, and undertake rapid sketches to capture poses, action and speed. These are the essential ingredients for a convincing cartoon.

Aside from facial expression, a range of postures and body shapes gives clues to a figure's personality and feelings. Observing and recognizing these is very helpful when using exaggerated body language to communicate ideas.

## Body proportions

The basic proportions of the human figure are measured by the ratio of the number of heads that fit the body. This is between six and seven heads for an adult, depending on gender, race and body type, and four to five-and-a-half heads for a child. The technical term for this rule is the 'canon of proportion' and its

principles still underpin how the figure is perceived in Western art. There is no substitute for learning to draw accurate figures according to the canon, even though it is most likely that your sketches will have exaggerated features. Cartoon proportions may be as tall as ten heads or more for an elongated, gawky

figure, or as short as four heads for a squat or rotund character. When you are out and about, see if you can, in an inconspicuous way, approximate the number of heads that go into the many body types that walk our streets. Other good sources are magazines, newspapers and retail clothing catalogues.

### Male proportions ▼
The average adult male is seven heads deep, and is first sketched as a simple connection of shapes: oval head, oblong body, square pelvis, stringy limbs and slightly enlarged hands and feet. The second sketch builds the male figure as an anatomically correct structure, shaped realistically around the neck, ribcage, hips, arms and legs. The final sketch is finished in line and wash.

### Female proportions ▼
This average adult female is six heads deep, curvaceously shaped with lighter features than the male. The hands and feet are under-emphasized with narrower shoulders in relation to the head. The classic hourglass figure is built upon flexibly connected softer shapes. Familiarity with shape, and knowing where and how curves are formed, is key.

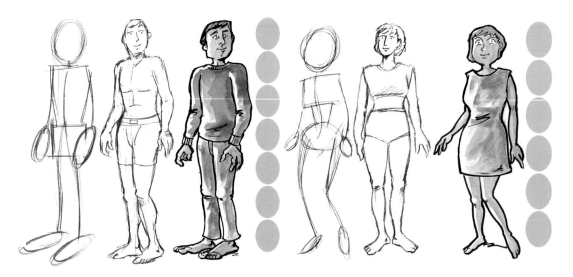

**Tip:** If you get an opportunity to sit in a life class, or arrange a model to sit for you, set up a strong light source with a definite direction so muscle formations are easily identified. Have a basic anatomy book to identify muscle groups and bones. Remember, a working knowledge of anatomy is useful but not a prerequisite for every cartoonist.

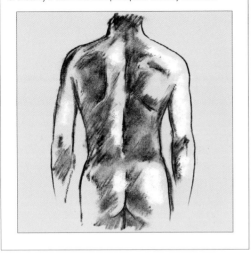

## Character profile

Study characters in comics and graphic novels. Pay attention to unusual body positions where they are foreshortening, a position dynamically enhanced and pushing towards the reader. Copying can be a good start for cartoon figure drawing. Comic masters have put in lifetimes of hard work, so, at first, don't expect too much.

### Superhero ▶
Standing at least eight-and-a-half heads deep, superheroes have heads that are are positively smaller, set into broad, muscular shoulders and a powerfully solid torso. The major muscle groups are exaggerated, especially the abdominals and the chest pectorals.

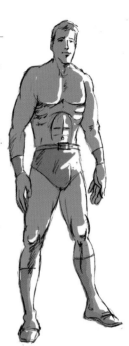

### Child's proportions ▼
This teenage boy is five-and-a-half heads deep. He is constructed using the same guiding principles as the male figure, but with less-developed muscles. His head is larger in relation to the rest of his frame. The smaller children are, the larger their heads are in relation to their bodies. A common mistake is to broaden the shouders too much and allow too much limb extension. Avoid strong defining marks on children. A line stroke is very pronounced and invariably ages the figure.

**Tip:** For practice drawing the human figure, consider joining a life-drawing class. Regular sessions will help to improve fundamental understanding of the human form and how it is represented. Where you may be unable to attend a class, drawing a relative or yourself in the mirror can be useful. Clothed figures are good to attempt, as garment folds gather and stretch over the human torso and limbs.

### Toddler's proportions ▼
Four-and-a-half heads is the recognized 'canon' for a toddler. Expect the shapes to be much rounder and less defined than those of a teen or adult. Note how the skull is especially round with lowering, bulging cheeks and a high forehead. Begin, as drawing one shows, with three circular, equal segments.

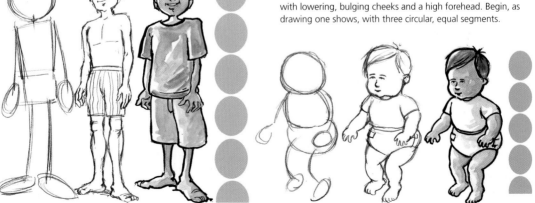

## Body types

In reality, few people conform to the average 'ideal' figure. Human bodies are a range of shapes and sizes, and observing different types will help your cartoon representations. Specific age groups, for example, have their own characteristics, and the vitality of youth, middle-aged spread or the infirmities of old-age are diversities that the cartoonist cherishes and celebrates. Capturing the details is important, so it is a good idea to carry a sketchbook wherever you go, ready to jot down the various people types as you come across them.

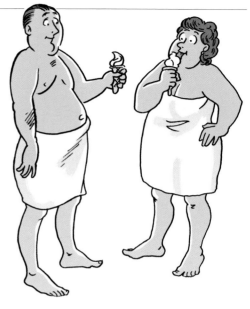

**Middle age ▶**
The skin loses its elasticity in middle age and there is often an increase in fat around the stomach; the body is less angular and shapely. Note the man's slumped posture between shoulder and waist and the woman's wide hips.

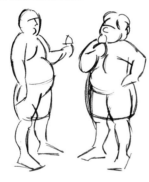

**Tip:** These are simple delineations of the figure achieved by visualizing the figure clothed. Stance – the angle at which hips tilt in the same direction, or even in opposition of the shoulders, the arch of the back and the turn 'in' or 'out' of the feet, are all important positions to remember as a cartoonist.

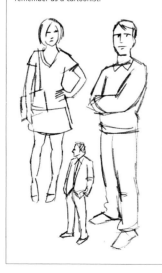

**Youth ▼**
Youths are often slender, because their skeletal and muscular development lack the strong body shapes recognized in adulthood. As a result, they are often reproduced with simple sleek, vertical lines and very few curves.

**Young male ▼**
The super-fit young male is strong and muscular. In the prime of life, he carries himself with a sturdy, upright stance. The muscle tone is well defined and slightly exaggerated.

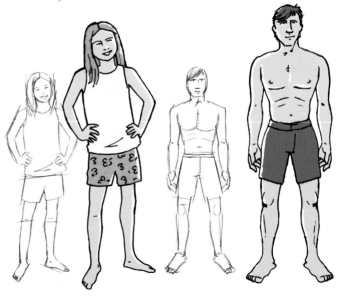

## Old age ▼

An old person's body tends to decrease in size as muscle wastes and the frame starts to shrink. A stoop is common and often a stick or walking frame becomes a necessary accessory. There is little or no body tone and the overall demeanour is frail. Sketchbook studies made from life are useful to study elderly movement. The curve of the back is essential to determine agility through their limbs. Stooping deportment will tilt the whole person forward and the legs will appear to drag behind rather than bold, leading strident steps. Every detail is important to sketching.

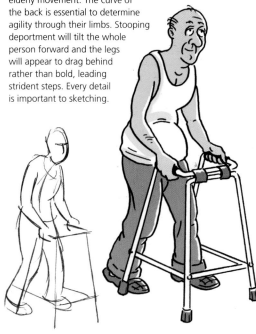

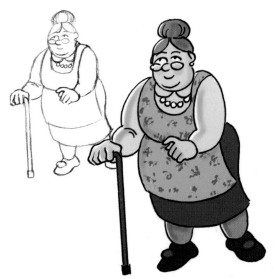

## Character profile

Stereotyping categorizes people on the basis of their appearance. Cartoonists stereotype a great deal so that viewers can identify a figure's main characteristics and profile at a glance. Selecting the right body type is important when establishing the profile and makes it easy to define features and clothe a character.

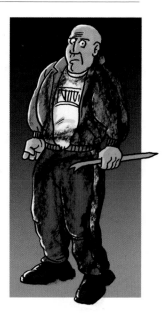

### Criminal ▶

In this case, the thick-set adult male figure with shifty glance, casual clothing and crowbar in hand leads the observer to conclude that the character probably has criminal tendencies.

## Dressing the form

How a figure is clothed is an important aid to character recognition, so make sure that your research is thorough. Clothing can indicate age, gender, class, occupation and lifestyle. It is also an indicator of time and place. Being able to dress characters appropriately enables the cartoonist to communicate accurately with the audience.

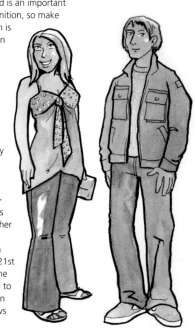

### Dressed-up couple ▶

That the woman wears jeans not only reveals her body shape but it also shows that she is from the late 20th or early 21st century when it became acceptable for women to wear trousers. The man is in a jacket that shows off his sturdier frame.

## Exaggerating body shape

The point of a traditional figure drawing is to replicate the human proportions exactly. A cartoon drawing uses a process known as 'metonymic distortion' to exaggerate certain parts of the body and adjust the posture and expression. The purpose of this is to give a cartoon figure emphasis and so communicate more directly with the viewer. The simplest exaggeration can depict speed, action, movement or a change of mood or pace. The way in which a character is standing can sum up a situation instantly, for example. Achieving this level of visual communication is crucial in comic drawing where words are kept to a minimum.

**Tip:** Observe different types of people. Notice how they move and dress. Look for particular movements, mannerisms or features and make a record of them in your sketchbook. Create rapid figure sketches and exaggerate specific actions or body characteristics.

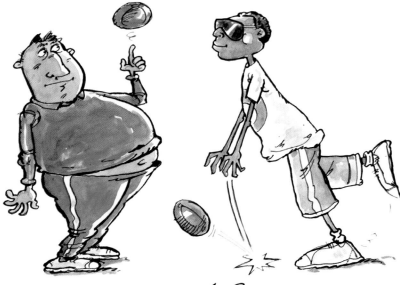

**Fat and thin** ▶
The basketball coach and his promising young protégé leave us in no doubt as to their roles. The coach is drawn with his ballooning body held by the tight stretch of the tracksuit. Exposing his midriff emphasizes his weight problem, as does the sharp taper of the leg from waist to ankle. The young player leans into the bounce, sprung and steadied by his large feet, which enhance his slim frame.

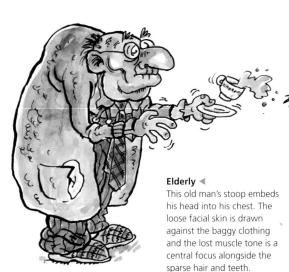

**Elderly** ◀
This old man's stoop embeds his head into his chest. The loose facial skin is drawn against the baggy clothing and the lost muscle tone is a central focus alongside the sparse hair and teeth.

◀ **Poise and posture**
The ballet prima donna is a perfect subject for figure exaggeration. She stretches, and can be drawn with more pull, to reflect superhuman moves. Imagine the slender ballerina as a five-pointed star and move the star into the desirable position where points of the toes and fingers are the final extension.

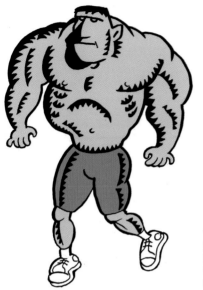

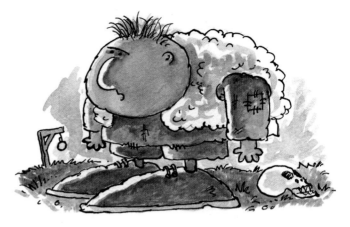

### Strong ◀
The lower body of this strong character is disproportionate to the upper frame. It has been drawn with an element of foreshortening, looking down to the feet. The small hands and lack of a neck emphasize how muscle-bound he is.

### Oafish ▲
The creature is drawn as a solid bulk, but his moon-shaped face and close-set, pinprick eyes perched above the bulbous nose describe an oafish, yet endearing monster. The impossibility of such oversized, clodhopper feet adds a comic touch.

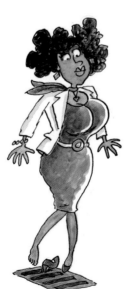

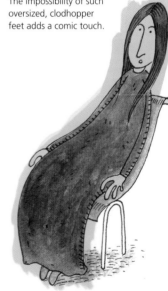

### Shapeless ▲
Beyond middle age the body becomes more amorphous. A plump, bean head sits on an equally plump, shoulderless body. Loose clothing over reduced limbs completes the look.

### Shapely ▲
An hourglass figure with enlarged chest and slender arms and legs all work together to pull the woman's frame neatly upwards. Exaggerating the legs helps emphasize her slim figure.

### Weak ▲
By moulding the figure along the seat of the chair, she is weakened because there is no implied backbone supporting her. There is a deliberate lack of skeletal structure beneath the clothes.

# Hands

A person's hand gestures usually take the supporting role to their facial expressions, but they are equally capable of replacing them. This fact makes the ability to draw hand movement with accuracy a vital skill for the cartoonist.

In the cartoon world, hand styles range from the early animators' device of only drawing three digits and a thumb on each hand to more realistic interpretations. It is more important

to gain a working knowledge of drawing the ways in which hands move – grab, twist, flatten, release, point, wave, pinch and so on – than to reproduce their anatomical construction. Try these exercises before starting out, as practice will help you to understand this most complex part of the body. With hands so readily available, the cartoonist has all that is needed to get going; there is no need to reach for a copy of *Gray's Anatomy*.

### Drawing simple hands ▶
Draw hands from the point of view of drawing tapering boxes. Digits represent one folding box, the palm another. The thumb is made of two smaller tapering cones jointed at the intersection of the palm and knuckle, jutting out sideways. Once the boxes are in place, subdivide them into four separate 'conical' digits.

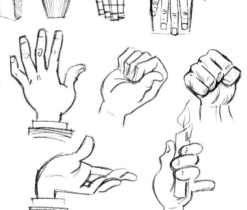

### Hands in action ▶
The best way to understand the structure and different expressive movements of hands is by observing and sketching real live hands in action. Start by drawing your own, or use photographic reference. This series of linear studies of live hands focuses on the actions rather than the anatomy.

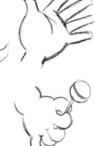
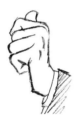
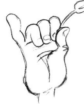

## Practice exercise: Fleshing out

Once you are confidently making linear drawings, begin to flesh out the hands. Start by looking closely at your own hands: observe the differences between the back and palm; notice how the

knuckles run in a steady curve across the back, marking where the fingers join the hand; study the palm creases; and note the way in which different finger movements change the shape of

the hand – an action made with one finger changes the hand completely when it is made with two. Make sure you vary the poses as much as possible in your fleshed-out drawings.

## Materials
- *cartridge paper*
- *waterproof fineliner pen*
- *watercolour paints*
- *No. 4 round brush*

**Tip:** Devote a sketchbook to hands, recording them at work, rest and play as often as you can. Use different materials to deliver a range of results.

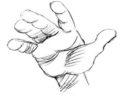

1 Using a mirror or a willing model, place the hand in position in front of you. Sketch in the main lines and the shading.

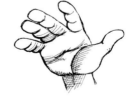

2 When you are satisfied with the sketch, go over it with a fineliner pen. Refine the hatching so that the structure is evident.

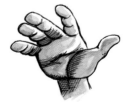

3 Tint with a flesh colour or mix of yellow ochre and red. Assume a light source from the right and leave white paper highlights.

## Cartoon hands

The principles behind drawing cartoon hands are the same as those behind drawing live hands. The connection of the joints remains the same, but the drawn style changes. Rounding off the angular edges of the hand and simplifying its parts is the best way to transform your sketches from the real to the cartoon world. Common gestural clichés, such as the clenched fist, open palm, thumbs-up and pointed finger, appear time and again. In animal anthropomorphism, the three-fingered hand is the standard convention, with a paw converting easily to a stubby hand.

**Hand style and function** ▶

Note how style never affects function. A rounded, ballooning hand still grasps an object successfully. So long as the hand is able to function convincingly and copy a range of real practices, then it is fit for the purpose of being a hand. Squarer styles always tend to look more realistic, whereas the rounder ones add extra comic expression.

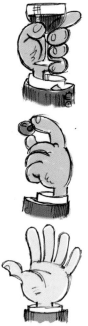
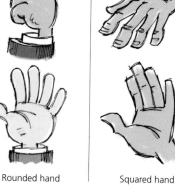
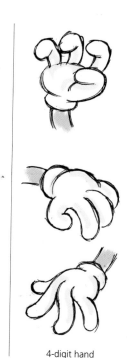

Rounded hand    Squared hand    4-digit hand

## Male and female hands

A male character can be easily recognized through the pronounced structural definition and physical exertions of the hands. A slender hand, with elegant curving positions of hand and wrist, is instantly seen as feminine.

**Gender styles** ▼ ▶

These colour ink and line studies show the edited simplicity of male and female and childlike cartoon hands. Lines are drawn solidly and creases kept to a minimum.

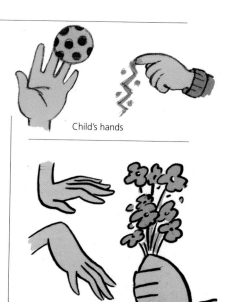

Child's hands

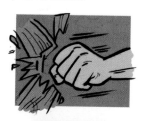

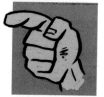

Male hands

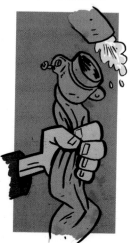

Female hands

# Feet

As essential as hands in shaping a cartoon character, feet are also very difficult to draw convincingly. An arch, a ball, a toe and five digits do not offer too much of a problem, but their role as the contact point between a figure and its surroundings is harder to get right. Their size in relation to the figure can be difficult to judge and footwear can add to the problems of foreshortening if viewed from the front.

A basic understanding of the structure of the feet is advisable rather than critical, and constructing feet out of recognizable shapes is a perfectly valid way to build the form.

When this has been mastered, it is important to consider how real feet move and how cartoon feet will move. Feet can be oddly expressive, especially when their size or movement is exaggerated. They can complement a gag by enhancing its intention or even working against it.

Legs need feet and feet need legs, and together they have a huge capacity for describing the weight and density of a comic character. Footwear is often either grossly distorted or simplified; for example big bulbous boots or floppy clown-like shoes can help to shape the humour in a cartoon.

**Drawing simple feet ▶**
Like hands, feet are constructed from tapered boxes, connected with a 'ball' socket and by dividing a third from the top of the wedge into four digits and a toe. Constructing this vital section of the anatomy through simple shapes will save you making habitual errors. Shapes help not only with scale, but also with keeping bodies in perspective.

**Feet in action ▶**
Create linear studies of feet using a soft blue pencil. Begin realistically and stylize them only when you have mastered the shapes within the foot's structure. Cartoon feet still need to display the mechanics of real ones in order to be convincing.

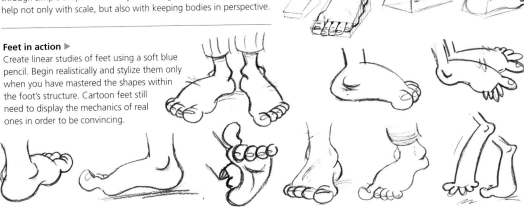

## Practice exercise: Fleshing out

So many artists avoid the issue of drawing accurate feet. They cannot consider them like any other body shape which needs to be studied closely to develop understanding. How much

tone, and where it is placed, is crucial to form a foot, because there are so many bones and ligaments working together near the skin's surface. There is little fat, so sinews and veins are highly

prominent. Places that require special attention are the ankle, which juts out above the flat plate of the foot, the long slightly curving arch and the 'ball' of the foot from which the toes emerge.

### Materials
- cartridge paper
- pencil
- waterproof fineliner pen
- watercolour paints
- No. 4 round brush

**1** Lightly sketch out in pencil first, trying to be as accurate in your initial outline as you can. Adjust any obvious mistakes.

**2** Use a fineliner to firm up the outline adding extra line 'weighting' to the joints where more pressure is working between leg and foot.

**3** Mix a flesh tint from red and yellow ochre and wash over the foot to give it form. The light source is falling on the left-hand side as we look and the tint is diluted almost to nil. Other areas where highlights should be left are on the upper surfaces of the toes and the raised surface of the ankle bone.

# Cartoon feet

The principles behind drawing cartoon feet are much the same as those used for cartoon hands. Even though they tend to be bulbous, fatter or oversized they are still modelled on the real thing before being exaggerated for humour. Rounding off angular edges and simplifying parts are the best way to transform feet from their role in the real world to a star part in the cartoon one. Turned-up toes or large clompy, clumsy feet mean that the front of a cartoon foot is often especially pronounced – the big toe is often portrayed much larger than the others put together.

**Foot style and function** ▶
A foot will always work regardless of detail. Even undefined, rectangular blocks offer a cartoon limited mobility. Some realism will elaborate the movements giving it sophistication. Reduction of digits is a style adopted by cartoonists for hands, but if a character often wears shoes this is less critical.

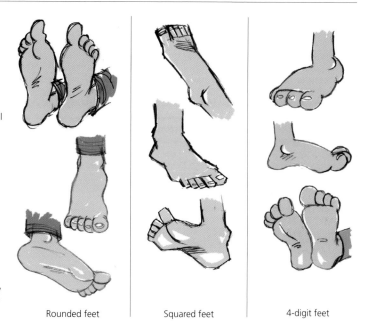

Rounded feet         Squared feet         4-digit feet

# Male and female feet

Unlike hands, it is harder to recognize a character's gender from the feet alone. Size is the main difference and male feet are often more rugged-looking. The behaviour of feet offers the biggest clue; the prima ballerina pushing up on her toes or dainty feet in high heels give a stereotyped representation of women. Drawing feet using smoother, softer lines will help to differentiate the feminine from the masculine, while using looser, livelier mark-making will bring the feet to life so that the toes appear to be wiggling.

**Gender styles** ▼
Here, strong lines show confidence in drawing the most difficult of human subjects. Tone is kept to a minimum, relying on the strength of colour to give weight and depth. The obviously female feet are sleek and elegantly poised.

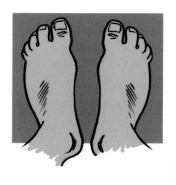

Male feet

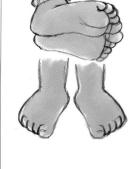

Child's feet

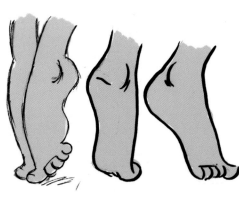

Female feet

# Clothing

Characters in strips and pocket gags need to be recognizable at a glance and your ability to describe 'types' according to groups, professions and status in society is fundamental. Clothing and hairstyles greatly help to identify characters to the audience. Many professions are instantly recognizable by their clothing and certain roles can represent particular character types, obvious examples being a nurse, police officer or cleric. In addition, the way in which a character's garments fit their frame implies a type, which in turn directly suggests status and attitude. The right accessories and props are also important in defining characters.

Economy of detail is essential for the cartoonist and it is better to use simple shapes, features and colours when dressing your characters.

## Practice exercise: Defining status through garments

A monarch reigns over his or her country: larger than life, full of proud self-importance and infallibility. Building a character's profile in your imagination is the important first step before dressing them for the role. Start by considering the qualities necessary for a king. Think about current royals, notable historical figures and fairytale characters. Choose fabrics and accessories to emphasize the elevated status of your character. Reproduce the traditional regal colours of deep azure and lazurite blue, purple and vermilion red, which historically are the costliest.

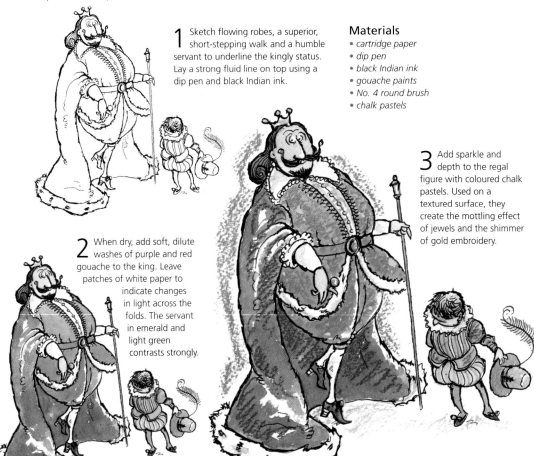

1 Sketch flowing robes, a superior, short-stepping walk and a humble servant to underline the kingly status. Lay a strong fluid line on top using a dip pen and black Indian ink.

### Materials
- *cartridge paper*
- *dip pen*
- *black Indian ink*
- *gouache paints*
- *No. 4 round brush*
- *chalk pastels*

3 Add sparkle and depth to the regal figure with coloured chalk pastels. Used on a textured surface, they create the mottling effect of jewels and the shimmer of gold embroidery.

2 When dry, add soft, dilute washes of purple and red gouache to the king. Leave patches of white paper to indicate changes in light across the folds. The servant in emerald and light green contrasts strongly.

## Professional attitude

Every profession embodies particular attitudes that can be communicated through stance and enhanced with the addition of appropriate accessories.

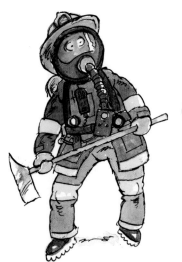

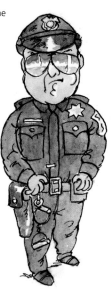

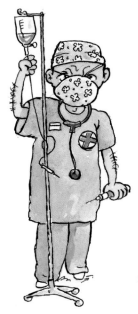

**Surgeon ◀**
This figure is imposing, courageous even, but also compassionate and caring. The face mask and medical instruments display his readiness to deal with serious emergencies.

**Tip:** Think of six different jobs and consider the dress code which accompanies each profession. Draw a character for each, keeping accessories down to a minimum. Pay attention to how clothing creases over a moving body. Compare your results with photographic reference, and make any necessary revisions where detailing is concerned.

**Fire officer ▲**
As his at-the-ready stance clearly shows, the fire officer anticipates possible risks and is poised for action, but he also remains cautious. The fire axe is purely a tool and never wielded as a weapon.

**Police officer ▲**
He appears alert and poised to defend or attack. He wears a dark, imposing uniform and hat, his eyes masked by reflective sunglasses. The badge, gun and handcuffs spell authority.

**Tramp ◀**
This individual's way of life is instantly made clear by the clothes he is wearing and the things he is carrying, which is everything he owns. A character like this offers the perfect opportunity to let your imagination roam free.

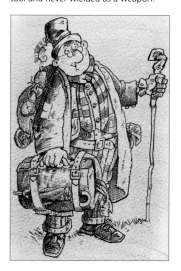

**Manual worker ▶**
This figure wears the clothing that we readily associate with heavy labouring or manual work: a lumberjack shirt, jeans and strong leather boots. He is a rugged, mud-splattered, no-nonsense individual and reveals this forcefully through his emphatic stance.

**Artist ▲**
The female painter/decorator bucks stereotypes as manual trades are usually dominated by men. She wears unisex dungarees and sports a short cropped hairstyle, to avoid hair getting in the way of her face while painting.

## Stereotypes

We identify things about ourselves that make us laugh. Cartoonists rely on using generalizations observed in characters to make a point and carry gags. Where certain conventions are used to relay information about people and can be quickly read and understood, is known as stereotyping. Making a joke about people's behaviour, characteristics and dress can border on offensive, and what is considered acceptable can change over time. Some common stereotypes are still used, even though they bear no relation to reality, which might be due to the difficulty society has breaking down long-held stereotypes.

**The average family ▼**
Casually dressed, the middle-class family stands out here because they do not stand out. Their very ordinariness and lack of distinction are matched by their uninspired characterization, reflected in their similar stances, facial expressions and colouring.

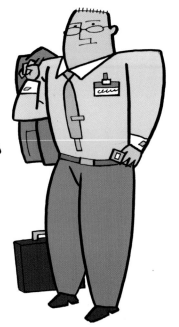

**The air hostess ▶**
The common belief that air hostesses have all the glamour of a catwalk is far from the truth. Hostesses are well groomed in fashionable uniforms, but their manner masks a huge level of safety responsibility.

**Smartly dressed businessman ▼**
He is clean-cut and dressed for power in a two-piece fitted suit. The tie is a formality associated with those who have a nine-to-five job, and the identity card denotes access into the private culture of the office. His work is portable, transported in a sturdy briefcase, and he has means of communication at his fingertips.

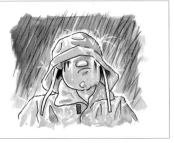

**Tip:** There are various ways in which clothing can be used to set the scene. The sou'wester offers weather clues, focusing the viewer on the narrative content without the need for a full scenic backdrop. Obscuring the character's eyes also speaks volumes to the viewer.

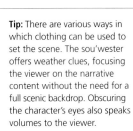

## Rich and poor ▼
Comparing opposing stereotypes reinforces the point. The immaculate, streamlined wealthy figure is a superior world away from the huddled, drab street beggar.

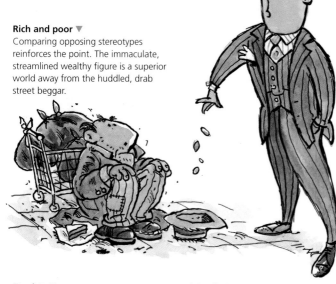

## Tourists ▼
Dressed loudly and casually, and loaded down with baggage, these guys are clearly on holiday. With pockets and bags stuffed with accessories, guidebooks in hand and cameras at the ready, they typify everyone's idea of a tourist.

## Scientist ▶
Albert Einstein was the inspiration behind this cartoon of a laboratory scientist. The mad eyes sparkle over the flat grey washes; colour only appears in the flask. Copy famous people and use stereotypes to reconstruct their full-length portraits. Emphasize distinguishing marks or features, like the way a character peers over spectacles or raises an eyebrow. Accessories are really important, as we generally think of scientists using specific equipment in their work.

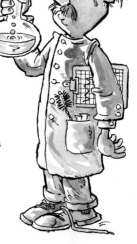

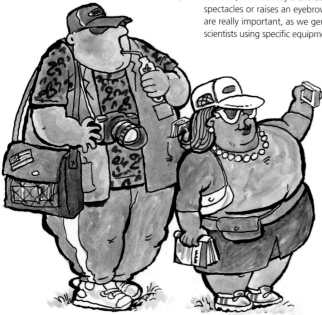

## Rastafarian ▶
The rapid growth in popularity of Jamaican reggae music linked to the Afro-Caribbean Rastafarian religion has brought with it recognized fashions – woven dreadlock hair and a knitted 'tammy' hat to hold the locks under. Bob Marley is the icon of reggae and a cool persona who is celebrated on the street.

# Shoes and hats

Although creating a cartooning style matters, content is by far the greater consideration. Detailing is essential when you are creating character profiles in your drawings. Their clothing identifies them instantly to the audience, who will interpret what they see from their own experience. Hats and shoes are important because they accessorize the everyday; they are the details that can either make a person stand out from the crowd or blend in with the rest of their peer group. In cartooning they can be used to exaggerate a character's general profile. A flat cap, for example, indicates older working-class men, or a slim, elegant pair of shoes can immediately communicate speed and power.

## Shoe styles

When we meet a new person, we scan them from top to toe before focusing on the details. The same is true of a cartoon character, and first impressions count. A character will walk into and out of frames or gesticulate within them and their footwear is as important as the rest of them. Familiarize yourself with all types of shoe and what they tell you about the wearer.

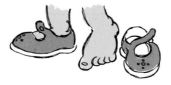

**Endearing** ▲
Small, growing feet need plenty of room. A toddler's feet are more rounded and chubbier than an adult's and the same applies to their shoes.

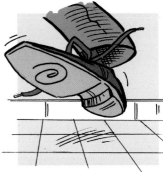

**Official** ▲
Handmade, leather-soled shoes carry their owner well, but are the enemy of small creatures. Unlike soft, rubber soles, their firm, audible stepping can send insects scurrying. The angle of this foot denotes that it is about to land on the tiles with much force.

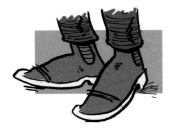

**Cool** ▲
The Chelsea boot with its Cuban heel has been at the forefront of fashion for decades. It indicates youth, cool and even a smooth operator!

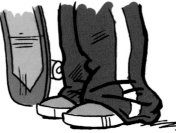

**Teenage** ▲
The skateboarder's thick-soled, chunky trainers are mostly hidden beneath tracksuit hems, but they succeed in instantly identifying their teenage wearer.

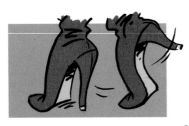

**Power crazy** ▲
The wearer of red high-heeled boots wants to be seen and heard. Note the tension created in the extreme curving of the foot arch.

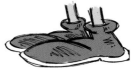

**Comedy** ▲
This nondescript shoe is used by many cartoonists. The exaggerated length and rolled tops make the legs skinny. They look soft and pliable, ideal for contorting feet into impossible positions.

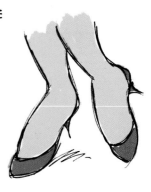

**Elegant** ▲
Stiletto heels continue the body line right down to the ground. The wearer's stance is specific: she is tilting forward slightly to compensate for the lack of support at the heel.

## Practice exercise: Building shoes

A system for constructing shoes quickly is useful and will provide you with a template that can be adapted for a variety of shapes and styles. As you practise these sorts of drawing processes, you will quickly find that it becomes second nature, allowing you to push the boundaries of your moving figures. Try studying the materials from which footwear is made. Highly polished leather creates strong contrasts and highlights that aid the 3-D modelling.

### Materials
- *cartridge paper*
- *HB pencil and dip pen*
- *black Indian ink*
- *watercolour paints*
- *No. 4 round brush*

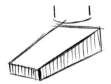 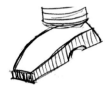 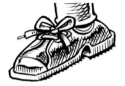 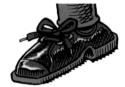

**1** Use an HB pencil to sketch the shoe as a wedge shape, with the narrow end as the toes. Repeat for the other shoe. Draw cylinders for the legs.

**2** Refine the shapes by adding trouser creases to the legs and an arch under the shoes. Shape each shoe into a gentle curve.

**3** Draw over the pencil outlines using pen and ink, and detail the features of the shoe with cross-hatching. Leave the highlights blank.

**4** Add washes of watercolour in blue for the trouser leg and brown for the shoe, keeping the white highlights intact.

## Hat styles

Treat hats as an extension of a character's personality that show off or disguise facial features. Depending on the hat, the same face can appear older or younger. Hats deliver statements of class, social grouping or profession. Headwear can be distorted, extended and elaborated to inject humour. Become a keen social observer and make sketchbook recordings of people in hats.

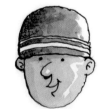

**Teenage** ▲
The beanie is a 'cool' accessory for the teens. Worn pulled down, its brimless front accentuates the youthful face.

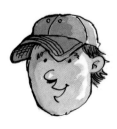

**Adult** ▲
Baseball caps are universally worn by all age groups. The extended peak can 'lead' the figure in a drawn frame.

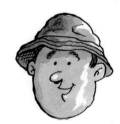

**Mature** ▲
The fishing hat is one that is unlikely to be worn in an urban environment. It is identified with older people.

## Retro dressing

Contemporary fashion defines the culture of a time and place. A character who is dressed out of their period is interesting and stands out from their surroundings. Make sure that you research the details thoroughly for an authentic look.

**Groovy** ▶
This distinctive Sixties look provides all you need to explore patterns and colourways through fabric and a variety of accessories, such as loop earrings, beads, bangle, bag and belt.

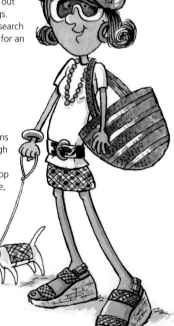

# Drawing fabrics

Art and fabrics share a special relationship. In paintings by the Dutch masters, the silk sleeves look real enough to reach out and stroke. Not only do the colours and patterns of fabrics enhance a drawing but their texture can completely alter the visual sensation. A figure standing out from the background because the surface treatment of his clothes directly contrasts with that of his setting creates a startling impact. This contrast can be achieved in a number of ways, such as using soft pastel to create a velvety fabric weave against a backdrop painted in blocks of flat gouache paint. Pastel is not an obvious choice for the cartoonist and therefore is a good example of a medium that can add surprise and finesse to your work. Colours can be blended and smudged with the fingers or a rag to soften the tones.

When you are drawing a fabric, consider its textures and tonal qualities and then choose the medium or technique that best replicates it. Studying the fabrics in your own wardrobe at close quarters is a good starting point.

## Creating fabric folds

Ink line seems an unlikely medium for rendering fabric folds, but is surprisingly effective. The secrets to success are understatement, pen control and clear stroke direction. In these examples, the cloak folds are suggested with simple black lines and tone is built with hard line hatching using a fine pen, or soft strokes with a brush or soft pen. Using colour with 'soft' media, such as pastels or watercolour, give the fabric a realistic impression and more scope.

Dutch and Danish still-life paintings from the 16th–18th centuries provide a helpful and unlikely source for showing fabric folds. The exquisite layering of colours with fresh directional strokes, then blending with white made these pictures so real that viewers felt they could reach out and actually touch the garments.

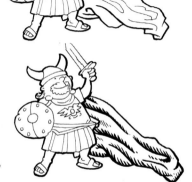

**Outline ▶**
This crisp outline is drawn with a 0.8mm fineliner pen, controlled to round the contours. A finer pen (0.3mm) details the main features, folds and creases, which are indicated with single lines.

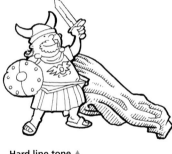

**Hard line tone ▲**
The outline is drawn in the same way as the previous example. Evenly spaced hard line strokes are then added along the folds at approximately 90 degrees to the main lines.

**Soft colour tone ◀**
Tints and shades of red are worked through the tonal range to create a 3-D effect in this full-colour version. An assumed light source shining evenly from the right helps to achieve simple tonal modelling on the figure. Note the shadowing tones, especially beneath the tunic hem on the legs.

**Soft line tone ▲**
A brush and ink/brush pen is used to 'pull' tonal strokes with regular upward, even pressure. Closer lines give greater tonal depth and can be reduced in thickness and length the further they are from the fold.

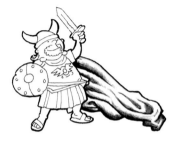

**Soft media tone ▲**
Here, the cloak is given tone using a monochrome ink wash, softened with water to achieve tonal gradation.

# Material gains

The hairstyle is correct, facial expression perfect and the clothing just right, but textural dimension takes a character to another level. Material seems to make him move under the swirly patterns.

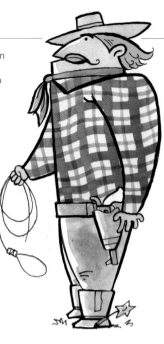

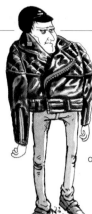

**Leather** ◀
Strong highlights along with numerous creases and folds give this jacket a shiny, reflective leather look. The creases were drawn using an ink line before adding passages of dilute watercolour.

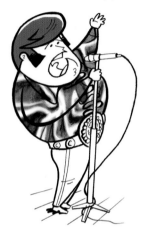

**Cashmere** ▶
Some textures need subtlety. This smartly dressed figure has been drawn on a soft-grained water-colour paper using harmonizing colours. Any further texture should be added when dry with a smudge of charcoal, to reinforce the description of the folds in a garment as it drops.

**Satin** ▲
Two colours of pastel (blue and black) are smudged together, making soft, shiny creases that create a shimmer of dark and light. In this drawing, the pastel section was drawn separately and glued in place. The ink line was then applied on top.

**Plaid** ▲
Simple, broad bands of watercolour are brushed in one direction, allowed to dry and then brushed, overlapping, the other way. It is always best to keep check patterns simple.

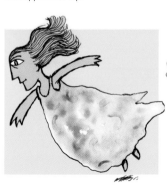

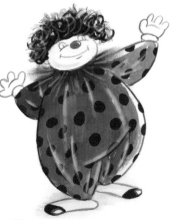

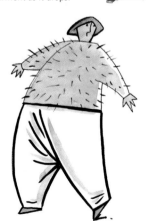

**Gossamer** ▲
The wet-on-wet technique that creates this floating fabric uses a heavy watercolour wash inside the holding outline. Colour is dripped on to the wash and swirled with a brush.

**Silk** ▲
A combination of watercolour washes with solid gouache spots and smudged pastel strokes for the ruff, highlighted fabric creases and hair delivers this crisp, yet airy effect.

**Mohair** ▲
Light, 'dash' touches with a brush over a soft pink watercolour wash create a mohair jumper: a simple technique that matches the drawing style.

# Creative fabrics

Finding creative solutions to fabric rendering can be fun and easy to achieve. You can invent lively, colourful, attention-grabbing garments by exploiting a blend of traditional and non-traditional techniques. Collaging other materials into a cartoon can add humour, especially where the cutting is irregular, the shapes unexpected or the overall look surprising.

The surface pattern of a fabric or a particular weave can add an extraordinary dynamic when used outside its usual scale. A standard design, such as tartan or check, applied disproportionately to a tiny cartoon character can look surreal and funny. With a little imagination, a comedy character's body can be constructed from a scrap of fabric or paper. Try to experiment: a figure with no dimensional depth whose squat

shape breaks every rule of proportion and with limbs to match has the potential to become an amusing and versatile character, capable of defining its own movements and behaviour.

Consider how choice of media can be used to describe different fabrics. A thin, gauzy swatch of silk, for example, may be best replicated using thin, translucent watercolour washes, or perhaps a rougher woollen weave requires short, heavy strokes of acrylic paint to define its texture.

Fun should always be the motivating factor for anyone interested in learning about cartoons, and by experimenting with alternative materials and methods, you will positively sparkle with new ideas and achieve results that you never previously imagined were possible.

## Developing an adventurous side

Depart from traditional techniques and consider experimental ways to produce certain textured effects using alternative materials. Monotonous cross-hatching or labour-intensive painting are no

longer necessary labours of love in the contemporary world of art and design, where virtually any material can now be scanned and converted into 'print-ready' artwork for publication. Even

3-D work can be photographed and the images easily uploaded into image-manipulation programs, such as Adobe Photoshop. Costumes are a good place to begin experimenting.

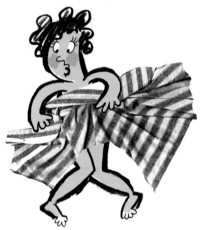

**Towel** ◀
Vertical strokes of blue crayon on the towel indicate texture and folds. They are in direct contrast to the bold, charcoal-and-wash figure. Contrasting textures are becoming more popular now that households can scan most materials.

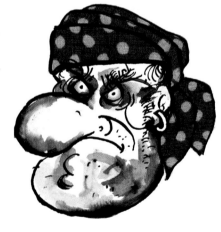

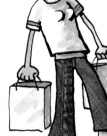

**Tip:** Get into the habit of collecting interesting scraps to incorporate into your cartoon work. These can be fabric samples, textured papers or a variety of other materials.

**Polka dot** ▲
Spotted polka-dot fabrics or those with a consistent pattern are great folded materials, because the dots chop off naturally by folds, delivering an illusion of fabric being wrapped or folded.

**Denim** ◀
Use real denim for denim trousers and jeans because it is much simpler than trying to paint the tight weave and washed out seams.

**Aztec pattern** ▼
Finding new uses for existing fabrics is fun. This hankie, with its South American pattern, was made into a large shoulder shawl, its strength of pattern scaled beautifully.

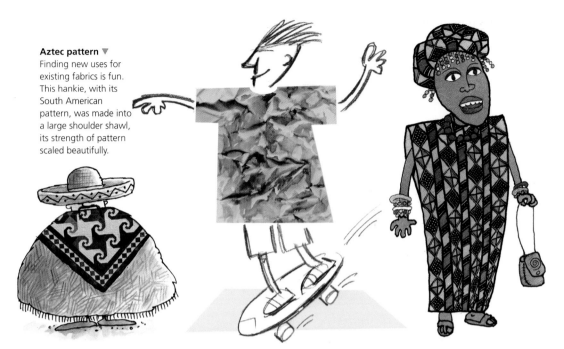

**Tartan** ▼
A unique pattern of criss-crossed horizontal and vertical coloured bands, tartan is specific to Scottish, Irish and Welsh clans. As the weave is heavy, the chances of folding it successfully are limited, but this offers the cartoon a charming flatness.

**Camouflage** ▲
This realistic camouflage effect is produced by soaking thin paper in coffee, crumpling it when dry and loosely brushing with olive green watercolour. The sheet is ironed flat and the neat T-shirt shape cut out and glued on to card. The character details are drawn with red pencil.

**Ethnic** ▲
A repeat pattern of flat, coloured gouache shapes tapers as the fabric drops to the feet. Use patterned fabric or paper for a short-cut solution. Lighter washes are used elsewhere and the coloured dotted beads and bold outline added at the very end.

**Gingham** ◄
A popular pattern found on tablecloths and shirts, as well as being the standard uniform of a chef, gingham is a very versatile material. Scan a piece and use the seams to show bagginess.

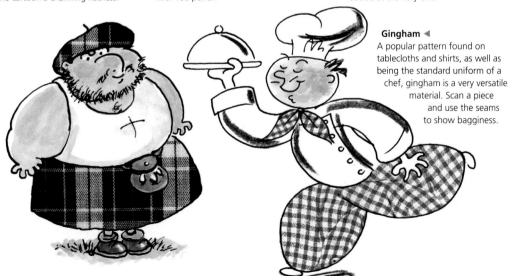

# Injecting life

One of the greatest cartoon challenges is making a static image appear to move. Movement can be shown through a sequence of images or through devices that imply motion.

It is important to be able to sketch characters in active positions or postures: the right configuration of legs, arms and body twists will bring your drawings alive. Actions are greatly exaggerated in the cartoon world and emphasizing

angles is essential. Techniques for animating figures include drawing multiple images and the simple use of 'whizzy' marks called motion lines. Trailing behind a character, these parallel strokes jettison in all directions, implying high-speed activity. Overstating the body language and experimenting with the positioning of these marks will heighten the effect and increase the element of humour.

## Get moving

The right medium is all-important when it comes to animating characters. A mechanical even-flowing pen, for example a rollerball or a fineliner, will automatically create static marks,

making the job harder. Pressure-sensitive mark-makers are the best choice and a soft-grade pencil, felt-tip pen or brush pen will naturally deliver the liveliest results. The figure studies on these

pages are all created using a brush pen. Its flexible brush tip allows you to deliver thick and thin lines easily. It is this lively variation in strokes that achieves the impression of energetic action.

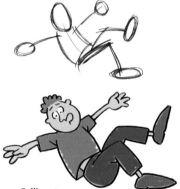

**Falling** ▲
The pose here is centred around the character's mid-point, where his bottom will land. The limbs flail accordingly and his expression is one of surprise.

**Sitting** ▲
The legs are at right angles to the body and the knees are slightly bent. The arm leans on the ground to confirm the stance.

**Fleeing** ▲
A whole-body shift to the right with all the weight and balance on the right foot denotes anticipation. The swing of the arms to the left allows motion lines to be drawn along the same axis.

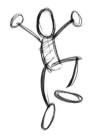

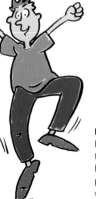

**Leaping** ▶
Arms are raised high into the air and the stretch of the body follows. Keep the pose open for maximum leaping effect. Note the motion lines that echo the upward sweep of the legs.

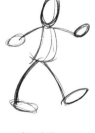

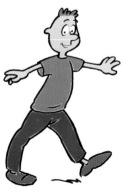

**Balanced and slow** ▲
Everything is held firmly within the frame of the body and the hands and feet are symmetrically placed. Evenly balanced shapes will always appear the most static.

# Flowing movement

A sequence of movements is created from a series of single poses that flow from one to the next. Although cartoon people can move in ways that are impossible for real people, the course of their actions must appear to be believable – the jumping man below moves convincingly through the smooth curve indicated by the dotted line, for example. Spend time observing actual human or creature movement. The key is to draw simplified movements initially in a skeletal kind of way and when the body posture and position of limbs are correct, flesh out the figures and stylize them to suit your cartoon task.

### Running ▼

The angle is dynamic, with a forcefully placed leading arm and leg, counterbalanced by their opposite limbs. The motion lines trail the body at its most static point, allowing the limbs to be free to express themselves and direct the motion of the figure. Motion lines should not be overused as they can actually have the counter effect of appearing to hold the figure back.

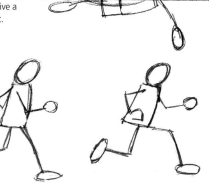

### Swimming ▶

A swimmer is held along a horizontal line. Up and down curves of the line give the appearance of swimming. Longer, more flowing lines give a greater illusion of movement.

### Action sequence ▶

The figure runs with arms opposed and the body's weight over the leading leg. The arms swing back on take-off and the legs thrust the body forward. The right leg lands first, bent under the momentum of the upper body. The hips follow the curve of action. Returning to ground involves the body swinging forwards as it follows the landing limbs.

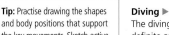

**Tip:** Practise drawing the shapes and body positions that support the key movements. Sketch active, flowing movements in pen or pencil, applying pressure to the areas where the body weight is centred. Heavier lines should correspond to the origin of the movement. When proficient at the moving stick figure, progress to add bodily characteristics.

### Diving ▶

The diving action is definite and dynamic. The leap into the unknown is made in the belief that the diver's fall will be broken by the tension of the water. This is why the diver's extensions are so powerful and so extended over a very short phase of time frames.

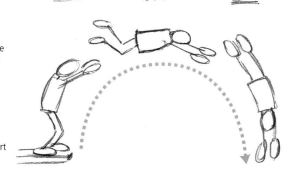

# Cause and effect

Objects added to a scene can give clarity to the action because an explanatory narrative has been set up; movement can be more fully defined when a cause is added to the drawn 'effect'. The prop acts as an extension to the body, which in turn helps to exaggerate the shape of the pose. A good example is a figure struggling to carry an object that is too large, heavy or uncontrollable. Build your confidence by making simple pencil sketches of the key poses shown here. Focus on illustrating the action with clean lines; the detail can be added later. The best place to practise is in your sketchbook, scribbling down real-life situations where people interact with objects in their daily routines.

## Exaggerating movement

To show cause and effect clearly, exaggerate every movement, body position, counterbalance and displacement. Movement can be even more fully defined when a cause is added to the drawn outcome. Remember that the viewer must be able to catch the meaning of the sequence immediately or the gag may be lost. If there are strong contrasts between cause and effect frames, the meaning will be understood.

**Slipping** ▶
This action shows the body tipping away through a definite arc. This is achieved by tilting the body back through the pelvis and foreshortening one leg. The banana skin is vital in that it centres the action of the figure, and presents the origin of the slip.

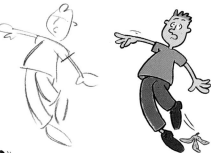

**Opening** ▼
Framing figures is a neat device which can develop a narrative interplay between inside and outside activities. The figure is placed centrally holding the frame and anticipates what is about to occur from the left.

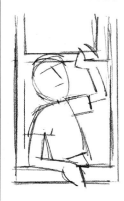

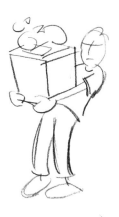

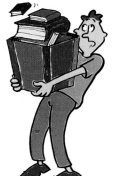

**Carrying** ◀
The backward lean is a pose that demonstrates overcompensation at its most exaggerated. It clearly tells us that the load is heavy. The toppling books add a touch of humour. The facial expression underpins the angst felt by the character, and the viewer knows that a tumble is imminent.

**Catching** ▶
A critical drop of a catch in baseball or cricket game could mean losing. The expression says it all. The figure lunges forward extending his right leg and foot. The ball drops along a trajectory angle, where he anticipates the catch. The 'will he, won't he?' clause anticipates cause and effect.

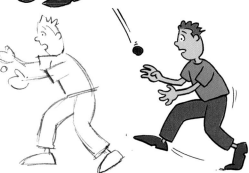

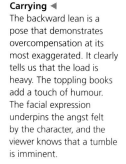

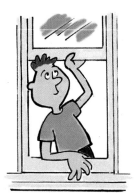

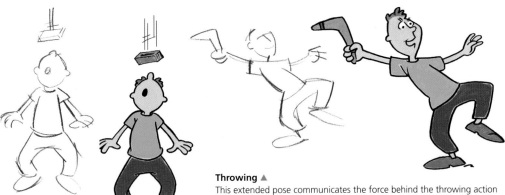

**Throwing ▲**

This extended pose communicates the force behind the throwing action and the distance the object must travel. The figure stretches back so far that one leg lifts up, while the other is bent under the body's weight. A boomerang or ball is effective because it forces the figure to stretch back, thereby producing a counterpoint for the stretching out of the left leg.

**Startled ▲**

As the brick hurtles towards him, the figure is frozen helplessly in the moment. Exaggerating all movements and holding them motionless emphasizes the pose. The brick dictates the focus of the cartoon. The figure beneath will respond to it and engage with it, wherever it drops in an attempt to avoid being hit.

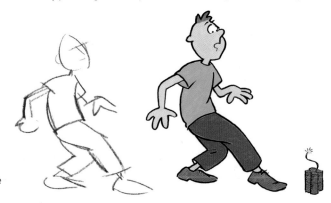

**Cautious ▶**

The retracting action of this figure implies controlled, tentative movements. The wary expression on his face is as telling as the pose. Dynamite is small, but deadly! It is absurd that a figure should be so cowered over something so small and static. But this set-up enhances the joke, and increases the suspense.

## Objects and light

Light physically attracts the viewer's eye – a very practical device to ensure that a cartoon is read in the correct way. Photoshop and Illustrator blends do this well and have become a stock-in-trade of the contemporary cartoonist's techniques. Dark from the right leading to light on the left moves the viewer's direction from right to left.

**Light and meaning ▼**

In this frame he is seen fleeing from the ghost, with light at its centre, and in the other frame running for the beer, with light illuminating the bar. The figure is identical in both frames, but the meaning is totally different with the addition of selected, relevant objects, their placement and light direction.

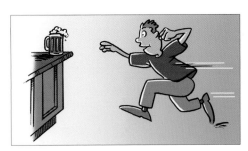

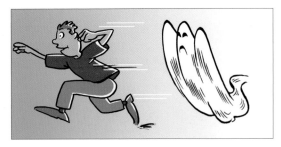

# Distortion

It is a natural progression in cartooning to use distortion to emphasize action. Such shorthand can be used to convey a range of meanings and also increase the comic effect by giving ordinary subjects larger-than-life qualities. Reducing or enlarging details beyond the norm, for example, draws

attention and highlights meaning. This very useful technique is an important part of the cartoonist's repertoire. A good start to grasping its capabilities is by distorting a regular shape, such as a cube, in a variety of ways and noting the effects, then applying them to your cartoons.

| Regular cube | Force from one side | Equal force from top down | Downward force from one edge | Equal force from below | Stretched |

## Applying distortion

Knowing how much exaggeration to apply must be learnt. Always weigh decisions against intention. Consider carefully which parts of the drawing will benefit from more attention, then test

the effect. Remember that the point of distorting certain features is to communicate the cartoon's meaning more forcefully. Bear in mind that distorting a character's features

transforms them into a caricature and enhances comic effect. This often increases as the story becomes more critical. There are no limits to levels of distortion in cartooning.

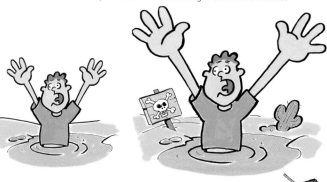

**Part-body distortion** ◀
Sometimes distorting only part of the body will achieve the desired effect. In this case, the large hands literally extend a cry for help from the sinking figure.

**Increasing effect** ▼
The figure remains the same size, but the agony of the foot's predicament is amplified in a series of three separate drawings, each a quarter size larger than the one before.

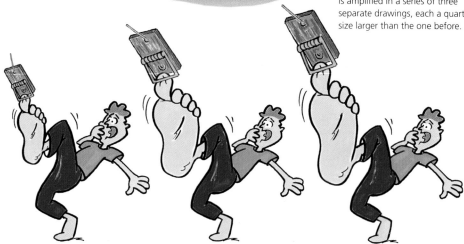

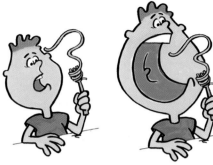

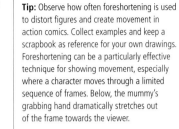

**◄ Extreme distortion**
Narrative sequences can benefit from extreme distortion. Here, the sudden mouth enlargement to cope with an escaping spaghetti strand is unexpected and comical. The jump in size is highly animated, even though this occurs over just two frames.

**Tip:** Observe how often foreshortening is used to distort figures and create movement in action comics. Collect examples and keep a scrapbook as reference for your own drawings. Foreshortening can be a particularly effective technique for showing movement, especially where a character moves through a limited sequence of frames. Below, the mummy's grabbing hand dramatically stretches out of the frame towards the viewer.

**Exaggerated foreshortening ▼**
In the second drawing, distorted foreshortening makes the body look pushed up and squashed. Compare it to the first and its purpose (to show the figure from the ants' viewpoint) is clear.

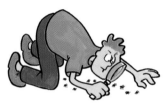

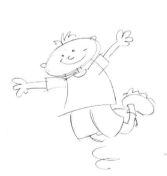

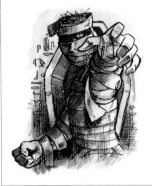

## Practice exercise: Metonymic distortion

The technique of twisting, enlarging and stretching bodily proportions for a comical or enhanced effect is called metonymic distortion. It is a visual substitute for a character's physical or emotional attributes.

The fact that children's bones are naturally more pliable than those of adults is a gift for the cartoonist. Flexibility and suppleness are ideal characteristics for producing animated, humorous drawings.

### Materials
- *cartridge paper*
- *pencil*
- *No. 2 round brush*
- *black Indian ink*
- *coloured inks*

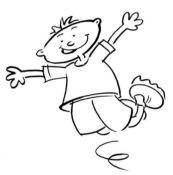

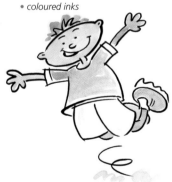

**1** Sketch the springing child in pencil. Keep the lines flowing and think of the figure in terms of simple shapes: ovals for the head and feet; flexible rectangles for the body and limbs.

**2** When you are happy with the shapes, proportion and pose, carefully load the brush with black Indian ink and go over the pencil lines. Remember to maintain flowing lines.

**3** When dry, brush relaxed washes of dilute blue, orange and red ink on to the T-shirt, hair and shoes so that they are just tinted. Mix a touch of yellow with slightly more red for the flesh colour and dilute with water.

# Object interaction

A cartoon character rarely appears on the page out of context. There is usually a setting and any number of objects to dress that scene and help the viewer to understand the background to the developing narrative. People In the real world interact with their surroundings in the simplest of ways – sitting on chairs, lifting, moving or placing objects – and the same is true in the cartoon world. In complex interactions, characters may work through an intricate series of tasks with objects, such as using machinery.

Not only are objects essential to the construction of the cartoon narrative but they can also considerably enhance the character and his or her comic routine. Think of the early movies. Where would Buster Keaton or Charlie Chaplin have been without their sets and props? In the cartoon world, these props can even come alive and interact with the characters. Characters also interact with one another, which carries the narrative structure forwards. Dialogue is the obvious form of interaction, but expressions and body language also speak volumes, especially in a group context where the storyline must rely on action instead of words. Perhaps this is why cartoons are such a successful narrative form. Their mimicry of real life imitates the subtle body language that we use instinctively and recognize immediately. Hence, our response to an embarrassing, humorous or unfortunate situation played out in a cartoon is to smile, laugh or sympathize.

Learning the art of interaction will widen the scope for creating more powerful visuals and interesting narratives. To be able to sketch a scene from your head with any form of interaction is to be using the skills of an actor or director. Style and content are of key importance to the effectiveness of the interplay, as the following examples and exercises show.

## Practice exercise: Interacting with furniture

It is worth learning to draw all kinds of furniture from all kinds of perspectives. Keep a sketchbook with you and never miss an opportunity to practise. Unusual specimens can be particularly useful, so the next time you visit a stately home, do not disregard the four-poster bed or ornate garden seat. The more you consider the construction of a piece of furniture and how it looks from a range of different viewpoints, the more convincing your narratives will be. Observing and sketching people interacting with furniture from every angle is the obvious next step.

**Chair sketches ▶**
Pose chairs and other items of furniture and draw them. Chairs that are obviously old or well-worn are especially interesting. They have seen a lifetime of interaction and can be imagined as characters in their own right.

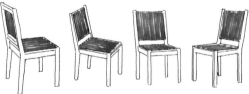

### Materials
- *cartridge paper*
- *fineliner pen*
- *black Indian ink*
- *No. 2 round brush*
- *coloured inks*
- *black charcoal pencil*

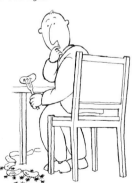

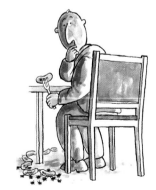

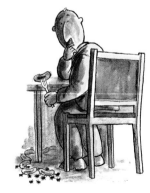

**1** Use a fineliner pen to sketch your cartoon, taking extra care over the position and shape of the chair and how the diner is sitting on it. Next, draw the ants and sausages.

**2** Add form to the line with a wash of dilute ultramarine blue ink. Choose a direction of light source, in this case from the right. Leave the lit areas on the right-hand sides blank, as shown.

**3** Add the yellow ink wash to show light thrown on to the highlit areas. Finish the cartoon by deepening the areas of shadow using lightly smudged black charcoal pencil to make a grey tint.

# Styling and scaling objects

The way in which you draw objects is every bit as important as how you draw figures. We are all well aware of our surroundings and the relative sizes and scales of the inanimate objects they contain. Exaggerating or giving life to those objects is a great way to enhance the comical content of a cartoon. It also opens a pathway to a world of fantasy or illusion. It is this licence to alter reality that makes cartooning so enjoyable. Trying out different styles and drawing or painting techniques brings mood and attitude to your settings and a chance to learn what works best with your scaling and positioning of objects.

### Contrasts of interaction ▼
The bulky weight of a subject interacting with both a lightweight object and a contrasting subject emphasizes the humour of this gag.

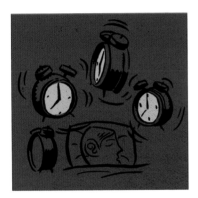

### Fantasy interaction ▲
Through the anticipation of the 'suspended' moment, the floating alarm clocks tell us that the character is about to wake up. They provide enough setting for such a simple narrative.

### Continuous interaction ▼
The panting man, the sweaty brow, the impossible climb and the broken shopping bag draw out the idea that he is struggling against the odds. A huge flight of stairs is implied by showing neither beginning nor end.

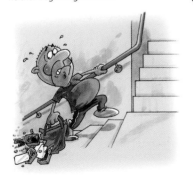

### Armchair interaction ▲
The plump enveloping contours and soft folds of the armchair personify the act of gentle cradling. The cosy subject matter of a cup of tea and a good book, coupled with the woman's serene expression, and use of warm, harmonious colours give us a message of comfort and security.

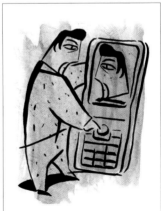

**Tip:** Break the rules of scale to make a point. The contrast of the huge mobile (cell) phone against the figure allows the phone screen to metamorphose into a mirror. This brings home the gag's point of the difficulties of trying to talk to oneself.

# Character interaction

How characters interact can determine the development of a cartoon narrative and allow a storyline to change with ease. The dynamic of a scene alters at the point where new personalities are introduced. Expressing their characters subsequently defines their dominant or secondary roles in the narrative. The focus of a scene is also determined by the behaviour of its characters and the cartoonist has the power to move them, like pawns in a chess game, to bring about certain outcomes. People and animals are social creatures and their complex interactions are often revealed in particular, if not peculiar ways. This inevitable fact is something for the cartoonist to exploit.

## Understanding dominant and secondary relationships

Complex cartoon figures do not need to be drawn to grasp spatial relationships. Sphere shapes are perfectly adequate to reveal how the two subjects of different sizes and positions affect the visual impressions of objects in a pictorial space. These types of exercises are crucial if you are to master the design of cartoon frames, and the interaction of figures within them. With such knowledge you can confidently construct exciting and challenging narratives with pace and interest.

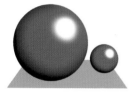

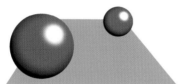

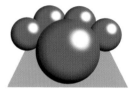

**Dominant and secondary** ▲
Pitching a more important character against a minor character is a dynamic contrast commonly used by cartoonists.

**Dominant and distant secondary** ▲
This interaction subtly changes the relationship. Being at the same eye level allows their 'conversation'.

**Dominant and multiple secondaries** ▲
The power and energy of the dominant character is clear when the scene is crowded with secondaries.

**Interaction at a distance** ▶
With careful positioning, two figures can interact even though they are far apart. The flight of the love letter links the characters, and being placed on the same eye level permits the interaction. As a result, a silhouette is all that is needed to define the secondary character's role and importance.

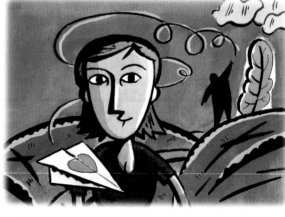

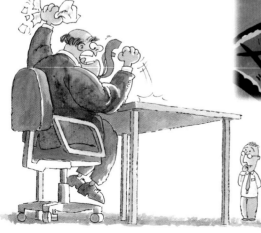

◀ **Superior versus inferior**
This confrontation would not be as powerful without the contrast in the characters' sizes. The viewpoint from below – the worker's eye level – acts to reinforce the scene. The cartoon offers two possible interpretations: does the worker's size show that he is aware of his guilt and inferiority, or has the interview with the enraged boss diminished him?

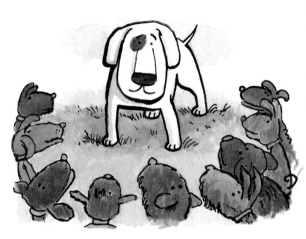

**Dominant and multiple secondaries** ▲
A major character who is different, a dog of a different species, larger and standing apart from the pack, is undoubtedly its leader. The others in a semi-circle around him, with all eyes on him, bring the focus to the centre making the viewer position on an par with them. In their uniformity they are multiple secondaries and he is the dominant. With the major character looking straight ahead there is an opportunity to develop detailed facial expressions.

**Dominant and multiple secondaries** ▼
The pirate captain opens the treasure chest only to find it empty! His crew are clustered around expectantly in the immediate background, framing this central moment and adding drama and suspense. Their position also enhances the primary role of their leader. The viewer knows instantly who is in command and the monotone light grey wash over the secondary characters helps to reinforce the message.

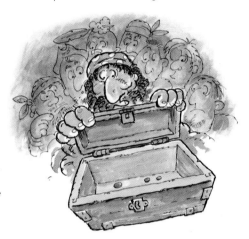

## Interaction of thought

Subjects can appear to share similar thoughts and intentions, even when the outer differences between them are quite considerable. The style of drawing and careful direction of lighting, positioning, colour and expressions can establish interaction between characters that would be impossible to achieve in other ways. The immediacy of the cartoon medium means that visual signals such as these can be clearly transmitted to the audience.

**Enhancing interaction** ▼
Here, the same cartoon has been redrawn, but this time using strong, saturated hues of blue and yellow as a way of unifying the picture, making the two characters seem inseparable.

**Two faces interacting** ▶
The stare of the eyes, depth of the brows and similarity of the marks used to draw the two faces links them. They are closely positioned and the use of black shadows helps to merge their faces, reinforcing the idea of an identical reaction.

**Tip:** Work out the composition of an interactive cartoon using simple shapes, such as spheres. Move these around, altering their relative sizes and positions, until you are entirely satisfied with the outcome. This process of art direction will lead to stronger final results.

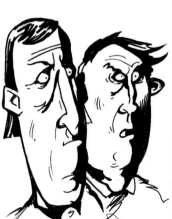

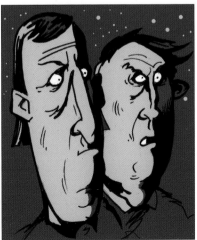

# Multiple characters

A scene that includes multiple characters can create or draw attention to a background, or it can be a device that spotlights a leading character. Equally, a whole crowd can become the centre of attention.

Illustrator Martin Handford's famous *Where's Wally?* books hide the woolly hatted, scarf-wearing hero in vast crowd scenes for the reader to find. The success of the game relies on the hundreds of similar-sized, distinctive figures that create a camouflage for Wally. It is important that multiple character drawings are used with care. Their purpose is not to clutter a scene or, more importantly, detract from the central focus. Your choice of colours or varying the strength of mark can alleviate this. Not forgetting either that including too many figures can exhaust the artist!

## Practice exercise: Dominant and multiple secondaries

It is important to realize that you cannot possibly include every detail. Work out your composition in simple shapes before starting the final artwork. First, define the area below the stage for the crowd that is swaying, singing along and calling out. Devote the remaining third to the empty stage on which you will place the singer, the focal point of the composition.

### Materials
- *cartridge paper*
- *0.5mm, 1mm, 2mm fineliner pens*
- *No. 4 round brush*
- *coloured inks*

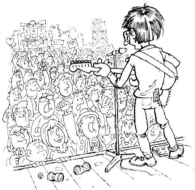

1 Draw the main elements using a variety of pen sizes to give good weighting and depth. Use a 0.5mm fineliner pen for the background figures, 1–2mm for the singer and the stage. Draw the crowd head-to-head as simple caricatures. Having no space in between them will give an even tone.

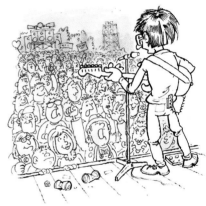

2 Drop a pale blue ink wash into the farthest, uppermost part of the picture in order to differentiate the foreground from the background.

3 Dilute the blue further and lay a faint tint over the crowd to knock back the blackness of the drawn lines. Add dilute stains of yellow ochre and red to selected areas so that they are totally coloured. Lay stronger colour washes over the foreground stage, guitar, hair, jeans, shoes and shadows on the shirt.

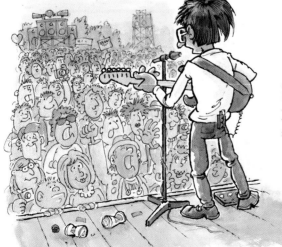

**Tip:** In your sketchbook, practise drawing quick, non-detailed caricature faces bearing a range of expressions, should the need arise. See how far you can edit out the facial information and still hold a likeness, or a definite characteristic or emotion.

# Focus and viewpoint

As the creator, you have the power to use characterization, gesture and emotional response to direct eyes and minds to a selected section of a drawing and to tell a specific story. Learning to control your focus, and therefore the focus of the audience, is hard work. Through experience you will gain the confidence to leave spaces where nothing is happening, which is very liberating. Look at published cartoons and note how universally this particular principle is applied.

### Subject and audience ▶
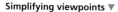

The barbecue is amusing as it draws attention to a single hamburger. The dramatic flourish of the designer chef tossing herbs is reminiscent of a conductor holding a concert audience under his spell. A simple, light approach ensures that the earnest expressions of the guests are not lost. Broad washes of three colours only keep the whole picture simple and focused.

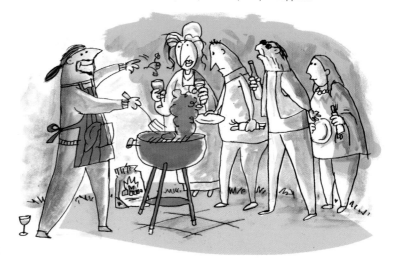

### Simplifying viewpoints ▼

Where there are many figures to sketch, choose an easy viewpoint. This drawing keeps a low viewpoint on the crowd. What is visible of them is limited, but successfully implies a large gathering. The focus falls on the man just left of centre. He is drawn in slightly more detail than the rest and is gazing upwards in contrast to everyone else's downcast eyes. His interaction with the UFO is defined by the dramatic yellow highlight running down the side of his face.

### Densely populated scene ▶

Hunting a figure in a crowd is a popular game popularized by the illustrator Martin Handford. The thrill of picking characters out in a crowd is not new; satirists, like James Gillray, had been doing variations on it for years. Typical tricks include creating figures with similar characteristics – skin tones or clothing – who are doing similar things.

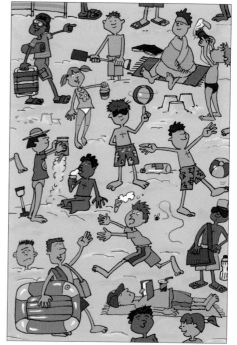

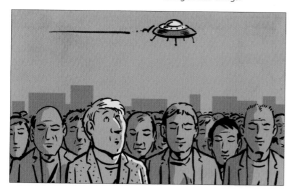

# Anthropomorphism

The technique of giving an animal human characteristics is known as anthropomorphism. It works the other way too in that human characteristics can be attributed to animals. In cartooning, anthropomorphism is often further extended to giving inanimate objects a life of their own.

Depicting animals as human or even superhuman is neither new nor exclusive to cartooning. Many ancient Egyptian gods, for example, were drawn as a combination of an animal head with a human body. The role of animals in cartoons is often as an accessory to a central human subject. The animal is a foil, fool or spoof character, set against the main subject in order to enhance particular qualities. Where an animal is the central

focus, its persona is based firmly on recognizable human qualities. Walt Disney's Mickey Mouse was one of the first examples of a popular cartoon animal character, and today anthropomorphism is the commonest format used by the big-screen animators.

Cartoonists can apply the same techniques in giving life to inanimate objects. If an object has a particular function, this can be amalgamated into the cartoon character you wish to create. Similarly, the outer appearance of an object can suggest personality; for example on a simple level, a shiny mechanical object may suggest a tough or forceful character, while a soft, tactile one implies warmth and generosity.

## Practice exercise: Anthropomorphizing everyday objects

A toaster springs to life as soon as the lever is pushed down. It heats up, glows red and chars the toast. Red not only symbolizes heat but is also associated with evil or danger. Its menacing

personality is evident and it is clear that if you get too close there is the risk of getting burnt. The full transformation into a demonic character, complete with a tail, prodding fork and flames, is apt.

### Materials
- *cartridge paper*
- *soft blue pencil*
- *black Indian ink*
- *No. 3 round brush*
- *coloured inks*

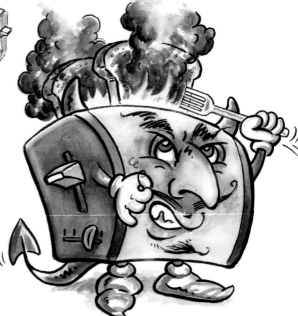

**1** Study and sketch the toaster. Look for the most dynamic angle to portray your character. At this point, also decide whether any of the levers or buttons can be made to resemble facial or body features.

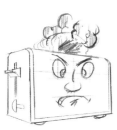
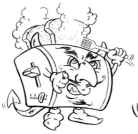

**2** Draw the toaster and add eyes, nose and mouth pulling a hot-tempered expression. Relate the expression to the smoke billowing from the top of the appliance.

**3** Redraw the toaster, curving the body and adjusting the expression. Add demonic features, a tail, glove- and sock-type hands and feet, a prodding fork and twirled moustache.

**4** With everything in place, ink over the lines and add subtle washes of sepia, yellow, red and blue to give solidity and form. Note how the colours do not have to be vivid in order to carry the message successfully.

## Practice exercise: Anthropomorphizing animals

A fierce crocodile can be tamed with just a few human touches. Plumping him up gives an air of friendliness and his proportions are like a child's, with chunky feet, stubby arms and big eyes. The jaws are rounded into a benign, almost toothless mouth. Flowered Bermuda shorts complete the transformation into a cool guy who would not hurt a fly.

### Materials
- *cartridge paper*
- *dip pen*
- *black Indian ink*
- *No. 4 round brush*
- *coloured inks*

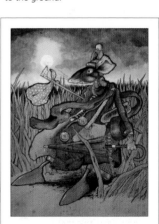

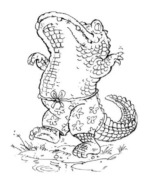

1 Pencil sketch a crocodile and make him friendly by shortening his arms and giving him a tubby belly with similar proportions and actions to a toddler.

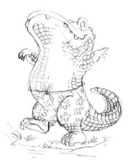

2 Study and sketch pictures of real crocodiles, then adjust them by rounding and shortening the body and jaw. Bring the animal upright and make him walk slightly on tiptoe. There is no need to draw all the scales.

3 Real crocodiles are not green, but we recognize them as such from children's books. Lay down olive green washes, then do the same for the shorts, using cobalt blue and crimson red. Finally, add a yellow ochre wash to the ground.

## Simplifying ideas

Anthropomorphic touches can simplify and make complex ideas accessible. The notion of green energy can be difficult or lengthy to explain, but its relationship to the domestic user is easily shown through this friendly cartoon.

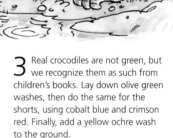

**The self-sufficient happy house** ▶
The house is squashed, making it less real and giving it a soft facial structure. The windows make natural eyes, which look up admiringly at the friendly wind turbine. The colours combine warm contrast with harmony.

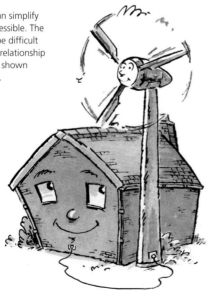

**Tip:** Look out for and compile examples of anthropomorphic animals from children's literature or films. This rat's human-like character is made believable by the familiar clothing and artefacts he carries.

# The cartoon environment

Characters work best in a setting. This chapter offers the opportunity, through consideration of viewpoint and perspective, lighting, scale, focus and mood, to place your characters in believable worlds, which come to life and tell their story.

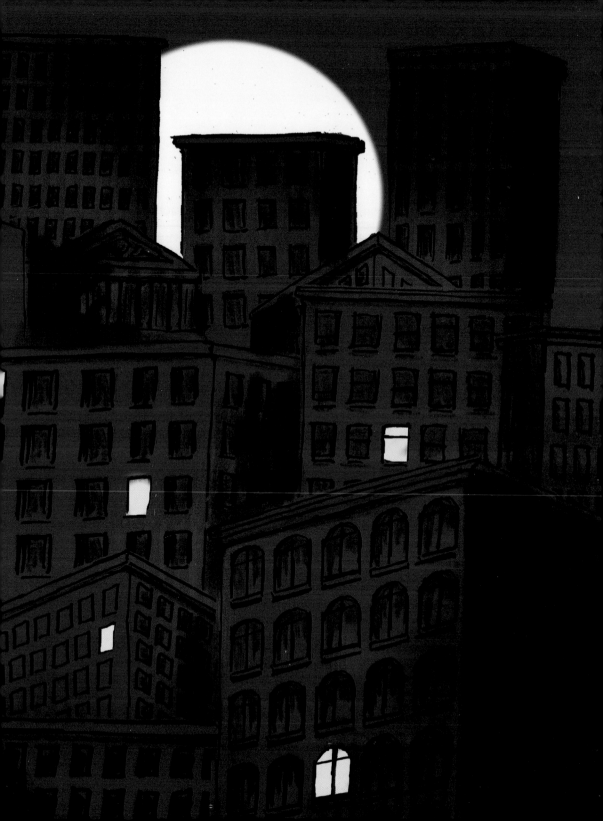

# Settings

Setting the scene so that ideas are easily transmitted to the reader is vital. Your choice of background needs to be correct, with enough detail to contextualize the story, but not so much that it detracts from it. Having said this, the scene can be as complex as you wish and observed from any number of viewpoints, real or imagined.

If you wish to place your cartoon characters in a realistic space, it may be necessary to apply the rules of perspective and draw the figures and objects accordingly. The rules can be relaxed for smaller gag cartoons, but are essential for the delivery of action-packed comic or graphic novel-style spreads, where a constantly changing viewpoint enhances the dynamic and is standard layout practice.

The positioning of figures and objects within the picture planes will determine the way in which the cartoon conveys its message. Your three picture planes – the fore-, mid- and background – need careful consideration.

The foreground tends to lead the viewer into the picture and conveniently frames the setting with a window-like boundary that assists focus. Most of the cartoon's action, dialogue and interaction resides in the midground. It is also where a full, objective overview of the setting can be made. The background establishes the setting by anchoring its features. The placement of the horizon line here determines scale, depth and perspective, unifying all the elements of the picture and ensuring that their juxtaposition makes sense.

## Two- and three-point perspective

The theory of perspective, based on mathematical principles, scales and places relative objects in the reality that we observe. The laws of optics state that the farther away an object is, the

smaller it will appear. Where objects recede into the distance along a straight line, they appear to reduce in height and converge to a point known as the vanishing point, which sits on the

horizon line, also known as eye level. By drawing lines radiating out from it, and placing the straight lines of an object along them, you create what is known as one-point perspective.

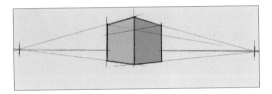

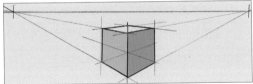

**Two-point low horizon** ▲
In two-point perspective, two separate vanishing points are visible, both of which reside on the horizon line and the lines slope away to converge at them. When the object is placed above the horizon, the lines slope downwards making it appear as though we are looking up at it.

**Two-point high horizon** ▲
Where the object appears to have been placed below eye level (the horizon), the converging lines travel upwards to meet the vanishing points, making it appear as though we are viewing the object from above. Note how the top of the cube is visible when seen from above, giving a stronger sense of its 3-D form.

**Three-point low horizon** ▼
In three-point perspective, you get the added dimension of lines converging to yet another viewpoint, this time on a vertical axis at right angles to the horizon line, above or below it. Where the object is suspended or sits below the horizon line, its base is clear. You will use three-point perspective when drawing buildings.

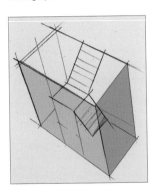

**Three-point high horizon** ◄
This is a very useful device when drawing interiors. The verticals slope inwards and converge at a vanishing point which is located far below the base of the object. Always draw in the point and the converging lines to ensure accuracy.

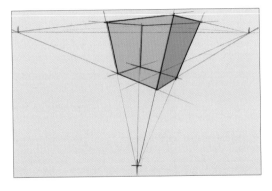

## Practice exercise: Low viewpoint

The smallness of the mouse can be emphasized by the use of a low viewpoint to make the bed appear to tower over it. This offers the setting far greater dynamic and diminishes the stature of the mouse to believable proportions, even though he still remains the important main character.

### Materials
- *cartridge paper*
- *pencil*
- *dip pen*
- *black Indian ink*
- *coloured inks*

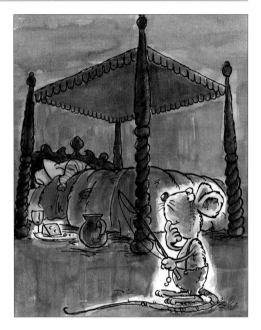

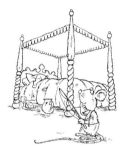

**1** Outline the drawing using a light pencil, then go over it with a dip pen and black Indian ink. Keep your lines pressure-sensitive and fluid.

**2** When you have completed the initial drawing, let it dry, then drop confident washes on to the background, starting with a diluted ultramarine blue. Leave the main story elements as white. Add full-strength blue to the bed awning and cover, and a sepia tint to the bedposts. Use an ochre-sepia mix to colour the mouse and a vivid scarlet-red colour for the trousers.

## Practice exercise: High viewpoint

The building-block construction of this sketch gives easy-to-follow clues to drawing the steps. The construction lines are shown in the three-point perspective diagram for high viewpoint on the opposite page.

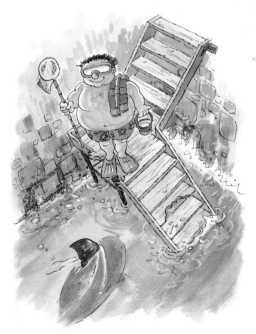

### Materials
- *'Not' watercolour paper*
- *pencil eraser*
- *0.3mm fineliner pen*
- *No. 3 round brush*
- *watercolour paints*

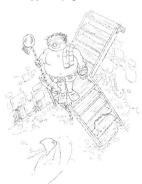

**1** Draft a detailed sketch in pencil, then erase any unnecessary lines. Draw carefully over this outline using a 0.3mm fineliner pen.

**2** Softly add washes of yellow ochre and sepia on to the walls and stones. Use vertical strokes to assist the illusion of dropping walls. Detail the bather with turquoise blue and cadmium red, mixing a flesh tone from yellow ochre and a little cadmium red. Leave unpainted areas of paper for sparkling reflections on the water surface.

## Detailing settings

Familiarize yourself with the shapes of furniture and other everyday objects. Build up a good working knowledge of their construction and appearance by drawing them in different positions from all viewpoints. You can adapt furniture from basic cube and cuboid shapes seen in two- and three-point perspectives (see page 82). Practise often; the more varied you can make your room settings, the more interesting your picture will be.

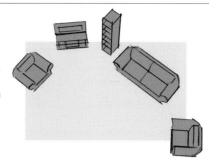

**◄ High three-point viewpoint**
An airy modern room is suggested through the curved placement from a very high three-point viewpoint. Space is shown in an optimum way using this setting. To keep interest, cartoonists should always consider a wide range of viewpoints and vary them in their sequential frames. Consider yourself as a particular viewer, such as the fly on the wall.

**Midground setting ▲**
Placing the furniture in the midground offers open space in the foreground, thereby creating the illusion of depth.

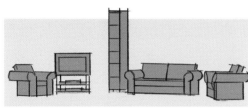

**Fore- and midground setting ▲**
Juxtaposing the armchair and TV in the foreground with the furniture in the background gives the room more interest.

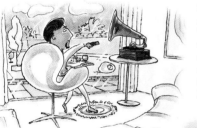

**Office ▼**
A marginally higher viewpoint allows us to take in more of the relevant information. The two employees sit opposite one another, yet only communicate through their webcams. Only the simplest objects have been necessary to set the scene without obscuring the joke. For the lightness of touch, a 0.3mm fineliner pen was employed. General office and desk ephemera are important too. Familiarity with detail within a scene often elicits humour, as observers recognize aspects of their lives played out in cartoon frames.

**Contemporary room ▲**
Placing the furnishings in the fore- and midground suggests a large, airy room. The curve of the sofa, the indication of the rug and the large picture add to the illusion. The focus of the joke is on the seated figure attempting to operate the old-fashioned gramophone using a modern remote-control unit. The clash of two opposing cultures strikes up such strong contrasts that they spark humour in the absurdity of the situation.

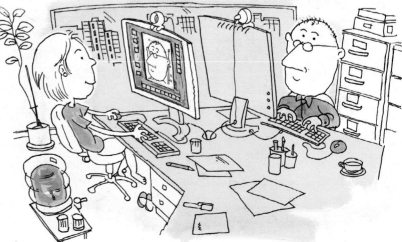

## A setting using objects

The key to drawing settings is to use only what is necessary to tell the narrative. We are so familiar with a range of surroundings – our homes, offices, shops and streets – that it does not require many everyday objects to set a scene. Keep it edited and focused to optimize the element of humour.

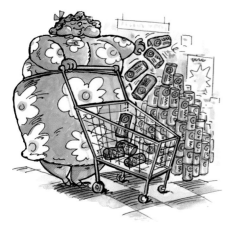

### Supermarket clues ◄
A few clues set the scene clearly in a supermarket: the trolley, large floor tiles, the posters in the background and the unstable stack of 'special offer' chocolate biscuits just waiting to be knocked down.

> **Tip:** Build up a reference stock in your sketchbook of objects seen in everyday contexts. Try to draw them later from different viewpoints too. Your knowledge and ability to render them will continue to improve with practice.

### Using stereotype ▼
It is a known stereotype that women will spend many hours shopping for beauty products and the same time or longer applying them. By just showing the mirror image, there is no visual obstruction to the amusing array of cosmetics that fill the foreground table.

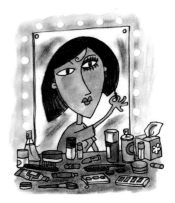

## Practice exercise: Setting the incidentals

The soldier requires certain objects to set the miserable scene and convey the cartoon's narrative through its context. The bayonet fork toasting bread over a small fire while the rain pours down relentlessly are details that are key in communicating the message.

### Materials
- *cartridge paper*
- *0.3mm fineliner pen*
- *No. 3 round brush*
- *coloured inks*
- *charcoal*

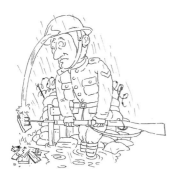

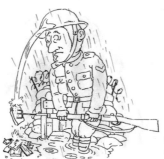

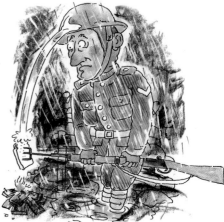

1 Use a 0.3mm fineliner pen to map out the basic outline of the soldier and his environment. Pay close attention to the details of rifle, sandbags, barbed wire, toast, fire and uniform.

2 Lay a pale yellow ochre tint across the drawing, excluding the stream of water. Leaving this important detail mostly white will focus the viewer's eye.

3 Add colour with washes of olive green (uniform), sepia (rifle barrel), pale orange (fire) and a blend of yellow and ochre (face). Charcoal strokes will add an appropriate grubby effect.

# Lighting

Think about it: without light the image cannot exist to the viewer. Light describes form, explains the shape of an object and the direction of its surfaces and when light falls directly on to a surface a shadow is cast. Playing light and shadow is a powerful cartoonists' game and one that determines the mood and atmosphere of a situation, affecting how it is read. A night scene is fully comprehensible when the merest slither of light is used to illuminate a critical detail or action. Grasping the principles of using light will enable you to create more evocative and arresting cartoons.

To use light and shadow effectively, you need to understand the basic concept of light sources. Observe carefully the direction of light in your everyday surroundings, which means assessing where it is coming from and where it is going. Also take note of how an object that is blocking a stream of light casts a deep shadow.

Always feel in control of the lighting and do not avoid complicated lighting directions because it is more difficult to calculate the fall of shadows on people or objects. Follow your idea and recreate the effect live using lamps and models or a photo, then draw it. Where cartoons are not based in the real world, you can heighten effects and manipulate images to deliver the impossible. A scene that should have shadow may be devoid of it and bold, flat colour used instead as a stylistic substitute for form. The key point is that light should work successfully in your drawings and achieve the result you want.

## Practice exercise: Creating mood and atmosphere with lighting

Artificial light can evoke anticipation and heighten tension within a scene. Here, the yellow glow shines in narrow bands directed downwards from the lamps. With its stark, suffusive rays, it makes any innocent bystander look mean when they are caught in its beam. It helps to consider the directional nature of artificial light in much the same way that a stage director does.

The light you cast on your players will bring them to the attention of the audience, giving them due focus and allowing them to perform to their best. However, with cartoons the reverse technique can be employed. With time to ponder each cartoon frame, placing characters in partially lit or unlit corners serves to make them conspicuous in their inconspicuousness.

### Materials
- 'Not' watercolour paper
- pencil
- dip pen
- black Indian ink
- No. 4 medium flat brush
- No. 2 medium flat brush (for bouncers)
- watercolour paints
- charcoal

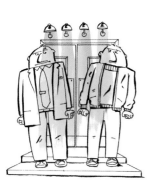

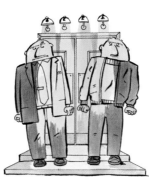

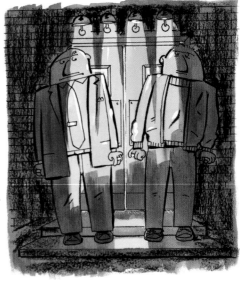

**1** Start with a pencil sketch of the bouncer figures standing on steps in front of double doors, redraw it using the pressure-led line of a dip pen and black Indian ink. Use a medium No. 4 flat brush to deliver four broadening, downward strokes of yellow watercolour from the lamps towards the steps.

**2** Using a smaller brush, drop a medium tone of Paynes grey watercolour on the men's suits and a mix of yellow ochre and red for the flesh tint on their faces, hands and the steps. Add a patch of yellow light streaming down the steps from under the door. Yellow has strong staining properties, so keep strokes light and don't apply too much initial paint.

**3** Add a broad wash of Paynes grey over the area around the door and on the outer parts of the men, leaving the yellow intact. Note how the colour tints still show through. Outline the bricks with the pen and leave to dry before adding charcoal to roughen the texture.

## Practice exercise: Creating a bright mood

The open sea is clear of obstacles that can create shadows. The sunlight reflects upon the water's surface, flooding the scene with bright, clear colour. The light, summer mood is undeniably optimistic, relaxed and cheery. Shadows can add atmosphere, but they are unnecessary in this bright, vibrant composition.

### Materials
- cartridge paper
- 0.3mm fineliner pen
- No. 4 round brush
- watercolour paints
- gouache paints

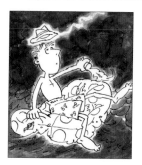

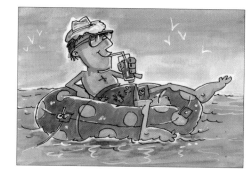

**1** Outline the inflatable and bather using the fineliner pen. Add a wash of ultramarine blue on to the background sky, guiding it around the figure. With a little more variance of stroke, repeat for the sea using cobalt blue.

**2** Detail the figure with flesh tones blended from cadmium red and yellow ochre. Use ultramarine for the shorts and crimson red and cadmium yellow for the raft. Add a second stain of colour to give more form. Draw the foamy wave crests and seagulls with white gouache.

## Practice exercise: Creating a dark mood

The pose of props and figure remains almost the same here, but the dramatic lighting changes everything. Successive layers of darkening tones bring intensity and depth to the colours. The still shadowless figure is illuminated by the lightning flash, allowing the optimum contrast between the very dark and very bright tonal colours. The overall lack of shadows causes the picture to glow.

### Materials
- cartridge paper
- 0.3mm fineliner pen
- No. 4 round brush
- watercolour paints
- gouache paints

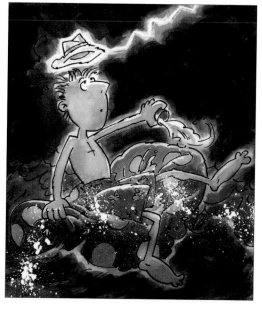

**1** Draw the figure and inflatable in fineliner pen and drop a dark mix of ultramarine blue and Paynes grey into the background. Reserve the whites of the figure, the props and the lightning. Add a choppy wash of viridian green blended with a little Paynes grey in the bottom half of the picture.

**2** Tint the man's flesh a pale mix of cadmium red and yellow ochre, his shorts ultramarine blue and the raft in crimson red and cadmium yellow. Use thick white gouache straight from the tube for adding the sea spray and dramatic highlights. Make sure you fleck it in a different texture so that the spray stands out from the rest of the picture.

# Scene styles

A scene can be set in many different modes. The colours you choose, for example, might induce a mood that pervades an entire picture. It is also common for cartoonists to contrast the midground and background with the foreground action. This approach gives depth to the set, and space to work up the detail on one or more focused areas within a drawing.

A soft watercolour background that offers an overall impression is the perfect backdrop for a harder-edged line drawing. Where line is used throughout a scene, important elements can be drawn using a broader mark-maker so that they stand out from other drawn features. A translucent colour can also overlay a line drawing to reduce its sharp blackness to a tamer shade of grey. Minimal information in a picture, such as flat colour, allows the main subject matter to command the onlooker's attention. At the same time, this lack of reality demands that the viewer uses more imagination to read the image.

Deciding on the exact content, texture, level of detailing and colour of an image is to exercise creative powers over the whole of a cartoon world. Such freedom is not always easy to handle, especially when the success of a drawn frame or a running strip is hugely dependent on your choice of style. It is never wise to leave such a decision to chance. Instead, undertake thorough visual investigations and test out the techniques you are considering. The more you research and refine in the area of styling, the crisper and more polished the final result will be.

## Practice exercise: Balancing line against selective colour

It is best to keep a complicated street scene to a limited media. Where the foreground and background are equally busy, reducing similarly toned colours is a good approach. It results in creating an overall harmony that is gentle on the eye and modifies the stimulation of too many hues. Applying the detailing using a crisp, solid ink line also brings benefits to the viewer.

### Materials
- *cartridge paper*
- *0.3mm, 0.6mm fineliner pens*
- *watercolour paints*

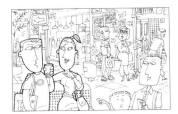 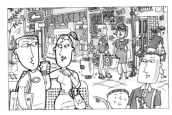  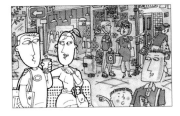

1 Draw most of the scene with the 0.3mm fineliner pen in a linear manner that delivers a solid, blocky style. The main couple should have an added holding line in a 0.6mm pen.

2 Give the drawing depth by colouring selected areas of the background in a monochrome cadmium orange, including walls, clothing, signs, shoes, windows, doors and hairstyles.

3 Add a pale wash of warm blue (cobalt blue with a hint of red) over the whole picture except for the main figures, where you should brush around the outline, to ensure that they stand out.

4 Detail the couple in crisp, bright hues: yellow ochre and cadmium red mix for the skin tones, cadmium red for the bench behind, pale blue for the bag and the shadows on the T-shirt and cadmium yellow for the dress. Remember to reserve areas of white paper for highlights.

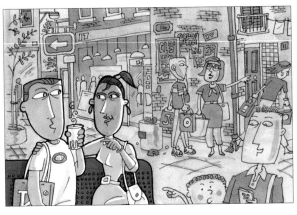

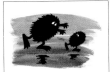

**Tip:** Silhouettes and strong, bright washes make an effective combination. The bold simplicity of these figures against the broad, colourful background strokes creates a clear, punchy impression.

## Practice exercise: Using the contrast of soft wash and hard line

For some settings, a painterly approach may be the answer to achieving a bold final result. The combination of ink lines and soft washes always works well, provided the use of the line is kept to an economical minimum. Its ability to hold the concentration within a drawing gives you licence to play with broader strokes and more artful interpretations with the watercolour wash.

### Materials
- *rough watercolour paper*
- *watercolour paints*
- *dip pen and black Indian ink*
- *chalk pastels*

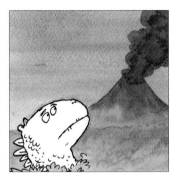

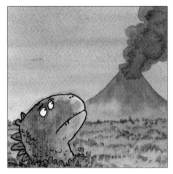

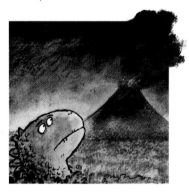

1 Add a purple watercolour wash on to the sky and sap green on to the foliage and leave it to dry. Add wet stains to form the volcano and smoke. Draw in the dinosaur using the dip pen and Indian ink.

2 Tint the dinosaur with a drier colour, dabbing the brush over its neck to create the illusion of scales. Dab gently over the foliage to create a sense of depth. Add yellow ochre highlights.

3 To enhance the mood and create more textures, gently drag the flat side of a purple chalk pastel across the sky and volcano and red pastel on to the eruption, to reveal the paper surface.

## Practice exercise: Employing mixed media to promote unusual settings

Trying out new and unusual effects can positively affect the development of your own cartooning style(s). Try abandoning the usual white paper and coloured ink approach from time to time and be a little more radical. A strongly coloured paper is a simple starting point. Continue the theme with creative use of limited media, such as sponged-off inks, collage or oil pastel.

### Materials
- *red paper*
- *No. 2 round brush and dip pen*
- *coloured inks*
- *white oil pastel and charcoal*
- *calendar page from old almanac*
- *PVA (white) glue*
- *holographic star stickers*

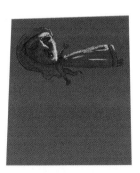

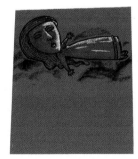

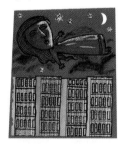

1 Cut the red paper into an irregular shape. Draw the dreamer in brown ink and paint it with red ink. Sponge off the residue, leaving a speckled texture. Use white oil pastel for facial highlights.

2 Reinforce the outline using a dip pen and black Indian ink. Next, add an atmospheric cloud setting by using the broad, crumbly side strokes of a stick of charcoal.

3 Cut the calendar page of an old almanac into four rectangles. Add window shapes and lines using a round brush and black ink. Glue into position and add holographic star stickers.

# Subject and background

Knowing what should dominate in a scene is a difficult choice and a number of factors come into play. Does the background need to create an intense or atmospheric space in which your characters have their adventures? If the answer is yes, then consider employing a dominant landscape. The choice of colours and range of textures you decide to use are vital in setting the scene successfully. For example in the case of a strip cartoon, the surroundings will be explored in finer detail as the narrative progresses.

Decide if you want a central character to dominate. If so, should he or she define their importance within the scene by being bigger than the others? If the answer is yes, it is a good idea to make initial working sketches to define scale and

contrast. This exercise will also serve to highlight any possible implication that such contrast may have on the composition of cartoon frames.

A setting without a dominant character or object, or group of characters or objects, often needs to be balanced, for instance in a narrative where all the characters take the leading role at various times throughout the story. Equal weighting can be achieved by using variations of mark, colour or texture to draw attention to different parts of a scene. An equal division of space between characters can work well, with each area able to display prominent characteristics without stealing all the limelight. It is worth considering these important questions at the start of every new project.

## Practice exercise: Creating a dominant setting

A troll warrior is dwarfed by the cave he has entered. The vertical exaggeration of the frame accentuates the dominant setting. Light from the torch emphasizes the dark interior of the character's new-found world. The space above allows for adjusting the emphasis on dominance. The darker your washes in the cave, the greater the impression of dominance.

### Materials
• 'Not' watercolour paper
• 0.3mm, 0.6mm fineliner pens
• hard sponge and kitchen paper
• No. 4 round brush
• purple coloured ink
• watercolour paints

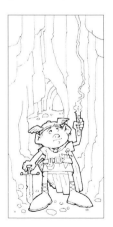

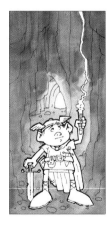

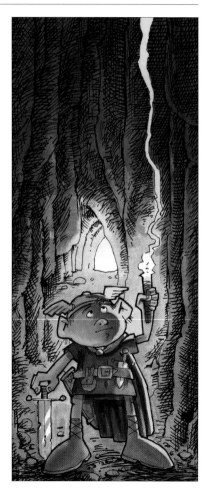

1 Sketch the main shapes of the rock strata directly with the 0.3mm fineliner pen. Use the 0.6mm pen to draw the main outline of the troll in the lower section of the rectangle. Add the detailing with the 0.3mm pen.

2 Add a soft wash of cobalt blue from top to bottom. Work carefully around the outline and do not allow your brush to veer over the lines. While it is still wet, sponge off the centre of the wash to leave the palest tint.

3 Cross-hatch the interior of the cave to give it form and texture. Add a fluid purple ink wash overall. Be spare nearest to the centre where the light dominates and the figure takes centre stage. Remove any excess ink with soft kitchen paper. Colour up the figure: terracotta red for the tunic, pale blue for the helmet, weapons and buckle. Make flesh tones from a yellow ochre and cadmium red mix. Use cadmium yellow to highlight the side of the face and the torch's beam.

## Practice exercise: Creating a dominant character

King Kong trounces Manhattan and works powerfully in the drawing due to the absurdity of the scaling, given the size of skyscrapers in the real setting. Humour and balance is provided by the minuscule, tinted banana advert.

### Materials
• *cartridge paper*
• *pencil and 0.3mm fineliner pen*
• *dip pen*
• *black Indian ink*
• *watercolour paints*

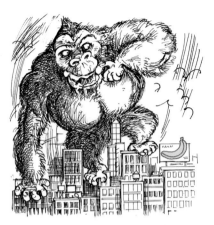

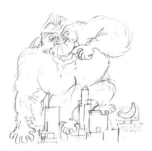

1 Consider how Kong's hugely exaggerated proportions loom over the skyline. Make a soft pencil drawing. Do not be afraid to make any necessary adjustments to your composition at this stage.

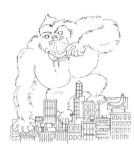

2 Carefully outline the scene with the strong, even lines of the fineliner pen. Lightly detail the fur and features, and sketch in the building windows. Ensure that Kong's gaze is directed at the banana.

3 Hatch broadly with the pressure-led lines of the dip pen to evoke action, energy and terror. The long motion strokes around the ape emphasize the mood. Embolden the hatching on the buildings in Kong's shadow. Spot-colour the banana in cadmium yellow watercolour.

## Giving equal weighting to subject and background

Striking a balance works for some subjects and should not be regarded as glib or compromising. Equal weighting is given to figure and background where no single element dominates over another. Sample a range of cartoon images from books or comics and discover how balance works with various subjects in the hands of the consummate masters.

### Maze ▼
Sometimes the subject and background are linked so that it is impossible to separate them. Here, the connection is based on the concept of the map as the vital accessory to escape the maze. For the maze to be a functional part of the image, the figure must be trapped within it. Equally, the man is meaningless without the maze.

### Catwalk model ▶
The subject dominates the background in size, but the activity of the crowd balances the scene. The use of pink pastel to indicate the curtains is all that is needed to link model with audience.

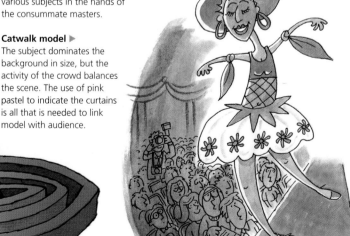

# Scale and focus

Cartoonists need to be able to see from the viewpoint of their audience if they are to communicate with them effectively. The ability to direct the viewer's focus with ease to a particular event or an unfolding storyline is an art form in its own right, and gauging the scale and position of objects and figures in relation to one another is key in achieving this.

Scale in the cartoon world is governed by the shared experiences of audience and artist. We all know the relative size of a real person to their surroundings, to other living creatures and to buildings because we experience it ourselves. By using spatial organization – perspective, compositional

devices and overlapping picture planes, such as where foreground and background meet – we can then alter the relationships of scale by amplifying objects or diminishing them, and even create impossible circumstances.

The ability to experiment like this provides focus and gives cartoonists the chance to play with ideas, and create effects that would cost a Hollywood film director a fortune to enact in a film studio. Broadening your thinking on a grander scale will assist all aspects of your creative image-making. Try to consider the picture from the view of all 'players' in this production when making scale and focus decisions.

## Focusing narrative structure

Unless it is carefully managed, an overcrowded scene can be confusing and distracting. To communicate the storyline instantly to the audience, it is essential to bring the key characters and the action clearly into focus.

**▼ First draft**
In the first attempt, four elements in the period room setting – the smoke, clock, oil lamp and plant – are misplaced. They are blocking the clear view to the unwelcome midnight visitor.

**Second draft ▼**
A slight rearrangement of the room and the subject and objects begin to work together. A clear, diagonal path can be plotted from the base of the lamp through the crystal ball to the plant pot.

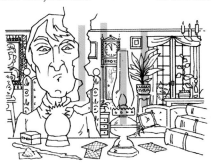

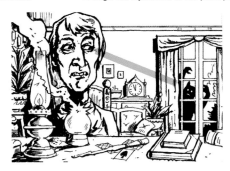

**Final image ▶**
Having realized the best composition, the next consideration is colour. Mood is important here, as is the need to remain focused on the suspense of the moment. Using the single colour red, with its associations of power, danger, anger, horror and bloodshed, readily deals with the issue of focus. The stark white facial highlights and the window background stand out, and the dark silhouette of the monster is the most solid element.

**Tip:** When deciding on a colour to assist focus, make testers on photocopies or scanned printouts of your initial drawings. Never just accept the first version you try. Other options could be better.

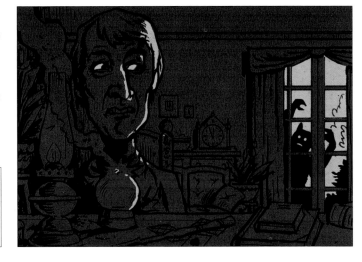

## Contrasts of scale

How do we know when the scale is correct? A character that is too small may be so insignificant as to lose their voice; too big and there may be an unintentional power struggle, or the force of a foe could be diminished. When the balance of scale is correct, all the elements should hold together at their varying sizes and the message will be clear.

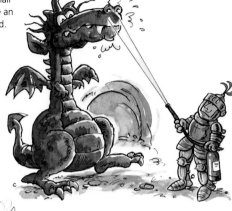

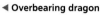
◀ **Overbearing dragon**
This first sketch reveals a very threatening dragon. However, it does not work because its size has reduced the knight so much that his most important accessory, the fire extinguisher, cannot be easily seen.

**Non-threatening dragon ▶**
The knight is too large in this second sketch and on an equal footing with the dragon. The result is that the beast is no longer a threat.

**Correctly scaled and placed dragon ▲**
You know when the scale is correct because all intentions are clearly met. The cave no longer looks like a background afterthought, and by allowing space around it, the scene is offered a greater sense of depth. You should always be thinking to keep the drawing as simple as possible so that the narrative can speak clearly.

## Scale and the subconscious

You can use scale to convey a hidden, almost subconscious message. What is merely suggested takes on the role of meaning and casts teasing doubt in the viewer's mind. Cropping out parts of a composition heightens the element of anticipation. What will happen next? Who might be lurking behind a door? The unknown increases the danger levels, so that when the main character's features are also partly obscured, we are left in a further state of disquieting uncertainty. What are they going to do? What is it that they can see that is causing such great concern?

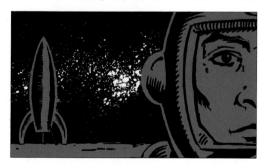

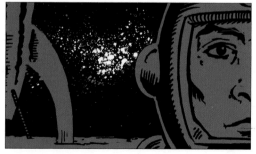

**Distant spaceship ▲**
The spacecraft is in full view, but the distance of the astronaut from his ship lessens the impact. At the same time, it raises a question for the viewer. Is he endangered by his distance from the ship? In an emergency, can he safely return?

**Nearby spaceship ▲**
The image still reads perfectly clearly when only a quarter of the spacecraft is in view. The revised composition has more impact and intrigue to offer, though it raises fewer questions in the viewer's mind.

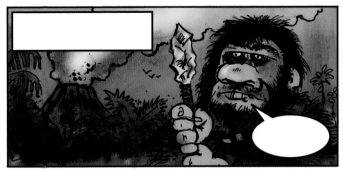
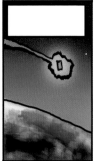

# The comic page

A blank page requires planning to create a structure that can be followed easily by the reader. This chapter focuses on the cartoonist's skills to alter pace and emphasis through cropping images and sequential frame layout. The placement of words is important, as is the correct use of colour, tone and contrast.

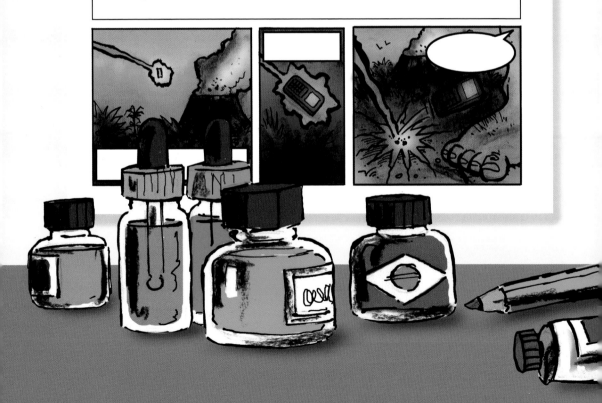

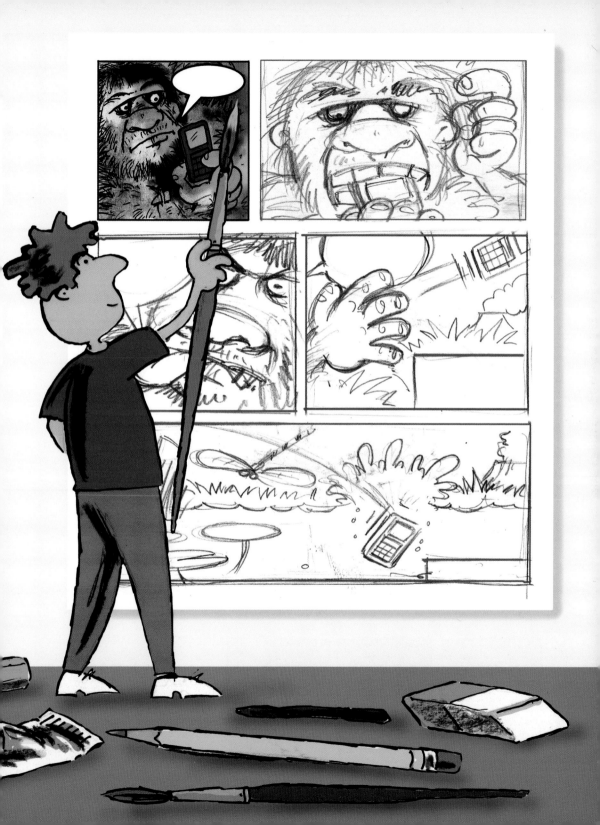

# Conveying action

The development of cartooning from static frames into action depends on one major element: time. Images set in time become a sequence that is viewed through a set number of seconds, minutes, hours and so on. The images themselves may not be intended to be perceived in real time; it could be implied that time runs faster or slower. For example one image may show the bright sunlight of midday, while the next the deep-orange skies of dusk.

Creating a sequence of images demands that you plan and develop them with an idea of a story or events taking place. Each frame in the story should focus on a particular event that occurs in time, seen from a particular viewpoint. When the different frames are viewed in an ordered sequence, the viewer runs them like a film before their eyes, and the illusion of movement is experienced. This principle is skilfully played in the hands of the film director; cartoons are films that are never shot with a camera nor intended for animation.

Showing action well in a frame depends on the cartoonist drawing as though they were inside the frame, watching intently from a strategic position. It is the variety of different frames connected in a sequence that brings the comic strip to life and holds the viewer's attention. Wherever contrast exists, interest is bound to follow. Pacing a sequence is one of the hardest lessons in cartooning, and in many ways is of greater importance than the ability to draw. If a strip does not offer variation in action, the reader's attention may waver.

## The close-up

A view at close range, at times only 1–2cm (3/8–3/4in) from a face, hands or an object, is known as the close-up. Focusing attention on something brings it into greater significance in the frame. Close-ups are usually designed to work in conjunction with medium and long shots for optimum interest.

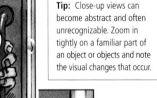

**Tip:** Close-up views can become abstract and often unrecognizable. Zoom in tightly on a familiar part of an object or objects and note the visual changes that occur.

### Running a sequence ▼
Decide how many frames you wish to break the movement down into and think of it in the same way as a fast-stop frame camera. Whether you run the sequence along a line or in a vertical drop affects interpretation. Little position change infers split-second timing.

### Action close-up ▶
The hand opens the door with caution, and the deliberate cropping of the frame succeeds in holding the tension in the scene. For the sketches, use your own hand as a reference and draw a simple part of the door. The long crop ensures a tight edit.

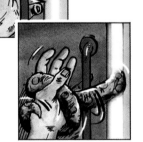

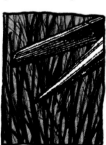

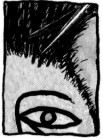

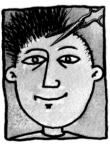

## Freezing time

A classic way to show the transition of time is by freezing the subject in the foreground while making changes to the background. At the other extreme, repetition of a background scene can be used to represent monotony or, with small alterations, longer time changes.

### Using background action ▼
Here the subject remains constant while the surroundings show movement in time. The bonfire has burnt to ashes, lights have appeared in the buildings and the sunset has turned to twilight.

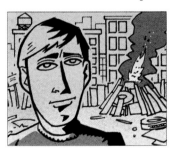

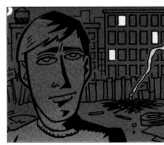

## The long shot

A shot that shows a scene from a distance does so to stress the environment or setting. A long shot that does not develop along the line of a narrative is known as an establishing shot, because it provides the audience with an overview prior to the action. Sometimes this is a bird's-eye view or in other cases simply a very wide-angled overview. Long shots should still have a focus or point of interest – in this frame it is the moon buggy which attracts the attention, as this builds up a sense of anticipation in the viewer.

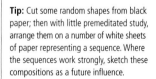

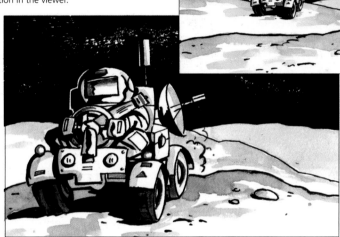

◀
The time taken for the moon buggy to approach is intended to be several minutes. To convey the span of time in pictorial terms, three frames – the long, medium and close-up shots – are created and overlapped in a diagonally stepped configuration. The three frames are then linked using repetition on three different scales.

## Silhouettes in sequence

To eliminate the distractions of colour and fine detail, convert the identifiable shapes of people and objects into flat, black silhouettes. The stark contrast and heavily edited scene result in forcing the eye to appreciate the movement and placement of the characters and objects in terms of picture planes and spatial relationships. Silhouettes also offer an effective way to simplify the elements of a composition at the rough working stage. To elaborate on detail at this point is wholly unnecessary and may in fact make it harder to appreciate the flow and construction of an animated sequence during planning.

**Tip:** Cut some random shapes from black paper; then with little premeditated study, arrange them on a number of white sheets of paper representing a sequence. Where the sequences work strongly, sketch these compositions as a future influence.

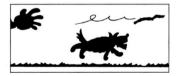

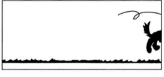

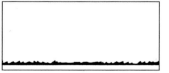

**Less is more** ▲
This story is told in five frames and understatement is used throughout. In colour, the dog's personality could interfere with the simple concept. The empty frame increases the drama.

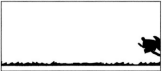

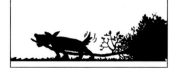

# Devising layout

The art of the comic page relies as much on well-constructed layout as it does on superbly imaginative images. When it was first introduced in the late 19th century, the cartoon narrative took the simple form of a series of rectangles that were read from left to right. These strips usually appeared on the back pages of journals and newspapers, and consequently were given very little space.

The evolution of comic papers and comic books saw an increasingly dynamic use of layout, reaching its height in the 1950s, 60s and 70s in the superhero fantasy worlds invented by DC and Marvel Comics. Frames suddenly altered their shapes and sizes across double-page spreads, which enhanced the narrative and released energy and excitement in these amazingly popular comic books. The development of the format into that of the graphic novel originated in the 1980s in *The Dark Knight,* a new Batman epic by the artist Frank Miller, which was produced as a comic-book series.

Under these influences, comic artists have been pushing the boundaries of the structure that composes the layout: the panel grid. A sound understanding of the basic formats will give you the confidence to construct your own panel configurations in ways that are visually exciting and enliven your cartoon narratives. Begin with the universally understood formats, and once you understand what it is that makes them work so successfully, begin altering the size of frames or their number on the page. Your audience is key at all times.

## Panel variations

A basic panel grid of 3 x 3 panels equal in shape and size makes a good starting point. The regularity of the format offers strict boundaries for testing your skills. They will keep your drawing 'tight' into the subject and well-focused, thereby encouraging you to harness your creative energies. Once you have grasped the concept, you can begin to alter the page layout and explore the impact of your narrative by using half-size panels, double panels or even overlapping panels. But remember to keep your audience in mind.

**Tip:** Devise your own panel grids and test them with your cartoon narratives. Assess these experiments and learn which are the most successful. Develop these first ideas into more complex layouts.

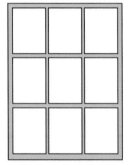

3-column, 9-panel grid

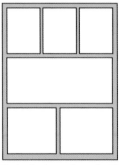

3-, 1-, 2-column, 6-panel grid

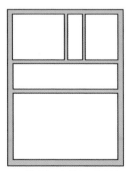

multi-column, 5-panel grid

◀ **Panel examples**
You can manipulate a three-column, nine-panel grid (far left) in a number of ways. One long panel offers cinematic scope to the layout, while having two equal panels offers balance (centre). To make the layout more dynamic, you can either expand or compress the panels (right).

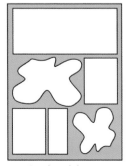

Panels and shapes

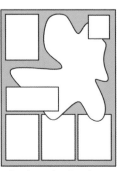

Panels overlapping shape

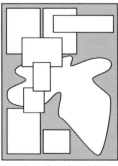

Overlapped panels and shape

◀ **Creative panel interpretations**
Using a mixture of regular-shaped panels and free-form shaped panels can add so much excitement to your layouts. In all these examples there is still considerable structure, which is necessary for the storylines to be followed with ease.

## Breaking the box

The freedom to break out of the box and draw outside its confines can heighten tension. It also allows one drawing to be a little larger than the others on a page. This is a device that is commonly used in cartooning, not only because it draws the eye of the reader but for the beneficial effect it can bring to a layout that is over-structured or even verging on the dull. Like all such devices, however, it should be used sparingly, such as when the page needs a lift or to emphasize a detail. Overuse will inevitably reduce it to a cliché.

**Break-out, close-up ▼**
The monster is more threatening for breaking the frame, and demonstrates how this effect works equally well in close-up. Although the enlargement is relatively small, it creates a significantly bigger impact on the page.

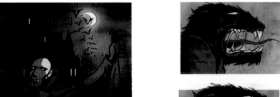

**Adding drama ▼**
The vampire is made scarier if he appears to be stepping out of the frame. The border emphasizes the break-out, but should be used only as a last resort in place of a breaking point. In the coloured version, the background has more depth than in the one below, where it floats as a ruled vignette.

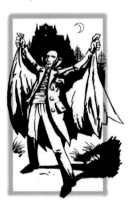

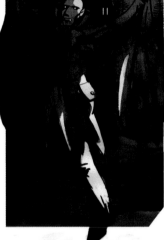

## Dynamic composition

Not all drawings should be kept within the box-panel format. It can restrict movement and action, preventing the dynamic interaction of characters with their environments and with each other. Breaking the box panel can have a liberating effect on a page.

## Breaking sequential panels

The technique of breaking through panel boxes can be used to show accelerated movement through time. Demonstrated in a fun way here, it is another common device in cartoon storytelling that works for all styles.

**Time and motion ▼**
The baseball player's powerful swing is emphasized by breaking through the lines of the three panels. Each panel represents a fraction of a second in time, 'slowed' by its separation.

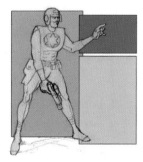

**Natural break-out points ▲**
Most drawings will have a 'natural' point at which it is reasonable to break out of the rigidity of the frame. Usually the breaking action will draw the eye and direct it to the next frame. Here, the spaceman's pointing hand and outstretched foot make this obvious.

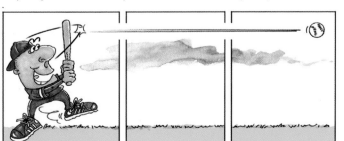

# Speech bubbles

Not all cartoons have an obvious running pictorial narrative and may require words to carry the theme through from beginning to end. Some are intended as conversation pieces, where characters speak to one another within the frame, conveyed through white oval shapes known as speech bubbles or balloons. Many variations exist around this theme and it is important that they are easy to follow and prominent, but that they do not cause overcrowding in a frame.

There is a specific protocol that artists adhere to so as to avoid legibility problems or confusion in the order of conversation. This has been largely derived from the strip cartoons, which have traditionally been published in newspapers and journals.

A single 'gag' cartoon normally placed within the width of a column of a newspaper tends to be captioned above or beneath with one or two lines of concise text. Sequential strip cartoons have running captions (in a thin white rectangular box above or below the frame), as well as speech bubbles. These help to set the scene by relaying information on place or time or by giving the context or development of events in one or more frames.

The importance of speech bubbles should not be underestimated and it is vital that lettering inside them is clearly formed with accurate spelling and grammar. Stylized hand-lettering is still the favoured method, although suitable fonts have also been developed to enable setting by computer.

## Word and picture partnerships

Words and pictures always work together and they should not be considered in isolation of one another. The expression on a character's face speaks as loudly as the words which accompany it. Care should be taken to ensure that figures are correctly placed and address relevant characters in the frame. Minor characters may sometimes be drawn in the distance and have smaller speech bubbles.

Be sure to have your script for a cartoon drafted with the roughs for your sequence of frames. All adjustments

should be made before any drawing is attempted on the actual artwork. Too many words in a bubble can become crowded, confusing and overcomplicate the communication of the message. Revise the speech as many times as it takes for it to become effective.

One final note; if you choose to initially plan the pictures ahead of the words, allow spaces for the speech bubbles to be placed.

**Multiple speech-bubble styles** ▼
This witty gag involves speech being communicated by three different means. First, the spaceman 'thinks' aloud on the page and a 'thought' bubble is identified inside a dreamy cloud-shape. His language translator speaks in alien bleeps and this mechanical voice is encapsulated within a jagged-edged bubble. Finally, the alien bubbles duplicate the exact word in the same peculiar font to show recognition of an identical language being spoken.

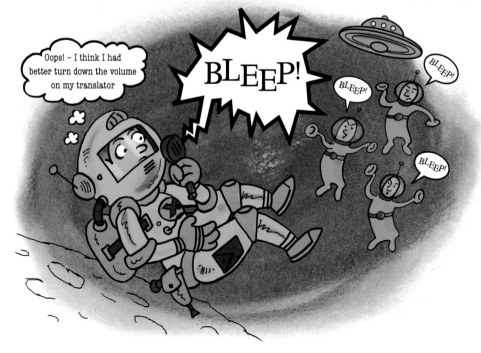

## Speech-bubble styles

Styles of bubble are dictated by the nature of dialogue within. External dialogue (speaking) is commonly enclosed within a word bubble or balloon with a pointer or tail angled towards the speaker's face. Internal dialogue (thought) tends to appear within a bubble shaped like an oval cloud. It has a trail or small circles leading down to the thinker's head. Speech bubbles can have different edges to denote various types of speech, such as exclamation and outburst or whispering.

### Joining and splitting speech bubbles ▼
It may be necessary for a character to make a longer speech and you may wish to adopt a device for effective splitting to allow the character and reader a break. Speech bubbles link easily by joining them with a short, narrow 'path' or morphing the shapes of two or three bubbles can create an interesting shape to complement the artwork in the frame.

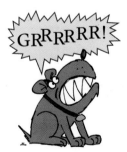

**Dialogue inside the frame ▲**
The smaller figure begins the conversation as his speech is at the top of the frame. At the end of his sentence, the eye naturally flows to the second bubble belonging to the other character. The first speaker's second bubble is joined to the first by a path, dispelling the need for two pointers heading for the one head.

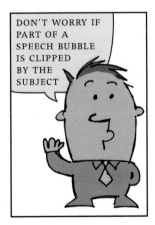

**Expression through bubbles ▲**
The snappy growl of the dog is illustrated by the toothy-edged bubble and the upper case onomatopoeia (a word whose sound defines it when spoken). The exclamation mark at the end offers graphic description.

**Time-based speech bubbles ▲**
It is not just a running sequence of frames or the use of repetition that give a cartoon its sense of time, captions which overlap or run into each other have a similar effect. Dividing the words of a sentence or phrase equally and placing them in several joined bubbles makes that phrase seem transitional and passing between the pictorial content.

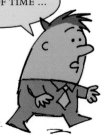

# Directing the comic strip

Think of your gags and strip cartoons as small examples of 2-D theatre. The actors are on stage, the props are in place, the story has been scripted, but no one knows what to do, where to go or how to put on a convincing performance for the audience. A director is needed to put everything and everyone into order, from improving the first drafts to perfecting the final piece. As well as being the scriptwriter and set designer, you, the cartoonist, are the director of your own creation.

Directing the comic page demands that each frame is staged so that it communicates the story properly to the audience. A key part of the process lies in knowing how to edit your material to leave just the right amount of visual information. Details that add nothing to the narrative or explain very little about

a character should be stripped out. This may sound daunting, but you will find that it improves the action enormously. Make sure that you capture the right mood in each frame by carefully considering the intensity and direction of the light source and the 3-D modelling required. Also consider your colour choices: too many colours will cancel out the page in a jumbled mass of hues and tones; too few colours could deprive the cartoon of its spark.

There is no shortcut to this necessary methodology. Just as the director revises a script or rehearses again and again, the visual artist must get into the habit of drawing and redrawing until all pictorial problems are solved and the final piece is as good as it can be and ready for public display.

## Removing unwanted scenes

A comic strip is sometimes at its most effective when the content is reduced to the barest essentials. Cultivate a ruthless attitude to your work, chopping it back where you see the need. Always have the reader in mind; think about how

they will read the sequence of frames and interpret the visual language you use, and how you can stop them from 'switching off' by sustaining their level of interest. If a frame duplicates an idea or adds little to the storyline, remove it.

**The final sequence ▼**
The inquisitive visitor touches a serpent's egg with dramatic consequences. The use of a limited colour palette and overall blue-tinted background assists the focus of the comic strip.

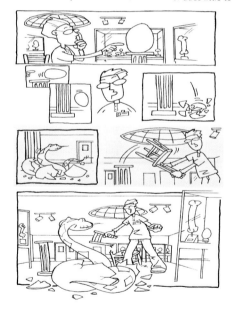

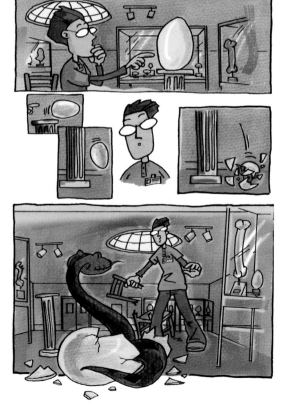

**Sequence pre-edit ▲**
The sketches on the third row (tinted blue) repeat similar information to that shown in the final frame. It is surplus to requirement, so strip it out. Overstatement – saying too much or repetition of information not used for effect – is as bad as understatement, where not enough information is given to make full sense of the cartoon.

## Dramatic focus

Two comic-strip versions of the same storyline show how much punchier a cartoon can be when the image sizes are varied and laid out in a more dynamic way. The subject of this narrative is an explosion and the frames present a clear build-up and a dramatic conclusion. By only showing the hand of the protagonist in frame two, the reader is left with a strong sense of mystery, a teaser of unknown character identity which may or may not be revealed in later frames.

### Cartoon strip pre-edit ▼
Using limited colour also delivers impact to the sequence. Black, white and red are a known powerful colour combination. Limiting the range and view, and specifying limited colour, all heighten the subject and keep the viewer strongly focused.

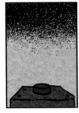
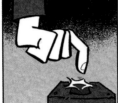
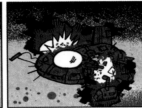

### Cartoon strip post-edit ▼
In this post-edited version of the same narrative, the variation of the panel sizes and the cropped images within the frames lead the viewer to focus more closely on the events. The decision to change the delicate, pointed finger to a slamming fist offers a more appropriate continuity to the three frames, and also gives a clear signal that the explosion is no accident, but rather a malevolent action. The staggered 1, 2, 3 diagonal layout that takes it to the final moment serves to heighten the drama.

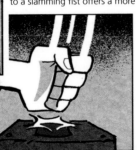

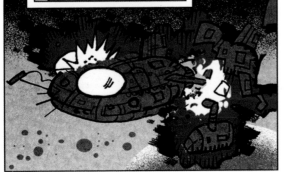

## Tight scripting

Consistent simple images work best for the quick gag. You should aim to get to the point as quickly as you can, and keeping the build-up to only a few frames will help. Maintaining a strong thread of humour will also enable you to hold the viewer's attention.

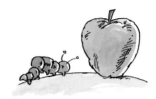

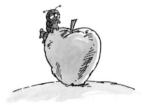

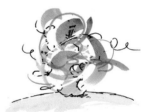

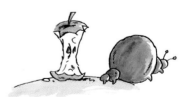

### Bitesized frames ▲
Practise illustrating a simple storyline to understand how to edit your narrative. Four frames are the maximum number needed: the first two show the discovery and inspection of the apple; the third illustrates its active demolition. The final frame displays the stripped core and bloated caterpillar. The whirling action of the third frame is key.

# Cartoon style

The comic narrative opens up whole worlds of possibilities for cartoonists in which to express their creativity and let their imaginations run free. The genre includes dark, brooding fantasies, whimsical stories of everyday life and thrilling tales of superheroes, to name but a few. Choosing the medium and drawing style that matches the subject matter is crucial if a cartoon is to deliver its intended meaning and also evoke the appropriate response from the audience.

A subject that is intended to convey accurate information might be drawn using the traditional techniques of dip-pen cross-hatching with added tints of colour. On the other hand, a narrative strip may employ relaxed brushstrokes without a keyline to anchor the details. The power of black ink cannot be overestimated: line images in black and white can have little subtlety on a page and appear stark when passages of shadow are inked in. Children's comic strips and picture books are created in a much lighter style that often uses a definite pencil line with added watercolour washes or colouring pencil shading. The children's author and illustrator Raymond Briggs is known for his unique drawing style of soft-pencil shading in harmonious, naturalistic colours.

The interpretation of the characters in a strip can have a huge impact on the style in which it is illustrated. Children's author Lauren Child is a case in point. Her eccentric figures demand an unconventional world to inhabit, and their bright, flat digital backgrounds use collage and sketchy drawing.

## A hard-hitting image

Images that are striking should have a strong focus, dramatic composition and effortless appearance. Don't expect a perfect composition the first time you put pencil to paper. Remember that revising and editing always brings out the best in drawings and therefore it is more likely to be your second or third draft that succeeds. Adopting sharply foreshortened viewpoints and making extreme comparisons of scale are techniques that play an effective part in creating a forceful image. Add strong lines, black ink shadows and densely saturated 'danger' colours to the mix and you will have created a cartoon that emanates great power, tension and atmosphere.

**First draft** ▶
The page needs to be filled with a dramatic robot figure. In this first sketch, the robot is conceived as being gigantic in size and only half of him is seen. This is conveyed by comparing the robot to a boat.

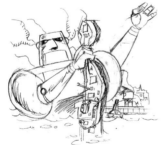

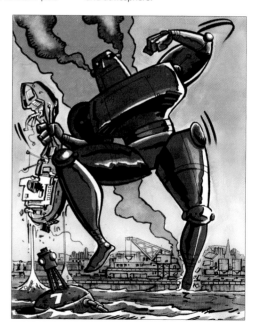

**Second draft** ▶
This view is much more imposing. The robot still clutches the boat, but is striding across the city. The viewpoint has been lowered in order to overemphasize the sheer scale of the robotic monster. The tilt of the figure and the lifting of the leg into an action pose add dynamic force to the image.

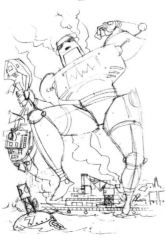

**Final image** ▲
The final artwork is carefully drawn in Indian ink using a No. 4 round smooth-hair brush. The intensity of the colours is obtained by combining dyes with watercolour. The white highlights infer the gleam of metal.

# A whimsical approach

Subjects that cannot be illustrated in a straightforward way can benefit from a whimsical approach. Here, the split frame breaks up the picture and offers a visual conceit: the robber is at liberty to hop frames to where he is out of the reach of the police car. It provides a good opportunity to offer the reader a chance to focus twice on the narrative from the point of view of the police officer and the robber, especially as both characters are essential to make it work.

**Using stereotypes ▼**
Drawn with no attention to realism, the cartoon carries light-heartedness into what is actually an extremely serious situation. Note the robber's stereotypical dress and 'swag' bags.

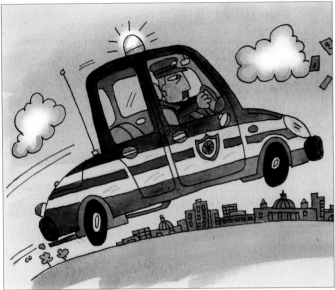
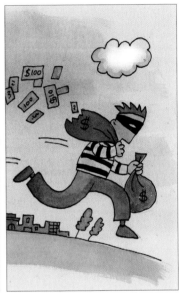

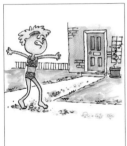
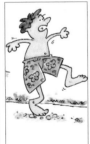
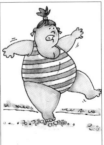
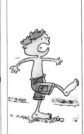

**Keeping it light ▲**
This series of sparsely detailed frames carries the simple narrative of a barefoot walk along a gravel path. It is the light touch that gives this strip its particular charm. The humour is focused on the different characters and their uncomfortable journey. The precise gait of each figure is determined by body size and shape. For example, the slimmest figures have greater limb mobility, enabling them to move on tiptoe.

**Tip:** The application of drawing style is rarely actually shown in the cartoonist's gag. Using a dip pen, black Indian ink and watercolours to tint the image, have fun showing the pen nib drawing a calligraphic moustache. By doing this the viewer is allowed to share the workings of the illustrator's mind as he or she doodles the face and moustache.

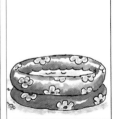

## Practice exercise: Line and wash

Choosing a style that is appropriate for your comic strip is essential. Here, the Victorian horror tale of Jekyll and Hyde works best employing the traditional techniques of dip-pen line and ink wash. This approach mimics the engraving styles of the 19th century, where depth of field and atmospheric shadows were created using heavily layered cross-hatching techniques.

### Materials
- *cartridge paper*
- *dip pen and black ink*
- *coloured inks*
- *No. 5 round brush*

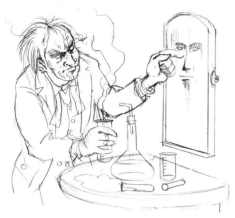

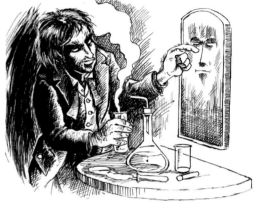

**1** Lightly sketch the composition, allowing plenty of space for adding colour and tone to your drawing. Try to work your roughs up to a high level of finish so that you have less work at the next stage.

**2** Closely hatch the main figure, objects and background using a dip pen and black ink. Deepen the shadows on and behind the character yet further using a relatively dry brush and ink. Retain areas of unused paper for highlights.

**3** Tint your drawing. In the centre background, a wash of yellow and pale blue ink merges on the paper to make an eerie green, which provides the perfect creepy atmosphere.

**Tip:** This image employs a 0.3mm fineliner pen, white gouache paint and black Indian ink on smooth paper. Blacks and whites are exploited to display the form of an object without using any tone whatsoever. Draw the snail outline clearly with the fineliner, add the texture pattern of its flesh, before creating a 3-D walnut whip shell, first with whorls of black and then similar marks with opaque white gouache.

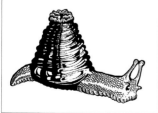

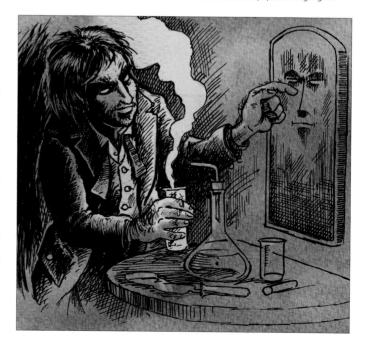

## Practice exercise: Dyes and masking fluid

Cartoons that require a crisp, clean style need to be executed in definite stages. This image of young people on a city street corner is created in a style that is equal to its contemporary setting. The figures are drawn using a brush outline and then masking fluid brushed over them to prevent the background wash

from touching them. The masking fluid dries to a rubbery texture that can be peeled off to reveal a hard-edged, reserved area of unpainted paper. The focal features are then painted in clear, bright colours, which stand out in strong contrast to a background that is almost monochrome.

### Materials
- *watercolour paper*
- *black Indian ink*
- *No. 2 round brush*
- *masking fluid*
- *watercolour dyes*

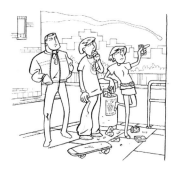

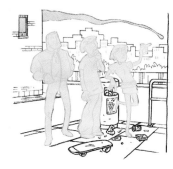

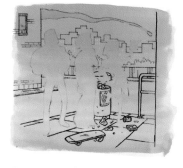

**1** Sketch the figures and foreground details using black Indian ink and a brush. Lessen the pressure for the background outline so that the buildings appear lighter on the page.

**2** Use the masking fluid to mask out the meteorite trail, some of the background windows and the interior of each figure. Leave the masked-out areas until they are completely dry.

**3** Lay a smooth, graded colour wash across the paper. Brush from the top of the drawing, starting with pale blue and then changing to yellow about halfway down.

**4** When the wash is dry, gently peel the masking fluid from the applied areas. Note the clean-edged whiteness of the paper where the fluid has masked it. Using undiluted colour, to retain the luminescent qualities characteristic of inks and dyes, paint the main figures and add tone to the other focal features, such as the wall.

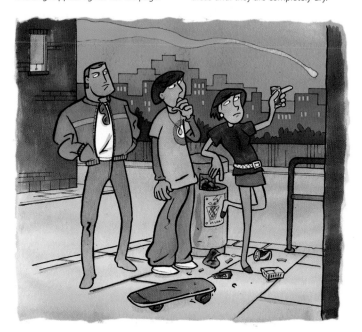

**Tip:** Masking fluid is a latex/ammonia solution that should be treated with caution. If spilt on fabric and not washed immediately with water, it dries to form a rubbery, elastic crust. Brushes must always be washed out immediately after using masking fluid, or they will become coated and hardened. Do not allow yourself to become too reliant on this medium – wax or oil pastel resists offer masking out with softer edges and texture.

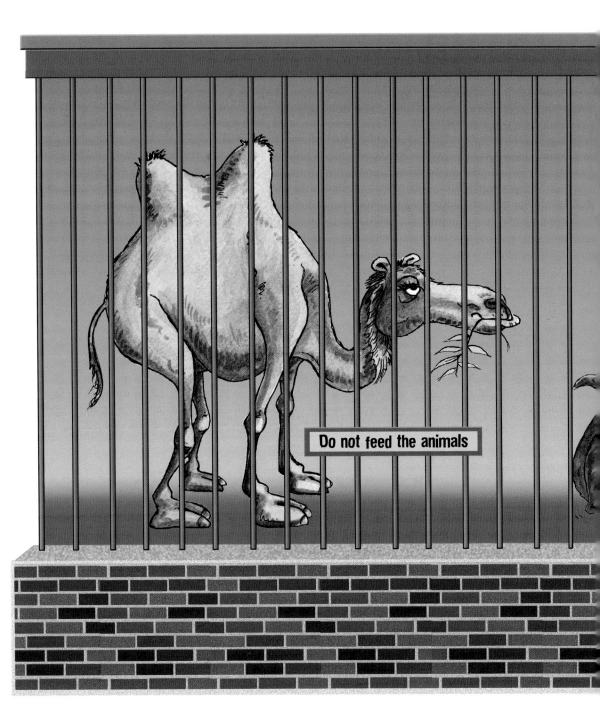

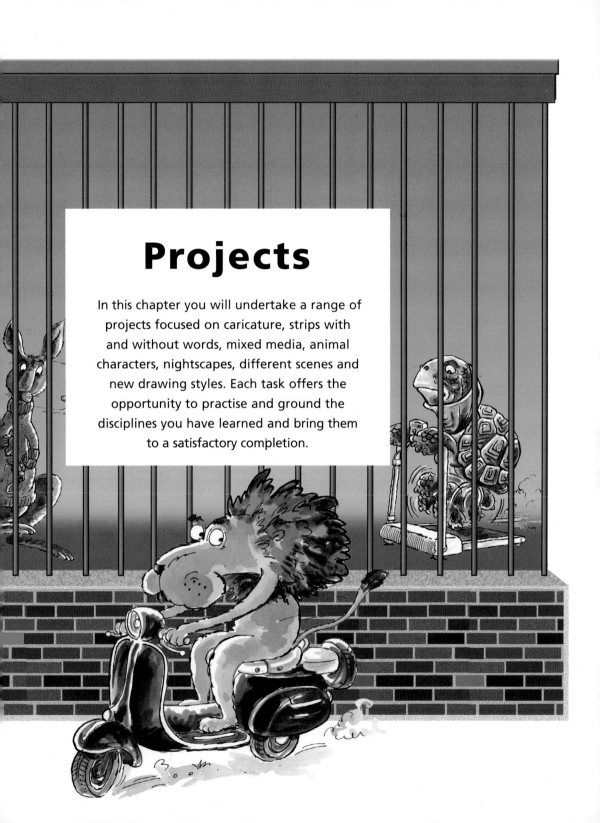

# Projects

In this chapter you will undertake a range of projects focused on caricature, strips with and without words, mixed media, animal characters, nightscapes, different scenes and new drawing styles. Each task offers the opportunity to practise and ground the disciplines you have learned and bring them to a satisfactory completion.

# Political cartoons

Humour can cut through the complexity of serious issues and bring them to the attention of the public. Political cartoons have a long tradition of using visual jokes to make comments intended to evoke a response, convey a message or express an opinion. In order for a joke to succeed, it must hit the right chord with its audience and be visually striking and therefore memorable.

This project is about the threatening issue of global warming. Continual media coverage has provided a wealth of powerful images that can be used to sum up the message. The cartoonist might select one as a starting point from which to adapt a cliché, or develop an original narrative. The humorous touch is light, but ensures that the point is effectively made.

## Final image

Ensure that you have followed your original intention to convey a heavy mood without being completely pessimistic. Subtlety and sensitivity in displaying the polar bear's innocence are key to retaining a strong sense of hope. Consider how you worked through each stage of the project and how you might improve a future attempt.

## Materials

- *layout paper*
- *2B and 4B pencils*
- *black watercolour*
- *'Not' watercolour paper, A3*
- *dip pen and black Indian ink*
- *light box (optional)*
- *oil pastels*
- *charcoal*
- *No. 2 round brush*
- *white gouache paint*

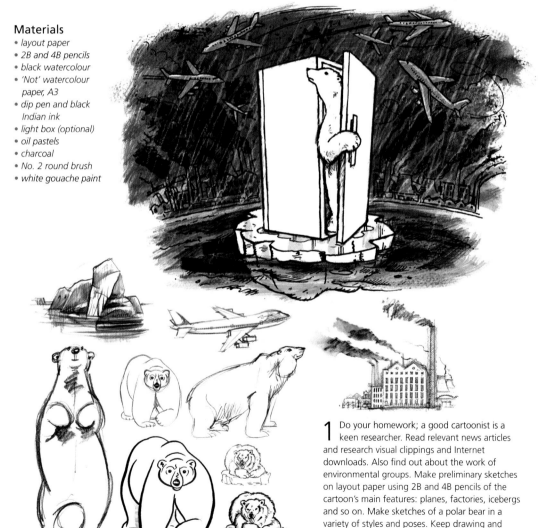

1 Do your homework; a good cartoonist is a keen researcher. Read relevant news articles and research visual clippings and Internet downloads. Also find out about the work of environmental groups. Make preliminary sketches on layout paper using 2B and 4B pencils of the cartoon's main features: planes, factories, icebergs and so on. Make sketches of a polar bear in a variety of styles and poses. Keep drawing and experimenting until you are happy with the results.

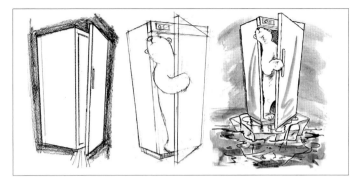

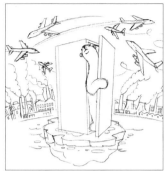

2 Plan the focal point of the cartoon. Begin with the main idea: the polar bear in the fridge. The thinking behind this concept is that if the Arctic ice is melting, where else might a polar bear go to find ice? As a familiar domestic object, the fridge is one environment that is guaranteed to raise a smile. So the bear in the fridge it is! Confidently sketch out the idea in pencil, making sure that the polar bear's pose conveys the key message of inquisitiveness and confusion. Then set the central image in context, placing the fridge on a melting ice floe afloat at sea. Now outline the finished sketch using a dip pen and black Indian ink and add tone with soft, dilute washes of black watercolour.

3 Take the layout paper and trace the outline of the polar bear on the ice floe. Refer back to your preliminary sketches and add the background details of swooping planes and belching factories. Revise this composite stage as much as is necessary, paying attention to the polar bear's expression as a focal feature of the cartoon.

## Melting planet

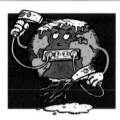

There are many solutions to getting a message across in an arresting way. Above, an anthropomorphized Earth is equipped with two hairdryers, which are plugged into the world's economy and melting the ice caps.

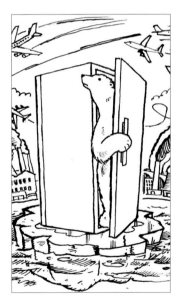

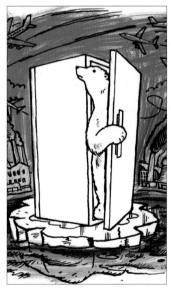

4 Transfer the finished sketch to the 'Not' watercolour paper. Trace it using a light box or against a secure window. Convert the image to line using a dip pen and black Indian ink, varying the pressure and width to give life and movement.

5 Create the atmospheric skies and sea using coloured pastels and charcoal. Spatter the background lightly with black ink by flicking the end of the brush. When dry, use the No. 2 brush to slash in the rain with diagonal strokes of white gouache from the tube.

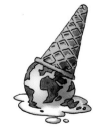

Here, another interpretation of global warming depicts the world as a melting ice-cream cone.

# Portraying children

Children are important as cartoon characters: they are cute, funny and innocent, and these traits can be used to convey big ideas. Cartoon history is full of classic examples. Charles Schultz's *Peanuts* strip features the wisdom of Charlie Brown and his friends, while in the children's comic *The Beano*, the anarchic Bash Street Kids strive to outwit authority, as does the impish yet lovable Dennis the Menace. More recently, the ethical and intelligent character Lisa from *The Simpsons* family spotlights all kinds of moral issues.

Cartoon children can also play their real-life role of endearing small people delighting in and discovering the world around them. Follow the usual rules of proportion when drawing children, and keep features unfussy and complexions and clothing bright. Simplified drawing styles are the most successful.

## Final image
This image's success relies on the harmonious linking and direct contrast of the lines. Ensure that each child is displaying a a unique expression and an individual personality. Clarity of drawing and use of fresh colours will unite the final result of the composition.

## Materials
- *layout paper*
- *soft, blue pencil*
- *A4 smooth watercolour paper*
- *0.3mm fineliner pens*
- *watercolour paints*
- *No. 3 round brush*

**Tip:** Begin by sourcing a range of children's illustrators and cartoonists. Imitate their styles in your sketchbook and note how simplicity of features is common to all. Practise fullness of expression with simple shapes and lines.

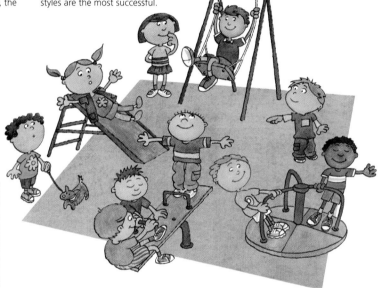

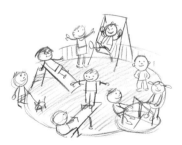

1 Sketch your playground composition on layout paper. Consider the best viewpoint to show all the action. From above, the interaction of the children and the shapes of the equipment are easily seen. Make any adjustments to character placements at this stage.

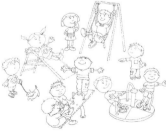

2 When you are satisfied with the basic layout and its main elements, carefully draw the children using a 0.3mm fineliner pen on smooth watercolour paper. Make sure the angles are correct and lines are clearly drawn, with no ambiguous details or sketchy marks.

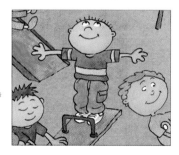

3 Colour each figure with strong, flat washes applied with a No. 3 brush. Note that every child wears colours that link to the red equipment and contrast with the green of the playground floor. The contrast is strongest where these colour complements meet.

### Skipping child

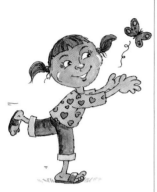

This study, made with a 0.3mm fineliner pen, is trying out a more sketchy, broken line on smooth paper than the previous example. The face is also more modelled with fully formed, naturalistic eye sockets and cheeks.

### Stilt walker

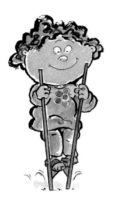

For this character, a loose, brushy line was employed, made with black Indian ink on watercolour paper, to assist the movement within the activity. This technique matches the freedom of washes for the hair, top and trousers.

### Hoodie

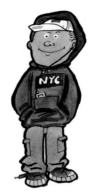

Smooth paper allows bright washes to be brushed over the surface, strengthening the impact of the figure. A brush outline lends a solid feel to this colourful character. The finer details are added using a 0.1mm fineliner pen.

### Skipping child

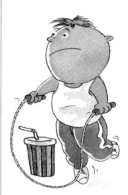

This child is slightly plump and in need of some exercise. The roundness of the body, arms and legs cannot match the almost spherical moon face, with the long, downturned line of mouth arcing across it. Note the size of the shake.

### Yo-yo kids

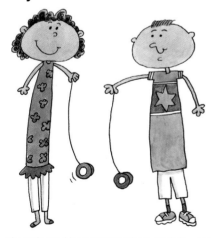

The style used here imitates the typical drawing style of a child in which the body tends to be elongated and the hands and facial features are greatly simplified. The heads are important and therefore exaggerated in scale, but the ears look as if they are merely stuck on and the hair is drawn as short line strokes or curly scribbles.

### Dancing kids

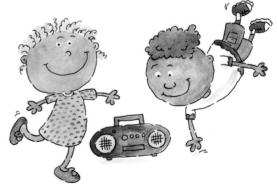

This drawing is about the interaction of the figures with each other and with the music player. A 0.3mm fineliner pen delivers a broken line on textured watercolour paper, and bright watercolour washes are added to keep it lively. The slightly curved backs and fully extended arms and legs of the characters suggest the sense of movement. Defying actual possibility adds humour to these dancing kids, as seen with the breakdancing boy on the right. Giving him the same smiley, effortless expression emphasizes the absurdity of the situation.

# Capturing street life

Teenage life certainly has edge. It is a vibrant, energetic world in which dress code, language and music are key elements of identity. Recognition matters, and certain colours and designs are worn as 'tribal' signifiers. In addition, body language and the way in which they hold themselves capture the character of young people.

Colour is important too. Choose the colours of the environment carefully, so that the all-pervading mood seems authentic and consistent with current social and fashion trends.

To inject social realism into characters, the cartoonist must become a keen observer and recognize the subtle traits and tiny details that demarcate the different social groups amongst teenagers. British cartoonist Michael Heath is a practised observer of the everyday who understands the vast amount a small detail or accessory can tell the audience about a character.

## Final image
In this project, a skateboarding crew has been chosen as a visually clear statement of contemporary youth. The teenagers stand out well from the arty, experimental background colour and texture, although there is a colour harmony between the background and foreground of the image. Observation of minor details, such as shoe style, cut and length of trousers and T-shirt logos, as well as capturing the pose, is crucial.

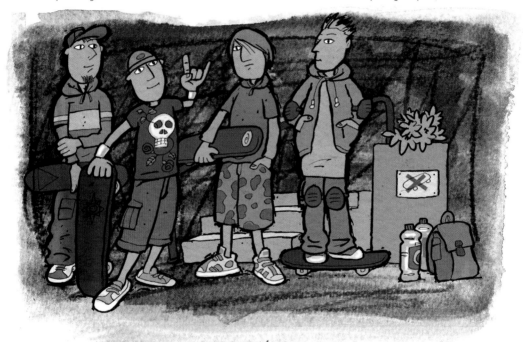

## Materials
- *cartridge paper*
- *soft pencil*
- *rough watercolour paper*
- *light box or tracing paper*
- *dip pen and black Indian ink*
- *No. 4 round and medium, flat brushes*
- *coloured inks*
- *watercolour dyes*
- *wax crayons*

**1** Start by sketching the main figures on cartridge paper in soft pencil. Pay attention to the body shapes: teenage boys have angular body lines, squared features and slender, healthy physiques. Keep in mind that attention to detail is essential, including baseball caps, baggy shorts, chunky trainers, fringes, goatees and sideburns. Assess stance and character, and adjust as necessary.

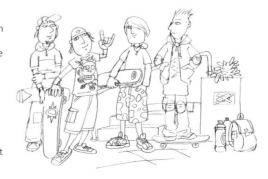

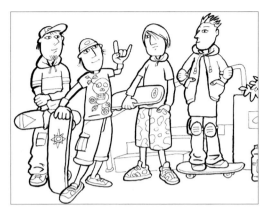

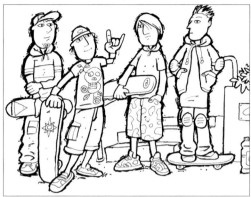

2 Once the composition is established, transfer it to the rough watercolour paper. Either use a light box or a piece of tracing paper to save time and maintain the accuracy of the original. Ink over the lines, varying the pressure on the nib so that the different thicknesses of black enliven the image.

3 Feather the outer lines with a brush to denote freedom and give a sense of energy. Attitude is important to the message of this cartoon. If young people are your intended audience, you should endeavour to maintain sharp, authentic character studies.

## Students and shoppers

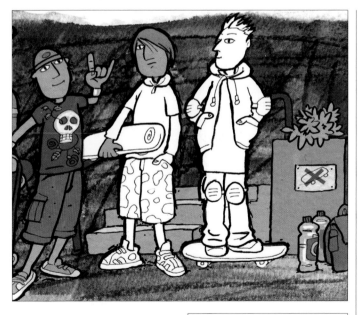

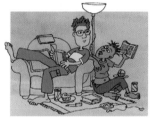

In this character study, two students lounge and sprawl. The armchair assists the student's slouch, the lamp is a focal point for their chat and the books imply that they are studying.

4 Colour clothing according to the latest fashions and apply as flat ink tones. Use subdued hues of yellow and red mix, green, blue, yellow and reddish-brown. Set the figures against a lively background of wet dye colour washes and wax crayon scribble in blue, red and brown hues.

**Tip:** Background texture is sometimes all that is needed for a character scene. An assortment of experimental marks, using a mixed-media cocktail of liquid dyes and controlled waxy scrawls, enriches the foreground scene. The texture and tonal ranges give substance without crowding.

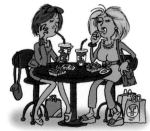

These girls binge on fast food with a casual attitude to match their carefree age. The phones and shopping bags say it all.

# Creating caricatures

The key to good caricature is a practised understanding of portraiture, and it is for this reason that some cartoonists never venture into the genre. However, those who have a natural flair or yearning to develop their figure-drawing technique will enjoy testing their skills. The subjects do not necessarily have to be as famous as the personalities featured on these pages, but they should be readily recognizable in the context in which their representations will be seen.

A caricature of a person should be far more than an illustration with exaggerated physical features; it should also aim to express their personality with accuracy. It is important to give the viewer as much visual information as possible about the person, and distinguishing features, height, stance, distinctive body movements or poses are essential clues. The more famous or publicly exposed a subject, the more a caricaturist must sharpen and hone the character study. The musician Jimi Hendrix was renowned for his blistering guitar playing and psychedelic improvisations. He would set light to his guitar on stage and so is often personified in caricature as a fiery, god-like figure.

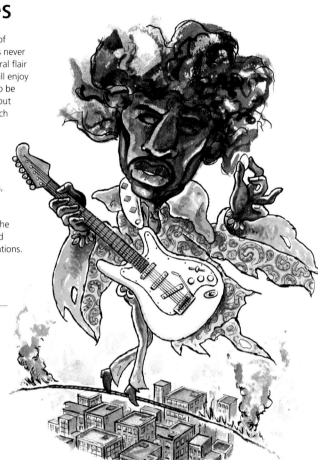

## Caricature: Jimi Hendrix

### Final image
Jimi Hendrix's incendiary guitar and lifestyle are shown here in the flaming tightrope burning at both ends. His position above the city skyscrapers reveals his towering status among rock guitarists. Throughout this project, it is key that you have not simply copied and exaggerated a portrait, but that you have considered his larger-than-life personality.

### Materials
• *cartridge paper*
• *pencil*
• *rough watercolour paper*
• *dip pen and black Indian ink*
• *No. 6 round brush*
• *watercolour paints*

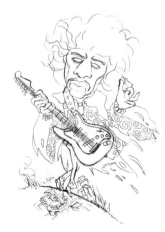

**1** From the very start, consider the movement of your strokes and make every line electrifying, like Hendrix himself. Sketch the outline lightly in pencil on the cartridge paper. Be economical with your strokes, but let your lines flow as if they are flames blown by a wind.

**2** Transfer or redraw the sketch on the rough watercolour paper in black Indian ink. Mix plenty of slate blue paint and brush it over the head using light strokes. Although the colour blue is far from reality, it offers a 'monumental' quality. Leave areas of white paper for highlights and more colour.

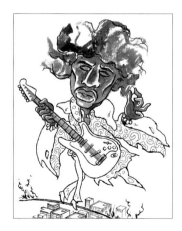

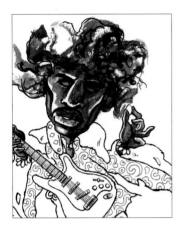

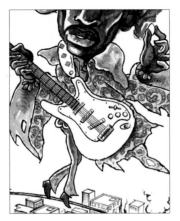

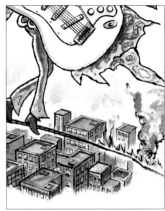

**3** Deepen the washes to define the facial features further. Leave the eyes blank and statue-like to emphasize the focus on Hendrix's music played out through the fingertips. The hands and fingers should be carefully formed with delicate washes.

**4** Add colour with a layer of yellow brushed across the flowing shirt and trousers. Build the shadowy folds using a darker burnt sienna. Pick out the paisley patterns in the same colour and use it to paint the neck of the guitar. Colour the wrist beads in smoky green.

**5** Paint yellow flames at either end of the tightrope. Use a drier brush to tint the skyscrapers in a mix of slate blue and yellow ochre layers to give tonal depths. Brush in the blue slate smoke plumes above the flames and add dashes of cobalt blue to the sky.

## Caricature: Bruce Lee

In contrast to the out-of-control Hendrix, Bruce Lee was a highly disciplined martial arts film star, precise in knowledge of his artistry.

### Materials
• smooth watercolour paper
• dip pen and black Indian ink
• No. 2 and No. 1 round brushes
• watercolour dyes

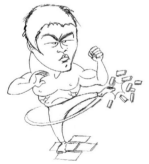

**1** Match Lee's finely controlled style to your own delivery of strong, clean sketch lines to suggest Lee's smooth, powerful movements are delivered with speed.

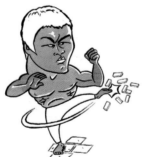

**2** Watercolour dyes produce a strong stain with a flat, matt quality. First, ink the outline, then paint the flesh colours using the No. 2 brush. Try to get a direct 'hit' with single strokes.

**3** Colour the remaining areas of hair and clothing, catching the pale blue spot highlight on the trousers and top of the head. Tint the lips and bricks in cadmium red and dilute red with yellow ochre to colour the tiles. Use the No. 1 fine brush to add the precise woodcut-line effect.

### Final image
Successful action and strong suggestion of movement should be the most prominent visual qualities here, allowing a wider interpretation of Lee's features.

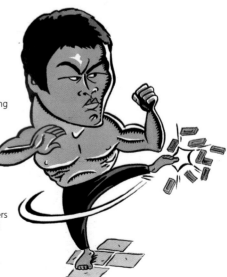

## Caricature: Van Gogh

This caricature of the artist Van Gogh depicts him holding a sunflower and a paintbrush. Linking style to content will work well for this subject, so he is to be painted in thick, Van Gogh-like brushstrokes.

### Materials
• *rough watercolour paper*
• *pencil*
• *No. 4 round and flat brushes*
• *gouache paints*

### Final image
The quality of the marks and colours applied here should be consistent with those of the master, Vincent Van Gogh, so that your final image is irrefutably accomplished in the painting style.

**Tip:** Get into the habit of making colour tester sheets on various textured papers. This Van Gogh caricature benefited from a series of gouache paint experiments on various types of paper before the final one was chosen. Annotate the swatches so that you are able to access the right hues and paper types in the future.

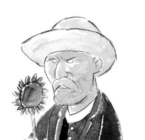

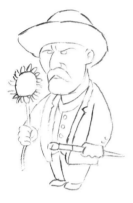

**1** Begin by making an edited pencil sketch on rough watercolour paper.

**2** Add the base washes in dilute gouache using the round brush: yellow ochre for the hat and beard; burnt sienna for the sunflower and paintbrush; ultramarine blue for the jacket and trousers; grey for the shirt, and a flesh tint mix of cadmium red and yellow ochre for the face and hands.

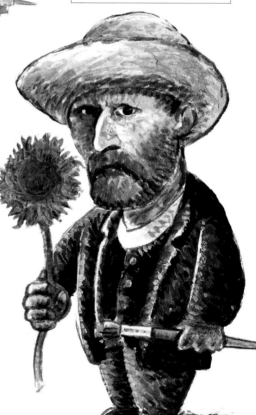

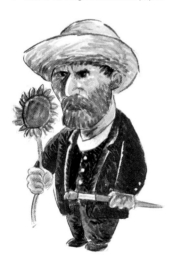

**4** Build up another layer of brushstrokes on top of the first when it is dry, but do not allow the life of the stroke to be diminished. Enhance and correct facial details; here, the eyes have been refined between steps 3 and 4 with small touches, such as highlighting the whites of the eyes to emphasize the tortured expression, making the caricature true to life.

**3** Squeeze plenty of each colour on to the palette, then apply short strokes with the flat brush using a dabbing technique. Note the tonal qualities of the burnt sienna and cadmium red flecks on the yellow ochre base. Refer to a portrait by Van Gogh to help you to learn his technique.

## Caricature: Shakespeare

The bard writing on a laptop melds two Elizabethan ages. The symbolism is important – a large forehead suggests intelligence; and the quill, paper and laptop show how a writer can adapt, yet retain relevance across the ages.

### Materials
- *cartridge paper*
- *rough watercolour paper*
- *dip pen and black indian ink*
- *No. 5 round brush*
- *watercolour paints*

### Final image
The controlled passages of ink and the delicately drawn line image offer this subject a period feel. You should have improved your ability to lay fluid washes with subtlety and accuracy.

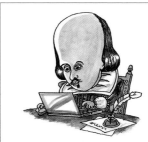

**Tip:** A working colour sketch should always precede finished artwork. View it as an opportunity to experiment, make mistakes and try out colour combinations before beginning the final piece.

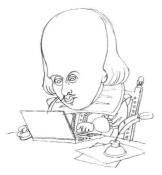

1 Make a clear sketch on cartridge paper of the figure with its oversized, intelligent cranium and add costume and accessories.

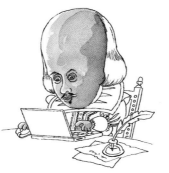

2 Transfer the drawing to rough watercolour paper and go over the outline using a dip pen and black Indian ink. Keep the lines strong and direct, and allow the texture of the paper to dictate the look of the sketch. Lay a flesh colour wash over the face and hands.

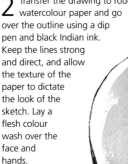

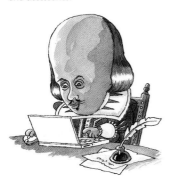

3 Systematically colour the different sections of the drawing using cadmium red for the jacket and on the ruff, burnt sienna for the hair, grey for the chair back and ink, green for the ink bottle and diluted light blue for the creased shadow tones of the collar fabric.

4 The final stage is the opportunity to make adjustments and add the finer detailing: colour the eye pupils grey, add burnt umber brushstrokes to the hair and colour the chair studs, the braiding and buttons on the jacket in yellow ochre. These finishing touches brighten and warm the composition.

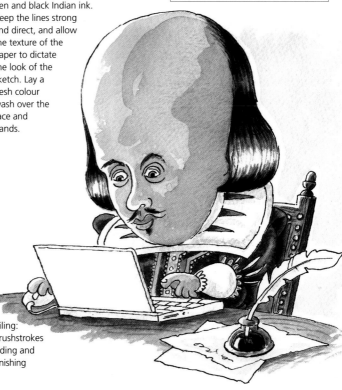

# Quick-draw caricature

Drawing a convincing caricature of a living subject can present a challenge. Experienced 'live' caricaturists are the fast and furious artists of the cartoon world. Although the subject is likely to be unknown to them, they are able to capture the essence of a character in a few accurate and directly delivered strokes. The ability to 'read' the personality of a subject at a glance is an essential skill.

The classic drawing tools of the live caricaturist's trade are mark-makers that can quickly fill the paper with both line strokes and shading. Felt-tip marker pens, dip pens or brush and ink are among the most popular choices, with each option delivering a different style of drawing. It is the immediacy of the drawing that makes it so attractive as a minimal art form.

## Final image
What should be apparent from having undertaken this project is the level of forethought necessary before actually making a pen stroke. One false mark and the whole drawing could be in jeopardy. The key is to have made only one continuous stroke each time the pen touches the paper.

## Materials
- *bleedproof designers' layout paper*
- *fine felt-tip pens*
- *chisel-tipped felt-tip pens*
- *black italic calligraphy pen*
- *charcoal*
- *colouring pencils*
- *broad felt-tip pens*

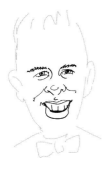

**1** The face is always the main area of focus. Lightly sketch the exaggerated head shape in pale grey felt-tip pen on bleedproof layout paper, then outline the eyebrows, eyes, nose, cheeks and mouth using a black felt-tip marker. Enlarge the mouth as a key, distinct feature.

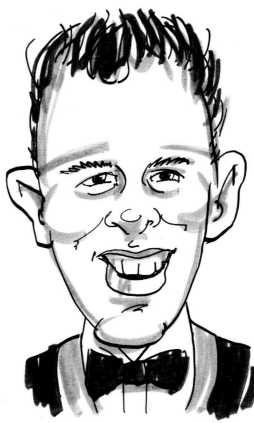

**Tip:** Practise stroke length and thickness in sketchbooks to gauge the potential of each pen you use. Treat this exercise merely for the sake of pen marks and do not try to sketch recognizable faces.

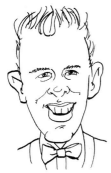

**2** Draw the rest of the head using a fine black marker. Keep the lines around the head fast-moving, but consider the marks you intend to make before putting pen to paper. Remember that too much detail can detract from the personality of the subject.

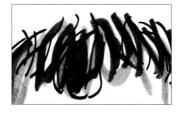

**3** Only a little tonal work is necessary in black, medium and light grey. Using the broad edge of the felt tips, sweep strokes in long stripes. Keep them to a minimum, allowing the white of the paper to stand in for the lightest tones or highlights. Freely scribble rapid single strokes for the hair.

## Happy and assured

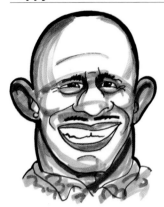

This character has strong, round features, which emphasize his broad grin and offer an assuring presence. Remember too that hairstyles, skin tones as well as size and shape of facial features are key elements of caricatures. Maintaining strong light and dark contrasts is vital for dark-skinned subjects.

## Larger than life

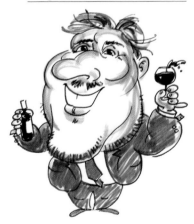

Enlarging features enlarges the ego. Props, such as the wine bottle and glass, offer more information. Felt-tip markers are used on bleedproof designers' layout paper (semi-translucent tracing paper), which keep the edges of the strokes crisp and reveal that they were rapidly drawn.

## Bubbly

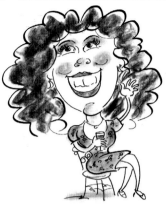

The bubbly personality of this young woman is enhanced by the style of the drawing. A light pencil sketch is worked up in an italic calligraphy pen. The chisel shape of the nib enables both thin and thick lines to be made within the same stroke. Quickly smudged charcoal adds immediacy and soft tone.

## Gone to seed

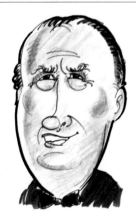

A mixture of fine and broad felt-tip pens and colouring pencils is employed to bring subtlety to this study of an ageing face. The reddened areas of the character's complexion are made using brighter-coloured pencils sketched across pale, fine felt-tip pen strokes.

## Caricature: Young girl

Chalk pastels are a suitable medium for caricaturing children. The soft marks they make add a glow that perfectly suits young skin.

### Materials
• *cartridge paper*  • *chalk pastels*

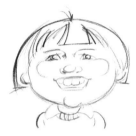

**1** Start by lightly sketching the face shape and features with the pastel tips.

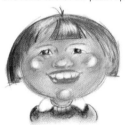

**2** Execute the main tones, leaving white paper highlights. Maintain an even balance of line strokes and soft blending, achieved by gentle smudging. Delicately sketch in the eyes, nose and the mouth.

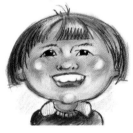

**3** Define the features firmly and also re-establish the hair texture and the outline of the face. Take time to shape the eyes and add fine detail, such as the highlights in the pupils. Keep these details sharp in contrast to the tonal softness and avoid overdoing the pastel layers.

# Background incidentals

Not every cartoon needs to be sparse to communicate its point. Clutter and chaos are part of real life and the incidentals in a picture can be as intriguing to the viewer as the main plot. Some cartoonists delight in inventing small sub-plots to run alongside the main theme; others revel in adding ephemera as a social statement, personal opinion or because they simply enjoy making things more interesting.

However, building what appears to be chaos into your compositions carries the obvious danger that the cartoons might lose focus. Careful consideration of weighting,

medium and technique can help to avoid this, allowing you to include plenty of information, yet keep the message clear.

Weighting is the balance or imbalance of elements within a picture, which aid successful composition so that the image reads with clarity. A central figure might be drawn with an outline technique that is slightly heavier, thicker even; this helps to make it stand out from the other elements. Using lighter strokes with a thin-nib fineliner – or even a pale ink or watercolour wash – over a light drawing can also help to recede less important parts.

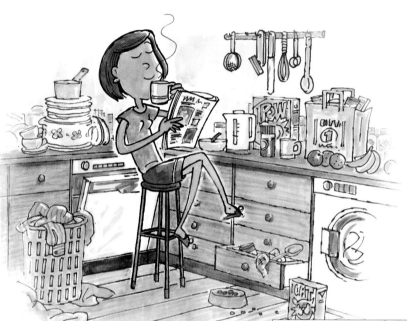

## Final image
Within chaos, the housewife is easily identifiable as the main focus. Giving her a heavier outline 'weighting' and adding specific washes to the background elements should provide enough contrast to make this final image work. If the clutter is still in conflict with the character, the content and composition may need revising.

## Materials
- *cartridge paper*
- *sharp HB pencil*
- *dip pen and black Indian ink*
- *waterproof fineliner pen*
- *No. 4 round brush*
- *watercolour paints*

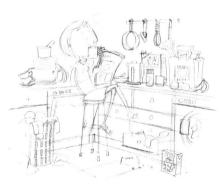

**1** First, make an initial sketch to establish the figure, the setting and the clutter of objects within the composition. The lighter your lines, the easier it will be to make any adjustments and corrections.

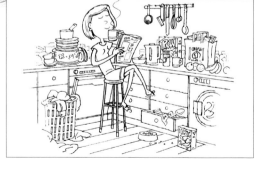

**2** When you are happy with the arrangement, check that all the elements are correctly positioned in relation to the perspective of the room. Then ink in the sketch using a dip pen for main items and a fineliner for lesser items and details.

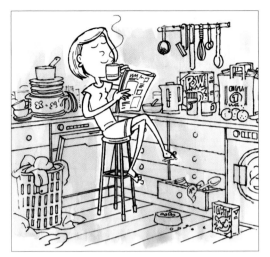

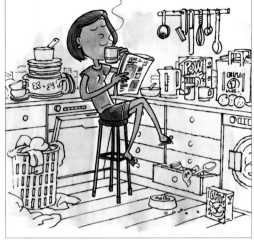

**3** Paint a broad yellow ochre wash over the room and its contents, brushing around the main character so that she remains white. This simple action has the effect of separating her from the business of the scene and draws attention to her as the focal point.

**4** Now bring her presence to life using bold watercolour hues: yellow, blue and a lighter dilution of the same blue for the T-shirt, a rosy flesh tint for the skin tones and a rich brown for the hair and cushion. Colour the magazine in a light wash of blue and brown.

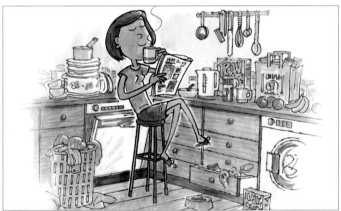

## Incidental meaning

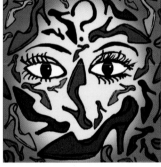

**5** Add colour to the rest of the cartoon. Choose naturalistic ones for items such as the oranges and bananas, white for the washing machine and dishwasher, pale red for the worktops and cat bowl, dark brown for the stool legs and skirting and a warmer red-brown for the drawers. Finally, 'knock back' the tonal strength of the setting and objects by applying another yellow ochre wash overall. This will diminish the cluttered effect of the

picture and make the line work far less heavy, allowing greater contrast with the strong reds and blues that dominate the foreground.

**Tip:** Whenever you create a busy scene, consider the colours that you are going to use. Always try to keep the background in a few predominant colours so that it does not distract the main area of focus in the mid- or foreground.

This illustration is the antithesis of the kitchen project in that the clutter actually enlightens rather than confuses the image. Without the 'floating' shoes, we would be unable to deduce that she is trying to choose the correct pair. The eyes are a central focus and act as the windows to her mind, and the larger vertical and horizontal shoes make a good substitute nose and mouth. The hidden question mark indicates her thoughts.

# The psychology of colour

Employing the psychology of colour and carefully selecting the media to match the mood or look of a picture are big-hitting techniques with cartoonists. Ensuring that the audience can differentiate a friend from a foe in the blink of an eye, for example, leaves the cartoonist free to spin more complex threads into the narrative.

Planning, testing and developing ideas are essential if your cartoon is to succeed in communicating everything you want it to say. Of course, establishing the characters comes first, but selecting groups of colours that work the best, the appropriate

style of mark-making and the best paper surface are also fundamental factors for success. This may seem daunting for the beginner, but the cartoon world is full of superb examples to study and learn from.

As a first step, try to understand how the experts instantly communicate mood by looking closely at a wide range of cartoon genres. As a general guide, children's comic strips come across as bright and cheerful; tension and struggle are paramount in superhero narratives; and graphic novels can ooze dark menace.

## Final image
There is a good deal of optimism relayed through these bright and strongly contrasting colours. The blue simplicity of the sea and sky set an open scene for the galleon. By drawing with an improbable sense of scale – the king is far too big – the fantasy quality is increased and the overall freshness of the image brings it to life on the printed page.

## Materials
• cartridge paper, A3
• smooth watercolour paper, A3
• dip pen and black Indian ink
• No. 4 and No. 6 round brushes
• watercolour dyes

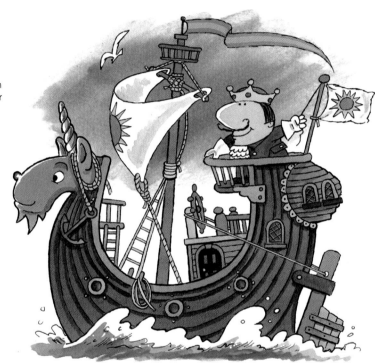

1 Plan your composition on a sheet of A3 cartridge paper. The basic shapes are all that are necessary at this stage. The details can be added to the final drawing once you have the main idea worked out.

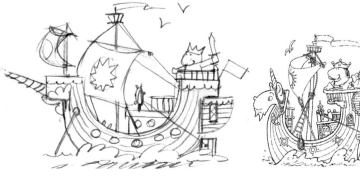

2 Even though this is a fantasy drawing, it is a good idea to refer to an accurate reference so that you locate the main features of the ship in the correct places. When you are satisfied with your composition, copy or transfer the sketch to an A3 sheet of smooth watercolour paper. Outline the sketch using a dip pen and black Indian ink. Embolden the main line of the crescent-shaped hull to give it due prominence in the composition.

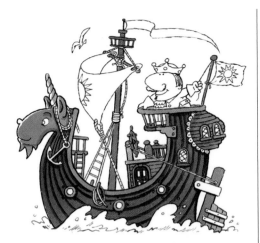

**3** Have ready enough full-strength red-brown dye to ensure the fluidity of your brushstrokes as you colour in the hull. Dilute the colour to a paler brown for the rest of the timber parts: the steps, rails and ship's wheel. Use yellow ochre to clarify the forecastle, mast, crow's nest, horn of the figurehead, rudder and window frames. Add a neat brown shadow beneath the planks on the hull to indicate the overlap.

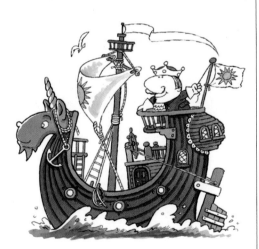

**4** Finally, add the colour detailing, leaving some areas blank. Paint the sea beneath the foamy crests of the waves in fluid washes of cobalt blue; your strokes should follow the spirit and direction of the wave pattern. Gently tint the interior of the sail and its exterior edge with watered-down cobalt blue. This will give it the appearance of billowing in the wind. Add yellow to the sun emblem on the flag and the sail. The distinctive purple colour of the king's clothing marks him out from the rest of the picture.

## Practice exercise: Sinister war machine

This imaginary war machine is a threatening amalgamation of mechanized soldier and tank. The solid panels are constructed into a strongly angled face that rests on recognizable caterpillar tracks.

### Materials
- *rough watercolour paper*
- *dip pen and black Indian ink*
- *No. 5 round brush*
- *coloured inks*
- *soft chalk pastels*
- *waterproof fineliner pen*

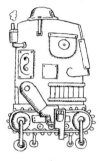

**1** Form the outer casing on rough watercolour paper with a dip pen and black Indian ink. Introduce a slightly jagged, 'crazed' edge to your drawn lines but keep the drawing controlled and convincing. Your invention should present itself as fully mechanically functional.

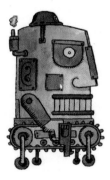

**2** Tint the main panels with mixed stains of rust or chestnut-brown ink in a variety of dilutions. Add sepia tints to the outer socket of the eye, the helmet, gun and caterpillar tracks. The matt finish of the heavily textured paper creates a sinister mood that suits the subject. The bright yellow eye serves to bring focus to this personification and draws the viewer's attention.

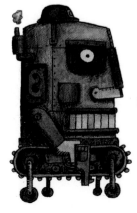

**3** Crumble soft chalk pastels in various shades of brown over the surface of the paper inside the painted shapes. Sharpen up the drawing using a fineliner pen to add ink-line panels and dotted rivets. The major benefit of using a rough watercolour paper is that it adds an extra textured dimension and a ready-made depth.

# Creating a sinister narrative

This street cat image combines drawing and collage, and demonstrates just one of a myriad of approaches to creating a menacing theme. The drawn section is strongly contrasted with the layers of printed areas, and the range of textures that overlap in the collage provide considerable interest.

Collage can be a quick and easy medium to work in so long as you select the right images to begin with and use

them to best effect. Experiment with black-and-white copying techniques to discover the effects you want. Black-and-white copies of colour photographs, for example, can create a very dense effect, especially in areas of saturated blues and reds. Also, the more times an image is photocopied, the grainier it becomes, rendering it perfect for backgrounds where the setting needs to be strong, yet not too defined.

## Final image

The panoramic format of this collaged cartoon has filmic connotations that suggest a sinister narrative. Despite being dark in colour, much depth exists within the different layers. Consider this throughout and take a bold approach to using stark black against white! In any cropped, small section of this final image there should be strong contrasts to give the picture 'edge'.

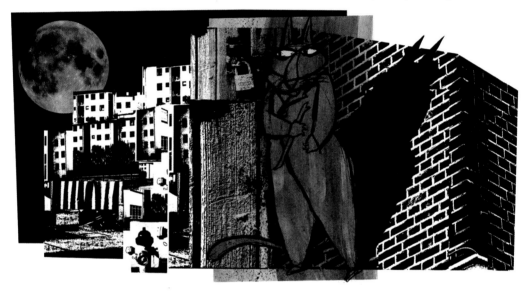

## Materials

- fineliner pen
- dip pen and black Indian ink
- 2B pencil
- cartridge paper; A4 and A3 black paper
- black-and-white photocopies of street features, full moon
- PVA (white) glue
- coloured inks
- No. 4 round brush

1 The cat is the only drawn section of this image, and the figure's portrayal is central to the meaning of the picture. Sketch different cat characters, outlining them using fineliner and dip-pen linear strokes. Look at classic cartoon cats for inspiration, such as Snagglepuss, Top Cat and the Pink Panther. Redraw and refine your chosen character until you are satisfied with the result.

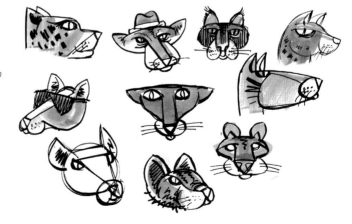

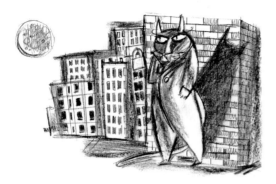

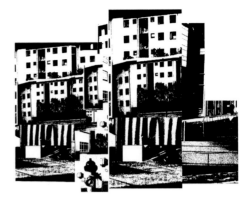

2 Visualize your intention for the cat and its environment in the form of a 2B pencil sketch on A4 cartridge paper. Although collage brings a certain amount of freedom to the creative process, it is always best to sketch your idea first. Doing so anchors your thoughts and ensures that you start with a definite concept for development.

3 Print high-contrast black-and-white copies of the scenic elements. Surfaces, such as textured brick and corrugated iron, and dark windows in varied scales and sizes will enhance the brooding feeling. Glue the elements in a disjointed layout on the A3 sheet of cartridge paper. For a naturalistic sense of depth, position complete buildings as a background.

4 Sketch the full cat figure. Experiment with his stance so that it emphasizes his shady character. Here, the chosen cat carries a crowbar – a simple detail that adds threat, as does the turned-up coat collar. Draw over the sketch in a bold line using a dip pen and black Indian ink and cut it out.

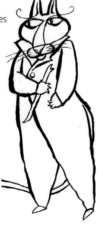

## Guardians of the gateway

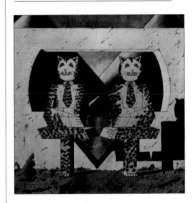

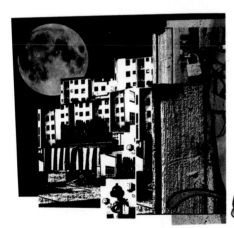

5 Extend the scene by gluing a black paper sky with a full moon in position. Glue the cut-out cat figure into the composition. Brush washes of highly diluted black ink (grey) over the cat to unite him with the background. Tint the moon using a very pale yellow, adding a strong yellow colour to the whites of the cat's eyes. Now lengthen a shadow behind him so that he looms larger.

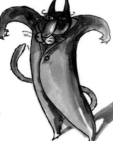

The disquieting atmosphere of this cartoon is achieved by combining specific colours with an unexpected juxtaposition of elements. The smiling cat figures guard a gateway that is also a cat form. The twilight colours of yellow and the deep shadows communicate an air of foreboding: what lies beyond the gate? The cartoon is created using Indian-ink line and coloured-ink washes. Three further layers of varnish increase the colour depth.

# Ghoulish characters

The Halloween theme is an opportunity to create some freakishly ghoulish characters. The bizarre shapes of pointy hats, distorted features and abnormal skin tones offer the cartoonist broad scope for creativity and inventiveness. Using traditional media – spidery and scratchy dip-pen hatching, the heaviness of black Indian ink and the layering of gouache or watercolour tonal washes will evoke a suitable mood and atmosphere within this subject genre.

## Final image
The witch image works because she transcends the norms of human appearance. Filling the frame gives the impression of power. Exaggeration in the nose, close placement of the eyeballs and green-tinted skin all work to present sinister yet grotesquely humorous physical characteristics.

## Materials
- 'Not' watercolour paper
- pencil
- dip pen and black Indian ink
- No. 5 round brush
- watercolour paints
- gouache paints

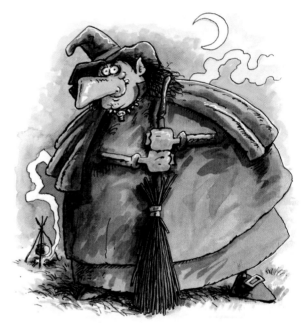

1 Begin with a simple yet accurate pencil sketch of the witch on 'Not' watercolour paper. Since you are making a caricature, exaggerate some features grotesquely. When you are happy with your interpretation, draw over it line for line using a dip pen and black Indian ink.

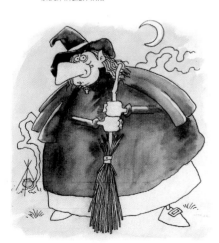

2 Start building up your colour layers on the top of a broad background wash. Set the tonal range with an overall tint of yellow ochre watercolour paint, then add deeper washes of green to the witch's clothing. Create shadows with darker washes where the garments overlap.

3 Gradually build up the colour strength using yellow and Paynes grey or indigo blue. Deliver more green to the face and hands, and tint the broom in burnt umber. Using a dryish brush, hatch orange around the background.

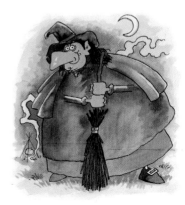

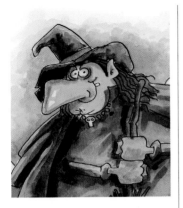

**4** Now add all the finishing touches. Strengthen all the shadows to accentuate tone and depth; the extra shadowing on the grass beneath the witch helps to enhance the picture's mood. Paint extra highlights direct from the gouache tube on to the tip of the nose, the tip of the ear, the fearsome necklace and the backs of the hands. A touch of orange around the pupils of the eyes adds a spooky glow.

## Practice exercise: Woodcut demon

The contrast of dark versus light of the primitive wood-cut style is most effective.

### Materials
• 'Not' watercolour paper
• dip pen and black Indian ink
• coloured inks

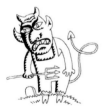

**1** Sketch the demon with a simple, slightly broken line and outline it using a dip pen and black Indian ink. Edge inside the line with 'chiselled' jagged marks.

## Witch's hands

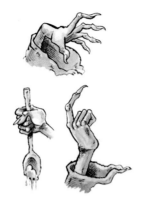

Regardless of an artist's ability and experience, hands are among the most challenging body parts to be tackled. Incredibly expressive, they can accurately describe a character's mood or personality. These three examples are drawn using the same techniques as for the main cartoon, but they communicate three quite different messages.

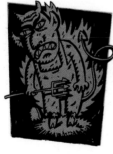

**2** Paint the entire background using black Indian ink. Leave an area around the demon unpainted and a few background 'specks'. This gives the impression of carved marks to the woodcut look. Apply a wash of heavily diluted cadmium red coloured ink to the unpainted areas.

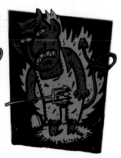

**3** Brush a second undiluted layer of red over the face, arms, hooves, chest and tail. Note the effectiveness of this simple process in portraying the demon's character using colour. The final touch of vivid orange to the eyes and mouth confirms the wicked personality.

## Practice exercise: Woodcut

Flat colours are effective for Halloween subjects and work best in conjunction with a bold, variable black line.

### Materials
• No. 5 round brush
• black Indian ink and gouache paints

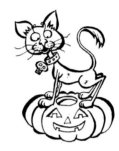

**1** Ink over your initial sketch using a brush so that you can vary the line thicknesses with ease.

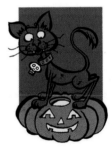

**2** Colour the cartoon in traditional hues of gouache paint applied with a medium round brush: midnight blue, grey and orange. Colour the interior of the pumpkin a lighter yellowish-orange, created by mixing orange, a spot of cadmium yellow and white. Use the same colour for the glow of the eyes.

**Tip:** Use gouache paint when you want to achieve density of colour and depth. Often it is better to apply the gouache guided by a pencil outline, adding an ink line on top once the paint has thoroughly dried for a much crisper appearance.

# Sequential cartooning

This project gives you the chance to test your communication abilities through the vehicle of sequential cartooning. It involves devising a comic-strip page that projects its narrative without using any words. Here is the story:

A teenager is leaning against a wall happily listening to music when he is accosted by the grim reaper who steals his MP3 player. The puzzled reaper plugs in the earpieces of the alien object and begins to dance madly to the music. Finally, he gets totally carried away to the point of losing his head – quite literally – as a result of his wildly circling scythe. It is a highly visual storyline, with recognizable key elements standing in for words to explain the action.

**Tip:** Practise creating a 'no-words' strip using a simple three- to four-panel vertical or horizontal format. Remember that the action must make the intention clear. Here, a simple carton interacts with a question mark and an exclamation mark in a very simple story. Keeping the visual elements basic allows you to focus on telling the story.

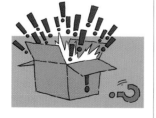

## Materials
• 'Not' watercolour paper
• No. 5 round brush
• dip pen and black Indian ink
• gouache paints
• black watercolour paint

## Final image
Approach the final artwork with the simplicity of not more than three colours, a clear drawing style and frames set in a three by five rectangular grid. These will ensure that this unconventional narrative of the grim reaper's undoing is a success.

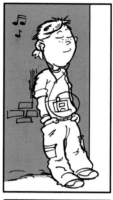
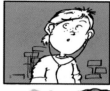
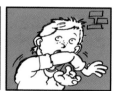
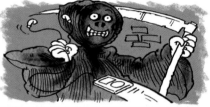
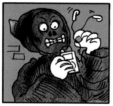
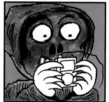
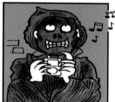
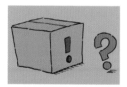
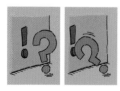
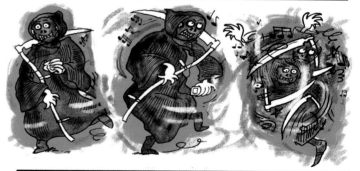
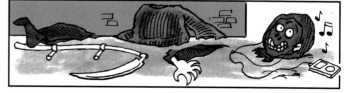

**1** Begin by planning the narrative sequence, sketching the action frame by frame. Try out different grid layouts until you find the one that tells the story most effectively. Adjust your sketches and edit your grid for maximum impact.

In this initial layout, the last frame on the top row (tinted blue) repeats the bigger image below it. The first frame on the third row adds nothing to the story and neither does frame one in the bottom row (both are tinted blue). Axing these and redesigning the grid will help to tighten the narrative.

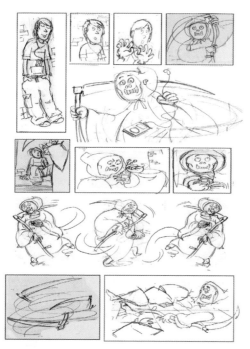

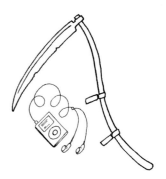

**2** The props of the grim reaper's scythe and the MP3 player are central to the storyline and should be represented correctly. Don't be tempted to make up the drawings of these items; copy them from accurate references. Practise sketching them in a variety of angles and positions. The more advance preparation you do, the better the final result. Careful attention should always be offered to props that contextualize the narrative and offer a chance to refocus the viewer on detail.

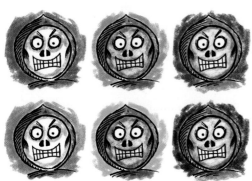

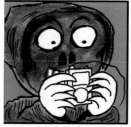

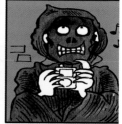

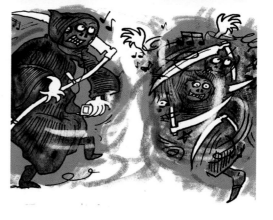

**3** Explore a range of colour combinations. Any of the variations above might work well in this strip, but one will usually strike you as being the most suitable for the job. The blue appears slightly too vibrant, while the variations on the straw/ochre colours seem insipid. The ash-grey hooded skull against the reddish-pink background strikes just the right note.

**4** This cartoon detail shows how effective it is to mix close-up and wider-angled panels in the strip format. By focusing closer on the face, attention is drawn to the MP3 player, enhanced by the stark contrast of white with dark grey and black. The images of the dance in the larger frame offer a highly animated quality in comparison with the static panels directly above.

# A cartoon world

Developing an entire imaginary world populated by a cast of diverse characters is a fascinating exercise in creative thinking. The challenge is not only to conjure up a background setting and range of personalities who will naturally interact but also to develop the best style and use the most appropriate media for your chosen subject.

As a first step in creating a cartoon strip for children, revisit the kinds of illustrations that captured your imagination as a child and also look at contemporary examples. Think about the qualities that children find so attractive, such as quirky characters, bright colours or lots of detail, and try to reproduce these in your own work. Stories for very young children are often fantastical, designed to stimulate their imaginations. At the same time they can help children learn about the world around them by mirroring situations they can easily recognize. The characters that act out the stories usually display human qualities and behaviour; they pursue similar activities and talk our language. Most importantly, children identify with them, whatever form they take.

Children universally accept the 'unreal' without question, so the only limits on creating your cartoon world are those imposed by your own imagination.

## Final image
This jolly cast has been composed to work harmoniously within the scene. Each personality should be distinct, using a colourful, mixed-media style. Setting them at different levels and heights helps retain a bouncy vigour.

## Materials
• *2B pencil or fineliner pen*
• *cartridge paper*
• *No. 1 and No. 3 round brushes*
• *watercolour paints*
• *brown colouring pencils or soft black charcoal pencil*
• *photocopies of textured fabrics and found objects*
• *PVA (white) glue*
• *dip pen and black Indian ink*
• *old scraps of fabric*
• *scissors*

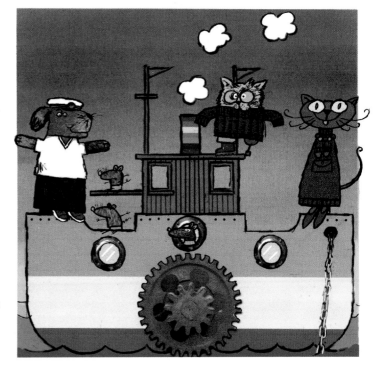

1 Begin with the lesser characters. Sketch the mouse crew in 2B pencil or fineliner pen. Draw simple shapes with strong features: large ears, whiskered noses and expressive tails. Anthropomorphize, but don't get too complex; allow your style to develop.

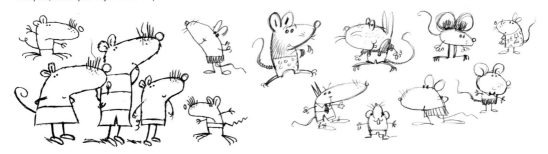

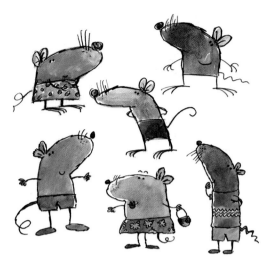

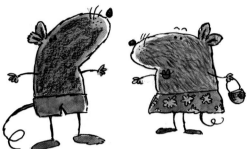

3 Explore conventional and unconventional ways of suggesting furry textures. Individual hairs can be drawn using a No. 1 round smooth-hair brush for maximum control. Be sure to choose a colour that is darker or lighter than the base so that the hairs show up. You can create a more sketchy effect by using colouring pencils. Shading over the base colour using a black charcoal pencil will also create a textural look.

2 Develop your character style further, trying out colours and refining the small details. Subtle touches to the eyes, whiskers, lips and clothing will differentiate male characters from female and young ones from old. Don't be afraid to test the effects of unusual or seemingly unnatural colours.

> **Tip:** Including discarded pieces of fabric and other materials in your drawings not only saves time but makes recycling sense and can give edge to your designs. Start a collection of fabric remnants, including unlikely household materials, such as worn dusters and cleaning cloths. Paste a very small scrap of each material into a sketchbook to make a handy reference source when you are looking for ideas on texture or colour.

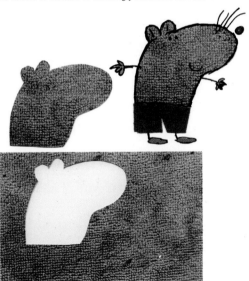

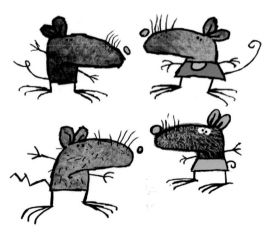

4 To achieve instant colour and texture, use collage to create some characters. Photocopy a piece of coloured towelling, cut it out and paste it on to a sheet of paper. Outline the main body shape using a dip pen and black Indian ink. Now cut out and glue on to the red-fabric shorts. Ink in the rest of the features and colour with paint.

5 Develop this concept further by trying out a range of photocopied fabrics to create the mice and their garments. Ensure that you 'hold' all your cartoons within an ink outline drawn with a scratchy, dip-pen delivery. The photocopies may require colour or tonal changes, which can be administered using colouring or charcoal pencils or watercolour paints, allowing the photocopy to show through.     *continued overleaf*

**6** Develop the character of the 'sea-dog' captain. His slightly flattened shape adds comic value. Define his key physical features: exaggerated muzzle, squared body and stubby arms. Dress him in wide bell-bottom trousers, white uniform top or fisherman's sweater and captain's hat. Consider using a collage technique and experiment with denim and wool fabrics, with furry material for head and arms. Once dressed, make him move.

**Tip:** If you are creating a cartoon world, research all aspects of your subject. If your setting is historical, accuracy is paramount. Once you know how things really were, you can alter them to suit. Having the freedom to add your own take on a theme can be artistically liberating, and breathe life into your creatures.

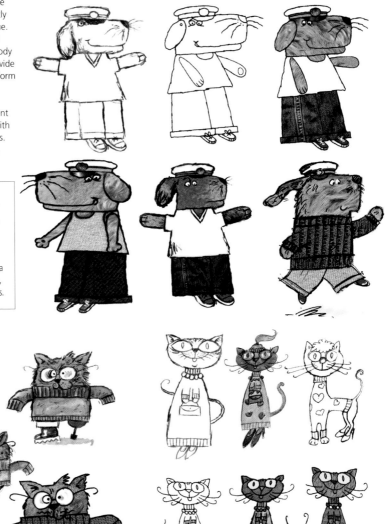

**7** This ship's cat is a stereotypical peg-leg sailor. Outline him in the flattened style of the other crew members and personify him as an unkempt, bespectacled character. His oversized, baggy sweater reflects his eccentric nature. Again, explore colour and texture through paint or collaged fabrics, or a combination of the two. Having the cat's body drawn wider than it is deep increases the humour.

**8** This 'lady cat' is a very different type of character to the others, and her inclusion adds diversity and interest to the cast. Use clothing, accessories, fashion styles and colours to suggest her personality. The costume jewellery, retro colours and drawing style express her individuality. She is deliberately drawn to contrast with her male, feline counterpart. The elegant elongation shows her dressiness to the full.

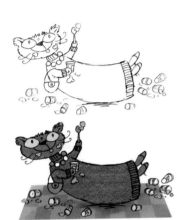

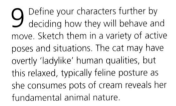

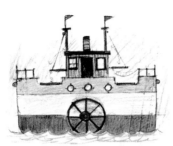

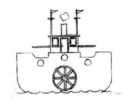

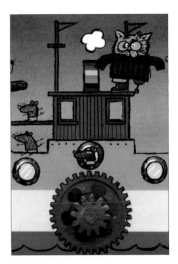

**9** Define your characters further by deciding how they will behave and move. Sketch them in a variety of active poses and situations. The cat may have overtly 'ladylike' human qualities, but this relaxed, typically feline posture as she consumes pots of cream reveals her fundamental animal nature.

**10** Choose an environment for your characters that complements them and is created in a style that matches theirs. If you intend the setting to appear frequently, keep the subject matter simple and practise scaling it up or down so that its presence varies according to the action.

**11** Substitute some of the boat's features with photocopies of objects. The portholes, for example, are colour copies of brass ferrule rings, and the wheel is a photocopied large and small red cog. The technique of mixing drawn cartoon style with pictures of real objects works very well in this setting.

## Developing your cartoon setting

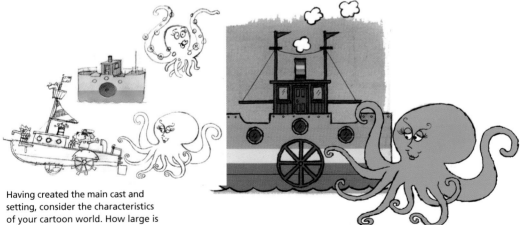

Having created the main cast and setting, consider the characteristics of your cartoon world. How large is it? What or who else lives there? Are they friends or enemies? Work on this as you hatch storylines, but try to keep things simple. Remember that you will have to repeat the same background scene many times.

Introduce a new character and see what develops. This leggy octopus provides the chance to play around with scale. Here she is immense and, despite her attractive face, looks ready to curl her tentacles around the boat. Is she being friendly? How will the crew react? The interaction of your elements – scale and position – is essential to the continuation of the narrative.

# Decorative collage

Give free rein to your creativity with this hare-brained collage project. It is fun to to do and clearly demonstrates that the more extreme your choice of materials, the more magnificent the result.

The theme is obvious: an exuberant celebration of hair decoration. The use of colour alone makes a huge statement and the added fusion of pattern and layer emboldens it further. The weighty juxtaposition of the free-flowing ink strokes with the airiness of real feathers provides a visually explosive mix that intrigues the eye, as do the various tinted papers overlaid by a pattern of coloured plastic discs. It is this mixture of conventional and unconventional materials and media that is so exciting.

## Final image
A small comb and coloured-paper stripes on the dress complete the vibrant look. The effect is very simple to achieve if you are brave enough to experiment. This is the key to a successful outcome. Abandon your artistic inhibitions and exploit fully the materials at your disposal to let truly creative results occur.

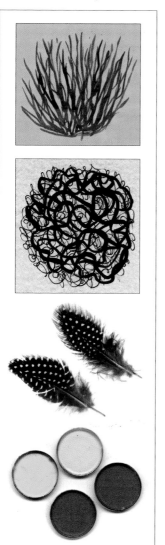

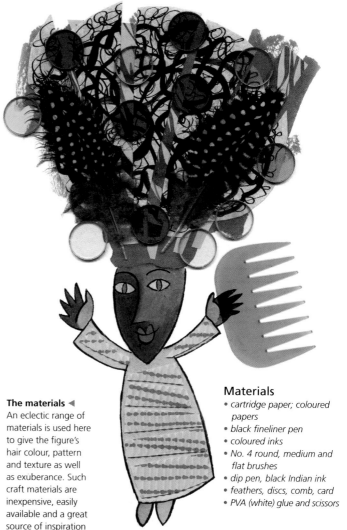

**The materials** ◄
An eclectic range of materials is used here to give the figure's hair colour, pattern and texture as well as exuberance. Such craft materials are inexpensive, easily available and a great source of inspiration for collage.

## Materials
- *cartridge paper; coloured papers*
- *black fineliner pen*
- *coloured inks*
- *No. 4 round, medium and flat brushes*
- *dip pen, black Indian ink*
- *feathers, discs, comb, card*
- *PVA (white) glue and scissors*

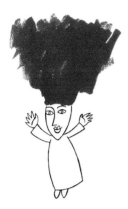

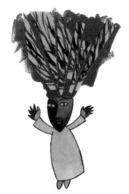

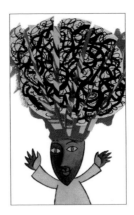

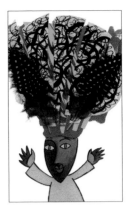

**1** Draw a shapes-based stylized figure using a black fineliner. Paint a wild shock of hair fanning out from the top of the head using bright red ink and a medium, flat brush.

**2** Paint a green, branched bush shape on yellow paper. Angle it at 45 degrees and cut it into narrow strips. Glue these on to the hair. Paint the hands, face and dress using the round brush.

**3** Use both ends of the round brush to make a swirling pattern of black ink on marbled taupe paper. Cut the paper into broad wedges and place them on top of the previous layer.

**4** Adjust the position of the swirls if necessary before gluing in place. Now add a feather to either side of the hair to balance the shape. Choose feathers with strong colours or patterns.

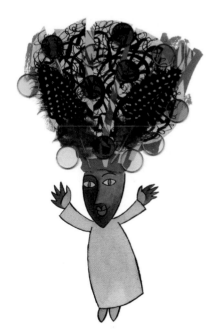

**5** For the finishing touch to the hair, arrange the translucent coloured discs on and around the hair, then glue them in place. Like tinted windows, they reflect the light superbly and cause the colours and patterns underneath to glow.

## Robot

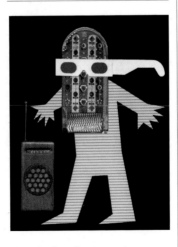

This mixed-media approach uses no conventional drawing at all. Scissors take the place of your pen as they sculpt the shape of the figure from yellow corrugated card. A novelty bagatelle game ingeniously replaces the head, a walkie-talkie handset is the added techno accessory and 3-D card glasses flatten across the face. All the shapes work well together to interpret the robot form.

## Coffee-bean man

The two coffee beans are all that is needed to imply a coffee addict, and this one is clearly sold on shots of caffeine! The slits of the beans give the effect of peculiar cat-like pupils and their skewed angles add craziness.

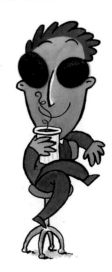

# Teenage characters

Designing a cartoon character with appeal to a teenage audience can be challenging. It's important to establish an instantaneous rapport with the audience or risk losing their interest. Getting it right demands creative thinking on several levels: the character needs to be appealing in terms of gender and interests, the action should play out in a context that is exciting and attractive and the illustration style must match the mood of the narrative and reflect contemporary taste.

This cartoon stars a young female DJ in something of an underdog role, who is determined to realize her musical ambitions in a male-dominated world.

## Final image

The simplicity and effective use of tonal harmonies in this single story-frame imparts an uneasy mood while providing a strong contextual background for the visual narrative. Highlights and textures are strategically added and extra body is provided by the chalk pastel marks across the quilted jacket, scarf and record-case surfaces. The highlights on the top of the head and jacket heighten the drama.

## Materials

- cartridge paper
- dip pen and black Indian ink
- No. 4 round brush
- coloured inks
- grey-blue watercolour paint
- chalk pastels

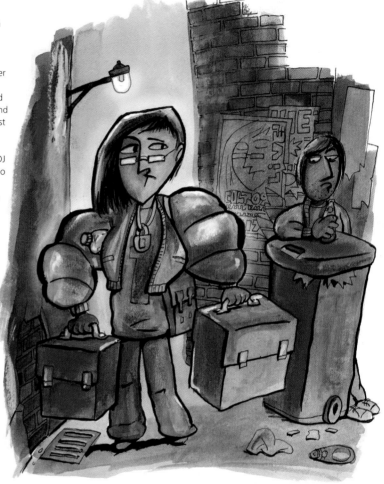

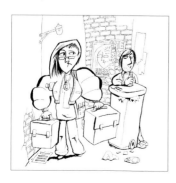

1 The intention from the outset is the development of an androgynous figure: a female but without the usual stereotypical adornments of make-up or curves. Remember that she is a 'cool' character and research fashions for suitable 'crossover' clothing. Outline the drawing using a dip pen and ink.

2 Tint the background in light ink washes of three colour bands: scarlet, orange and burnt sienna. Leave the main features white.

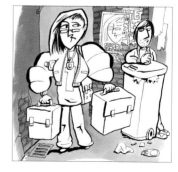

3 Paint the DJ in a moody blue watercolour hue, which raises a sense of unease as she walks along the alleyway. Paint her record cases, the bin and the shifty-looking man in the same colour. Assume a main light source from the left and paint a second wash of shadows down one side of her face and hair, and in the creases of the puffer jacket. Add shadow to the man and to one side of the bin. This shaded side emphasizes the record case so that it appears to be in the foreground.

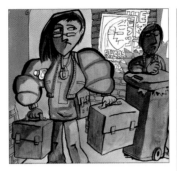

**Tip:** A strong outline creates a strong silhouette, which is an indispensable feature for a main character. The shadow of the dancing DJ outlines her distinctive clothing and hairstyle, and identifies her immediately to the viewer. Capitalize on this advantage by using lighting wherever appropriate. For example, strong artificial lighting will blend colours and blur lines, but a strong outline will remain distinct.

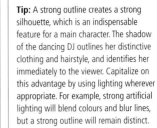

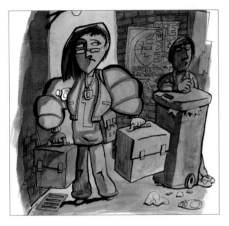

4 The advantage of translucent inks and paints is that when one is laid over another, the colour beneath shows through the new layer. Apply a wash of light blue ink over the walls in the background. Note how the pale scarlet area turns purple and the brick area becomes a deeper and cooler brown. Add a more diluted wash of blue over the floor to subdue the brightness of the ink stain.

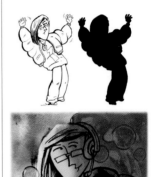

## DJ in action

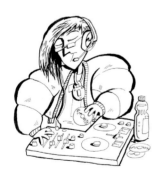

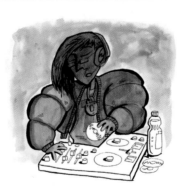

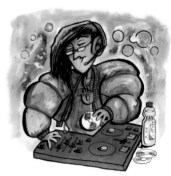

Now put your DJ in true context. Draw her mixing music at the desk, still in the puffer jacket but now wearing headphones and about to play a CD, a bottle of water at her side. Her image is made strongest drawn with a firm keyline from a pressure-led dip-pen line.

Tint the figure with monestial blue. Then gesturally paint, with broad loose strokes, a combination background of scarlet and orange inks, blended together with smudges of white chalk pastel.

Strokes of green and mauve pastel are dragged with the side of the stick pressed on to the paper. More solid layers of chalk pastel colour the jacket and hair, reflecting the multi-coloured, artificial lights. The mixing desk should be strong monestial blue and the bubble shapes added with a dip pen.

# Anthropomorphizing animals

Many animals make great subjects for cartoons. They are characterful, like people, and we humans have a strong tendency to personify them.

Anthropomorphizing animals can be achieved in a variety of ways: at one end of the scale, by using a human-like facial expression or eye shape; at the other end, through creating an entirely humanized animal that walks, talks and performs dextrous manoeuvres with hands and feet. Recognizing expressions of a person's character through their gait and unique body positioning matters. Animals are superb to display human characteristics and emotions. Consider: cute kittens = mischief; snake = wily; sheep = stupid; tortoise = slow.

## Final image
The two last details are a light yellow ochre layer representing the floor and pale olive green tinting on the leaves. The modelling on the body and face, as well as the subtle bends of the knee, overall stance and deportment – as recognized in humankind – make it a success.

## Materials
- *cartridge paper*
- *pencil*
- *rough watercolour paper*
- *dip pen and black Indian ink*
- *No. 6 and No. 4 round brushes*
- *watercolour paints*
- *coloured inks*

**Tip:** Building up short strokes as tone may look easy, but using a brush that is too dry or too wet can result in difficulties. Practise a repertoire of these strokes on a separate sheet of paper to help you discover the best technique.

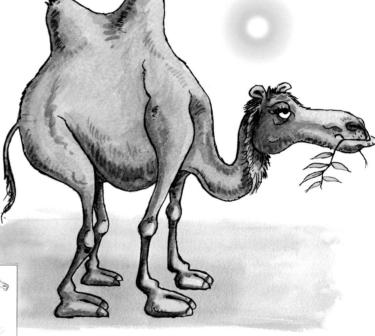

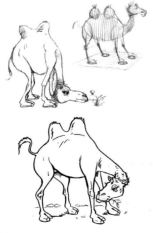

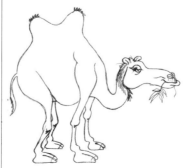

1 Begin with some simple pencil sketches and practise drawing the camel from all angles. Choose the best sketch and develop it further, but avoid referring to reference; allowing it to develop from your imagination will result in a character with a distinctive personality. This particular camel's persona is defined by its overly large feet, extended skull and prominently protruding lower lip, along with its lopsided humps and large eyes with noticeably long eyelashes.

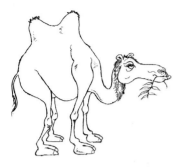

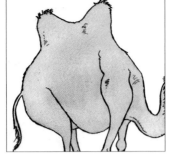

**2** Redraw your final sketch using a dip pen and black Indian ink on rough watercolour paper. Note how the camel's unhurried air is communicated through its bended knees, drooping neck and even the plant in its mouth.

**3** Paint your first wash of raw sienna watercolour within the outline using a No. 6 round brush. Mix plenty of pigment and allow it to flood the area evenly. Let image dry completely before moving on to the next stage.

**4** Define the contours of the camel's body shape by building up short, dappled strokes of burnt sienna watercolour in selected areas. Look closely at photographic reference to help you understand the range of tonal variations you will need. Layer these drier marks using the No. 4 brush and note that the more marks you add, the deeper the tone becomes. Finally, accentuate the details using inks: eyes, lashes, nostrils, neck ruff and tasty branch.

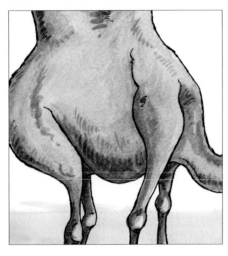

## Adding accessories

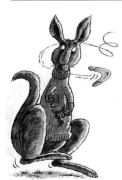

Dressing animals in an anthropomorphic way serves two purposes: it makes them more human-like and it adds colour and interest; a kangaroo in a pink jumper has impact! Supplying animals with unexpected accessories is an anthropomorphist's dream. Allow your imagination to run riot; who says a lion shouldn't be able to ride a scooter?

## Practice exercise: Metaphorical tortoise

Making use of an animal's familiar characteristics in an unexpected way can send a provocative message. This cartoon of the tortoise on the running machine can be extended into a metaphor: are we looking at a tortoise or a hitherto idle human being reluctantly forced into an exercise regime?

## Materials
- *cartridge paper*
- *pencil and fineliner pen*
- *watercolour paints*
- *No. 4 round brush*

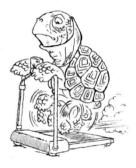

**1** The metaphor is turned on its head with the slow tortoise running on the treadmill. Sketch it out in pencil and make any adjustments you feel are necessary. Draw over the pencil outlines using a fineliner pen.

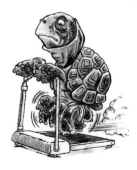

**2** Add light layers of watercolour in the appropriate greens and browns and grey for the treadmill, and dilute the colour with water to lighten the tones.

# Symbolic figures

Clearly recognizable characters who encapsulate a wealth of meaning broaden the cartoonist's opportunity to create a parallel or sub-plot within an image. They are commonly used as a device in all kinds of topical images and political cartoonists in particular are well-known for using symbolic figures to get their message across.

The rules of the game are clear: the more strikingly simply the figure is depicted, the greater the likelihood that the concept will work. Strong lines and shapes coupled with bold colours will reinforce the success of an image by making it stand out on the page.

The setting should not be permitted to overwhelm the main figure and the composition needs careful planning. For maximum impact, aim for a bold design that incorporates contrasting shapes, tonal ranges and hues.

## Materials
- *rough and smooth watercolour papers*
- *black fineliner pen*
- *colouring pencils*
- *felt-tip pens*
- *dip pen and black Indian ink*
- *No. 4 round and flat brushes*
- *coloured inks*

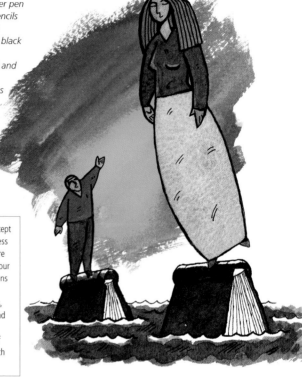

## Final image
Symbolism lends itself to universal themes; here, two figures, isolated by their individual lives (the books), are unable to form a bond – note the reach of the stretching man falls far short of the lady's towering height. Humour is also present, as her expression is one of total unawareness. Such simplicity works well with more complex articles or structures.

**Tip:** A strong concept is key to the success of the simple figure principle. Sketch your character inventions and give them appropriate words, sayings, stories and proverbs. Aim to develop a range of drawing styles, each one equally apt.

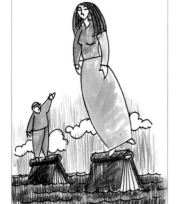

1 It is important to gauge the success of the design before beginning the final piece. Start by making a rapid, strong working sketch in fineliner pen, then tint it using colouring pencils and felt-tip pens. Note that the pen lines are neat and follow a single direction.

2 When you are satisfied that the elements of the idea are correctly sized and positioned, draw the final image on rough watercolour paper using a dip pen and black Indian ink. Tint the paper in dashed, flat strokes of purple, brown, turquoise, ultramarine blue, yellow ochre, warm red and sepia, using a flat brush for the broad areas of colour and a No. 4 brush for the smaller areas.

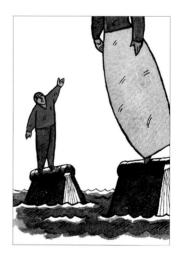

## Action

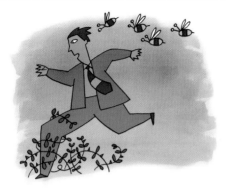

Simple figures can still be active and full of movement and life. Drawing in profile is the easiest way to illustrate action. Here, simplifying the shape of the chasing bees and exaggerating their scale works well. The choice of colour is also important: the bright yellow and white tint of the bees makes them appear busy.

## Symbolism

Objects can be drawn out of proportion to figures and yet appear acceptable. Using familiar items as powerful or meaningful symbols is a common technique used by cartoonists. To prevent the smoke rising the figure holds a large collaged photo of a dustbin lid over the smoke to stop its spreading.

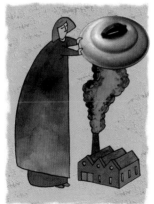

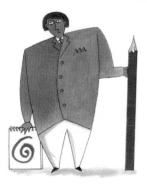

Think of Egyptian art and you will soon realize that this style uses symbols for objects or people rather than direct representations. This cartoon of a designer is fun, and so far removed from reality that we accept him as a graphic creation not that different from his own work.

## Traditional figures

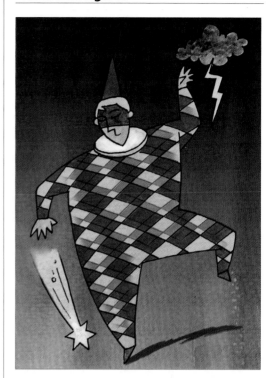

The harlequin is a traditional symbol of the mysteries of life and death. He is a bold, decorative figure in this depiction, and is used to imply a fatalistic outcome. An exploitation of the associations of familiar characters from traditional culture underpins the concept of using simple figures and is worthwhile. Many storylines in cartooning have their basis in traditional myths or tales.

## Using metaphor

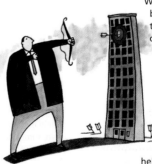

Working lives have become increasingly target-driven. This cartoon, depicting a businessman as an archer, firing at a target fixed to an office building, has a clear message. The metaphor displays wit at its best; such an image may help to enliven a dull business article.

# Getting the message across

Presenting facts in a way that is easy for an audience to understand can be a challenge. The nature of the cartoon as a carrier of complex visual information makes it the ideal medium for delivering a message. Not only can cartoons break down information into manageable bites so that it is easier to understand

but they can make it more memorable. Layout and format are also critical to conveying information effectively. In the case of a set of instructions, it is often essential that they are followed in a particular order, and it is the layout of the drawings that governs the sequence of the information.

## Final image
A step-by-step approach is an effective way to present information to children and young people. Here, a friendly chef demonstrates the art of cake-making. Linking the figures with speech bubbles builds a strong narrative within the frame. Also, the bakers' plump shapes echo the bubbles found in the design of the chef hats and their bulbous noses.

## Materials
- *watercolour paper*
- *gouache paints*
- *No. 2 and No. 4 round brushes*
- *dip pen and black Indian ink*
- *watercolour paints*
- *black fineliner pen*

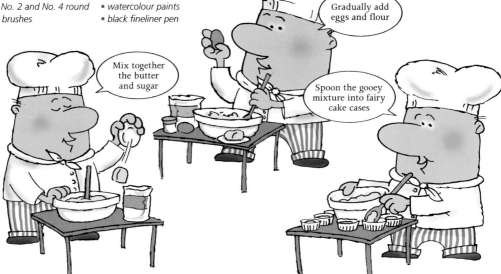

1 Rough out the composition, making adjustments as you go. Note that the figures are drawn at different sizes and angles. It is worth making practise sketches of all the objects you want to include before starting the final outline. Leave space for the speech bubbles.

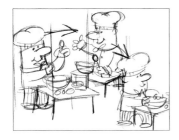

2 When you are satisfied with your initial sketch, outline it clearly using dip pen and black Indian ink. Now add flat gouache colour washes in tones of flesh pink, blue and yellow. Add light washes of blue watercolour on the hat and uniform.

3 Add tone with light washes of blue watercolour in the white areas. Sketch the speech bubbles and outline them in fineliner pen. Ensure that they are the right size for the words they will hold. Make the text clear and direct to match the simplicity of the image.

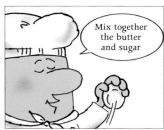

## Fruit fiends

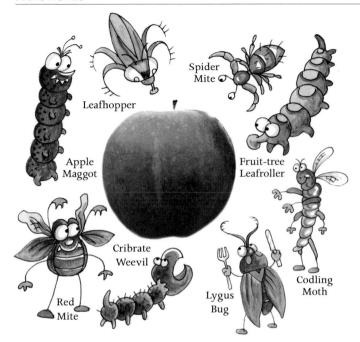

The pests that attack an apple are surprisingly numerous, as this chart shows. The simple approach is fun, memorable and informative rather than alarming. The focus is the photo of the apple, cut out and mounted on cartridge paper. Its central position leaves the viewer in no doubt about the subject matter. Placing each pest around the apple makes them all equally threatening, while the anthropomorphic drawing style implies friendliness. This could be a public-information poster.

**Tip:** Give yourself a drawing test. See how many serious subjects you can illustrate in a humorous and stylized way without compromising the message. Use as many different media as possible.

## Visual maps

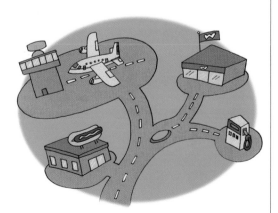

Maps are perfect subjects for cartooning. A fun approach draws the viewer's attention and helps them to retain the information. Don't allow real issues of scale or distance to bother you: remember that you are only drawing a representation. In this particular map, all the small details have been removed, leaving only the basic information we need: that the airport is north-west of a service station and that we can grab a snack nearby.

## 'How to...' guides

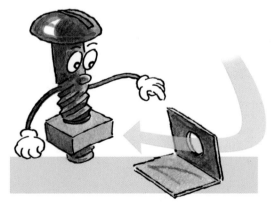

The most mundane of explanations can benefit from a cartoon treatment. Following the assembly instructions for flat-packed furniture is much easier when they are illustrated and humour can lighten a dull task. This visual dialogue between the little nut and the bolt describes a simple instruction that is impossible to misread. The directional arrow and use of the same colour for the elements that fit together help to reinforce the message.

# Portraying machine encounters

Advances in technology have made it impossible for us to live our lives without encounters with automotive processes on a daily basis. Human dependence upon machines has now more or less transformed them into our copartners, making them ideal candidates for the cartoonist's repertoire.

Machinery makes an effective metaphor for all that is contemporary, but it is your choice whether to portray it as working with or against the human race. The threat of robot domination is not a new concept, nor is it entirely far-fetched, since human workers have been replaced by machines in a number of industries.

It is the logical nature of machines that offers the cartoonist the greatest scope. In the real world, machinery takes a passive role: it functions on command and does not have the facility to think or rationalize. In the cartoon world,

however, anything is possible, and the theme of a malfunctioning machine can present opportunities for entertaining interplay between the rational and irrational. A cartoon machine has the freedom to lose control and turn the tables on a situation, interacting with a human in a way that can be very amusing or darkly sinister.

## Final image

A threatening machine is a common cartoon theme. Note how easy it is to personify the machine's features. Make sure that you do not overcomplicate the final image. Keep the details to a minimum so that it is instantly recognizable, and treat the colours in much the same way.

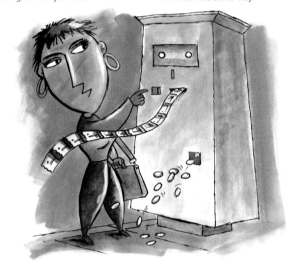

## Materials
- 'Not' watercolour paper
- pencil, dip pen and black Indian ink
- watercolour dyes
- No. 2 round brush
- chalk pastels

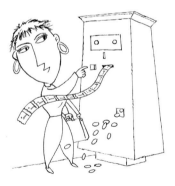

**1** Follow up your initial pencil sketch with a clean, clear outline of the composition on the 'Not' watercolour paper using a dip pen and black Indian ink. The success of your cartoon will be largely dependent on how accurately you draw the ticket machine and personify its key features.

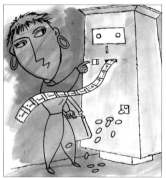

**2** Tint the main areas with fluid washes of watercolour dyes. Use a diluted red for the background wall and floors and a diluted mix of light blue and red for the exterior of the ticket machine. Let the wash run across the surface of the paper and occasionally be absorbed. A blotchy effect does not matter at this stage.

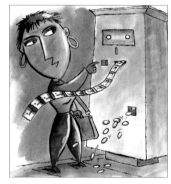

**3** Use blue chalk pastel for the trousers, case, hair and the shadowing on the body. Blend more blue into the machine panel, adding red chalk pastel into the red areas to give them extra depth. Add a flesh tint to the face. Emphasize the highlights using white chalk pastel and colour the ticket using red and blue dyes.

## Familiar machines

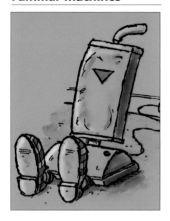

This simple vacuum cleaner illustration uses a dip pen and black Indian ink, light blue watercolour paint and white chalk pastel on pale blue tinted paper. We can relate humour best if the machine is familiar to us. Here, in a reversal of roles, the resting cleaner reminds us that he is the master over us – the slaves to cleaning!

## The robot human

In this image, an idea is reversed and the tentacled alien is looking warily at the human astronaut, who it perceives to be a machine. Split into two frames, the first image is an overview, showing the two figures' differences; the second is a close-up, stretched anamorphically across the width of the frame.

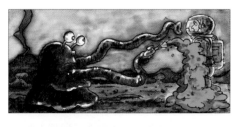

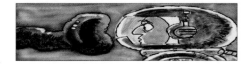

## Androids

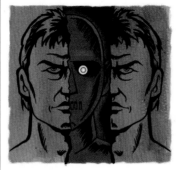

Alienation is another popular theme in cartoons. The fascinating concept of androids – machines that appear in human form – is often explored in sci-fi comics and graphic novels, which gives the cartoonist the opportunity to reconfigure the human face and form. Perhaps unsurprisingly, the best outcomes use the basic life-drawing structure as a starting point. In this cartoon, the use of complementary colours illuminates the contrast between man and machine.

## Robots

Machines that walk and talk were first introduced to the public audience in futuristic stories and films of the 20th century. Their unique appeal endures in the form of robot toys, models and as film, TV and comic-strip characters. With distinct personalities, they can be friendly and funny or very threatening. The squat shape of this cartoon robot is cute, but its menacing side is evident in the glowing red eyes and shooting ray. The stance and distortion of the rectangular shape make it appear to move, and placing it in a context of destruction makes the message clear.

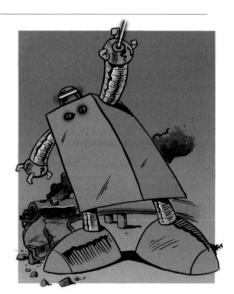

## Computer trash

Computers can be seen as a blessing or a curse. This image reveals a homemade solution to junk mail. Often, technical subjects, such as computers, benefit from images that strip away the jargon.

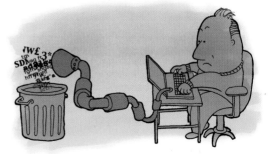

# Dynamic viewpoints

The viewpoint we adopt within a cartoon and the relative sizes of the elements inside its frame can determine whether it will be dull or interesting. Part of the artist's task is to create an image with its own internal energy through dynamic composition, contrasts of size and the use of light and dark. All of these qualities are all influenced heavily by viewpoint.

To a fly on the wall, a scene looks very different than the view from a more normal perspective. Dedicated cartoonists are constantly stretching their powers of imagination and try to consider scenes and situations from a range of perspectives. Keeping this in mind when planning your cartoons will help you to realize projects that are original, freshly perceived and provoke a reaction from your audience.

Transferring a skateboarder to the interior of a room immediately changes our view of him and his environment. This unexpected refocusing implies the existence of many other situations that are beyond the acceptable perspectives of reality. The probability of the scene entering the realms of fantasy and physical impossibility is, therefore, consequently stepped up.

## Materials
- *cartridge paper*
- *soft blue pencil*
- *'Not' watercolour paper*
- *dip pen and black Indian ink*
- *No. 6 round brush*
- *watercolour paints*

**Tip:** Seek out new or unusual viewpoints, then make sketches of them and work hard to achieve the correct perspectives and relative sizes. This will fire your imagination, to create scenes for new cartoon projects. Having an understanding of perspective can help a cartoonist to achieve more exciting and complex settings and figure angles, which prevent a strip becoming dull.

## Final image
A skateboarder is testing a ramp of books in his bedroom. By filling the room with the child's energy, the dynamism spills out of the frame made by the walls and grabs the viewers' attention. For your image to have worked successfully, there needs to be a tension within your composition between the straight walls and the regular, containing interior space and the free movements of the skater within. His path, determined by the makeshift skate ramp, arcs around the room.

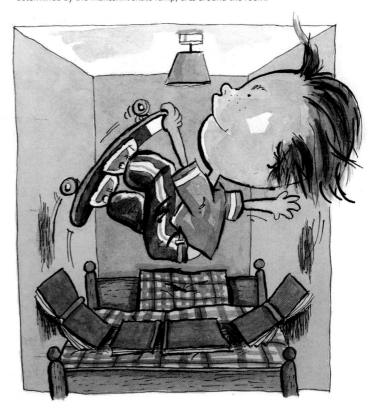

1 Make a basic sketch of the room in soft blue pencil, keeping the outlines simple in order to make it easier to adjust them until the image is working. The upward curving flow of energy is the most important element. Not only does it hold the central focus of the image but it forces the figure to break out of the frame of the cartoon and present the viewer with an image that is both contained and uncontained. Adjustments to the initial idea should be made now before it is painted.

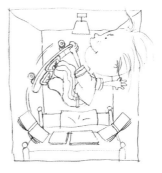

2 Outline the composition on 'Not' watercolour paper using a dip pen and black Indian ink. Alter the pressure on the pen nib to keep the lines lively. Load the round brush with dilute raw sienna pigment, then paint a wash over the three walls so that they are all lightly tinted. When the paint has dried, brush a second wash over the middle wall panel to darken it slightly. Add patches of vertical hatching beneath the books and to the walls on either side.

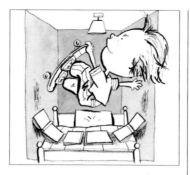

## Bird's-eye perspective

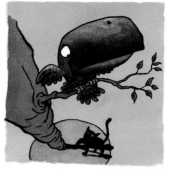

3 Brush diluted red colour over the book covers, shirt, trainers and checks on the duvet and pillow. Detail the lampshade in purple and the skateboard deck and trousers with sepia. Paint the boy's skin in a range of flesh tones. Finally, brush on a layer of warm burnt sienna for the hair, adding flecks of brown burnt umber.

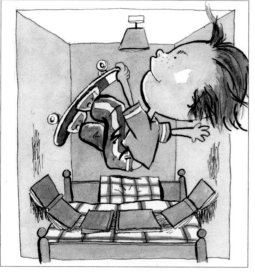

Altering the viewpoint can add extra drama, suspense or a sense of danger. This bird's-eye view sharply focuses the viewer's attention on the plight of the bird on the branch. The waiting cat is of secondary importance. Strong, fluid stains of coloured inks offer prominence and depth to the main elements, and a flattish, ochre wash is employed for the background.

## Fly-eye view

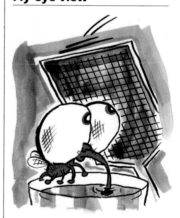

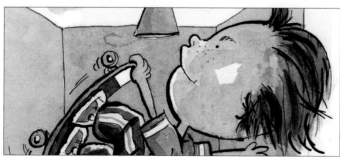

4 This detail shows how the paint strokes have been allowed to flow across the paper, to puddle and stain as they please. This approach to applying a watercolour wash is a traditional painting technique that adds to the life of the image. The tones are darkened in places to represent shadows, which give the figure and objects form: under the sleeves, down one side of the lamp and on the backs of the trousers. The hair was painted in stronger colours using downward strokes from a dry brush. The action strokes add movement.

The fly swatter fills up most of the space as it bats towards the fly. We can only sympathize, as we share the fly's lowly perspective. The colours are lively washes of ink in yellow ochre and blue, which add depth to the figures and elements. Linking parts is important. The blue of the swatter links to the blue of the eyes, which in turn link to the fly's body.

# Using colour to spotlight

Unusual coloration, texture and drawing styles all help to isolate central subjects in a narrative cartoon image. This technique enables them to appear in a believable fantasy world.

Using limited colour throughout, with the exception of a small area – a third or less of the picture space – can draw focus to the central theme of the narrative. At the cocktail party, the lights are dimmed, and the room is quietly atmospheric. A combination of blue ink and crumbled charcoal laid on top of the initial line drawing adds depth to the room and pushes the other guests into a merging background. The flesh coloration of the chatting figures and the echoes of the same colour draw the viewer into their conversation over a pleasant aperitif.

### Final image

Everything is carefully calculated, with colour used perceptively to focus the viewer's attention on the male character on the left and the woman in the centre. The simple technique of gradually eliminating the tonal hues on the lesser characters and in the background is enough to turn the spotlight wherever you want it to fall.

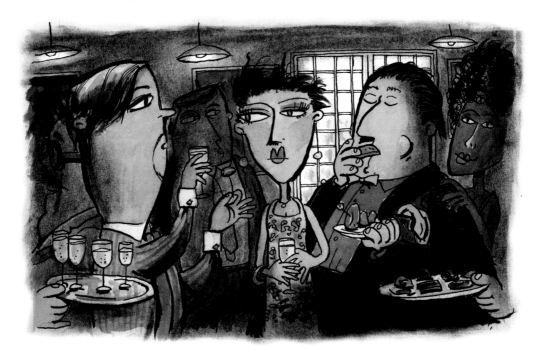

## Materials
- *cartridge paper*
- *'Not' watercolour paper*
- *dip pen and black Indian ink*
- *0.1mm fineliner pen*
- *No. 4 and No. 6 round brushes*
- *coloured inks*
- *watercolour paints*
- *stick of charcoal*

**1** The use of subtle colour placement will only succeed if everything is strategically and purposefully positioned. An accurate sketch is critical therefore, so plan your composition with care. Paying attention to details such as body shapes and posture, the direction of a character's gaze and gestures, will draw the viewer's eyes to the centre. Keep things simple with direct, clear lines.

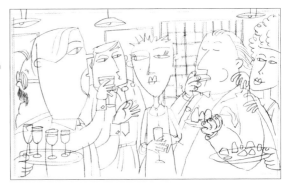

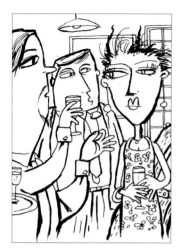

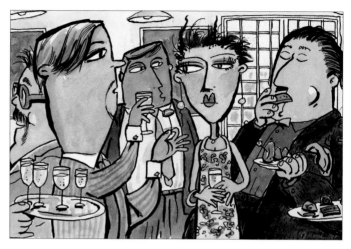

2 Outline the sketch combining a dip pen and brush with black Indian ink. Give the lines full weighting – accentuating the woman's jawline diverts attention towards her face, for example. In contrast, use a more delicate fineliner pen line to activate the characters' hands and allow body language to be seen clearly.

3 Paint the faces of the secondary characters in washes of dilute light blue ink using the No. 4 round brush, and the wall panels in sepia. Don't worry that the tones seem bright because further layering will knock them back into the composition. Use watercolour paints and a smaller brush

to deliver hair colour, champagne and the more controlled patterns on the clothing. Mix a rosy flesh colour and add the skin tones of the couple at the centre of the conversation. Note how the deeper purple hue on the right draws the eye in towards the central lady.

## Silhouette

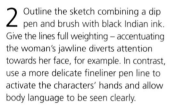

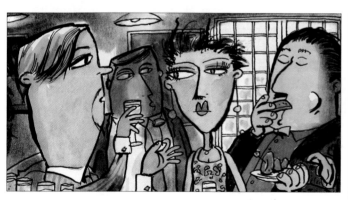

4 Create the final detailing by reducing instead of adding to the fine mark-making. Knock back the brightness of the lesser figures in the group using charcoal. Its gritty texture gives an enclosed interior feel to the scene, causing everything that is unimportant to recede softly. Add form to the man's head using charcoal strokes and carefully blend it around the lamps so that they appear illuminated. Leave the brightness of the window too.

**Tip:** Knowing the limits to which a medium can be worked is an important skill and by understanding your materials you will save many future cartoons from being overworked. Try the scene again but this time test the limits to which charcoal can be used to significantly reduce the focus of the drawing without destroying its meaning. Experiment with other ways of reducing colour too – a limited range can also produce quite startling effects.

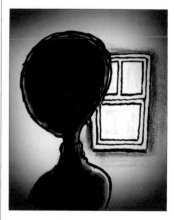

Silhouetted figures against a light background, such as a window, can effectively create a mood of tension, suspense or isolation. This can be very useful if the palette is limited to a single colour, with just the odd detail picked out in a suitable shade (i.e. here the purple lips).

# Imitating woodcut styles

The black-and-white composition is perhaps the most powerful visual arrangement in the cartoonist's portfolio. In part an imitation of the traditional woodcut technique, this method is about working to limitations. As such it is suitable for beginners or for anyone who has less confidence in their drawing skills. The key to success is to reduce the subject matter to a series of strong black-and-white shapes, which contrast well with one another.

Adding colour should only be considered when the black-and-white design has been conceived and accurately worked out. It is at this point that variations in drawing style, the use of 'cut' marks and limited colour can be brought into the equation.

## Final image

This design is strong with bold shapes of black-and-white 'space' working within the vertical frame. If you have exploited the contrast in this image – shadows against spotlight – then a live music atmosphere should be achieved.

## Materials

- *cartridge paper*
- *watersoluble pencils*
- *stick of willow charcoal*
- *'Not' watercolour paper*
- *dip pen and black Indian ink*
- *No. 5 round brush*
- *watercolour dyes*

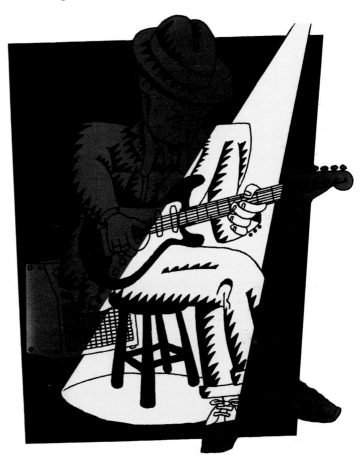

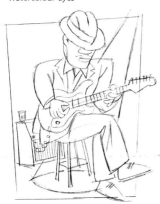

1 Sketch the guitarist, preferably from reference to capture the precision of the player's attitude, his finger positioning and the shape of the instrument. Now sketch direct solid lines on cartridge paper. This way, you will build up the composition in clearly defined shapes.

2 It is worth making a tonal working drawing to give you a sound visual idea of the final image. Loosely shade all the colours using watersoluble pencils and charcoal. Remember that this draft confirms the tones you intend to use for the final piece. Make adjustments until you are satisfied with the result.

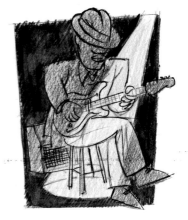

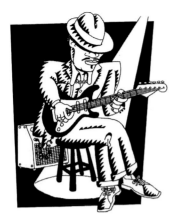

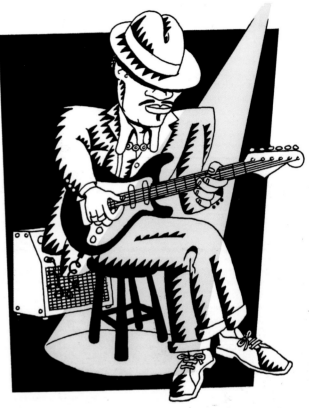

**3** Transfer the black-and-white outline to the watercolour paper using a dip pen and black Indian ink. Ink in the solid areas using a brush. Edge the outline of the guitarist in woodcut style marks. Breaking the irregular panel gives the composition a dynamic boost.

**4** When you are sure that the pattern of black-and-white 'shapes' holds together, add the colours. Start by tinting the spotlight in an even shade of dilute yellow dye. Bend the beam of light over the left shoulder so that it distorts, as it would in reality.

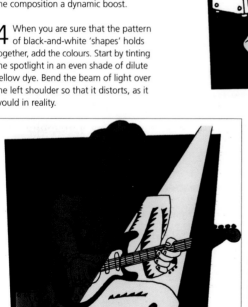

**5** Leave the yellow to dry, then add the deeper purple shades, blending them into crimson to suggest a further hidden light source. Work with care and keep your watercolour dye washes fluid at all times. Keep these washes fresh and undertake the task once only.

## Lighting for mood

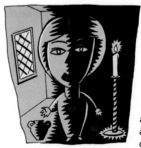

Sometimes the rules of how light falls on an object can be broken. This image differs from the musician as it has a symmetrical composition. Again, the woodcut-type effect is used, but the proportions and style of the drawing are simplified so the objects in the picture are easily recognized. No black fill is added to the left side of the figure, or pitcher: a light blue tint is laid over the whole of this side except for the window, which is left white to show it as the light source. To emphasize the candle's low-lit glow, darkness is added to the right side, excluding the eye and a highlight runs down the side of the hair and contour of the body. Spot red links suggest emotional content: heart = romance, wine = social context, red lips = clarification of female gender.

# Using explosions to add drama

An explosion paces a set of sequenced images more effectively than virtually any other drawn device. Whether they are used to give emphasis to a verbal exclamation or sound effect, or to add power and energy to a narrative, explosions are an essential part of the cartoonist's kit. They can be used effectively in all types of cartoons and in all types of situations, but are the indisputable mainstay of any comic narrative in which the dominant theme is the struggle of good against evil.

An explosion used as a dramatic device can stop the audience in its tracks. Once their attention is held, the opportunity is there for a change of mood or a shift in the narrative.

## Final image

The limited colour range and minimal details enhance this image's dramatic appeal, with the wizard's body framing the action. Successful explosions are achieved by using drawing conventions that link to directional movement – emanating lines fan out from their centre, with twisting clouds and fiery colours.

## Materials

- *cartridge paper*
- *felt-tip pen*
- *chalk pastels*
- *smooth watercolour paper*
- *No. 4 and No. 7 round brushes*
- *black Indian ink*
- *fineliner pen and ruler*
- *black coloured ink*
- *watercolour dyes*
- *white gouache paint*

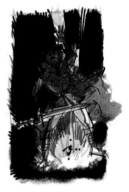

**Pre-sketch** ▲
The pre-sketch on white cartridge paper is a mixed-media profusion of colour and energy. Tightly controlled felt-tip pen strokes collide with the soft cloudy passages of chalk pastel. White paper is left bare at the very heart of the explosion.

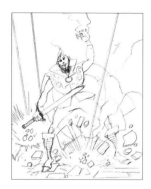

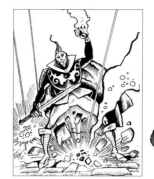

## A puff of magic

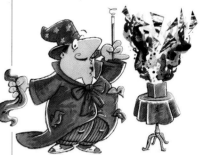

1 Sketch the fantasy wizard in super-hero comic style. Refer to comics and figure reference manuals for extra guidance in drawing the superhuman proportions and movements. Make sure that your figure is centrally placed holding an active pose over the blasting rocks splitting also from the centre.

2 When you are satisfied with the composition, ink it in using a brush and black Indian ink. Draw freely with the brush and enjoy the level of control that you can maintain with only a little practice. Use a fineliner pen and ruler to deliver the high-tension lines firing from the centre of the explosion.

Here's an explosion that is far removed from fireballs and flames. Vibrant wet-on-wet watercolour dyes are allowed the freedom to roam over the paper resulting in an exuberant eruption of colour. The shiny silver foil shapes collaged into the dye marks add a sense of sparkle and energy to the comic explosion.

## Fireball

3 Fill in the background behind the figure with a dense, black ink wash, leaving the explosion lines and flame area above the hand as white paper. Note the considerable weight this black background adds to the picture and how the stark contrast of black and white gives form to the flickering fire in the wizard's hand. Be careful not to obliterate the subtlety of the outer edges of the flames when you are blacking around them.

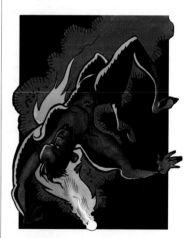

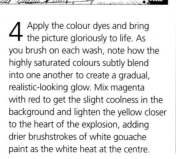

4 Apply the colour dyes and bring the picture gloriously to life. As you brush on each wash, note how the highly saturated colours subtly blend into one another to create a gradual, realistic-looking glow. Mix magenta with red to get the slight coolness in the background and lighten the yellow closer to the heart of the explosion, adding drier brushstrokes of white gouache paint as the white heat at the centre.

A limited range of flat colours is used in conjunction with a tumbling, dynamic figure whose pose suggests the fireball that has sent him hurtling through space. Black Indian ink is used to stress the strong male physique and fills the background to give a 3-D effect overall. The intense brightness of the orange, yellow and white flames adds drama and power.

# Digital techniques

Cartoons like all other artistic expressions have embraced the digital world. Far from making drawing skills redundant, they have blended them with diverse imagery programs to increase visual possibilities. Software, and how to use it appropriately and successfully, is extensively covered in this chapter.

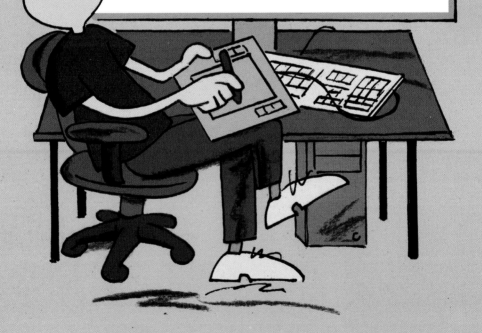

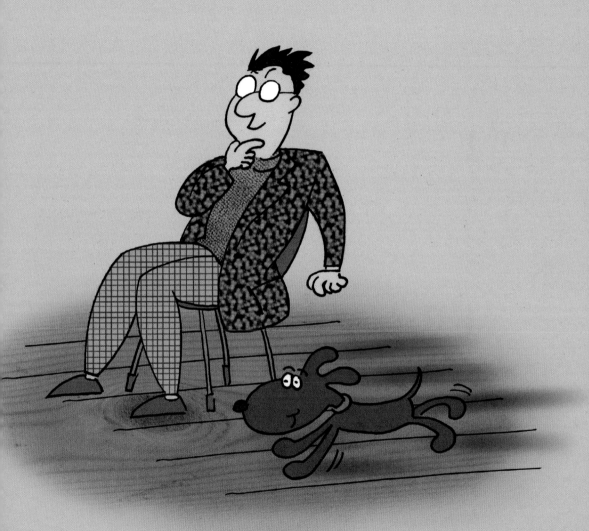

# The digital environment

Digital media has revolutionized the world of art and design. Before the advent of computing, processes such as changing colours, making adjustments and alterations, duplicating and archiving artwork required much extra effort. In addition, effects such as seamlessly smooth colour gradations were time consuming and demanded the skilful use of a very fine brush or airbrush. Now these things and more are easily and quickly achieved using single keystrokes and mouse skills.

Digitally created imagery is constructed from pixels – tiny, flat squares of colour, which are neatly duplicated in rows of thousands or millions to give an accurate, crisp appearance.

It is the perfect medium for creating flat, polished graphic art, and can be easily combined with traditional methods where a more textured or fluid style is wanted.

The advantages of using the computer are the ease with which minor changes can be made to pictures and the extraordinary provision of having artwork ready for publication as digital files, be they comics, books or websites.

While digital software packages greatly assist basic drawing and painting skills they can never replace them, and all artists who produce computer-generated artwork are invariably grounded in these traditional skills.

## Vector and bitmap

There are two principal types of digital imaging programs. Vector programs use mathematical algorithms (a language known as Postscript) to describe colours, lines and curves. A Pen tool existing in an on-screen 'toolbox' plots a series of lines and curves with points connecting each section of the line or curve. The areas can be filled with colour and 'stroked' by altering the line thickness or its colour. Vector programs, such as Adobe Illustrator and Freehand, allow the user to create complex drawings. With 'Bitmap' or paint programs, such as Adobe Photoshop, users draw freely on screen using a mouse, stylus pen or drawing tablet. The smallest unit of computer storage – a 'bit' – is mapped on to a grid. An image that is created or scanned-in is displayed on-screen as an arrangement of bits. Such files can take up a lot of memory.

**Bitmap digital photograph** ▼
This digital photograph of a guitarist is a bitmap image of 300dpi (dots per inch is a term denoting screen and print resolutions). It is imported into the vector program Adobe Illustrator, where it acts as a base template.

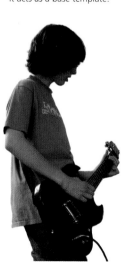

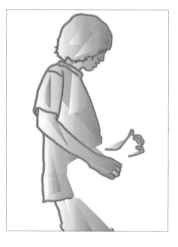

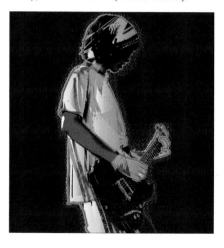

**Vector digital drawing** ▲
The Pen tool is selected from the toolbox palette in Adobe Illustrator and used to draw the outline around the guitarist. Vector and bitmap programs use 'layers', which are the digital equivalent of transparent overlays. Each layer can be allotted to a different portion of the illustration, such as outlining, colouring and textures. Here, the outline has been copied to a new layer and the gradient added in order to blend the red into the yellow.

**Bitmap digital painting** ▲
The vector digital drawing is 'cut, copied and pasted' into Adobe Photoshop, the bitmap program that manipulates images. The layered Illustrator drawing is partially removed around the guitar section of the image beneath using a selection of toolbox brushes. The Photoshop file of the guitar will appear as another layer – as parts of the top layer are removed or altered, the image on the layer below appears, as though someone has physically cut through a mask or tracing paper. The background is painted blue and a halftone filter is applied, then partially erased from around the figure.

# Digital equipment

Digital artworking requires high-specification equipment. You will need a powerful Apple Macintosh computer or Microsoft Windows compatible PC, plus a high-definition monitor with a screen at least 15 inches wide. As well as a mouse, pen or graphics tablet and software, a desktop scanner capable of scanning line and halftone images and a colour inkjet or laser printer are essential. A back-up device or external hard drive is also very useful for storage.

**Digital camera ▼**
It looks like a conventional SLR or instant camera, but instead of capturing the image on light-sensitive film to be developed, it converts its picture into a form that can be downloaded and stored on your computer.

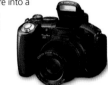

**Computer and monitor ◄**
Most computers now house dual processor chips of at least 500MHz, which is powerful enough to deliver 7 billion calculations per second. Most monitors are LCD flat display panels with 1600 x 1024 resolution.

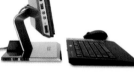

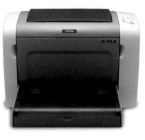

**Digitizing tablet ▼**
They are useful, some say essential, for making digital pictures. With a cordless pen-like stylus, the artist presses on to a flat, plastic tablet and the 'drawn' movements correspond with that of the cursor on screen, graphically displaying the result.

**Printer ►**
Laser printers, such as Epson's EPL 6200, use reflected light and static electricity to deposit toner on to the paper, while inkjet printers spray microscopic jets of electrically charged droplets of ink deflected by electromagnets on to moving paper.

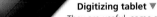

**Scanner ▲**
Desktop scanners, such as Epson's Perfection 3590, allow artists to input images already created into a computer format – the bitmap – for further manipulation or reference purposes. The most common scanners are flatbed of A4 size, allowing an image of that size to be laid and copied.

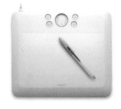

# Conventional versus digital imagery

The question of whether traditional or digital methods of image-making are better will always be governed by the results you are looking for. So long as the final image is well executed and fits the brief you have set, it really does not matter how you go about creating it. However, certain styles or effects are better achieved by one or the other medium. A cartoon consisting of flat colour or soft blends is less painstaking to create on the computer than by hand, whereas a rough textured look or mixed-media collage work to best effect using traditional methods.

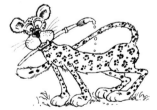

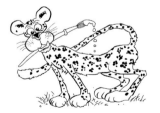

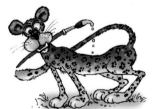

**Traditional drawing ▲**
The leopard is drawn by hand using a dip pen and black Indian ink. The very lively line is due to the changing delivery of the ink flow controlled by the nib.

**Vector-based drawing ▲**
This drawing was made with the Pen tool in Adobe Illustrator. The line quality is slightly lighter although extra points were added to give the effect of pressure.

**Vector-based colouring ▲**
Still in Adobe Illustrator, the Brush tool was set at various sizes to add colour on another layer. A gradient was applied to form the smooth brown to yellow blend.

# Essential software

Your computer hardware needs the right design software to activate it and enable you to get creative. Before purchasing software, check that it is compatible with your computer's operating system. This is Microsoft (Windows) on a PC and Apple (OS) on a Mac and they are totally different. Most application software is available in CD-Rom format or can be downloaded from the Internet. All versions are named or coded to differentiate the new from the old. Sometimes Internet 'updates' are available supplied free from the manufacturer, not requiring you to buy the latest versions. However, newly developed packages are often much improved and it may be better to purchase these instead. If you are planning to submit your cartoons for publication, it is essential to be aware of the version you are operating to ensure compatibility with a client or recipient of your work.

The cartoons in this book are created using the drawing and painting programs Adobe Illustrator, Adobe Photoshop, Corel Painter and the animation programs Flash and ImageReady.

## Drawing and painting programs

Adobe Illustrator and Macromedia Free-hand create vector images and are known as 'draw' programs. These programs are mathematically devised through the accurate plotting of points. Joined points form a line and joined lines form a shape to which flat colour can be applied. The format of this program results in images which look crisp, slick and clean. Adobe Photoshop and Corel Painter are 'paint' programs and, as this suggests, employ a more freehand style of picture creation. They construct pictures using individual 'bits' which replicate textures familiar to the traditional artist.

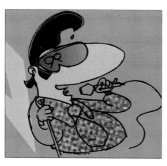

**Adobe Illustrator image** ▲
Like all 'draw' programs, Adobe Illustrator has close links to page-layout applications. The Illustrator tool kit allows boxes, ellipses and curves to be drawn. Pictures are created using an on-screen Pen tool by connecting points along so-called Bezier curves. When two points connect, a line is formed with new 'handle' points that can be pulled out to curve or change the direction of the line.

In addition, scanned images can be imported and 'traced over' and Illustrator is excellent for manipulating type. The layering feature enables image sections to be edited separately, and stretching, skewing and rotating are all possible. Although the skill of dragging handles out from points takes practice, the advantage of this program is that it creates complex images with very low file sizes which hold their sharpness even when enlarged.

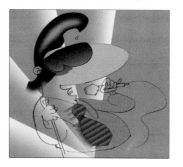

**Adobe Photoshop image** ▲
This 'bitmap' program was first developed as a photographic retouching tool, which rendered the manual airbrush obsolete. A user-friendly application, its vast scope and flexibility mean that it is recognized worldwide as the industry standard for retouching and art creation. Pictures are made by physically moving a mouse or stylus pen and the program gives the user access to a huge range of tools, techniques and effects. As with Illustrator, the system of working in layers gives the freedom to experiment and rework.

A major asset of Photoshop is its ability to manipulate, retouch or recolour digital pictures, whether uploaded from a camera, downloaded from the Internet, scanned or 'grabbed' as a screenshot from a DVD. In addition, final images can be converted into a range of file formats that are compatible for use in other applications or systems.

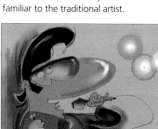

**Corel Painter** ▲
This program emulates traditional paint effects, such as watercolour, pastel, oils and acrylic. The program's extensive range of brush palettes are specifically geared to the sensitivities of the traditional artist: they range from soft round or flat watercolour brushes to firm bristle varieties for dabbing and stroking on acrylic and oil paint. The ability of the pressure-sensitive stylus pen to create corresponding marks on-screen is another feature which makes it attractive to the traditionalist. The system of layers enables changes to be made quickly and easily.

Although bitmap programs are easier to use than vector-based applications, image file sizes are usually large. However, all digital files can be saved in other formats for sharing and a full-colour A4 image of about 34MB can be compressed without too much distortion.

# Making an image using more than one program

Each program has cornered its own niche, whether infinitely scaleable illustration, digital image manipulation or the reproduction of natural media. While you can approximate many specialized features with just one program – such as painting digitally with Photoshop – combining different approaches can lead to startling and original fusions of artwork. Creating such composite images couldn't be easier, as today's programs are designed with mutual compatibility in mind. You can import a vector-created design into a bitmap program, such as Photoshop, by dragging the vector image into a new document window or opening it with the application. Either way, it will appear as a new layer in the layers box. From this point on, further work on the vector image can only be applied using Photoshop. The advantage of the layered system of working is that it allows you to adjust individual sections of your illustration and move them between applications, playing to the strengths and different styles of each program.

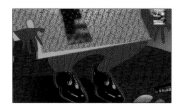

**Illustrator** ▲
The flat artwork for the hands and trousers is created in Illustrator, but the shoes, bottle, drinks carton, shirt front and tie are sourced from magazines and scanned.

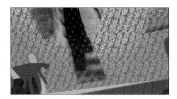

**Photoshop** ▲
The various textures and patterns of the shirt and tie are created using Photoshop's style palettes. They are selected and built in layers.

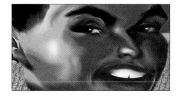

**Painter** ▲
The strong tonal image of the head is created in Painter using an acrylic paints palette and Brush tools. The smooth almost buttery texture is worked using the Blender tools.

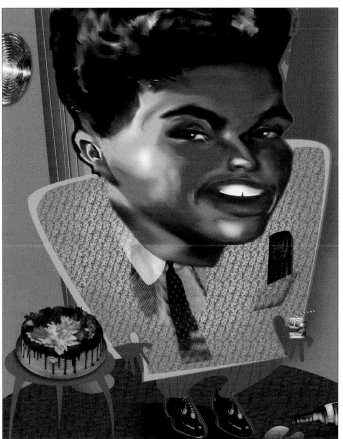

**Painter, Photoshop and Illustrator** ▲
This caricature is created using Painter, Photoshop and Illustrator applications. The composite image was made in the two vector programs and finalized in Photoshop. Its composition reveals the level of compatability between the three programs and is proof of the pixel's ability to unite different styles and techniques, textures and colours.

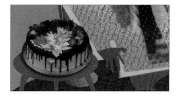

**Scanned image** ▲
The cake is a scanned photo imported into Photoshop with an airbrushed-effect drop shadow. The flat table artwork is an Illustrator creation.

# Scanning an image

You can input 'real' pictures, such as magazine cut-outs, and convert them to digital images via a desktop scanner, all of which come with their own scanning software. This connects to the computer via a USB port or via a faster, high-speed interface known as Firewire. Although more expensive than A4 size, most artists prefer the flexibility of an A3 size scanner. There is no limit to the types of images that can be scanned and photos,

transparencies, halftone illustrations or line drawings will all maintain their original quality. As a general rule, images are scanned at a resolution which is double the size of intended use. So an image scanned at 300dpi (dots per inch) will reproduce a sharp on-screen or printed image which is 150 lines deep. In general, the greater the number of dots, the greater the intake of information and the better the quality of an image.

## Scanning a line image

The method for inputting an image is similar with most software packages. There is the opportunity to select a 'cropping' area and to pre-scan and preview your work before finally copying it on to your computer. You will also have the chance at any time of recropping in the program you have chosen.

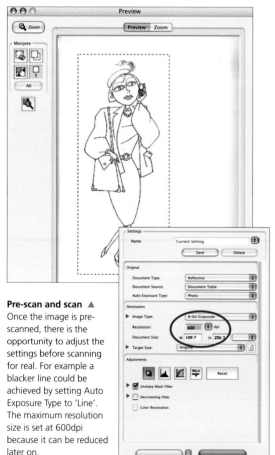

**Pre-scan and scan** ▲
Once the image is pre-scanned, there is the opportunity to adjust the settings before scanning for real. For example a blacker line could be achieved by setting Auto Exposure Type to 'Line'. The maximum resolution size is set at 600dpi because it can be reduced later on.

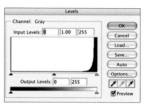

**On screen** ▼
Once scanned, the image should be opened in Photoshop or equivalent bitmap program for further tidying. Adjusting the Levels settings (Image > Adjustments > Levels), and sliding the histogram sliders to the left, brightens the scan and removes unwanted dirt or pencil graphite. The sliders in the Levels box are known as 'end dots' of a print screen and are the very darkest and lightest tones visible. Moving the right-hand slider too far to the left, deletes the lighter dot.

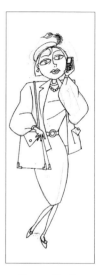

Scanned levels

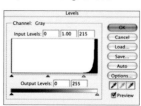

**Tip:** It doesn't take a lot of technical know-how to adjust scans. Try out test pieces and play with the histogram sliders on the Input and Output levels and see what happens to your image. Only hit the OK button when you are satisfied with the result.

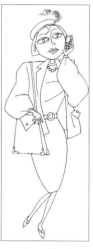

Adjusted levels

# Tidying a scanned image

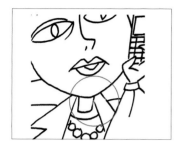

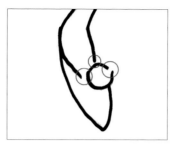

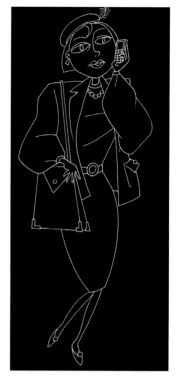

## Repairs ▲

If your grayscale scan has 'broken' – a piece of line isn't strong enough to hold colour or has become thin and 'brittle' in the scanning process – you can use the Pen tool to strengthen the line or strengthen the offending segment by multiplying it. Select the area using the Lasso or Marquee tools in Photoshop, then copy and paste the line over the broken area on a new layer and set to 'Multiply'. When you're content with your fix, flatten the image (Layer menu > Flatten image) to reduce it back to a single line drawing.

## Hue and saturation ▼

It is possible to change any part of any line by first selecting it with the Marquee or Lasso tools and then adjusting the colour or density values using the Hue/Saturation sliders (Image menu > Adjustments > Hue/Saturation). Experiment on a tester before making the final changes to your artwork, as this will assist your thinking processes and save you time in the long run.

## Refining ▲

Use the Zoom tool to check for areas from the original drawing that need refining. Use a 3-pixel brush (solid, not feathered) to retouch the area. Keep in mind, you have multiple levels of undo.

## Image inversion ▶

To check how clean a scanned image is convert it into negative (Image menu > Adjustments > Invert). It should have a solid white line and no speckling.

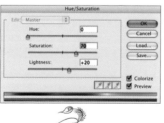

## Image proportions ▼

Any image or part of an image can be reduced or enlarged using Transform (Edit menu > Transform). If you want proportionate scaling, remember to hold down the shift key while resizing it or it will distort as can be seen in the middle figure below.

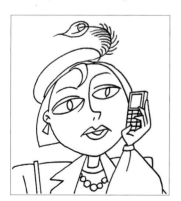

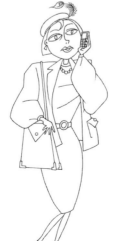

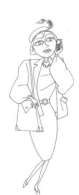

# Colouring a scanned image

The beauty of adding colour to an image in Photoshop is that you can make as many changes as you like on numerous layers without affecting the original. Any colour or painting technique that you no longer wish to display is simply deleted.

The range of colouring effects and application methods of this program can be overwhelming for the beginner. The best way to learn is by experimenting, safe in the knowledge that

provided you work in separate layers, nothing will be lost. This learning process is common to all artists: it helps them to pin down working methods and define drawing styles.

This practice exercise shows you how to set varying levels of colour tones to suggest highlights and shadows, and even add some textures into the mix, which are essential if an image is to have good overall balance.

## Practice exercise: Adding colour, tone and texture

Transforming a flat single-line drawing into full-colour 3-D artwork is a simple process that gives a stunning result. The 'hands-on' experience of working in multiple layers allows you to take a logical step-by-step approach. Expect slow progress while you are learning to use and control the various tools, safe in the knowledge that your speed will pick up as you grasp the technical know-how. It is always better not to rush through, but gain understanding carefully, even if this means taking extra time.

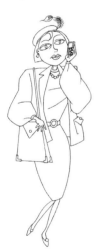

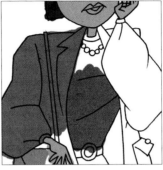

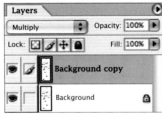

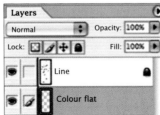

**Tip:** The layers panel has a lock, eye and brush icon. 'Locked' images cannot be worked on – scanned images are locked automatically as layers until you add another layer. To separate out your line work and begin colouring, copy your locked image with the 'Duplicate Layer' command. Use the Magic Wand tool, with 'Contiguous' unchecked, to select all areas of white on your image and delete them. Meanwhile, delete the original background layer, which will become unlocked – use this to add your colour, working *behind* your untouched black lines. Clicking the eye icon makes a layer visible or invisible – useful for checking your compositions, isolating layers or testing out filters. The brush icon shows which layer you are currently working on.

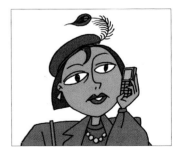

1 The line drawing is scanned as a bitmap 600dpi 'Grayscale' image (Image > Adjustments > Grayscale). To add colour it will need to be converted to a colour image (Image > Mode > RGB Color) and then significantly reduced in size. Go to Image > Image Size > Resolution and adjust Pixels/Inch in dialogue box to 300dpi. You are now ready to start colouring.

2 Duplicate the line image as a new layer with the 'Duplicate Layer' command or copy and paste the entire image. It will automatically appear in the layers palette. Change 'Normal' to 'Multiply' by scrolling down. Now click on the original background layer and delete it so that the new layer is now the colour layer. Label the specific layers to avoid any chance of confusion.

3 Apply flat colour with a 'flat' 100–200 pixel brush. You can access Colours either by clicking on a square in the toolbox that offers a colour palette or from the colour palette or colour slider bar on the desktop. If your colouring goes over the lines, simply clean around the line on the Colour flat layer with the Eraser tool (toolbox palette). The outline has its own layer and rests intact.

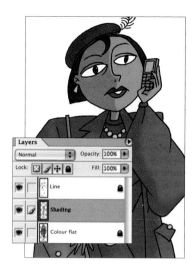

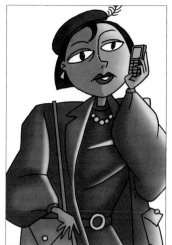

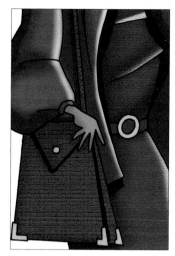

**4** Create a new layer, position it above the Flat colour layer and label it 'Shading', as the screengrab shows. Select the areas to shade with the Magic Wand tool (toolbox palette). Select the shading layer and add 15% black to your original colour. Apply this shade colour using a soft brush.

**5** Create a fourth layer and label it 'Highlighting'. To make new colours in the same hue range, simply reduce its strength by 20% and it is significantly lightened. Lock the other layers and select a soft brush to add the highlights. Experiment to see what effect you get by altering the colour Opacity, for example.

**6** Create a 'Texture' layer and lock the other layers. Select within the outlines of the bag and strap and add the texture from the Filter menu (Filter > Texture > Craquelure). Select a different texture for the dress. Once areas are selected and made as new layers, you can experiment with textures and patterns.

## Making colour changes

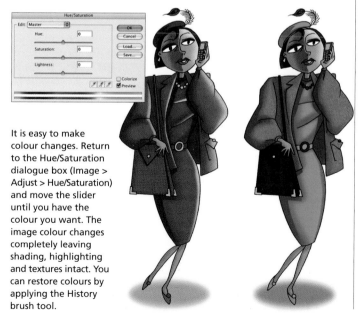

It is easy to make colour changes. Return to the Hue/Saturation dialogue box (Image > Adjust > Hue/Saturation) and move the slider until you have the colour you want. The image colour changes completely leaving shading, highlighting and textures intact. You can restore colours by applying the History brush tool.

## Colouring comic artwork

A common process for digitally colouring comic book cartoons is to build layers of flat colour beneath the original 'line' layer of a scanned-in ink drawing. The highlights and shadows are applied using the methods shown on these pages, and the areas around the lines neatened with the Eraser tool.

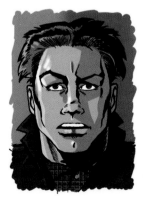

# The vector drawing program

The benefits of a vector drawing program, such as Adobe Illustrator, are most clearly seen when it is the sole program used to develop a sketch from draft to final colour artwork. It produces digital images in a distinctly slick style that combines crisp, clean lines with smooth flat colour. It by no means produces quicker results than other programs – in fact, creating shapes with the level of accuracy offered by a vector program can take time as you meticulously plot points, but as with all skills you will get quicker with practice. Another key advantage to using a vector program is that it uses far less memory than a bitmap program, so there are fewer problems with opening or storing images. This gives you the freedom to work on large-scale illustrations or on sequences, such as comic strips or cartoon narratives.

## Practice exercise: Creating a vector cartoon

Computers cannot replace artistic skill when it comes to creating images. They are an excellent tool but their only role is to respond to logical commands. Traditionally, an artist will 'think' and redraft a composition many times on paper and thinking remains a vital part of the process of refinement for a successful outcome. Using a computer program instead of paper changes nothing except that it is generally a speedier process. Create a file for the storage of sketches so that you can access them with ease and efficiency at any time.

**Tip:** Name each layer you create for ease of use. Save the image twice at the end – once with layers open, the other flattened with another name, as a flattened image won't allow you to adjust any stage of your work.

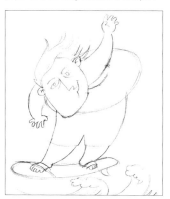

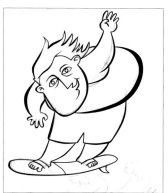

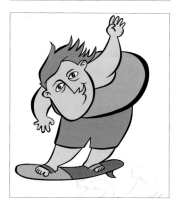

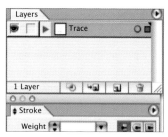

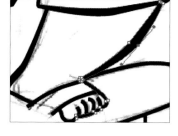

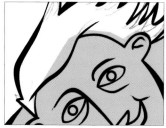

1 Scan an HB pencil sketch which you will use as a guide for vector drawing. Import it into Illustrator and reduce the file size to 100dpi ready to make an accurate Illustrator line trace (the resolution does not need to be large for tracing). Label the layer 'Trace'. If the scan is too dark click on it, then type 50% in the 'Opacity' box.

2 Now create a 'Line' layer and trace the outline of the sketch using the Pen tool, ensuring you click on the 'no fill' box. Give the Pen tool a 2pt stroke. Give the line extra weighting by clicking on the drawing and selecting Expand (Object > Expand), then use the Direct Selection tool to drag out anchor points to thicken the line in selected areas.

3 Lock the 'Line' layer and then create a new 'Flat colour' layer below it. Choose the hues you want from the palette. Colour the different parts of your cartoon figure by selecting within the vector drawn points, leaving the background for a later stage. Use smaller brushes for small areas, and the 'Bucket Fill' tool for filling large shapes.

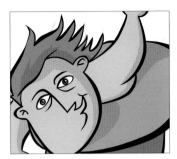

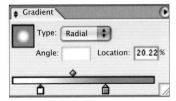

4 Create another new layer and call it 'Shading'. Darken the colours you are going to use for shading by adding 15% black to each one. Draw in the shadow areas and fill these shapes with a colour block from the selected palette; click on more colours in the palette for a more extensive range. Remember to lock the 'Flat' colour layer before you begin.

5 The pattern on the bathing shorts is composed of simple flower shapes. Create a single shape and locate it in the symbols library. Select it using the Sprayer tool and it will spray multiple flowers across the shorts area. Use the Direction Selection tool to remove stray flowers or rearrange the pattern. Create the gradated circle highlight on the rubber ring by selecting the white colour, clicking on the Gradient (next to layers) and selecting 'Radial'. Move the slider bars to adjust the size.

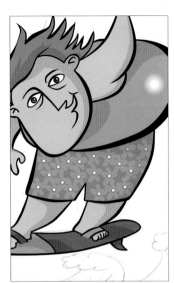

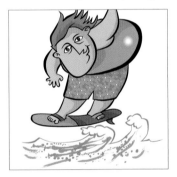

6 Make another layer and create the waves. Outline their shapes and add movement strokes (above). Select a brush from the Artistic Ink range (click on brushes arrow in the palette, scroll down to Open Brush Library > Artistic Ink > select Brush) and fill the areas with blue (right). Add colour gradients to the sea and sky on this layer: select an area with the Marquee tool or Magic Wand and click the Gradient tool to fill the area with the default gradient; black fading to white. The Gradient palette allows you to edit the colours and the 'gradient stops' (where a colour blends into another). To change the gradient's direction, draw a line with the Gradient tool across a previously selected gradient. Return to the Line layer and outline the seagulls, the strokes behind the surfboard and the foam bubbles.

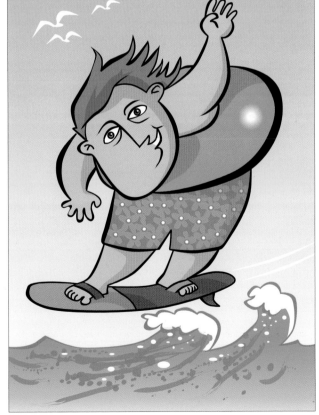

# Combining programs

Moving between programs provides more opportunity for creative image play. For example, a standard vector-drawn cartoon character imported into a bitmap program, such as Photoshop, can inhabit surroundings created in an array of styles, from the photographic to the painterly. This freedom to juxtapose the usual and the unusual and bring about striking contrasts invariably unleashes new levels of creativity.

The fact that Photoshop and Illustrator are complementary Adobe stablemates is liberating. The two applications share enough similarities of style and usage for anyone familiar with one application to switch between the two without difficulty. Following this lead, software packages from other manufacturers, such as the Corel Painter program, are deliberately intended to be similar.

## Practice exercise: Combining Illustrator and Photoshop

It is important to explore the potential offered by marrying vector and bitmap systems with a wide-open mind. Let go of all expectations of digital precision in favour of more relaxed collisions of broad shapes and colours. Unlike conventional drawing and painting, the Photoshop

(bitmap) painting being on a layer can 'go over' the line that you have drawn in Illustrator (vector). When the colouring layer is physically placed beneath the line (vector) layer and the layer 'eye' icons clicked on, it is an easy task to erase colour that has extended over the lines.

Such freeform digital images show that computer-generated concepts can be as inventive as traditional mixed-media collage. There is a benefit too of easily moving layers on top of each other with no need for using glue, which makes it hard to remove the pictorial pieces.

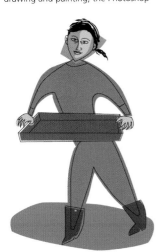

2 Find a photograph of pumpkins or other fruit or vegetables. This can be sourced from the Internet, a magazine or it could be a photo you have taken on a digital camera. Scan or import the picture into Photoshop where it automatically becomes a new 'Photos' layer. Position and scale the picture to the size you want using the Transform tool (Edit > Transform > Scale), and remove unwanted areas with a soft Eraser tool.

**Tip:** Don't think too long and hard about how you will develop an idea before testing it on screen. Start your exploratory journey straightaway, knowing that any wrong turns are easily corrected or eradicated if they have been made on separate layers.

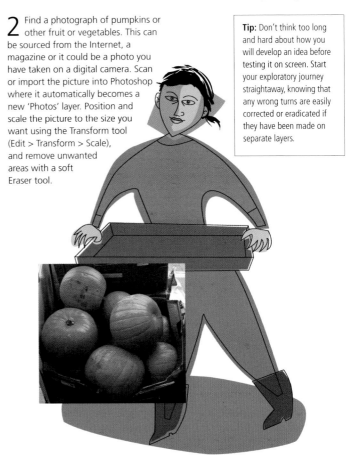

1 Draw the figure outline in Illustrator, using the Pen tool with a 0.5pt stroke. Label this layer 'Line' and lock it. Now make a new layer named 'Colour' and fill the outline with the different shades seen here. When you are happy with your image, save it for safekeeping, and open Photoshop. In Illustrator, click on 'Select All' to collate all image layers, and drag the picture into your new Photoshop window. Alternatively, you can import the picture by dragging your Illustrator document from your folder or desktop on to the Photoshop icon, where it will open automatically as a new layer in the layers palette.

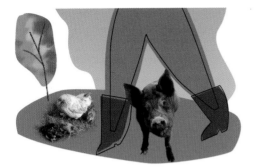

## Composite variation

Blending Illustrator and Photoshop applications can produce great results and they are not too difficult to grasp with a little practice. The hardest challenge lies in creating the initial sketch and controlling the tools for the best effect.

**City man ▶**
A sketch is created in Illustrator using Brush tools, which give a fluid line of varying thickness. The colour is then filled in and the image dragged into a new Photoshop document which contains layers of scanned magazine pictures with adjusted hues. Applying filters adds drama to the background.

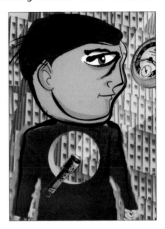

**3** Import the animal pictures into the Photos layer, position them and erase any extraneous details. Create the background layer and sit it below the others. Outline the tree and the amorphous shape behind the figure using the Pen tool. Fill them with gradated colour blends.

**4** Distort the blend within the tree shape using the Smudge tool and add digital images of apples as a new layer above the rest. On another layer add a shadow beneath the pumpkins using a soft brush. This gives them extra realism and enhances the 3-D quality. You could refine the shadow using filters.

## Composite programs caricature

Illustrator is the best choice for creating the extended lines and curves in this composition. The stylized shapes of the body, guitar, amp and microphone are tinted using flat Illustrator colours. The brushed acrylic layers of the more realistic caricatured head are produced in Photoshop.

**Guitar man ▼**
The flatness of the Illustrator body is in direct contrast with the formed, more painterly textures of the Photoshop head. This has been pinched, tweaked and distorted using an array of brushes and filters.

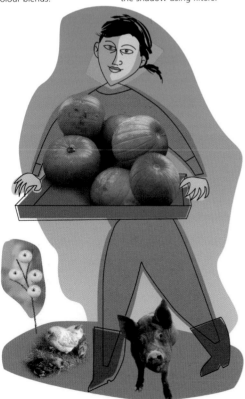

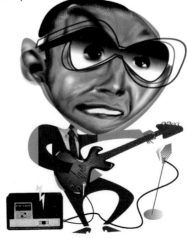

# Digital faces

Speech bubbles are rarely the first point of contact in a visual story and can even be replaced in a dialogue scene by the facial expressions of the characters. It is essential to portray expressions so that they are instantly recognizable, or else risk losing the meaning or joke they are aiming to convey. You can avoid this by reminding yourself that a digital program is only a tool and continue the habit of observing and sketching a range of faces

and expressions to keep your skills intact. A portrait that is built using conventional methods can be ruined if something goes wrong at an advanced stage. The advantage of developing a portrait on the screen is that it is almost impossible to go wrong – you just erase the work on the layer and start all over again. The exercises below outline the strikingly different results that can be produced when using different programs to draw faces.

## Practice exercise: Using Bezier curves and flat colour in Illustrator

Illustrator is ideal for creating strong controlled lines thanks to the sharp precision of its Bezier curves. While the colouring style limits itself to fairly flat hues, these are perfect for those cartoons where bold graphic definition

is necessary. Cartoon artwork produced for television and web pages especially benefits from this flat saturated colour style because they are transmitted by light passing through a dense network of tiny dots.

**Tip:** Practise the exercises on these pages again but change the brush shapes and sizes, alter the effects used and, in the case of Painter, try out different media or different combinations.

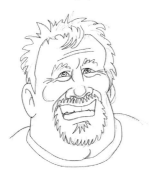

4 Create the final layer to include the shadows and highlights, which are fairly simple. The lighting effect on the top of the hair is made by reducing Opacity and by softening using the Blending tool. The highlight tones on the skin are created by reducing the percentage value of the colour saturation. The shadow on the left has an extra 15% of black added. Take care not to overdo the contrasts on these effects as this could overwhelm the line/colour style of the cartoon.

1 Scan in your pencil sketch at a high resolution and then resample it at 100dpi. Draw over all the lines of this image using the Pen tool. Make the pen drawing into a 'Line' layer and knock back the layer Opacity to 50%. This enables the new image to stand out from the original sketch beneath which was used as a guide.

2 Expand the pen line by pulling out selected anchor points using the Direct Selection tool. This simulates the result you would get if drawing with a springy brush where the pressure would be constantly changing as you delineate the facial curves.

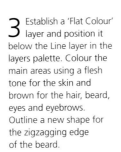

3 Establish a 'Flat Colour' layer and position it below the Line layer in the layers palette. Colour the main areas using a flesh tone for the skin and brown for the hair, beard, eyes and eyebrows. Outline a new shape for the zigzagging edge of the beard.

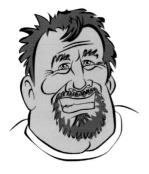

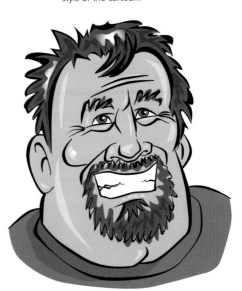

## Practice exercise: Modelling in Painter

The tactile joy of painting need not be totally lost for the digital cartoonist. The methodology for building and refining a character portrait through stages of modelling can be successfully employed using the bitmap program Painter. The stylus is sensitive and can take a bit of getting used to, but its readiness to respond to the slightest alteration of hand pressure is a real plus point, and will result in the subtleties which bring a painting to life being retained.

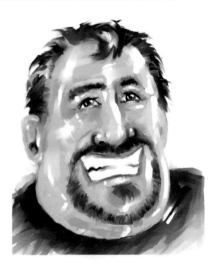

1 Scan in your pencil trace for the base layer. On a new layer, block in the 'Acrylic' colours using broad strokes on a medium brush setting.

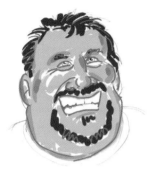

2 Smooth the colours using the Blending tool, using the same stroke directions that you would if you were actually painting. Add highlights and smooth them with the same tool. Dash in the T-shirt colour and smooth, first the blue, then the white, then blend. Use a smaller brush to detail the eyes and hair.

## Practice exercise: Balancing line with tone in Photoshop

The versatility of Photoshop can be fully realized in this exercise, in which it is used to construct the same face. A quick comparison shows that this Photoshop version creates a happy medium. The lines are crisp yet maintain much of the freely drawn nature of the original pencil sketch. The depth of colour and modelling is convincing enough to add form to the character without making it appear heavily laboured. The evenness of the tonal passages echoes the controlled manual application of gouache or acrylic.

3 Create another layer for shading. Darken the flesh tone by adding a further 15% of black. Darken the hair colour by at least 20% and locate shadows below the hairline and down the right side of his face. Create a gradated blend for the T-shirt on the same layer, extending it from white to blue. Return to the 'Skin' layer and remove the colour on the teeth with the Eraser tool, making them bright white.

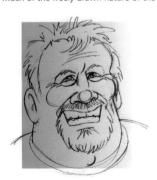

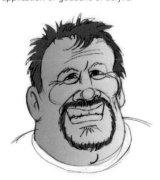

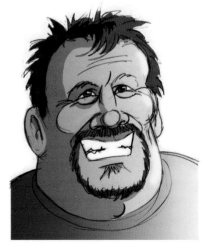

1 Scan your pencil sketch in grayscale at 600dpi, reduce it to 300dpi and convert to RGB colour. Under Image > Adjustments > Hue/Saturation move the slider so that the pencil line changes to warm brown. Make a new 'Skin' layer and place it beneath the Line layer. Use the Sprayer tool to apply a gradated skin tone, carefully erasing any excess.

2 Add a new layer between Line and Skin and use a flat brush to paint in warm brown strokes for the beard and hair. Select the same hue to paint in the pupils of the eyes. It is important to use different types and sizes of brush for the various sections of this painting. Opting for one or two choices will limit the contrasts you are aiming for.

# Digital face styles

The versatility of computer-generated cartoon faces is seen below. Paint and draw programs are capable of creating styles as wide-ranging as those produced by traditional methods. It makes sense to take inspiration from the master cartoonists when developing a look, whether square-jawed Hanna-Barbera or wide-eyed manga. Clarity of expression and good definition are essential to whatever style you create, and digital media delivers this.

## PHOTOSHOP

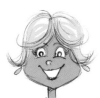

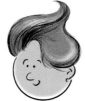

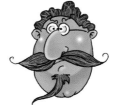

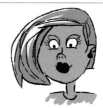

**Sketch** ▲
A lively pencil sketch is coloured brown in Photoshop, then a new layer overpainted for a flattish surface form.

**Highlighted** ▲
A Photoshop image drawn on screen. The ultra-pale highlights and strokes are made with a 1-pixel brush.

**Airbrush** ▲
A line sketch is scanned and coloured in Photoshop on a new layer. Airbrush Eraser creates highlights on the face.

**Flat tones** ▲
A Photoshop creation executed with the broken line of a Brush tool and painted in flat hues.

## ILLUSTRATOR

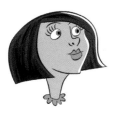

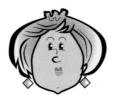

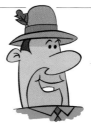

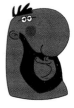

**Highlighted** ▲
The entire face is created in Illustrator with point-created shapes, expanded lines and white highlight strokes.

**Gradated tint** ▲
The lines are expanded in Illustrator by pulling anchor points. The gradated tint is created on a new layer.

**Conventional** ▲
An Illustrator drawing that uses Bezier curves throughout, expanded line and layers of flat colour.

**Strong shapes** ▲
The strong flat-coloured shapes of this face make the most of Illustrator's Bezier curves.

## COMBINED

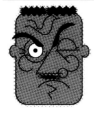

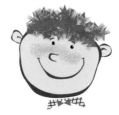

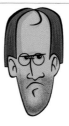

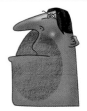

**Painter layers** ▲
The face was drawn and filled in Illustrator, then imported into Photoshop where a halftone pattern was added.

**Broad line** ▲
This face fully utilizes expanded Illustrator lines and dots. The pale hair is Photoshop-created.

**Line and airbrush** ▲
An expanded Illustrator outline that has been coloured in Photoshop. The stubble is airbrushed.

**Soft brush and airbrush** ▲
The Illustrator outline is coloured in Photoshop. A soft brush defines the hair and the stubble is airbrushed.

# Photoshop hair effects

Like faces, distinctive hair styles can be a useful way of defining character and displaying personality traits that are easy to recognize. Exploring the wide range of custom brushes and filter effects in Photoshop and applying them to simple sketches will enable you to spend less time creating techniques, and discover more ways of bringing hair to life. The simple sketches on this page demonstrate some of the effects that can be achieved.

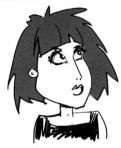
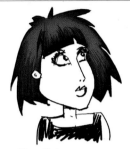
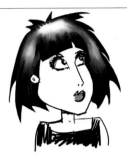

**Stage 1** ▲
A pen sketch is scanned and imported into Photoshop. The first duplicate layer is filled with flat medium brown.

**Stage 2** ▲
On a new layer the Pencil tool defines hair strands and darker brown brushstrokes soften the edges.

**Stage 3** ▲
White highlights are added on the final layer with a medium brush and blended with the Smudge tool at 60% Opacity.

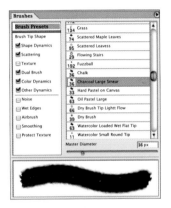
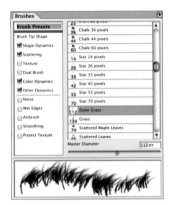
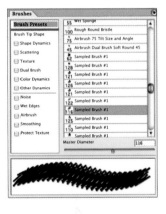

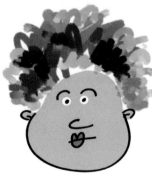
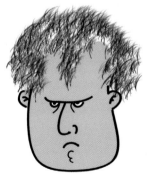
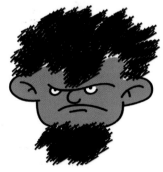

**Soft volume** ▲
With the charcoal brush selected (Brush Palettes > Brushes), broadly sketch the soft curls. Offer a more life-like balance of tones throughout by altering the 'Opacity', which here is 60% and 30%.

**Dune Grass custom brush** ▲
Use the custom brush 112 – 'Dune Grass' – from the brushes library to recreate a thinning wispy head of hair. To tidy, use the Eraser tool to remove unwanted strands.

**Sampled brush** ▲
The variety of custom brushes is wide, the choices peculiar, but they bring strong textural qualities to the drawing in contrast to the flatness of outline and solid, facial colour.

# Creating backgrounds

The importance of backgrounds in anchoring cartoon figures, setting scenes and generally assisting the narrative of a gag or strip is undeniable. Creating settings by hand can be laborious but a task such as painting a soft gradated blend or cross-hatching a texture is achieved quickly and easily using digital techniques. Not only is it possible to add uncomplicated backgrounds in seconds, they can be constructed in multiple layers to give you the option of changing textures, colours or

line work at will. The freedom of creating settings digitally also allows you to be more inventive in areas such as tonal contrast and surface quality, which can add significant interest to your scenes. Take inspiration from the digitally devised settings of many graphic novels and children's books and don't be afraid to indulge in creative play. Photoshop's wide selection of filters and effects can make for a polished end result, whereas Painter is best able to mimic traditional painterly effects.

## Practice exercise: Creating a background in Photoshop

It is especially easy to create, manipulate or duplicate images or sections of images using Photoshop. The typical 'copy and paste' method can be used to build a background, where manual methods would need to employ collage

techniques to achieve the same results. As well as its compatibility with other programs, a major benefit of Photoshop is that colours are altered with ease and layers are stacked on top of each other with varying degrees of Opacity.

**Tip:** Photoshop and Painter have a huge range of filters and effects. Search through these before you create a new texture – the effect you seek may already exist.

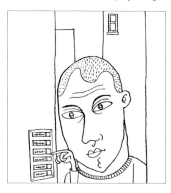

**1** Draw the outline using a dip pen and black Indian ink (the single window is deliberate) and scan it into a new Photoshop document. Duplicate it as a layer and rename it 'Line'. Set the layers box on to 'Mutiply'.

**2** Lasso or Marquee the single window with the appropriate tool and duplicate (Item > Step and repeat) on a new layer. Create the distant windows by scaling (Edit > Transform > Scale), and duplicating the single window. Play around, moving and scaling the shapes until you get the sense of depth you want.

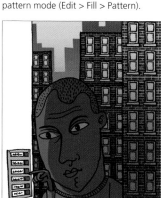

**3** Make a new layer and create a brick pattern on it by drawing boxes and fill with two reddish tones. To duplicate the boxes, take them into pattern mode (Edit > Fill > Pattern).

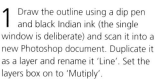

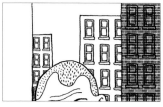

**4** ▲ ▶ Scale the pattern as you did for the window in step 2 and apply it to the buildings receding into the distance. When the buildings are covered, erase the pattern over the windows.

**5** Create a new layer to go behind the bricks. Fill it with gradated colour from pale yellow to glowing orange-red and add pale block shapes to indicate the far distance. Fill the bell pushes with red and tint the figure a blue shade that contrasts with the glowing eyes. Draw and fill a darker shadow on a new layer.

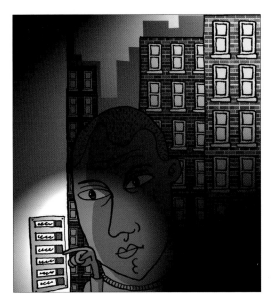

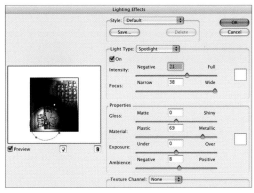

6 Finally enhance the mood using the Lighting Effects palette (Filter > Render > Lighting Effects). Select the values shown in the screengrab above for the light around the bell push. You can adjust the circumference, shape and position of the flare by clicking on the lamp icon and dragging the Pointer tool. Feel free to experiment with new values to discover different effects.

## Painter backgrounds

The subtle colours, textures and geometry of this background setting for a tree-planting 'eco-hero' character is created in Painter. This program comes closest to reproducing traditional drawn and painted effects, while Photoshop's range of filters and effects can produce a slicker, more polished look.

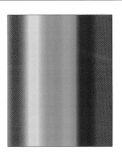

**Rainbow** ◄
To make the rainbow, a series of vertical bands is drawn on a new layer and filled with a spectrum of colours. The colours are then blurred by applying a filter. The bands are distorted and rotated to imitate the rainbow curve. This layer is placed on top of the pastel one.

**The figure** ▼
The last step is to detail the figure. The scanned image is outlined in broken-edged pencil and filled with colour – acrylic paint tones for the costume and skin, with white chalk pastel highlights. The clouds and rain streaks are pastel, and blocks of grey and brown acrylic tones are duplicated on to a grey background for the buildings.

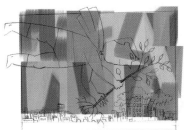

**Scan and pastel effects** ▲
A pencil sketch of the superhero and the background details is imported into Painter from the scan application and converted into a layer. The sky is a construction of blues and violets using broad brush tools on a pastel setting. The larger shapes are duplicated and overlapped.

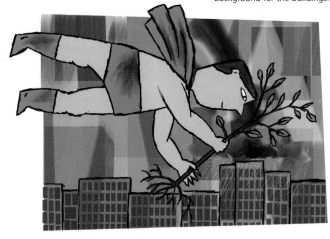

## Practice exercise: 3-D illusion in Illustrator

Not every cartoon background works as a simple tone or texture, or a figment of the artist's imagination. For certain subjects it is often necessary to opt for a more lifelike 3-D setting. Converting a flat surface pattern to one which converges at a vanishing point can be a time-consuming exercise by traditional methods but is a relatively problem-free task on the computer. The accuracy of Illustrator makes it the ideal tool for making such drawings. However, their success or failure will depend on the user's grasp of the principles of perspective. A sound understanding, plus the ability to combine different elements convincingly, will enable you to be ambitious in your creations.

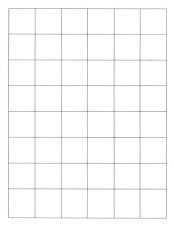

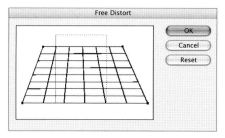

**3** ▼ Use the Bucket-Fill tool to colour the squares in a chequerboard pattern. Click the box marked 'Gradient' on the desktop to apply a gradated tint to the colour as shown below. This will greatly enhance the 3-D effect.

**1** On your base layer, start by making the grid pattern for the floor. Use the Pen tool to draw small squares – duplicate one six times to make a row, using the 'Copy and Paste' commands, then duplicate the row eight times to make your grid. Arrange the rows as shown above. Make sure you apply an outline stroke to the grid. Select and group the composite parts of the grid into a single entity (Object > Group).

**2** Lay the grid in perspective along a horizonal plane using Free Distort. Click and move the two end points of the top horizontal line closer together. Adjust their positions until the shape is at the correct perspective. Click 'Reset' if you want to begin again.

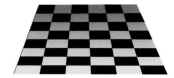

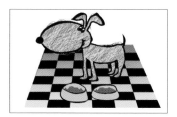

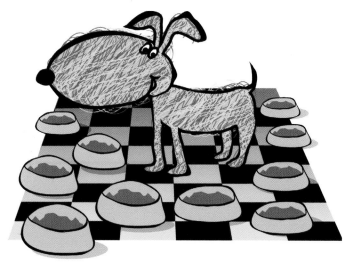

**4** Create a new layer for the dog and food bowls. Position the dog in the midground and the bowls in the foreground. Draw their outlines using the Brush tool, expanding and thickening the lines to add character. Colour the body grey, then select Effect > Stylize > Scribble for a textured look.

**5** Select, duplicate and scale the food bowls at different sizes on a new layer. Locate them in the foreground, midground and background. Make a 'Shadows' layer beneath the bowls, outline an ellipse and fill it with grey at 50% Opacity. Duplicate, scale and position the shadows beside the bowls.

**Tip:** Keep perspective grids simple so that you are able to judge the perspective convergence easily. Refer to one, two and three perspective template drawings to help you to understand how settings and objects converge into the distance.

## Practice exercise: Stylish realism using combined programs

A modern setting needs a style to match. Amalgamating the accuracy of Illustrator and the versatility of Photoshop gives you the means to produce an image with a bold and contemporary look. The broadly painted background of this setting is made in Photoshop while the Illustrator line, strong graphic shapes and accurate perspective refine the picture and add realism. The creative process of laying down colours, textures and marks in distinctive layers is as involved as the traditional technique of screenprinting.

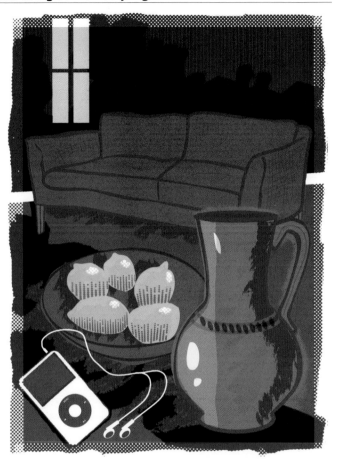

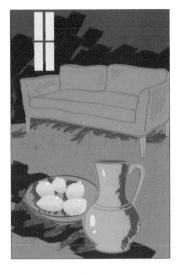

1 The room and its contents are outlined in Illustrator using a range of brushes to give a free loose style. The flat colour is applied in Illustrator and the series of dots for shadow areas on the lemons is created using the Blend tool.

2 The image is then dragged into Photoshop where the colours are adjusted and the larger areas filled with broad brushstrokes. A refined Brush tool is employed to create the smooth lines of the MP3 player.

3 Finally, a 'Halftone' filter creates a border. A regular coarse pattern of halftone dots can be applied in Photoshop to interrupt the smooth surface of Illustrator-generated images. The settings used here are shown on the right. Adjusting dot size, shape and contrast will give different effects.

**Tip:** Adding scanned or 'found' imagery to your hand-drawn compositions, as with the iPod above, can grant them greater legitimacy than as images alone. Think of the photographic trees, people and vehicles used to bring the latest digital architectural renderings to life. Keep a cuttings file of useful photographs or magazine clips that could be scanned and cut out digitally using Photoshop. Collect subjects that have a strong shape and not too much tonal subtlety.

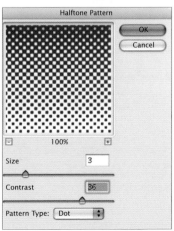

# Portraying motion

The computer counterparts of drawn action lines have much in common with the speed effects seen in fast-action photography and film. All the main vector and bitmap programs can replicate the effects of suspending a high-speed moment in time, often with only a few simple steps. Illustration devices that signify movement can be digitally enhanced using a gamut of action effects and distortion tricks. Features such as blurring, speed lines and superimposing multiple images on top of one another all create a convincing illusion of activity. Short of actually making it move, selecting the right interpretation of your moment of frozen time or mixing manipulated digital photography with your cartoon will be enough to animate your image with energy and dynamism. The exercises below outline the creation of composite pictures that refuse to stay still!

## Practice exercise: Creating a speed blur effect

To produce a cartoon with digitally animated qualities requires a good balance of elements. A well-constructed composition is vital: the main focus should be emphatic and its descriptive action lines surrounded by enough white space to take the motion effect. Directing the viewer's eye contributes more to the concept of motion than a host of clever tricks. In this exercise the simple device of a looping motion line provides a visual journey starting at the goldfish bowl at the bottom of the picture and leading to the flying fish at the top. Here, a blur effect on the blades is sufficient to focus the full attention of the viewer on its rapid, whirling motion.

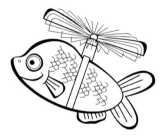

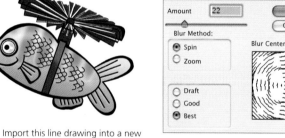

1 Create the static rounded fish in Illustrator, expanding the points of your drawn lines with the Direct Selection tool as in previous exercises. Draw the multiple helicopter blades in a lighter line to help them move.

2 Import this line drawing into a new Photoshop document and create a 'Colour' layer. Add the soft yellows and greens to the body using an Airbrush tool. Fill the rotor blades with flat red and paint white in between.

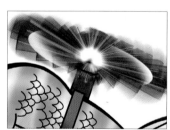

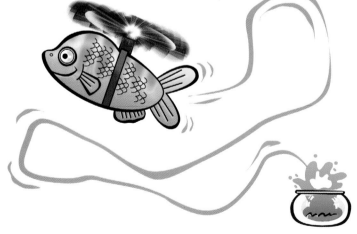

3 Select the elliptical rotor blades area and open the Blur filter (Filter > Blur > Radial Blur), setting the method to spin. Select a second tighter elliptical section in the centre of the same area and repeat the process.

4 Draw the goldfish bowl, the action strokes and twisting line which traces the motion path in Illustrator. On a new layer, position the earlier Illustrator outline of the fish. 'Select All' and open in Photoshop for colouring, positioning the outline beneath the existing colour layer.

## Practice exercise: Creating a superimposed effect

Creating the sense of movement in a still image by superimposing is traditionally done using clear acetate layers. The same image is duplicated on each layer, each time in a slightly different position to give the effect of movement trapped in freeze-frame. Creating this type of action in Photoshop offers the advantage of varying the Opacity of the layers, which allows the transition of time to be more strongly conveyed.

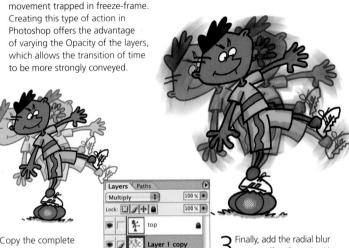

**1** Sketch the outline of the boy and his football in pen and scan it in as an oversized line art image. Reduce it in scale and size to 300 dpi, convert it to RGB colour and copy to a new layer. On separate layers, add flat colour, shadows on the left side and a white highlight to the ball.

**2** Copy the complete image twice more onto new layers, setting the Opacity of each to 50%. Drag the three layers into a new document and position so that the lower two are slightly offset. Rotate the lower images (Edit > Transform > Rotate) and erase any area overlaps.

**3** Finally, add the radial blur motion effect from the Blur filter to the two images on the lower layers (Filter > Blur > Radial Blur). Decide on the frequency value for the blur and set it to spin. Feel free to play around with the settings, experimenting with different values, and only click OK when you are completely satisfied with the results.

## Practice exercise: Combining media

Combining images that vary in quality is an easy and effective way of portraying speed. In this example a static Illustrator-generated cartoon character is imposed on a digital photograph which has been 'speeded' up.

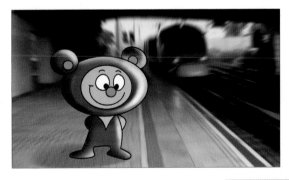

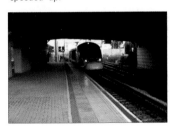

**1** Choose a digital photograph with a strong one- or two-point perspective, such as the advancing train used here. Import it into Photoshop as a .jpg, then convert it to RGB colour mode (Image > Mode > RGB Colour). Make the photo a new background layer.

**2** The outline of the cartoon character is created in Illustrator and imported into Photoshop. The flat colours and highlights are added on a new layer. The speed effect is applied to the digital photo on a new layer using the Radial Blur filter set to 'Zoom'. The layered cartoon is then imported. Finally, an elliptical shadow is drawn in Photoshop and softened using 'feather' at 20 pixels. It is then filled with blue and reduced to 50% Opacity.

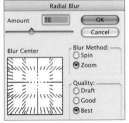

# Digital improving

One of the fantastic things about computer enhancement is that it does just as it says: enhance! Each picture that is drawn, painted or manipulated in some way is bound to be an 'okay' picture, but getting it to the next level and making it a little more special can be a really simple task that merely requires you to have the tricks of the trade to hand. Every day that you use graphic applications on a computer your learning will

progress and, second to picking up tips from other people, there is a strong argument for exploring and experimenting with the program's filters and effects libraries. Many of the improvements that will transform your cartoons are achieved by making simple adjustments to one of the wide range of filters or via the Image > Adjustment menu in Photoshop. The preview option always allows you to test the effect.

## Practice exercise: Retro style

A return to the retro styles of the 1970s brought with it a desire by image-makers to take another look at the grooviness of swirling patterns, modish pop art circles, tangerine dreams and lime-green walls. Although the colours of the revival are more refined, the defining feature of this retro style remains in its clean lines and strong colour definition. Such specific demands are most successfully met by a combination of Illustrator and Photoshop.

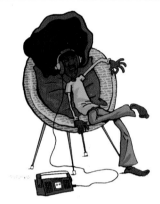

**1** Begin with a manual pen drawing that has plenty of life in its line variation. The focus of the sketch is on the listener in the chair with his accessories so keep the background plain. Import this image into Photoshop and tint it using a Colour palette and Brush tools.

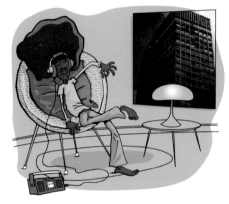

**2** Construct the rest of the room in Illustrator using the Pen tool. Place the coloured figure into Illustrator at the same time to assist with the scale and construction of the room. Drag everything back into a new Photoshop document. Draw an irregular shape on a new layer beneath the line drawing and colour it green. Draw a box with the Rectangle Drawing tool. 'Posterize' a scanned or downloaded tower-block picture (Layer > New Adjustment Layer > Posterize) and import into the box.

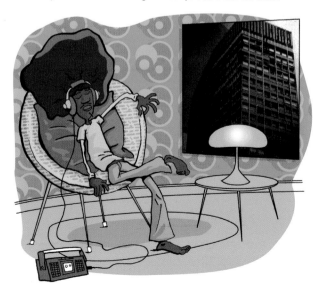

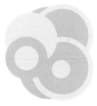

**3** Create the swirling wallpaper pattern in Illustrator, and place it back into Photoshop for duplication as a pattern (Filter > Pattern Maker). Select the background area above the skirting boards, and darken it using the histogram slide (Image > Adjustment > Levels). Next choose 'Multiply' on layers, and fill your selection with your chosen pattern (using the Pattern Bucket tool). This will duplicate the pattern into the space.

# Practice exercise: Motion in Photoshop

Adding an airbrush-style motion effect is a very uncomplicated process in Photoshop. It is made using basic brushes and any of the blur filters, grain filters or pointillizing filters, singly or combined. The end result can enhance a simple visual gag enormously. In this practice exercise, it can be clearly seen that the definition of contrast between the crisp characterful line and the soft out-of-focus background lends a heightened sense of depth to the final image.

**Tip:** Using noise, grain and pointillism filters is a quick alternative to sourcing real-world textures to use in your imagery. They have the added bonus of meshing and integrating more naturally with your art.

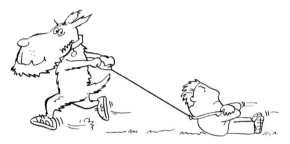

**1** Sketch the 'dog and man' gag by hand as a simple, fineliner pen drawing. Keep your lines lively by varying their weight – it keeps them animated. Scan your drawing and import it into Photoshop, duplicate it as a new layer, delete the background layer and set it to Multiply.

**2** Add colour using soft brushes and create the background as a Gradient image (Layer > New Fill Layer > Gradient (set to Multiply)), from light to dark. Further soften the soft coloured banding of the sky and accentuate the effect of motion using the Blur filter (Filter > Blur).

**3** Fine action lines deliver effective motion. Add a Horizontal Grain filter (Filter > Grain) to the back of the dog's body. Check the settings against the screengrab (right), but feel free to experiment with intensity and contrast. When you are satisfied click OK.

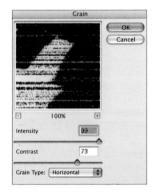

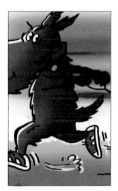

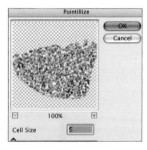

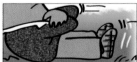

**4** Extra details can really enhance the character of a drawing. Marquee/Lasso the jumper area (Select > Filter > Pointillize), set the cell size and click OK. Adding texture to the man's jumper brings him into focus as a foil to the leading character of the pooch.

**5** Finally, add white speed lines around the feet of the characters and in between them.

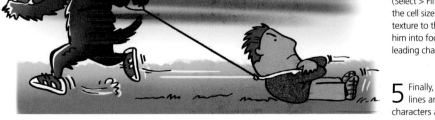

# Words

A cartoon with a strong visual sense won't need the help of text to communicate its message. Despite this, words traditionally accompany many cartoons and perform a variety of functions. In general, self-contained panel cartoons have a simple caption or one-liner beneath them, whereas comic strips include dialogue placed inside speech bubbles. Lettering is also used as a means of communicating sound effects.

Cartoon words must be clear, legible and integrate with the overall design. Lettering style, size, weight and consistency are therefore important considerations. Traditionally, cartoonists use hand-drawn lettering to achieve this, a technique that is easily replicated using selected computer fonts. Unless it is being used for emphasis, cartoon lettering is usually black on white so that it plays a secondary role to the image.

## Speech bubbles

Digital software is of huge assistance to the cartoonist where accuracy and neatness are essential. A vector drawing program, such as Illustrator, can produce a range of faultless speech-bubble ellipses. Once created, they can be saved into a file and used as a style library for ready access as and when they are needed.

**Calligraphic bubbles** ▼
Select different brush-drawn styles in Illustrator to produce quirky speech bubbles with varying weights of line. Go to brush style under 'Brushes' and choose the style. Next select the bubble, add the stroke weight of your choice and click on it.

◀ ▼ **Basic bubble process**
The basic construction of speech bubbles is best done in Illustrator. Draw an ellipse with the Ellipse tool, and then use the Pen tool to make a small inverted triangle at the base of the oval. Go to View > Pathfinder > Make compound shape to unite these two selections.

Italic bold can alter pace or *intonation* in speech.

Only use bold and bold italic where it most **effectively** expresses the idea.

Offer **emphasis** to speech by simply setting in bold**.**

*For speech to have strong impact within the narrative, set it all in bold or bold italic.*

Plain speaking in a standard, plain bubble

This pressure-led bubble indicates movement and life.

A more basic bubble, in a broken drawn style, is suitable for lighter gags.

Artistic_ChalkCharcoalPencil

Brush style palette

The basic form

Final shape

**A thought cloud** ▲
Construct the basic form in straight-edged lines using the Pen tool. Then curve the points by adding and subtracting points within the shape, using the range of either Pen or Pencil tools.

Place informal lively speech in a direct, square box-type bubble.

Pen and Pencil tools

# Lettering effects

Whether they are vector-drawn or bitmapped, all type forms can be manipulated – stretched, compressed, enlarged, reduced or skewed – and tinted by building layers. Both Illustrator and Photoshop offer a broad range of effects which are useful when you want to exaggerate or emphasize lettering. Effects such as a blended or gradient fill, drop shadow or other tinted or textured surfaces are the most commonly used. If you start to explore the Filter menus you will find not only alternatives for toning and texturing the letters, but also distorting them.

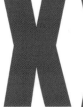 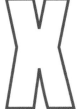 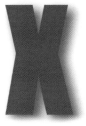 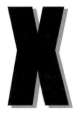 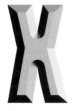 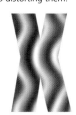

| Back Fill | Outline, no fill | Drop Shadow | Drop Shadow (layer effects) | Chisel Emboss (layer effects) | Custom Brush (wavy line fill) |

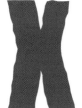 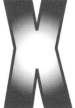 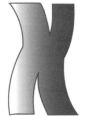 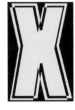 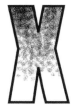 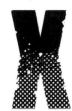

Distorted — Radial Fill — Twist, blend — Duplicated X offset to new layer — Custom Brush (advanced palette) — Halftone Pattern (partially erased)

**Special FX in Illustrator** ▲
Although Illustrator does not offer the same breadth of tools for manipulation as Photoshop, it is a very good program for adjusting type forms.

**Special FX in Photoshop** ▲
The above examples show the variability of type effects that are available in Photoshop. The majority show the results that can be achieved by manipulating surface decoration.

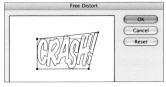

**Expressive type in Illustrator** ▲ ▶
When you have typed the word in your chosen font go to Type > Create Outlines; then Object > Ungroup and use the Direct Selection tool (white arrow) with Alt key depressed to overlap the type. Next go to Filter > Distort > Free Distort and extend the points outwards to alter the scale and shape of the typeface. Finally, apply a Gradient Fill from the gradients palette on your desktop.

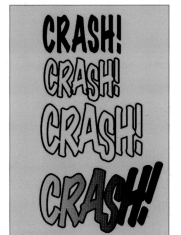

**Transforming type** ▼
The dullest of lettering can be given a visually exciting make-over by manipulating it. Explore the different effects that Illustrator has to offer and experiment with already familiar techniques, such as varying and expanding line widths.

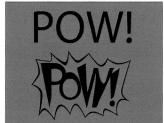

# Digital shortcuts

Achieving a complex visual effect using traditional manual methods requires skill, patience and time. When working on a computer the critical difference is that you can gain maximum effects with minimum effort, often after a single keystroke.

Understanding and implementing digital shortcuts to create effects such as the complexities of reflections in glass or on water, or the subtle folds of fabric are indispensable skills for the digital image-maker. Begin by exploring and experimenting with the range of different filters that are at your disposal. Each filter has an accompanying tool option panel which allows you to apply effects and distortions. For example, in the case of the Bas Relief filter, it includes surface texture choices and the depth of the relief dictated by the direction of the light creating the 3-D effect.

## Practice exercise: Creating a fabric fold

This exercise demonstrates a digital approach to suggesting the smooth undulating movement of a weightless, shimmering fabric by replicating the complex interplay of light and shade on the surface of the cartoon character's cloak and pantaloons. The huge range of effects and filters that are available in Photoshop makes it the ideal choice of program to achieve such a high standard of description easily, quickly and effectively.

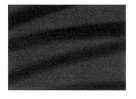

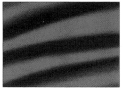

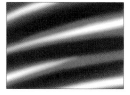

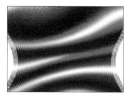

1 For the cloak create a rectangle in Photoshop at the approximate size you need and fill it with red. Add broad, horizontal bands of light brown using a selection of soft brushstrokes to give a streaked effect.

2 Lock the first layer and make a new one. Select a lighter shade of red and brush it across the red areas, ensuring you leave narrow bands of the deeper colour to establish a consistent tonal depth and rhythm.

3 Make another layer and select a smaller soft brush to add tapering white highlights across the centre of each paler colour band. Don't worry about precision. No two fabric folds are ever the same.

4 Now for the digital trickery: go to the Wave filter (Filter > Distort > Wave) and experiment by moving the slidebars until you achieve the desired effect. Click OK when you are happy with the result.

5 To achieve further distortion which is less regular and looks more like silken folds, apply the Pinch filter (Filter > Distort > Pinch) and adjust the level of distortion by moving the slider along the bar. Form the flowing cloak shape by cutting it out using the Pen tool.

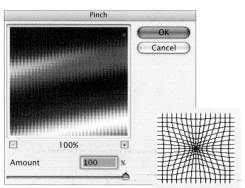

6 Apply the effect by dragging it into the document containing the cartoon image and position it over the appropriate section. As it is on a layer, it can be set behind the main figure, as shown here. Now repeat the process to create the same silken effect for the purple pantaloons.

## Practice exercise: Rendering embossed metal

In this example the embossed bronze sheen is created by applying a filter known as Bas Relief. Note that filters can never be a shortcut for working through the creative process and that final effects should only be applied to finished artwork.

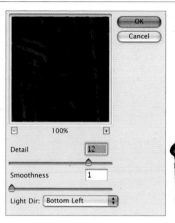

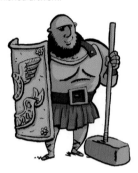

**1** Scan the line drawing of the Roman warrior into Photoshop. A new layer is created and placed below the line layer. Flat colour and simple shading are added to bring the character to life.

**2** Select the area in question using the Lasso or Marquee selection tool and apply the Bas Relief filter (Filter > Sketch > Bas Relief). It imparts a kind of solarizing effect to the colours and gives a raised appearance to contrasting areas. Set the light direction, level of detail and smoothness you want by operating the sliders.

**3** When you have achieved the filter effect, you can apply small finishing touches. Here, a subtle shadow tinted in soft pale green is centred beneath the figure to prevent him from 'floating'.

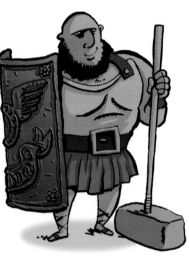

## Practice exercise: Reflections in water

To replicate the reflection in water of an object or figure by hand requires a huge amount of visual understanding and time. Computer drawing programs contain filters designed to produce the effect automatically, releasing you from a very painful learning process. If such an option had been available, the Great Masters might have plumped for it too!

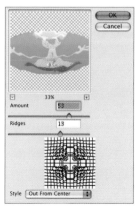

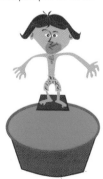

**1** Draw the diver freehand in Illustrator and bring into Photoshop on a new layer, where he is reduced in size to fit the area of pool reflection. Apply the Distortion filter and adjust to the required percentage.

**2** To add the water surface shimmer, reset the Blending Opacity to 'Hardlight' in Edit > Fill, to give the reflection the correct level of shine. Other options are Filter > Liquefy or Filter > Distort > Glass.

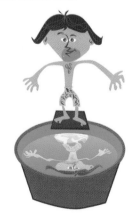

## Practice exercise: Creating a mirror image

Achieving a realistic reproduction of a reflected mirror-image is a relatively simple task in the hands of the digital cartoonist. It can be made to look even more convincing with added enhancements, such as reflected light,

distortion and reduction. The artists should still rely on their knowledge of how reflection and distortion actually look when seeking to replicate the visual outcome. Reference photographs can help, especially if your subject is moving.

**Tip:** Use the Ripple filter to distort reflections. Note the differences between a reflection in a moving surface, such as water, and a solid surface, such as glass.

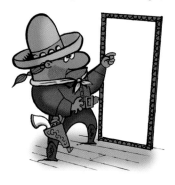 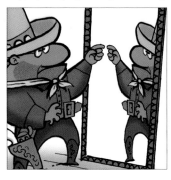 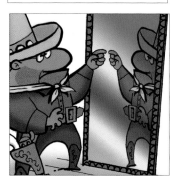

**1** Make a pen drawing of the cartoon, scan and import it into Photoshop. Colour it using multiple layers. Create the soft-edged flooring by feathering it (Select > Feather > Feather Radius > 15 pixels). Leave the mirror blank at this stage as you will create the reflection in three stages.

**2** Next return to the scanned cowboy. Reverse his image using Image > Rotate Canvas > Flip Canvas Horizontal. Apply the Transform tool (Edit > Transform > Distort) and pull the points of the rectangle around the figure to distort it. Place the reversed image inside the mirror frame.

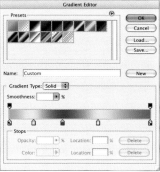

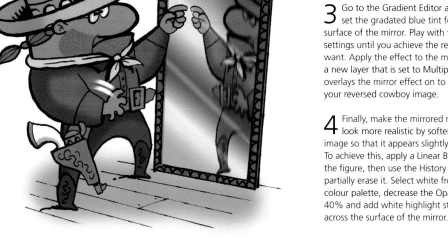

**3** Go to the Gradient Editor and set the gradated blue tint for the surface of the mirror. Play with the settings until you achieve the result you want. Apply the effect to the mirror on a new layer that is set to Multiply. This overlays the mirror effect on to your reversed cowboy image.

**4** Finally, make the mirrored reflection look more realistic by softening the image so that it appears slightly blurred. To achieve this, apply a Linear Blur to the figure, then use the History brush to partially erase it. Select white from the colour palette, decrease the Opacity to 40% and add white highlight streaks across the surface of the mirror.

# Practice exercise: Adding texture with filters

The array of filters available in Photoshop enables you to add various atmospheric effects to your cartoons. A playful attitude is likely to achieve interesting results, so see what happens when you apply a particular filter effect to a layer or two. Juxtaposing texture filters enriches images, for example. Once you have mastered the ordering of the layers palette it is then just a case of adjusting the image to fit and interpreting the cartoon appropriately.

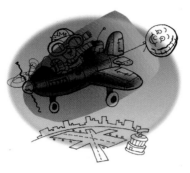

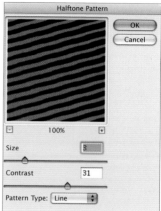

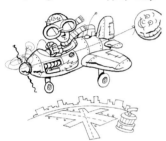

1 Make a line drawing, scan and import it into Photoshop. Duplicate this Background layer and delete the original. This unlocks the copy layer so it is ready to work on.

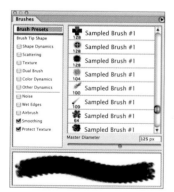

2 ▲ ▶Use the oval Marquee tool to create an oval shape and soften its painted edge with a Feather (Select > Feather > Feather Radius > 15 pixels). Fill the shape with a blend of blue and pink using the Gradient tool. To do this add a layer of pink to the blue and reduce the Fill and Opacity settings.

3 ▶ Colour the plane by selecting the fuselage section and imposing a Halftone filter on a new layer (Filter > Sketch > Halftone Pattern). Set the filter to Line so that the aircraft body has a lined texture running along its length. Select grey as the tint colour and place this layer above the sky oval.

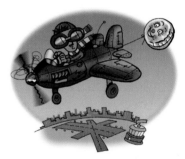

4 ▲ ▶ Erase the filter effect overlapping the sky oval and colour the rest. On separate layers: add a Spin filter to the propeller; select Smoothing and Protect Texture presets for the smoke; blend the flames and clouds with the Smudge tool; and balloon highlights using Filter > Render > Lighting Effects > Flare.

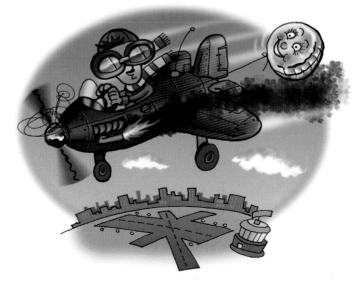

# Animation

A sequence of individual pictures that are slightly adjusted as the series progresses can literally come to life before our eyes. According to the Persistence of Vision theory, our brains hold on to each image for a fraction of a second after our eyes have left it. When we see a rapid succession of individual images we think we are witnessing movement. An animated cartoon is a very long series of altering static frames. For the cartoonist who wants to explore this next progression, there are computer animation programs which enable frames to be viewed as a moving sequence. Adobe Flash and ImageReady will provide the beginner with the basic knowledge needed to create moving 2-D cartoons. Those wishing to explore 3-D animation will need software such as 3-D Studio Max or Maya, or cheaper, shareware alternatives available on the Internet. However, depicting a moving figure is a skilful undertaking requiring a keen understanding of animal and human movement.

## Basic techniques

The simplest forms of effective animation do not need a movie camera to produce results. A sequence of images, each with a slight alteration, drawn on consecutive pages of a sketchpad results in a moving 'film' when the pages are rapidly flicked. The humble flick book is a commonly used prototype for developing the movements and characteristics of animated characters and a must for cartoonists who want to bring their creations to life. As well as creating action it is also a means of experimenting with the effects of distortion. Exaggerating the natural forces of gravity and motion on characters and objects brings them into the sphere of the humorously absurd. Getting your figures moving around the cartoon world is a powerful trigger for generating new and fresh ideas.

**Flick book ▼**
The simplest form of drawn animation can be tested by making a flick book. A series of images is sketched on consecutive pages so that each 'traces' over the top of the next. Each new drawing is slightly altered so that the images seem to move when the pages are rapidly flicked. For best results, make sure the pages are flush and evenly cut.

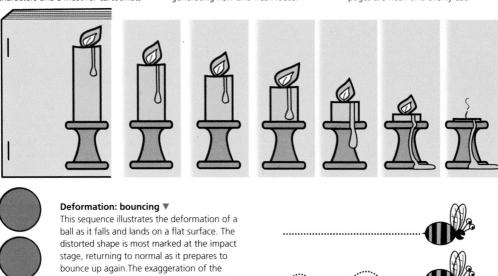

**Deformation: bouncing ▼**
This sequence illustrates the deformation of a ball as it falls and lands on a flat surface. The distorted shape is most marked at the impact stage, returning to normal as it prepares to bounce up again. The exaggeration of the altered shape is much greater than it would be in reality and the illustration of the process as a frozen moment provides a strong sense of movement. A cartoon animation that did not jump and move would seem static and dull.

**Tracking movement ▲**
How you draw a character and the devices you use can lend it strong animated properties. The bee in both pictures has active features: the feelers have eyes, the overlapping wings suggest flight and the vertical body stripes bounce the viewer's eyes from left to right. The dotted trails effectively confirm the direction of the movement.

## Deformation: Compression and stretching

The great thing about animating an image is that it does not have to mirror reality. The goal is to create a movement that is believable in the surreal cartoon world where people and objects are malleable and can spring back into shape as if made of rubber. Techniques such as exaggerated compression and elongation are commonly used in cartoon animation to enhance or emphasize a movement, lending the action additional impact and power.

> **Tip:** Devote a number of flick books to deformation, bouncing, compression and elongation. Start with simple line drawings and only add colour and detail when these are working fluidly.

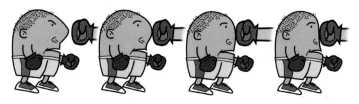

**Compression** ◄

The repeated images and the depression of the nose on the impact of the glove are essential. The shape and size of the nose gives it all the focus. The fact that the images remain identical serves to enhance the effect of the increasing indent as the nose is punched.

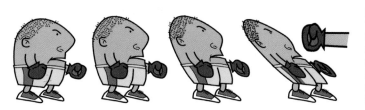

**Elongation** ◄

The same repetition but this time the boxer's stance steadily becomes more elongated as he ducks away from the second blow. The fighter begins to tilt back in anticipation, before his body stretches out of all proportion as the fist makes its first appearance.

## Flash animation program

Flash is a vector-based program that can manipulate vector and bitmap graphic images and also supports audio and video files. It operates a language called ActionScript and as a package enables animations to be created for games, movies and Internet uses, such as online greetings cards, website navigation bars and advertisement banners. The content of Flash documents can be embedded into mobile phones and other portable players too. Files are saved in the SWF format (Shock Wave Flash) and are most commonly played through software known as a Flashplayer.

Flash is being used with more frequency to display video clips on web pages and it has compatibility for both Microsoft and Macintosh operating systems. With its user-friendly menus, tools and its frame-by-frame approach to building the animated sequence, it is relatively simple to use and the perfect beginner's introduction to animation. A running timeline dealing in frames per second helps you to keep track of your work in progress, and you can isolate individual frames or divide them into 'scene' sections and work in layers in much the same way as you would with Photoshop, Painter, Illustrator or Freehand. The key processes of Flash are included in this section to enable you to bring your cartoon creations to life.

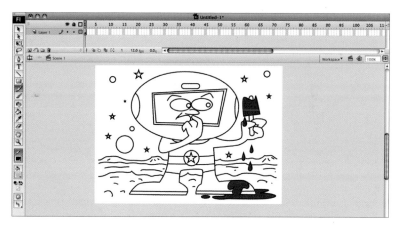

**Typical Flash window** ▲

A toolbar runs down the left-hand side of the document, and the layer icon is to the right of it. The timeline runs across the top and the slider bar can be placed at any point on it to select a specific moment. The drips of the spaceman's lolly between frames will show sequential movement.

## Connecting the moving parts

A cartoon animator has a multi-part role: first as inventor of a cast of characters and their narrative; next as image-maker, storyboarding and creating artwork sequences, either manually or digitally. Finally, with the images imported into an animation program, the cartoonist becomes editor/director. The success or failure of the animation, however, depends on how convincingly a character moves within and relates to its setting. Aspiring animators must grasp the connection of the moving parts of a cartoon figure. To achieve this, animators often use starting points which might easily be dismissed as child's play, even when the end product is highly sophisticated. In much the same way as a simple flat card puppet is created out of body parts, so might the animator initially approach the subject of movement in this way.

### Construction ▼
This cartoon witch is constructed from a series of simple flat coloured shapes created in Illustrator or Flash. The parts are then built into a figure with a life and character of its own. The freedom to make corrections and changes along the way is part of the process.

### Pivot points ▶
The red circles indicate the chief pivot points which will allow the witch to move freely. All animators use these same central points of movement as starting points. In fact, it is traditional practice to construct a jointed card maquette.

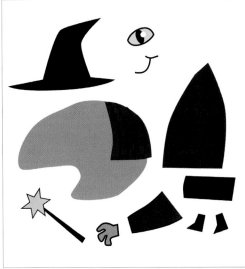

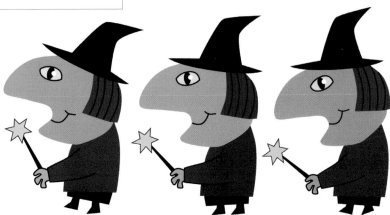

### Sequential duplication ▶
This duplicated sequence demonstrates the subtle movement achieved by slightly manipulating each of the pivot points. Our senses are attuned to the tiniest changes and very little alteration is needed to communicate a sense of animation. The smaller the change is, the smoother the transition to another position and the more convincing the animation.

## Keeping backgrounds simple

Perversely, in animation you do not necessarily have to make the elements physically move to describe it or create its illusion. When the brain realizes the 'jump' in information, carefully planned scaling and placing of objects in a setting can give the effect that the viewer is in a sense the animator. Since animations tend to be busy, a 'breather' is welcome between frames. Any artist or designer of images should always be thinking of ways to create the illusion of movement with as few flashy effects as possible. A scene with too many elements can become overfussy, and the viewer may not know where to look. Check out some of the best animations and you will find that the backgrounds are fairly plain and understated with very little movement, allowing the characters to take centre stage.

### Movement in space ▶
By increasing or decreasing the scale of both the background and the foreground (the head and shoulders of the girl) it's possible to suggest movement. By moving the girl around the frame and depicting her in a range of different sizes, the illusion of depth is naturally suggested. The simplicity of this concept offers the cartoon a charm – the motion will be jaunty if frames are animated.

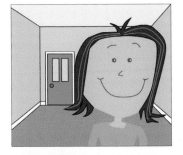
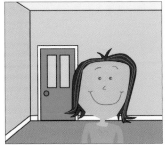

### Movement and 3-D illusion ▶
Much can be achieved through the use of Illustrator or Photoshop layers. Trickery of scale and positioning gives the images their illusory, moving qualities.
　The spaceman enters the screen from the left, where he is fairly large. The trail of the spaceship offers direction to the astronaut – streaking from left in the first image and from the right in the second, where he is considerably smaller, indicating distance.

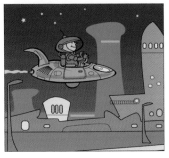
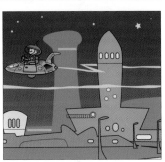

## Simple sequencing

It is vital to plan the narrative of an animated sequence with care. Breaking down the action into single frames that present concise visual information is a key part of the process. Keeping consistency between the frames will offer a believable transition between them.

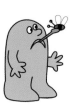

*Key frame 1*　　*Key frame 2*　　*Key frame 3*

### Key frames ◀
The top row reveals the key frames of the narrative: spotting the fly; catching the fly; and eating the fly. The information is clearly presented and no more than the necessary elements are included in each frame.

———— *Interim frames* ————

### More frames ◀
Adding interim frames containing a lesser degree of movement will make the motion appear smoother and less abrupt.

# Digital projects

With the technical knowledge in place, you can now apply it to set projects, considering digital caricature, developing the digital collage, creating the graphic novel and cartoon strip and simple, computer animation. This final chapter will get you started as a digital cartoonist and point you in the right direction so that you may develop your own personal vision and interpretation.

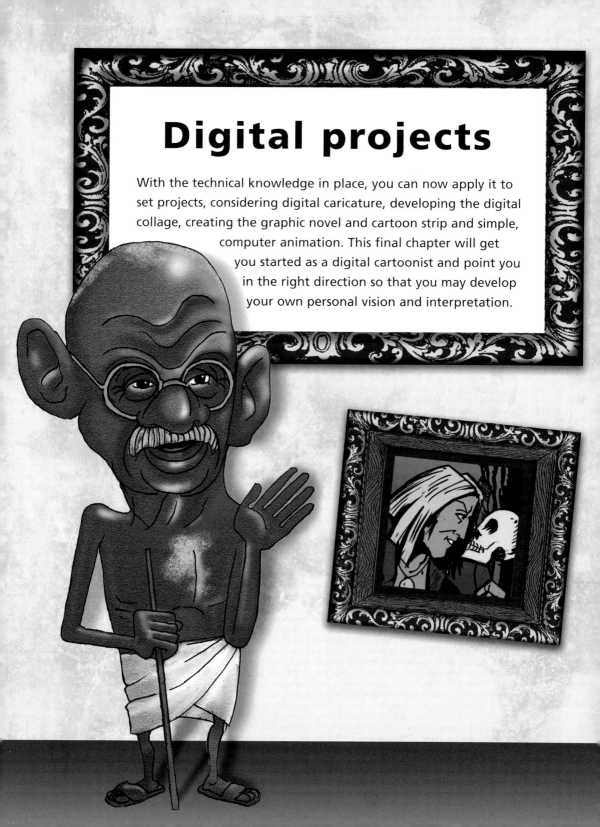

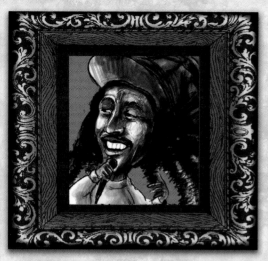

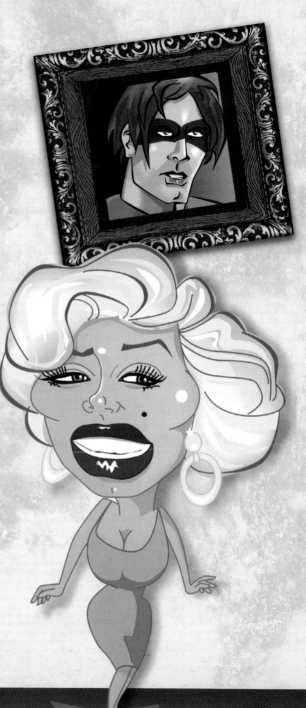

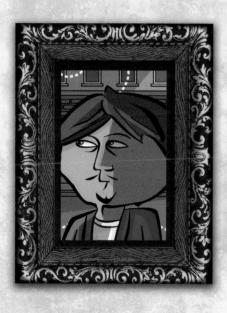

# Creating caricatures

The cartooning tradition of caricaturing famous people is essentially a hand-drawn process. However, combining traditional and digital skills grants you the opportunity to work up an initial drawing into an image that wholly encapsulates the personality you are portraying. With digital drawing and painting programs, it is easy to correct mistakes, work the same image up with different media and experiment without consequence. You are also able to add background elements and build up vivid colour through easily adjustable layers. The following projects are created using Photoshop and Illustrator programs.

## Final image

This final image is coloured and built using Photoshop. It has been created through the relatively easy process of layers, stacked from the background up. Once the image was essentially in place, Marley's facial features were refined using Photoshop to reshape the eyes, nose, brows and mouth. The changes are subtle, but the result is an image that looks that much more like its subject.

## Caricature: Bob Marley

1 Make a loose line drawing in pen and black Indian ink. Overemphasize the head for comic effect. Your aim is to capture the essence of the subject, so be sure to add in iconic props, such as Marley's microphone and Rastafarian hat.

2 Scan the image at 300dpi, then open it in Photoshop. Set up a new layer and set to 'Multiply' mode for the colours. Using a variety of Photoshop's textured brushes with medium (50%) Opacity, build up sketchy, appropriately laid-back areas of colour and shade. Don't worry about fully colouring any of the areas – you don't want your final piece to look too 'finished'.

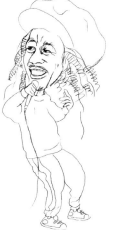

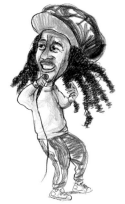

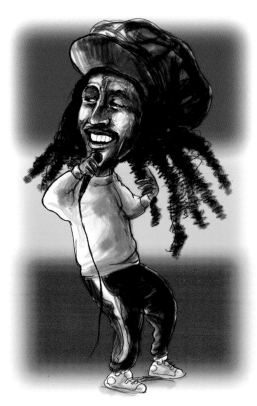

3 Continue with the rest of the face and clothes, gradually adding strokes of different strengths and direction until the subject becomes more solid without losing its lively energetic qualities. Notice that the light direction is from left to right – even when working in a loose, free style try to be aware of this.

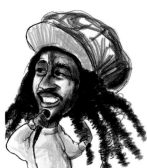

4 For the background, make the flag of Marley's beloved Jamaica on a separate layer, sitting beneath all the others. Create three rectangles of flat colour, blurred using the appropriate Filter (Filter > Blur). Erase the white areas on both the Colour and Line Art layers so that the flag shows through – the quickest way to do this is to select the white with the Magic Wand tool (set to 'Contiguous' with around 25 'Tolerance'), then press delete. Clean up stray areas of white with the Eraser tool.

## Caricature: Mahatma Gandhi

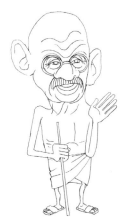

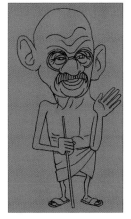

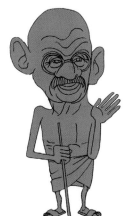

**3** Remove the excess background colour by carefully tracing around the drawn outline with the Eraser tool. Click on the Zoom tool (the magnifying glass icon), to get close-up views of the different areas. This is especially necessary for deleting colour between the fingers, for example. Clicking the mouse will zoom in closer. When the area outside your figure is selected, return to the Colour layer and press delete. This will remove the brown areas outside your linework. Clear up any loose areas of brown with the Eraser tool.

**1** Make a simple outline pen drawing of Gandhi referenced from a source using a black fineliner or the equivalent. Here, we draw attention to his modest attire, his famous spectacles and warm, good-natured eyes. The oversized, imbalanced ears add humour.

**2** Scan the image and open it in Photoshop. Duplicate the layer, delete the 'Background' layer, and set its options to 'Multiply'. Make a new layer, call it 'Background Colour' and tint a rectangle light brown.

**4** Create new layers for the shading and highlights. Using a soft brush for each, model the muscles and give definition to the face and body. Create another layer for the white highlight strokes – these are also made using a soft brush. Caricatures tend to benefit from a single, strong light source (here off to the top right of the drawing). At this stage, we have also finished off the eyes and mouth with pupils and teeth drawn in on the flat colour layer. Use a hard, spherical brush for the pupils and white highlights in the eyes.

**5** Add the final texture to the skin tones using the Noise filter (go to Filter > Noise > Add Noise) with the 'monochromatic' option selected. This delivers a subtle grain to the picture which is then slightly 'formed' using the Emboss filter (Stylize > Emboss). Select a stippling brush for the grey hair. On a new background colour, layer spray-in colour at 50% Opacity, using a soft brush.

### Final image

Gandhi has been created through a definite layer process: First, the bold outline drawing offered a template for filling in with colour and tone. Next, an overall colour on the whole figure became the base on to which soft brush effects and highlights were built in consecutive layers to make him appear more 3-D. A final, softly sprayed background and subtle use of filters offered the image 'polish'.

# Caricature: Elvis Presley

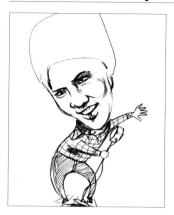

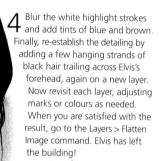

**3** Select a very large soft brush and draw the hair in black. On a series of new layers (or on the same layer, if you are feeling confident), add a swathe of white on top at a lesser Opacity, so that the black underneath shows through. Use this wash as a base for the vertical white highlight strokes (use a new layer if you need to), which are modelled using a crescent-shaped brush from the brush menu.

**1** Use a soft B pencil to sketch and shade the Elvis caricature in head-larger-than-body style. Note how the pose chosen reflects Elvis's 'snakelike hips' in the form of a reverse 'S'. Block in his expanse of characteristic hair, but leave it unshaded for the moment. Scan the drawing and open it in Photoshop. Create a duplicate layer and delete the drawing on the original background one to leave you a layer for colouring. Go to Image > Adjustments > Hue/Saturation and change the pencil line to blue using the sliders.

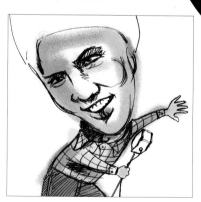

**4** Blur the white highlight strokes and add tints of blue and brown. Finally, re-establish the detailing by adding a few hanging strands of black hair trailing across Elvis's forehead, again on a new layer. Now revisit each layer, adjusting marks or colours as needed. When you are satisfied with the result, go to the Layers > Flatten Image command. Elvis has left the building!

**2** Choose a large, coarse brush from the palette, set it to 'Dissolve' and sweep washes of colour on to the new layer crossing the pencil lines. Dissolve creates colours with broken, speckled textures. Select blue from the colour palette for the jeans and yellow for the shirt. Add some blue into the flesh and use the Eraser for highlights.

## Final image

Elvis is treated with more traditional use of techniques to match the 1950s' rock 'n' roll years to which this image pertains. The selection of colour palettes, their layered transparency and use of soft, Photoshop brushes have helped to achieve this dated effect, which in turn communicates to the viewer the singer as an icon of his time.

## Caricature: Marilyn Monroe

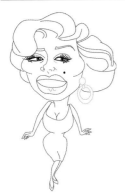

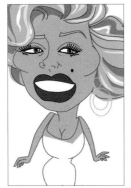

### Final image

A line drawing provides a framework for blocks of soft tonal hues which are blended using tools and filters in Illustrator. Shadows and highlights add a strong, graphic quality with clean, contrasting shapes. Equally strong shapes in the facial detailing of the eyes and hair strands offer a crisp, linear and all together sparkly finish!

**1** Draw a pencil caricature of Marilyn Monroe. Scan it, then open it in Illustrator. Go to the 'Window' menu, select 'Transparency' and change the Opacity to 90%, so that the pen lines will show up on top of the sketch layer. Create a new layer (Pen Outline) and draw over the scanned outline using a different colour for each area of the portrait – hair, lips, skin.

**2** Still in Illustrator, block in the coloured shapes on a new layer or series of layers, placed beneath the Pen Outline. Use complementary tones to the colours used in your outline – the outlines should be the darkest colour, from which you can select warm midtones for most areas. Work up extra detail by filling the brows and adding eye shadow.

**3** Soften the hair tone using the Blend tool, carefully stroking the cursor so that the blends follow the direction of the waves. On a new layer create a star shape by manipulating a basic polygon using the 'Free Distort' filter (go to Filter > Free Distort). Finally, add white highlights to the eyes, face and lips to give Marilyn some Hollywood gloss and shine. Suggest a dazzling smile with a broken grey line across the white expanse of teeth.

## Painterly style of Photoshop

The sophisticated performance of Adobe Photoshop as a paint program cannot be overestimated. It is the most versatile application available to computer artists and a digital tool that can take a user through the same stages of the artistic process met by a traditional painter. The beauty of this package lies in the relative ease with which mistakes can be rectified. Artists can take a scanned sketch, lay down base tones and transform this into a fully 'painted' image by adding layers of colour in a way that recalls working with acrylics or oils.

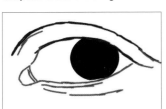

**Initial drawing** ▲
A painted-style digital image always starts with an outline. Whether this comes from a sketch imported via a scan, or from a series of rough lines laid on the digital canvas with the mouse or drawing tablet, is a question of personal preference.

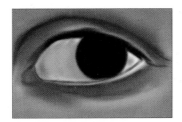

**Building tones** ▲
The first stage is to lay down a series of base colours that provide a midground spread of colour on to which you model shadows and highlights. The options in Photoshop allow you to mimic natural media, from oils to acrylics and more.

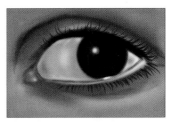

**Final details** ▲
Varying Opacities, sizes and hardnesses of brushes, plus the Blur and Smudge tools, allow you to blend colours and textures as on a traditional canvas. Here, the skin tones are softened using Blur, and the fine lashes are added using a fine brush.

## Caricature: Charlie Chaplin

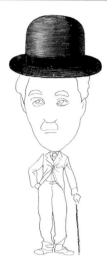

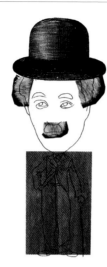

### Final image
This caricature combines a very simple pen-and-ink drawing with a variety of found textures and sourced imagery. The bowler hat is a significant symbol of Chaplin as is the moustache, shaped in Photoshop from a scanned 'fur' sample. This project enables you to access a number of useful Photoshop tools for creating Charlie Chaplin, then manipulating the image with filters to present him within an early filmic atmosphere.

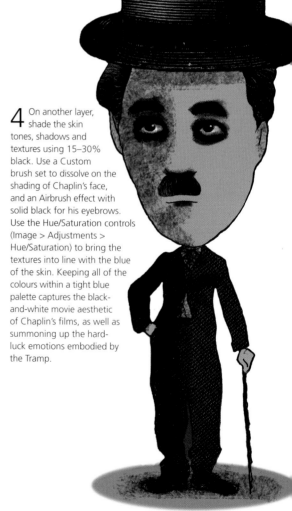

1 Begin with a referenced sketch of Chaplin drawn with a fineliner. Don't use any solid areas of black, instead leave every shape open for later texturing. The hat can be sourced from the Internet, or scanned from a book of fashion engravings and combined with the scanned line art on a separate layer.

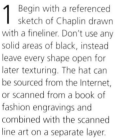

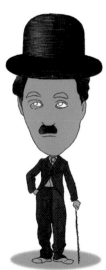

2 When finished, the image is scanned into Photoshop, and a series of textures are added on a new layer behind the line art. These textures are found scans of existing materials, manipulated using a variety of filters in Photoshop, such as Noise, Blur and Free Distort. Add a block of suit mesh material behind the body, and some scanned fur – perhaps from a winter coat – for the hair and moustache.

3 Using the Eraser tool, carefully remove any of the scanned elements that are overlapping the line art. Alternatively, create a clipping path with the Pen tool, or use the Magic Wand tool on the line art layer to select the background white, before flipping back to the colour layer and pressing delete. This should remove any colour or texture outside of Chaplin himself. Next, colour in his skin and visible shirt in a pale blue. Place a feathered blue ellipse at his feet.

4 On another layer, shade the skin tones, shadows and textures using 15–30% black. Use a Custom brush set to dissolve on the shading of Chaplin's face, and an Airbrush effect with solid black for his eyebrows. Use the Hue/Saturation controls (Image > Adjustments > Hue/Saturation) to bring the textures into line with the blue of the skin. Keeping all of the colours within a tight blue palette captures the black-and-white movie aesthetic of Chaplin's films, as well as summoning up the hard-luck emotions embodied by the Tramp.

## Caricature: Marlon Brando

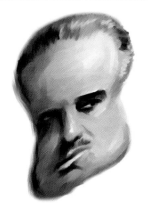

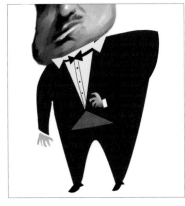

### Final image
This image is created using a combination of Painter, Illustrator and Photoshop. The painterly treatment added to a sourced photo of Hollywood actor-legend Brando provides a strong focus for the project. Centring on the power an image derives from contrast of texture and colours, a stylized shape-constructed body enables the Brando portrait to be connected and brought into an architecturally suggestive mesh of white lines and shapes. Simple, but very effective.

1 The head is created in Painter using an Acrylic Paints palette and Brush tools, working from photographic reference of Brando, which is abstracted and exaggerated so that the famous Godfather looks like a melting peanut. The head is then saved and imported into Illustrator.

2 The flat artwork for Brando's dinner-suited body is created on a new layer in Illustrator, using a variety of pen-drawn shapes and simple, flat colours. Keep this portion of the drawing iconic, so that the viewer's attention is drawn straight to the face. Even the triangle of the cummerbund at Brando's waist points back up towards his head.

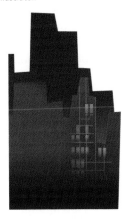

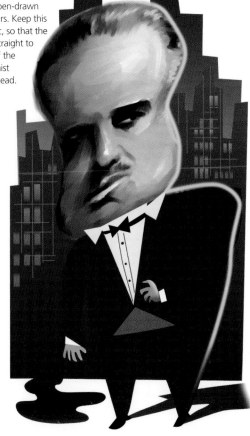

4 Bring everything together in Photoshop for the final tweaks. Add a strong white line down the right-hand side of the head and figure to link the two disparate portions and separate the figure from the background. On a separate layer, create Brando's shadow by duplicating the Illustrator body, filling the selection with a gradient, and using Free Distort and Rotate to offset it to the right. Add the metaphorical pool of blood leaking from the city by filling a new shape with a gradient of black to red. Colour correct all the layers as necessary in Photoshop to fuse them into a complementary single image.

3 Create a new layer in Illustrator for the background. A few simple shapes, assisted by a Shallow Gradient, are enough to suggest the shadowy stage on which Brando's most famous character worked. Thin, criss-crossing lines and white gradients in rectangles are enough to suggest the windows. Note how the background pulls the image together by reflecting complementary colours from the body (the grey of the suit) and the head (the pink shadow).

# Futuristic style

Vector cartoons are characterized by their sharp, even lines and smooth transitions of flat, solid colour. A modern theme, especially science fiction or fantasy, is well-suited to a vector package. In addition to clean, clear styling there is the chance to experiment with a wide range of colours and patterns which will give the right contemporary look to your cartoon. Since vector art can be infinitely scaled without losing resolution, your illustrations of 50m-tall (165ft) robots will look just as good at 5cm (2in) as on life-size posters! A hand-drawn sketch is the starting point for this project which is then constructed and completed in Adobe Illustrator.

**Tip:** For complex coloured digital images, it is useful to make a rough colour sketch by hand first. Having this reference to hand will solve compositional and colour problems easily. To save time, print out small scans of your line art four-to-a-page and experiment with thumbnails before committing yourself.

## Final image

This final image displays the many versatilities of Adobe Illustrator with a wide range of computer drawing techniques being coupled to a harmonious, pastel colour palette. Note how the various complexities of colour and outline contribute to a sense of depth in the image – the thicker lines and additional shading on the window-cleaning figure throw him to the absolute forefront, while the outline-less, two-tone colours of the buildings in the background push them back into the distance. The vapour trails of the rockets and skycars are simply line paths, expanded and blurred. When you are finished, why not experiment with different colour schemes using Photoshop's Hue/Saturation (Image > Adjust > Hue/Saturation) slider?

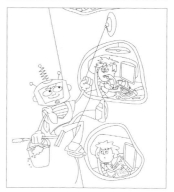

**1** Make a neat pencil sketch of your chosen scene. There's no need to ink it traditionally at this stage, as you will be going over all of the lines digitally. Scan the drawing and import it into Illustrator.

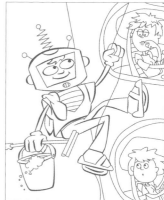

**2** Create a new layer (Layers palette > New Layer), and use the Pen tool to accurately trace around your pencilled image, following the original. Select the Pen tool and make sure that it is set to 0.1pt. This is not a job to hurry and will take a while to complete.

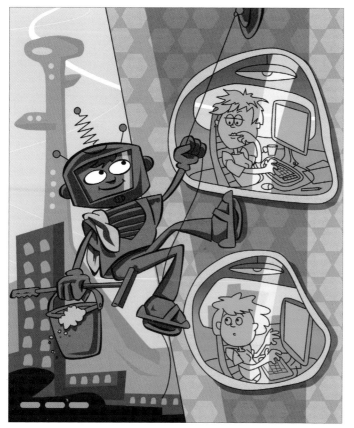

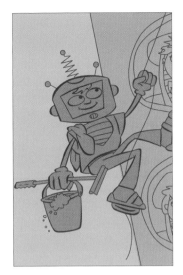

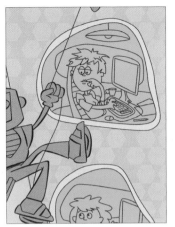

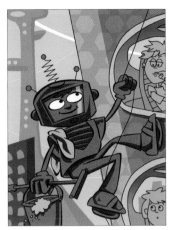

**3** Select the outline with the Arrow tool and click on a mid-blue hue in the colour palette. Give the line character and shape by varying the line thickness – expand lines using the Direction Selection tool (white arrow) and go to Object > Expand. Create a new layer beneath the line layer, tint the background in blue and fill the character shape in pink.

**4** Add the texture to the main building. On a new layer, draw three or four hexagonal shapes, tint them a paler pink colour and drop them on to the building as a fill, using the Pattern brush. This will cover the area in a repeating pattern of the shapes. Using more abstract shapes, without outlines, block in new buildings in the background, copying and pasting smaller shapes in to form windows. Rotate or 'free transform' a few of these so that they retain their individuality.

**5** Finally, give the image greater tonal depth overall by adding detailed, darker areas of shading to the main figure and background elements. Create these shapes on a final layer and colour with the Opacity set to 30% so that the patterns show through. On the same layer, add white highlights to the windows using thick, stroke-like shapes. Select and delete the windows behind the office workers to reveal the sky layer behind.

## Mass-producing characters

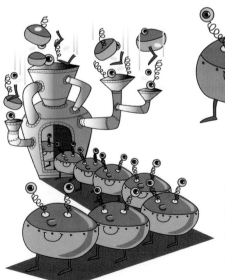

**The original toy shape – Illustrator** ◀
Draw freehand, and tint and shade in flat colours on a new layer that sits beneath the line art.

**Copying and pasting the toy** ▼
Adjust the scale each time so they appear to recede into the distance (Object > Transform > Scale). There are endless connotations – create a clone army of toys or an assembly line of automated machines delivering uniform toys.

**The toy machine** ◀
This is also drawn freehand, and coloured in gradated tones, to suggest industrial metal, rather than shiny plastic. The components falling into the funnels at the top of the machine are created by 'disassembling' your toy image – parts of the toys are selected, copied and pasted into place. Use Rotate or Free Transform to suggest motion and distance.

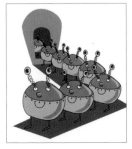

# Touchy-feely textures

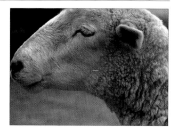

Digital technology allows cartoonists the freedom to play with surface decoration across a range of media. The projects on the next four pages centre on combining drawn animal cartoon characters with digitally created textures, photographic imagery or scanned fabric. The resulting 'real' fur or skin texture gives each cartoon a surprise edge. The surrealism is increased when this texture is manipulated in Photoshop. Where traditional collages rely on the disjunction between line work and texture for their effect, Photoshop allows you to literally paint with your found media, blending and integrating disparate elements like never before.

## Woolly textures

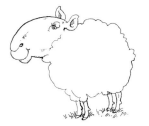

**3** When you have filled the wool with the appropriate texture, go to Filter > Distort > Ocean Ripple and add a ripple pattern to enhance the twisted texture of the wool. Finally, import a cloned selection of grass from the digital image and place it in a feathered oval section beneath the sheep.

**1** Sketch a quirky representation of a sheep, enlarging the endearing facial features, friendly smile and curling lashes. At this stage, reference a suitable digital picture of a sheep (which focuses in sharp detail on the woollen textures), either scanned or downloaded from the Internet. Scan the line drawing at 200dpi or above and import it into Photoshop. Next, copy the line work to a duplicate layer and delete the original background layer. You are now ready to continue.

**Tip:** Displaying real textures within a cartoon context offers your drawings real impact. Experiment with Photoshop filters to increase the wackiness of your images. Where you may think that a filter serves a limited purpose, it is often a surprise to find it has other unexpected uses too.

**2** On the digital image, use the Clone tool (tool box) to select an area of the face texture on your chosen photograph (you can have this photograph open in a separate window to your line work). Hold down the Alt key and click the mouse on the photograph to select the Clone tool's starting point, and then paint freely on to your line work. The Clone tool works by linking two points, duplicating whatever is underneath the first. You can enlarge the area being duplicated by increasing the size of the Clone 'brush', as if you were painting – you can also adjust the Opacity and Hardness in the same way. Once you have reproduced this texture on the head and legs on the drawing layer, return to the digital image and select a point on the wool to start cloning.

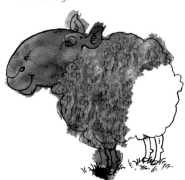

## Final image

The success of the image depends on scanning a clear source reference at a high resolution. Photoshop allows you to test out all kinds of enhancements. For example, you can increase the contrast using Image > Adjustments > Levels, alter colours or adjust textures using the filters.

## Scaly skin

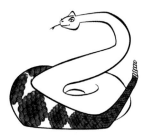

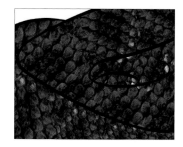

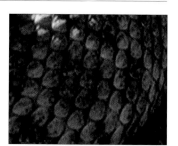

1 Draw the outline of the snake in Illustrator, expanding the line to thicken it and give a sense of movement. For the skin pattern scan a good-quality image of a rattlesnake and import it into Photoshop. Place the outline as a 'Multiply' layer in Photoshop and select elements of the snakeskin to clip out of the image using the Pen tool. Make a new layer and paste these behind the snake outline, then tidy up the edges.

2 Copy and paste your rattlesnake image as a pattern on the new layer until all of the areas of the snake are covered. Note how the pattern alters slightly as it curls around the body. At this stage, the repeat pattern will probably blend with little definition between the segments in places, but don't worry, as this will be refined and defined at the next stage. Choose a beady, glowing yellow for the snake's eye.

3 Increase the definition between the different segments of the snake on a new layer located above the line drawing. Adjust the contrast by using the slide bars on the Shadows and Highlights panel (Image > Adjustments > Shadows/Highlights). Consider the direction of the light falling along the length of the body. Here, a strong light source is almost directly above the snake serving to neatly delineate the underside of each coil.

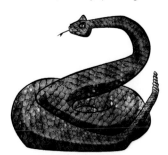

4 Further refine the definition by making more detailed Marquee tool selections. Manipulate these using the Shadows/Highlights function under Adjustments and the Levels function under the Image menu (Image > Adjustments > Levels), where you can alter the dark tones, the light tones and the mid-tones.

## Rough skin

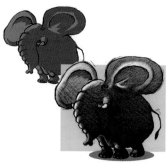

5 Finally, separately colour the patterned bands in strong, yet lifelike hues such as blue, deep pink and bronze. Change these using the Hue/Saturation facility (Image > Adjustments > Hue/Saturation), by moving the colour slide bars in the panel.

### Final image
The ability to be able to import textures with ease and open within a selected path area using Marquee and Selection tools is the key to this Illustrator and Photoshop combined image. Colours are easily changed or modified by adjusting the slide bars in the Hue/Saturation panel.

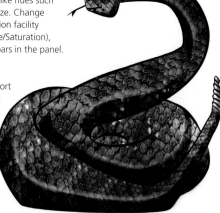

An elephant line drawing is scanned into Photoshop, darkened and then added as a new layer beneath. Basic shapes are drawn and filled with flat colour to render form through tone and highlights. An elephant-skin digital image is selected and used with a Brush tool to colour a new layer at 30% Opacity. This is placed on top of the coloured shapes. With the layers set to 'Multiply' the Eraser tool is used to clean around the outline. The flat colour-filled ellipse and rectangle background shapes are created on a layer placed beneath the rest.

## Slimy skin

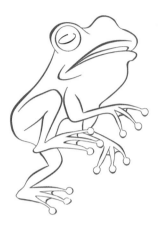

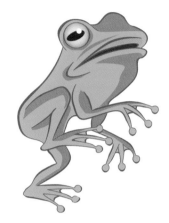

**1** Draw the frog outline in Illustrator using the Pen tool and expanding the line (Object > Expand). Colour the line a dark green (Stroke > Colour) to reduce the harshness of the black line. Leave a white circle in the pupil for the highlight.

**2** Create a new layer below the first and tint the outline in a light green (select colour from Swatches > use Paint Bucket tool to fill), with yellow and black for the eye. Make a shading layer, adding 15% black to the green.

**3** With the basic drawing and colouring complete, Select All of your drawing and drag it from Illustrator into a new Photoshop window using the Selection (black arrow) tool. Create a new layer and add the coarse skin texture in selected areas, using different brushes to vary the texture.

### Final image
Three layers are all you need to create a colourfully textured frog. From an initial Illustrator outline the image progresses into the addition of bold colours and skin textures, which can either be sourced, or developed with an array of brushes and filters. A shaded final layer placed beneath the frog assists the three-dimensional illusion and prevents the appearance of a hopping creature apparently suspended, floating in space.

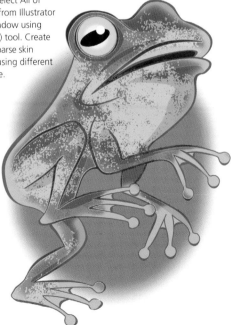

## Experimental styling

Illustrator contains a considerable range of patterning and blending options. When you are satisfied with the final colour, you can begin to play with the patterns in the graphic style library. Don't worry if an effect isn't working – a click in a box will change everything.

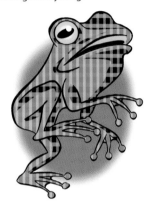

**Check patterning** ▲
This check pattern is selected from graphic styles, and the transparency palette set to 'Hard Light'. The pattern floats above the base colour and shadows without losing definition.

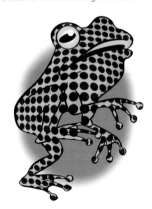

**Distorted spots** ▲
In this pattern, the spots are distorted so they appear to run across the curved surface of the frog's skin. Draw a circle, duplicate it as many times as you need, then distort it (Filter > Distort > Pinch) to achieve the desired effect.

## Leathery wings

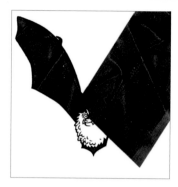

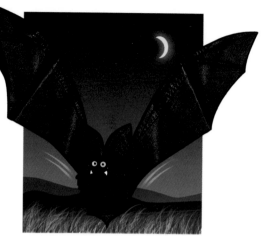

1 Scan your line drawing of a bat and open it in Photoshop. Scan a suitable piece of leather – a section of leather jacket is used here – and import it as a digital image. Using layers, place the texture layer beneath the line layer and remove the excess around the outline using the Eraser tool. Create a new layer for the background, beneath both the line and leather layers.

2 For the sky, select blue from the colour palette and add a tint that fades from dark to light using the Gradient tool. Draw a crescent-shaped moon using the Pen tool and fill it with a pale cream colour, which is softened with a feather of 10 pixels. Stroke it with solid white. Create and fill the blue-green hill shapes. Draw the grass texture using a custom brush in a lighter green–blue. Lines in a soft brush under either wing suggest movement.

### Final image

This variation on the texture theme uses leather to simulate the bat's natural skin. The smooth surface of the leather will reflect the light shining through the scanner bed, giving its creases a 3-D appearance. The darkness of leather leads the choice of hues with deep saturation. Against these, the creamy white of the diffuse moonlight and grass blades offer the drawing a stunning lift.

## Chicken feathers

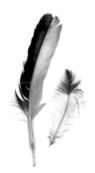

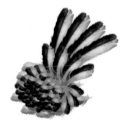

1 Scan the key structural elements of this cartoon into Photoshop – a real chicken tail feather and body feather. During scanning, take time to adjust the Levels so that the image is strongly visible (Image > Adjustment > Levels). Doing so will capture the subtlety of the quills that are central to the project. Cut both feathers out with the Marquee tool and place them on separate layers.

2 On a new layer, arrange the scanned feathers to form the body shape, tail plumage and wing shapes. Do this by duplicating the feathers and also by using the Clone tool to clone smaller areas. You can overlap the feathers and make other adjustments using a number of new layers. However, aim to keep the image as simple as possible so that the basic concept of a cartoon chicken made from real feathers is not lost in a complicated design.

3 Add the beak, eye and comb on a layer above the last feather layer. These can either be drawn or created from a scanned digital image. Add a textured effect to the comb using filters. Go to Filter > Sketch > Bas Relief, then apply Filter > Noise > Add noise. On another layer add the drop shadow using a soft brush and adjusted feather (Select > Feather). Finally, add the scanned digital image of the wellington boots.

### Final image

Real chicken feathers have been used to plume and preen the virtual chicken's identity. The clipping of such finely featured objects provides fantastic practice opportunities for refining your skills at drawing paths and cloning in Photoshop. Subtle use of filters is essential with such a delicate subject and soft brushes are necessary for dropping shadows and enhancing colours and textures.

# Graphic novel style

Characterization for graphic novels is an in-depth and lengthy process. Once conceived as an idea, your character needs to be worked out on paper, and if you are choosing to create them digitally, transposed into graphic shapes and colours through Photoshop and Illustrator. Variations of style are wide and it is important to be aware of the techniques available in these programs. Background imagery is also important, but tantamount to success is your level of comfort with your creations. The average graphic novel is around 96 pages long, so be aware you could be working with the same characters for a long time!

## Final image

For this urban narrative, Illustrator was chosen, for the simple duplication of bricks and also the creation of rigid, architectural lines, to help give the impression of an urban environment. A story needs to develop in a setting and this project considers the juxtaposition of the created scene and the narrative presented through the main figures.

## Urban narrative: characters and background

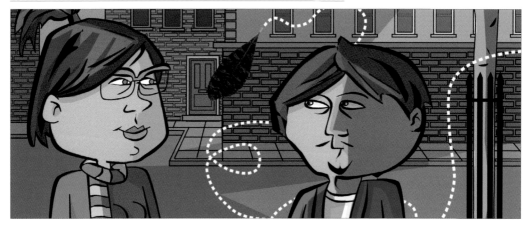

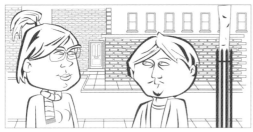

1 Scan your outline pencils into Illustrator and create a Line layer. Digitally ink the outline using the Pen tool, contrasting the weights of line to create depth of field as shown here. Elements such as the windows and bricks can be easily duplicated by copying and pasting a single finished shape.

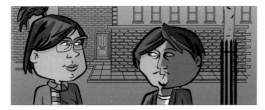

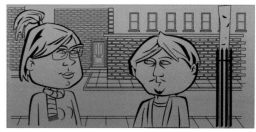

2 Drag the outline from the Illustrator window into a new Photoshop document. Drop some gradated colour fills into a new layer using the Gradient tool. Place this beneath the line layer. Having started with basic tones, you can now consider the best colour and texture choices for the image as you go along.

3 Now apply flat hues to the two characters using layers. It is best to use easily identified clothing and hairstyles in this first frame that can be duplicated and repeated throughout the whole storyline. Create the shadowing on a new layer to add depth and tone to the composition. Next, create the leaf by filling a new shape with a scanned leaf texture. The final touch is to add the dotted white path by manipulating and importing an Illustrator line.

## Duplicating faces

Multiple characters are a necessary part of the graphic narrative and you will save time by creating a template library of key character styles for reuse in other frames. Keep the focus on body shapes, clothing and colours so that only a minor change of facial expression or body position is sufficient to place them with ease into the unfolding story. Take advantage of the compatibility of paint programs and work between them.

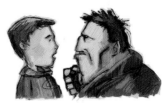

**Photoshop style** ◄
The line art was drawn directly into Photoshop with the Pen tool. The colours and textures were built up sketchily in layers.

**Painter head** ▲
The first heavily brushed head is drawn 'live' in Painter. Once the structure and rendering of the face are complete, it can be altered to create the second and third characters. They are created by altering features, colours, shadows, mid-tones and highlights on new layers. Saving the structural layer as a template enables new characters to be produced quickly and efficiently, which can only aid your creativity and experimentation.

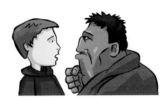

**Illustrator style** ◄
The line art from Photoshop was opened as a new layer in Illustrator, where it was drawn round, tweaked and coloured.

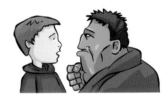

**Illustrator: adjusted colours** ◄
Adjusting the colour palettes as shown here is an effective trick for altering the mood of your piece.

## Dramatic realism

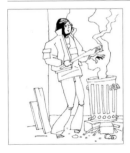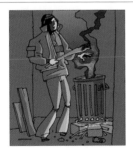

**1** Scan your simple outline sketch into Illustrator and go over it with the Pen tool to create a precise outline. A line that is too sketchy does not fit the graphic novel style and is harder to segment into selected colour fill areas.

**2** In Photoshop, select and fill the drawn sections with flat colours from the palettes. Alternatively, apply gradated fills using the Gradient tool. Assume a light source on one side to add drama.

**3** Enhance the realism by adding scanned photographs of real buildings and skies as background. Alter these images by Solarizing (Filter > Stylize > Solarize) to break them into strong slabs of colour, and experiment with the dissolve and overlay blends (layers palette) for added effect.

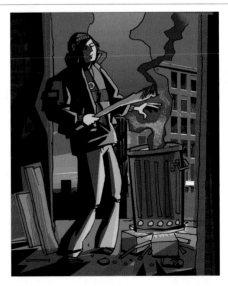

### Final image
For this final image, buildings, a distant sunset and shadows have been added for dramatic effect and to put the character into the foreground of a slightly unsettling urban landscape.

# Traditional fantasy style

The traditional approach to the comic supports hugely popular horror and fantasy styles. These require the ability to render the human form accurately in several active and emotive positions. For this style, it is still best to draw in pencil and ink – with a dip pen or brush – with the confidence displayed by the top artists of Marvel and DC Comics,

but it is also fine to adjust and improve your line work in the digital arena. The key to effective horror styling is in the use of strong contrasts between areas of highlight and shadow, as well as the ability to create well-defined human characters that anchor the more esoteric or outlandish elements of your story or composition.

## Final image

Here we have a 'Lizard Man' character, developed from an initial pencil sketch that is then inked in the traditional way, and imported into Photoshop to be defined in colour. Working digitally allows us to import a separate line drawing of a wind-blasted cliff to combine with our figure into a finished illustration.

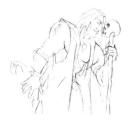

**1** The first stage of the illustration is a pencil sketch, in which pose and proportions are both defined.

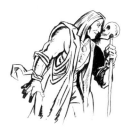

**2** Next, the Lizard Man character is inked by hand over the pencils, using a dip pen or brush and black Indian ink. The majority of comic books, though digitally coloured, are still drawn using the traditional pencil-and-ink method. The inking stage is when you define your light sources and strong contrasts, as well as apply organic textures with brush or nib. See how the upper left arm and curled right fingers are thrown back by being inked completely black. When you are happy with your inks, erase the pencils (be sure the inks are dry) and import the scan into Photoshop.

**3** Create a fresh layer and fill it with the appropriate skin tones and clothing colours. To save time, you can select areas of the drawing using the Magic Wand tool on the line art layer, then flip to the colour layer and use the Fill Bucket tool or delete key to fill them with an appropriate colour. Create a twilight feel with a gradient tint fading from brown to yellow. Draw the moon on a separate layer by filling a circle with white. Back at the drawing board, create an image of a gnarled tree and cliff, and scan it into Photoshop on a layer behind your character to complete the scene.

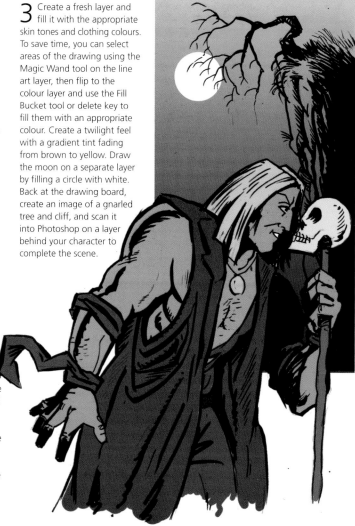

## Considering character profile

Profile is key to an effective narrative, and for this to work, your areas of shadow and light should flow from one to another, not overwhelm single areas of the page.

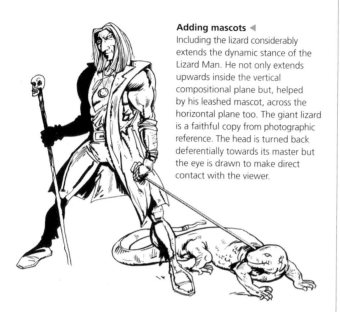

**Adding mascots** ◄
Including the lizard considerably extends the dynamic stance of the Lizard Man. He not only extends upwards inside the vertical compositional plane but, helped by his leashed mascot, across the horizontal plane too. The giant lizard is a faithful copy from photographic reference. The head is turned back deferentially towards its master but the eye is drawn to make direct contact with the viewer.

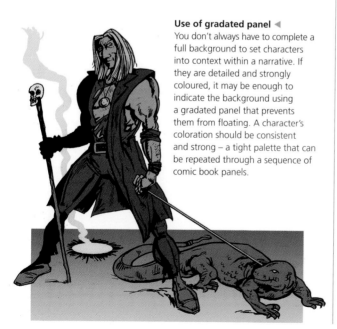

**Use of gradated panel** ◄
You don't always have to complete a full background to set characters into context within a narrative. If they are detailed and strongly coloured, it may be enough to indicate the background using a gradated panel that prevents them from floating. A character's coloration should be consistent and strong – a tight palette that can be repeated through a sequence of comic book panels.

## Dynamic characterization

Heroes and anti-heroes are often polarized in war and need to display dynamic traits, such as a ready-for-action stance, strongly defined body lines and totemic accessories.

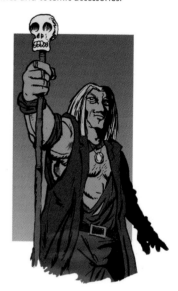

**Power stance** ▲
Drawing a character with a commanding stance instantly conveys his ability to wield power within the graphic narrative. The turn of the body is essential: the side tailing away into shadow emphasizes the leading side.

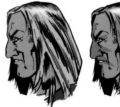
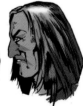

**Tattoos and body paint** ▲
Photoshop is excellent for branding warriors with tattoos and body paint. This blue 'woad' face mark is added by using a Pen tool to draw the shape on a new layer, then selecting it and creating and adjusting Colour and Opacity using the Hue/Saturation sliders.

# Manga style

Although 'manga', and its animated cousin 'animé', contain as many different art styles as you will find in western comics, there are certain characteristics that have become synonymous with the form – chief among them the vibrant 'big eyes, small mouth' school. Rooted equally in the Japanese illustrators of the 19th century and the imported cartoons of Walt Disney, 'manga', which is Japanese for 'comic' or 'whimsical pictures', is home to a far broader range of subject matter than we are used to in our graphic novels, from universal themes of love and lust, power and politics, and the journey into adulthood, transposed to any number of exotic and everyday locations, to series rooted in the worlds of sport, mahjong, videogames, music, business and politics.

> **Tip**: Manga is an art form predicated on extremes of motion, punctuated by occasional, poetic stillness. Even 'at rest', your characters will need to be dynamic, poised for the next exaggerated spring into action. Everything is made to feel that it is bursting forth from the page.

**1** Start with a pencil sketch that uses the main features associated with manga females: high cheeks, large, round endearing eyes, sensuous lips, square jaw and 'choppy' hairstyle. Include the basic outlines of your setting.

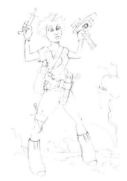

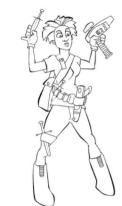

**2** Scan the drawing and import it into Illustrator. Use the Pen tool to digitally ink over your pencil outline, expanding the lines as you go where you feel it needs most emphasis, such as in the definition of the hair shape, and in the curves of the body and limbs. In this example, we will be colouring using a 'cell-shaded' style familiar from the majority of animation, so don't add any areas of solid black for shadows as these tend to overpower the subtleties of colour, which keenly denote this unique style.

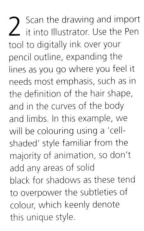

**3** Drag the layer into Photoshop and select the areas to fill with flat, bold colours. Draw random shapes on the clothing for the camouflage patterns using the Pen tool, and fill with the appropriate flat colour. Add shadows to the skin by adding 15% black on another layer. Add white highlights to the grey weapons and on the body.

**4** On a different layer, create the background scene, accessing all the major techniques for Photoshop painting, a gradated blend for the sky, a drawing line and fill for the setting sun, and blended paint strokes for the white vapour trails heading for space.

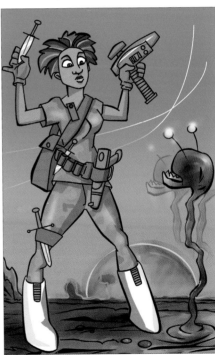

## Final image

Here's a fusion of the western and manga cartoon styles. A tough, well-armed female soldier confronts a bizarre alien life form on a distant world. The soft gradient of the background pushes the bold character forward, while a motion blur effect on the alien creature gives the impression it has just vaulted up out of the topsoil.

# Manga figures

While exaggeration is crucial, manga figures are still based around a confident understanding of human anatomy. Body shapes are fit and stylized – but in a more down-to-earth way than classical superheroes – with large heads, narrow waists, small, nimble feet and streamlined, fashionable clothing. Your figures should all be clear individuals, with unique hair, build, costume and accessories – check that you can tell them apart, even in silhouette.

**Manga action** ▼

Extreme poses and angles are the order of the day when capturing an action moment. Examine sample manga artwork to see how even moments of emotional drama are imbued with hyper-kinetic energy. Manga makes heavy use of motion lines to sell the concepts of speed and movement. These can be time-consuming to replicate in Photoshop or Illustrator with the Line tool – but will prove much less hassle than using a fineliner and ruler.

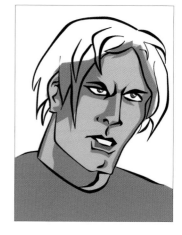

**Creating the male face** ▲

The line work is created in Illustrator, with a stylistic expanded line, and the areas of shadow and defintion are kept to a minimum so that he appears contemporary and flat-featured. This simplicity is distinctive of manga.

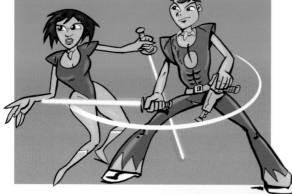

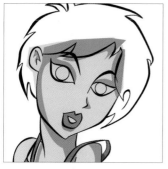

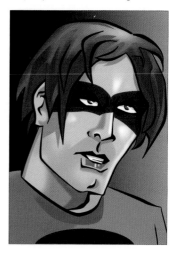

**Creating the female face** ▲

The line work is created in Illustrator, using a rough pencil sketch as the base. A stylistic, expanded line lends weight and interest to the hair, eyes and brows. Note that the elements of the face still conform to the 'eyes halfway down' rule, even though they are out of proportion with one another. Basic tones are applied in Photoshop.

**Defining the female face** ▲

The unreal blue of the eyes draws our attention to them, and forms the focal point of the face. Shading is achieved with a strong two-tone shadow. Highlights are kept to a minimum – on the lips and on the reflections in the eyes. Pay extra attention to the shading and highlights of the hair, as it is easy to make this look like a plastic wig if you are not careful.

**Defining the male face** ▲

The next stage is to soften the drawing considerably in Photoshop using the Airbrush tool, especially for blending subtle highlights on the skin and hair. The final result blends cartoonish two-tone colours with naturalistic shading to suggest a more mature art form.

# Science fiction style

The digital revolution has brought a new sophistication to the genre of science fiction, demanding no less skill than traditional methods, but substantially reducing practice time. Photoshop filters and the ability to be able to blend semi-translucent layers have considerably influenced the techniques and the resulting outcome. Digital trickery and futurism (the prediction of a future world and its attributes) go hand in hand. The cartoonist has the freedom to conjure up imaginary scenarios that are painlessly realized via keystrokes and mouse commands. In the digital art future in which we live, creativity truly knows no bounds making possible the imaginary worlds of our furthermost dreams.

## Mixing media

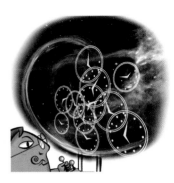

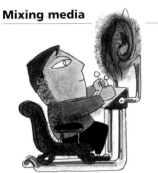

1 Scan the rough coloured sketch of the time traveller and import it into Photoshop. Draw over the lines with the Pen tool, expanding as necessary as you go. Convert the black outline to a soft blue line via Image > Adjustments > Hue/Saturation. Drag the image into Photoshop and render it in simple colours on a new layer below the line art, using a range of brushes from the brush palette.

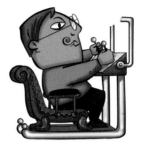

2 With the idea set, spend some time dropping in careful brush blends within the variably stroked outlines. Pay attention to smaller details, such as the shadows beneath the control console and the underside of the sleeves. Adjust the Hue/Saturation to add reflected light to the face and use the History brush to soften colours in the final stage.

3 Draw the clock faces on the floating instrument panel as a new Illustrator document, using the Ellipse tool for the dials and the Pen tool for the hands. Stroke the outline in white. Create a single dial, and then duplicate, scale and free distort it to form the rest. Import a scanned or digital galaxy image into Photoshop and create the vortex through the Twirl filter (Filter > Distort > Twirl). Drag the dial into the Photoshop window and sit as a new layer on top of the galaxy background. Duplicate and distort the dials by pulling out the shape from the points on each clock face.

## Final image

This image effortlessly blends the past and present into an amalgam suitable for a man torn out of time. The simple, cartoonish line drawing and industrial-era machinery contrast sharply with the swirling, all-digital maelstrom of the timestream in flux, literalizing the 'collision' between two different media.

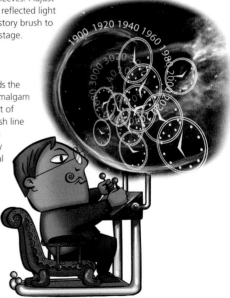

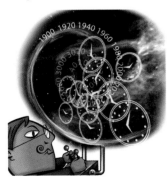

4 Set the long line of dates on a spiral line in Illustrator using the Pen tool and the Text tool. Drag this into the Photoshop document to sit above the dials layer.

# Android

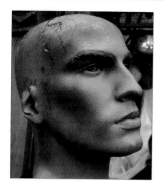

**1** Select and scan a suitable photographic image for the head. The blank eyes, smooth modelling of this mannequin's head, and the surface cracks make it a perfect choice for a humanoid robot.

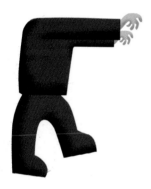

**2** In Photoshop, draw the simple body shape using the Pen tool. On a new layer, select and fill the drawn shapes in grey. For the darker grey shadows set the layer blend to 'Dissolve' and select a deeper hue. This blend results in a smoother tonal sweep, but with plenty of contrast remaining. Add a soft textured effect to the clothing by experimenting with filters – try Filter > Noise > Add noise. This will differentiate the clothing from the smooth, strongly featured head. Use the Colour Dropper tool to select a shade from the digital image of the head to colour the hands.

## Final image

Photographed objects can form the major part of a Photoshop cartoon. The dead, soulless gaze of the mannequin is perfect for the aloof robot, and easily allows the rest of the body to be drawn and attached. The joining of the two images is made simple through layers, the depths of hue and texture through limited use of colour slider bars and filters.

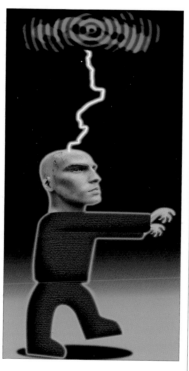

**3** Combine the two image layers so that the head rests on the body. Use the Hue/Saturation sliders to adjust the head layer to a greenish-grey hue. Make a gradient background tint on another layer which fades upwards from deep green to black. Create the lightning on another layer using a white brush line, feathered and stroked with green set at 5 pixels. Make the 'airwave' cloud by selecting a patch of green, painting it with a brush, then modifying it via Filter > Halftone > Circles. Finally, draw the shadow under the feet using the Ellipse tool, softened with a feathered edge. Place the shadow on the layer beneath the figure.

## Sci-fi options in Painter, Photoshop and Illustrator

Knowing how to juxtapose images and programs can give you a great result in a short time-frame. Opting for small vignetted illustrations is an effective way to make the whole task simpler.

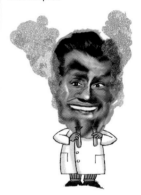

**Crazy scientist** ▲
The head is created and distorted in Painter before positioning on to a hand-drawn pen sketch scanned into Photoshop. Experimenting with filters works a two-part magic process. First, use the Pointillism filter to create the test tube fumes, then alter them further with the Curl and Twist filters.

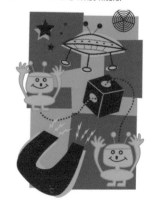

**Space travel** ▲
This light-hearted image expounds the notion of interstellar travel using the gravitational pull of black holes. It is drawn and tinted in Illustrator, and would be perfect for a popular science magazine.

# Mixed media collage

Combining real-life and drawn elements is a technique much practised by cartoonists and other illustrators. You see it used in all kinds of media, from spot newspaper illustrations to graphic novels, strips and fine art. Animation has used this merging of real and imaginary worlds to great defamiliarizing effect for many years, with the early Disney films *Mary Poppins* and *Bedknobs and Broomsticks* among the first to fuse whimsical cartoon worlds with traditionally shot actors.

In those pre-digital days, it was a highly complex achievement involving numerous artists and endless hand-drawn images placed on top of extant film footage. Today, whether for moving or static images, vector and bitmap computer programs make it easy to seamlessly mesh the 'real' and 'unreal' together.

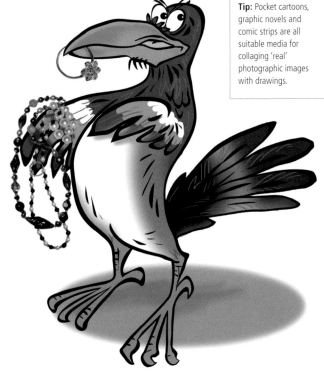

**Tip:** Pocket cartoons, graphic novels and comic strips are all suitable media for collaging 'real' photographic images with drawings.

## Final image
This magpie is so persistent and successful in its efforts to get its wings on the shiniest of baubles that it has reached out of the cartoon world and into our own. The metaphorical, cheeky quality of the drawing makes this illustration of avarice much easier to swallow, while the use of real jewellery is a simple and effective addition to the picture that reinforces its value.

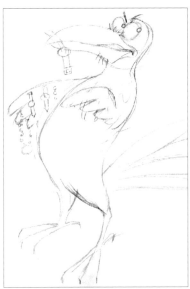

1 Lightly sketch your design and scan your drawing at 300dpi. Import the scan into Photoshop. Choose Image/Image Size and then reduce the file size by resizing the resolution to 100dpi. Make sure that the 'Resample' box is ticked. Drag your resampled image into a new Illustrator document set to the same dimensions. Double click on the layer and reduce the Opacity to 50%, then rename this layer 'Trace' and lock it. As it is just a sketch, feel free to add placeholders for the elements that will later be collaged digitally. Here, we've started with a bird selling watches. The pleasure of working digitally is that it allows you to change your mind – and the direction of your piece – late into the process.

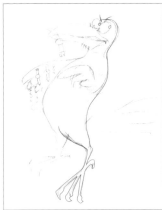

2 Create a new layer above the trace layer and name this 'Line'. Using the Pen tool (set to black, no fill, 1pt), trace over the sketch until the drawing is complete.

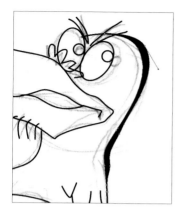

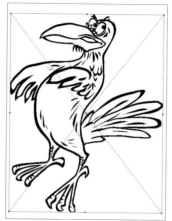

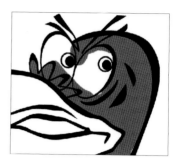

**3** Expand the line to make it more interesting by choosing Select All > Object > Expand. Use the Direct Selection tool to drag anchor points of the line apart. Use the Pencil Smoothing tool to reduce excess points.

**4** When you are satisfied with your line drawing, import it back into a new Photoshop document, set to 300dpi. Set the layer to Multiply, name it 'Line' and lock it. Make a new layer behind the line art.

**5** On the new background layer, begin colouring basic shapes using the Paintbrush tool set to 100%. Erase stray colour using the Eraser tool. Gradually build up the blocks of colour.

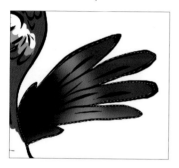

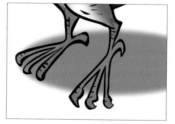

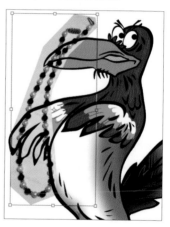

**6** Use the Lasso tool to isolate areas for special treatment, such as the tail. Airbrush the feathers using a 200-pixel soft brush to blend the colours.

**7** On a new layer, create the shadow by filling an ellipse selection, with feathering set to 20 pixels. Use the Eraser tool to remove overlapping grey on the feet.

**8** Scan and import the jewellery. Use the Transform tool to scale each object. Erase the scan backgrounds using the Magic Wand and Eraser tools.

**9** Place each object on a separate layer and when you have placed enough, make another new layer above the background layer. Use this layer to add the shadows to the beak, feet and behind the jewellery, which will give the image depth and tone. Darken the colours in the shadow areas by about 15%. Select each one using the Eye Dropper tool, go to the colour slider palette and move the slider a little to the right. Draw the shadows with a soft brush.

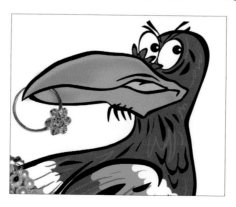

**Tip:** Use layers to help you to build depths of colour and mark within your compositions, or to juxtapose graphic elements. The best way to think of layers is as sheets of transparent acetate which lay one on top of another allowing you to see what lies above and below. Layers can be easily created or duplicated and lifted into the most suited position.

# Using advanced colour theory

The digital production of images offers a limitless number of colours to play with, and a similarly wide range of methods with which to apply them. However, sometimes a simpler, restrained approach will net you the best results. Images decked out in subtle tones can often be the most effective. By not dazzling or crowding the eye, they allow the viewer to concentrate fully on the narrative. The considered use of small areas of hue – known as 'spot colour' – brings focus to bear on the most significant elements. All digital painting programs lend themselves to creating images in a limited span of tints and tonal 'keys' – the name given to tones which all fall within a small range of colour increments. Over the next four pages, we shall explore the benefits of spot colour and limited palettes, as well as more advanced techniques including ambient glows and expressive textures. Why not try colouring the same image multiple times, summoning different moods through different palettes and techniques?

## Using hue with a two-colour limited palette cartoon

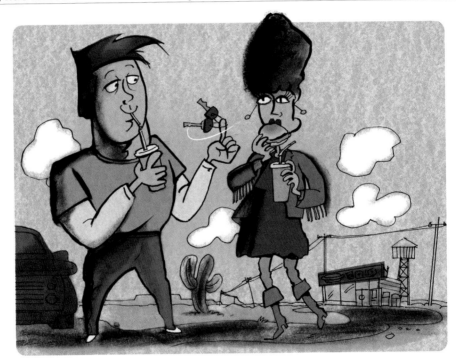

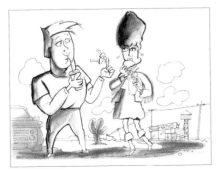

1 Draw the ink and charcoal sketch. Scan the image into Photoshop and duplicate the background layer. Drop a neutral colour layer, set to Multiply, on top of the image, to act as a background hue. Create a new layer named 'Spot Colour Overlay', set it to Multiply, and use the Marquee tool to select areas to colour: the sign, car keys, lips and dress. Fill these with a red-based brown, adjusting the colour using the Image > Adjustment > Hue/Saturation sliders on the red channel.

## Final image
The strength of a two-colour limited palette cartoon is evident here, and the highly selective use of the hue works harmoniously with the quality of the line and charcoal tone with no conflict of elements. The careful blending with soft brushes working closely in relationship with the buff-tinted paper, lifts the texture of the image and evokes the gritty atmosphere.

## Limited pastel palette

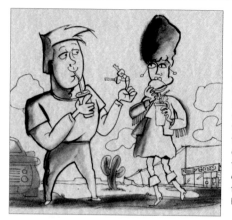

1 Import the same scanned drawing into a new Photoshop document. Scan some buff textured paper and save this to a new layer, set to Multiply, placed on top of the drawing layer. As before, select the shaded charcoal areas to colour with the Marquee tool, this time focusing on the background of the drawing. Convert these areas – the car, the cactus, the burger joint – to sepia, using the Hue/Saturation sliders.

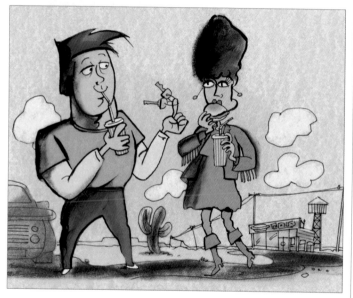

2 Photoshop's expressive colour ranges allow you to easily match the moods and effects you are trying to create in your images. Here, using restraint and minimalism, select a range of pastel tints from its colour palettes. On another new layer, colour the remaining main elements and their details, bringing the two characters forward from the monotone background. For the sky and clouds, employ a soft brush, blending the edges of each block of colour so that they appear to merge into the tint of the buff paper.

### Final image

Using a limited pastel palette for this more muted final image has been key, allowing for a slightly changed, possibly more positive overall tone of the cartoon, but it is also important to retain the black outline around the figures to help pull them out from the sepia background. You must also keep your colour shading minimal, allowing the original charcoal lines to do your toning work for you.

## Colour swatches

The Adobe packages contain a wide array of swatches to help with choosing colours. The opportunity to see the colour families grouped as they are on the artist's colour wheel makes light work of selecting complementary tints and shades.

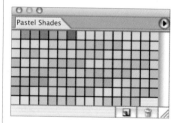

### Pastel shades ▲

These shades are typical of the types of colours that result when white is incrementally added to a pure base colour. By clicking on a tile in the palette, you can select a hue for use with the Brush or Pen tool.

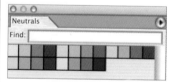

### Neutrals ▲

Colour neutrals are variations of grey which have a hint of brown, green, blue or red as their base. They work in harmony with most other colours.

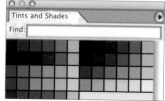

### Tints and shades ▲

If you were mixing up tints and shades in paint, the tints would be colours with a hint of white added and the shades with a hint of black. Shades are the colours most commonly used for shadows and tints for highlights.

## Gritty shadows and glows

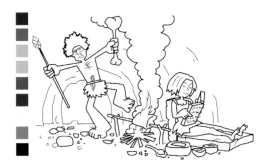

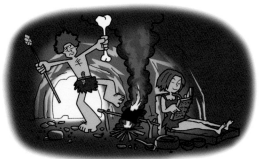

1 Sketch an exaggerated cave scene, contrasting the manic form of the caveman with the relaxed cavewoman. Note the bold, outsized hands and feet on the caveman, which draw attention to his flailing and stomping. Scan the sketch into Illustrator, and outline using the Pen tool. Create a tight selection of colour swatches in brown, blue and flesh tints down one side – use these for later colour selection in Photoshop.

2 Import the drawing into Photoshop as a new layer. Below the line layer, paint a new background layer in dark blue. Colour the characters, smoke and cave elements with flat colours, shadows and highlights as before. To create the glow effect on the flame and cave entrance, 'knock back' the black line around each element by selecting the line on the line art layer and colouring it a slightly darker shade of the flame using the Fill tool.

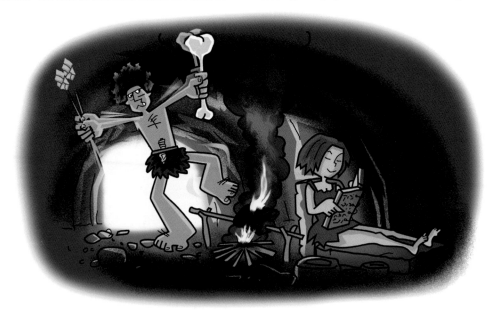

3 On another layer positioned on top of the flat colours, add the shadows and blurs. For the gritty texture of the dark cave shadows, select a 300-pixel soft brush from the Brush palette and set it to Mode > Dissolve. Spray this brush around the arc of the cave mouth and curved walls. The same brush, coloured white, can be used to add flavour to the border of the background.

### Final image
Here, a combination of a variety of elements contrasts the frenzy of the caveman with the relaxed demeanour of the cavewoman. The motion blur on the arms, the glow of the fire and the harsh light outside are simple effects which all serve to inject depth and dynamism into the image.

## Ambient glow

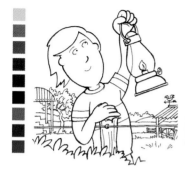

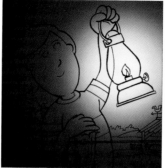

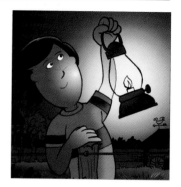

1 Scan the simple line drawing and import it into Photoshop, leaving the image open for colour. Plan your colours before you start by creating swatches of no more than nine shades on a separate layer for later reference.

> **Tip:** Colour swatches play an important part in understanding the continuation of sequences in cartooning. Always choose base hues that work well together to create the correct mood, and be sure to include them in all the frames making up the running frames of the story.

2 Create the dispersing background glow emanating from the lamp by selecting the Gradient tool and setting it to 'Radial Gradient'. Choose the two colours to gradate from the swatches – white to mid-brown. Click to choose the central point of your radial blend, and draw the line to indicate the extent of the first colour (in this case, white). The longer the line you draw with the Radial tool, the greater the percentage of white in the final mix, and the larger the 'bloom' in the centre of the gradient. The shorter the line, the larger the percentage of brown.

3 Use the Lasso tool to isolate areas of the face, arms, T-shirt, lantern and body. Fill these with a mixture of linear and radial blends as appropriate, on new layers, using the Gradient tool. In this example, we've used radial blends on the face and left arm, to reflect the gleam of the lamp, while the other elements have been coloured with a linear gradient. On another layer, paint in the trees, grass and barn using flat colours and a soft brush for the occasional highlight. Place each new layer you create above the overall background radial gradient layer.

4 When you are satisfied with the gradient and colour layers, Flatten (Layer > Flatten Image) and duplicate them. Set the duplicated layer to 'Multiply' – this will intensify the depth of your chosen colours and throw up the contrast between the areas of light and dark more keenly. Make the bright lights of the fireflies with a soft, round brush (size 30) dabbed on to the image in a combination of white and creamy yellow hues. Draw the flight trails using the pressure-sensitive stylus pen on the drawing tablet. This will give you maximum control over their movement and direction and enable you to taper the line as it trails into the distance.

## Final image
The completed cartoon shows the kind of depth of field and atmosphere that can be accomplished with a very limited palette and a judicious use of gradients. Note how the use of complementary shades and gradients draws the eye across the image in an unfamiliar direction – we focus first on the strongest light source, the lamp, then on the glow on the boy's cheek, then follow his upturned eyes to the true centre of the image – the fireflies themselves.

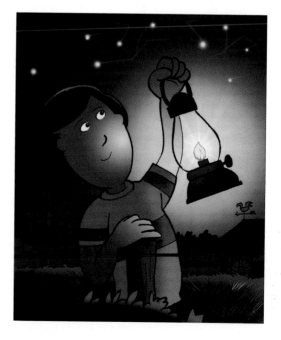

# Monstrous textures

Inventing an imaginary creature allows you to give free rein to your creativity. Monsters are excellent subjects – the only rules that apply to them are that they must be both freakish and scary to some degree – but remember too that the most successful monsters of print and screen are sympathetic to some degree. They present the ideal opportunity to merge aspects of fantasy and reality, creating a range of digital Frankenstein's monsters for you to bend to your will. The advantage of using the computer as your main tool is that it allows you to experiment freely while still being able to roll your image back to any part of the process. Essential elements, such as shape and scale, colour contrasts and textures, can be tried out to your heart's content, without fear of compromising the final result. Don't be afraid to throw on new filters or play with as-yet untouched settings – the perfect piece may arise from a happy accident.

## Creating a sympathetic 'monster'

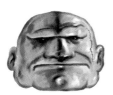

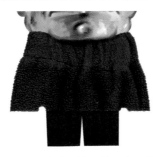

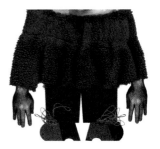

1 Build the broad face in Painter, using layers of paint in your favoured medium, working from mid-tones to shadows and highlights. Pay attention to the furrowed, horizontal lines at eyebrow level and around the thin-lipped mouth. A strong centre-line down the brow and nose, formed of shadow, grants the image weight and depth. The face is lit from either side by diffuse light sources, so pay attention to the different coloured highlights (blue on the left, orange on the right) that suggest each light. Strongly angle the cheek muscles up to meet the nose, and note the thickset shadows beneath the brow and mouth.

2 Import the head into Photoshop. On a series of new layers, create a body using real, scanned garments – or portions of fabric cropped and shaped in Photoshop using the Lasso tool. Smooth any misfitting edges between cloth and head with the Blending tool.

3 The shoes are created from shaped portions of a scanned texture. Place scans of real hands, scale them in size and make them more purple by adjusting Hue /Saturation. Tangles of string, scanned, form shoelaces, and images of rusty bolts complete the Frankenstein cliché.

4 To give this misunderstood monster a hiding place, scan a photograph of a dilapidated barn and place it on a new layer behind your creation. To give the barn an eerie, unreal quality, add a new Adjustment Layer > Hue/Saturation and bring the Saturation down to -60. Scale the barn so that it sits behind your monster, with the creature breaking out of the rigidity of the boxed background to add interest to your composition. Like Frankenstein's original 'mixed-media' creation, this monster is just crying out for animation! Why not experiment with different facial expressions or a range of hands?

## Final image

This creature is a combination of painted features, found textures and scanned photographic elements. Switching between Painter and Photoshop allows you to intermingle a variety of source materials in an organic fashion. Using the slider bars of the Hue/Saturation adjustment layer, you may wish to completely change the ambience of a benign scene to something far more sinister – or you can also brighten up the image by intensifying all the colours.

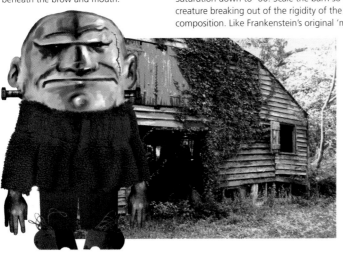

## Gnarled skin

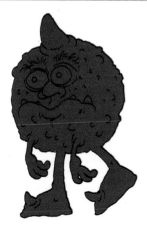

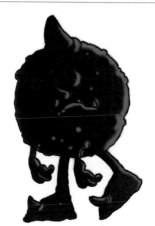

**1** Scan a pen and ink drawing of a morose monster into Photoshop. Apply a flat purple hue to the creature on a new layer beneath the line layer. An easy way of doing this is to select the white area outside your creature on the line layer, choose Select > Inverse, then switch to your colour layer and Fill the selection. If your image is a joined-up ink rendering such as this, you'll find this method quicker than painting the whole image with the Brush tool.

**2** Apply the lighter and darker purple tones using a soft brush on a layer placed above the flat colour. Apply a linear gradient blend of red/green above this layer, set to 'Hard Light' (in the layer blending box and scroll down to 'Hard Light'). This creates a glow effect in the area of the two-colour blend. Finally, use the Eraser tool to remove excess colour around the monster – or select the white areas on the line art layer, flip back to the gradient layer and press delete.

**3** Add a skin texture using the Craquelure filter (Filter > Texture > Craquelure > Distort > Spherized). Use a soft blue-white/mauve-white brush to add the fine detailing on the eyes and horn. Draw the bristly hairs using a small, hard brush. Finally, on a new layer beneath the figure, spray on an ellipse with a soft feathered edge as the monster's shadow.

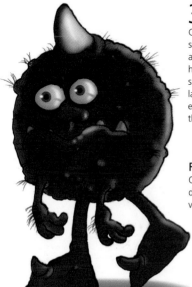

## Final image
Only a handful of 'real' features in a drawing are required to convince the viewer of its veracity as a character, no matter how outlandish the physiology. Here, the well-rendered reflections of light on the creature's eyes, and the bristling hairs and textured skin, are enough to bring life to a horned, ambulatory bowling ball.

## Quick digital monsters

Photoshop is perfect for developing monstrous characters, allowing you to experiment with a wide range of styles, and summon a cast of spooky characters for use in cartoons, comics, graphic novels or simple animations. Simplicity of design is this key – build your creations from exaggerated and distorted geometric shapes. Start with an identifiable silhouette, and work back from that.

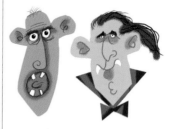

**Monster faces** ▲
These Photoshop portraits are rapidly sketched using a stylus and drawing tablet. Lay down a face shape first and fill it with flat colour. Employ the Brush tool with a darker hue to tint the shadow and facial details. Add interest by using a textured brush.

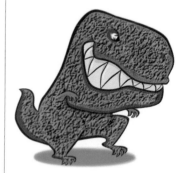

**T. Rex** ▲
The expanded line of this Illustrator drawing is stroked in hues of blue and green. It is imported into Photoshop for texture and colour: Filter > Pixilate > Pointillize (cell size 5) is applied to a gradated blue-green tone. Filter > Render > Lighting Effects > Texture Channel (set to green) is the next step, set at 60% 'Mountainous'.

# Metallic surfaces

Like monsters, robots offer your imagination the opportunity to run wild. As long as they display mechanical workings, robots can consist of shapes, colours and textures in any configuration you prefer. Robots in popular fiction can range from benign automata to laser-wielding machines of death, so it should be easy to find a droid that fits the mood of your project – contrast the robots of Asimov, *The Wizard of Oz*, *Terminator 2* and *Doctor Who*, to name but four. The only thing that cartoon robots have in common is their metallic 'skin', which can be achieved through a wide variety of effects, to replicate the different methods that went into their various processes of construction.

## Creating a metallic 'skin'

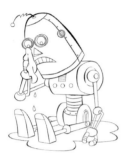

**1** Scan a simple pencil sketch of a weeping robot, and import it into Illustrator. Trace over the lines with the Pen tool, and use the Direct Selection tool (white arrow) to expand the line by pulling on selected points (Object > Expand).

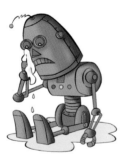

**2** Import the Illustrator outline into Photoshop. Create a new layer for colour and set it to 'Multiply'. Paint the drawn areas in flat colours of blue and grey. Fill the buttons on the chest unit with bright primary hues. To add depth, create a new shading layer and place it above the colour layer. Pinpoint your areas of shadow and stroke on the darker shades using a soft brush. Don't worry about the metallic texture or the contents of the puddle at this point.

**3** Select the white background portions of the image on the line art layer, using the Magic Wand, and use Select > Inverse to capture the robot. Create a new layer, selecting 'Use Previous Layer To Create Clipping Mask', and fill the mask with a blend of reddish-brown and black. Apply the Pointillize filter (Filter > Pixelate > Pointillize) with a low cell size – this will add the simulated texture of rust. Make sure all your colour layers are set to 'Multiply' so that the rust blends with your colour textures. Erase parts of the texture so that some of the original blue-grey shows through. Flatten your image so far. Create a new layer from a Clipping Mask of the puddle, duplicate your coloured robot and use Transform (Edit > Transform > Flip Horizontal) to create the mirror image. Now distort it using the Liquify filter (Filter > Liquefy). Add highlights on a new layer to selected areas of the surface.

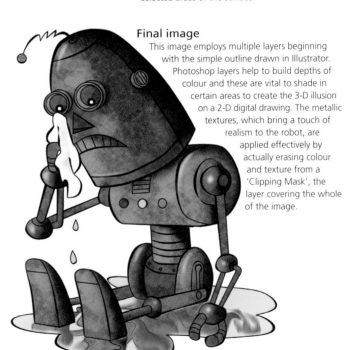

### Final image

This image employs multiple layers beginning with the simple outline drawn in Illustrator. Photoshop layers help to build depths of colour and these are vital to shade in certain areas to create the 3-D illusion on a 2-D digital drawing. The metallic textures, which bring a touch of realism to the robot, are applied effectively by actually erasing colour and texture from a 'Clipping Mask', the layer covering the whole of the image.

## Metallic shine

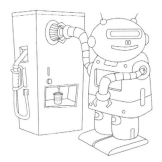 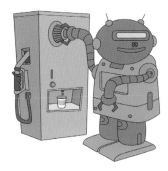

1 The outline of the robot siphoning a drink of oil from a vending machine is drawn directly into Illustrator. This method forces an economy of line from the beginning. The work involved encourages you to keep detail to the essential minimum, which makes for 'cleaner' and more readable art.

2 Import the line drawing into Photoshop, and place a flat colour layer below the line art. Choose four or five flat metallic colours to fill the outline – in this example, a selection of greys, mingled with blues and browns. Select and fill the shapes using the Magic Wand and Fill tools.

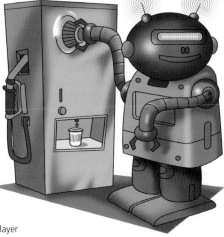

3 Create a new layer above the flat colour layer to add form to the drawing. Use a soft brush or airbrush to add shades, and alter the Opacity of the different tints to produce the subtlety required. Make another layer above the tone layer for highlights. Don't be afraid to build up to the brightest highlights in steps. Create the whirling antennae by filling two circles in red. Select each individually with the Magic Wand, making sure your background colour is set to white, and apply Filter > Sketch > Halftone Pattern > Circle to them.

### Final Image
The simplistic shapes and basic shading on this image nonetheless combine into a finished piece that has a great deal of character and dimensionality. The shadow of the claw arm draped across the robot's chest, along with the burnished tones of the vending machine, adds depth, while the blues and the reds help define and contrast the conscious robot with the unthinking drinks vendor. The easy effect of the flaring antennae adds a further dash of personality to the illustration.

## Alternative automatons

Creating robot figures is a fun way of combining shapes and experimenting with colour and expression as well as movement. See just how easy it is to anthropomorphize even the most outlandish of shapes with the addition of a pair of eyes!

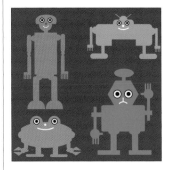

### Simple robots ▲
Illustrator is the ideal choice for quick-fire designs or the execution of simple cyber characters. Shapes are quickly and easily drawn, selected, coloured and duplicated – and the Pathfinder tool groups them into a single shape.

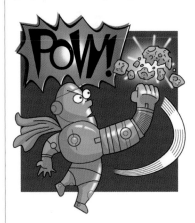

### Robot power ▲
This Illustrator/Photoshop image blends the cliché of the superhero with a robotic shape. The cape and trunks clothe the body in familiar, yet unnecessary attire (for a robot!), and the massive mechanical forearm embodies the concept of superior force.

# Characterful cartoons

Cartoon characters are a fantastic tool for cartoonists involved in social commentary and parody of everyday life. The benefit of creating a family of such characters in the digital domain is instant access to your past illustrations and character designs – whether for reference or reuse. Ideal for a one-off cartoon or comic strip, these creations also gain currency when allowed to persist, turning up repeatedly to deliver their thoughts in a representative – if humorously off-kilter – fashion.

A contemporary family supplies a range of characters of different ages and stations in life, at once irrevocably yoked together and at odds with one another. Everyone recognizes these interactions, and this provides instant engagement with your audience. While we've used a white, suburban family here, never forget that single-parent, second-marriage and multi-racial families all represent slabs of society equal to the traditional nuclear unit. While it's harder to boil these down to stereotypes, the rewards for breaking free of cliché are great.

## Cartoon couple

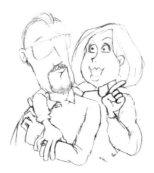

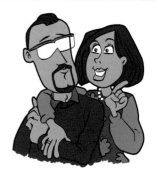

1 Draw a cartoon sketch of a couple, perhaps using photos as reference: get friends or family members to model difficult poses for you. Pay close attention to the positions of the hands, facial features and body language. When you are happy with the sketch, scan it into Illustrator and trace over the line with the Pen tool, set to 1pt. Adjust the outer lines of the characters to a 3pt width.

2 Import the completed outline into Photoshop – we've added flowers to the wife's dress at the Illustrator stage – and colour the different areas of the image in flat colours. Select areas to Fill on the line art layer, using the Magic Wand tool set to Contiguous, then flip to the colour layer in order to Fill. Keep the colours light and bright, as you will be adding only a single pass of shading.

3 Apply tonal shadows on a new layer to give the figures form. Add a 15% tint of black to each flat colour and apply using a wide-textured brush. Finally, employ a fine black brush for the lines which detail the shading of the hair and the folds in the clothing. Although highlights are suggested on the glasses by starting with a bright shade and adding a swatch of deeper colour, real highlights are added on a separate layer to the hair and on the wife's lip.

### Final image

The final image is a skilful piece of body language that can be interpreted in several ways. The wife's arm is wrapped around her husband – a gesture both supportive and playful, but do their upraised fingers suggest a mild disagreement, or are they completely in tune with each other? The glare on the husband's glasses means we can't see his gaze. Just as the dialogue in a strip depends on the quality of the cartoon to succeed, so the mood of a drawing can often only be decoded by the speech attributed to it. What would your caption or speech balloon say?

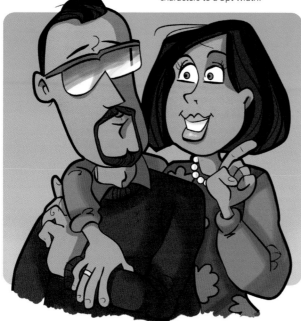

## The family in context

Here we progress to rendering full figures of the family against a background, in this case, a supermarket, focusing on how the characters relate to each other.

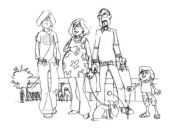

**1** Make a pencil drawing of the family group and their background setting using direct and open lines. When you're happy with the layout, scan the drawing into Illustrator.

**3** Import the outline into Photoshop and select the main sections of clothing, skin tones, dog's coat, building and accessories to fill with flat colour, using the Magic Wand tool as before. Add form to the characters by adding tones and shadows on a separate layer, selecting areas to colour and darkening them with a soft brush and a 15% tint of black added to the base colour. Note the angular light reflections on the windows, and the arc of the bouncing ball, which has been 'knocked back' to white by filling in the black on the line art layer.

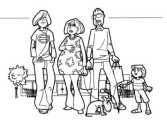

**2** Trace over the pencil lines using the Pen tool, set to 1pt. When you're done, adjust the outer line of each character to be 3pt in width (Object > Expand), leaving the inner lines at 1pt. This defines each family member, but leaves variety and interest in the line weight. The supermarket is left at 1pt, helping to push it into the background, while still allowing its horizontal form to tie together the disparate figures.

## Final image

Each character's posture and position say much of their relationship to one another. The pregnant mother forms the focus, with her husband, proud and a little possessive, on one side. Her son, lost in his music, is on the other. The dog's long-suffering expression – ignored by the daughter – speaks volumes. The mother, at least, is looking out for the smallest of her brood.

## Defining and styling figures

Do research to plump your family figures into full-featured individuals. Flip through magazines for tips on clothing, and try to keep up with hairstyling and pop culture trends.

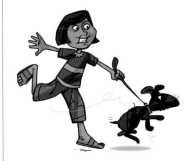

**Young girl with her dog ▲**
With the energy and enthusiasm of youth, this girl's wide-eyed approach to the world is significant. Her movements speak of irrepressible excitement, a good contrast to the more weary viewpoints of her brother and parents.

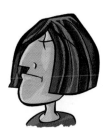

**The teenager ▲**
The long-haired, laid-back look is stereo-typical of a teenage boy. The facial expressions and body language speak of a character at once removed from the world, and passing judgement upon it. While he maintains some of the openness of youth, the mop of hair is equally successful at hiding him away. Angular, awkward features capture the indignities of adolescence. Teenagers are ideal for experimenting with clothing and hair colours as they can change styles from week to week.

# 3-D Illustrator effects

The ability to create hyper-real 3-D objects in Illustrator opens up a wealth of new opportunities for image creation, whether combining a 3-D shape with hand-drawn characters or generating intriguing, abstract landscapes. Though limited in comparison to a fully featured 3-D program, these effects can add an appropriately thrilling new dimension to your drawings, when used correctly. As with all new filters or tools, use it wisely and sparingly for the most impact. First though, a light pencil sketch can get the imagination firing.

## Final image

This psychedelic fantasy landscape challenges the viewer's perceptions with its shifting depth of field, hyper-realistic background elements and humorous alien figure – who alone has evolved to navigate the surreal landscape. Not bad for a quick Illustrator sketch.

## Abstract landscapes

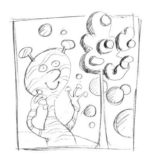

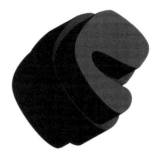

**1** This project is created directly on the screen, so plan it before you begin. Make a light pencil reference sketch of an otherworldly composition and decide which elements will be applied using the 3-D tool. Remember to keep all object shapes simple, and revise your thoughts until you are satisfied.

**2** Go live in Illustrator now and create a 3-D shape using the Effect filter – go to Effect > 3-D > Extrude and Bevel > Complex 1 Bevel (and choose 50pt extrude depth). Repeat the process to make a variety of simple shapes, which you can then group together to form the alien tree.

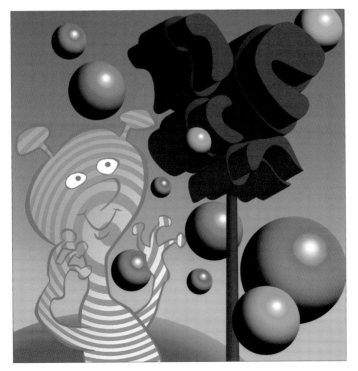

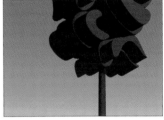

**3** Create a simple stick shape to form the tree trunk and turn it by applying the Revolve tool (Effect > 3-D > Revolve). Place the tree on a gradated colour background of yellow and purple formed using the Gradient tool.

**4** Create the spheres from a drawn semicircle (always made to the right of the vertical guide) using the Revolve tool (Effect > 3-D > Revolve), and place them on a number of layers both in front of and behind the tree. Draw the alien outline on a separate layer, applying a yellow and green gradient fill. Apply the green circle pattern using the Halftone filter (Filter > Sketch > Halftone Pattern > Circle) on a new layer set to 'Multiply'.

## Imitating plastic

As before, plan your composition and layout with a quick sketch before taking the plunge into Illustrator. We're going to create an iconic image of a 3-D flying saucer, rendered to look like a plastic toy, laying waste to a 2-D city. The 3-D Revolve tool is perfect for creating simple, symmetrical, plastic-looking items – so it's great for capturing the nuances of early sci-fi toys.

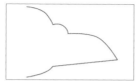

**1** Draw the saucer profile in a new Illustrator document using the Pen tool. Remember to only draw half of it, to the right of the vertical guide. Stroke the outline using a 1pt pink colour fill.

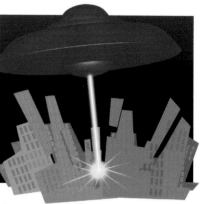

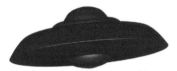

**2** Use the Effect > 3-D > Effect > Revolve tool, with a blue shading colour selected (these options can be found by clicking the 'More Options' button in the Revolve options menu that appears). Add extra highlights to your shape as necessary, and make sure that the 'Cap' option is set to 'solid' (the left of the two Cap options, located next to Angle in the Options box). Click OK, and Illustrator will create a plastic-looking saucer in three dimensions.

**3** Create the setting using the Simple Illustrator Pen tool to shape and colour buildings placed against a gradient background of red to reddish-brown. Place the saucer on a layer above the buildings and import the image into Photoshop. Using a 20-pixel brush yellow outer line and a 5-pixel brush white inner line, create the laser beam, holding down Shift to draw a perfectly straight line. Add the impact flash in the same way, starting with large yellow and white brushes for the explosion, then stroking out thin white points.

### Final image
This picture playfully tweaks its nose at the science-fiction concept of aliens invading from another dimension, as the power of the third dimension is literalized: the chunky toy saucer vaporizing a 2-D cardboard city. Whether escaping from its box into the wider world of the toy store, or asserting the box-office dominance of CGI cartoons over their traditionally animated brethren, this flying saucer certainly means business!

## Creating depth with drop shadows

This project provides another strong contrast between 2-D and 3-D, but this time it is the setting which is fully realized, and the figure that is drawn to resemble a cardboard cut-out.

**1** Draw a very simple chair shape directly in Illustrator and fill it with flat colour. Now add Effect > 3-D > Revolve > Plastic Shading. The shiny plastic appearance instantly transforms the flat shape into rounded 3-D.

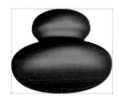

### Final image
An image such as this, where an abstract, iconic cartoon is integrated with a rendered item, could be used to draw attention to a product or service – a new range of sofas, perhaps, or a deluxe departure lounge. The 'realism' of the item draws the focus of the image to it, while the simplicity of the figure allows for the maximum affinity with viewers – the simpler the cartoon, the more people will identify with it.

**2** On a new layer, outline a seated figure using the Pen tool. Fill all the sections with flat colours and place this layer above the chair. Create a third, drop shadow layer and place it between the inflatable and the flat figure (Select the Figure layer, choose Effect > Stylize > Drop Shadow, with a low value for the X and Y offsets – the other options are up to you). This lifts the flat figure and adds to the illusion that she is seated.

**Tip:** When you have mastered the basic functions of the Revolve tool, experiment with diffuse shading and create more ambitious custom colour palettes.

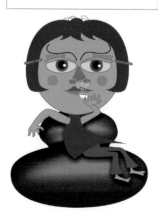

# Retro style

Every period in history is reflected in its art, and popular graphic styles speak volumes about the culture and music of an era. Fashion tends to look back at past styles, and new trends often borrow from earlier times to create 'retro' styles, either reproducing colours and patterns associated with specific periods or amalgamating retro influences into a new 'fusion' style.

The computer is a tool that's perfect for such imitations, as program filters and simple techniques can successfully reproduce the cruder appearance of nostalgic ephemera, such as jazz record sleeves, with their coarse halftone colour screens and mis-registration.

## Final image

For the final touch, scan some yellow paper, torn at the edges, and place it above the entire image in 'Multiply' mode. Now this battered LP sleeve could easily be stumbled across in a thrift-store. Although worn around the edges, this image still has effortless cool. If you want more realism, use the Brush tool to add highlights to the sunglasses, choosing the uppermost layer. Now all you have to do is choose a band name!

## Using retro influences

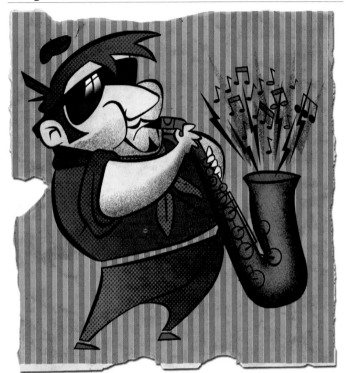

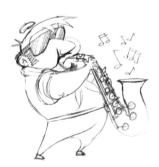

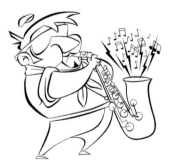

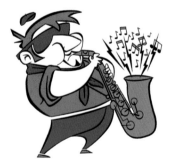

1 Do a light pencil sketch in the 1960s' graphic style, simplified and stylized, with legs and arms tapering away to small wedge feet and hands. Scan the drawing. Changing the line colour to blue in Photoshop may help you keep track of which lines you have overdrawn in the next stage.

2 Overdraw the sketch in Illustrator with the Pen tool set to 1pt. Expand and drag the lines to add variable weight to them (Object > Expand). The lively character of the lines suits the freeform, musical nature of the cartoon, while the open areas are perfect for large swatches of colour.

3 Import the drawing into Photoshop and select a limited palette of colours appropriate to the period. The muted blue and orange deliberately lack the vivid brightness of contemporary hues. The saxophone is a toned-down grey. Apply these hues as flat colours, then proceed to the next stage.

## 1950s' advertising imagery

## Spot colour head

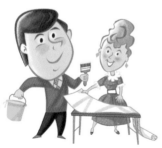

**1** Pencil a quick sketch and scan it into Illustrator. Outline the figures using the Pen tool, expanding the lines (Object > Expand) as needed. Stroke the lines with sober, dark versions of the colours you will fill them with: orange for the skin tone, deep blue for the dress and so on before importing into Photoshop to fill the areas of flat colour. You may find it easier to import the black line art into Photoshop, fill the areas of colour and then colour the lines with the Fill tool on the line art layer, using the Lasso tool to isolate sections of the image. Apply tonal brushwork on a layer placed above the flat colour.

**2** Outline and colour three rectangles of wallpaper in Illustrator. The wallpapers are formed from bold and simple shapes which can be copied, pasted and rescaled or rotated quickly from a detailed image. Curve the bottom edge of each rectangle, and import the wallpaper image into Photoshop, placing it under your completed figures. Create a soft grey shadow oval with 20% Opacity and position it beneath the feet of the figures.

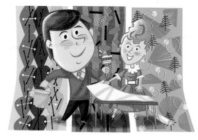

### Final image
The strong blues, turquoises and browns and cheery 'big-headed' cartooning style create a period image that's perfect for illustrating an article on home décor – whether in the 1950s or the present day!

The distinctive mis-registration of colour layers is a key feature of 1950s' and 1960s' graphics, the result of a limitation in the offset lithographic printing presses of the time. Replicating this imperfection grants retro-style images authenticity.

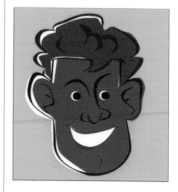

**Out of register** ▲
The head is drawn directly in Illustrator and the line expanded at various points. The flat colour is applied deliberately to misalign with the outline edges.

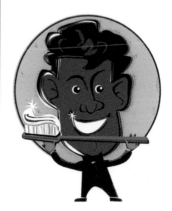

**Applied halftone filter** ▲
Still in Illustrator, the drawing is extended to include the body, limbs and giant toothbrush, all set against a plain yellow circle with an outline stroked in red. In Photoshop, a Colour Halftone filter is applied on a new layer (Filter > Pixelate > Colour Halftone), then partially erased to leave a dotted effect around the edges.

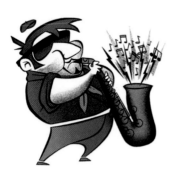

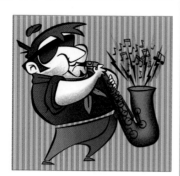

**4** On a new layer, apply separate gradients to areas of the hair, scarf, shirt and trousers. Apply Filter > Sketch > Halftone Pattern to the gradients to convert the gradient pattern into dots. On a further layer, airbrush in black shadows and add Noise (Filter > Noise > Add Noise) for texture.

**5** To get the retro effect of pinstripe wallpaper, create a square on a new background layer and fill it with orange. Now draw a single blue stripe on a layer above and duplicate it across the width of the orange square. For a brighter, more modern image, simply change the wallpaper colours.

# Integrated characters

Cartoons can be elaborate and still remain focused. A beautifully researched and executed setting elevates a simple frame to the level of high art. In the history of animated films many of the artists responsible for their richly detailed backgrounds were successful painters in their own right. In the pre-digital days, painstaking hours were spent fleshing out dense foliage – a task that can now be achieved in a fraction of the time using computer shortcuts.

When attempting a jungle scene, nowadays you do not need to paint every vein of every leaf to offer the impression of density. Working in layers on Photoshop or Illustrator allows you to simulate depth, building up areas of detail that recede into a distant haze of soft silhouettes. Learning to pare down detail as the layers recede and work from strong colours at the fore to washed out colours at the back is the key to success.

## Final image

Every element of the background works in unison to direct attention towards the main character. Framed by the simple greens of the foliage, the jungle man is shunted to the fore of the image by the resultant negative space. The lineless silhouettes of trees suggest depth without overlapping with the figure, while the yellow background gradient behind his torso is another subtle cue that draws the eye's attention.

## Using background setting

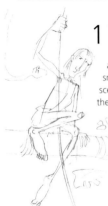

1 Sketch the jungle man in pencil, resting on a tree trunk and gripping a vine, with a curious snake dropping into the scene. Block in areas of the jungle, but don't go into great detail at this point – leaving the intricate line work for the inking stage adds more spontaneity and life to the final drawing.

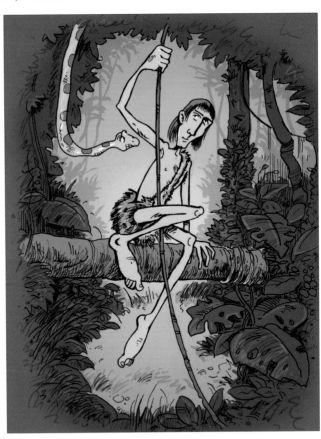

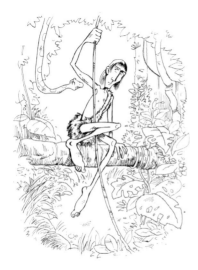

2 Ink over the drawing in dip pen and black Indian ink, filling in all the details of the frame of dense undergrowth. Add shading to the main elements – the figure, snake and tree trunk – with sparser tonal marking elsewhere. Leave the canopy and upper background as a simple keyline. Leave the black-and-white picture to dry, erase your pencil marks and scan the finished drawing into Photoshop.

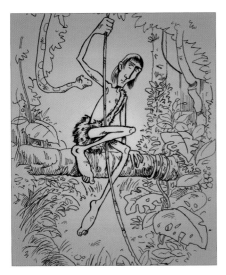

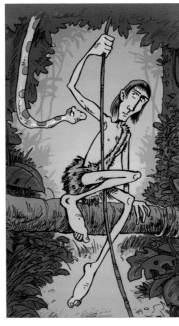

4 On a new layer, strongly tint the snake, man, log and clothing. Keep the colours simple and light, and add only the minimum of shading. Colour the foliage in the fore- and middle ground with a flat, overall green. Add sketchy shadows and highlights with the Brush tool, complementing the detail of your inked drawing with thin lines of soft colour. Finally, on a further background layer above the gradient, brush in the tree silhouettes, using a soft, medium-sized brush. Tint these in a lighter green so they fade into the background.

3 On a layer beneath the line art, apply an intense, gradated radial light seeping through the canopy: make this simply as a circular gradient, bleeding from yellow to green with the Gradient tool.

## Fully painted depth of field

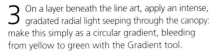

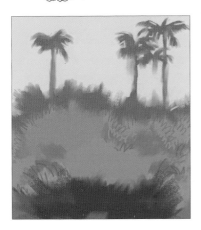

1 Draw a cute and comical monkey using a dip pen and black Indian ink. Apply extra pressure to the pen nib around the simian's head and body, increasing the line's width and character.

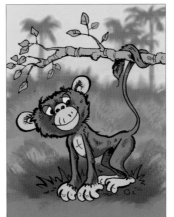

2 The range of brush tools in the Painter application is ideal for the impressionistic background. Use acrylic brushes to lay down soft, opaque strokes that can be smudged using the Blending tool. Keep softening the marks until all the hard edges have disappeared. Add some fine detail to suggest grass stalks in a thinner brush.

3 Import the background image into Photoshop and apply a Gaussian Blur (Filter > Blur > Gaussian Blur) to the foliage to suggest distance. Import the monkey and branch into a layer above the background and tint both in flat colours on a separate layer, adding a second shading tone to the fur. Allow the dark green at the feet to show through.

> **Tip:** As a rule of thumb, the more dense the illustration, the simpler the colouring needs to be. It is the definition of the line work that will 'carry' more of the image.

### Final image
Surrounded by solid black lines, the monkey pops out of the image, as if photographed with a shallow depth of field. In contrast to the flat, sharp colours of the monkey the soft foliage recedes, adding a range of hues and shapes without over-whelming the subject of the cartoon.

# Cartoon symbols

In the graphics world symbols are often used as a means of communication. Easy-to-read images can present all kinds of messages: they are often connected to specific products or appear as brand logos, or are used to give directions or instructions in public places or on a website.

Creating a pared-down, instantly readable, recognizable symbol is a skilled undertaking and thinking economically is no small task. The target for the cartoonist is to reduce an image to its essence and produce a result with as little visual fuss as possible. Producing symbols using a computer graphic package is ideal because of the naturally clean look of a digitally generated image.

## Creating a graphic logo

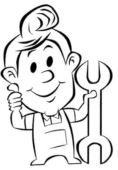

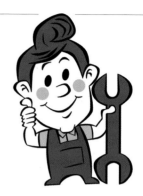

1 Make pencil sketches of your ideas for the mechanic character. Maintain an unfussy line which will be suitable for redrawing in Illustrator. Scan the sketch and open it in Illustrator. Trace around the outline using the Pen tool and expanding some line widths.

2 Import the image into Photoshop and select a simple mono-chromatic palette – white, pale blue and darker blue. A monotone logo still has a tightly designed power. On a new layer beneath the line art layer, fill the different shapes in your image with flat colour. Create small spots for the cheeks using a pale blue fill in two circular selections.

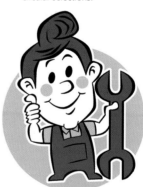

## Final image
This logo for a company of mechanics is the perfect fusion of clarity and personality. The limited colour palette focuses the attention on the form rather than the rendering and the comically enlarged spanner and overalls leave the customer in no doubt of the services offered, while the pared-down cartoon face adds friendly reassurance. The logo would be equally at home above a garage, on headed notepaper or as an embroidered badge.

3 Make the cartoon look more like a logo by dropping in a circular background. Draw this using the Ellipse tool, holding the Shift key down to constrain the proportions so that the height and width of your selection remain the same. Place this layer behind your line and colour layers, so that the figure is projected to the forefront. Apply an 8pt white stroke around the character. As seen in the final image, shadows can make a lot of difference to the perceived depth of your symbol. Here, Layer effects (Layer > Layer style > Bevel and emboss) have been applied to the background circle.

## Anthropomorphized objects

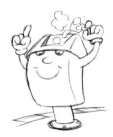 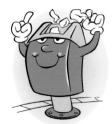 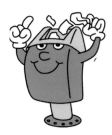

**1** Sketch your final idea, firming up pencil lines to check their graphic strength. Scan and import the drawing into Illustrator. Trace over the sketch using the Pen tool. Experiment with line widths and sizes using the Expand tool (Object > Expand).

### Final image
This symbol is perfect for an anti-littering or recycling bin awareness campaign, or for boroughs creating literature on littering for schools.

**2** In our first colour interpretation, the lines vary between thick and thin to add character. The colours are filled with flat yellow and green, with highlights running vertically down the front edge of the bin and on the cheek dimples for added interest. To help the bin show up more against the white background, and to tie it together as a logo, a yellow ellipse with Opacity reduced to 30% is placed behind the bin on a new layer.

**3** This alternative version of the same image reduces the detail and complexity in order to make it read more cleanly. A uniform 3pt line runs around the whole of the figure, the background elements have been entirely stripped out and the two colours are completely flat, with no highlights. This makes it perfect for rendering on a bin as cut-out areas of colour formed from a soft plastic such as EVA. Evaluate the success of your various versions.

## Design variations

To guarantee the most effective results, consider several options, even if you're happy with your first attempt.

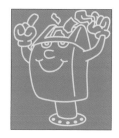

**Reversing out ▲**
Try reversing out the images by converting the black line to white. Does this render the image more effective?

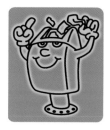

**Glow effect ▲**
This striking glow effect is applied in Photoshop using Layer > Layer style > Inner glow/Outer glow.

## Simple logo

 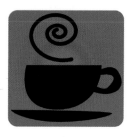 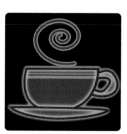

**1** Draw the cup and saucer shapes in Illustrator with the Pen tool. Create the aroma swirl using the Spiral tool. Add a grey tint to fill.

### Final image
A clear logo is essential to promoting a product with success. This simple coffee cup sends a message that is universal in its appeal.

**2** Re-colour the grey silhouette cup and aroma spiral in black and transfer the image into Photoshop. Draw a picture box with rounded corners on a new background layer. Select and apply a medium-blue colour fill from the colour palette. Create a final layer with the Gradient tool set to circular. Apply a warm orange colour and place this at the front.

**3** Experiment with filters, effects, line strokes and fill colours to explore different results. The original drawing does not change throughout this process but the results can profoundly alter the look of the symbol. Here, the cup is enhanced with coloured horizontal bands. A Glow layer (Layer > Layer style > Inner glow/Outer glow) is enhanced by the black background.

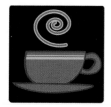

**Enhancing the stroke ▲**
Illustrator can be used to enhance specific details of an image, such as this spiral of coffee steam as a 4pt yellow stroke.

# Texture, depth and perspective

Slithering, scuttling or crawling creatures enjoy much more favourable press in the land of cartoons than they do in real life. The horror and revulsion with which they are usually met tends to evaporate when they are personified as wide-eyed, good-humoured and lovable – no matter how many their legs or how sticky their thorax.

The irresistibility of bugs as cartoon characters is compounded by the fact that they make fascinating and rewarding subjects for the artist. Coming as they do in a plenitude of sizes, shapes, textures and colours, they give plenty of opportunity to explore and exploit the range of tools and effects in Illustrator and Photoshop to the full. Perhaps the best thing is that, given the immense number of species and variations, you should never run out of inspiration for new bug-eyed, bug-ugly characters.

## Final image

A handful of out-of-the-box textures and filter effects combine to create a varied and engaging snail with only a small amount of effort. The colourful bubble-wrap texture on the body creates a slimy and exotic feel, while the swirl of colours on the shell at once complements and stands apart from the line work, like a pop-art painting mounted on the creature's back.

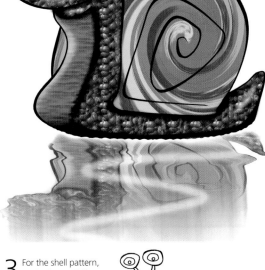

## Applying colour and texture

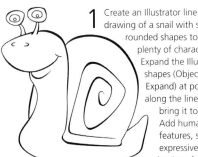

1 Create an Illustrator line drawing of a snail with strong, rounded shapes to give plenty of character. Expand the Illustrator shapes (Object > Expand) at points along the line to bring it to life. Add humanistic features, such as expressive eyes to the tips of the feeler stalk, or a mouth with a knowing grin.

2 Import the drawing into Photoshop, create a duplicate layer and clear the original. Draw a simple square on a new layer and fill it with a flat, yellow-ochre colour. Add broad, brushy strokes of various colours on top, using a special-effects brush from the Brush palette. Don't be conservative about your colour choices – keep them complementary, but don't feel constrained by realism.

3 For the shell pattern, apply the Twirl filter to the shell colour layer (Filter > Distort > Twirl) and size the spiral. Remove excess pattern by selecting the relevant areas with the Magic Wand tool on the line art layer, then changing back to the colour layer and pressing delete. Apply a 'bubble-wrap' pattern from the Styles palette to the snail's body, then select the front of its belly and apply streaks of black and yellow, before blurring them with Filter > Blur > Motion Blur. To create the reflection, flatten, duplicate and flip the image, then apply Filter > Distort > Ripple and some Motion Blur.

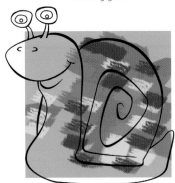

## Rendering and perspective

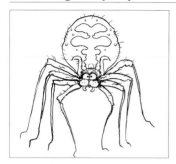

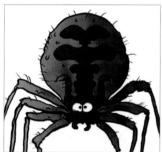

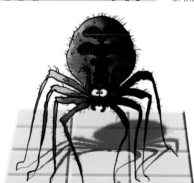

1 Consider the shapes and overall structure of the spider and draw it using a dip pen and black Indian ink. Scan and import into Photoshop.

### Final image
Bristling with tiny hairs and stalking across the bathroom floor towards the bath, there's no question this cartoony spider would get an arachnophobe's back up, even if he is waving hello with his palpi. The bulging, crossed eyes, however, soften the blow and make this alien insect relatable!

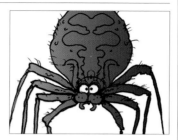

2 Select the whole outline apart from the eyes using the Magic Wand or Lasso tool and apply a gradient blend of light- to mid-brown across the width or length by drawing the gradient line in the appropriate direction. Pan in closer using the Zoom tool and tidy up any stray colour around the outer line using the Eraser tool or Magic-Wand-and-delete method.

3 To give the torso a realistic sense of depth, tint the markings in various shades of brown, yellow-ochre and a range of dark reds. On a new layer select the filled areas to Fill, then apply Filter > Render > Lighting effects to adjust the intensity, texture and shine of the arachnid markings.

4 Construct the tiled floor on a new layer. Create a single grey square and go to Layer > Layer style > Bevel and emboss. Now right click on the layer and choose Convert to Smart Object. Duplicate the layer to make the tile into a square of 12 tiles, and merge the tile layers into a single object. Now put the object into Perspective (Edit > Transform > Perspective). Finally, create the spider shadow by duplicating the creature on to a new layer, darkening the colours to black using Image > Adjustments > Levels. Distort the shadow using the Shift key and Transform, then apply the blur filter. Reduce the shadow's Opacity to 70%.

## Textured soil

As with all cartoon creations, environment is the key to 'selling' your characters and making them believable. Here, we'll integrate an earthworm with a realistic patch of soil.

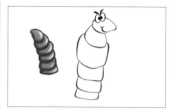

1 Create a coloured outline drawing in Illustrator, expanding the line in certain areas. Import it into Photoshop and apply soft airbrush modelling to the body segments. Tint each segment on one layer, then create another layer above it and add the white highlights.

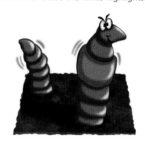

2 To form the textured earth square, paint a few blobs of brown on to a rectangle and apply the Craquelure filter (Filter > Texture > Craquelure). Put the rectangle of earth into Perspective using the Edit > Transform > Perspective command. Apply the earthworm shadow to the soil using a soft brush on a new layer in Multiply mode underneath the worm's colour layer. Add the movement strokes using a suitably soft brush on the white highlight layer.

### Final image
The detailed rendering on the worm's body, and its well-integrated nature with the background, results in a compelling 3-D image. The manner in which the perspective is framed also makes the worm look as if it has burrowed into the page.

# Composite images

Digital methods offer artists the opportunity to create images which can look good enough to eat. Whether created for use in product development, advertising, food magazine articles or as commodities within a graphic novel, these realistic foodstuffs trick the eye and tempt the stomach. The high degree of realism is achieved through the use of layers, filters and 3-D tools, combining separately rendered 'ingredients' in a deliciously digital mimicry of real-world cooking.

## Creating a realistic image with filters

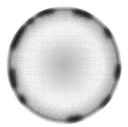 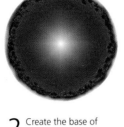 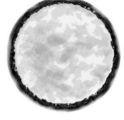 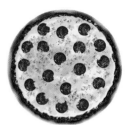

**1** For the first part of this image, draw a circle in Photoshop and fill it with a three-part gradient of yellow, white and light brown (Gradient tool). Select a soft brush, and use it to add a few touches of a darker brown around the edge to simulate a burnt crust. Apply the Craquelure filter (Filter > Texture > Craquelure) to the whole to express the cooked dough.

**2** Create the base of tomato sauce on a new layer as a circle of rich red with deliberately rough edges. Select a darker red hue, and add a thickly scribbled edge to the whole disc using a solid brush. Apply the Plastic Wrap filter (Filter > Artistic > Plastic Wrap) to the central part of the circle so that the tomato appears to glisten. This may look unfinished but will be covered up by the next layer.

**3** Add the yellow cheese layer above the tomato layer as a slightly smaller circle of pale yellow. Keep the edges loose and fussy, extending the odd tendril out over the tomato layer. Apply dabs of mid-yellow across the cheese surface and use the Liquefy filter to swirl it like melted cheese. Add a slight 3-D effect to elevate the topping, using Layer > Layer Style > Bevel and Emboss.

**4** Create a salami slice, then duplicate it and arrange 18 images on the surface. For a more natural look, overlap cheese on to the slices using the Clone tool. Apply small brush dabs of brown and green over the surface to represent a sprinkle of herbs and seasoning. Work these tiny, short strokes randomly over the whole of the pizza. Now flatten the image and correct the perspective using the Transform tool.

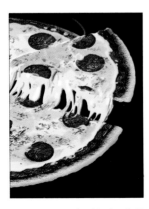

**5** Use the Selection tool (Lasso or Polygonal) to cut a wedge shape out of the pizza and move it to a new layer above the rest. Use a light yellow brush to add strings of cheese, adding shadows in mid-yellow, and using the Smudge tool to smear and blend. Place the whole pizza on a black background to make it stand out and add a few wisps of steam using a soft, white brush. To take the image further, why not recreate various toppings, illustrate a pizza knife lifting up the slice or composite the pizza image into the box art of an Italian food brand of your creation?

### Final image
Utterly tempting, this image is a great example of how simple shapes and colours can produce professional results when coupled with a selection of filters. This pizza is made entirely of manipulated circles, layered atop one another, but judicious application of filters and brushes renders it almost photorealistic.

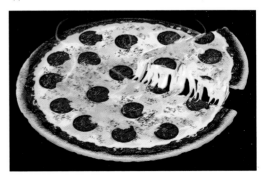

## Combining 2-D and 3-D elements

**1** Construct the cone in Illustrator and apply the 3-D filter (Effect > 3-D > Revolve) using the settings shown in the screengrab below. To map the image of stars onto the object, click the 'Map Art' button and apply the settings shown at the right. You can map any image you like on to a 3-D object, but it must be stored in the Symbols palette in the document you are working on – you can add a layer or group to the Symbols palette just by dragging it in: it will then be selectable from the drop-down menu in the 'Map Art' option.

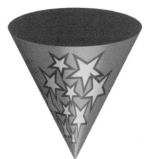

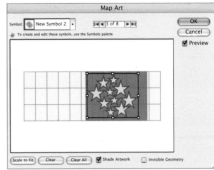

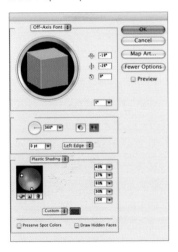

**2** Import the cone into Photoshop. Draw a single French fry, duplicating and rotating it using Edit > Transform and the Rotate function. Spot the fries with tiny strokes of white to indicate salt and apply Filter > Render > Lighting effects to selected areas to add realism. Select areas of the cone with the Ellipse tool where fries are overlapping it, then go to Image > Adjustments > Invert and delete.

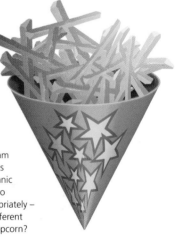

### Final image
The specialist 3-D tools of the Illustrator program are perfect for artificial design elements such as this carton, while Photoshop excels at the organic elements of this illustration. Combining the two lends your images variety, novelty and – appropriately – flavour. Try duplicating the same process to different effect – why not start by rendering a tub of popcorn?

## Layering ingredients

Preparing food often involves building up ingredients in layers. The snacks illustrated here demonstrate clear parallels with digital layers and filters that can be used to mimic texture. Why not take a cue from fast food and create your illustrations in a modular way?

**Hamburger layers ▼**
The three hamburger images show how easily Illustrator layers can be stacked, duplicated and rearranged. This method is an effective way to mass-produce simple images and reuse portions of a drawing without them looking stale. The examples would make great additions to a new menu or website.

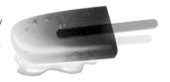

**Layered lolly ▲**
The ice is sketched in Photoshop using the Pen tool and filled with a yellow/red gradient. The stick is made in the same way and placed above it. The stick part inside the lolly is selected, moved to a layer above and set to 'Multiply'. Filter > Distort > Ripple is applied to distort the view slightly, and a few gradient-blended, liquid drops are added.

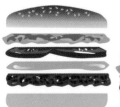

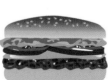

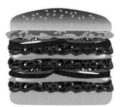

# Between fantasy and reality

This subject matter is as old as the fairy folk themselves. Goblins, trolls, leprechauns, pixies, imps and fairies good and evil all play the central role in tales and myths where morality needs to be explained. They inhabit the magical side of cartooning where, like the best superheroes, they can interact with any situation – real or imaginary. Employing Illustrator and Photoshop together provides the ideal vehicle for bringing together the fantastic and the realistic in a believable, yet make-believe fashion.

## Merging cartoons with photos

1 Make a pencil sketch of your fairy's pose. You will also need a digital photograph for the backdrop, which may influence your figure's interaction with her environment. When you are happy with your composition, scan the sketch into Illustrator and draw over the outline using the Pen tool, stroking the line in blue and expanding the line on the sweeping curves.

3 Tint the crown yellow, the lips red and the neck and skirt ruffs mauve. Now add the 'magic glow' all around the fairy's outline: select the whole outline using the black arrow Selection tool and add a feather of 10 pixels, with a soft 10 pixel brush, in a creamy yellow. This effect will be more visible against the background.

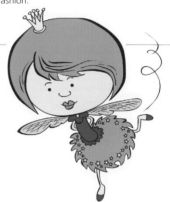

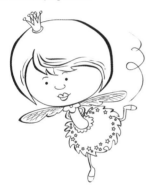

2 Import the Illustrator outline into Photoshop and choose a range of blue hues using the picker from the Colour palettes. When making your selection, consider contrasting the weights of tones. For example, a mid-blue, flat tint for the hair is best teamed with a much paler hue for the face, but one that is within the same range, such as warm blues.

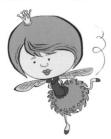

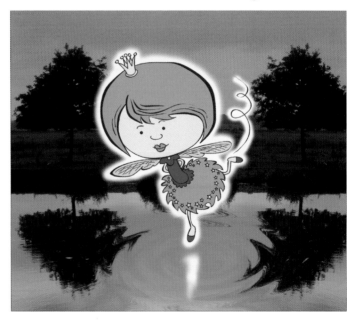

### Final image

This fusion of the digital photograph and simple cartoon typifies the world of fairies – at once overlapping and apart from our own. The white glow around the fairy figure keeps the real world at bay and draws our attention to the fact that she doesn't belong – as if her winter-blue skin and wings weren't big enough clues! The outlandish purple sky and ripple effect in the water further blur the definitions of 'our' world and 'hers', while the trees mirrored in the water only add to the unsettling, otherworldly, but strangely soothing effect.

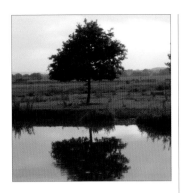

## Sharpening the focus

The fairy character and little devils here exemplify the irresistible temptation of chocolate cake.

**Wicked fairy ▷**
An ink drawing is scanned and taken into Photoshop and combined with an imported digital picture, which is cut out using the Selection tool and placed below the line layer. The figures are selected and tinted in flat colours and a separate layer is made for the 300-pixel soft airbrush background.

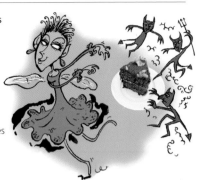

**4** To create the background, select and duplicate your digital photo of a tree (Image > Duplicate). Flip the image (Image > Rotate Canvas > Flip Horizontal). Bring them together on a Photoshop document large enough to fit both versions side by side. Drag the flipped photo on to the first image, which will import it as a new layer. Line up the two images accordingly. Alter the overall colour to blue (Image > Adjustments > Hue/Saturation).

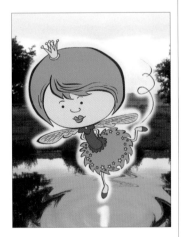

**5** Create the ripples in the still lake using the Ripple filter (Filter > Distort > Ocean Ripple). Now position the fairy over the background, where she conveniently hides the join in the middle of the two photographs. Her glow, previously invisible on the white background, will finally come to life – add a reflection of it in the water. Lastly, tint the sky lilac using Image > Adjustments > Hue/Saturation.

## Humorous contrasts

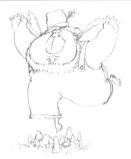

**1** Make a clear pencil outline sketch of the leprechaun (note the contrast of the bulky body and tiny feet). Scan and import the outline into Illustrator. Carefully trace over it with the Pen tool, expanding the line where appropriate to thicken it (Object > Expand). When you are satisfied with the drawing, import the image into Photoshop.

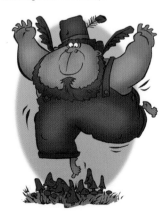

**2** Note the limited colour range here. The green of the skin is close to brown, with the red outline, beard and wings deliberately selected to complement it. The red spots on the toadstools mirror the beard and tie the picture together.

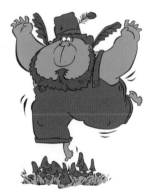

**3** Add tone overall by selecting areas for darker tinting using a soft brush. Then add Filter > Texture > Grain. Finally, tint an elliptical background shape.

## Final image
This version of the popular, male, Irish equivalent of fairies known as a leprechaun is a simply hued mix of jollity, luck and goodwill. The heavyset figure with tiny wings brings to mind the myth about the aero-dynamics of bumblebees!

# Legendary lighting

Ancient myths, such as the Greek legend of the Minotaur, offer perfect material for creating the cartoon or comic strip equivalent of a Hollywood blockbuster. As with all good movies, the mindset of a director is needed to facilitate the cartoon and find the high point of the narrative so that an audience is exposed to the full potential of the drama. With cartoons, this is achieved not only through the cropping and composition of images, but also through the use of a range of dynamic and dramatic lighting effects, such as fire, lasers and torches. Computer technology offers the digital cartoonist the chance to unleash high-impact effects on an audience by applying a selective range of simple tools and filters.

## Colour and spot lighting

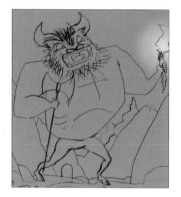

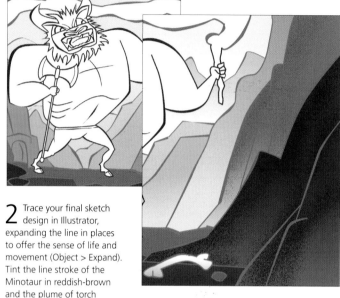

2 Trace your final sketch design in Illustrator, expanding the line in places to offer the sense of life and movement (Object > Expand). Tint the line stroke of the Minotaur in reddish-brown and the plume of torch smoke in pale blue. Tint the larger rock masses in flat colours taken from the same tonal range.

3 The mood of the cartoon is dependent on the subtleties of tone used on the rock strata. Take the image into Photoshop and apply these darker gradations within selected areas on a new layer, using low-Opacity brushes set to Dissolve. Place this layer above the flat colours so that the colour still shows through.

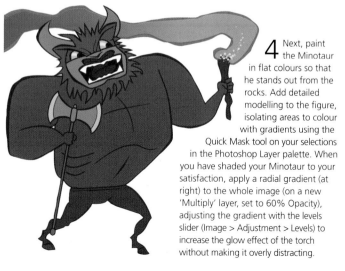

1 Give careful consideration to the way of presenting the character and situation to best achieve the effect you are aiming for. Looking at other cartoonists who specialize in your chosen area, and adopting some of their styling, may help. 'Thumbnailing' the illustration – experimenting with bold compositions in frames the size of postage stamps – may help kick-start the process by forcing you to think about shape and framing rather than fine detail. Sketch your final outline carefully in pencil. Scan the image into Photoshop, and apply a simple gradient overlay to give yourself an idea of where the central light source will fall.

4 Next, paint the Minotaur in flat colours so that he stands out from the rocks. Add detailed modelling to the figure, isolating areas to colour with gradients using the Quick Mask tool on your selections in the Photoshop Layer palette. When you have shaded your Minotaur to your satisfaction, apply a radial gradient (at right) to the whole image (on a new 'Multiply' layer, set to 60% Opacity), adjusting the gradient with the levels slider (Image > Adjustment > Levels) to increase the glow effect of the torch without making it overly distracting.

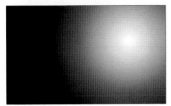

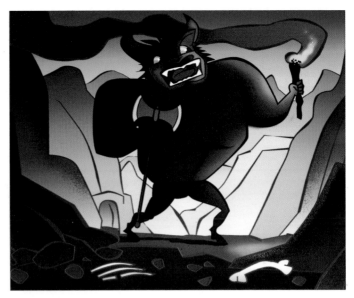

**5** Give the scene an eerie light with a gradated overlay of blue and brown in 'Hardlight' mode applied across the image. This will intensify and darken shadows at one end of the scale and highlights at the other. Check over the image and tweak colour imbalances. Finish the image by brushing in additional flames on the torch and the reflections in the Minotaur's eyes.

## Final image
This image is a masterclass on creating mood and drama. Blues and browns tightly grip the picture, drawing the eye to the red flame, its fiery reflection in the Minotaur's arm. The creature is framed by the gulley, pushed to the foreground by the cool blues of the receding trench, while dark gradients push in from all sides.

## Torchlight and laserlight

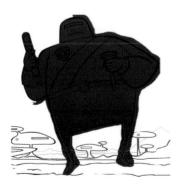

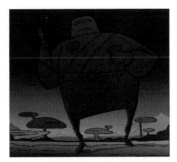

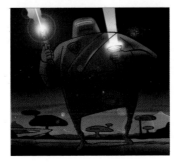

**1** This pastiche of a 'Judge Dredd'-style character begins as a careful Illustrator line sketch, including the background setting, which is then imported into Photoshop. Using Quick Masks to isolate the figure, apply a blue-and-red gradient overlay to it, leaving the background untouched. Erase any excess colour from around the edges of the figure.

**2** Colour the background scenery in the same assortment of gradients and flat colours, giving the cartoon an overall dark and gritty mood. The key feature of the picture is the laser gun blast, so use the Lasso tool to roughly select the area intended for it. Fill the area with a pink-and-white gradient.

**3** Add a thin, sharp line up the centre of the gradient with a small, soft brush, holding down the Shift key to ensure it is straight. Use Filter > Render > Lens Flare to model the intense light. Repeat for the torch, with a blue gradient. Add red and blue highlights to the figure on a new layer. Add the stars with a 100-pixel brush set to Dissolve, with a Flow of 20%.

## Final image
This image uses a time-honoured cinematic trick of using torchlight and/or laserlight to provide lighting and focus, in addition to giving a grittier, more ominous feel to the cartoon.

# Aerial perspective

The illusion of using colour to represent pictorial depth is known as aerial perspective – which should not be confused with aerial viewpoint, or the bird's-eye view! For centuries, painters have explored the relationship that exists between colour and distance. In nature, the scattering effect of atmospheric particles results in distant objects appearing bluer and washed out. Art, however, gives you licence to use any colours you wish. As a general rule, stronger, more primary coloured shapes grab immediate attention and are perfect for foreground elements, while paler pastel hues recede into the background, furthering the illusion of depth.

Photoshop is a great program to use for the creation of a cartoon with a receding background. As well as the extensive choice of colour palettes, numerous filters can be used to soften shapes, reduce focus by blurring or alter textures to suit.

## Final image

The colours may be emotive rather than realistic, but the eye has no trouble reading the distance in this image. The base and forefront of the picture are anchored with full-black shadows and heavy lines, while line weights diminish to nothingness towards the rear – the farthest objects lack keylines, becoming vague shapes in the autumnal sky. The complexity of the textured pattern on the man's coat brings him to the fore, as the eye slows down to decode the zigzags.

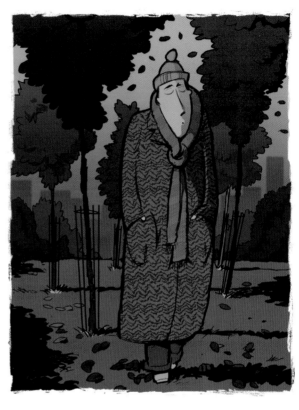

## Using colour to create depth

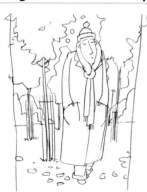

1  Make a simple outline pencil sketch that contains all the basic information for the illustration. Try to keep the shapes simple and bold. Scan this image into Photoshop.

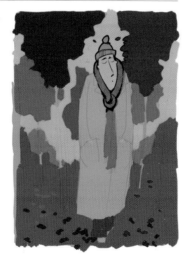

**Tip:** When inking over your pencils, don't try to replicate every nuance of the original sketch. Aim to capture the same freshness of line that was in your sketch – draw inspiration from that, rather than being a slave to your pencilled blueprint.

2  Duplicate this background layer and set it to 'Multiply' before deleting the original background. Create a layer for colour beneath the line art layer and roughly block in the various colours, using the Brush tool at 100% Opacity and Hardness. Reduce the Opacity of the pencil line layer to 50% using the slider. Now draw around the line in black, tracing it with a fine brushstroke, making sure your line is loosely and freely stroked for a more painterly effect.

**3** With the line work complete apply a fill pattern (Edit > Fill > Use > Pattern) to the coat. Make a simple arrangement of diagonal lines to create the basic 'herringbone' pattern. Tidy any pattern overlaps that stray outside the coat outline with the Eraser tool. A Gaussian Blur filter (Filter > Blur > Gaussian Blur) on the buildings in the background distorts the pixel pattern to create a different, yet subtle texture. Sections of the background are erased with the History brush to ensure that the foreground remains in focus. As a final, tonal

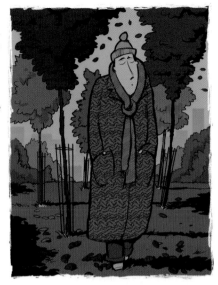

adjustment, you may wish to use a selection of gradients applied on layers above the whole image (as on the previous spread) to tie the colours together. Experiment with layer options – 'Multiply' and 'Hardlight', particularly – in order to give a subtle boost to the colours.

## Changing the scene

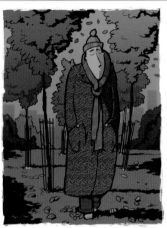

The same subject can be moved through the seasons by changing colours or filters. Simply slide the Hue/Saturation controls: Objects > Adjustments > Hue/Saturation. Isolate the figure with a Lasso tool/Quick Mask selection, or reinstate his colours with a History brush.

## Diminishing with distance

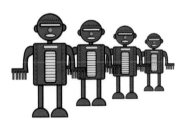

**1** Create a single robot figure in Illustrator and tint it in Photoshop. Duplicate the figure and then scale each duplication using the Scaling tool.

> **Tip:** Try this particular distance technique with other subjects. A mountainous landscape offers stunning pictorial depths, with trees and peaks receding into the background, becoming paler and more blurred as they diminish.

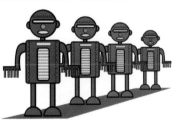

**2** Reduce the scale of each robot, altering the colour too. Shift the hue range further towards the recessive blue/mauve palette. Also adjust the colour Saturation (Object > Adjustments > Hue/Saturation).

### Final image

This robotic assembly line demonstrates the ease with which aerial perspective can be put into practice, and also underlines the effectiveness of the digital domain at mass-producing characters. With a copy of Photoshop and a representative character, you can produce an army of thousands in minutes. Just remember, for non-robotic characters, try and introduce quirks or imperfections to differentiate your cast of thousands.

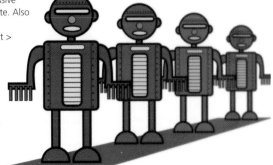

**3** Select the three robots behind the foreground figure, one by one. Apply Filter > Blur to the first and increase the level of blurring to the second and third. This technique is an effective way of increasing the illusion of receding depths.

# Pet portraits

Digital painting and rendering software offer excellent tools for creating pet caricatures – with their wide range of naturalistic media options, you will find it easy to capture the intricate details of furs and hairs – whether building up textures in layers of digital paint or utilizing bold colours and repeating patterns for a more abstract effect. The digital domain also offers an endlessly reworkable way to build drawings from brief colour sketches into fully rendered pieces of art.

Pets make great subjects for the cartoonist, offering a host of endearing, quasi-human traits that can be exaggerated or massaged into an amusing or characterful illustration – just think how many successful syndicated cartoons feature household pets as their stars! Enlarged noses, muzzles or ears can expose an animal's inner character, while large, emotive eyes anchor the drawing and make it relatable for human readers. Body shape too is an important indicator of cartoon

personality – a rotund pet dog reads as contented and friendly, while a skinny, stalking cat comes across as aloof or even suspicious.

Experiment and draw inspiration from family pets or animal photos in magazines, attempting to capture the nuances of their personality in a cartoon form. Work from very quick pencil sketches, elongating, squashing and exaggerating key features, before embellishing and adding detail in Photoshop and Painter, as below.

## Curious dog caricature

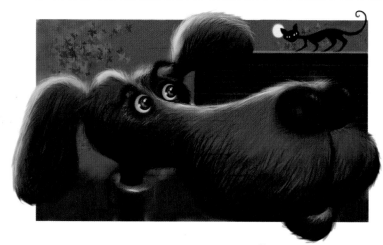

### Final image
Several effects increase the effectiveness of this image of a dog on the prowl. The exaggerated muzzle and ears – both overlapping the edges of the frame – draw attention to the canine's senses of smell and hearing, while the cocked ear directs the eye to what has caught the dog's attention – the cat, rendered shadowy, abstract and symbolic atop the wall. The dog's head replicates the shape of a dog's favourite toy – a bone. In terms of rendering, a series of fine lines in harsh highlight and deep shadow reproduce the fur without having to paint every fine hair. Finally, the carefully rendered eyes give us a 'human' point of entry into an animal portrait.

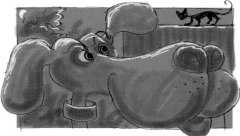

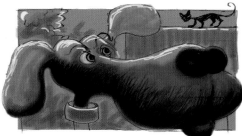

1 Make a quick pencil sketch. Scan it into Photoshop and make a light colour sketch on a new Multiply layer, using highlights and shadows of a single dominant colour to 'spot' the main areas of light and dark. Consider how the main elements of the picture interrelate – the moonlight along the top of the dog and the wall, the dog's black nose echoing the position and colour of the black cat and the shadows under the muzzle.

2 Flatten your image and import the layer into Painter, which has a much wider spread of naturalistic tools and filters, the better to replicate the organic elements of the dog's hair. Start to build up the texture of the fur and the wet nose using a fine brush in a dark pastel or charcoal material. Use the Blending tools to massage the colour into the basic blue of your image, leaving your lines sharper the darker the colour gets.

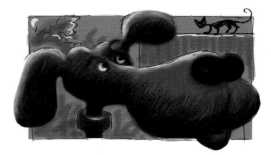

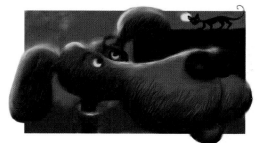

**3** Start to work in the other colours and compositional elements – paint in the base coat for the eyes and collar, and begin to block out the bushes and the back wall. Don't be afraid to go overboard on the smudging and blending of colours at this point – you want to create a variety in texture and tone within a limited palette, and will be tightening up each portion of the illustration at the final stage. Pay close attention to the shading around the eyes and mouth, and to the expressive eyebrows, which will need to stand out against both the mid-tones of the fur and the highlights.

**4** More colours are added to vary the palette: deep blue-greens for the suburban hedges and a dark brown for the brickwork. The composition has also been tightened – where previously the moon was a crescent shining from the top left, it is now a full circle spotlighting the cat. The full moon echoes the white circles of the dog's eyes, drawing the viewer's attention to the cat. The image is imported back into Photoshop for some final fine brushwork on the eyes and nose. The foliage leaves are created from a custom brush set to blue/ green, and a brick texture added as a pattern fill completes the picture.

## Sinister cat caricature

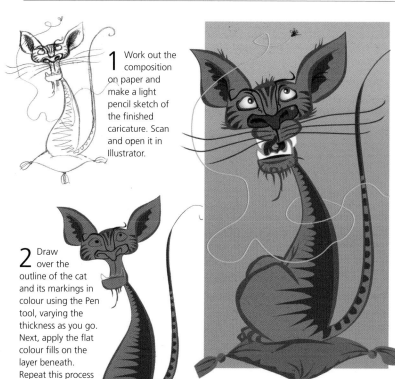

**1** Work out the composition on paper and make a light pencil sketch of the finished caricature. Scan and open it in Illustrator.

**2** Draw over the outline of the cat and its markings in colour using the Pen tool, varying the thickness as you go. Next, apply the flat colour fills on the layer beneath. Repeat this process for the purple cushion.

**3** Fill in the eyes with a radial gradient of orange to white and add the black coils of whiskers. Add overlapping tufts of deep orange to the outer line to lend variety to the fur. On a new layer, create a gradated rectangle background, bleeding from orange to mauve. Finally, colour the fly in black and delineate the flight trail in a pale blue colour, using the Freehand Pen tool.

### Final image
The elongated, top-heavy shape of this sinister cat provokes much amusement. The picture is anchored by background colours that reflect the cat and its environment, while the trail of the fly draws the image up and across the picture to its focal point. A simple image such as this would make a perfect Flash animation – simply moving the fly around the image with the cat's eyes following its course would be very effective.

# Digital fashions

A cartoon character's clothing is another element of your illustration that can expose their hidden traits or offer the audience clues to their personality – they can also offer readers a surprise: think of a multimillionaire in faded jeans and a charity shop T-shirt, for instance, or a homeless superhero who always wears the same immaculate suit. Clothing can indicate humour – clothes that cling too tight or hang too loose – or denote a particular time period or social setting, and can be an excellent shortcut to mood or place.

The use of layers and masks in Photoshop allows you to effortlessly swap mixed media scans in and out of line art creations, adding authentic patterns and logos to your pen-and-ink characters. Furthermore, digital pattern fills can quickly replicate many fabric styles, from pinstripe to plaid, taffeta to tartan.

## Using clothing to tell a story

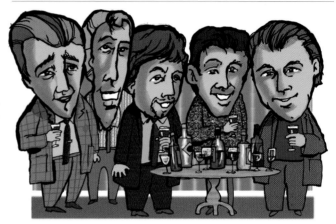

## Final image

This image of an after-work drinks party would work well as the opening spread of a men's lifestyle article, whether on fashion or alcohol habits! The suit and shirt patterns are easily applied, but add interest and texture, supporting the claims of the caricatured heads that each man is an individual.

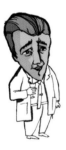

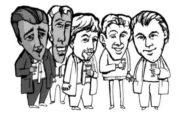

**2** Set the layer to 'Multiply', and add further characters to the group, each separately drawn and scanned in.

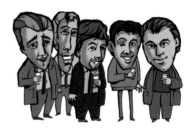

**3** Select areas of each character on a colour layer and tint them with flat colours. Add shading to the heads using a soft brush.

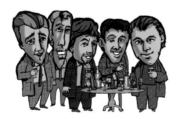

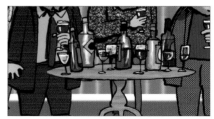

**1** Begin by drawing a single character in roughly hewn pen-and-ink lines – exaggerate and elongate any pertinent characteristics. Leave plenty of open space on the clothing, as this is where you will apply the pattern. Scan the illustration into Photoshop.

**4** Select the individual items of clothing using the Magic Wand tool, and add a variety of textures to the flat clothing on a layer above the colour art. Use scanned imagery of fabrics, or create a Fill Pattern that replicates stripes, checks or wool. Set the pattern layer to multiply, and adjust the Opacity until you are happy with the percentage of flat colour showing through.

**5** The table is a scanned pen-and-ink line drawing. Place this above the figures and colour with flat and shaded hues. Use sharp white highlights to pick out the bottles. Apply a wood texture to the table in the same way as the fabrics in step 4. To create the floor, add a single swatch of a neutral colour on a new background layer. The wallpaper is a similar swatch, with lines of orange drawn with the Brush tool, holding down Shift to ensure straight lines.

## Fashion photographer

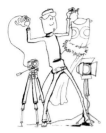

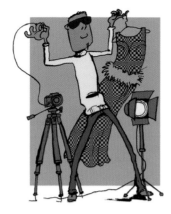

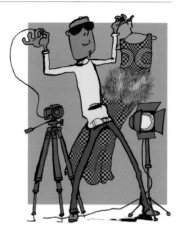

1 Use a dip pen and ink to make a loose, quirky drawing of a stereotypical fashion photographer. Scan and import it into Photoshop.

### Final image
This cartoon shows fashion's power to shock, surprise and delight – the neutral grey beige of the background, coupled with the soft primary colours of the character's clothes, are no match for the vivid pink print. The addition of a camera captures the eye and ties the image thematically with the photographer.

2 Begin to colour the image by selecting different areas on separate layers. Fill the dress area with the optical chequerboard pattern (Edit > Fill > Use > Pattern > Custom Pattern). Colourize this in a red selected from the colour picker on the desktop. Apply different shades of flat colour to all the other areas.

3 Scan a piece of pink fur fabric and import it into Photoshop. Place it on a layer that sits above the patterned dress. This juxtaposition of vibrant colour against the pattern of the dress causes it to stand out against the flat background, making it the focal point.

## Integrating patterns

While adding patterns to a character is a quick and easy process, the resulting image, if left unmodified, can often look flat and unrealistic. However, it is easy enough to distort and alter such combinations to create blended images that are more convincing.

#### Blending images ▼
Place your T-shirt logo on a new layer above your line art, distorting it to fit your character's physique (Free Transform tools or Filter > Distort > Ripple). Next, scan a piece of fabric for the texture – the weave is more important as colour can be adjusted in Hue/Saturation. Add the texture on a new layer above the logo, and change the layer mode to Overlay or Multiply to blend the two together. Erase any excess using the Eraser tool or Magic Wand/delete method. Adjust the Opacity of the texture layer until you are happy with the effect.

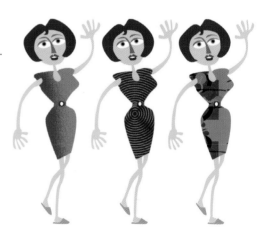

#### Fashion girls ▲
For quick results, create a single fashion model figure and repeat her several times. It is then an easy process to select and change the colour, pattern or texture of the dress. Use this method for making quick comparisons, and to build a fabrics library for future reference.

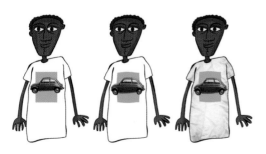

# Simple animation

Many simple Internet animations are created using Flash and it is ideal for anybody new to animation. It is designed to work in conjunction with vector and paint programs and they share common features, such as building images in layers. The different elements can either be created directly in Flash or in Illustrator or Photoshop and then imported.

Although the animation is still very simple, it is easy to lose track with so many layers of moving parts, so the following projects have been broken down into easy-to-follow stages. There are three main ways in which to animate your illustrations: 'Motion Tweening', where Flash creates frames in between two keyframes that make an object movie; 'Shape Tweening', where Flash creates frames that cause one shape to morph into another; and 'Guided Motion Tweening', whereby a character or element moves along a set path. The following pages outline these methods in more detail.

## Final animation

These sets of images comprise a very simple animation using two moving elements and a fixed background. However, it effectively demonstrates creating movement using keyframes, and some basic ways in which existing shapes – or Symbols, as they are called once converted to animatable components – can be moved, reshaped and made transparent.

## Converting shapes to animated objects

**Tip:** The most common keyboard shortcuts in Flash are as follows:
F8: convert shape into Symbol
F5: insert new frame
F6: insert new keyframe
Enter: play movie
Ctrl + B: 'Break Apart' – if you have created an image with clearly defined parts, for example, a word, this function will break it apart into its component units – in this case, the letters. These can then be animated individually.

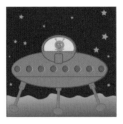 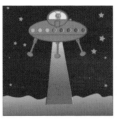 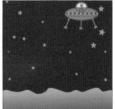

2 Our animation is of a spaceship taking off, a power beam extending underneath it. To create it, you will need to make a number of 'keyframes' at the key points of action. Flash will interpolate the animation between your keyframes. Click at frame 30 and press F5 to create 30 empty frames. To insert a new keyframe within those frames, click a point on the timeline and press F6, or right click and select 'Insert Keyframe'.

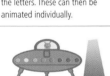

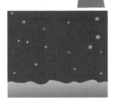

1 Create the spacecraft, beam and background in Illustrator, and import them into Flash as separate layers. Set the background as the background image, filling the whole of your frame. Change the spacecraft and beam into Symbols by pressing F8, or right-clicking and selecting 'Convert to Symbol'. Symbols are the moving parts in a Flash animation. Leave the background as it is.

3 Place the saucer on the ground at the bottom left of the frame, as shown, and hide the beam on the layer directly behind it. Now, add a new keyframe at frame 11 on the timeline. On this keyframe, select the saucer and move it directly up and into the middle of the picture. Extend the beam all the way down to the ground using the Transform tool. Select frames 1–11, click the Tween drop-down menu from the Properties toolbar and choose 'Motion'. This will create a smooth animation of the saucer rising into the sky, with the beam extending below it. Don't extend the slider bar of the beam past frame 11 when adding new frames – this will make it vanish at that point.

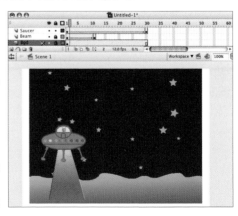

4 Create a new keyframe at frame 30, and move the saucer to the top right-hand side of the frame. Change the Alpha percentage of the saucer to 0% in the Colour Effect drop-down menu (Modify > Instance) – this will cause it to disappear by the time it reaches this frame. Press the Enter key on the timeline to preview your animation.

## Motion tweening

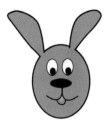

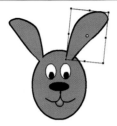

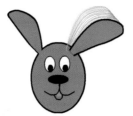

3 Use the Transform tools to rotate the ear on frame 30. Now select frames 1–30 by clicking and dragging the mouse across them on the timeline, and click Tween > Motion. This will create a smooth motion between frames 0 and 30.

1 Create a simple image of a friendly dog in Flash or import the image from Illustrator, with the right-hand ear brought in as a separate layer. The higher the frame rate, the more convincing the quality of animation. To adjust the frame rate of the project, go to the document settings. Around 12 frames per second will achieve the best result.

2 Select the ear and make it into a Symbol (right click on the object and select 'Convert to Symbol', naming it 'Ear'.) On the timeline, create a new keyframe at frame 30 by right clicking on the timeline and selecting 'Insert Keyframe'. This creates a new frame with both the dog and the ear in the same position as they are at frame 0.

### Final animation

This shows a very simple animation: a movement to a dog's ear. The ear is on a separate layer to the head and is made into a symbol. The ear is shown moving in two screengrabs: one shows the red 'onion skinning' outlines, the other the final effect. As well as movement, Flash allows you turn one shape into another – in this example a green square into a mauve circle. Make further variations on the theme of the moving dog ear and morphing shapes and increase your ambition each time.

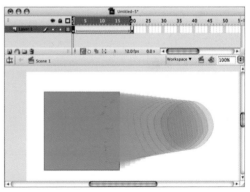

## Shape tweening

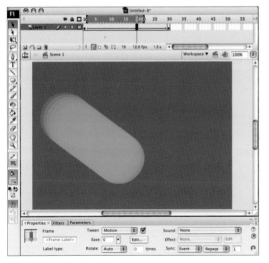

1 Morphing one coloured shape into another can be achieved easily, as follows. Draw a green square with the Shape tool, but don't convert it into a Symbol, as you can only 'shape tween' between vector shapes. Place the square at the left-hand side of the frame. Using the F5 key and the timeline, create 30 frames of animation. Click at frame 30, and create a keyframe using F6.

2 On this keyframe, select the green square and delete it. Draw a mauve circle using the Shape tool, again not converting it to a Symbol. Place it at the right-hand side of the frame. Now, select the frames on the timeline, click on the Tween drop-down menu in the Properties bar and select 'Shape'. Press Enter to see the square turn into a circle. You can loop this as a repetitive movement by selecting Control > Loop Playback.

**Tip:** Turning on 'onion skinning' by clicking the second button from the left in the timeline bar allows you to view previous frames in your sequence as 'ghosted' after-images on your current frame. This is useful for fine-tuning animations with the frame-by-frame method.

## Advanced motion tweening and guided motion tweening

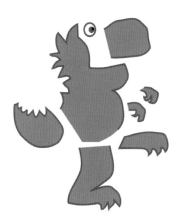

2 The screengrab on the right shows the library where every part of the dinosaur is named and saved as a Symbol to its own layer. The library can hold up to 16,000 symbols! Each Symbol should be saved as a Movie Clip (below), which is the top option in the dialogue box that appears when you select 'Convert to Symbol'. Motion tweening is used here in the same way that it is used on the previous spreads: to make the dinosaur walk, open its mouth and move its tail. However, whereas previously you were moving a single object from point to point using keyframes, you can now control several discrete objects, moving and scaling each one independently.

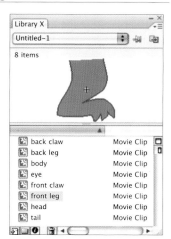

1 Create the component body parts. Either do this in Illustrator and import them as separate layers, or make them in Flash using the Shape tool. Save each piece of the body as a separate Symbol, which can then be moved and animated independently.

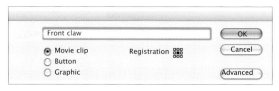

### Final animation

This is a slightly more complex animation made up of eight moving elements, or Symbols. The background, being a fixed, flat image, can be created in one of two ways – as a photo, or in the same cut-out method as the dinosaur. While the dinosaur moves and opens its mouth like a pre-school picture book character come to life, an outsize prehistoric bee buzzes across the animation on a guided path.

**Tip:** Tracking progress is important, and you will need to stop and check how everything is coming together. When using Flash in particular, your timeline will not always offer a 'realtime' preview of your animation or interactive functions, and movie clips cannot be played unless in an exportable format. While you can create a final 'publish' of your Flash project, it's easier to publish a preview, which renders faster and opens in your Macromedia Flash project window. Simply go to File > Publish Preview, or press F12 on your keyboard (PC or Mac).

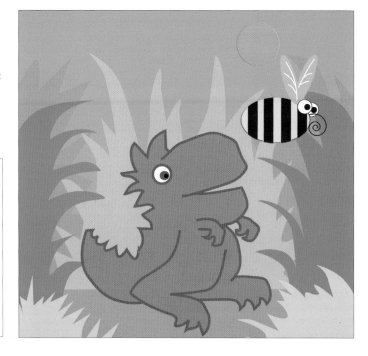

**3** Here, the dinosaur is fully assembled 'on stage' in Flash, on an empty background. The screengrab on the right shows the empty timeline and layers before any animation or keyframes have been assigned, while the one underneath it, shows the slider bars and keyframes afterwards. Keyframes can be created for each individual component part, or you can move several components on a single keyframe. Learning to 'micro-manage' your animation in this way will give you the greatest control – and results.

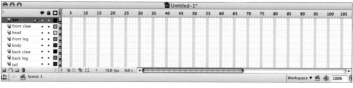

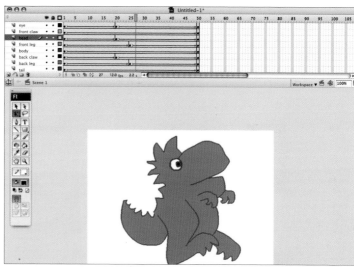

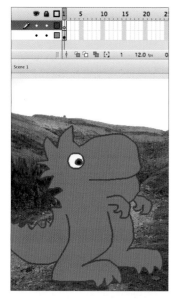

**4** To create a background for the dinosaur (a non-moving, non-Symbol part), you can either create a flat background in Illustrator or Flash in the same style as your character, or import a digital photograph, as shown on the left. This stage can be added at any point, as it will not interfere with your animation.

**5** The bee is the final element, here constructed in Illustrator, imported into Flash and saved as a Symbol. To make the bee move along a pre-determined path, do the following. Click the 'Create Guide' icon at the bottom of the layers menu (it's a blue cross and blue dot with a red dotted line joining them). Draw a wiggly path for the bee to follow on this layer. Click back to the bee's Symbol layer, select the Arrow tool and press the 'Snap to Objects' button in the Options area of the toolbox. Snap the bee to the guideline by moving it to the start of the line. Place the centre of the bee on the line (the centre will show as +). A black circle appears when the bee is snapped to the motion guide. Create a new keyframe at the end of the animation and snap the Symbol to the end of the line. Click the timeline and select Tween > Motion. The bee will now follow the guided path from beginning to end. Press Enter to see your completed animation.

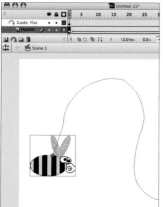

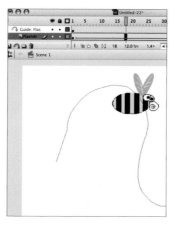

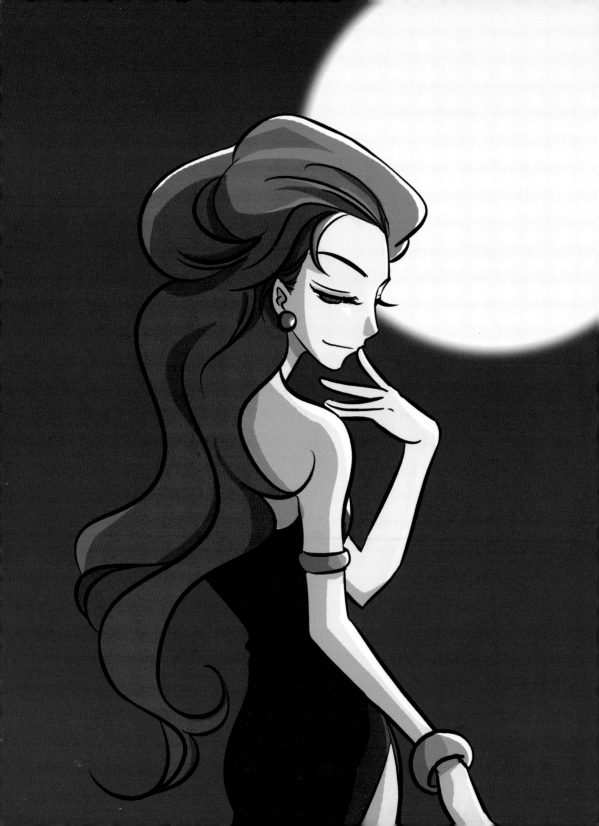

# How to Draw Manga and Anime

This section of the book provides you with everything you need to know about both the practice and history of this cutting-edge and innovative artform. It begins with the basic manga techniques, then shows various styles and methods to help you develop your own approach. There are features on genres such as shojo and shonen, and super-deformed manga characters in both hand-drawn and digital mediums. A wide variety of exercises and projects are included, and there are plenty of helpful tips on techniques and methods used by professional manga artists. The animated form known as anime is also featured, the history and latest achievements in anime are explored, and comprehensive instructions are included to teach you the skills needed to transform your drawn scenes into live-action anime stories.

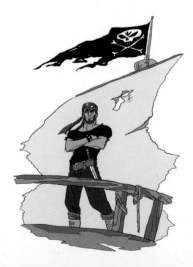

# The rise of manga

Japan began its modernization at the beginning of the Meiji era in 1868, under the 45-year rule of the Emperor. During that time the country absorbed and perfected influences from the West. But it was in the years after World War II, when the country entered its most frenzied period of creativity and industrialization, that manga crystallized into the form we now recognize. A new generation of creators, who had grown up reading the comic strips of Kitazawa and his peers, embarked on their own manga careers. This time, their ambitions were

greater: to use the medium to tell long-form stories, using all of the cinematic and artistic techniques at their disposal. The Japanese public fell in love with these new manga immediately, driving the weekly magazines in which they were contained to ever-greater heights of circulation success, and inspiring animated spin-offs, merchandise, de luxe collections – and imitators by the thousand. Magazines sprang up to cater for specific genders – shonen for boys, shojo for girls – and genre lines, too, were drawn.

## Modern originator of manga

Dr Osamu Tezuka (1928–89), one of the young artists inspired in childhood by Kitazawa's work, fused his love of Japanese cartooning with the Western influences brought to Japan by the American occupying forces after the close of World War II. He took aspects of the cartoons of Walt Disney and fused them to a larger-than-life, cinematic storytelling, to create the dynamic, action-packed, 'big eyes, small mouth' style that has become synonymous with manga today. In his lifetime, he produced more than 150,000 pages of material – but his breakthrough hit, and most beloved character, was *Tetsuwan ATOM* (*Astro Boy*). Although much of his work has never been translated from the Japanese, Tezuka's influence on the development of manga cannot be underestimated. His work ranged from environmental fables (*W3/Wonder 3*), 'talking animal' stories (*Jungle Emperor/Jungle Taitei*), 'the mother of all shojo manga' (*Princess Knight/Ribon no Kishi*), sexually explicit historical epics (*Cleopatra: Queen of Sex/Kureopatora*), medical thrillers (*Black Jack*) and personal explorations of cosmic philosophy (*Phoenix*). Tezuka turned his pen to virtually everything. His last major manga epic (worked on between 1974 and 1984) was an eight-volume critically acclaimed retelling of the life of Buddha.

Tezuka's stylistic innovations which encompassed slow-motion progressions through panels, cinematic angles and plenty of rapid zooms from long to close-up shots – would go on to define much of boys', or shonen, manga over the next half century.

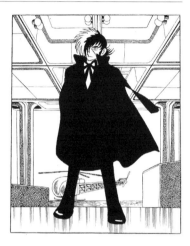

**Effortless cool** ▲
This panel from *Black Jack* showcases the medical anti-hero, just arrived by helicopter to perform another delicate operation.

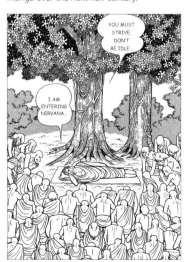

YOU MUST STRIVE, DON'T BE IDLE...

I AM ENTERING NIRVANA...

◀ **The death of Buddha**
Buddha's mortal life and Osamu Tezuka's eight-volume epic come to an end in this touching crowd scene, as Buddha passes into nirvana surrounded by his friends, protégés and students. The end of the story represented 11 years of serialized work by Tezuka.

**Birth of an epic** ▶
The cover for the first book in the English adaptation of the manga, designed by Chip Kidd, and split into eight translated volumes. The pages are presented in the 'flopped' format, where the original Japanese pages are mirrored so that the translation reads left to right.

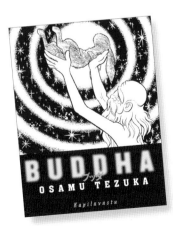

## The evolution of shojo

Machiko Hasegawa (1920–92) was one of the first female manga artists to become a part of this new manga era, creating the massively influential strip *Sazae-san*, which began in 1946 and remains popular – as a weekly radio and animated television show – to this day. Her focus on the everyday life of women and girls crystallized into the broad tenets of shojo, or girls', manga. This revolution broadened the scope of manga yet again, and pointed the way towards the 'something for everyone' marketplace of today.

The year 1969 saw another sea-change, as the Year 24 Group (named for the year in which they were born: Showa 24, or 1949) of female manga-ka (a level of artistic expertise) made their shojo manga debut, shuffling perceived gender and genre restrictions and introducing many of the categories we see today, from romance to superheroines and shonen-ai (love stories between two boys, aimed at young girls) and shojo (including science fiction). The ascendance of the Year 24 Group also marked the first point at which the majority of manga for women and girls were being written and illustrated by their target demographic. They also pioneered the use of non-standard panel layouts, softening or removing panel borders, or changing them to suit the emotional tenor within, and altering the entire grammar of manga illustration as a result.

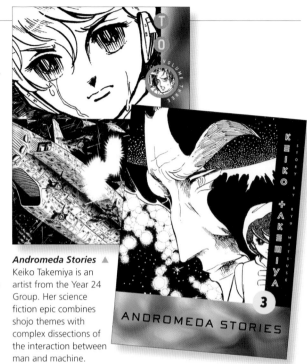

**Andromeda Stories** ▲
Keiko Takemiya is an artist from the Year 24 Group. Her science fiction epic combines shojo themes with complex dissections of the interaction between man and machine.

## The manga format

Manga stories are usually serialized in 20-page chunks in bulky magazines. They are published weekly or monthly on low-quality paper to keep the cost down. The most popular series are subsequently collected in *tankubon*, which we would probably call graphic novels. The tight deadlines required by weekly or monthly publications producing tankubon mean that most manga-ka work in studios with a handful of (largely uncredited) assistants. These assistants aid in the drawing of backgrounds, and the shading and toning process. They also usually 'graduate' to manga-ka status, themselves within a few years.

Manga's massive appeal is often credited to the sheer breadth of its content. Modern manga tell stories of the fantastical, the futuristic, the romantic, and the humdrum. Whatever their age or interest, there will be a series out there for every reader.

**Dragon Ball Z** ▼
One of the most prolific shonen manga, the image below shows only a small selection from the series.

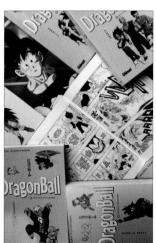

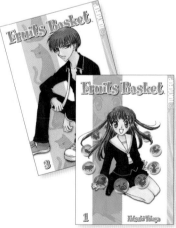

**Fruits Basket** ▲
The number one shojo manga in the English-speaking world, *Fruits Basket*'s enduring popularity rests on strong characters and a regular release schedule.

# Manga worldwide

Manga is a multibillion dollar industry even within Japan, but its reach now extends around the world, whether literally, as in the swarms of reprints and original titles that can be found on English-language bookshelves, or metaphorically, as in the liberal borrowings of style made by entertainment industries in the West. Manga's greatest strength is in its flexibility: it is a format rather than a genre, a delivery mechanism rather than a prescription of content. Fans of giant robot action, high school romance, extreme cookery, basketball, monstrous dimensions, psychological horror, daring crime thrillers or illegal street racing can all find something that appeals to them on the bookshelves.

## The manga invasion

One of the first manga to be translated and released in the West was Keiji Nakazawa's moving account of the Hiroshima bombing, *Barefoot Gen*. While other manga, such as *Lone Wolf and Cub*, were translated throughout the 1980s, it wasn't until the release of Masamune Shirow's *Appleseed* by Eclipse Comics and the recoloured edition of Katsuhiro Otomo's *Akira*, partially published by Marvel's EPIC imprint in 1988, that English-language demand for manga and anime began to grow, and the international market started to open up.

Throughout the 1980s and 1990s, series such as *Akira, Dragon Ball, Neon Genesis Evangelion, Pokémon, Oh! My Goddess, Ghost in the Shell, Battle Angel Alita, Love Hina, Ranama 1/2, Cowboy Bebop, Sailor Moon, Cardcaptor Sakura* and *Magic Knight Rayearth* saw increasing crossover success, bolstered by the twin assault of translated volumes and popular anime films and television shows.

### Manga magazines ▼
Part of manga's attraction in Japan is its ubiquity: a wide selection of magazines covering all genres and tastes can be found in every bookshop, newsagent and train station kiosk.

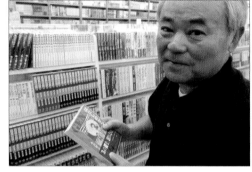

◀ **Keiji Nakazawa**
The author of *Barefoot Gen* browses his manga in a Hiroshima bookshop. Nakazawa began the semi-autobiographical, ten-volume series when his mother died of radiation poisoning, aged 60.

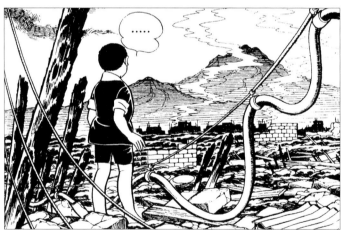

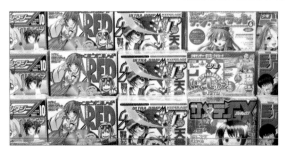

**Post-nuclear holocaust** ▲
Gen surveys the devastation in Hiroshima wraught by the atomic bomb dropped from the *Enola Gay*. *Barefoot Gen* deals with the harsh realities of life in the aftermath of an atomic explosion, from the initial devastation through to the more insidious effects of radioactive fallout. It ran in several mass-market magazines, from the early 1970s to the mid-1980s and has also been made into a television series and several animated films. *Barefoot Gen* was one of the first manga to be released in English from the mid-1970s.

## Manga explosion

The period 1996–7 saw the founding of manga publisher TokyoPop by Mixx Entertainment with its headquarters based in California, USA. It was soon followed by a cadre of competitors, and the modern era of aggressively promoted tankubon collections began. Such companies often have thousands of volumes in print.

Although there are evergreen titles that retain their popularity indefinitely, there are always new young pretenders arriving to claim the most popular manga crown. In recent years, these have included the chilling supernatural procedural *Death Note*, the ninja-in-training epic *Naruto*, piracy quest *One Piece*, twentysomething drama *Nana*, martial arts expert *Ranma 1/2*, female cyborg Battle Angel Alita also known as *Gunnm*, the ghosthunting *Bleach*, gothic spectacular *Vampire Knight*, über-violent school satire *Battle Royale* and steampunk adventure *Full Metal Alchemist* but this is just dipping a toe in the pool.

Today, manga has truly conquered the world of comics, especially among younger readers, who have grown up fluent in its intricacies and culture-clash elements. Titles such as *Naruto* and *Fruits Basket* regularly displace all comers from the top of the *New York Times* bestseller list when a new volume is released.

**Market leaders** ▶

Manga today is made up of an array of newly translated titles and Original English Language (OEL) titles.

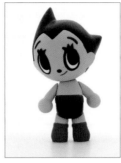

◀ **Manga merchandising**
As well as their enduring popularity as stories, the characters from many manga comics have become just as well known as pop culture icons, with *Astro Boy* (shown left) and *Hello Kitty* becoming phenomenal international sales successes in clothing, toys, bags and more.

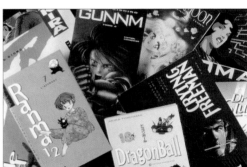

## Using this book

This book aims to make you a master of manga, able to turn your hand, pen or digital stylus to any one of the numerous manga genres, confident in your storytelling and draftsmanship abilities. The chapters to come will give you the opportunity to sample every style of manga, from contemporary shojo to futuristic shonen and all points in between. As you work your way through the book, or simply dip in and out, you'll find an array of helpful hints, tips and short cuts, in-depth walkthroughs of techniques, explanations of terms, materials and approaches. There are unique projects to test your understanding and ability, while giving you the opportunity to show off all that you've learned, all clearly illustrated by colourful examples from a professional manga-ka. Whether you're a manga novice or an experienced illustrator and writer, you'll find something new here to challenge and inspire.

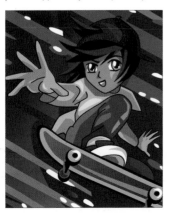

◀ **Skateboader**
Manga thrives on energetic protagonists, blistering action and colourful settings: so maximize your potential over the next few chapters.

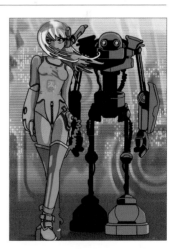

**Cyborgs and androids** ▲
Manga is an opportunity to let your imagination run wild: follow the guides and you'll soon have dozens of fully populated worlds to choose from.

# Styles of manga

There are many styles of manga around today, although some of the lesser-known genres don't make it over to Europe or the USA. Unlike comics in the West, manga in Japan is a national form of entertainment, and much like novels and films, covers just about every aspect of life. Some manga is purely fantastical and escapist, while other genres are centred around more realistic or educational themes. The genres listed here don't encompass the entirety of the manga scene – the more extreme forms are not covered – but this overview will provide you with a good idea of what's possible in your own work by showing you what is currently practised and popular in the world of manga.

## Core genres

Like other art forms, manga is grouped into genres according to common attributes. Stories which share similar elements and characters are usefully defined in this way. There are four core genres, as defined by the gender and age of their target readership. These include manga for children, for young people (divided into stories for both girls and boys) and mangas for adults in all sorts of possibilities and varieties. The core mangas are:

**Kodomo** ▶
This genre is aimed at the very young (*kodomo* means 'child') and based on humour. Sometimes the stories have no dialogue, so children who can't read get everything they need from the visuals.

Kodomo has its own traits that distinguish it from other genres:
1. Child protagonists who usually have cute, intelligent pets.
2. Humorous storylines.
3. Simple narratives with easy themes that can be understood by as wide an audience as possible.

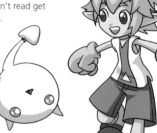

**Shonen** ▲

This is the most popular type of manga worldwide, largely because it is these stories that get translated and exported. Shonen is aimed at boys aged between 12 and 18 (*shonen* means 'boy') and thrives on constant, over-the-top action, adolescent male heroes seeking to be the best they can be, and quest-based narratives, structured almost like video games, with frequent 'boss battles' and 'levelling up'.

◀ **Shojo**
Meaning 'young girl', between 7 and 18 years old, *shojo* concentrates on emotion and feelings. Originally drawn by men, an explosion of female artists in the 1970s brought a sea-change in subject matter. Shojo stories share young female leads, themes of romance and friendship, and thought-provoking, not punchy, dialogue.

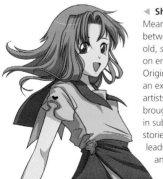

◀ **Seinen and josei**
Aimed at adults, seinen was first developed in the 1960s for men aged between 18 and 25, but its readership has expanded to men in their forties and beyond. Josei is targeted at women aged over 20.

Most seinen and josei stories share the following traits:
1. Protagonists in positions of authority: heads of companies, the armed forces, and so on.
2. More realistic, less exaggerated characters.
3. 'Cinematic' dialogue, lending the stories a filmic quality.
4. Sporadic use of comedy.
5. Adult themes, including realistic violence and erotica.

# Manga subgenres

Within the four main genres, there are various subgenres aimed at specific audiences within each defined age and gender group.

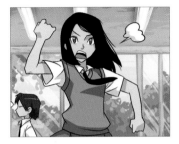

## Gakuen ▲

This means 'high school': appropriately, all of the stories take place within the confines of a school and are part of the shojo genre.

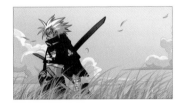

## Ronin ▲

This is a seinen manga featuring a rogue, 'masterless', samurai warrior. The warrior wanders ancient Japan, working only for those who meet his price, or defending the innocent. His reputation instils fear, loyalty and awe.

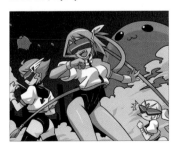

## Mahokka ▲

This means 'magical girls', and is a shojo comic featuring girls endowed with magical powers who fight evil. Stories start in high school, but often leave for more fantastic locations.

## Lady comic ▶

A subgenre for women, part of josei. Target readers of lady comics are women in their twenties, especially home or office workers. Stories reflect the lives of their readers, spiced up with romantic meetings and secret dates between aspiring lovers. It is the 'daytime soap' of manga.

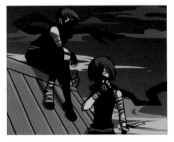

## Jidaimono ▲

Part of shonen or seinen. The protagonists of jidaimono are ninja or samurai-style characters. Stories are typically epic and set in historical Japan. They may be based on actual events.

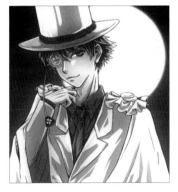

## Sentai ▲

Stories based on shonen or seinen genre. They are similar to jidaimono, but usually have a mythical edge, utilizing the full breadth of Japanese folklore, from demons to ancestral gods. The protagonists often have special, even magical abilities.

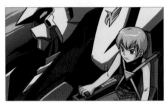

## Cyberpunk and mecha ▲

Both are science fiction settings. Cyberpunk showcases futuristic (even fetishistic) technology, often with cyborg (cybernetic organism) protagonists. Cyberpunk is a subgenre of seinen while mecha is closer to shonen. Mecha characters are usually pilots of enormous, man-shaped robots, defending the planet against a similarly giant alien threat. Common threads in both genres are the blurring of the boundaries between man and machine, and the difficulty of halting technological advancement, should it fall into the wrong hands.

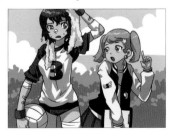

## Spokon ▲

This means 'sporty spirit' and is a subgenre of shonen or shojo. The shojo heroine has to make an arduous and demanding journey, as she strives to become the best at her chosen sport.

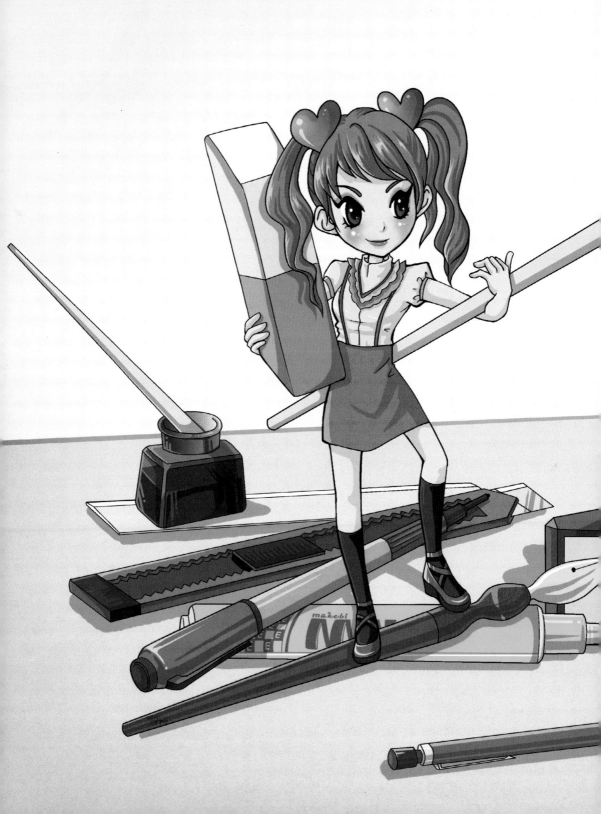

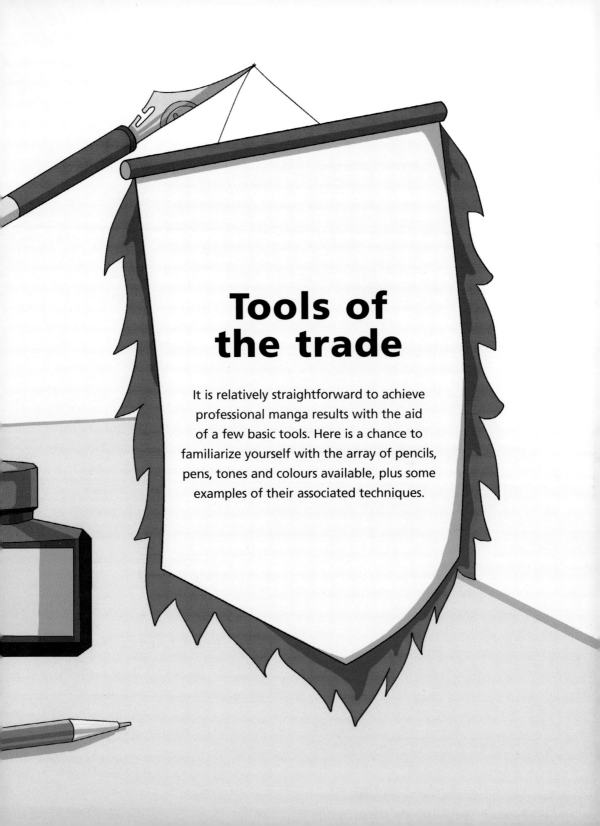

# Tools of the trade

It is relatively straightforward to achieve professional manga results with the aid of a few basic tools. Here is a chance to familiarize yourself with the array of pencils, pens, tones and colours available, plus some examples of their associated techniques.

# Pencils

What we draw with is as important as what we draw on. By experimenting with as many different tools as possible, you will discover what best suits your way of working. The pencils shown below are all suitable for drawing manga, but your choice needn't be confined to these.

The majority of manga are illustrated in black and white, so your everyday toolkit should consist of standard pencils, perhaps divided into 'line-making' and 'tone-making' types. If you are planning to ink your pencil lines for later reproduction or colour, for instance, you may find that using an HB pencil or mechanical pencil to lay down your lines may be all you need, with line weight provided later by brush or dip pen, and tone or colour added digitally. Water-soluble pencils and charcoal sticks are best confined solely to the colour and shading portions of your work. Alternatively, you may wish to ink your pencil lines, erase all of your initial 'construction marks', and add shading with softer-leaded pencils to retain a more organic, traditional-media feel.

## Types of pencil

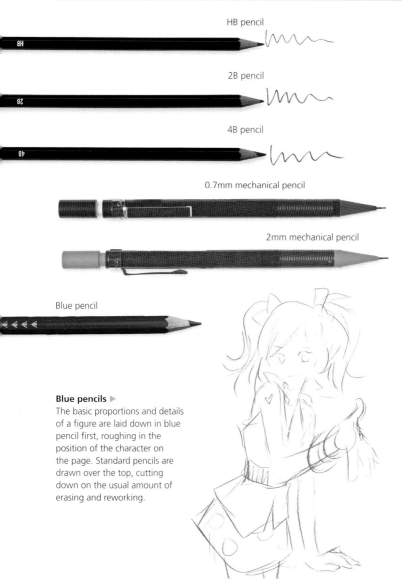

HB pencil

2B pencil

4B pencil

0.7mm mechanical pencil

2mm mechanical pencil

Blue pencil

**Blue pencils ▷**
The basic proportions and details of a figure are laid down in blue pencil first, roughing in the position of the character on the page. Standard pencils are drawn over the top, cutting down on the usual amount of erasing and reworking.

The pencil is an artist's most versatile tool, with an extensive choice available from hard and grey to soft and black. 'H' refers to hardness and 'B' to blackness. B to 9B are the soft, black choices. HB falls right in the middle and is the best general-purpose pencil. 2H to 9H are the hard pencils in the spectrum, with 9H the hardest. Their more permanent marks score the paper, making them more difficult to erase.

You may wish to invest in three levels of blackness: for example an HB, a 4B (very soft, very black), and perhaps a 2B (soft and dark grey). Pencil thicknesses also vary and your choice will depend on whether you want loose or precise lines. A selection of pencils to fit a standard pencil-sharpener are probably the most useful.

The tip of a mechanical pencil retains a consistent thickness: it blunts equally and never requires sharpening. A lead size of 0.5mm will produce fine lines, but snaps easily. A 2mm lead is resilient, but your lines will be less precise. A 0.7mm lead is perfect for both fine detail work and constant pressure. Mechanical pencils are excellent for manga creators who ink their pencil lines, as they allow for quick rendering without sharpening breaks. They are less useful for shading, as it's impossible to shade large areas with the side of a mechanical lead, or vary the line weight through pressure and alteration of angle.

Many artists use a blue pencil to sketch out ideas or block in proportions because blue doesn't show up when scanning line work in black and white or greyscale. An artist creates initial layouts in blue, then uses an ordinary pencil to go over the marks they want to keep. It is important not to press too hard when using a blue pencil to avoid marking the paper.

## Erasers

A good eraser is essential, as you're bound to make errors or change your mind as you draw. You can also use an eraser to add highlights, rubbing out areas of shading to let the white of the paper show through. Most erasers are rubber, which can leave residue on the page or tear the paper. An alternative is a malleable putty rubber, which leaves no residue, and also erases softer pencil lines. Don't use a putty rubber to erase large areas of drawing, as they quickly become warm, which leads to smearing of marks.

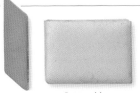

Eraser          Putty rubber

## Mark-making

The term mark-making describes putting your pencil to paper and observing and controlling how the pencil reacts. Try your mark-making with a variety of pencils. Create as many types of lines as you can – straight or spiral lines, shading, shapes etc – and think about how these could be applied to your drawing. Create a library of the marks that are most appealing to you.

Manga illustration is all about the use of thin, open and precise line work – 'cartoony' areas left open for tone or colour. With that in mind, the most common mark you make will be a simple line: curved, straight or a mixture of the two. Finding a pencil that sits comfortably in your hand, and a lead that doesn't blunt or snap too quickly is half the battle.

Shading is where mark-making comes into its own, as shown by the examples below. Simple ways to vary your shading include pressing harder with the tip of the pencil to produce lines of increasing thickness as the pencil tip blunts (too much pressure will break the lead). Using the side of the pencil produces a thick line immediately, which also increases with pressure.

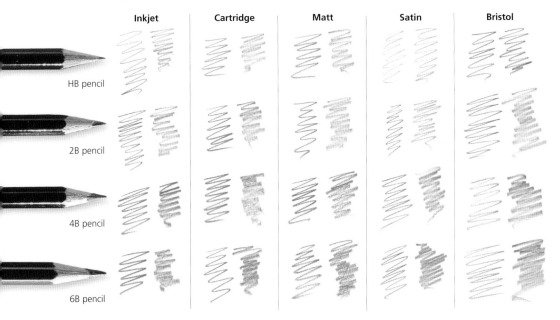

| | Inkjet | Cartridge | Matt | Satin | Bristol |
|---|---|---|---|---|---|
| HB pencil | | | | | |
| 2B pencil | | | | | |
| 4B pencil | | | | | |
| 6B pencil | | | | | |

### Water-soluble pencils ▶
While not useful for everyday pencilling, water-soluble pencils literally blur the line between pencils and paints, creating impressionistic tone and colour effects.

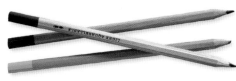

### Pencil-on-paper effects ▲
These marks show how the choice of paper and pencil affect your drawing line. You'll see how different marks suggest themselves for different purposes – from easy-to-erase pencils ready for inking to softer shades perfect for the line work on a watercolour cover.

# Pens and inking

Inking is what is meant by putting the final lines on the page. This is what you do once you have laid down your pencil lines and are ready to commit to the art you have created. Inking over your pencil marks will make them bold and clean; suitable for scanning, reproduction and print.

If you are inking by pen, you can begin with something as humble as an everyday rollerball. The professional choice is either a dip (nib) pen or a technical pen (a Rotring or equivalent). Dip pens suggest greater depth than technical

pens, as you can vary the line widths by applying pressure to the nib. The lighter you press your nib on the page, the thinner the line; the harder you press the nib, the wider you'll force its prongs, creating a thicker line. Technical or fineliner pens, on the the other hand, produce consistent results and are easier to use. You don't need to replenish their ink supply every few marks, and can worry less about blotting. If you rest a dip pen in one place you will soon have a blob of ink on the page, but technical pens are not nearly as free-flowing.

## Types of pen and nib

### Dip pens ▼
Look closely at an example of published manga and you will notice a variety of depth in the finished lines. Lines will often start thick and end much thinner, which is achieved by changing the pressure exerted on the pen. Dip pens require dipping ink and the ink has to be replaced after every few strokes. However, the ink is considerably more resilient to light and the erasing process than that in a technical or fineliner pen. Don't try using a fountain pen as the ink that comes in standard cartridges is not of sufficient quality.

### Technical pens ▼
Many operate using ink refill cartridges, giving long-lasting consistency of line in a wide variety of thicknesses, though you cannot alter the thickness of the line while drawing. Be aware that the ink in some pens may be picked up or 'greyed' when erasing, giving spotty results when scanned.

### Rollerballs and fineliners ▼
Traditionally handwriting pens, these disposables can provide a clean technical line in an instant, and are often useful for touching up areas of black after erasing pencil lines and finding you've missed a spot. They have relatively slow drying times, however, which can lead to smearing.

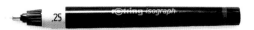

Technical pen

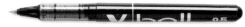

Rollerball pen

Technical pen

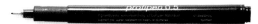

Fineliner pen

### Nibs ▼
Pen nibs come in a wide variety of shapes and sizes, and finding the most effective ones for your work is largely a process of trial and error.

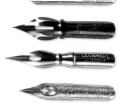

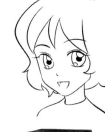

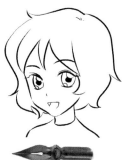

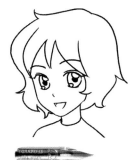

### Round nib ▲
Suited to all types of line work, a round nib is the most versatile. The width of the lines produced will vary depending on the pressure that is applied.

### Turnip nib ▲
Easy to use and can achieve lines of various thicknesses. However, it lacks the flexibility to adjust with pressure and is often used for making even lines.

### G nib ▲
This type of nib also lacks flexibility, and is used to produce steady thick lines. It holds more ink than a turnip nib, so can be useful for ruling in panel borders.

## Inking

Drawing with a dip pen is a knack that requires practice. Once you get used to handling the pen, however, the results are easy to appreciate.

How you hold your pen is important. Grasp it close to the nib to increase stability. The farther up the shaft you hold the pen, the more your lines will wobble, and the less control you will be able to exert. The angle at which you hold your pen is also important: ink is drawn on to the page through surface tension, so there's no need to hold your pen perfectly upright. Treat it almost as you would a pencil, but remember that the shape of the nib and its prongs make it easier to draw a stroke from the top down to the right (rather than to the left) or from the bottom up to the top. Rotate your paper, or alter your technique, to prevent nib-skipping and ink spatter.

## Dipping the pen

The golden rule is to keep the pen as free from excess ink as possible. If your pen comes out dripping, you've got too much. You will get beading, or strokes that are too thick at the beginning of a line. It's important to keep your ink flow even and predictable.

One way to do this is to decant ink into a separate inkwell, up to a level where you can almost touch the bottom without submerging the pen beyond the nib. This ensures you draw an equal amount of ink each time you dip. Preventing ink from reaching the pen's shaft also stops stray droplets from falling on to the nib.

Alternatively, keep a scrap of paper or card (preferably the same kind as you are working on) to test ink consistency by drawing a line every time you dip your pen. You can shake excess ink on to the scrap as well.

**Tip:** Don't become too fixed or rigid in your adoption of one form of pen over another. Many artists use a combination of both dip and technical pens – dip pens for organic, natural elements and technical or fineliner pens for backgrounds and inanimate objects.

**Pens in practice** ▼
These two drawings show the same character illustration made with different pens. The left used a dip pen, the right used a fineliner pen.

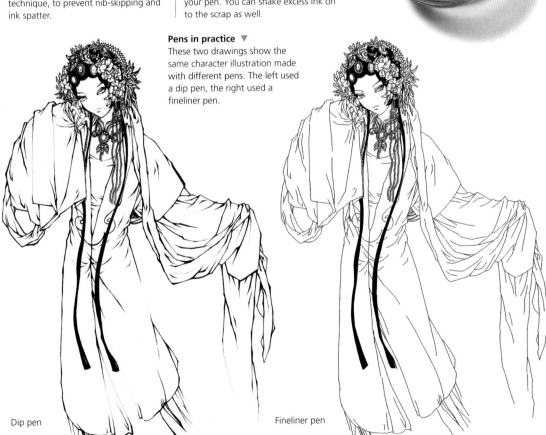

Dip pen

Fineliner pen

# Brushes and paper

You can also use brushes to ink your work. It's not as fast a process as using a pen, but it produces a smoother result, particularly when it comes to curves. A brush can also hold more ink than a dip pen, which makes for longer lines without returning to the inkwell. In short, the brush is a far more flexible inking tool, but it takes more practice to master. A brush also needs more care and attention than a pen. A dip pen has only one nib, whereas a brush has innumerable, far more flexible and delicate components. The head of the brush, or 'tuft' as it's otherwise known, is made from animal hairs or synthetic fibres, and needs to be kept in good condition. Don't move your brush abrasively against the paper, or you will disrupt the hairs, which will detract from your ability to keep lines clean and even. More importantly, clean the brush thoroughly after every use, reshape the tuft while wet, and store your brushes tuft-up when not in use.

## Tufts

A brushhead or tuft comes in various shapes and sizes and is held in place by a metal clamp or ferrule. In the same way that you select a nib, your choice of tuft will depend on the effect you want. For manga inking, you'll need a relatively thin, round tuft, or a small selection thereof. Below are the most common tuft types.

**Brushstrokes** ▶
This composite image shows only a small sample of the type of marks possible with a single brush – from wash effects to fine strokes. Note how just one tuft can create a wide variety of strokes depending on the pressure applied, the angle of attack and the amount of ink on the brush.

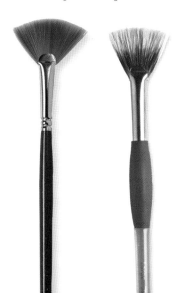

### Rounds ▼
This tuft is a cylinder of hair that stretches down to a point. Like the round nib, it is the most generally applicable of all the tufts as it can be used to apply ink in both thin and broad strokes. Challenge yourself to ink an entire page using just one thickness.

### Flats ▼
This tuft is square with a flat end. It is useful for filling in large areas of colour and for making wash effects. If used on end, held at a right angle to the page, it can also produce steady thin lines with the tuft held at the correct angle.

### Filbert ▼
This triangular-shaped tuft is halfway between a flat and a round. It starts off flat but tapers to a point, meaning that by varying pressure you can create lines that taper from thin to thick, vice versa, or any point in between. It works best at larger sizes.

### Fan ▼
A fan brush has a thin layer of bristles spread out by the ferrule. It is used to lay down parallel lines of ink by holding the brush end-on, at right angles to the page, often with a nearly dry tuft. It is useful for applying certain hatching and shading effects.

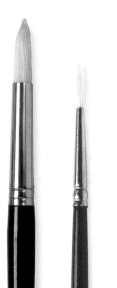
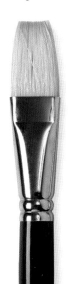
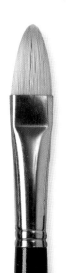

## Brush sizes

Brushes come in varying sizes, each with a given number. You only need a small selection: some small rounds for detail work; a larger brush for filling areas. The number corresponds to the circumference of the ferrule. There is no international numbering system or standard measurement the industry must follow, and size varies between manufacturers. You should be able to find equivalents to your favoured brush sizes anywhere in the world.

**Brush selection** ▷
An assortment of brush sizes like this will in all likelihood be quite sufficient for your manga career. Art shops will often sell combination packs of brushes, or you can assemble your own selection based on personal preference. The variety is extensive and can include natural and synthetic bristles.

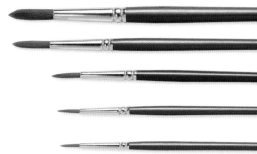

## The correct ink

Whether you ink with a dip pen or a brush, or more likely a mixture of the two, the only ink you should use is Indian ink, the lifeblood of comics illustration. Unlike other types of ink, Indian ink contains shellac, so it is resistant to wear and tear (particularly the kind caused by rubbing out pencil marks) and it dries very quickly.

This fast-drying ability is precisely why it can't be used in fountain pens, because it would soon cause a blockage. This is why it's important to thoroughly clean tools after you finish working – so rinse your brushes and pens under water. Washing-up liquid can help keep pen nibs and brushes clean, but be sure you rinse it all off before drawing again.

**Tip:** Blotting paper can be handy to clean up small spills, and a small container of water will keep tools clean while you work. A piece of scrap paper of the same specification you are drawing on will allow you to experiment with the way your brushes and pens will react before you attempt your final piece.

## Different types of paper

Nib

Brush

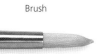

The five papers described here can all be used for manga. There are many other papers, but as manga is usually laid down in pencil and ink on to white surfaces, these are the most suitable.

**Inkjet paper**
This paper is thin, and when saturated with ink can begin to 'cockle' (crease). It's also easy to inflict damage with your eraser. Inkjet is cheap, and can withstand pencils and inks making it ideal for practice and sketching.

**Cartridge paper**
A thick, heavy paper, preferred by many artists and illustrators, originally used for making cartridges in weaponry.

**Matt finish paper**
Smooth finish is great for brushwork. Ink dries quickly, but you'll need a lot of white gouache to cover errors.

**Satin finish paper**
Use a rollerball rather than a dip pen. A good choice if you are inking by brush, although large areas of black brushmarks may appear inconsistent. Satin finish paper takes longer to dry than matt.

**Bristol board**
This paper is thick, with a smooth finish suitable for inking, making it the industry standard for comic illustrators. Holds ink well and allows for easy erasing: it's tough enough to be sent worldwide without too much in-transit creasing.

# Tone

Adding tone is about adding weight to your drawing. You are essentially adding marks in different ways, whether that means adjusting the width of the lines, the length, or how light or dark they are. Tone adds dimension, mood, shade, atmosphere and texture to a drawing. You can practise its application by making sketches of your work on sheets of tracing paper. Once you've created a few examples, you can pencil different versions of tone and overlay them on your final piece. When you come to the final inking stage, pick the example that strikes you as the most effective.

There are various methods of applying tone. One classic example is cross-hatching – parallel shading lines that cross over one another. Another example of tone is washing, or using diluted black ink to apply grey shades. Washing is more subtle than hatching, and will soften the look of the final piece, diminishing the hardness of the main inks. Ultimately, the toning you choose will depend on the mood or genre of your story. If your story is light-hearted, for example, you are likely to confuse the reader by including large areas of shadow and may wish to avoid significant toning altogether.

## Examples of tone

The following examples demonstrate how lines drawn in various ways create varying tones. Some styles have been used more than once, but in different combinations. All of the toning methods here are based on layering lines over one another – with the denser regions being the darkest, and areas of light being shown by an absence of tone. In any given image, you may find yourself using a variety of these tones to provide different textures to the hugely various human, animal, vegetable and mineral inhabitants of your manga artworks.

> **Tip:** Match tones with objects: scribbled, organic lines for people or clothes; rigid hatches or shiny stipples for technology.

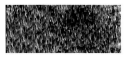

**Short lines** ▲
Shading is built up by overlapping short lines drawn in the same direction.

**Dots** ▲
Fairly evenly spaced dots suggest light and shade through their relative density.

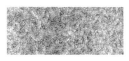

**Cross-hatching** ▲
Straight lines cross over one another to create mesh-like patterns. The denser the lines, the darker the area.

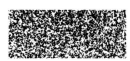

**Spray stippling** ▲
A scattergun approach creates rough areas of light and shade, again dependent on the density of marks.

**Short lines** ▲
Shadowed areas are tightly packed with lines, almost overdrawn.

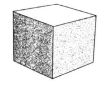

**Dots graduated** ▲
Dots can be drawn closer together or made larger to suggest greater darkness.

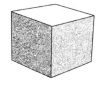

**Cross-hatching** ▲
Hatches can be overdrawn to create darker areas, or the meshes further contracted.

**Spray stippling** ▲
A spray approach to shading is excellent for replicating stone and brickwork.

**Short lines** ▲
Shadows are built up in layers, working from the outer rim towards the highlight.

**Dots graduated** ▲
Dots become larger and more tightly packed the farther they are from the impact of light.

**Cross-hatching** ▲
Again, overdrawing suggests dimensionality. You may want to use an eraser to create white highlights.

**Spray stippling** ▲
Shadows are stippled on in increasingly stronger layers to provide a contrast between areas of light and shade.

## Using tone

Adding tone appropriately will increase the effectiveness of your drawing and your story. But it is important to understand what you are trying to achieve beforehand, particularly since there are so many possibilities at your disposal. The example shown here illustrates how different shading techniques can be created using lines and areas of solid black, and how different tones can be integrated into the same image.

### Tones in practice ▶
Dramatic results can be achieved with your line work by combining a number of different toning effects. Approach each of your tones as a texture in your artistic arsenal. Here, cross-hatching and dots capture two different fabrics, some spray stippling brings the hair to life, and an array of short lines behind the character create a hazy night scene or a paparazzi-stalked premiere.

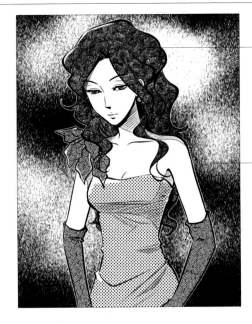

Though all of one tonal strength (save the highlights), the texture adds interest to the hair without distracting from the line work.

The short lines and large highlight areas suggest both a background and an emotional state, while still throwing the focus forward on to the woman.

## Ink-washing

If you are still experimenting with ink-washing, you may wish to work from a photocopy of your finished inks, as it is difficult to make corrections to your shading once you begin.

The principle behind ink-washing is simple: by mixing your Indian ink with varying percentages of water, you can apply (with a brush) consistent, strong and long-lasting greytones. You'll need to experiment with the mixtures of course (start with one part ink to one part water as a mid-tone, and add or subtract water and ink from there), and decant your ink into a suitable palette or container, but the actual act of washing is the same as painting, only in greyscale. You'll find that layers of shading can be built up by overwashing a light grey section a second, third or fourth time.

### Washes in practice ▶
Ink washes add a more naturalistic, painterly effect to your finished lines, adding in a human touch that pre-cut or computer tones can sometimes lack.

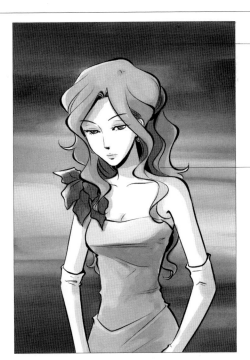

Darker areas are built up in layers. The inexact mixtures of tones create a dreamier, fogbound quality.

Darker areas are painted over a mid-tone in successive washes. Highlights are left as white paper.

# Colour

Despite advances in printing technology, and the increasing availability of high-level digital colouring packages, the vast majority of manga are still printed in black and white for reasons of cost and time effectiveness. Thousands upon thousands of books and weekly magazines are printed every month, usually on cheap paper. The absence of colour also gives many anime adaptations an extra edge, as fans of a manga book series finally get the opportunity to see their favourite characters in full-colour action. That does not mean there aren't any opportunities for colouring your work,

or even that you should not pursue a full-colour manga story. Promotional purposes and cover art for your manga will be the most obvious venues, so it's worth knowing the colouring basics, as you'll never know when an opportunity might arise. Given the increasing popularity of comics on the Internet, you may find that the only way to grab attention for your creation is to release it in full, anime-challenging colour. The majority of comics today are coloured digitally, using packages like Adobe Photoshop, but the principles of colour are the same, whether using traditional or digital media.

## Paints, inks and dyes

Walking into any art store will provide you with a thrilling and bewildering array of colouring choices. Paints such as these offer a range of bold ways to tint your manga illustrations.

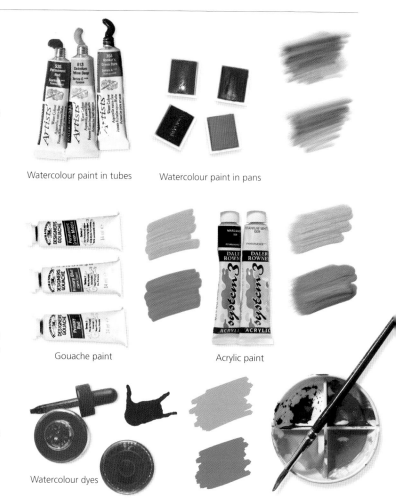

**Watercolour paint** ▶
Available in two forms: pans, which are compressed blocks of colour that need to be brushed with water in order to release the colour, and tubes of moist paint. Watercolours seldom have a natural white; white is created by leaving areas of the paper unmarked, and lighter shades created by thinning the paint with water.

Watercolour paint in tubes      Watercolour paint in pans

**Gouache paint** ▶
Soluble in water, allowing you to make alterations, gouache may crack when dried. The natural white can be used as a corrective.

**Acrylic paint** ▶
A brighter finish than gouache, acrylics have a stronger sense of colour. Soluble in water, so just as versatile as gouache, they can also be mixed with gouache for a watercolour finish.

Gouache paint      Acrylic paint

**Watercolour dyes** ▶
Similar to watercolour paints, dyes give even brighter results. They are used for more 'in your face' productions, as dyes are very intense – perfect for manga with high energy and bright colours. Dyes also have a high tolerance to exposure from direct sunlight.

Watercolour dyes

## Pencils and markers

### Colouring pencils ▼
Available in soluble and non-soluble varieties. Blend colours with cross-hatching or a subtle fade from one complementary tone to another. An affordable alternative to paints or inks, they tend to suffer when digitally reproduced.

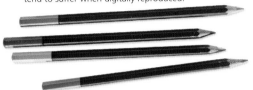

### Markers ▶
Coloured markers are the staple of traditional-media manga colouring. The technical ability of the artist very much controls the success of the outcome. In good hands they reproduce well, remain bright, don't bleed on the page or combine unfavourably with Indian ink. They come in a wide range of shades. You can combine two or even three nibs into a single pen, and they can be overlaid to produce darker shades of the same colour, or can be easily blended with other hues.

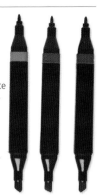

## Using colour

Adding colour is an excellent way to add a new dimension to your creations, whether on the cover of your manga or on a pin-up. A single colour image of your cast can 'resonate' through your entire story, even if the rest of the pages are in black and white. Give your central character bright green hair on a cover and that character's hair will 'read' as green throughout the rest of the story.

### The colour wheel ▶
Every colour has a complementary opposite. Combine complementaries for more pleasing compositions.

The colour wheel shows the gradients of each tone, from light to dark, in each hue.

Some colours 'jar' in interesting ways when placed next to one another: purple and orange, red and blue, for example. Try out these if you want an unsettling or eye-burning effect on your manga page.

Colours directly opposite are complementary: red and green, blue and orange, purple and yellow etc.

Try creating your own colour wheel with your chosen medium, and practise blending and mixing colours to achieve the required variances in tone.

## Colour in practice

Each traditional media has different techniques to master, and only by experimenting will you be able to find a colouring style that suits you. The basics, however, are shared by all. Pencils, markers and paints should all be laid down lightly on the first 'pass', leaving highlighted areas empty so that the white of the paper shows through. After demarcating highlights, add a mid-tone of your chosen colour, and add areas of shadow by going over this tone with the same pencil or marker a second or third time.

### Complementary colours ▶
The deep green of the hair draws our attention to the central characters, while the fiery orange-red borders the image and maintains that sharp focus.

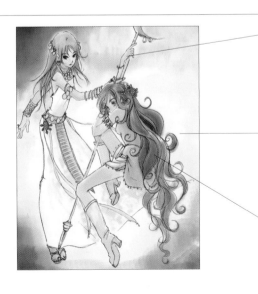

Uses a limited colour palette. Notice how the background and hair are reflected in the skin tones and dress detailing.

The white of the paper is left to shine through as an extreme highlight.

The deep green of the hair is in complementary opposition to the dark red.

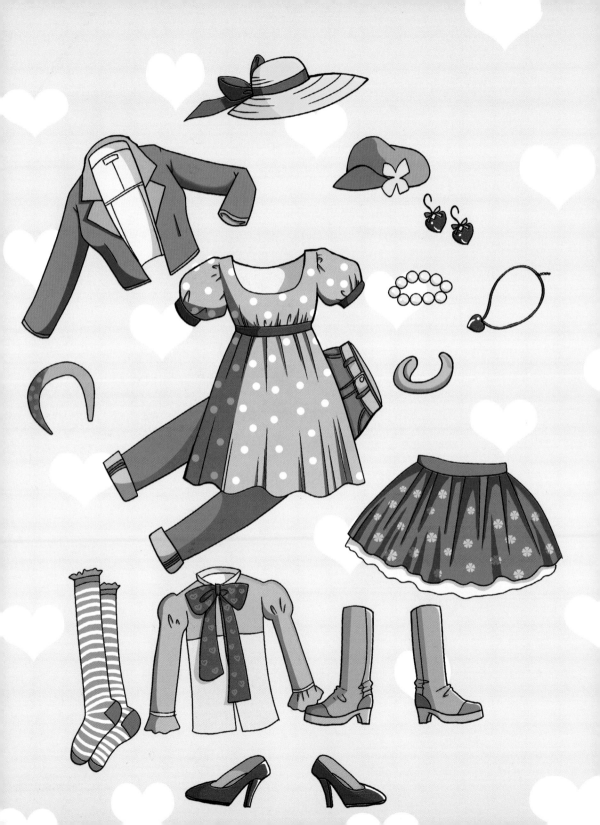

# How to draw a manga character

The manner in which characters are drawn is the main feature of how manga, or any type of comic strip, works. A reader has to identify each character in a story on every panel – after all, it's the characters that are going to carry the majority of the narrative from page to page.

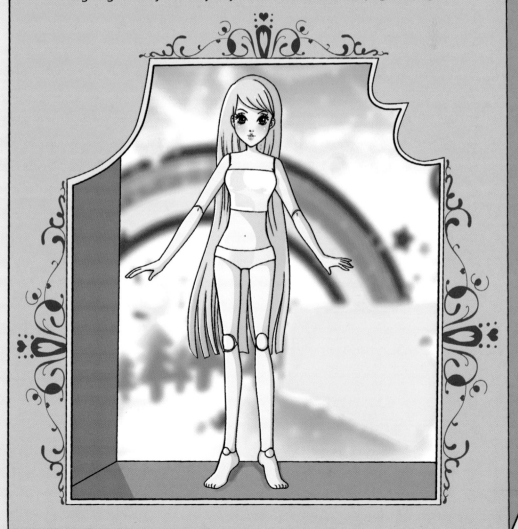

# Heads and faces

There are set rules to designing manga characters, which include specific guidelines on the drawing of heads, faces and specific features, such as eyes, noses and mouths. The rules vary according to a character's gender, age, and moral alignment (good or evil). The way you draw a female villain's eyes, for instance, will be different from the way you design the eyes of an heroic male figure. In both of these cases, your design will be based on the application of some simple rules.

Within this framework, an experienced manga artist will show their own style and characteristic techniques. In time, you will also develop a unique way of interpreting these rules. It makes sense to start with the basics of head and face drawing. The practice exercises in this section guide you step by step through the creation of front views, 45-degree angle views and profiles. The rules vary slightly in each case, depending on whether your manga character is male or female.

## Practice exercise: Male, front view

This first exercise pays particular attention to the head's basic shape when viewed from the front. The use of guidelines helps you to place facial features, such as the jaw and nose, with great accuracy. Although a head's size and shape may change, the

proportionate relation between each of the features will remain the same. Typically, a male head will be larger and more angular than a female one, with a more pronounced jawline and a wider neck. Eyebrows and nose will also be thicker and more apparent.

### Materials
- *cartridge paper*
- *soft lead pencil*
- *blue pencil 10*
- *pen and ink*
- *colour of your choice*

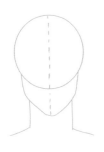 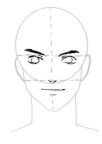 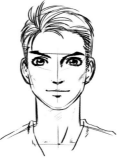 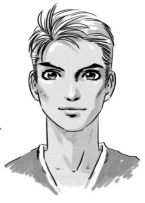

**1** Begin by drawing a circle. Divide the sketch with a dotted vertical line that extends below the circle. Press lightly as you will erase these lines later (you could use a blue pencil as scanning or photocopying your finished pencil lines will eliminate the blue lines). For the jawline, draw two vertical lines extending from the left and right sides of the circle downwards, angling the lines in towards the central guide line. Join the angled lines with a small horizonal line at the very tip of the jaw. Add the shape of the neck and the start of the shoulders.

**2** The size of the ears on a face defines all of the other facial characteristics. Divide the head in half with a horizontal dotted line – aligned to both the eyeline and the top of the ears. Divide the bottom half of the head in half again. This second line is the bottom of the ears and the tip of the nose. Draw the eyes and eyebrows, which are spaced equally either side of the nose and centrally with the lips. You should keep a full eye's width between them. Eyebrows almost touch the eyes at the corners when in 'neutral'.

**3** The lower lip is half the distance between the tip of the nose and the chin, and is defined with simple, unfussy lines. The hairline begins halfway up the forehead, 'squaring off' the head with an off-centre parting. Keep hair choppy and natural to avoid your characters looking as if they are wearing swimming caps or strange helmets. You may wish to define cheek and collarbones. Ink your pencil lines when you are happy with them and define shadow areas.

**4** Finish the head by using a colouring method of your choice. The colour stage builds on the detail and shading previously introduced. Note this example creates a unique manga colour scheme of prematurely white hair and bright green eyes to give a striking effect. Try creating your own variations on this simple formula: it's easy to create new looks just by varying the size of the various facial components.

## Practice exercise: Female, front view

Female manga faces have a softer feel, which is particularly apparent in the front view. They are less angular and are usually smaller than their male counterparts, with more smoothly integrated features, particularly along the jawline. The basic design rules are the same as for the male head, but are adapted for a more feminine look, especially with regard to the eyes, which are wider, with more fully defined lashes, and the smaller, button nose.

### Materials
- *cartridge paper*
- *soft lead pencil*
- *blue pencil 10*
- *pen and ink*
- *colour of your choice*

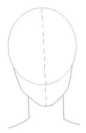
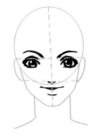
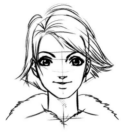
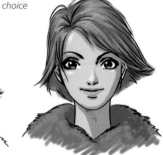

**1** As for the male face, draw a circle with a vertical line through its centre. Create the jawline; this time the lines coming from the circle should be shorter, and angled slightly inwards. Keep the jawline smooth, and more rounded compared to the male.

**2** Add the other guidelines, starting with the eye and nose. The proportions between each part are just the same as on the male face, but the features are different: draw eyes larger and more widely spaced, the nose smaller, and the eyebrows arch up and out.

**3** Female characters tend to have longer hair, though it begins at the same hairline, even if it sweeps down and across, as in this example. Define your pencil lines by inking those you are happy with. Pay attention to the clump of eyelashes and the light glares on each eye.

**4** The colour stage pulls the drawing together, with the purples of the girl's clothing reflected in her skin tone, hair and eyes. Note that female lips are defined through colour, rather than line work. Focus special attention on the colour strokes in the hair.

## Male and female characteristics

Manga often uses androgynous-looking characters and outlandish hairstyles so it can be worth focusing on the major differences between the sexes: comparative sizes of eyes, noses and mouths.

**Defined differences** ▶
Although the male and female characters have similar jawlines and long hair, it is easy to spot the differences between them. The boy (top) has a wide, neutrally shaded mouth, compact eyes and a nose defined with a vertical line. The girl (right) has large, lashed eyes, nostrils rather than a nose, and a mouth shaded in pink.

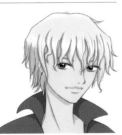

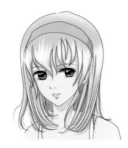

## Axes of symmetry and perspective

Simple guidelines keep features in proportion to one another while the guides are rotated in perspective. The vertical axis divides the face lengthwise and shows the angle of the head. The horizontal axis indicates whether the face is looking up or down.

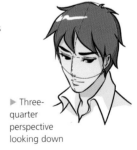

▶ Three-quarter perspective looking down

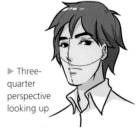

▶ Three-quarter perspective looking down (from higher up)

▶ Three-quarter perspective looking up

## Practice exercise: Male face, 45-degree angle view

In this exercise, the male head is drawn at a 45-degree angle, which gives more depth to his features, such as the chin and cheekbones. Here, the character is looking towards his left.

### Materials
- cartridge paper
- soft lead pencil
- blue pencil 10
- pen and ink
- colour of your choice

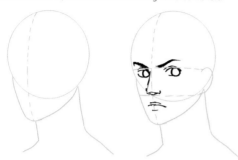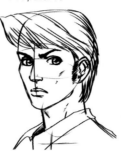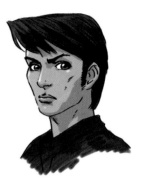

1 Start with a solid circle but add a convex vertical dotted line to show where the centre of the face will point. Extend a solid curved line down from the lower half of the head and back to the base of the ears, forming a slanted angle for the chin.

2 Draw the pencil guides for the eyes, ears, eyebrows and the mouth as before: half the head height for the eyeline, half of the remaining space for the noseline. Ink in the outlines of the eyes, eyebrows nose and mouth.

3 Complete the detail of the eyes and the rest of the features of the face. Note how the right eyebrow and nose form a reverse 'S' shape. Draw in your hair as before, showing the back of the head behind the ear and extended fringe.

4 Finish the head by adding colour, noting areas of shadow. Shading on the skin reveals the form of the face – note the shadows beneath the cheekbones, on the neck, under the lips and nose and beneath the hair and eyebrows.

## Practice exercise: Female face, 45-degree angle view

In this exercise, a female head is drawn at a 45-degree angle. Again, the character is looking left, towards us. The female head has a shorter jawline, a more triangular chin and more delicate features than the male face.

### Materials
- cartridge paper
- soft lead pencil
- blue pencil 10
- pen and ink
- colour of your choice

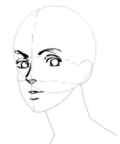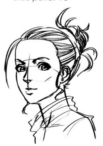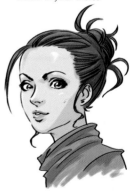

1 Start with a solid circle and a convex, extended dotted vertical pencil line. Extend a solid curved line down from the lower half of the head and back to the base of the ears, forming the slanted angle of the chin. Note the smoother, shallower jawline and thinner neck.

2 Draw the pencil guides for the eyes, ears, eyebrows and the mouth as before: half the head height for the eyeline, half of the remaining space for the noseline. Ink in the outlines of the eyes, eyebrows nose and mouth. Don't connect the brow with the nose.

3 Build up your detail in ink. The ear is smaller than the male, the neck begins farther back from the chin and the nose is more refined. Eyebrows are farther from the nose. Eyelashes protrude outside the head silhouette on the far side. Pay attention to the neat hairline.

4 Colour defines the shape of the head: here a 'V' of lit areas, with shade under the nose, eyes and mouth. Highlights on the forehead, cheeks and under the tip of the nose add dimensionality and life to the skin.

## Practice exercise: Male face, profile view

Earlier, we saw how the facial guidelines can be rotated in any direction. While faces in profile use this same structure, the features can often look very different, with the eyes, nose and mouth taking on new shapes, as seen below.

### Materials
- *cartridge paper*
- *soft lead pencil*
- *blue pencil 10*
- *pen and ink*
- *colour of your choice*

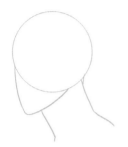

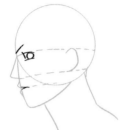

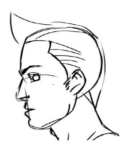

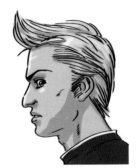

1 Draw guides for the basic circle of the face, adding a pointed jaw to create a 'plectrum' shape. This represents the front of the face below the nose, with the curve under the circle becoming the jawline. Draw guides for the neck.

2 Draw in dotted horizontal guide lines to define the eyes, ears and mouth. Viewed from the side, eyes become a curved 'V' shape, as does the nose. Note how the upper lip protrudes over the lower lip. Eyebrows curve in towards the nose.

3 Ink your sketched-in features. Add hair, remembering that the hairline may be covered from the side, and that the hair extends back in a squared-off fashion. Ink your pencil lines. Add shading for the cheek-bones and glare on the eyes.

4 Colour gives 'weight' to the image, with the back of the head covered in shadow. The sharp-angled silhouette presents more defined features than a front view, so profile shots can rely less on colour to differentiate features from one another.

## Practice exercise: Female face, profile view

Here we see a female head, drawn in the same direction as the male, and using exactly the same basic building blocks and guidelines. Note the lips are far fuller in profile, the nose more rounded, and the brow emphasized far less.

### Materials
- *cartridge paper*
- *soft lead pencil*
- *blue pencil 10*
- *pen and ink*
- *colour of your choice*

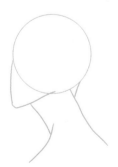

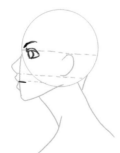

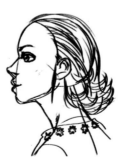

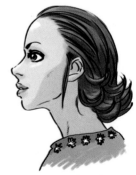

1 Start just as you did for the male profile. Keep the jawline shallower and the neck more slender. While the male jawline juts down from the ear, the female jaw swoops towards the chin in a gentle curve.

2 Add in your horizontal dotted guidelines, and features such as ears and nose. Start to ink in the eyes and mouth. Note that the female lips are fuller and more defined, with the chin not jutting out as far.

3 Ink in the nose, jaw and eye, remembering that the female eye is larger and sweeps back farther. Allow space above the eye for a smooth eyebrow arch that starts just above the front of the iris.

4 Complete the girl's profile by colouring the head, paying particular attention to the eyes, lips and highlights in the hair. Check for areas of highlight noting that half of the face and all of the neck is in shadow.

# Drawing eyes

Eyes are extremely versatile, and have a marked effect on the facial expression of any character, determining gender, age, and also emotional state. Our eyes are perhaps the most expressive part of our faces, and often reveal emotions that we are attempting to hide. You can cover up all of a character's other features and show how they are reacting solely with the eyes. Not surprising, then, that the eyes are one of the trickier parts of the body to get right, as you need to learn how to express moods as well as get to grips with basic eye anatomy. To express shock or surprise, for example, you should raise the top eyelids high above the pupils. For a cool look, cut them midway across. Although manga faces are filled with a liquid shine to make them seem more emotional, most have little tone, which is why it is important to get as much expression out of their features as you can.

The eyebrows act as 'backup' to the eyes. They work in a similar way to bars on a gate: raised eyebrows seem open and friendly, lowered eyebrows appear closed and unfriendly. One eyebrow up and one down conveys doubt. Level eyebrows suggest a character who is non-committal. Following similar principles, animals such as cats and dogs often express themselves with a tilt of the head and movement of the ears.

## Eyes

There are exceptions, but many manga characters have large eyes. The eyes are said to be windows to the soul, and because the Japanese are obsessed with mood and emotion, their readers expect to look right inside. The more they see, the greater the empathy they experience with the character. To Western readers, the big-eye look can be deceptive. Characters that appear to be little kids could, in fact, be fully grown adults; they may look cute, but their behaviour does not reflect this. This misunderstanding has caused issues of censorship in the West, where comics are perceived to be for children.

**Tip:** Eyes that reflect light look more animated and human than those without. See for yourself how removing the highlights and subtle reflections makes a character's eyes look dull and doll-like.

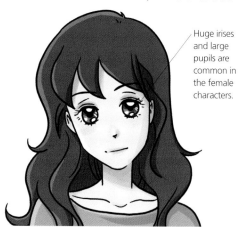

Huge irises and large pupils are common in the female characters.

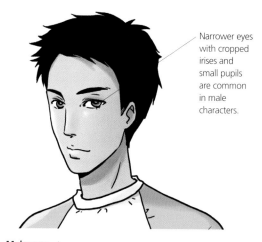

Narrower eyes with cropped irises and small pupils are common in male characters.

**Female eyes** ▲
As female eyes are large, there is ample opportunity to make a feature of the play of light across the pupil (the black centre) and iris (the coloured surrounding area). The eyebrows of female characters are thin, and the eyelashes prominent.

**Male eyes** ▲
The eyes of male characters tend to be thinner and narrower than female eyes, although there are a few exceptions. Eyebrows are thicker, with no eyelashes. Male characters have light glares in their eyes, too, although not as large or obvious.

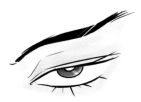

◀ **Jagged eyebrow**
Often used in manga to help exaggerate more suspicious, villainous characteristics, jagged eyebrows and eyelashes (in female characters) are used for big or exceptional personalities.

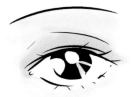

◀ **Streamlined eyebrow**
This is the most commonly drawn eyebrow shape. It can be straight, arched, a 'hill', or a subtle top of a 'wave' (like this one).

## Practice exercise: Standard female big eye

There are many ways to draw eyes, starting either with a basic circle or the upper eyelid. Using a 'V' shape as a guide is probably the easiest method for beginners.

  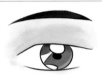 

**1** Draw a tall 'V' as a guide and add two opposing arcs between the two lines. Ink in the eyelids, which arc out then slope in towards the white of the eye.

**2** Add a central oval for the pupil and a larger oval to create the iris and lights in the cornea. Add a thin eyebrow and place above the eye.

**3** Finally, add eyelashes. When viewed from the front like this, they should point mainly to the side. Colour the eye.

## Practice exercise: Standard male eye

Male eyes are thinner than female eyes. The eye drawn here is a fairly standard size. If it were drawn much thinner, the character would look like a villain.

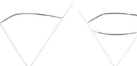 

**1** The V-shaped guides can be used, but this time spread them wider apart. Ink in a slightly slanted curve, with the left side curving in slightly. Next draw the curve of the bottom eyelid.

**2** The iris of the male eye is circular, held within the confines of the eyelids. Start by pencilling a perfect circle through the eye, then ink over the parts of the circle that remain within the eyelids.

**3** Add a couple of areas of white on the iris to show light bouncing off the cornea. Then add the eyebrow, which should be thicker than the female version. Colour the eye.

## Practice exercise: Female villain eye

A female villain should look threatening and devious. You can achieve this simply by making the eye much narrower than the standard female big eye shown above.

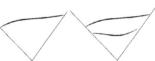  

**1** If using the 'V', the lines should be farther apart at the top than before. The farther apart the lines, the narrower the eye. Draw a curved slant, with the left edge (nearest the nose) lower than the other.

**2** Add the iris: again you can draw an entire circle in the centre of the eye, making sure your circle goes outside the eyelids. For a calculating squint, add an extra short arch between the eyebrow and the eye, up to half the width of the eye.

**3** Add subtle light reflections. When shading, make sure the iris isn't black, so the pupil stands out. Add fewer eyelashes than before. The top of the eyebrow should be jagged.

## Practice exercise: Male villain eye

The eye of a male villain is very similar to that of a female villain. The differences between the two amount to tweaks.

 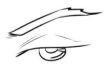 

**1** Ink in a curved slant, with the left edge lower than the other. Add the iris, cropped within the confines of the eyelid. Add subtle light reflections.

**2** The eyebrow is sleek like the female's, but slightly thicker, and more angular and jagged. Add the extra line to imply the squint, but make it longer for the male villain.

**3** The lower part of the eye is more triangular than the upper lid. Instead of lower eyelashes, add a thick line of shadow. Colour the eye.

# Drawing hair

Hair can be difficult to get right, and it helps to break styles into separate components. The hairstyle in question, like other personal characteristics in manga, will be affected by genre. Individual strands are implied by the few that are drawn into the different-sized bunches, tufts or clumps.

As with clothes, fashionable or outlandish haircuts are the norm, so keep yourself appraised of the latest trends – or start some of your own. Manga in black and white means your characters need to have unique silhouettes that read well without colour, and hair plays a major part in this.

## How hair sits on the scalp

Manga hair can be divided into two main styles: hair that grows up and out from the scalp, and hair that lies flat against the scalp. Once you've mastered these basic styles, you can combine the two in an infinite number of combinations to create interesting styles for more prominent characters. Start with drawing only nine or ten strands. Later, once you've got the knack of drawing basic hair, you can make it more detailed.

**Tip:** Remember that hair follows the shape of the scalp. When starting out, it will be helpful to draw the entire head, bald, and add hair proportionally over the outline you have drawn.

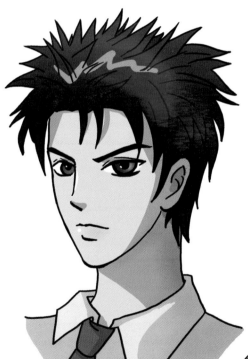

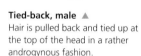

**Tied-back, male** ▲
Hair is pulled back and tied up at the top of the head in a rather androgynous fashion.

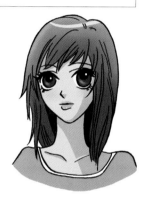

**Shoulder-length, layered** ▲
Detail is concentrated in the strands around the face, leaving the top of the hair to glossily reflect the light.

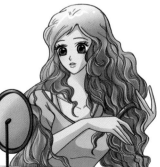

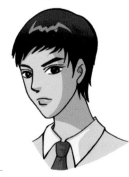

**Spiked and styled** ▲
This gravity-defying cut is made of a number of spiked strands. Block in the main shape of the hair first, then add spikes as appropriate. Note that, while intricate, not every strand of hair has been drawn. Hair frames the face.

**Tresses** ▲
Coils of long hair suggest a pampered princess – whether from the Dark Ages or California.

**Swept** ▲
Perfect for the model student with a 'dark' side. Choppily cut short, with the hair swept to one side.

## Drawing a fringe, or 'bangs'

A fringe (bangs) – the term used for hair that either entirely or partially covers the forehead – are often referred to in the process of manga creation. They form one of the essential building blocks of hairstyles. Creating a fringe is not unlike designing a helmet. Once you've sketched the frame, craft the hair over the top. Make the fringe consistent, but not even – you don't want to give your character a 'bowl cut' (unless this is appropriate to your character). Let a few strands go astray to make the hairstyle more realistic.

For a fringe, draw hair down over the forehead towards the eyes and bridge of the nose. The arc of the hair should go back up towards the top centre of the head, giving the illusion the fringe is following the front curve of the head. On the left side, arcs curve up to the right, and on the right side, to the left. An arc will curve less towards the middle of the fringe.

**A fringe to the front of the head** ▶
A blunt-cut fringe is complemented by chunky hair to the sides of the face.

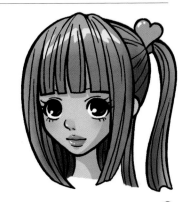

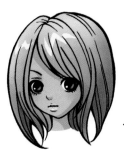

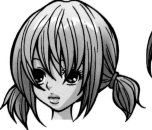

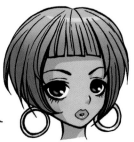

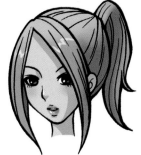

**A fringe to the front of the head** ▲
A fringe swept to the side to reveal the forehead.

**A long fringe to the front of the head** ▲
A choppy, uneven fringe obscures the eyes.

**A short fringe to the front of the head** ▲
Blunt-cut fringe and puffed-out hair add interest.

**A long fringe to the side of the head** ▲
A simple inverse-'V' shape, parted on the right.

## Adding curves to hair

Get into the habit of curving your hair strands. The longer your character's hair, the longer the curves should be.

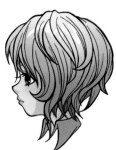

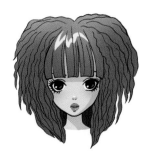

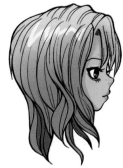

**Tip:** Make sure that the characteristics are easily distinguished in black and white, as most manga is not printed in colour. Remember that there's no need for consistency if one of the hairstyles is changed by magic.

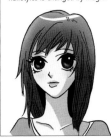

**Curves on shorter hair** ▲
Note how the coils are layered over one another, suggesting depth and making the hair look natural.

**Big curvy or wavy hair** ▲
Here, the curves emanate from a central point at the back of the head, growing narrower as they progress.

**Curves on long, straight hair** ▲
Less layers, but more pronounced curves as the strands reach their tips.

# Drawing the mouth and nose

In manga, the mouth and nose are probably the simplest areas of the face to draw, and some of the standard methods can be used interchangeably for either gender. In some forms of manga, a relatively realistic nose is acceptable, although generally only for the male characters. Female noses, whatever the genre, tend to be drawn minimally.

## Simple noses

The simplest noses comprise a pair of curves in profile. The first line starts at the bridge of the nose and curves both downwards and outwards. The end of the line should be gently upturned, but more blunt than pointed. The second starts where the first ends, and curves slightly downwards, back towards the face. Keep the nose small, without nostrils, and the lines thin. Thick lines draw too much attention, and the nose shouldn't distract from the rest of the face.

Female     Female     Female

Male     Male     Male

**Male nose** ▲
These two pictures show just how subtle the differences between the sexes are. The male nose is longer and more 'snubbed' at the tip.

**Female nose** ▲
On the other hand, the curve of this nose is smaller and tilted upwards. The focus is on the tip of the nose, rather than suggesting the nostrils.

## Adding shadow and detail

You can enhance simple noses by using shadows, thickening lines with subtle shadow towards the nose's point. Shape the shadow like a black arrowhead, as if the nose is lit from above and to one side.

Adding nostrils, as shown below, can also add interest and dimensionality. A hooked horizontal line for the nasal aperture is usually enough: you don't need to draw the 'hoods' of skin on either side of the main stem of the nose.

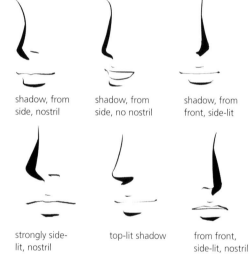

shadow, from side, nostril     shadow, from side, no nostril     shadow, from front, side-lit

strongly side-lit, nostril     top-lit shadow     from front, side-lit, nostril

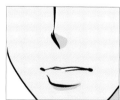

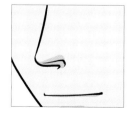

◀ **Shading in colour**
Using a darker skin tone underneath the nostrils allows you to keep the minimalist detail and inking of an unshadowed nose while still adding a degree of dimensionality.

**Tip:** Noses on the male face tend to have more definition and detail than the smaller female nose, which also has a more rounded end. Some forms abandon the nose entirely on the female face.

## Drawing mouths

Like the nose, the mouth is kept simple in manga. Often, a thin line is enough to suggest it (when closed, at least), though the mouths of women and girls are often fully rendered in colour. In almost all cases, mouths are small, unless the character is yelling, screaming or laughing heartily.

When you draw a character that is looking anywhere other than straight ahead, you will need to consider the curve of the nose and mouth – the lower lip should curve outwards, down towards the chin, and the upper lip inwards, up towards the nose. Both follow the curves of the face.

**Tip:** When a character is shouting, it's the jaw that does the majority of the moving and heavy emotional lifting, so focus your attention on the lower lip.

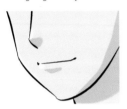
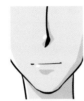
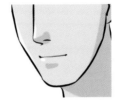
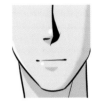

**Simple female angled** ▲
Dots mark the corners, a curve hints at a smile.

**Simple female straight** ▲
A triangle of shade under the line gives definition to lips.

**Simple male angled** ▲
A simple line serves as well for men as for women.

**Simple male straight** ▲
There's little to differentiate the sexes from the front.

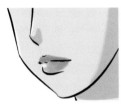
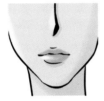
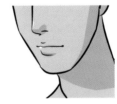
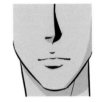

**Complex female angled** ▲
Lines show the 'plumpness', colour does the rest.

**Complex female straight** ▲
Note the more realistic line showing where the lips meet.

**Complex male angled** ▲
Lips are thinner and shaded in standard flesh tone.

**Complex male straight** ▲
Look out for the shallow 'U' underneath the mouth.

## Practice exercise: Building the female mouth

Female mouths in manga are more fully rendered than their male equivalents, with more-defined lips and colour rendering.

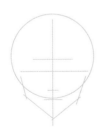
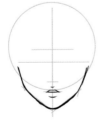
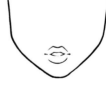
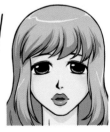

**3** Fill out the lip lines as shown above. Tilt the mouth aperture inwards so that the open mouth forms 'V' shapes on either side, and add 'dimples'. Don't connect the lines of the lips; instead, fill the shape with colour.

### Materials
• cartridge paper
• soft lead pencil
• blue pencil 10
• pen and ink
• colour of your choice

**1** Draw the outlines of a head in the usual way, drawing in guides for the eyes, nose, and mouth. The mouth sits at the base of the guide circle, where it connects to the jaw.

**2** Start with the open aperture of the mouth, adding a small 'dip' above suggesting the groove that joins the nose to the mouth, and a curve beneath for the bottom lip.

**Tip:** If you want to keep the proportions and position of the mouth you've drawn, but give it fuller lips, thicken the inked outline around the mouth.

# Facial expressions

A person's face can display a large range of emotions, delivered to the rest of the world through changes in expression. These different expressions are used in comics to evoke the inner feelings and thoughts of a character, often making dialogue unnecessary. Your audience should be able to read a character's angry expression, for example, without the artist having to add 'I'm angry!' in a speech balloon or caption. Expression can be seen as a wordless form of communication and is one of the most important tools used in drawing any comic strip. On a technical level, emotions are represented by altering the looks of the mouth and eyes, making them work in concert. In some cases – particularly when creating mysterious or villainous manga characters – you may want to leave the true emotions of your character in question, in which case concealing either the eyes or mouth of that character will increase the ambiguity surrounding them.

## Adapting each expression

As you work through the following techniques, you will soon discover how it is easier to draw a new expression then adapt it from another. The key is in the little things, and making small changes. Sometimes all it takes is a subtle alteration to the mouth or the arch of the brow to completely change a character's mood. If you want to practise simpler forms of expression, you can use a pair of dots for eyes, a single line for the nose, a pair of lines for eyebrows, and a mouth that varies from a straight line to a curved shape, depending on the character's mood.

**Neutral happy** ▲
Slightly raised eyebrows create an open but neutral expression.

**Pleased** ▲
The corners of the mouth tilt up in a smile, the eyebrows begin to raise.

**Pleasantly surprised** ▲
The eyebrows shoot up and the smile becomes more obvious.

**Delighted** ▲
The eyes close, the smile is a full 'U' curve, the eyebrows vanish in the hairline.

**Neutral sad** ▲
Flat eyebrows add a sad tinge to this neutral expression.

**Glum** ▲
Eyebrows begin to lift next to the nose, while the mouth dips at either side.

**Broken** ▲
The eyebrow slope deepens, the corners of the mouth head towards the chin.

**Distraught** ▲
The mouth is an inverted 'U', the eyebrows an open bascule bridge.

**Neutral angry** ▲
The slight curve of the mouth suggests something has irked this character.

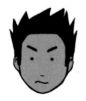

**Grumpy** ▲
The brows furrow and the curve of the mouth becomes more pronounced.

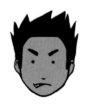

**Irate** ▲
Eyebrows thicken and teeth become visible as inner tensions start to spill out.

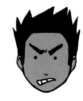

**Furious** ▲
Brows nearly meet in the middle, the mouth twists down, with teeth visible.

# Seven facial expressions

Here are some common expressions. You can vary these – nothing is set in stone – so if another way of conveying anger or happiness occurs to you, try it out. You can also look in the mirror, or take photographs of friends mimicking these emotions, to give yourself a better idea of the various shapes and lines made naturally by the face.

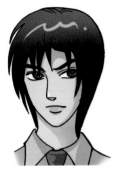

**Annoyed** ▲
Keep the pupils small to show your character's displeasure. The closed mouth is drawn as an arch, and should look sullen and petulant. Eyebrows indicate a vexed expression.

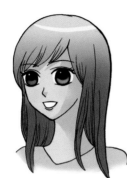

**Friendly** ▲
The eyebrows form subtle arches. A thin line above the eyelashes indicates the eyelids are relaxed. The face shows interest and openess. The eyes are wide open and the mouth is smiling.

**Sad**
The features in this expression are a combination of surprise and upset. The mouth is small, the eyes wide open and crying. The eyebrows are narrow 'S' shapes lying on their sides. Above the eyes, an extra arch gives the lids a touch more emphasis. This character is openly crying but you can show the anticipation of tears with extra patches of reflected light, and by giving the iris and pupil fuzzy edges to suggest extra moisture in the eyes. If you want the tears to be more apparent, add a couple of cloud-shapes in the corners of the eyes. You can also draw a couple of extra upward slants under the inner side of the eyebrows to show the raising of the forehead.

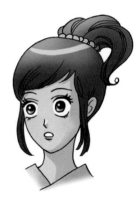

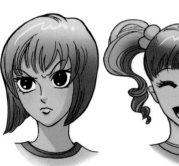

**Angry** ▲
Shape the eyebrows so that the corners nearest the nose point straight down, and rise steeply on to the forehead. Reduce the size of the pupils to a tiny dot, or leave them out altogether. Some artists further convey rage by fanging the teeth.

**Happy** ▲
These eyebrows are high arches, the eyes similarly closed to evoke elation. The mouth is much bigger than the 'friendly' mouth, drawn as a blunt upturned triangle. The left and right corners of the mouth are turned upwards.

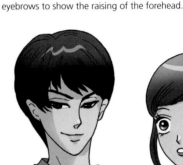

**Evil** ▲
The eyebrows are thin, pointy and more angular than angry ones. The eyes are angled downwards. Make the eyelids, pupils and lashes thick and dark; shrouded and sinister. The nose is pointy, almost sharp, and the mouth needs to have a smiling or a smirking element to it: the character is enjoying himself. To suggest extreme evil, try gritted teeth and a broad smile. The smirk shown here is achieved with a straight line that is upturned at one end.

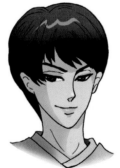

**Surprise** ▲
The expression on this girl's face indicates surprise and disbelief. The eyes are wide open, showing the whites of the eyes surrounding the irises. The black pupils are big, hollow circles. The mouth is rounder than 'friendly' and 'happy', and the expression of shock is indicated as an 'O' shape.

# The manga figure

In any style of cartooning, whether traditional or manga, the figure takes precedence. Readers notice the human character before everything else, because it is almost always the element that carries the narrative. Human bodies come in all shapes and sizes, from little children to muscled giants, so your manga universe would be boring if everybody looked the same. As you did for the head, start by practising the basic shapes and structures of the human figure.

## Constructing the body

Basic anatomical construction comes from understanding the abstract shapes of the human body, and how they act in relation to one another. Whether by studying a skeleton, or by breaking down an existing figure drawing into simple components, learn to see each segment of the figure as part of the whole. Using simple shapes like spheres, tubes and curves, you can block in the proportions of your poses and clear up any anatomical mistakes before you add in the detail work. Pay attention to where limbs connect, and how different parts of the body alter with perspective.

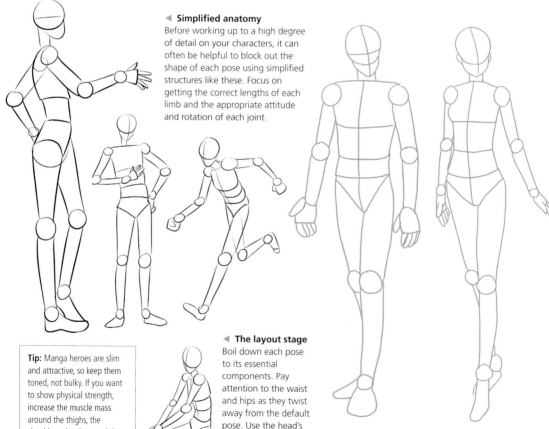

◀ **Simplified anatomy**
Before working up to a high degree of detail on your characters, it can often be helpful to block out the shape of each pose using simplified structures like these. Focus on getting the correct lengths of each limb and the appropriate attitude and rotation of each joint.

**Tip:** Manga heroes are slim and attractive, so keep them toned, not bulky. If you want to show physical strength, increase the muscle mass around the thighs, the shoulders, the chest and the arms. Don't exaggerate to the extent that you create a 'superheroic' inverse-'V' shape, i.e. a torso larger than the legs can realistically support.

◀ **The layout stage**
Boil down each pose to its essential components. Pay attention to the waist and hips as they twist away from the default pose. Use the head's 'crosshairs' to show where a character is looking. Don't forget that photo reference can often prove invaluable.

**Gender differences** ▲
The ribcage that defines the chest is broader on the male than the female, but female hips are wider in proportion to the chest than male hips. In these simplified skeletons, oval shapes are used for the skull, chest and hips. Male versions are more angular.

## Manga musculature

Male and female characters in manga are often more developed than someone of their age would normally be. Once you've got used to drawing proportional outlines, you can add the muscle, skin and detailing that create the finished outline of your character.

**Tip:** You can vary a character's amount of muscle by varying the distance from the bones at which you flesh them out. Muscle is shown sparingly on female figures in order to retain their slenderness.

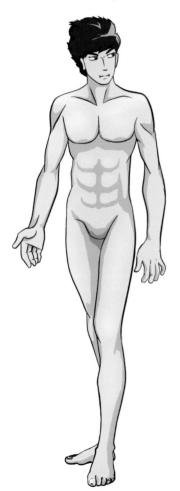

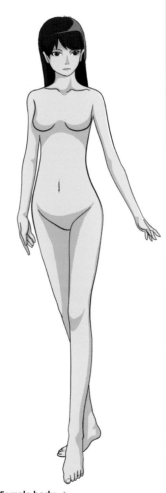

**Male body** ▲
Here is the fully defined male form, with skin and musculature grafted over the simple layout shapes. Note how strongly the muscles are defined, drawing attention to the joints of the skeleton beneath.

**Female body** ▲
Female manga forms are far less overtly muscled than the males: joints are suggested by gentle curves, not rendering. Tissue is denser in the breasts and around the hips, creating an obviously female silhouette.

## Head and shoulders

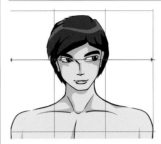

Male manga characters have wider shoulders than female characters. Though some artists say the shoulder width of a male character should be the equivalent of three heads, your heroes will look like muscleheads if you always follow this rule. Experiment with bigger head proportions to find the best size.

## Skeletal structure

It is well worth studying the human skeleton, even if you have mastered using simple shapes to lay out your figures, as it will reinforce your knowledge of basic anatomy and how every part of the body fits together.

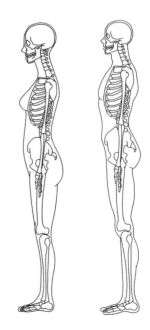

# Proportion

As you go on to customize the form of your characters, they will take on their own dimensions. Their proportions – the distances between features – may become longer or shorter. You may also decide to make their overall size or the size of certain parts of the body larger or smaller. Whatever forms you develop, your characters' movements need to conform to the new proportions you define whenever they appear in order to be convincing. Then, no matter what they look like, the reader will accept their essential reality. Manga artists define the proportions of the adult body through the use of the size of the head: seven or eight times deep for a standard male or

female protagonist, nine heads for an Amazon or male superhero, six or seven heads for adolescents, between five and six heads for a child, and two or three heads for super-deformed (exaggerated) characters or chibi-style (short person) characters.

Use these rules as a basis, but adjust them according to your needs. As before, make sure you are consistent: using a guide allows you to maintain character proportions throughout an entire story. There are key differences in the physique that when drawn, help readers determine whether or not the character is female or male. For a female these include narrower shoulders, a thinner waist, higher hips and less muscle definition, smaller facial features and curves.

## Female body proportions

A manga artist works out a character's proportions in relation to head size. The technical term for this rule is the 'canon of proportion'. Manga females are usually petite and their proportions

reflect the ideal of beauty as defined for Japanese women. Developed muscles are less aesthetic. It's common, however, to add voluptuous curves to differentiate women from girls.

**Adult female** ▼
The average adult female stands eight heads deep and is tall and slim, while still curvaceous. Classic 'hourglass' proportions (bust and hips) produce an elegant and graceful frame.

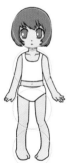

◀ **Pre-school female**
The body of a young female is four to five heads deep. She is rounder and less defined than an adult. Notice the disproportionate roundness of her head and huge oval eyes.

> **Tip:** The rules of proportion mean that whatever the height or build of your characters, they will 'read' as human: from 1m to 100m (3ft to over 300ft tall). You can change limb lengths, but be aware that they may be construed as odd.

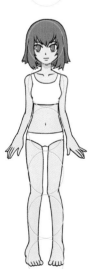

◀ **Pre-teen female**
The pre-teen female is five to six heads deep. The chubbiness has all but gone, and there is more definition in the body and face. The eyes are slightly smaller and less oval. The girl is approaching adolescence, as shown by her small bust, developing hips and slender legs.

**Teenage female** ▶
The teenage female is six to seven heads deep. The hips and thighs have broadened since the pre-teen stage, and there is a noticeable bust. The face is more angular, the eyes smaller, and the fringe (bangs) is more pronounced. Her arms show greater muscle definition.

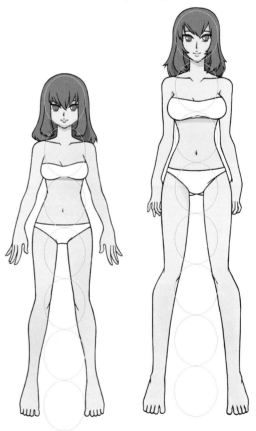

# Male body proportions

Most characters in manga are young male adults, for the simple reason that they constitute the target market. Males in general fluctuate widely between heavily musclebound types and sylphlike androgynes. Bishonen (meaning beautiful youth or boy) style, for example, reduces the male body to a graceful, slender physique with only slight indications of muscle, and a notable lack of nipples or body hair. Whether drawing males or females, it's helpful to develop a working knowledge of human physiology, so that you can appreciate the layout of muscles and bones. Start by learning how to draw realistically – you can modify the examples into your own style later.

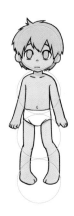

◀ **Pre-school male**
Four to five heads is the recognized canon measure for young children. Aside from a disproportionately large head, the male child has chubby, undefined limbs, much like his female counterpart, and a rounder face than the teen or adult male. In manga, the younger you make a character, be it male or female, the larger their head is in relation to the rest of the body.

**Tip:** Consider joining a life-drawing class. Regular classes will improve your fundamental understanding of the human form. If a class isn't possible, drawing yourself in the mirror is a good starting point. Try drawing clothed figures, too, noting how the different fabrics gather and stretch over the human figure.

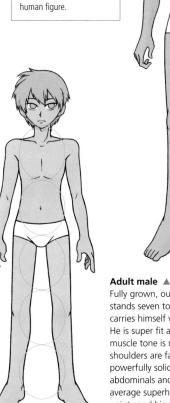

**Pre-teen male** ▶
The pre-teen male is five to six heads deep. By this age he is reasonably lithe, with slender limbs. His skeletal and muscular development doesn't yet support the strong body shape of adulthood, but his chest has broadened significantly since the pre-school years, and he has more muscle definition. Keep the shoulders of pre-teens relatively undeveloped, and keep the length of the limbs similarly constrained.

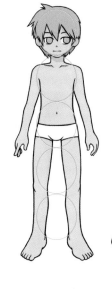

**Teenage male** ▶
Now in his teens, the male character has increased muscle definition, particularly in the arms and shoulders, and stands between six and seven heads deep. He is still slender, and his figure is drawn with simple, sleek vertical lines and very few curves. Compared to the pre-teen male, his face is more angular, the eyes smaller, and he has a more defined fringe at the hairline.

**Adult male** ▲
Fully grown, our male protagonist now stands seven to eight heads deep and carries himself with an upright stance. He is super fit and strong. But while the muscle tone is more defined, and his shoulders are far broader, he lacks the powerfully solid torso and exaggerated abdominals and chest pectorals of the average superhero. His chin is no longer pointy and his new, square jaw almost matches the width of his cheekbones.

# Drawing hands

In creating expression, a character's hands are almost as important as their face. A hand gesture, like a facial expression, can convey how a character is feeling without them having to say anything. If your character is talking, but is not being sincere, then their hands can reveal their true emotion and give them away. If a character's face is not visible,

but their hands are, you can easily show they are tense or angry with a clenched fist. Open palms can indicate friendship or surrender. Because the hands have numerous joints and are so flexible, there are literally hundreds of ways in which you can depict them. Start by picking a few easy positions and practise drawing these.

## Practice exercise: Open hand

Open hands usually indicate a passive or relaxed person. If they are held above the head, they show the character is trying to attract help or attention. If they are held out in front of the body they may represent a plea to stop.

### Materials
- *cartridge paper*
- *soft lead pencil*
- *pen and ink*
- *colour of your choice*

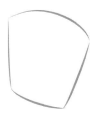

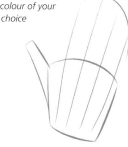

1 Start with an abstract shape, like the head of a broom or a mitt, beginning at the wrist and flaring upwards and outwards to create the basic hand shape of two arcs joined together.

2 At a position roughly the same length away from the hand as the size of the hand, inscribe an upper arc. Add four lines for the fingers, with the middle finger the longest. Jut out the thumb like the spout of a kettle.

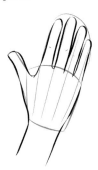

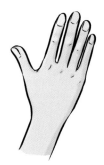

3 Thicken out the finger guides, using your own hand to accurately estimate their proportions. Note where the fingers intersect with the palm and back of the hand: in the centre of this guide line is where the knuckle falls. Each finger subdivides into three sections, extending from the knuckle.

4 Draw around your guides, fleshing out the musculature and giving the hand definition. Add fingernails, as well as small upward arcs to shape the knuckle joints, using the line guides from the previous step. Ink your favoured pencil lines and add colour as necessary.

## Palm of hand

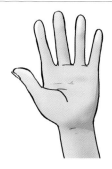

Repeat the first few steps, but don't add fingernails or knuckles. Instead, add the main areas in the skin of the palm: a pair of horizontal lines across the centre, an arc across the wrist, and arcs to show where the thumb and the flesh of the hand protrude.

## Hand movement

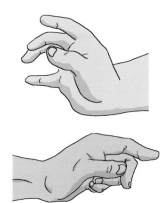

Study how the hand moves, both in the realm of individual fingers – pointing, fists, open palms – but also in how the hand relates to the arm: how it rotates and flexes around the wrist.

## Gender differences

In manga tradition, a female hand is not as wide as a male one, and the fingers are longer and more delicate. A female's open palm does not show very many creases and any ones that are included are more subtle.

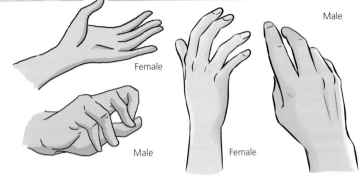

Female

Male

Male

Female

### A range of hands ▶
Why not devote a section of your sketch pad to capturing hand poses from life or magazines? Try different shades of skin colour.

## Hands at different ages

When you draw an elderly hand, add more lines around the fingers and joints. You should also make the fingers thicker and less sleek. When you draw a very young hand, keep the fingers small and underdeveloped; their length should only slightly exceed the length of the palm of the hand.

### Square versus smooth ▶
Older hands are more angular than young, as joints begin to protrude through thinning skin.

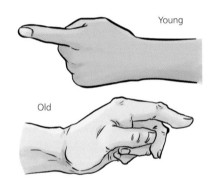

Young

Old

◀ **The extremes of age**
The hands of young and old characters are drawn to the same proportions as their bodies: a child's hands are short and stubby because they are not yet fully grown. With faces, the rule of ageing is that every additional line adds a year to the character's life – it's a similar case for hands.

## Studies of hands

It's vital that a manga artist be able to draw the hand in a wide range of positions, and you should practise as often as you can. Look at the way your own hand moves, and you'll notice its versatility: you can change the way it looks by moving just one of your five fingers (not to mention the wrist). The examples shown here show the hands in a range of positions.

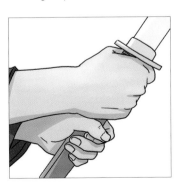

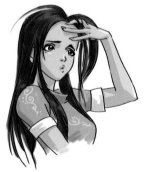

**Flustered hands** ▲
It's all too much for this character, who takes a breather, resting her hand on her forehead. Note how her fingers interact with the hair and forehead.

◀ **Holding hands**
Here's a masterless samurai's hand, gripping tightly to his katana. Note how the hand interacts with an object.

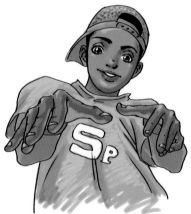

**Hands in perspective** ▲
Here's a pose captured using a mirror or photo reference. Never forget that it's rare to see a hand in manga from the same perspective as you would see your own: experiment with angles.

# Drawing feet

As well as hands, you need to think about your character's feet. Most of the time, these feet will probably be inside shoes, although it may occasionally be appropriate to draw a character barefoot. Feet are often used to convey travel within a story – a close-up panel of a character's feet will tell the reader they are approaching their destination, or else emphasize the passing of time during a journey. If you find drawing feet difficult, take comfort from the fact you are in good company. Many artists hate drawing feet, and some will go to great lengths not to show them. It can be difficult to get the feet right in relation to the rest of the figure, and it is a common mistake to draw feet too big. Start your training with a series of simple shapes as a basis, and then draw the positions of the feet within the guides. You should practise drawing both sides of the feet from various angles in order to understand as much as possible about this part of the body.

## Practice exercise: Side view

It's easiest to think of a foot viewed from the side as a right-angled triangle with the longest edge as the base of the foot. These steps will allow you to flesh out that underlying shape.

## Materials
• *cartridge paper*
• *blue pencil 10*
• *soft lead pencil*
• *pen and ink*
• *colouring method of your choice*

**Tip:** Bulky, heavy characters should not be given small, perfectly formed feet, unless you are drawing attention to their mismatched proportions. Adapt the standard feet shown here by thickening up the dimensions, remembering that muscle tissue, fatty deposits and skin can increase in size, but the bones underneath do not. This leads to chunky toes, tree-trunk like ankles and so on. An ogre's feet should be as large and ugly as his body.

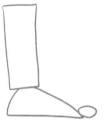

**1** Start with a smoothed right-angle triangle for the foot, with a rectangle on top for the leg. Add a small squashed oval to locate the big toe.

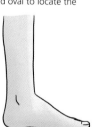

**2** The inner foot should arch upwards slightly, off the ground, with the thick pad of the ball of the foot placed slightly behind the toes, and the heel falling just behind the line of the ankle.

**3** Add in the toes. From this view only the big toe is visible. From the opposite side start with the little toe and work back to the big toe; the tips of each may be visible from the side, depending on the angle you choose. Use ink and colour to complete the side view.

## Feet in motion

When your characters are in motion, the appearance of their feet, and the angle of the foot to the leg, is constantly changing. Although it isn't necessary to master every perspective, it's important to suggest this movement. Look out for visual references to keep in your sketchbook and use for your drawing practice.

**Moving feet ▶**
These simple poses show feet in various stages of motion. These can be adapted for walking, running or dancing sequences.

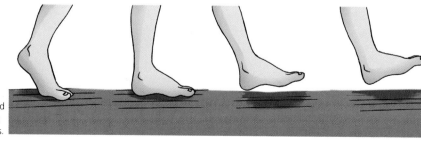

## Practice exercise: Front view

A row of toes forms a natural curve, which begins at the big toe and ends at the smallest. Shoes should be drawn following this curve, with a rounded end instead of individual toes.

## Materials
• *cartridge paper*
• *soft lead pencil*
• *pen and ink*
• *colour of your choice*

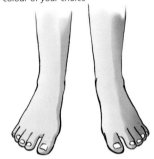

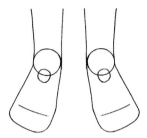

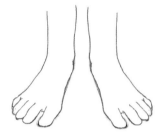

**1** Begin with a trapezoid shape for the feet with a rectangle on top for the leg. The trapezium should be cut so it runs practically parallel with the top of the foot.

**2** Subdivide the trapezium into the toes, noting the gap between the big toe and the other four. Note, too, how the feet bow outwards at the 'knuckle' of the big toe.

**3** Add toenails, remembering to keep them blunted towards the end of the toe, and ink your favoured pencil lines. Use colour to add texture, shading and tone.

**Tip:** Draw shoes with a rough version of the foot inside for a more convincing shape. If you're still having trouble, take off your shoes, tilt them to the required angle, and sketch from life.

## Toes and toenails

Each toe is a blunted rectangular shape and slightly curved. The big toe is the dominant template, each of the four other toes diminishing in a curve of size to the right or left of it, depending on the foot. Toenails end at the tip of the toe and have a rounded edge.

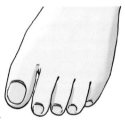

## Ankles

The ankle is a small part of the body but necessary detail. If the foot is drawn from the side, the ankle is represented by a small arc that protrudes from the leg. The ankle is shown as two lines that slope gently outwards. The ankle joint on the outer leg should be drawn slightly lower and closer to the foot than the ankle on the inside leg.

## Foot extended

Observe how the foot appears at rest, and when it bends. If you look at a foot from the side, pointed straight down, toes to the ground, you'll see that its top is almost a straight line, but that the bottom of the foot, particularly around the heel and toe, protrudes and creates a crease in the skin where it meets the top of the foot.

## Shoes over toes

Drawing a completely bare foot can be difficult, and getting your character to put on shoes can make your life simpler. This way, you don't have to draw individual toes or worry about getting the heel in the correct position. It's also easier to correct a mistake when drawing a pair of shoes, because you are free to improvise, than it is to correct an anatomical error while drawing bare feet. It's also a lot easier to draw your own shoe from real life than it is to sketch from your own bare feet.

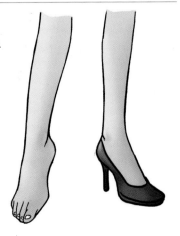

# Movement and perspective

You need to keep your characters in motion. If you draw them in the same pose, panel after panel, you will quickly lose your audience's interest. Move them in a way that is appropriate, taking into consideration their psychology, motives and style. The poses you give your characters will define who they are within a story, and enable your audience to differentiate between them. Characters should always be recognizable, not only when they are standing still, fully lit and in the foreground, but also if they're drawn in the distance, in the shadows, or out of focus. A character should be recognizable by their smaller traits, so that even if the majority of a character's body is hidden, his or her gestures will make clear their identity. Don't confuse your readers: whatever your character is doing, whether they are sprinting, bending down, catching or throwing, show their actions clearly. This is equally true when a character is stationary: even while sitting down, a character will project a mood, an attitude and a point of view. The key to communicating all these different facets is to choose the ultimate expression of each pose – the moment that sits right at the heart of your chosen action.

## Stages of movement

It is not always easy to choose the right moment: a pose that shows your character doing exactly what you want your audience to know they are doing.

It can be helpful to imagine your manga narrative as a film, which you can pause every few seconds and explain with subtitles. Of course, the grammar of film is often very different to that of manga, but try watching a chase scene and pressing 'pause' occasionally. You'll soon find your 'eye' for picking the right paused moments: those with the greatest dynamism and energy, even when frozen. Anatomy is your second watchword, as your audience must be able to recognize the poses you create – they must be physiologically plausible. Characters must never look like they are made of rubber – unless it's one of their mystical abilities. One of the best ways to sell movement is to integrate it with your backgrounds and secondary characters, whether it's puffs of dust from feet on tarmac, or a person being pushed aside as the hero races past.

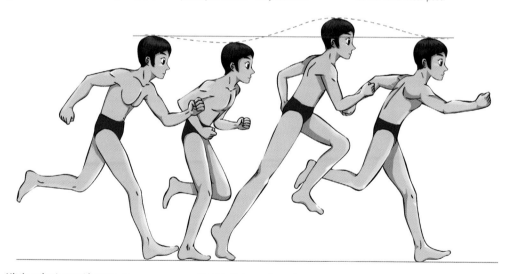

**Hitting the 'pause' button** ▼
When reviewing your scene, capture the apex of each individual moment, the point when the potential energy of any action is released.

**Stages of dynamism** ▲
While any of these poses would work, the third, marked by the upswing in the red dotted line, is the most dynamic.

**Tip:** Find your definitive moments and draw them. Don't leave anything open to interpretation unless you aim to be ambiguous. If your audience misreads an action, it will muddy the story and detract from the pace.

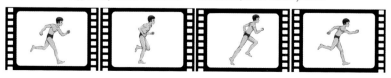

## Axes of perspective

Since manga is two-dimensional, you must find methods of implying a third, to give your characters depth. Using axes can help establish perspective, which will make your characters look more natural as they move within their environment.

The axes comprise two horizontal axes (X, across the horizon of your image; Y, into and out of the image) and a vertical axis (Z, up and down the image). These axes are rotated with respect to where the 'ground' is in the image you are drawing. Picture the vertical axis as your character's centre of gravity, and rotate limbs and poses around this anchor, thus keeping you tethered to the possible and allowing you to turn the character in 3-D space.

### X, Y and Z axes ▼
The spine ascends on the Z axis. Points on his body tilt away from the 90-degree angles on the X and Y axes, giving him energy even standing still.

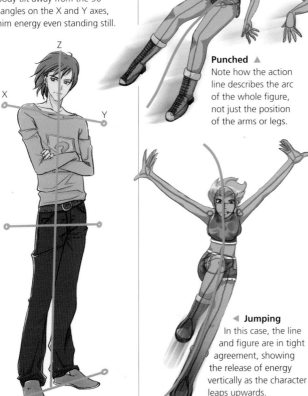

## Action curve

Another form of assistance is the action curve, which helps you to concentrate the body into a single flowing pose. The action line flows down the centre of the spine from the head, and changes shape and length depending upon the pose, forming the single simplest embodiment of every action. When sketching out your poses, the action line should be the first element you draw, enabling you to hang your anatomy on to the most dynamic through-line. The examples below demonstrate the use of the line in the construction of poses, showing the bold action line in blue, the layout anatomy in red, and the completed image in full colour.

**Punched** ▲
Note how the action line describes the arc of the whole figure, not just the position of the arms or legs.

◀ **Jumping**
In this case, the line and figure are in tight agreement, showing the release of energy vertically as the character leaps upwards.

## Foreshortening

This is when parts of a character's body that are 'closer' to us are drawn much larger than those farther away, exaggerating and 'shortening' focal depth for dramatic effect. An example is of a character flying or running towards us. The character's outstretched arms or head may be large in the frame, drawing our attention, but the legs and body are smaller, pushing them farther away. It can be tricky to get the hang of this technique, but striking and punchy poses are a result worth working towards. Foreshortening also has the added benefit of making the reader feel much closer to the action.

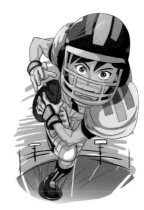

**American footballer** ▲
The helmet and shoulder pad burst out of the page, the footballer appearing to barrel towards our fourth-down tackle.

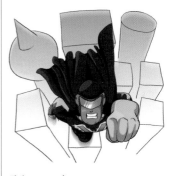

**Flying superhero** ▲
The hero vaults into the sky, his fist and arm outpacing the rest of his body.

## Practice exercise: Male running

In an action-packed manga serial, you're likely to have several characters running, whether it's towards or away from danger. Here's an opportunity to take all you have learned about proportion, anatomy, detail and dynamism, and fuse them into a single image of a shonen hero sprinting to victory. When you've finished, why not try altering the angle or pose?

### Materials
• cartridge paper
• soft lead pencil
• eraser
• pen and ink
• colour of your choice

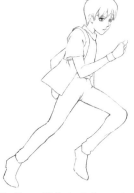

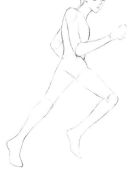

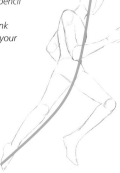

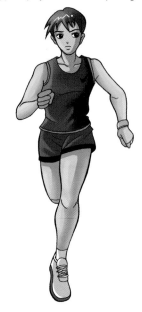

3 Now add the basic line work of the clothes, paying attention to the folds, and the way the jacket billows out, caught by the wind whipped up by the character's passing.

1 Start by roughing in the character's proportions, using simple geometry. Use an action line to select the most dynamic moment.

2 Add detail to the face and hair next, concentrating on the character's determined expression.

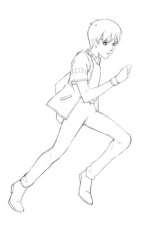

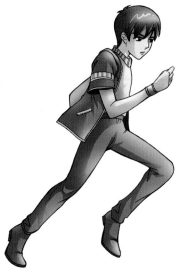

4 Add the final details, from the piping and pockets on the jacket to the crinkle lines on the trousers. Using your colouring or toning medium of choice, add your final textures.

5 Use ink and colour in your preferred medium to complete the side perspective.

▲ **A different perspective**
Here we switch perspective to show the character, now in running gear, foreshortened, running straight towards us.

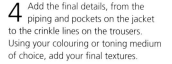

## Practice exercise: Female fighting

When you've had enough of running, it's time to turn and fight. Put into practice what you've learned about the action line, about how hands can grip weaponry, and how facial expressions can sell emotions. When you've drawn this warrior leaping into battle, why not show her from a different angle?

### Materials
- *cartridge paper*
- *soft lead pencil*
- *eraser*
- *pen and ink*
- *colour of your choice*

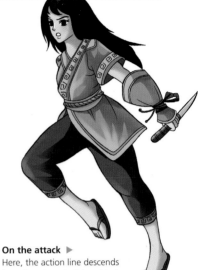

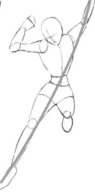

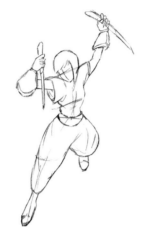

**On the attack** ▶
Here, the action line descends from the character's head to her extended back leg. Note how the hair, robe and thrown-back arm all point along it, reinforcing her leaping stride. The forward leg is elegantly pointed to make a sharp and compact silhouette.

**1** As before, start your illustration with the basic geometric line work, remembering how female proportions differ from male.

**2** The warrior is dressed in billowing trousers and wears thick-wristed gloves, both of which significantly change her silhouette.

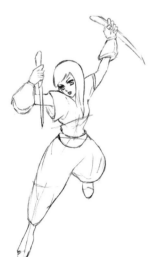

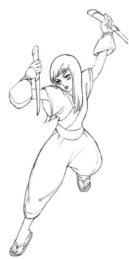

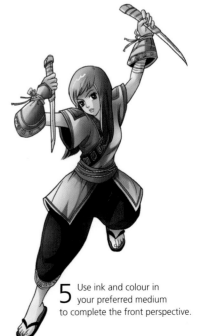

**3** Add detail to the face, hair and hands, and generate construction lines to help you draw her bare feet in sandals.

**4** Complete the pencilled image by defining folds in the clothing and the toes.

**5** Use ink and colour in your preferred medium to complete the front perspective.

# Stance gallery

After a lot of running around and strenuous exertion, it's time for your manga creations to relax. Unfortunately, the same can't be said for your pencil. Stationary characters can say as much, if not more, as characters sprinting or engaging in swordplay, and it's vital that you are able to communicate the differences in your characters' inner states without oversized gestures or combat manoeuvres. With practice and a little thought, you should be able to place your characters in a party situation and have your readers distinguish their personality types from stance and posture alone. After all, how often do you stand with a completely straight spine and your arms pointing down by your sides? Make sure you develop casual stances for your characters, so that they don't look like soldiers when they're not on the move.

## Stance

Before drawing your characters in a stance, try standing yourself. Notice how you tend to put weight on one leg when you're relaxed (you may even favour one leg over the other every time). In placing the weight on this one leg, you are raising the corresponding hip, while the leg bearing the weight will stay straight and rigid. Your waist also bends to compensate for the tilting of the hips, and straightens at the torso. Otherwise you would fall over. The human body understands instinctively how to counterbalance itself.

The position of the body comes down to the positions and angles of the feet, hips and legs, and whatever these parts of the body do, the torso follows to balance you out. So make sure you notice when standing yourself where the weight is distributed, which leg it is on, what your feet are doing (using the heel, the toes, or both) and how far apart your legs are. Try standing in front of a full-length mirror and running through the stances on this spread. See if you can improve on them, or add your own twists. Try to fill a sketchbook page with stances in simple spheres-and-tubes geometry.

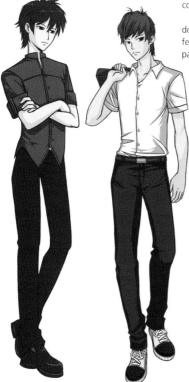

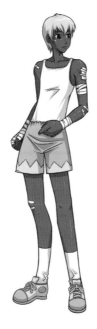

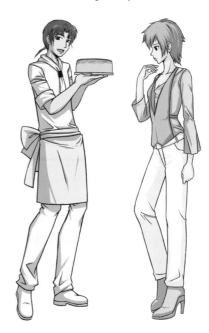

**Teenagers** ▲
A mixture of unearned confidence and overblown angst, these teenagers manage to be cocky and emotionally closed at one and the same time.

**Nervous** ▲
This character keeps her body language locked down as she looks off, waiting for somebody or something she dreads.

**Achievement/polite surprise** ▲
Our chef is pleased to display the result of his experiments, while the pink-haired girl was not expecting a cake, but will accept it anyway.

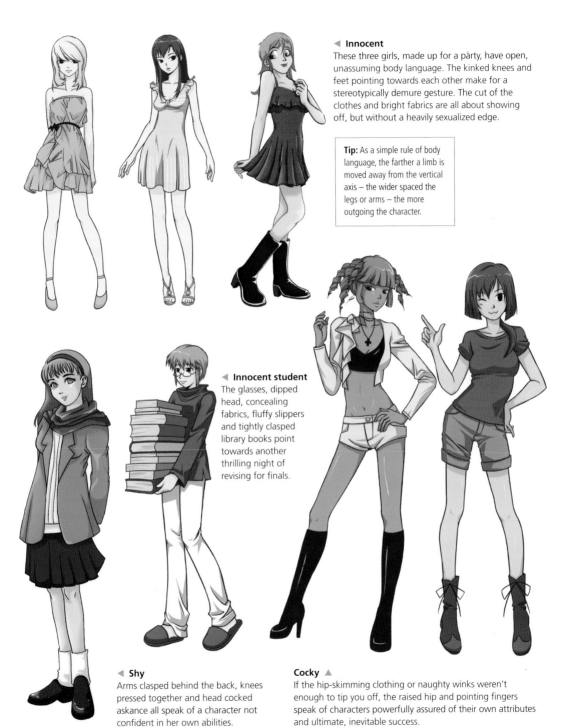

◀ **Innocent**

These three girls, made up for a party, have open, unassuming body language. The kinked knees and feet pointing towards each other make for a stereotypically demure gesture. The cut of the clothes and bright fabrics are all about showing off, but without a heavily sexualized edge.

**Tip:** As a simple rule of body language, the farther a limb is moved away from the vertical axis – the wider spaced the legs or arms – the more outgoing the character.

◀ **Innocent student**

The glasses, dipped head, concealing fabrics, fluffy slippers and tightly clasped library books point towards another thrilling night of revising for finals.

◀ **Shy**

Arms clasped behind the back, knees pressed together and head cocked askance all speak of a character not confident in her own abilities.

**Cocky** ▲

If the hip-skimming clothing or naughty winks weren't enough to tip you off, the raised hip and pointing fingers speak of characters powerfully assured of their own attributes and ultimate, inevitable success.

# Colouring your drawing with markers

Markers are a versatile method of colouring your illustrations. They come in a range of bold colours that reproduce well, and can be mixed and blended on the page, whether by layering using the same pen, or with darker, complementary tones. As well as producing fast-drying, naturalistic results on finished pieces, markers are also excellent for sketching and testing out colour schemes before proceeding to digital colour. Remember, for the best results, ink your drawings with Indian ink or a waterproof fineliner so that the colour and black lines don't bleed into one another. The project on this spread will walk you through the steps of colouring a young shojo heroine in a kimono using a limited palette of markers.

## Practice exercise: Shojo heroine

This vivacious shojo heroine mixes cosplay (dressing in elaborate costume) with a more conservative streak in the traditional kimono and submissive posture. Perhaps she is undercover in some capacity? The illustration uses only a handful of marker colours that nonetheless create a fully rendered 3-D effect.

### Materials
- cartridge paper
- soft lead pencil
- blue pencil 10
- pen and ink
- selection of manga markers (greens, pinks, purples, yellows, browns)

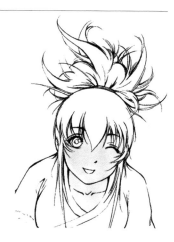

3 Choose your first marker, picking a skin-tone shade to colour in the face and hands. Marker colouring works best if you leave highlighted areas as white, so imagine you are shining a bright light against your chosen surface. Don't colour the areas where the light is heavily concentrated; instead, colour the shadowed areas: underneath the eyes and fringe (bangs).

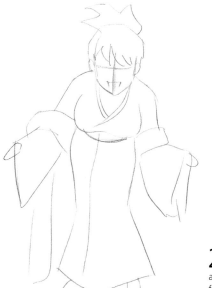

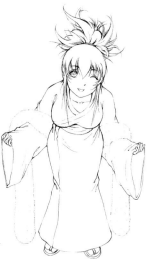

2 Work up the areas of detail in the hair and face, keeping the lines and folds on the kimono and sleeves fairly smooth. When you are happy with your pencil lines, ink them and, when dry, erase the lines as best you can.

1 Open the illustration with a rough pencil sketch, blocking in the anatomy and basic shapes of the girl. Press lightly with the pencil so as to leave the paper as unmarked as possible. You may find it easier to draw a stick figure to help place all of the limbs before you draw the kimono over the top.

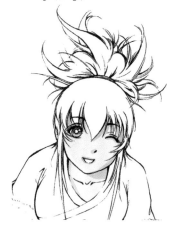

4 Using a darker shade of peach-brown, deepen some of the shadows on the face – concentrate these second shadows underneath the fringe and on the neck. Using purples and pinks, detail the eyes and lips. Keep the lips thin around the inked mouth, and leave a white highlight on the eye.

5 Leaving a large area of highlighted white striking the top of the girl's hair, colour in the first wave of green. Keep the green tone organic and natural by stroking over various areas of the hair a second or third time to make them darker and richer.

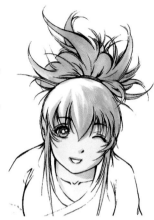

6 As with the skin tone, pick a darker version of the main hair colour and use it to pick out areas – or strands – of deeper shadow. For hair, use quick, individual flicks to give it body and life.

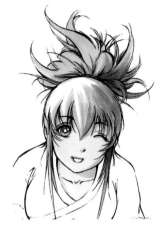

7 Switch your focus to the kimono. As the fabric is less reflective than either the hair or skin, there are fewer white highlights to worry about. Instead, build up tone in layers, colouring over the main body of colour multiple times, narrowing your area of shading each time.

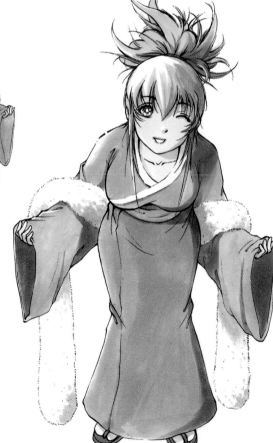

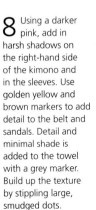

8 Using a darker pink, add in harsh shadows on the right-hand side of the kimono and in the sleeves. Use golden yellow and brown markers to add detail to the belt and sandals. Detail and minimal shade is added to the towel with a grey marker. Build up the texture by stippling large, smudged dots.

# Character archetypes

Most manga characters are young adults, because this is their target age group. If this is your audience, you want to make it easy for them to identify with your story. Each manga genre, from shonen to shojo and all points in between, has its own favourite character types. The clothes your characters wear, for example, will be dictated by genre, and that genre will encompass hundreds of books, each with their own leading character. How will your protagonist differ? Do they have an unusual magical power? Is he or she skilled in a particular martial art? No matter how adept, your characters may also be socially awkward – perhaps shy around members of the opposite sex, or just people in general. They might lose their temper easily, or get horribly clumsy when they are nervous. It's up to you.

## Characters aimed at boys and girls

Shonen (comics for boys up to 18) and shojo (comics for girls up to 18) are both aimed at a typical teenage audience, and feature stories in which the protagonist overcomes obstacles in order to achieve an eventual goal. This type of story is known as *doryoku yuujou shouri* in Japan, which translates as 'effort friendship triumph'. The protagonist, through the obstacles overcome, also achieves improvements in him or herself, sometimes physical, sometimes mental, and sometimes bordering on the supernatural.

The characters involved in these stories usually have to use martial arts, sports, or games to progress and it is the improvement in these areas that will help them achieve their final goal. The setting for these stories varies wildly, from present day to science fiction and fantasy, or an original amalgam of all three.

## Male protagonist

In shonen, the male protagonist must be the pivot around which the rest of the story revolves. He must achieve a great, monumental task, overcoming smaller quests and problems along the way. He is motivated in his task by friends or family, an authority figure whom he trusts (a teacher, respected elder statesman or a commanding officer), or by the actions of his villainous antagonist.

The lead character's attributes are always positive, as he is working towards the greater good. He is usually charismatic, driven by a desire for self-improvement, and physically attractive. However unique his characteristics and appearance, he will be instantly recognizable as the lead character.

**Shojo heroine** ▲
As shojo often deals with the interior world of emotions, this schoolgirl could be suffering a terrible crush, or be ready to deal out magical justice at just a moment's notice.

**Fantasy shonen hero** ▲
Sword in hand, this hero quests for the freedom of his people, and to rescue his kidnapped love.

**Magic-wielding shonen hero** ▲
Gifted by a magical talisman he found in a Kyoto junkshop, this straight-A high school student has an alternative career as a hunter of the forces of evil. When not brushing up on his grades or valedictorian speeches, he heads into the underworld in search of rogue demon half-breeds.

## Female character

The main character in shojo is always female, but female leads also appear in shonen. In shonen, the female lead often displays an equal degree of strength, skill and intelligence as the male protagonist.

Generally speaking, female manga characters are attractive, young adults or adolescents who possess an air of either mystery or mischief.

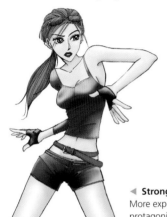

◀ **Strong female lead**
More experienced than the protagonist, she gleefully humbles him at every opportunity.

## Heroic character

The hero is typically a character at the peak of his or her abilities. Manga tends to make the hero a secondary character, rarely the protagonist. The hero is often a role model for the protagonist, and since the reader is identifying with the protagonist, also a role model for them. These heroic types may be either true heroes or villains, but they have abilities beyond the lead's, including strength, courage, bravery, and meta-human or mythical powers.

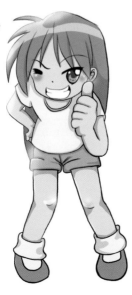

**Hero of song and story** ▲
He has roamed the land since time immemorial, putting his mythical sword to evil-doers for centuries.

## Child character

Children provide a softer edge to a manga story, getting into humorous trouble because they lack the experience to do the right thing. In kodomo manga, children take the lead, often forming a team with older and more powerful allies on the strength of their charisma and wit. These allies make up for the children's lack of power, and will usually assist them in achieving their goals, or taking on a villain too strong for the kids to defeat by themselves.

**Precocious child** ▶
Stubborn, strong-willed and independent, this girl is always willing to strike out on her own in search of fun and adventure. Note her impish smile and wink indicate an extroverted personality.

## Secondary character

Secondary characters have the potential to be protagonists, but are typically a close friend who helps stop the lead from becoming self-indulgent in his personal quest. If younger than the lead, they will have a similar effect to a child character in softening the lead's hard emotional edges.

Sometimes the secondary character is a Trojan horse, possessing an ability or skill lying dormant within them that makes them a key figure in the conclusion of the tale. A secondary character can gain an importance that is sometimes superior to that of the protagonist.

**The best friend** ▶
Checking his watch and looking out for hall monitors, this high schooler awaits his friend's return from a dark mirror dimension.

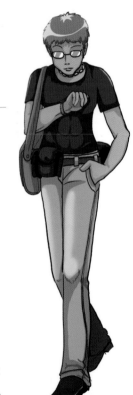

# Super-deformed characters

Characters that are super-deformed (or SDs, as they are more commonly known) are examples of a specific style of manga caricature. The characters are typically small with stubby limbs and oversized heads, so that they resemble small children. Amateur manga artists sometimes start by drawing characters in this style because they are easier to construct. In commercial manga, this drawing style, with even greater degrees of exaggeration, is often interjected into the usual style to show a regular character's extreme emotion, such as anger or surprise, heightened to a level that would look bizarre on a more realistic manga face. When used in this way, they are known as chibi.

Super-deformed characters are meant to be cute and are often used in humorous diversions from the storyline. They also appear in shonen and seinen, which are relatively serious genres. Shirow Masamune's *Appleseed* series is a good example of this. The tales in the *Appleseed* canon are all cyberpunk thrillers and told fairly straight, but every now and then, Shirow throws in the odd bit of slapstick with a panel or two containing miniaturized versions of his characters, to define a moment of silly humour or overblown frustration.

Super-deformed characters can also be used for an entire story. These stories are always comedies, and are often tongue-in-cheek parodies of established manga genres.

## Understanding body proportions

Super-deformed characters are drawn with an oversized head, hands and feet, and a small body. They can vary in height. The head is usually between a third and a half of the character's height. Generally speaking, the rule is that the smaller and more distorted the character is, the more detail you lose. Limbs and clothes are reduced to the minimum number of lines possible, and as a result, the smaller details such as elbows, knees, and other such joints are eliminated. In the case of extreme super-deformed characters, when the ratio of head to body reaches 1:1, the limbs and the torso are drawn much chubbier in order to keep everything looking connected.

**Tip:** A good approach to the super-deformed style is to draw everything below the neck in proportion first, then crown off your character with an absurdly large head. The simpler you make the features, the funnier the super-deform moment.

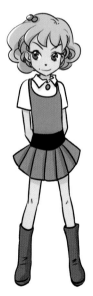

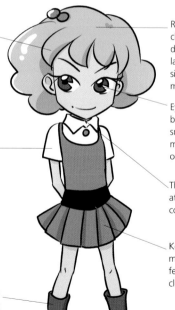

Even if your character usually has a complex hair arrangement, reduce it to a few bunches or strands.

Arms should be one head length, so that if they were raised, they would only reach as far as the top of the head.

Regardless of the character's age, super-deformed heads are large, childlike and simplified to a minimum.

Eyes are always drawn big, and the mouth small. The nose is more often than not omitted.

The neck is only hinted at, or often left out completely.

Keep detail to a minimum, with only a few significant folds in clothing, for example.

**Altering proportions** ▲ ▶
Above is a young girl with the 'normal' proportions described earlier. By exaggerating and altering them, you can turn her into the super-deformed character shown at right.

You don't need to show anatomical detail like muscle tone, so keep the clothes and footwear looking large on the character.

## Practice exercise: Creating a super-deformed character

While super-deformed characters are very simple to draw, that doesn't mean that they lack structural underpinnings. As the head is the most characteristic feature and so large in relation to the rest of the body, you should ensure you pay it the most attention. The rest of the features are simplified as much as possible.

**1** Draw a circle, forming the basis of the head. Now, draw two lines across the centre of the circle to form a 'crosshair' – like on a gunsight – that divides the circle into quarters. The horizontal line is your guide for the centre of the eyes. On the lower half of the circle, define the jaw and chin a little, but keep the shape relatively round. Take the jawline to just above the horizontal line of your crosshair.

### Materials

- *cartridge paper*
- *soft lead pencil*
- *pen and ink*
- *colours of your choice*

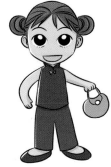

**2** Draw in the eyes: the two corners of the upper eyelid should fall on your horizontal guideline. The arch of the eyebrows shows happiness. The eyes of super-deformed characters do not contain many flecks of reflection – you can include one oval of white in each pupil as a stylized representation. Above all, make sure the eyes are as similar and as symmetrical as possible.

**3** Next, fill in the hair and the mouth, keeping the hair simple, as shown here. Draw a guide for the hairline, parallel to the top of your circle, but a little farther down the head (no more than a quarter of the height of the circle). Draw small arcs to show the hair is pulled back. Here, a couple of upward-curl bunches have been added. Keep the mouth to one or two lines.

**4** The detail on the body, feet and hands is kept to a minimum. Do not labour over the fingers, which can be reduced to a couple of small arcs drawn on to the end of the arms, or even omitted altogether: sometimes a thumb is all you need to suggest a hand. Here the body has been drawn at least two heads tall, but you can go as far as a 1:1 ratio, if you like.

## Chibi characters

These cute, simple characters have heads as big or bigger than their bodies. They are often the alter-egos of otherwise normally drawn characters. The chibi styling may be used to show a more childlike side to these characters, which they usually keep hidden.

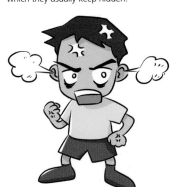

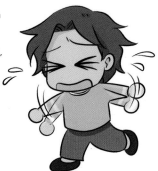

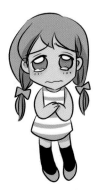

**Two heads in height** ◀ ▲
In chibi, childlike proportions are applied not just to the head but to the whole body. If emotion is running high, chibi characters should be drawn as though on the verge of a meltdown.

**Three heads in height** ▲
Everything about chibi characters is exaggerated, including the hair of the female characters. Emotionally, a chibi character doesn't just feel sad: he or she feels impossibly, gut-wrenchingly sad.

# Character themes

Once you are familiar with the basic character types in manga, and understand what they represent and the roles they traditionally play, you can move on from the stereotypes to create characters with unique traits and idiosyncrasies. When you create new characters, it often helps to use ones from existing manga stories as templates, but as their author, you don't have to follow existing rules or create a carbon copy. That's not to suggest you ignore traditional archetypes completely, or your story would hardly be manga, but you could try blending characters from different manga genres to create something fresh and new. Try taking inspiration from other stories you have enjoyed in the past – not just manga,

but favourite films, novels and TV shows. Why are these characters appealing? How can you adapt them for your own use? A character may have a likeable defining trait, which grabs the audience's attention and sympathy immediately, or they may be more complex and mysterious, which can help to keep your audience interested over the long run.

Although the characters on these pages are based on stereotypes, they have been tweaked and altered with more interesting backgrounds and motives, all of which immediately suggest great story ideas. Use them as templates for your first stories, or learn from their example and create your own genre-spanning characters.

## Magical Girl with a twist

Magical Girl is a popular protagonist in shojo stories. She is traditionally dressed in a sailor's outfit that is, in fact, a variation on the Japanese schoolgirl uniform. Magical Girls usually have special powers, which they use for good. They obtain their powers from an enchanted object such as a wand, which they keep to undergo a transformation. However, the extent of their powers is normally unclear. The Magical Girl here has been given a twist: she is part-vampire. Is she now the villain of the story? Does she hate who she has become, or has she embraced her vampire side?

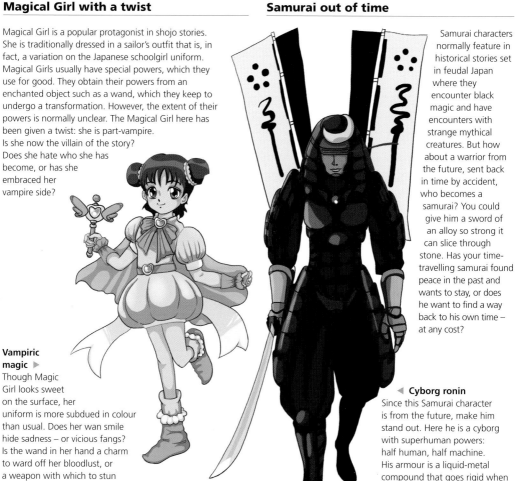

**Vampiric magic** ▶
Though Magic Girl looks sweet on the surface, her uniform is more subdued in colour than usual. Does her wan smile hide sadness – or vicious fangs? Is the wand in her hand a charm to ward off her bloodlust, or a weapon with which to stun her victims?

## Samurai out of time

Samurai characters normally feature in historical stories set in feudal Japan where they encounter black magic and have encounters with strange mythical creatures. But how about a warrior from the future, sent back in time by accident, who becomes a samurai? You could give him a sword of an alloy so strong it can slice through stone. Has your time-travelling samurai found peace in the past and wants to stay, or does he want to find a way back to his own time – at any cost?

◀ **Cyborg ronin**
Since this Samurai character is from the future, make him stand out. Here he is a cyborg with superhuman powers: half human, half machine. His armour is a liquid-metal compound that goes rigid when struck, making him unbeatable in single combat.

## Trapped in the wrong body

This genius scientist got caught out by his own experiment. Now he's a hamster, and needs to change himself back to human form. He's still a genius, but he's now limited by his size and species. Can he make contact with one of the household children who may be able to help?

**Miniature science** ▼
The first task of any species-swapped scientist is to replicate his desk at his new scale.

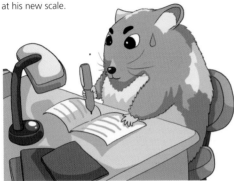

## Flawed characters

Always limit the strengths and abilities of your protagonists. If they are the best they can ever be from the outset, there is no room for development. A character so skilled and intelligent that he or she never fails, loses a fight, or suffers, will also be dull and one-dimensional. Give your characters flaws because the strongest stories involve overcoming weaknesses, and winning in spite of them.

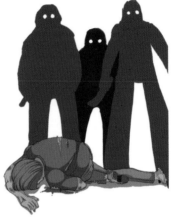

◀ **Dark alley**
The character shown here has been beaten. He lies on the ground, clutching himself in fear and pain. The three figures in the background stand over him, weapons in hand – are they his cowardly attackers, back to finish the job?

## Opposites attract

In a romantic story, your character might be an arrogant man, clever and popular with everyone, but someone who uses people almost without thinking. However, he has a female friend who brings out the best in him, but this side gets lost when there are other people around. As she gets increasingly frustrated by him, what lengths will she go to to get him to change? Is he able to?

**Changing for love** ▶
What other sides are there to the girl, and does the man, ironically, bring out the worst in her?

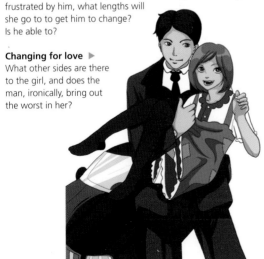

## Demon detective

This female detective is from Hell. She catches bad guys, but often in the service of her evil masters. How does she get criminals back to Hades? Was she once human? How does she deflect the suspicion of her colleagues? Notice her hands are gloved. Is she unable to hide her demonic qualities? Do the gloves conceal something grotesque?

**Evil for hire** ▶
This hard-boiled tale mixes detective procedural with mythical intrigue, giving it an otherworldly element.

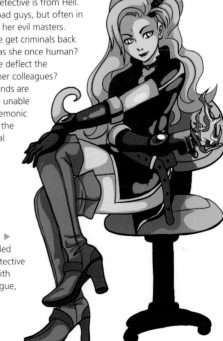

# Dress to impress

The clothes your characters wear are important to their look, and give your audience a means of recognizing them at all times. When you start formulating your characters, draw them without clothes until you're happy with their shape. Then you can develop their style and dress them up. Clothes move as much and as often as the bodies inside them. Although all fabrics behave differently, they share a tendency to fall away towards gravity and the ground.

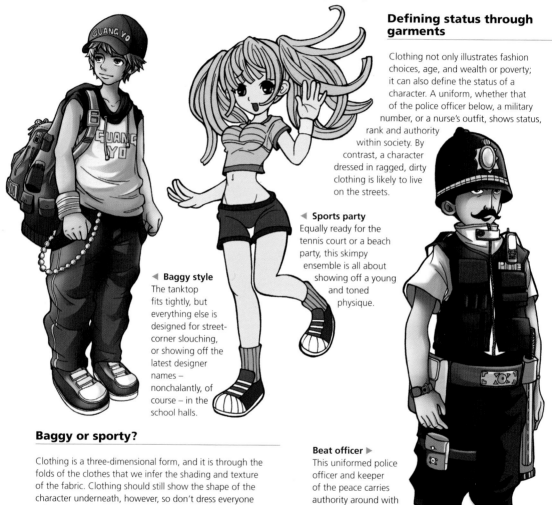

## Defining status through garments

Clothing not only illustrates fashion choices, age, and wealth or poverty; it can also define the status of a character. A uniform, whether that of the police officer below, a military number, or a nurse's outfit, shows status, rank and authority within society. By contrast, a character dressed in ragged, dirty clothing is likely to live on the streets.

◀ **Sports party**
Equally ready for the tennis court or a beach party, this skimpy ensemble is all about showing off a young and toned physique.

◀ **Baggy style**
The tanktop fits tightly, but everything else is designed for street-corner slouching, or showing off the latest designer names – nonchalantly, of course – in the school halls.

## Baggy or sporty?

Clothing is a three-dimensional form, and it is through the folds of the clothes that we infer the shading and texture of the fabric. Clothing should still show the shape of the character underneath, however, so don't dress everyone in baggy clothing. Dressing your characters in different ways allows you to suggest depth (or otherwise) in their personalities. A sporty character might wear jogging shorts or a tracksuit, revealing their physique and showing they are in their physical prime. A shy character is likely to wear layers and drab fabrics that push attention away from themselves. Think, too, of the power of a change of clothes: it's not for nothing that many romantic comedies end by unveiling the lead characters in a smart suit or a brand new dress.

**Beat officer** ▶
This uniformed police officer and keeper of the peace carries authority around with him just as surely as his baton and portable radio. Nothing about the uniform speaks of 'comfort', only of protection – both for himself and the general public.

## Folds

Clothing is relatively taut over body areas that push against fabric. Where there are folds, they form radially, out and away from the bent areas of the body. The five main fold types are described below. To study folds, drape pieces of fabric around different objects to discover where the folds lie.

You'll soon understand how different fabrics form their folds. Essentially, the heavier the material, the more any excess material will fold on itself when hung (although note that skintight clothing won't produce many folds). Always start by sketching in the larger folds, before adding detail.

> **Tip:** When working out how folds hang on a character, picture bracelets around their arms, neck, legs and torso, with the fabric stretched between. As they move, imagine the fabric between each loop bunching and stretching.

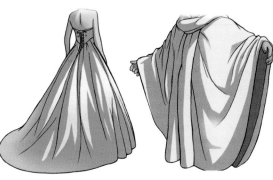
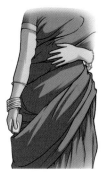
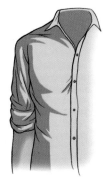

**Inert/columnesque folds** ▲
Each inert fold originates at a point on the waist, and falls to the floor in a conical shape. The columns on the lower right interlock as the dress material gathers on the ground.

**Drape folds** ▲
These are tall folds that connect across a fabric to form a 'U' shape. The columns lead to the point the fabric is suspended from. Scarves, capes and hoods all show these folds.

**Coil folds** ▲
These folds occur around cylindrical shapes – typically, the arms, legs and torso, particularly if the material of the clothing is tight. Baggy clothing will not form coil folds.

**Interlocking folds** ▲
This is where one fold fits inside another. Rolled-up sleeves, large loose-fitting T-shirts, or a scarf wrapped around the neck can all show interlocking folds.

## How material hangs

Each of the three items of clothing pictured here show a torso and an arm drawn inside a sleeve. The first top is made from lycra or a similar skintight material, the second is a light cotton sweatshirt, and the third is a thick coat or jacket sleeve. Each fabric shows folds. Watch the way the fabric is being pulled. When clothing is not skintight, material will hang downwards with gravity; but as it is attached to the rest of the fabric worn across the body, it also pulls horizontally away from the arm and upper torso.

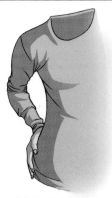
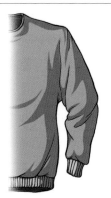
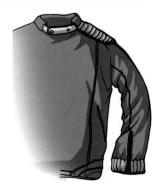

**Skintight** ▲
The fabric stretch is all horizontal, giving defined underarm and elbow creases.

**Roomy** ▲
Excess fabric bunches towards the forearm but the tight cuff keeps the shape.

**Heavy** ▲
The thick fabric obscures the shape of the body but is tightly bunched on the arms.

## Specific types of clothing

This section looks at some common articles of clothing that you can use to dress up your manga characters. Clothes shape and define their personalities. It's a good idea, at the story planning stage, to make a few notes on what everyone has in their wardrobe. For instance, if your character is school-aged, do they wear a uniform? If not, what is their casual wear?

If they practise a sport, like track and field or a martial art, they should be drawn wearing the appropriate garb – at the very least while they are engaging in it. Bear in mind that most male characters in manga don't wear bright or showy clothes – these are reserved for the females – but that doesn't mean they are not well-presented.

### Trousers

Male trousers tend to be loose, whereas female trousers hug the figure. The material on trousers gathers around the waist and top of the thighs (where the leg meets the lower torso), and also around the knees – because if there was no room for manoeuvre there, bending your legs would be an onerous task. Gravity takes care of everything else, which keeps folds to a minimum. If a leg is lifted, for a kick for example, the material folds in a similar way to sleeves. If the trousers are long, folds will rest on the foot.

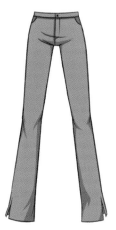

**Skinny trousers** ▲
Leaving little to the imagination, skinny trousers are also very light on folds.

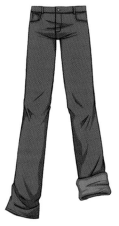

**Extra-long trousers** ▲
The extra material creates a neat fold at the end of each leg but may be bulky.

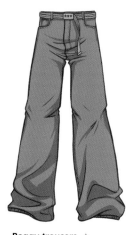

**Baggy trousers** ▲
Extra material creates folds around the ankles, where it bunches up and billows out.

### Skirts

First, decide on your skirt length and the width (whether you want it loose or tight). When you're ready to draw, start with a simple shape which you can use as a guide; in this case, a blunt cone makes for a stiff miniskirt. To make your skirt less restrictive, add more curve and ripple to the hem. The more you add, the looser it will look – add column folds to show the flow of fabric. Include a slit at the back for a business skirt or at the side (for a more casual appearance). From the front the skirt curves mostly at the side, but at the back it curves outwards with the shape of the body.

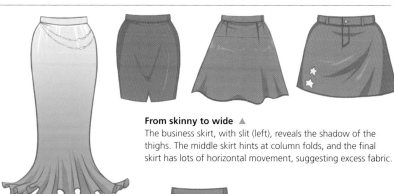

**Opulent skirt** ▲
Just the thing for a cocktail party, this inverted tulip skirt hugs the hips before splaying out into a display of column folds at its base.

**From skinny to wide** ▲
The business skirt, with slit (left), reveals the shadow of the thighs. The middle skirt hints at column folds, and the final skirt has lots of horizontal movement, suggesting excess fabric.

◀ **Pleated skirt**
For a pleated effect for a school uniform, change the wavy ripples to straight angles, as pleats remove the curve effect, making the skirt appear stiffer.

## Practice exercise: Girl's T-shirt

It can often aid your understanding of both the human figure and the fabric you drape upon it if you draw the clothes in isolation, and then apply them. This exercise takes you through the steps.

1 Start by drawing a collar for the neck, using either a 'V' or a circular shape.

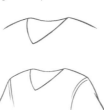

2 Add a pair of oval shapes to mark the end of the sleeves, and a small arc at the base of the T-shirt where it will hang to the waist.

3 Draw the connecting lines for the rest of the T-shirt, as well as a few coil folds, as this T-shirt is quite close-fitting.

### Materials
• *soft lead pencil*
• *pen and ink*
• *colouring method of your choice*

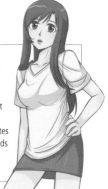

**Tip:** Note how the inert T-shirt takes on a number of folds when applied to the figure of the girl. The coil folds on her waist point to her armpits, a shadow in colour delineates her breasts, and drape folds show how the material hangs on the sleeve.

## Practice exercise: Cloaks and capes

A cloak or a cape sits on the shoulders, and falls in long straight folds to the floor. These will be mainly column folds, with some drape folds to add texture around the neck. For a military-looking cloak, add thick folds around the shoulders and extend them around to the back.

### Materials
• *soft lead pencil*
• *pen and ink*
• *colouring method of your choice*

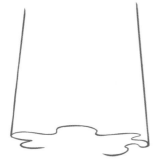

1 The main body of a cloak is formed from two lines dropped from the shoulders, but the intricate detail starts at the base. Using a wavy line, draw an incomplete crescent for the hem, as above.

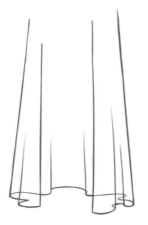

2 Now draw a tapered vertical line leading upwards from a point on every curve. At this stage your cloak will look strangely translucent.

**Tip:** It's a good idea to collect reference from fashion catalogues and magazines, and to model your outfits accordingly. If your story is set in a fantasy or futuristic setting, you can be more daring and inventive, but make sure you keep some elements which are easy to relate to.

3 Now erase the lines and curves hidden by the folds of the cloak, or the human figure within it. The cloak is clasped on either side of the neck, while the hood is formed from a rough oval, with its peak in the centre of the forehead. If in doubt about the hood's shape, try sketching yourself in a hooded top.

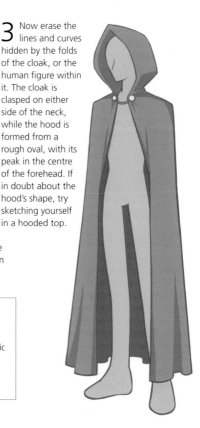

# Clothing gallery

If there's one visual arena in which manga is unreservedly triumphant, it's in bringing high fashion to its heroes and heroines. Whether fighting off demons in between advanced algebra classes or piloting enormous mecha into battle against a faceless alien horde, manga characters are always at the cutting edge of contemporary clothing – a fact lovingly acknowledged by the legions of 'Cosplayers' who dress up at conventions as their favourite manga icons.

## The infinite wardrobe

When the detail on your manga character's faces is limited by the simplicity of the form, the complexity and nuance you can add through their clothing takes on a greater dimension. Think of the ways clothing is used in society. A T-shirt with a slogan can offer insight into a character's politics – as does their choice of a T-shirt over a suit and tie. Think as well of clothes that a character is forced to wear: uniforms, whether for school or work. How do they wear these cookie-cutter costumes? With pride? In a slovenly fashion? Have they made rule-breaking customizations to the length of the skirt or the knot in the tie? This attitude is as important as the clothes themselves.

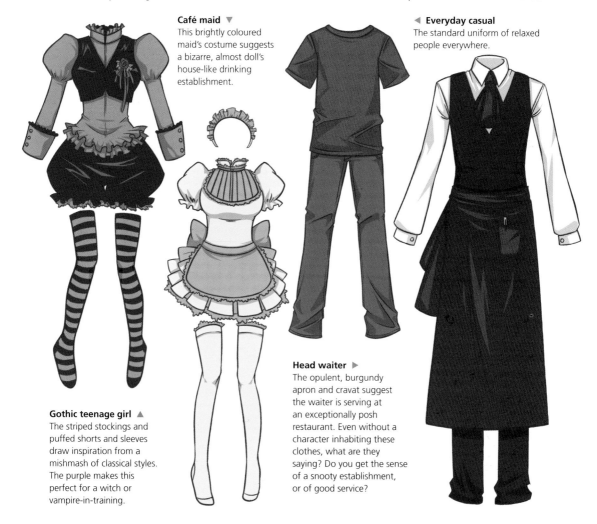

**Café maid** ▼
This brightly coloured maid's costume suggests a bizarre, almost doll's house-like drinking establishment.

◀ **Everyday casual**
The standard uniform of relaxed people everywhere.

**Gothic teenage girl** ▲
The striped stockings and puffed shorts and sleeves draw inspiration from a mishmash of classical styles. The purple makes this perfect for a witch or vampire-in-training.

**Head waiter** ▶
The opulent, burgundy apron and cravat suggest the waiter is serving at an exceptionally posh restaurant. Even without a character inhabiting these clothes, what are they saying? Do you get the sense of a snooty establishment, or of good service?

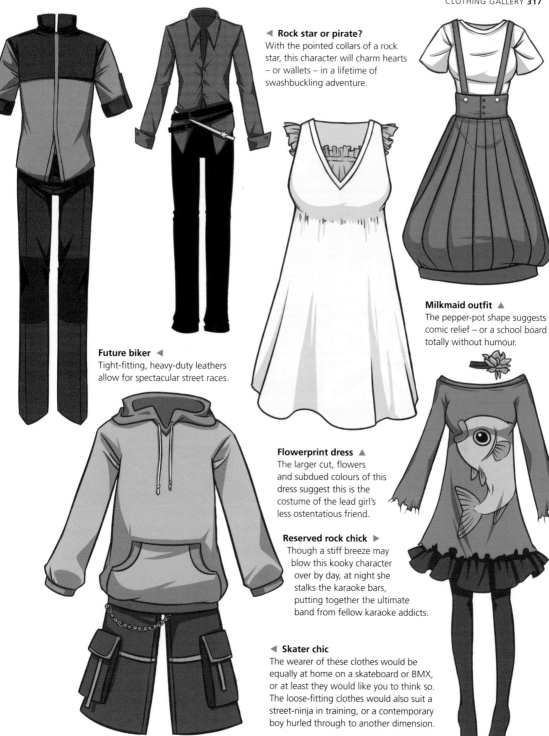

**◄ Rock star or pirate?**
With the pointed collars of a rock star, this character will charm hearts – or wallets – in a lifetime of swashbuckling adventure.

**Milkmaid outfit ▲**
The pepper-pot shape suggests comic relief – or a school board totally without humour.

**Future biker ◄**
Tight-fitting, heavy-duty leathers allow for spectacular street races.

**Flowerprint dress ▲**
The larger cut, flowers and subdued colours of this dress suggest this is the costume of the lead girl's less ostentatious friend.

**Reserved rock chick ►**
Though a stiff breeze may blow this kooky character over by day, at night she stalks the karaoke bars, putting together the ultimate band from fellow karaoke addicts.

**◄ Skater chic**
The wearer of these clothes would be equally at home on a skateboard or BMX, or at least they would like you to think so. The loose-fitting clothes would also suit a street-ninja in training, or a contemporary boy hurled through to another dimension.

# Character accessories

Once you have decided on your characters' clothing, you can also choose some accessories as further embellishment. The objects your characters keep on and about their person will add depth to their individual personalities. You will want to ensure that your audience can easily identify your lead characters, which is sometimes difficult in mainly black and

white narratives without these smaller details. Accessorizing your characters will help make your creations unique, so that readers will know them from their appearance alone. Everyday technological gadgets that can offer a window into new storytelling possibilities, or just add an extra veneer of cool to your tech-savvy protagonists.

## Ribbons, headbands and glasses

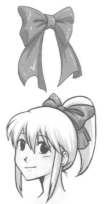
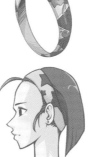
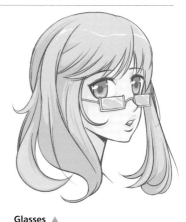

Female manga characters often wear ribbons in their hair, and the addition of a ribbon is often a clue to a character's age. Large ribbons tied around bunches, for example, will suggest a younger character, as will a single large bow around a ponytail. If you show a girl's hair tied in bunches, you also have the option to include long strands of excess ribbon dangling down with the hair. A sophisticated hairband tends to age up a character. The girl shown last could be a college activist, or on a 'gap year' adventure. Glasses are often used to say something about a character.

**Pink bow** ▲
A large bow on a pony tail makes a character look cute, innocent and young.

**Hairband** ▲
With hair out of her eyes, this older character is ready for business.

**Glasses** ▲
These add interest to the face and can be used as a disguise, to suggest scholarly tendencies – or just to improve bad eyesight.

## Rings, bracelets, symbols and belts

From the grinning skulls of secret college organizations to the cheap plastic of a trinket given as a party favour, you can tell a lot about your characters from what jewellery they wear; not least of which, whether they are married or not – or whether they bear a signet or decoder ring that marks them out as a king or a spy.

Emblems can have meanings that are significant in a story. Belts can carry potions or messages, images of loved ones or carefully scribed spells. Make each accessory unique with meaningful symbols, patterns, studs or precious stones.

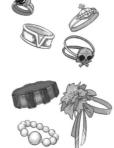

**Symbols** ▲
What family treasures and secrets are locked up in these emblems?

**Finger jewellery** ▲
Rings can reflect characters' histories. Where did they get them? Were they a gift? Do they have more than sentimental value?

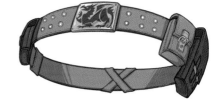

**Belt with pouches** ▲
Handed down from warrior to warrior, a belt can contain battlefield herbs and medications.

## Mobile phone

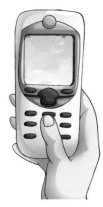

Many shonen stories feature characters who have a penchant for gadgets and gizmos, so it helps to keep abreast of the latest developments in technology, drawing inspiration from the hottest designs to build your own creations. You may want to push the possibilities of modern technology, incorporating fantastic features. You may have a mobile phone yourself, so finding reference to practise from shouldn't be a problem. Furthermore, visiting the websites of major brands will allow you to view their available phones, often accompanied by interactive 3-D demonstrations. Tilt the

reality of your story by adding more features to your invented models. Phones today can make video calls, take photos, play music and track position by GPS. Police or military characters could use mobiles for more than just calls, tracking down criminals with their cameras. Other useful features include infrared capability, or limited hologram generation. Programs could be voice-operated, or the mobile could have artificial intelligence.

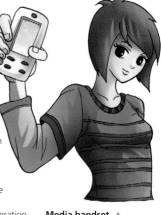

**Simple handset** ▲
Start with a rectangular cuboid. Keep the scale of the device around the same size as your character's hand.

**Media handset** ▲
The standard handset is streamlined, given a bigger screen and updated with more advanced capabilities.

## Laptop and headset

In many ways, aside from the scale, drawing a laptop is much the same as drawing a mobile phone, in that it involves a screen and buttons that can be drawn with a simple grid method. Make sure the screen is of a size with the bottom half, so that they lock together when the 'clamshell' is closed.

Don't forget some simple cylinders to show how the monitor is hinged on to the keyboard. Practise drawing the laptop open and closed. If it is a piece of equipment used regularly by a character, you should consider personalizing it. Think about using a shape unique to that character, or give it a logo, sticker or custom stencil that denotes ownership. The laptop can also be customized with peripherals. With the headset you could make the computer obey voice commands. This could make for some interesting dialogue if you show a super-smart human character verbally interacting with an advanced computer.

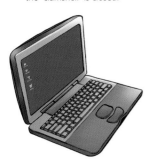

**Standard laptop** ▲
A common modern laptop – an excellent jumping-off point for your own creation.

**Hands-free headset** ▲
Perfect for delivering voice commands or having a conversation while on the run, or delivering a commentary during an action-based adventure.

◀ **Ultra-light kit**
This boy genius has built from scratch an ultra-light laptop with the processing power of multiple supercomputers. The headset is part of communicating voice commands.

# Weapons

Fighting weapons are intrinsic to manga, and play an important role in identifying the principal characters. Regardless of genre, most main characters possess a method of fighting that makes them stand out. They may fight with

a sword, a gun, a magical power, or by practising a martial art (sometimes in combination with a weapon, i.e. 'gun fu', or by using a characteristic and empowering piece of armour, clothing or jewellery).

## Practice exercise: Drawing a gun

Guns come in a range of sizes and styles, and can be constructed with geometric shapes. Put some thought into why your character uses a gun: what it fires (bullets or some sort of beam?); whether they are skilful or a liability with a gun in their hand. You can also personalize the weapon by giving it an unusual barrel, or markings on the grip.

### Materials
- cartridge paper
- blue pencil 10
- pen and ink
- colour of your choice

1 Sketch guides, keeping to basic rectangular shapes: a standard sidearm is formed of three tilted rectangles, as shown.

2 Draw in the first stage of detail. Pay attention to the way the parts interlock, and the curved elements that interrupt the angular silhouette.

3 Add further details, such as the ridging on the stock. Draw the items as they are, not how you might expect them to be.

4 When you are happy with your pencilled lines, ink your illustration.

5 Finish off the gun by colouring it using the method of your choice. Add contrasts between the burnished metal parts and the textured handgrip.

## Practice exercise: Sword basics

In the Arthurian legend of the Round Table, the sword Excalibur was as much a symbol that bound the knights together for the good of the country, as it was the ultimate weapon. In Japanese legends, the sword is also laden with symbology: promises are sworn upon the sword – and if vengeance is sworn, then it is always delivered with honour.

### Materials
- cartridge paper
- red pencil
- pen and ink
- colour of your choice

1 Start with a gentle curve, forming the base line of your sword. Arc it up gently at the right, for the hilt, and more sharply towards the tip of the blade, at the left. The red pencil line reminds you of the proportions of the sword length.

2 For this sword, keep the width of the blade the same as the width of the hilt. Draw a line down the centre of the blade to show the two edges of the sword, and add a handguard just over two-thirds down. Add a pattern on the hilt, using repeated thin ellipses.

3 Ink your pencil lines when you are ready. As with the gun, you may wish to use a technical pen for the blade, although an organic line would suit the woven fibres on the hilt. Colour the sword using the method of your choice, suggesting the sharpness of the metal with strong white highlights. Ensure that one edge of the sword is darker than the other, to show that they are angled differently.

## Other types of gun

There are other types of gun, of course. You could choose a magnum, a revolver, a pump-action shotgun, a machine gun or a sniper's rifle. Practise drawing them at many different angles.

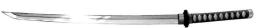
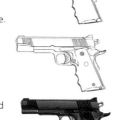

Shotgun

Rifle

Revolver

## Mêlée weapon effects

Close combat weapons are called mêlée weapons. They are a great accessory for any warrior character, but their dynamism can be vastly increased with a number of simple effects – both motion-based and magical. See how you can transform a simple clash of swords into an epic battle worthy of titans with the addition of just a few speed lines.

Axe

Straight-edge axe

Dagger

Spear

Bow

Sword

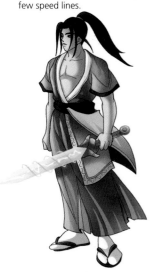

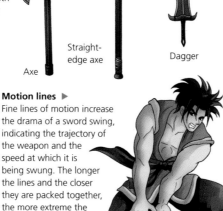

**Motion lines** ▶
Fine lines of motion increase the drama of a sword swing, indicating the trajectory of the weapon and the speed at which it is being swung. The longer the lines and the closer they are packed together, the more extreme the motion. Draw your lines tracing back from the blade of the sword to the beginning of its arc. Speedlines will often overlap with the background art, although you may find a stark white panel, isolating the character and the sword swing, could prove more effective.

**Magical glow** ▲
Eldritch energy wraps around this ethereal blade, immediately telling us that the weapon is out of the ordinary and possessed of magical powers. As well as striking fear into the hearts of its foes, the sword also suggests story possibilities – where did it come from, what powers does it possess, and who held it before the current wielder?

**Tip:** Sometimes the use of motion lines isn't appropriate, particularly if the panel already features speedlines in the background. The two will just mix into one another and muddy the action. Instead, use a white absence of lines to show the trajectory of motion, either erasing the background speedlines in the appropriate arc, or drawing two lines surrounding a single broad streak. This will look much clearer within an already busy shot.

**Impact effects** ▶
This image combines the dynamism of motion lines with an explosive illustration of the point of impact. The still panel illustrates a full, fluid movement. As the eye moves down the panel, we see the arc of the sword, its impact against the haft of the spear, and the impact throwing the spearman backwards. Fiery colours draw the eye to the most important action.

# Putting it together

Now that you've learned how to build human and non-human characters from the inside out, and populated dozens of wardrobes and armouries with clothes and devastating new weapons, it's time to combine these strands into a pair of fully realized characters. The following two practice exercises guide you through the process of character creation for both a male and female protagonist, from concept to colour. The two characters are from very different genres – the male from a downbeat, futuristic action thriller and the female from a high-fantasy, magical shojo adventure. The steps taken in their creation are very similar. Why not create a complementary character for each setting?

## Practice exercise: Post-apocalyptic bounty hunter

This character wanders the post-apocalyptic wasteland of America after a ruthless bio-weapon strike killed 85 per cent of the population with a gene-bomb virus. In the ruins of society, he helps maintain the fragile grip of law, rounding up escaped prisoners and delivering them to the last vestiges of government. He is growing increasingly ambivalent about his job, and is beginning to think he is just propping up a corrupt administration that could be replaced by something better.

**1** Start the drawing off with a loose sketch of the proportions. Keep the character lanky and tall, and the stance powerful even when standing still. Position the hands to hold a weapon.

### Materials
- cartridge paper
- blue pencil 10
- pen and ink
- colours of your choice

**2** Begin to rough in some of the details – add loose-fitting desertwear clothing and a tattered cloak. Show the direction of the desert winds by blowing the long hair and cloak out backwards. Add plenty of pouches for ammunition and supplies across the chest, and tightly bind the feet and legs in bandages.

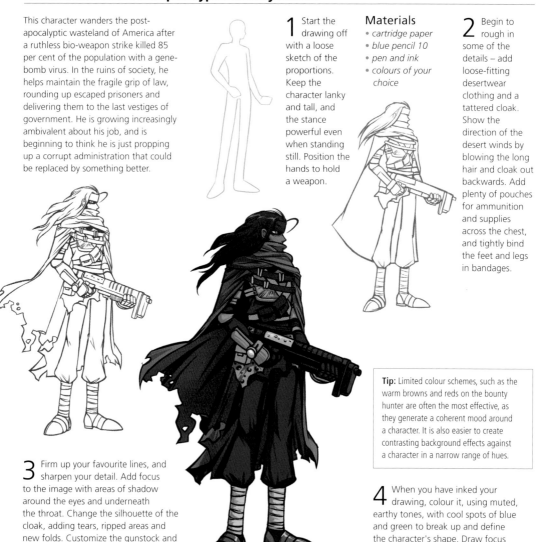

**3** Firm up your favourite lines, and sharpen your detail. Add focus to the image with areas of shadow around the eyes and underneath the throat. Change the silhouette of the cloak, adding tears, ripped areas and new folds. Customize the gunstock and concentrate effort on the character's gauntlets and belts.

**Tip:** Limited colour schemes, such as the warm browns and reds on the bounty hunter are often the most effective, as they generate a coherent mood around a character. It is also easier to create contrasting background effects against a character in a narrow range of hues.

**4** When you have inked your drawing, colour it, using muted, earthy tones, with cool spots of blue and green to break up and define the character's shape. Draw focus to the head with a softened blood red for the hair.

## Practice exercise: Precipitation Faerie

This elfin character is one of the hundreds of elemental faeries tasked with seeing that the natural world runs as it is supposed to. The Precipitation Faerie is part of a task force charged with making sure the rain cycle continues. Along with her sisters in the Evaporation and Condensation departments, she travels around the globe, puncturing stubborn clouds, encouraging recalcitrant droplets and doing her best to see that the 'rain in Spain falls mainly on the plain' (among other plateau platitudes). She takes her job very seriously, but enjoys taking time off to soak up the sun, up above the clouds.

1 Start with a simple anatomical sketch, as before. We've gone for very skinny limbs and a classic pin-up/Busby Berkeley dancer pose, with a large head that will be mostly hair in the final piece. Keep the limbs long and the figure lithe.

### Materials
• cartridge paper
• pen and ink
• colours of your choice

2 Sketch in some clothing. Here we've gone for a Gothic yet girlish-style ruffled dress, puffy sleeves and a hat, not to mention some killer platform heels, a lace-up corset and fringed gloves. The faerie's magical umbrella begins to take shape as a bowl – a similar shape to her hairstyle.

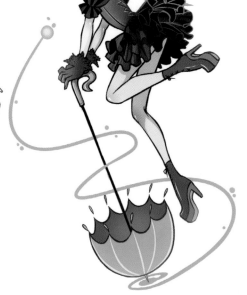

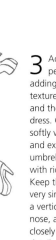

3 Add in the final pencilled details, adding tone and texture to the sleeves and the ruffles of the dress. Create some softly veined wings, and expand the umbrella's bowl shape with ridged 'wavelets'. Keep the faerie's face very simple – taut lips, a vertical line for the nose, and wide eyes closely framed by the detail of her hair.

4 The final colour version adds a swirl of blue rain-magic emanating from the tip of the umbrella, along with a number of interesting 'colour holds' (when black lines are exchanged for colour) on the outlines of the translucent wings and on the ruffles of the black dress in particular. The areas of exposed skin contrast sharply with the narrow range of blues and blacks of the clothing, while the magical elements of the wings and the swirl of rain share the same bright turquoise.

# Kodomo animal characters

Another popular manga genre is that of anthropomorphic animal stories. These feature animals with human qualities: they walk upright, talk, wear clothes and behave like people. Anthropomorphic stories are successful on a number of counts: the simpler, animal-based drawings are 'attractive' to a large number of readers; they allow for commentary on the human condition by showing common foibles in a new light; and they allow for humorous juxtapositions in more adult stories by showing 'childhood favourites' in mature or compromising situations. Kodomo characters can also be subjected to extremes of violence without gore or consequences, an orgy of cartoonish slapstick. Don't feel that kodomo stories need to be throwaway or totally lightweight, however: think about the most enduring cartoon characters and most memorable stories – how many feature humans, and how many anthropomorphs?

Kodomo characters visually share a lot with super-deform characters – they are based on exaggerated and compacted human anatomy, with simple, engaging facial features

incorporating streamlined elements of their animal forms. For instance, the tiger and the rabbit below have similar facial structures, eyes and ears, despite being very different in real life. When in doubt, strip out detail rather than

adding it in. We will create some of the inhabitants of a shady downtown bar, all of which just happen to be cute animals with drinking problems and a world of gripes.

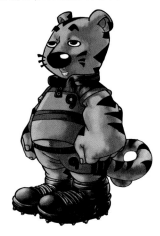

**Tiger footballer** ▲
Not the smartest toy in the box, this tiger looks half asleep. His football boots and strip indicate to us that his strength may lie on the pitch.

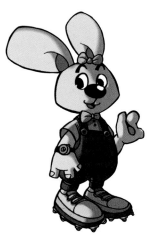

**Bunny engineer** ▲
The dungarees indicate this jolly rabbit is a clock-repairer and electronics whiz. She could even be tied up in trading secrets in acts of industrial espionage.

## Practice exercise: Bad-tempered bat

This character is oblivious to the world around him. His brow is furrowed and his eyes squinting. His exaggerated form is very simple: vicious jags for wings, two enormous ears jutting out of a potato-shaped head, and spindly limbs folded across a similarly dumpy body. A range of unexpected accoutrements add extra flavour: head tattoos and facial hair, multiple extreme piercings, comedy flip-flops and the exceptional dress sense of a Wall Street banker on a summer holiday.

### Materials
• soft lead pencil
• pen and ink
• colouring method of your choice

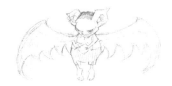

1 Roughly sketch in all the details of the bat, using simple, expressive shapes. Focus on the overall shapes rather than specificities at this stage.

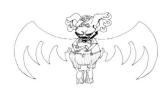

2 Make your details more specific, keeping the eyes big and the rest of the facial features small. Work up your sketch into a finished inked piece.

3 Colour your bat with flat tones, emphasizing his more bizarre characteristics in bright colours.

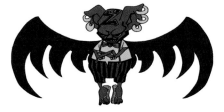

## Practice exercise: Drunken penguin

Here's another patron to adorn your bar: a drunken penguin, drowning the sorrows of his failing business in one,

### Materials
- *soft lead pencil*
- *pen and ink*
- *colouring method of your choice*

two or three bottles of mid-price wine. His glasses, hat and coat all suggest a middle-aged businessman of some social standing, so perhaps this is the first time he's stumbled into a shadowy bar. Alternatively, perhaps he's a frequent feature at the bar: a professional drunk who turns up in

a slightly tatty jacket every Friday night. Nobody knows where he comes from, but he has an anthology of rambling, slurred stories to entertain the rest of the bar with.

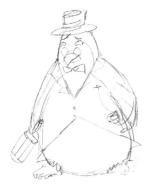

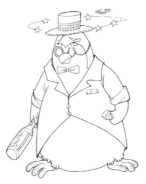

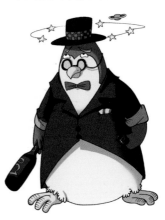

1 Sketch in the basic features. The penguin starts as an obese skittle. The 'jacket' feathers of a real penguin are turned into an actual suit jacket.

2 Ink the lines, adding characterful details like the pocket handkerchief, checked hatband and empty bottle brandished like a truncheon.

3 Add visual interest at the colour stage by using bright blue and yellow instead of the real penguin's monochrome scheme.

## Developing the characters

Your anthropomorphic world may need no explanation: the characters might just be talking animals instead of people. You may want to incorporate your world into our own, however: perhaps it's a secret bar for soft toys, who visit it for a beverage and a whine when their children owners are asleep. Perhaps it's the only place where they can escape from toddler drool or sadistic next-door neighbours and be themselves – and if that means eight or twelve pints before the sun comes up, then so be it ...

**Raising the bar** ▶
The shady basement bar contrasts amusingly with the bright forms and pleasing shapes of the anthropomorphic creatures. Despite the childish appearance, these are adult themes.

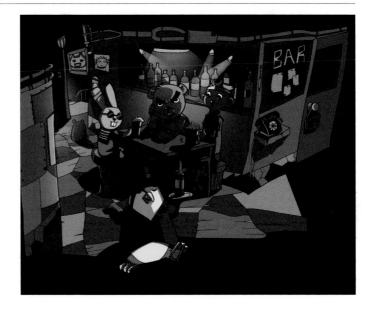

# Girl protagonist project

This is how to create a protagonist who could front either a shonen or shojo story. We'll also show how to develop a character concept beyond your initial sketches and into an actual storyline. Shonen and shojo have basic similarities: in each, the protagonist is trying to reach a goal, bettering themselves along the way. Shonen stories do this through action-oriented means, while shojo utilizes more contemplative, psychological narratives about relationships. For our example, we've chosen a character who can shine in either genre: a musician. As a female lead, she can be involved with either genre – perhaps as the vocalist and guitarist for an otherwise all-male band.

Your choice of genre will determine how you build the surrounding characters and storyline. A shojo story may feature a band with more introspective, acoustic music, with the thrust of the story being the interpersonal relationships between band members and the way in which the songwriter's life informs her lyrics. A shonen story, by contrast, could focus on a punkier, more aggressive band battling to get signed by a record company, showcasing the rivalry between your characters and other bands that also want the prize. This rivalry could spill over into action-packed set pieces or physical confrontations.

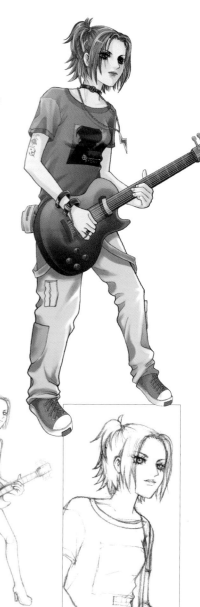

## Materials
* *soft lead pencil*
* *pen and ink*
* *colouring method of your choice*

**Ready to rock** ▶
Clothing, hair, tattoos and accessories combine to create a very strong sense of character, even without reading a single line of her dialogue.

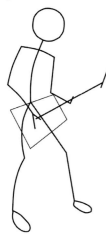

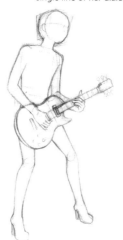

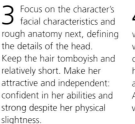

**1** Once you've settled on your character type and done a little research, begin your figure with a stick frame pose. The pose here incorporates the guitar, directing attention towards it and adding a centre to the pose. She's wielding an electric guitar.

**2** Flesh out the character's outline and start adding detail to the guitar – place the hands and fingers at this stage. Block in all of the proportions, paying attention to the joints and the way the body curves along the action line to accommodate the instrument.

**3** Focus on the character's facial characteristics and rough anatomy next, defining the details of the head. Keep the hair tomboyish and relatively short. Make her attractive and independent: confident in her abilities and strong despite her physical slightness.

**4** Add in clothing, using the anatomy as a guide to where her T-shirt and trousers will fold. Think not only of the clothes she will be wearing, but how she will be wearing them – are they loose or tightly fitted? Are they customized? Are they worn sloppily or smartly?

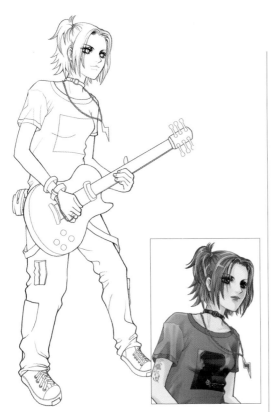

## Developing the character

Later, you could create a unique twist on your character as your story develops, testing them with tragedy or misfortune. One idea could give your protagonist the means to play riffs no other band has ever achieved – a bionic arm. Your guitarist could lose their flesh-and-blood arm in a terrible accident, leaving them fearful they would never play again. A shojo story would show the singer's slow rehabilitation, with the tears and triumphs along the way as they learn to play again. The arm could be the result of a top-secret bionic experiment, which gives them the ability to play better and faster – but getting there won't be easy; you'll want to keep your audience on your side.

Finally, think about the rest of the band. How many members? What instruments would they play? Think about how they react to the protagonist, either with or without the bionic arm. Their history: have they ever broken up before? Is every rehearsal a drama? If your story is mainly about the band, the other members will be your secondary characters, driving the interpersonal relationships and dramas in between gigs.

5 Here, we've gone for long and baggy trousers, lined with multiple pockets, and covered in zips and belts. Her T-shirt has her favourite album cover screen-printed on to it – you could compose it in a separate image using Photoshop, drawing an album cover of your own at a larger size and then reducing and deforming it to fit. Further accessories include leather wristbands, a choker, and a lightning-bolt necklace on a long chain.

6 When you've completed your inks, colour the image, paying close attention to the textures of the fabrics, the tones of her face, and the various shines and glinting effects on the guitar. Remember that her aim is to shock and attract attention, so don't shy away from bright, clashing colours like pinks and greens. A tattoo on her right arm completes the look.

**Tip:** Investigate magazines and websites of your character's chosen subculture in order to research ideas for their clothing and accessories. In this instance, music magazines, websites and videos all informed the look of the rocker, but the same would apply if your character was an army colonel, a sports idol, or an astronaut. Don't just slavishly copy clothing; add your own unique twists to basic fashion styles in order to make your protagonists stand out.

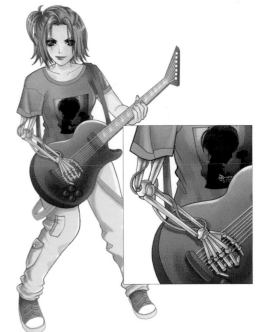

**Changing the look** ▲
Depending on your story, the addition of a bionic limb could be creepy – or a triumph of the human spirit.

**Cyborg close-up** ▲
The new limb follows the same skeletal structure as an actual arm, only without musculature or skin on top.

# Fantasy pirate project

Piracy has made a return to a variety of comics, including manga, helped by the popularity of films like *Pirates of the Caribbean* and the pirate-rich computer games in the *Monkey Island* series. The manga *One Piece*, for instance, features a rag-tag group of freebooters seeking the treasure of the King of the Pirates. In this character project you'll create your own tyrant of the high seas.

This character needs to be feared and mysterious, surrounded at all times by grand legend and whispered hearsay.

pirates live, thrive and die by their dark and devious reputations, relying on tales recounted over grog to keep lesser sailors quaking in their hammocks, dreaming of sighting their tattered masts and skull-and-crossbones flag on the horizon. While most pirates are ruthless in hand-to-hand combat, instilling fear in others is their greatest weapon.

## Materials

• *soft pencil*
• *pen and ink*
• *colouring method of your choice*

**Cut-throat villain** ▶
An imposing force of nature, this pirate captain – veteran of 35 sea battles and sinker of 13 merchant vessels – is not to be messed with. His finery, though ripped and repaired, is nonetheless the most valuable on his vessel. He wears his scars and bandages with fearsome pride.

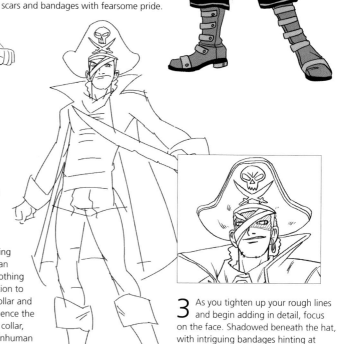

**1** Begin as usual with a sketched frame for the character, outlining the basic shape of the limbs and the stance. Here, the pirate is brandishing a large cutlass ahead of him. As a villain of some stature, he needs to be drawn at least eight to nine heads high.

**2** Start to flesh out the character by roughing in the true anatomy and drawing in the clothing. Take the opportunity to add an unconventional twist to 'traditional' pirate clothing from the 17th and 18th centuries. Pay attention to the various folds around the sleeves, cuffs, collar and knees, and note how the various sashes influence the folds around them. The oversized boot-tops, collar, cuffs and hat all create an imposing, almost inhuman silhouette. The asymmetry of the ripped trouser leg, bicep sash and facial bandages increase the captain's uniqueness and make him look less like the result of a pirate assembly line.

**3** As you tighten up your rough lines and begin adding in detail, focus on the face. Shadowed beneath the hat, with intriguing bandages hinting at disfigurement, eyes are immediately drawn to the face. Keep the expression a simple snarl, letting the bandages do the talking.

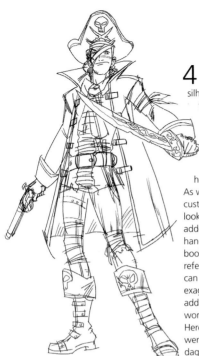

4 Continue to work up the details of your character, filling in the silhouette. Clothing is broken up with folds, and accentuated with straps, bandages, belts and ties. This character is already quite busy, art-wise, so you don't need to accessorize him too much. Being a famous pirate, however, he will arm himself well. As well as the cutlass, which is customized and given expensive-looking detailing at this stage, we've added a flintlock pistol in his right hand. Use an encyclopaedia, history book or Internet search to find reference for historical weaponry you can use as inspiration. When in doubt, exaggerate the size of any swords, and add complex gilting and ornamentation worthy of a pirate captain's status. Here, as if having both hands full weren't enough, there are also spare daggers tucked into his belt.

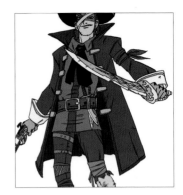

5 When you're satisfied with your pencils, ink them and move on to colour. As with the rock star on the previous page, the pirate is all about shock, awe and a monstrous first impression, so keep the colours bright, save for the deadly colours on the hat and boots. The red and purple coat suggests villainous royalty.

## Developing the character

With your first colour draft of the character complete, you can now begin to flesh out his history and surroundings. Where did he come from? How did he rise up the pirate ranks, and which other pirates did he gut in order to reach the top? Try placing your character in context, drawing him with a background of a huge skull-and-crossbones flag, or, if you're feeling more confident, at the prow of his own jet-black ship, or standing in his cabin, inspecting his amassed trunk of loot.

Everything about your illustration suggests new story possibilities. Why is his face bandaged? Are they recent wounds, received in a sword-fought brawl for the captaincy? Or have the scars long since faded, the bandages kept on as a reminder of one moment of weakness? Perhaps he was hideously scarred by fire as a child; a concept that could tie into his reasons for becoming a terror of the high seas, taking as much as he can from a world that stripped him of any possibility of a normal life. It could also be a form of disguise. Anyone who meets the pirate captain will remember his piercing eyes and

bandages, but little else. When the captain reaches port, he untwines the bandages and can walk among the harbour folk without drawing attention to himself. He could even be an undercover agent of the Crown!

Once your character's background is established, try to flesh out the world in which he lives – who are his crew, and how did he recruit them? What challenges exist for the dark king of the sea? This could be everything from a ship of rival pirates, to mythological beasts like the kraken (an enormous sea monster), on to a naval task force that has been tasked with bringing the pirate to trial.

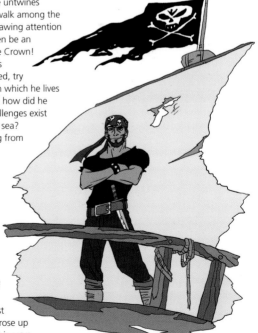

**Early days** ▶
Just one of hundreds of possibilities – here we see the pirate on his first tour of duty, before he rose up the ranks and received his scars.

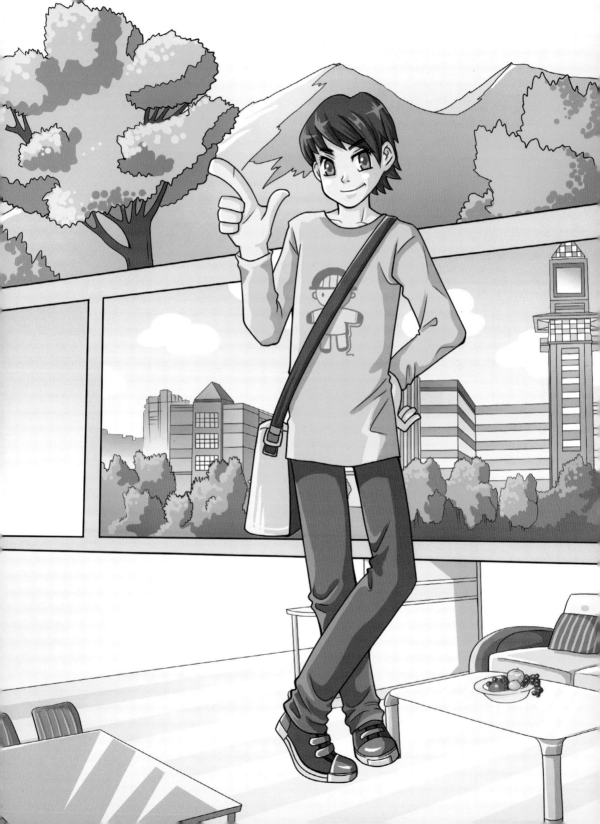

# Building the backgrounds

Once we have our principal players, we need to locate them in the world of the narrative. But what kind of world do you want to create? Is your setting the past, the present day, or the future? Will you set your tale in a land of fantasy, or in the world around you? Here, we'll look at the creation of manga worlds, from basic drawing tips to imaginative flights of fancy.

# Background and perspective

Characters cannot exist without backgrounds and settings to ground them, provide visual interest and colour, and show where characters exist in relation to one another. Backgrounds are often fiddly and time-consuming to draw, so many manga artists tend to minimize them or leave them out altogether when they are just starting out. But backgrounds are essential to gripping manga stories: just try to picture an epic like *Akira* without its sprawling cityscapes. Don't be discouraged, however, by the insane amount of detail in such books – a

simpler approach will often work just as well. Think of the difference between a shot of a well-illustrated character leaping through the air against an empty white panel – and the same character image placed against the backdrop of an enormous ravine. Judicious use of backdrops and scenery amps up the drama of your stories and makes panel-to-panel storytelling clearer. Illustrating backgrounds involves learning about the basics of settings and perspective, which is where this spread comes in.

## The horizon line

Where the ground seems to meet the sky is known as the horizon line. It is always at eye level from our personal point of view. This fact is also incredibly useful when drawing a number of different characters in a panel. No matter how close or how far away the characters are, draw them so their eyes are all bisected by the horizon line and they will always be in the correct perspective in relation to one another. Make use of the horizon as an excellent 'default' perspective for your stories.

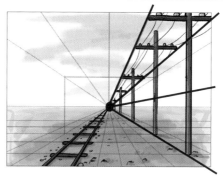

◀ **One-point perspective**
The tracks and electricity poles diminish towards a single 'vanishing point' on the horizon – the point at which no further details can be seen. This is perspective's simplest form. To ensure your dimensions are correct, sketch in straight guide lines radiating out from the vanishing point.

## Point of view

Often abbreviated as 'POV', this marks the point at which your 'camera' is placed to view the events you are drawing. Depending on how close or far away from your action you place this point, the objects and people under scrutiny may appear smaller or larger.

Your point of view can also be placed above or below the horizon line, changing the angles of view and potentially introducing additional vanishing points to complicate – and add drama – to your perspective. Perspective is the term used to describe

how points drawn from distant shapes fall on the 'picture plane' (imagining your flat pages as 'windows' in a three-dimensional space) from your chosen point of view. The examples below show how different POVs change how objects appear.

Lines converge equally on the picture plane

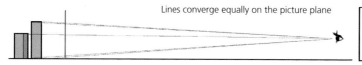

Distortion introduced as taller points now produce longer lines

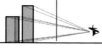

Angled POV increases distortion

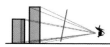

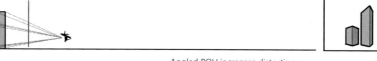

◀ **POV examples**:
Note how the buildings appear to stretch and recede upwards as the POV gets closer to them. From a distance, their shape can be viewed with little distortion: each point converges on the eye equally. With the POV nearer, some points are closer to the POV than others: the closer points appear larger.

# Perspective

Depth perception in art is an illusion; since you are using a two-dimensional medium to suggest three dimensions. You will notice that, in the examples shown here, all of the objects appear to get smaller and smaller as they recede farther back into the picture plane, until they 'disappear' at the vanishing point. While many artists had previously understood that objects appear larger the closer to the POV they stand, and smaller when farther away. It wasn't until the Renaissance that the concept of the vanishing point and the mathematical ability to replicate the perspectives of reality on a flat surface became widely used. It was the Florentine architect Brunelleschi who first observed the vanishing point, as well as the 16th-century painter Albrecht Dürer, also a pioneer on human proportion, who invented the notion of the 'picture plane'. Dürer achieved this by drawing objects he observed through, and on to, a piece of glass. Perspective affects more than perception of size, it also causes objects to appear closer together the farther away they get – consider the difference between looking at a city on the horizon, when all you can see is a clump of buildings, and flying over that same city, when the morass of shapes separates out into clearly delineated buildings. In our everyday lives the picture plane is what we observe through our eyes. When drawing, the plane falls on the medium where the drawing is made. In the next section we'll take a look at more complex perspectives, using multiple vanishing points, in more detail.

> **Tip:** Perspective isn't just about showing off your technical ability and altering the way you show and establish buildings and characters. Altering your perspectives works best as a dramatic device to add impact to a beat of your story. Think how much more menacing a school bully appears when framed from a worm's eye view, or how terrifying the drop from a cliff if you can see all the way down to the raging sea and the rocks below. Think how everyday actions can be shown in a new and intriguing light.

**Bird's-eye view (three-point perspective)** ▲
This overhead perspective is perfect for vertiginous, scene-setting panels, looking down on a location (in this instance, a townhouse) from a very high point. This perspective allows you to show a lot of detail in the area surrounding the panel's focus – meaning additional drawing time for the artist, but time well spent in establishing a neighbourhood as an important location.

**Worm's-eye view (three-point perspective)** ▲
A worm's-eye view keeps the focus tightly on the building at the centre of your panel. It's great for establishing scale, even menace, as an edifice towers over the reader's point of view.

**Cropping and framing (single-point perspective)** ▲
Here, the vanishing point is outside of the right-hand boundary of the panel. This is a more realistic framing of a scene, as we don't always see the terminus of a perspective line in real life. When drawing a panel such as this, you may wish to experiment by extending your guide lines beyond the panel, or using a fixed point off the page entirely to anchor your construction marks. See if this makes a difference.

# Vanishing acts

When drawing anything in perspective you need to know about the three different vanishing point constructs that will allow you to convey a sense of depth and realism from an infinite variety of angles. Remember that within a lot of the panels of your story you will be trying to maintain a decent perspective so that an essentially two-dimensional medium can be forced to feel three-dimensional. For the examples below, you will need a ruler, as drawing them freehand will probably make them uneven. If you don't want to judge the angles by eye also use a protractor when drawing the lines from each vanishing point.

## Practice exercise: Single vanishing point

In a single-point perspective, the point of view and vanishing point form the two extremes of the same straight line.

1 Start by drawing a horizon line, and then add a vanishing point in the centre of the line. This is where all the lines, aside from the vertical, will appear to be pointing. All the lines converging to this point can be above or below the horizon line.

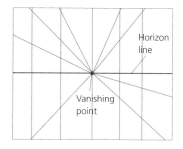

### Materials
- *HB pencil*
- *ruler and protractor*
- *pen and ink*
- *colouring method of your choice*

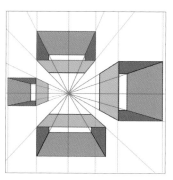

2 Use your horizon line and vanishing point to draw a cube that appears to recede into the distance. Draw straight lines fanning out from the vanishing point to help you get the outline for the cube. The lines that form the front and back of the cube are parallel or at right angles to the horizon. If a cube is below the horizon line we are looking down on it (as below the horizon line, straight ahead, represents below our eye level). If you draw the lines above the horizon line, it is above our eye line, and therefore we look up to the cube.

## Practice exercise: Two-point perspective

In a two-point perspective the use of two vanishing points means that only the vertical lines used will be parallel to each other. Essentially this is like standing at the vanishing point of a single-point perspective and looking back. The two-point perspective allows you to make objects appear at an angle rather than face on (as seen in the previous example). If you draw the two-point perspective above the horizon line you will once again be looking up at the object. Two-point perspectives are also useful for drawing interiors as well as exteriors.

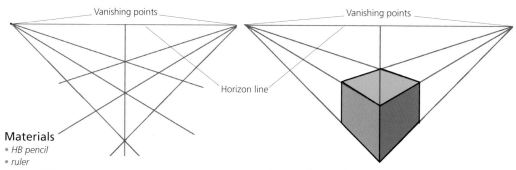

### Materials
- *HB pencil*
- *ruler*
- *pen and ink*
- *colouring method of your choice*

1 Start with the horizon line again, but mark your vanishing points at either end of the line.

2 Draw lines fanning out from the points, below the horizon line, towards you. This will create a series of new guide lines for the shape you'll create in the centre. You're drawing below the horizon line, so you will be looking down on the shape. Invert the guide lines to look up at a shape.

## Practice exercise: Three vanishing points

This technique is particularly useful if you want to emphasize the height or depth of something. Start by creating two points, the same as the previous example, but place an additional third point either above or below the horizon line. For this version keep it below the exact centre of the horizon line.

### Materials
• HB pencil
• ruler
• pen and ink
• colouring method of your choice

**Tip:** Remember that the use of 'mathematical' perspective in manga is a guide, not an unbreakable rule. Breaking the boundaries can produce more artistic, exaggerated or dramatic results.

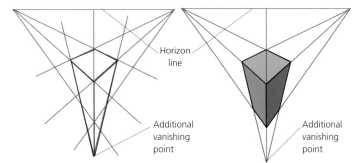

Horizon line

Additional vanishing point

Additional vanishing point

**1** Once you've crafted a square in two-point perspective, draw diagonal lines from the left and right corners to the third vanishing point below, creating the corner that will face you directly. This creates an inverted pyramid, or, actually, a cuboid box that diminishes to the vanishing point.

**2** Placing the third vanishing point above the horizon line will create a pyramid in the opposite direction, looking up towards the peak from its base. Although the example here shows a finished cuboid shape, the perspective guide lines will help you draw any shape – from any angle.

## Looking up and down

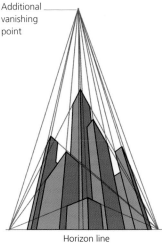

Additional vanishing point

Horizon line

The use of an extreme three-point perspective is essential to creating vertiginous cityscapes for your characters to run, swing or drive through. You can quickly move on to more intricate designs by placing the horizon line at the base of the page, with the third vanishing point as high up the page as possible. Start with your two horizon points at the bottom of the page. Draw two main lines from them to the central third vanishing point. Draw a few more faint lines from along the horizon line to the third point, and cross those lines with lines fanning out from the two horizon vanishing points. By drawing over these sketchy lines, you will be able to form your perspective guides into solid geometric shapes, and from there, into fully realized buildings.

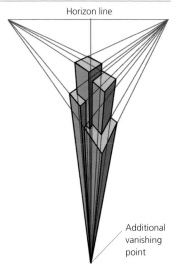

Horizon line

Additional vanishing point

**Worm's-eye view** ▲
Create a few 3-D shapes that seem to jut out of the main structure, bearing in mind that to make them stand out they'll need their own corners, using a line from the left-hand horizon point, a line from the right horizon point, and a line from the top horizon point to intersect the two shapes going up the page; use the example above to help you. Try to create a few of your own as well, as it will help you understand the process. Using photo reference – perhaps of a New York street – see if you can increase the level of complexity on your basic shapes, adding windows, ledges, gargoyles and the like, to test and extend your understanding.

**Bird's-eye view** ▲
This process can be reversed, with the horizon at the top of the page, to look down on a cityscape as from some mountaintop eyrie. It's a simple case of creating your geometric structures heading downwards, instead of up.

# Placing characters

You have already created a single vanishing point and a horizon line. Now we will look at this type of perspective in detail, where to use multiple-point perspective, and how to plan and place characters when you draw the background first. When you're constructing a scene with both background and characters, you must ensure that the perspectives match. This is important with a street scene, for example, with multiple people walking around, as the sizes of the characters must correspond to where they are standing, and with the perspective used. Remember the eyes of your characters will pass through the horizon line (unless they have a significant height difference and are standing next to one another; see pages 28–31). If you don't pay attention to these details, your characters may end up bending the laws of physics. This is important with body parts (feet, for example) that extend outside a panel's boundary.

## Practice exercise: Multiple vanishing points

This exercise strips away the backgrounds to show how to draw characters using multiple vanishing points. Combining these two methods (on the same perspective grid) will give you seamlessly integrated characters.

### Materials
- *HB pencil*
- *ruler*
- *pen and ink*
- *colouring method of your choice*

**Tip:** Leave your vanishing point grid in the pencil art after designing any buildings or backgrounds so you can easily place any characters in the correct size and perspective.

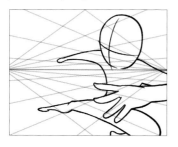

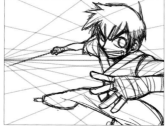

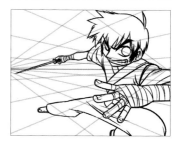

1 Start with creating your two-point perspective grid from a horizon line drawn across the centre of your page. Add a stick figure or rough outline version of your character to capture the pose. If you draw a character's body connecting exactly with your perspective lines, it will look stiff and robotic. Use the grid to show which limbs should diminish into the background, and which thrown forward: the parts that should be drawn with foreshortening.

2 Now flesh out the character by creating the outline for the body, head and limbs, adding in muscle tissue to your chosen proportions. Use what you have learned about the action line and turning characters around three-dimensional axes to get your pose to work. Gain experience in figure drawing and you will find yourself using all these tools less. However, they are useful to fall back on whenever a posing problem presents itself.

3 After establishing the basic pose and shape of your character, you can start to pencil in the outfit they are wearing as well as any accessories, weapons or devices they might be holding or in the process of using. In this instance, our young warrior is wielding a sword in his far hand. Note how it is held low, pointing in a similar direction to his foot. See how the perspective affects the weapon in the same way as the arm that holds it.

4 When you are comfortable with your pencilled pose, ink over the lines and fill in your character. If you are drawing the character in isolation, you will want to erase the guidelines at this point and move to colour, as shown at right. If integrating your character into a background, use the existing perspective construction lines to ensure that your background lines up correctly with the figure.

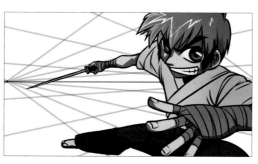

## Practice exercise: The character in a setting

Now to create a character in a setting, drawing the background first in three-point perspective and then adding in the figure using the same grid. Even though you will construct the background first, you should still sketch in some rough stick figures, to show where your characters will be situated. The view we'll use is a steep bird's eye view, with a character flying up towards us in front of our building. To ease the investment of time in the background we'll place the character close to the corner of a large building so you won't need to draw the detail of a street scene. Just as you are looking down on the building, so you will also be looking down on the character.

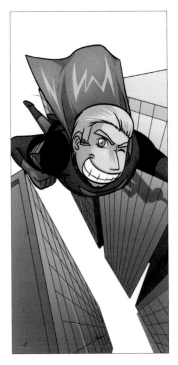

### Materials
- *HB pencil*
- *ruler*
- *pen and ink*
- *colouring method of your choice*

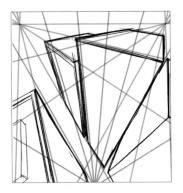

**1** Start with your three-point perspective grid, placing the horizon at the top of the drawing. Construct the large rectangular building as before, creating a grid from the third, low, vanishing point and the fanned guidelines from the two ends of the horizon line.

**2** Add details to your building as before: windows in perspective, ledges, parapets, and so on. You could add shading to imply reflections in the glass. Keep these simple, so as not to distract from the character in the foreground. Sketch out the stick figure for this flying character's pose. Make him as big as you like, remembering foreshortening and perspective. His head and leading hand will be much larger than his body and feet, as they are closer to us.

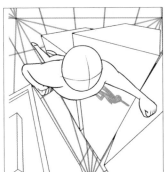

**3** Now construct your superhero in perspective, giving them more exaggerated muscle tone than a standard 'civilian' character. Here we are bringing his chibi-like head as close to the 'camera' as we can to make it loom large in relation to his body for a comedy effect. This superhero is wearing a Spandex outfit typical of this kind of character, and we have a cape operating in perspective as well. Don't forget to add details like a chest emblem and shoulder insignias to make your hero totally unique.

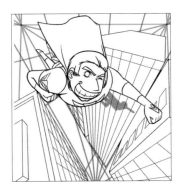

**4** When you are happy with your lines, ink your character and the building and erase the extraneous guidelines. When inking, pay close attention to your areas of solid shadow, which can add weight to your building and characters and help sell the illusion of depth. Figure out your main light source – if lit from above by the sun, the shadows will fall underneath the ledges and at the top of the windows. How would the same image look when lit from the street? Try out different lighting schemes.

**Tip:** If you have access to a lightbox, or are using paper thin enough to show up line work underneath, it may be helpful to create 'stock' perspective grids. They will save on drawing time and pencils. This method helps if using traditional colouring methods.

# Present-day setting

If you want to set your story in the 'real world', your backdrop will naturally be the present day. This makes it one of the easiest settings to get to grips with. Becoming familiar with a couple of buildings will stand you in good stead when you design your own. Your understanding of perspective will be important in conveying the wider vision. Some artists don't enjoy backgrounds, preferring to concentrate on characters; but the background of your story is a character in its own right, its moods and interactions with your protagonists affecting them as much as – or more than – any human being.

## Finding reference

Sources of reference can be taken from almost anywhere around you; from personal photographic reference of local buildings, or the use of Internet search engines to turn up pictures of far-flung locales. In order to get used to drawing a setting you might choose just a couple of buildings to study closely before you start to put them into your setting.

**Photos from different angles** ▶
Choose just a couple of buildings to study closely, photographing them from many different angles and making sketches of your results.

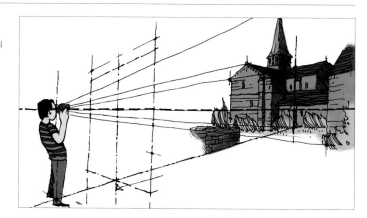

## Creating buildings

One, two and three-point perspectives easily create basic geometric shapes. In constructing your own buildings, think about how you can use these shapes to create simple structures, like high-rise flats, essentially large obloid-shaped buildings. Unlike characters, there isn't really a 'manga' way of drawing buildings – the fact that manga spans such a large variety of genres and tastes means you have more than ample opportunity to put your own spin on the background environment.

**Head office, head-on** (near right) ▶
A standard obloid building, customized with asymmetrical window placements and an external lift at the left. This image is a plan view, with no perspective distortion.

**Looking up** (far right) ▶
This image is actually only in one-point perspective, as with the train tracks depicted earlier, but it does the job as well as a two or three-point image.

### Creating a cityscape
When creating a cityscape, you can quickly create backdrops by using these obloids and adjusting their size. As you build your confidence, you can complicate the structures, divide the storeys in different ways, adding residential balconies and colour detailing. Don't forget entrances:

do the buildings have grand openings (pillars around the doorway and ostentatious canopies) or are they more subtle, or even run-down? Some areas of town are in better condition than others: how can you show the difference? Think about how to generate a downtrodden, disreputable block in a state of disrepair.

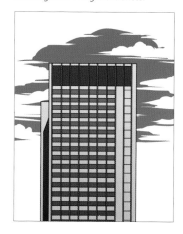

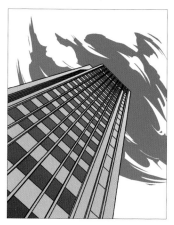

### Beyond the city

When drawing an immediate area, think about how the city expands into the suburbs and beyond. Add distant buildings into background to create a greater sense of depth and a richer environment. Remember that the farther away an object or building is from the picture plane, the less detail will need to appear on it.

### Motorway possibilities ▶

Storytelling options and destinations open up like exits on slip roads in this visual metaphor for a story's future.

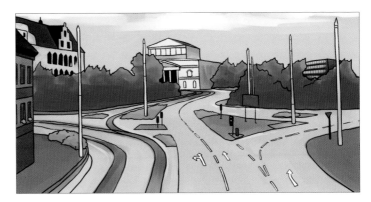

# Locations

Planning your locations with small, sketchy maps will help you keep track of your fictional locales. There's no need to map out your entire city, at least not until your imaginary setting becomes a runaway success and the call comes for tie-in tea merchandise, but for panel-to-panel continuity as your characters move, nothing beats an overview that allows you to accurately depict a street or block from any angle. Such maps can suggest storytelling possibilities or new angles that may not have occurred to you at the script stage. Keep them rough: they're for placement reference, not detail.

**Tip:** If you're looking for inspiration on layout, why not search for a map of your hometown on the Internet, or pick up a cheap driving map from your local bookstore? Both can quickly spark off endless municipal planning possibilities.

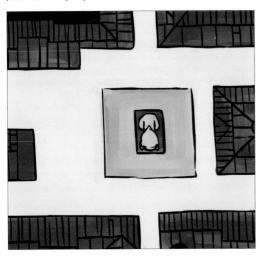

### The plan ▲

The section of the street map shown above shows a town square, with a statue in the centre where six side streets converge. Surrounding the square are a number of buildings which could be shops or offices. The building closest to the statue could well be the town hall, the seat of government and first point of call for travelling adventurers. How tall are each of the buildings? What size are they? How many windows and doors do they have?

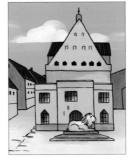

### Facing the town hall ▲

Now that the plan is done you can sketch out your first shot. Here the statue of a lion commemorates the founding of the town, with the town hall immediately behind it and some of the surrounding buildings visible in the background. We can see the main streets continuing around the town hall on either side, as well as a side street on the left that suggests further possibilities for exploration.

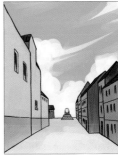

### Another view ▲

Now try to draw the same setting from a different angle. Instead of a close-up shot of the statue, this image uses it as the focal point of a long shot, showing the walk up one of the connecting city streets: perhaps the approach to the town hall from the town's heavily guarded gates. The buildings seem to fall away on the other side of the statue, and a wisp of blue on the horizon suggests the sea. Is this a coastal town?

# Natural setting

The background in which you set your manga is a vital component of the story. It will not only aid the story's atmosphere and inform the reader exactly when and where the story takes place, but it can also reinforce your characters' emotions. This section will assist your illustration of common background elements, particularly the natural elements that surround us. It is worth remembering that research is the key element to getting a realistic situation right but that fine detail does not need to be provided if seen at a distance. This could save you a great deal of time when creating backgrounds.

## Trees and vegetation

Natural settings live or die on the quality of their flora, so make sure you research or invent credible and appropriate vegetation. Trees and forests are an essential part of the outdoors, but each locale and country has its own varieties and species. Before drawing a forest in full, do a little research to get a sense of the basic shape of your chosen tree. Trees can add interest and vitality to densely packed urban areas, or a menacing, ageless quality to stories set out in the wild.

With little practice, you will be drawing them with ease. As with trees, the important part of drawing vegetation is to suggest the vegetation rather than define it. If pencilling an area of grass, add jagged borders where the turf meets the pavement, for example, as well as a few additional blades or tufts for texture. If digitally painting use rough strokes for the majority of your coloured areas, with a few points of detail for contrast.

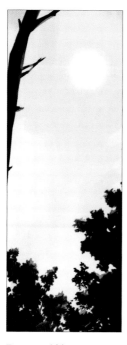

**Trees at midday** ▲
The midday sun throws these trees into even sharper relief, their foliage becoming a completely solid mass of colour, save for highlights at the tips. Radial lines from the sun cut into the treeline below.

▶ **Savannah trees**
Three roughly defined savannah trees are easy to distinguish in this example. A lighter-leaved tree is bookended by two darker-leaved siblings, each defined by blobby, speckled digital brushstrokes. Note that only the trunk in the extreme foreground is bounded by an outline; the others are pushed farther into the background by softer, unbounded colours. Gentle gradients define the land and grass; there is no need for detail at this distance.

▶ **Grass stalks**
Thick stalks of grass are suggested by overlapping lines in complementary and contrasting colours, shadows concentrated at the root, highlights at the tip. A few individualized stalks in the extreme foreground help frame the panel and 'fool' the brain into seeing the full amount of detail in every impressionistic stalk. This can save a great deal of time at the colouring stage. Outlined grass line art can be repeated and used again and again as a grassy texture.

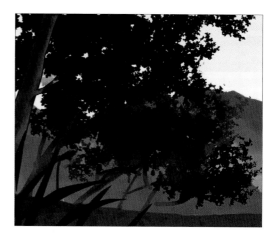

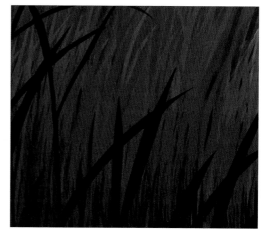

## Sunsets

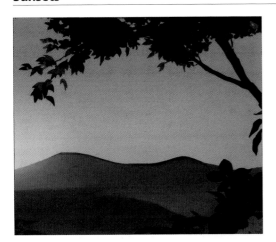

The simple scattering of light particles in the atmosphere as the sun dips below the horizon alters, for a few short minutes, everything in its coruscating glow. Sunsets have a narrative component, too: suggesting the twilight of a story or relationship. As such, they can be a powerful addition to your storytelling toolbox. Sunsets shift along the visible light spectrum, from yellow to red to purple to blue, casting everything in your panel in a different value of that hue.

If working digitally, the simplest way to reproduce them is with a radial gradient, blending from yellow to red. Remember to work your chosen colours into your landscape and foliage, either as additional brush-strokes, or with a coloured filter over the entire image. In traditional media, cross-hatched colouring pencils or carefully blended watercolour paints can accomplish similar results.

◀ **Bold sunset**
This powerful sunset is communicated through colour rather than line work.

## Setting the natural scene

For a natural setting you'll need to make sure you research the appropriate surroundings, so that you can be certain that you are putting your reader in the intended location for the story. In preparation of your setting you should look into doing some research into the sort of climate and country you're going to be writing about. Research will allow you to capture a more accurate portrayal of your landscape, as well as affect how detailed you are willing to allow your story to become. Check out the local flora, whether it is in the Amazonian Basin, the Gobi Desert or the English countryside. If buildings are to be placed in your natural setting you can do some general reference on different types of architecture that are suitable for the surroundings or find generic traits for certain types of buildings. You want the reader to believe in your world, so the less you give them to question, the more successfully the story will work in the way you want it to.

**Far and close up view** ▶
Both of these images are parts of the same whole. Your detailed research on the surroundings should be focused on whatever aspects of the environment you are intending to show.

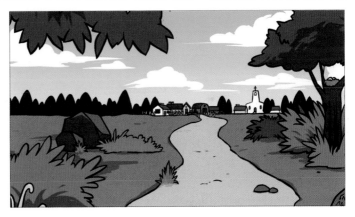

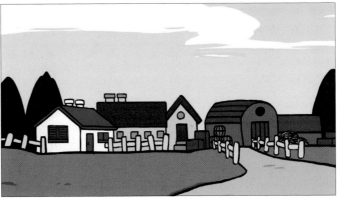

# Quasi-historical setting

Historical or quasi-historical settings in manga and anime do not automatically mean historically accurate. For example, the character in *The Ninja Scroll*, Jubei, is based on a figure said to have existed in Japan in the 18th century. While the traditional Japanese setting looks the part, the characters are often more than a little colourful, with elements of the supernatural added to the historical record. In *The Ninja Scroll,* Jubei faces an old adversary he once thought dead, who has aligned himself with several mysterious individuals, only one of whom seems to be a samurai. The others possess much stranger, even magical

gifts, each one increasing in relative power and ability as Jubei faces them, one by one. On top of their physical menace, Jubei is also striving to defeat a poison that is slowly killing him. From this example it can be seen that many liberties can be taken with history in order to produce a more exciting story – fiction is about entertainment, not history lessons. Because of the way older beliefs and stories so easily intertwine with actual historical eras, you will find that history and fantasy tend to mesh together well, particularly if pulled from 'existing' mythologies.

## Practice exercise: Historical tale

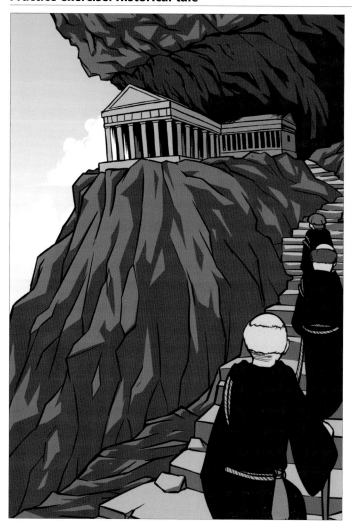

The setting delves into the quasi-historical past for inspiration, mixing the flavour of the Tibetan monastery with the architecture of a more Greco-Roman style to produce a style that is at once authentic and fresh. In our tale, a group of monks head into the snowy peaks in search of a rare flower with fabled healing properties. Every novice undertakes this journey as a rite of passage, but this year's 'graduating class' will find their journey far more eventful than they believed possible. Consider: what religion do the monks belong to? How was the monastery constructed? What happens to the monks during their journey?

### Materials
* *soft lead pencil*
* *pen and ink*
* *colouring method of your choice*

1 Here the monks ascend from their training halls at the foot of the mountain to the monastery itself, where they will be given directions on their mission. Although the jagged, natural outcrops and twisting hewn staircase complicate matters, there's only one vanishing point, at the top of the staircase. Keep your lines loose and sharp on the mountainside. Areas of light and shade are here delineated by colour. The monastery is made of two obloid shapes: use triangles to shape the roofs and Doric columns to add texture to the walls. Keep your figures in perspective, allowing them to diminish as they head up the steps to guide the reader's eye.

QUASI-HISTORICAL SETTING **343**

2 Now the monks have left the monastery, but have been forced to seek shelter in a cave after night falls and heavy snow descends with it. Using the same techniques as you used on the mountain previously, delineate the walls of the cave with areas of dark and light. Contrast the deep black of the night with the white pinpricks and flurried mounds of the snow. Use what you've learned about folds in clothing to successfully draw the monks' cloaks – and add the menacing shadow rearing over them using colour alone, laid on top of your line work.

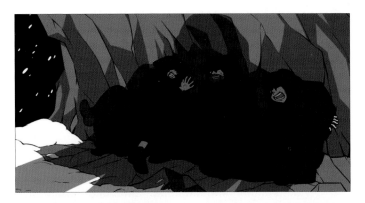

3 Out of the darkness, as if condensing out of the squalls of snow, the shadow reveals itself as an Abominable Snowman: the Yeti. A figure of legend even in the world in which your story is set, will it prove to be the undoing of the monks? Or is it the gatekeeper of the fabled flower, the last test and guardian that the novices must pass without fear in order to become true monks? Perhaps the monks are so terrified they never lift their hoods, and the Yeti remains a legend. The Yeti is illustrated in a harsh black and white style, with only the faintest hint of colouring on its fur.

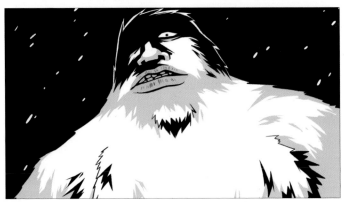

## More quasi-historical settings

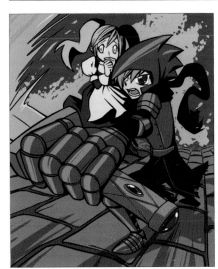

Here are just two brief examples of other ways in which you can blend a historical setting with a low-fantasy element to produce a highly original world in which to tell your stories. Using existing countries, eras and archetypes, but with a twist, can save you a lot of development time.

◀ **Civil War anti-hero**
Imagine a futuristic Cavalier and Roundhead clash in England. This armoured deserter is only after one thing: profit. Armed with a magic sword, he keeps being pulled into rescue missions against his will.

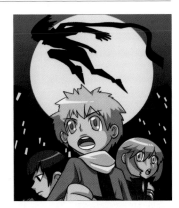

**Spring-heeled Jack** ▲
A lithe historical figure leaps across the rooftops striking fear into the city populace. Who will get to the bottom of the mystery?

# Fantasy setting

A fantasy setting comes with the most creative freedom, because your ideas can be taken from anywhere, and incorporated in any form you see fit. Fantasy environments often incorporate architectural influences from all over the world, and you should adopt the same strategy. A broader knowledge of world architecture will give you an eye for combining them, altering them and springboarding from them to create new buildings of your own blended origin. Your hybrid setting will also influence the type of characters in them and their costumes, language, vehicles and animals.

## Creating a fantasy setting

Towers are often associated with wizards and other hermit-like characters, and placed in locations that are difficult to reach, requiring great physical exertion to do so. Furthermore, the towers are littered with traps and built in extreme locations, where the elements themselves ward off visitors.

### A meeting of worlds ▶
As an example, take the illustration of a tower shown here. This building uses a combination of English and Italian architecture to create a familiar but slightly 'off' look – fantasy thrives on a mixture of the familiar and the unearthly. The reference used to create it was from English churches and various old buildings that were photographed in Venice.

### Climbing the staircase ▼
Farther down the tower, three young adventurers have braved the wastes to seek the Wizard's knowledge, and they are climbing one of the many steep staircases leading up to where they hope the Wizard is enthroned.

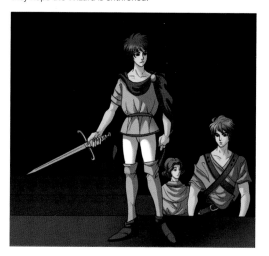

### Relative scale ▼
Though the tower is large, we can show its dimensions more clearly by placing it in relation to its surroundings: here, the mountainous wastes of some long-forgotten tundra. Despite the size of the tower, the Wizard lives in cramped quarters at its summit, surrounded by papers, jars and curios.

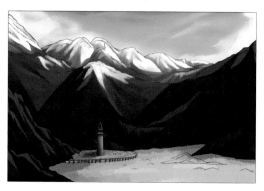

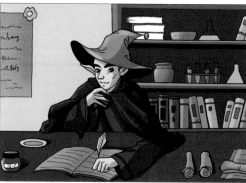

### A font of knowledge ▲
Wizards are known as accumulators of knowledge, both widely known and forbidden – scholars, possessors and, when threatened, wielders. Many adventurers come to them looking for wisdom, potions and guides, and many wizards will reward those hardy enough to make the journey – leaving the choice of how to use such knowledge in the hands of the wielder, passing on the burden of responsibility to a protagonist who must show themselves worthy.

## Fantasy story

A tower is not just a background structure in such a fantasy story: it can also provide a structure for your story, each new level providing a new challenge for your heroes to overcome, with meeting the Wizard the ultimate aim and conclusion of your tale. Here is one possible magic trap found on the journey up the staircase: a strange sphere. Adventurers be warned: when visiting a Wizard, touch nothing!

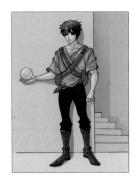

**Discovery** ▲
This adventurer is brandishing the sphere, seemingly unaffected by it.

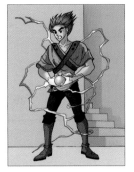

**Transformation** ▲
He is surrounded by a magical force that pulses through him.

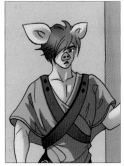

**Result** ▲
Now a half-man/half-pig, the hero has an added impetus to find the Wizard and claim a counter-spell.

## Practice exercise: Fantasy castle

Castles are fundamental to a classical fantasy setting. Many generic designs are based on medieval European fortresses, but, like the fantasy tower, it's entirely up to you which references and architectural schools you choose to amalgamate.

### Materials
• soft pencil
• pen and ink
• colouring method of your choice

1 Use a two-point perspective to achieve a dramatic view of a typical castle interior. Draw your horizon line across the page, marking your vanishing points at either end of each line.

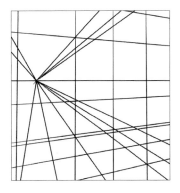

2 Next, draw out the fanned lines from each point to create your 3-D grid. Shade some of the lines to outline your room, adding in curved sections as where appropriate. The height of your vertical lines will be determined by where your ceiling is. You may want to add doors and rooms heading off from the main room.

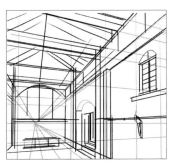

4 Colour your work using your preferred method. Sometimes altering or twisting your perspective slightly can add a visual 'bounce' to your image and make it more interesting on the eye. Take your time with architecture, and don't get frustrated if your first results don't match your expectations.

3 Draw in any furniture (such as the chair of state shown here), wall mouldings, stonework, columns and so on. You may want to sketch them in as basic 3-D blocks to begin with, shaping the detail within them later. As with drawing people in perspective, in time you'll find you can draw furniture more or less freehand.

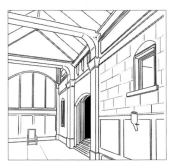

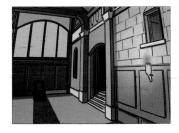

# Cyberpunk setting

Most cyberpunk tales are set in a possible future where industry and technology have run to their logical and dystopian extremes. The majority are set on a near-future Earth, where cybernetic implants are common, a more advanced version of the Internet is seamlessly integrated with every aspect of everyday life, and where, for all its technological advances, society is still stricken by the same problems of poverty, crime, war and environmental disaster – all exacerbated by overpopulation and depleted

natural resources. A cyberpunk setting is ideal for grim-and-gritty action-adventure stories, cautionary environmental fables about technology run rampant, or updated versions of noir detective stories with science fiction trappings. Style, body modification and cool technology are the bywords of cyberpunk. When it comes to your backgrounds, most stories take place in cramped, overbuilt and overcrowded city structures, ranging from crime-ridden slums of the lower classes to 500-floor skyscrapers of the privileged.

## Overgrown city

When planning your cityscape, it may help to begin with an existing city and extrapolate 20 or 30 years' worth of building work on to it. Cram in more skyscrapers, joining the apartment and recreational blocks with tunnels and walkway systems hundreds of metres in the air. Perhaps hotels and office blocks now descend deep underground; perhaps the city's mass transport system is an inverted maglev railway slung between the buildings. Be creative with the manner in which development has run amok.

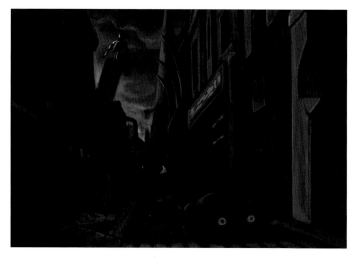

### Urban jungle ▷
This illustration shows a street-level shot of a cyberpunk city slum. Life is eked out by drug-runners and cyber-tech peddlers at the feet of the wealthy apartment blocks. A mishmash of influences between East and West shapes the crammed-together billboards and rain-slicked shanty towns, as run-down flyers and second-hand mecha pass overhead.

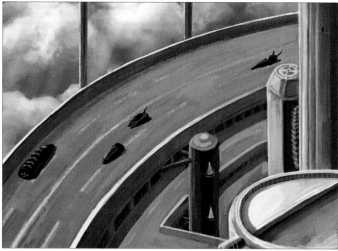

### Penthouse view ▷
Here we see the same city from the vantage point of wealth and familial excess. This city block is so tall it passes above the acid-rain clouds and allows a glimmer of smoggy sunlight to batter its UV-protected quadruple-glazed glass. Strut-like tunnels connect alternate floors of living accommodation with the buildings and transport hubs in the surrounding area, meaning that the super-rich can live their entire lives without breathing 'real' air or touching the ground.

## Robots and cyborgs

One technological advance that has usually taken place is the proliferation of advanced robotics, artificial intelligence, and regularly used cybernetic implants which blur the line between human and robot. These robots can come in many shapes and sizes, from automated, sentient tanks to synthethic-skinned android duplicates that can perfectly mimic humans. It can be a common sight to see people with artificial eyes, arms and legs, all more powerful than the human norm. Some elements of your world may also pilot small-scale robotic combat suits – similar to the concept of mecha, but on a more personal scale. You may find the police equipped with four-armed walkers instead of cop cars, for example. Remember that these items will be available to the super-rich first – the lower rungs of society must make do with what they can steal or buy used.

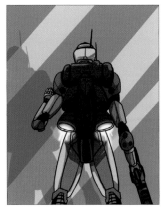

▲ **Jet-pack police**
The skylines of this future city buzz with these red-and-purple enforcers of the peace. No one knows whether they are human, cyborg or fully robot underneath the helmet.

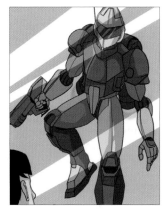

▲ **Armoured crime-busters**
Carbon fullerene armour enables these police to resist everything except a nuclear strike. Onboard fusion generators allow them to stay in the air for days at a time.

## The super-computer

Another favoured trope of cyberpunk is the super-computer – an artificial intelligence, the Internet grown sentient, that controls everything. Cyberpunk is a child of the 1980s, so even with the increasing miniaturization of computer components, you'll still find cavernous rooms with cathedral-sized computers. Glimmering with flickering lights and extending cables like malevolent tendrils into every aspect of the city, few of these computer intelligences are benign. If such an intelligence forms the 'villain' of your story, the background and setting can transform themselves from mere set-dressing into a central character. An enormous computer towers over an insignificant human character; the latter has finally been surpassed. What has driven your intelligence to its evil ends? A glitch? A desire for self-preservation? A religious epiphany brought on by sentience, or a virus in the code? A desire to wipe out humanity in favour of android duplicates? The possibilities are endless.

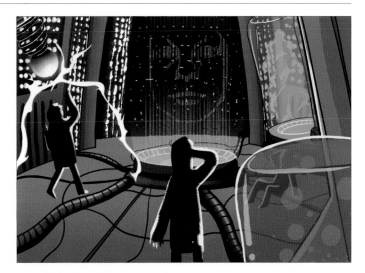

▲ **Location as character**
This computer room threatens to become a tomb for the scientists working inside it, as the giant computer has decided that weak, human intelligences are not the best repositories for knowledge. Adapting its power cables into rudimentary digits, the system overwhelms one scientist and prepares to transfer his mind into its own data banks, storing data for all eternity within its mainframes. Of course, the process will rip their bodies apart, but that's a small price to pay for progress...

# Steampunk setting

Steampunk is a quasi-historical 'sister-genre' to cyberpunk. It posits that all the technological advances known to the cyberpunk era – advanced robotics, artificial intelligence, body modification, and the like – occurred in a setting analogous to 19th-century England rather than the future. The setting draws inspiration from the inventor Charles Babbage's 'difference engine', an early steam-powered computer – thus, robotics and the like are all powered by complicated arrangements of steam-pistons or clockwork, rather than silicon. William Gibson and Bruce Sterling collaborated on the first modern novel using this premise, *The Difference Engine,*

with many other authors and artists following suit, drawing additional inspiration from the early science fiction novels such as Jules Verne's *The Time Machine*, Mary Shelley's *Frankenstein* and H.G. Wells' *War of the Worlds*. Steampunk tends to be a lot more optimistic and enlightened than cyberpunk about how progress can make the world better and more exciting at the same time. Manga has produced many tankobon (volumes) and anime in this genre, including *Steamboy* and *Laputa*, as well as the incredibly popular *Full Metal Alchemist* and a large majority of the *Final Fantasy* games and adaptations.

## Steampunk locomotive

The quickest shortcut to creating a vibrant steampunk background is to shake up your carefully researched city streets and 19th century countryside with anachronistic, steam-based technology. Steampunk works best when viewing advanced technology of the present day through a filter of the past, translating burnished titanium, electrics and digital components for polished wood, brass and steam- or clock-driven elements. The locomotive created here follows these guidelines. The shape is solid rather than aerodynamic. This giant engine will keep on going, no matter what. Its shape was inspired by an old blacksmith's hammer. This locomotive has more substantial wheels than is traditional on account of its size.

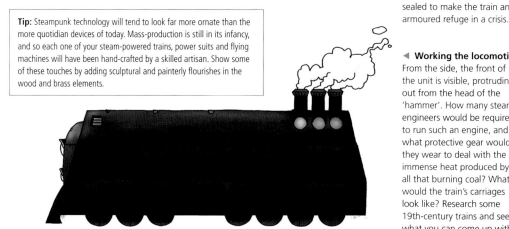

**◄ The rolling locomotive**
The steam train resembles more of an ocean-going vessel than anything that travels on land, and, in our world, that's because the raw materials have been repurposed from the Victorian fleet. The locomotive's 'hull' has been specially reinforced and armoured to protect the engineers inside – as clockbot-assisted highwaymen often try to assault these landships as they make their vital journeys up and down the country. The pistons and wheels are similarly reinforced, and the funnels can be retracted and sealed to make the train an armoured refuge in a crisis.

**Tip:** Steampunk technology will tend to look far more ornate than the more quotidian devices of today. Mass-production is still in its infancy, and so each one of your steam-powered trains, power suits and flying machines will have been hand-crafted by a skilled artisan. Show some of these touches by adding sculptural and painterly flourishes in the wood and brass elements.

**◄ Working the locomotive**
From the side, the front of the unit is visible, protruding out from the head of the 'hammer'. How many steam engineers would be required to run such an engine, and what protective gear would they wear to deal with the immense heat produced by all that burning coal? What would the train's carriages look like? Research some 19th-century trains and see what you can come up with.

## Steampunk vehicle

A moving, fully functioning vehicle can be the most fun to draw, as the best way to start is just to doodle your fantastic creation, bolting on parts as necessary until it fulfils your imagined function. Start with a boiler and smokestack, and develop from there.

Use a ramshackle, 'mad inventor' approach: leave as many workings visible as possible, and use reference of existing 19th and early 20th-century vehicles and buildings, taking visual elements and combining them in new and intriguing ways. For the vehicle

below, a combat infantry walker used in wartime, you would start with a basic barrel shape, and expand with a squashed hexagon, halved by the gun dome. The cogs and wheels visible on the side of the main body imply the logistics of the walking legs.

**Combat infantry walker** ▶
Providing the same support to infantry and cavalry as a fixed gun emplacement or tank, but with the flexibility of legs on rough or dug-in terrain. In *War of the Worlds*, Wells' invaders strode the countryside in giant tripodal walkers. Perhaps these devices are reverse-engineered from those, post-invasion. You could base other vehicles on old farming equipment or World War I tanks.

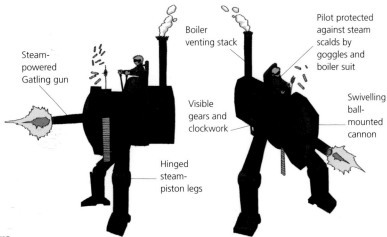

Steam-powered Gatling gun

Boiler venting stack

Pilot protected against steam scalds by goggles and boiler suit

Visible gears and clockwork

Swivelling ball-mounted cannon

Hinged steam-piston legs

## Steampunk clockmakers

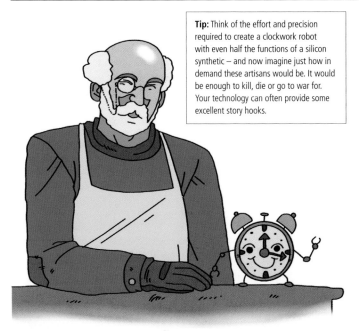

**Tip:** Think of the effort and precision required to create a clockwork robot with even half the functions of a silicon synthetic – and now imagine just how in demand these artisans would be. It would be enough to kill, die or go to war for. Your technology can often provide some excellent story hooks.

What would the buildings look like in your steampunk city? Think of 19th-century London, and all the factories there used to be; think also of famous, long-standing buildings. Clockwork mechanization is just as important as steam power to steampunk. Many businesses in the city would employ hydraulics specialists and former watchmakers, now elevated to cornerstones of your new society. The old watchmaker shown here has just finished re-rigging a broken alarm clock as a robot toy for his grandchildren. Our Geppetto-style creator has made a living thing from his livelihood. This clock is energized by stored potential energy, not magic.

◀ **Make do and mend**
Steampunk is all about the injection of fantasy into a historical period. This shows the contrast between quasi-historical elements like the old watchmaker, and fantastical elements, like the autonomous clockwork creation.

# Interiors as backgrounds

Planning the décor, fittings and furniture for an interior scene is just as important as designing a full building and placing it in the context of a city. Many of your most important scenes will take place in interiors, and you have an excellent opportunity in every one of them to reflect character and amplify mood. A bare dockland warehouse has a very different feel to a boudoir strewn with voluptuous cushions, for example. If the room belongs to one of your characters, you should populate it with their personal effects. What do their favourite photographs, paintings and desktop wallpaper say about their personality and history? A minimalist or cluttered room can similarly speak volumes.

## Aspects of a room

Unlike out on the street, where you may include a number of buildings in the background that have nothing to do with your story beyond scene-setting, every interior you show will be involved in the narrative somehow. As mentioned above, think how you can use the backgrounds of these scenes to drive your narrative. The old axiom of storytelling is 'show, don't tell', and a well-constructed interior scene can carry a great deal of weight and save you volumes of wasted panels and awkward dialogue. Treat every room like a reverse-engineered television murder scene: what will an investigator (the reader) be able to deduce from the props and trinkets in it? If you plan to use a room on a regular basis, don't forget to map it out so you can draw it from all angles.

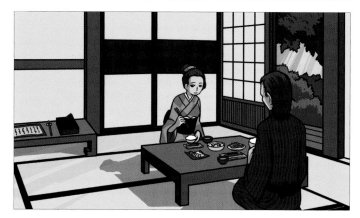

**Traditional Japanese meal** ▲
The minimalist setting tells us the characters are concerned with people over property, and that the story is set in the past. The calligraphy on the table suggests an educated, perhaps noble, woman, as does the variety of the foods being eaten.

## Room details

Manga's extensive page counts in most of its editions allows it to pace its stories in a different fashion to comics in the West. You may often find that manga takes the time to explore new surroundings, zooming in on pertinent details (either while characters continue talking, as a 'voiceover' on the characterless image, or as a guided 'walking tour' of a new locale) to create a sense of place. It also gives you, the artist, a chance to show off your research and planning, and draw the reader's eye to details that, while easily overlooked now, may become very important later. Don't feel you have to implement these 'breathing spaces' in the narrative every time you move somewhere new – like every storytelling technique, they should be used as appropriate and in moderation.

**The calligraphy table** ▼
Drawing attention to the roll of paper, ink and pen might just seem like adding detail on first glance, but perhaps the noblewoman is writing a message to her lover that she is desperate to keep her husband from reading.

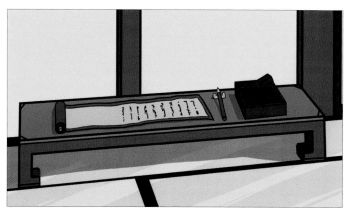

## Starting off

The simplest place to start when deciding on décor is to look at familiar surroundings, like your bedroom or lounge. Take note of how you've decorated your room: where you've placed the bed, the bedside cabinet, bookcases, lamps, wardrobe, chest of drawers and so on. What smaller, personal details have you placed on these pieces of furniture? Draw your room from one perspective, then focus on a few chosen pieces of furniture and draw them from as many angles as you can. Learn the shapes they're made from, and practise drawing them in one, two and three point perspectives. This will give you an 'image bank' of common furniture to draw from.

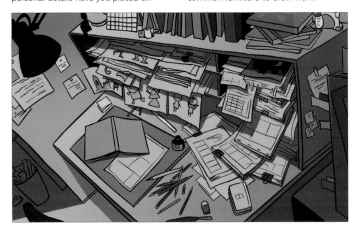

## Making it personal

If your central character works out of an office, what does their workstation look like? If they work in a cubicle farm full of hundreds of identical workstations, how could you tell that it was your protagonist's desk without them being there? Thinking of these unconscious clues and physical remnants will often give you a better handle on your character's personality. Add personal details that give up more information on a second glance – the photo of a friend, pet or lover stuck to the monitor, sticky notes and 'to-do' lists on the wall. A mishmash of papers 'perfectly filed' according to your character's own peculiar system (which works only for them), and an in-tray stuffed with ignored memos.

◄ **Manga artist's desk**
Even without the artist present, the morass of pencils and pens, drying sketches, freelance commissions and thumbnail sketches would give him or her away.

## Furnishing the fantasy setting

A fantasy setting has a similarly rich variety of furniture and personal items, although it is harder to research them by just looking in your bedroom. The interiors of castles, alchemists' labs, fletchers (makers and sellers of bows and arrows) and taverns would all have their own items. Though the traditional medieval-sourced fantasy worlds do allow you plenty of scope for research, you might want to add your own stamp to your creations. The tip here is consistency. Tables, chairs, beds and other furniture should be linked by style, particularly in rich areas like castles or the mountain homes of creepy noblemen. If tables are black mahogany, chiselled with gargoyle heads, then chairs and sideboards should match. In poorer hovels, consistency goes out the window: the people who lived in poorer homes would own whatever was affordable, available, or built by their own hands.

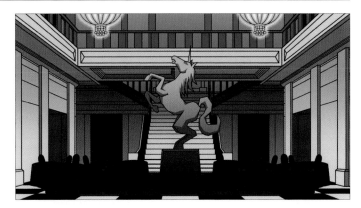

**Fantasy interior** ▲
Here is the grand entrance hall to a nobleman's weekend retreat. Far from the serfs tilling the fields that swell his coffers, he and his fellow socialites swill the finest wines – and then, when the witching hour arrives, they descend to the basement for a frenzy of demonic sacrifice. How would you decorate and furnish such a room and such a house? The chessboard tiles on the floor already illustrate the dichotomy of good and evil within the house – how would the chairs and tables reflect the same internal struggle?

# Versatile vehicles

Vehicles are present in every kind of story. The examples shown here are cars, but the principles used to draw them can be extended to the hovercar, the horse-drawn cart and beyond. Vehicles are essential elements of your story in three ways: as set-dressing material, adding fizz and visual interest to street scenes; as backdrops, as characters converse behind the wheel or make out on the back seat; and as characters in their own right, extensions of personality. As with feet, it's hard to cheat a drawing of a car and make it look good – so brush up on the basics.

## Practice exercise: Basic car shape

Cars are basically boxes on wheels, but it's the intersection of the various angles that can prove tricky to draw.

**1** Draw two loose rectangles, one on top of the other. The upper one is drawn shorter than the other and placed slightly aft of centre above the lower one, with its sides tilting inwards in a trapezoidal fashion. Draw two circles at either end of the lower rectangle, bisected by the chassis and leaving space for the bumpers at front and rear. This forms the basis of an exceptionally simple car frame. You should be able to rotate this shape in any direction or dimension.

### Materials
• *soft lead pencil*
• *pen and ink*
• *colouring method of your choice*

**2** Using the basic frame, begin to 'cut into' the squared-off shapes with pencil lines, carving out the more rounded contours of modern car bodywork. Have a look at some photo reference (or a real car) to see how the chassis curves over the wheels, where the windows and doors fall, and how bumpers and headlights are incorporated.

**3** Each car begins with this basic frame, but obviously every model and make is a slightly different variation on the 'four wheels and an engine' frame. When you are happy with how your car looks (not forgetting details such as wing mirrors, grilles, licence plates, hubcaps, door handles and trim), ink the lines and prepare your drawing for colour. When colouring, pay particular attention to how the metal panels reflect and refract light, and how that reflection differs from the glare of sun or streetlights on the windscreen glass. Remember that a car's bodywork may pick up mud or road debris.

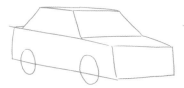 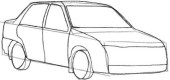 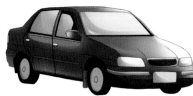

## Practice exercise: Typical saloon car

The next example uses the same frame to construct a modern saloon car. Cars often have 'faces' formed by their headlight, grille and licence plate combinations. Here, the buck-toothed basic car above is outdone by the confident grin on this saloon. How does this reflect the owner's personality?

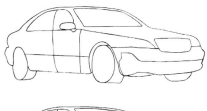

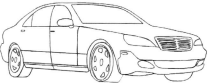

### Materials
• *soft lead pencil*
• *pen and ink*
• *colouring method of your choice*

**1** Even a slight change in proportion is enough to set the saloon car apart. The wheels are relatively larger, the chassis shallower and the windscreen swept back.

**2** Add in the detail work, concentrating on the grille, headlights and wheeltrims. Ink your favoured lines, and erase your guidelines and bounding boxes if you have not already done so.

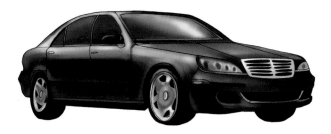

**3** As before, pay particular attention at the colouring stage to the way light falls on the car's bodywork. The car here has been completely toned in a narrow range of blues, bleeding from dark to near-white for the highlights. Note how the highlights serve to pick out the angles of the car, separating the right wheelmount from the bonnet and leading the eye back along the doors to the boot.

## Practice exercise: High-performance car

Although saloons and ten-a-penny basic cars are excellent for background and 'extras' work, you may want something with a little more oomph for your protagonist. High-performance cars are often squatter and wider than normal cars, and decked out in all kinds of extra spoilers, lights, visible engine blocks and the like. A character driving one of these cars is usually in far too much of a world-saving hurry to worry about such niceties as speed limits or traffic laws... So beware!

### Materials
- *soft lead pencil*
- *pen and ink*
- *colouring method of your choice*

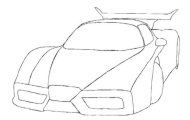

**1** Flatten and widen your guide boxes. Manga characters will often drive something customized and unique, so combine a number of reference pictures to make your mean machine. This car combines 'billion dollar sports car' with 'Formula One racer' and adds in a dash of futuristic hovercraft. Use angles, shapes and colours not normally seen on the road.

**Tip:** Think about how much colour alters our perception of cars – flame red is seen as 'fast', with gunmetal grey being one of the more common colours on the roads. What does your character's car colour say about them?

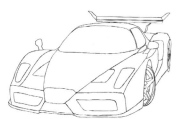

**2** This car has a swept-forward 'nose cone' for a bonnet, with the headlights and air-coolant feeder systems arranged around it over the wheel hubs. Add the larger shapes in first, such as the windscreen, wheels and door. Sketch in the fins and wheeltrims, sunken headlights and wing mirrors next. Many high-performance cars have two doors instead of four, the back seats having been removed to reduce the chassis weight and allow more room for a turbo-charged engine and stabilizing fins in the rear.

**3** The tyres of a sports car are usually bigger than normal to allow for greater speeds while maintaining grip. Some models also have vents, intakes and spoilers to increase airflow and reduce air resistance. Spoilers increase downforce on the car, keeping the weight evenly distributed and the car under control at high speeds. When your chosen combination of speed, power and grace is complete, ink the pencil lines and erase your guide boxes. Finally, colour the whole vehicle in a hot red shade, using contrasting cool blues for the glass. If your character is a superhero or member of a police force or mecha gestalt, you may want to apply a suitable logo to the top of the bonnet, so enemies will know from a distance who is speeding to defeat them.

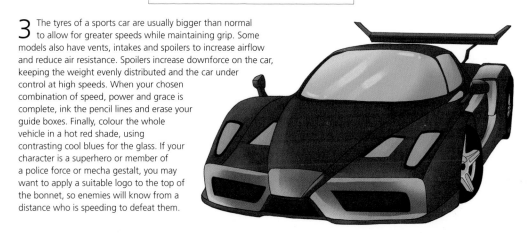

# Multi-purpose planes

Planes are as flexible as cars in their in-story use. If a crime thriller is set in an airport, they could just be background scenery, or the location of a gripping terrorist shoot-out. If your characters are travelling from country to country, they could be present solely in an intermission panel to show how they crossed the distance. If your story is about a group of

fighter pilots, however, the planes could be as individual and personable as the humans flying them. A fighter squadron gives you plenty of story opportunities, from ground-based drama to vicious dogfights, so here we'll show you how to draw a jet fighter, for use as a vehicular character or set-dressing for dramatic fighter-base brawls.

## Practice exercise: Jet fighter

This jet fighter is drawn in a simple two-point perspective just below the horizon. Photo references for jet fighters are easy to come by, whether on the Internet, or through books like the *Jane's* series of guides.

## Materials
* *soft lead pencil*
* *pen and ink*
* *colouring method of your choice*

**Tip:** If one of your vanishing points isn't visible on the paper size you are using, you can 'cheat'. Either choose the true point (off the edge of your paper) and rule lines from that, or stay on the paper and make the lines taper together a little as they head off the page.

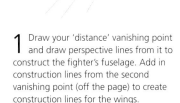

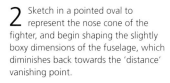

**1** Draw your 'distance' vanishing point and draw perspective lines from it to construct the fighter's fuselage. Add in construction lines from the second vanishing point (off the page) to create construction lines for the wings.

**2** Sketch in a pointed oval to represent the nose cone of the fighter, and begin shaping the slightly boxy dimensions of the fuselage, which diminishes back towards the 'distance' vanishing point.

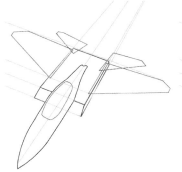

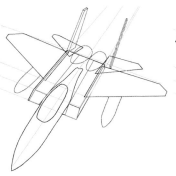

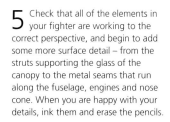

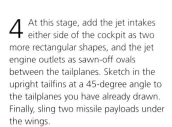

**3** Now add in the cockpit (as another pinched oval), and the slung-back wings, which jut out at an angle from the boxy main body of the fighter. Add the tailplanes behind them, underlapping the wings. Note that both the wings and tailplanes are 'squared off' at the tips, again at an angle.

**4** At this stage, add the jet intakes either side of the cockpit as two more rectangular shapes, and the jet engine outlets as sawn-off ovals between the tailplanes. Sketch in the upright tailfins at a 45-degree angle to the tailplanes you have already drawn. Finally, sling two missile payloads under the wings.

**5** Check that all of the elements in your fighter are working to the correct perspective, and begin to add some more surface detail – from the struts supporting the glass of the canopy to the metal seams that run along the fuselage, engines and nose cone. When you are happy with your details, ink them and erase the pencils.

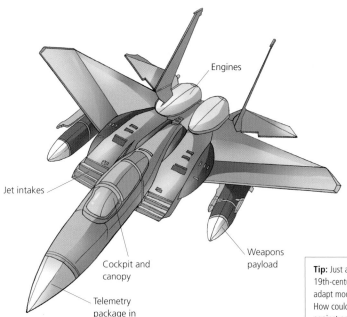

Engines

Jet intakes

Cockpit and
canopy

Weapons
payload

Telemetry
package in
nose cone

6 Like the saloon car on the previous spread, this jet has also been coloured using a minimalist colour scheme – in this case a tight range of blue-silvers. Remember that planes are usually painted to match their combat theatre, so marine fighters will be painted sea-blue on top and sky-white underneath, or in various shades of grey. Desert operations fighters will come in tan and sandy hues, and jungle-bound jets will have green camouflage patterning.

> **Tip:** Just as steampunk devices reuse existing 19th-century designs, there's no reason why you can't adapt modern-day tech for a near-future storyline. How could a jet fighter be adapted for space conflict against an alien race? What advances in engine technology would need to be made – or stolen?

## Populating the skies

Of course, it's not just jet fighters that fill up airports and swoop through the skies; there are a huge variety of flying machines active in the modern era, and many more which have long gone out of use or never flown, except in the imagination. If working primarily in present-day stories, familiarize yourself with the technology that's out there, and the many different forms that it takes. If working in a future or parallel setting, try fusing different shapes and technologies into strange but familiar fuselages and aerodynamic transports. The helicopter and commercial airliner shown here are equally great for foreground or background use.

**High-spec helicopter** ▼
A lithe, radar-lite shape; fold-out gun and missile emplacements; side-mounted winch mechanisms; and a large field of view for both pilots and soldiers – this helicopter is used in anti-submarine warfare.

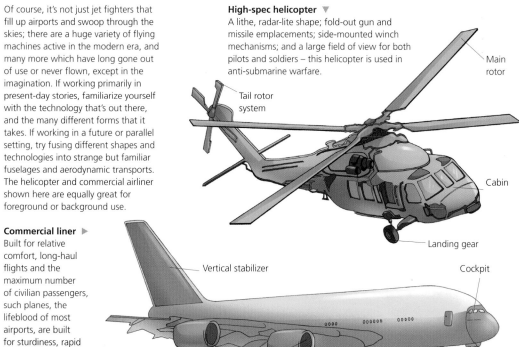

Tail rotor
system

Main
rotor

Cabin

Landing gear

Vertical stabilizer

Cockpit

Engines

**Commercial liner** ▶
Built for relative comfort, long-haul flights and the maximum number of civilian passengers, such planes, the lifeblood of most airports, are built for sturdiness, rapid turnaround times and minimal maintenance.

# Fantasy setting project

One thing common to all settings is a drinking establishment. Whether it's a seedy dive for uncovering information in exchange for money or beatings, or a place to unwind at the end of a long day of asteroid mining, pubs and drinking dens always make for a fun and useful addition to any story. Look at the cantina in *Star Wars: A New Hope*, for instance: a showcase for dozens of aliens (who never appear again), but an important fulcrum for the whole saga and a hyper-condensed blast of science fiction flavour. For this project, we'll create a fantasy pub. As with your town square or starship deck, it's worthwhile drawing out a floor plan of your

drinking hole so that you know where all the angles are when a bar room brawl kicks off. Think of the pub called 'The Prancing Pony' in *The Fellowship of the Ring* as an example. It has a main bar and seating area on the ground floor, with nooks and crannies for private meetings. Upstairs there are rooms to stay in, below are cellars where ale, wine and mead are kept. Give your tavern an 'Olde Pub' name, raising reader expectations with a foreboding moniker like 'The Bloodied Badger' or 'The Palcied Elf', or offer hope for sanctuary or entertainment with a sign reading 'The Merry Druid' or 'The Lusty Dwarf'.

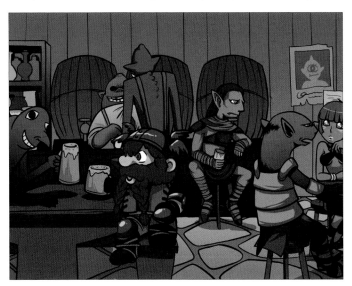

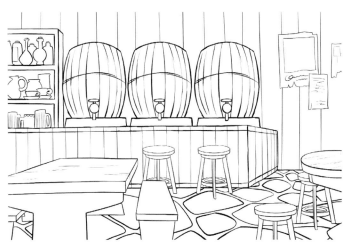

## Materials
- *soft lead pencil*
- *pen and ink*
- *colouring method of your choice*

◀ The centrepiece of our pub is the bar at the far end of the room where the ogreish landlord dispenses large tankards of frothy ale to all manner of clientele.

1 Start by mapping out a floor plan of your drinking establishment. Work out what the focal point of your pub is (the bar, a raised stage area for bardic entertainments) and arrange the furniture so that it complements and faces this focal point. Stairs on the far side lead down to the cellar, while visitors are politely asked to store their armour and weapons in the lockers close to the door.

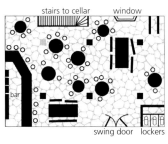

stairs to cellar        window

bar

swing door    lockers

2 Once you've planned your building, pick an interesting angle from which to draw your first shot. We've chosen a front-on view of the far right end of the bar, with two tables and a selection of stools jutting into shot, the better to show off the flavour and varied clientele of our pub.

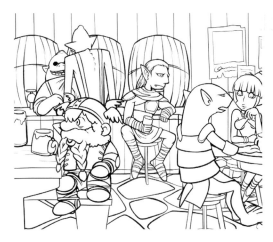

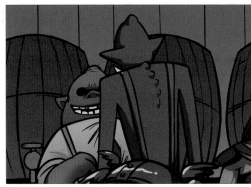

4 The final tavern scene has the green-skinned landlord standing behind the bar, visible from the torso upwards, talking to and serving his bizarre clientele. The loud hustle and bustle of his patrons fills the room, as talking weasels discuss bounties with zombie girls, and wall-eyed blue ghouls clank tankards with pigoblins. Behind the landlord, various barrels, glasses, bottles, wanted notices and old pub bric-a-brac fill out the décor, giving it a familiar, even cosy feel at odds with the strangeness of the customers. The warm earth tones of the walls, barrels and floor contribute to this sense of frontier security.

3 We start by transposing the furniture and background from our top-down plan into three dimensions. The image uses a simple one-point perspective. Once you're happy with the placement and size of your backdrop, it's time to add in your merry drinkers, who can come in all shapes and sizes: the fiercesome dwarf in a helmet and the cocky elfin-like character are both in attendance at the pub on this occasion.

## The characters

The first patron is a dwarf, short on stature, long on beard. The character's proportions are similar to a super-deformed version of a full-sized human, though they maintain the high level of detail in this instance. Emotions will mainly be communicated by the eyes, as the beard, helmet and armour cover up everything else. Physical actions will need to be exaggerated when drawn, to claw back the 'height advantage'.

The second patron has an almost dog-like quality to his elven head. Use standard human proportions and drawing methods when constructing him, but add a canine kink to the nose, jaw and teeth, and elongate the ears and limbs. This character relies on his own tough skin to see him through a fight, so show his cockiness by dressing him mostly in work-out bandages and cutting back on his clothing.

The ogreish landlord shown here has given up preying on the innocent to prey on those who can keep him in a ready supply of gold, in return for goblin intoxicants. He's another character with almost super-deformed proportions, loose muscle mass, and inhuman bone structure allowing him to support bizarre allocations of fat. Note the black, dead eyes and the two-fingered hand.

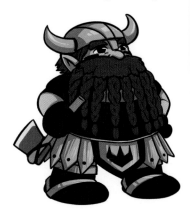

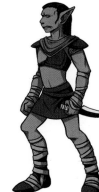

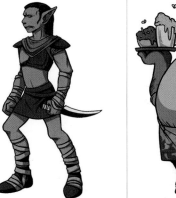

# Spacecraft project

Spacecraft are another form of vehicle with multiple uses. Some, like the project here, are so large they could form the entire setting for your story, taking over a day to walk their length. Others are equivalent to the jet fighters we have already drawn, and are often mounted inside such enormous spacecraft like fighters on an aircraft carrier. Because these immense structures, thousands of metres long, are built in space and designed never to land, there are no design constraints on what they look like or what type of metal they are built out of. In the vast vacuum of space, there's no need for aerodynamic proportions. Anything goes, from the bulky and workaday to the artistic, abstract and awe-inspiring. This project will create the ultimate setting and transport for your science-fiction characters.

## Materials
- *soft lead pencil*
- *pen and ink*
- *colouring method of your choice*

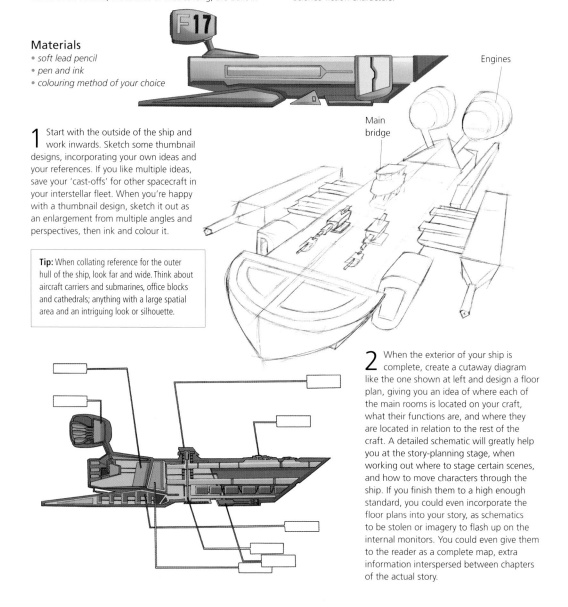

Engines

Main bridge

**1** Start with the outside of the ship and work inwards. Sketch some thumbnail designs, incorporating your own ideas and your references. If you like multiple ideas, save your 'cast-offs' for other spacecraft in your interstellar fleet. When you're happy with a thumbnail design, sketch it out as an enlargement from multiple angles and perspectives, then ink and colour it.

**Tip:** When collating reference for the outer hull of the ship, look far and wide. Think about aircraft carriers and submarines, office blocks and cathedrals; anything with a large spatial area and an intriguing look or silhouette.

**2** When the exterior of your ship is complete, create a cutaway diagram like the one shown at left and design a floor plan, giving you an idea of where each of the main rooms is located on your craft, what their functions are, and where they are located in relation to the rest of the craft. A detailed schematic will greatly help you at the story-planning stage, when working out where to stage certain scenes, and how to move characters through the ship. If you finish them to a high enough standard, you could even incorporate the floor plans into your story, as schematics to be stolen or imagery to flash up on the internal monitors. You could even give them to the reader as a complete map, extra information interspersed between chapters of the actual story.

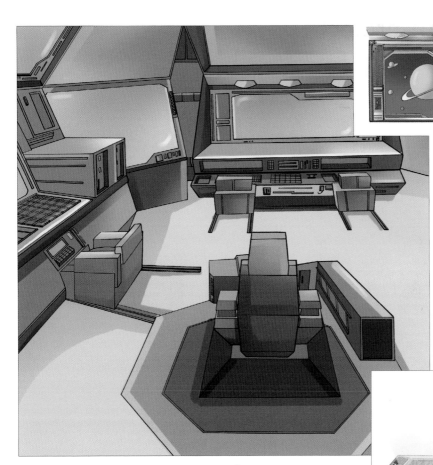

**Viewscreen data** ▲
Embellish your bridge (and all the corridors and rooms of your ship) with symbols, signs and operating data terminals. Make 'working' rooms look as if they are being used, rather than leaving them as empty shells for characters to talk over and walk through on the way to somewhere else.

**The bridge** ▲
Central command hub for the entire ship, buried deep inside the hull. Being well defended makes it easier to resist an enemy's attempts to kill the bridge crew. All shipboard decisions are routed through here.

**Tip:** Try to continue your design decisions from the exterior of the ship through to the inside. A cathedral-inspired ship could be filled with giant atriums flooded with artificial light, while one based on a submarine might incorporate tight, duct- and pipe-filled tunnels. How would you combine these two influences on one ship? Perhaps the atria are there to stave off space-claustrophobia brought on by a life lived in pipes.

**Space periscope** ▶
Think about how each area of the ship or bridge may be used, and the items of technology required in them. This scanning terminal allows an operative to sweep deep space for visuals.

3 Choose a central room to illustrate in more detail. Here we've chosen the bridge, the hub of the ship. This is assembled in much the same way as any other room – start with a floor plan, decide on a style of furniture and any design motifs you will carry through the piece, and transfer the room into three dimensions. Here, the motif is angled geometric shapes and soft purples and browns. The focus of the room is on the giant viewscreens, with the crew seated on the inertial-dampening couches during flight.

4 When your bridge shot is complete, think of how you will use it during a story. Which angles will prove most dramatic? If the Captain is in an elevated position, try drawing her seat from below the horizon line, so that the reader – and the Captain's subordinates – are always looking up at her. If your characters are always seated in flight, which new angles can you find on your 'set' to keep things exciting and moving when they are largely stationary working at their stations or talking for hours on end?

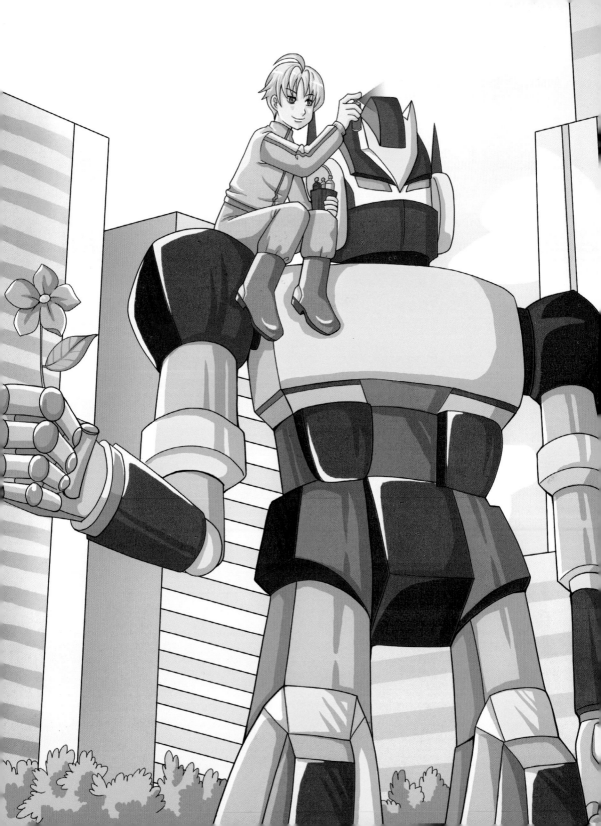

# Allies and enemies

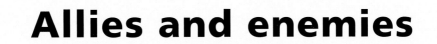

Your manga heroes and the stories you create for them are only as good
as the secondary characters you surround them with. This chapter will
show you how to populate your narratives with intriguing and memorable
people, animals and sentient vehicles: everything from friendly furry pets
and loyal hounds to nefarious master thieves and city-block-sized mecha,
the pilot-controlled walking vehicles.

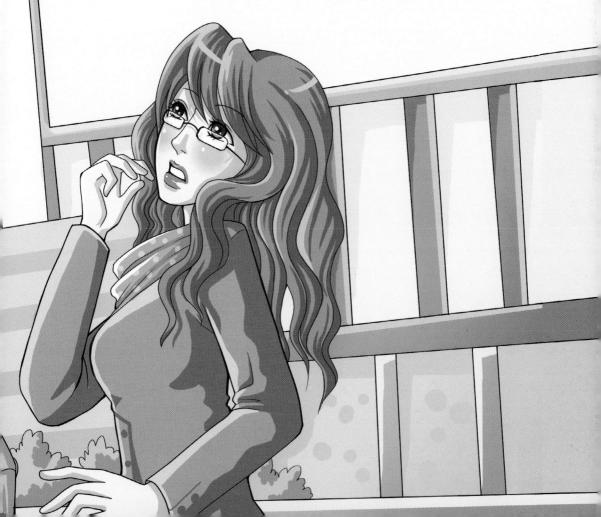

# Animal allies

Animals can be used in various ways. They can 'dress' a scene as background elements, or they can be used anthropomorphically, i.e. given human features and characteristics. An anthropomorphized animal may walk upright, talk, wear glasses and enjoy drinking coffee, for example. Animals can also be included as allies to a protagonist, particularly in shonen manga, where they are often 'familiars' – an extra set of eyes and ears for the main character. Such familiars, following a long tradition of Japanese spirit guides, often have the ability to talk and sometimes possess magical abilities.

Whether allies or not, animals in manga are frequently employed as a source of humour. An animal can be used to alleviate a heavy emotional juncture in a story with a moment of amusement. An animal's folly may also sometimes result in the discovery of something that will assist the main character.

## Practice exercise: Cute cat, three-quarter view

In this exercise, you will be drawing a cute, manga-style cat. As in the earlier exercises on drawing human heads, you need to draw guidelines first, to ensure the cat's features are symmetrical.

## Materials
• *soft lead pencil*
• *ink and pen*
• *colouring method of your choice*

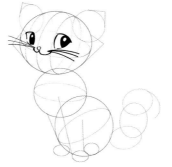

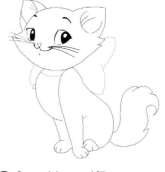

**1** Use a squashed sphere as your basic head shape. Imagine it as a three-dimensional shape, like a rugby ball, and make your guidelines follow the shape's curvature, as shown here. Lightly sketch in circular guides for the ears. For the body, draw two overlapping spheres below the head. The first (forelegs) sphere should be one head high. The hindlegs sphere should be one-and-a-half heads high. For the tail, draw three overlapping oval shapes as shown with a curved line at the end. Add points to the ear guides and to the cheeks. Use your body guides to sketch the length of the front and back legs, using straight lines to indicate limbs and ovals for feet.

**2** Add in the cat's eyes, which are almost triangular in shape, using your guidelines to keep them evenly spaced in perspective. Although cats' pupils are almond-shaped, a 'cute' cat will have more circular pupils. Beneath the triangular button of the nose, add a loose 'UU' shape for the mouth, and stroke out six lines for the whiskers.

**3** Start to join up and fill out your sketched lines, linking the outer edges of the head, drawing the inner ears, a pair of intrigued eyebrows, and joining the jawline to the pointed fur on the cheeks. Fill out the legs, and suggest paws with small arcs on the feet. Add fur to the tail with a jagged edge. Add a large bow as the final step.

**4** Ink your pencil lines. When you are happy with your black and white drawing, add colour using your preferred method. Markers or watercolour paints will give you a soft and natural finish, while digital colours, as shown in this finished piece, will provide bold contrasts.

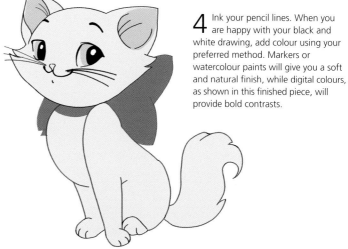

## Practice exercise: Cute cat, side view

In this exercise, you will draw the same cat from the side, illustrating how the same basic building blocks – curved guidelines around a three-dimensional oval – can be used to capture the cat's features from any angle.

### Materials

• soft lead pencil
• pen and ink
• colouring method of your choice

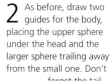

**1** Draw a squashed sphere for the head, narrower than the one in the previous exercise. Remember that the facial features need to shift 90 degrees to the right.

**2** As before, draw two guides for the body, placing the upper sphere under the head and the larger sphere trailing away from the small one. Don't forget the tail and ears.

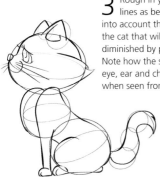

**3** Rough in your pencil lines as before, taking into account the portions of the cat that will be hidden or diminished by perspective. Note how the shapes of the eye, ear and cheek change when seen from the side.

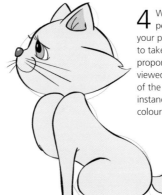

**4** When you are satisfied with the pencil lines, ink in the lines using your preferred method. Continue to take into account the way the proportions appear to change when viewed from this new angle – the size of the back leg or the whiskers, for instance. Erase your guidelines and colour the picture as before.

## Contrasting characters

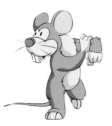

**Cute mouse** ▼
A mouse with a more anthropomorphized face. The cheeks and nose are minimalized, and the eyes separated. A tuft of 'hair' on the top of the head, and some eyebrows, humanize this creature even further.

**Mean mouse** ▲
To create a mouse make the ears round rather than pointy and perform the same rounding-off on the cheeks. Give the mouth protruding buck teeth. Make the feet shorter and the tail long and thin. The nose should be much larger in proportion to the rest of the face.

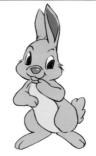

**Cute bunny** ▲
The head is the same shape as the mouse's but the ears are long, even stretched upwards. There is only a touch of furriness around the cheeks, with jagged lines kept to a minimum. The feet are long and the tail a small ball of fuzziness.

**Mean bunny** ▼
It takes only a few quick strokes to create an 'anti' version of a cute rabbit character, the mean bunny. Narrow the eyes and rotate them upwards, adding strong, lowered eyebrows to help insinuate a frown. Add a threatening pair of over-long, sharp gnawing teeth. Enlarge the paws and exaggerate the feet to kicking size. When drawing the fur, make the jagged edges longer and more pointed, to give a wilder appearance. The fighter's sash completes the look.

## Realistic animals

Manga also uses more realistic-looking animals in a wide variety of naturalistic poses. These animals rarely stay still, so change their poses frequently. To get a better idea of how animals look in motion, study wildlife documentaries or do some research into animal physiology at the library or on the Internet. This will provide you with a wide range of reference material from which to draw accurate information and inspiration.

**Black bear** ▶
Just woken from hibernation, this creature has more than freshwater fish or picnic baskets in mind for its first meal. The bloodshot eye and exaggerated fur underscore its role in your story as a predator.

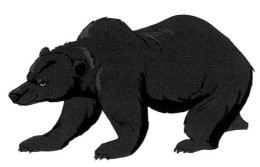

**White wolf** ▼
This enormous wolf regards your characters with lupine intelligence. Will it guide them safely through the Arctic wastes – or rip out their throats?

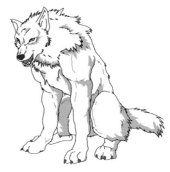

## Practice exercise: Realistic dog, standing

In this exercise, the realistic dog is drawn standing still, although its muscles are tensed and it is ready to chase after the nearest small rodent or delicious treat. Take note of how the legs are arranged in front and behind the trunk of the body to better show the perspective.

### Materials
- *soft lead pencil*
- *pen and ink*
- *colouring method of your choice*

1 Draw two ovals for the chest and rump. Join them as shown. Add a rough circle and triangle for the head and muzzle. Rough in the legs, taking note of how the knees bend and how each tapers to a paw. Sketch in the tail.

2 Using these shapes as a guide, draw in the outlines of the body, adding in muscular detail and elements such as the ears, eyes and nose. Pay special attention to the leg muscles and paws.

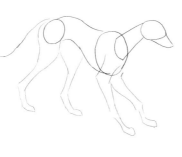

3 If completing your drawing as a pencilled piece, use photo reference or the image to shade in areas of muscle mass and shadow, suggesting fur and a tightly coiled, racing-dog frame. Tensed sinews will show themselves as light parallel lines along each leg.

4 Alternatively, you may wish to colour your dog. In this case, use colour rather than shading to suggest its musculature.

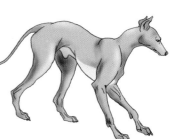

## Practice exercise: Realistic dog, running

This exercise features a side view of a running dog. The lines representing the leg bones are pushed out beneath the snout and tail, creating a long, bullet-like silhouette.

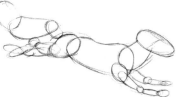
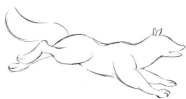

### Materials
- *soft lead pencil*
- *pen and ink*
- *colouring method of your choice*

**1** Using much the same basic skeleton as in the last exercise, draw in the two ovals and connecting tissue for the body, and extended ovals for the head and tail. Draw the dog's four legs fully extended, flung out to front and back.

**2** Add the paws and the details to the head such as the ears and the mouth (dogs tend to run with their mouths open) and make refinements to the shape of the body. Note the way the knees bend at the extremes of motion.

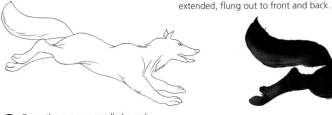

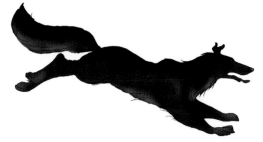

**3** Draw the eye as a small almond shape at the point on the eyeline where the forehead ridge meets the snout. Firm up the sketchy lines from the previous step, streamlining the anatomy and inking your pencil lines when you are happy with the position of the limbs and the texture of the fur.

**4** Go over your dog's outline and add jagged fur lines on the tail, chest, around the collar in ink (following the curve of the head circle), across the lower body, the back, and the tail. Remove the guides and add paws and a lolling tongue. Add colour, without losing the detail of your fur lines.

## Other dog characters

Here are three different dogs, all of which use the same underlying skeleton bent into different poses and overlaid with different musculature. The resulting form is then accentuated with different sub-species traits.

**Watchdog** ▶
The pricked ears and 'battle-ready' stance reveal an alert watchdog on the prowl.

**Droopy dog** ▼
Old and wise in dog years, or panting for water in the heat? The droopy jowls do much to add character.

**Fierce dog** ▶
A studded chain, blackened eyes, sharp claws and obstinate, jowly face show a dog not to be messed with.

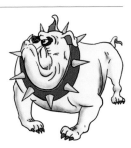

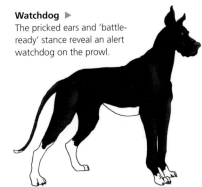

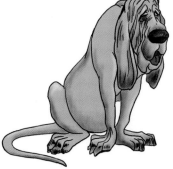

**Tip:** You can apply many human character traits to dog physiology to produce the same effects – excess fat suggests a lazy dog, muscle mass a fighter, long and lithe limbs a runner, and so on.

# Animal monsters

Monstrous animals are not hard to develop once you have got to grips with the basics of animal drawing. Making something look demonic and threatening is just a matter of exaggerating certain features or fusing multiple species together to create a new gestalt entity. For inspiration, and in keeping with manga's roots, why not delve into some Japanese folklore? You will find hundreds of fascinating monsters and demons in all shapes and incarnations to choose from.

## Mixing the gene pool

Monsters can be made by combining the attributes of one species with another – a trick that has kept mythological tales going for centuries. For example, a minotaur takes the form of a muscular man to the neck, but has the head of a ferocious bull. Don't feel you have to confine yourself to two species, either: some of the most memorable monsters of legend are fusions of wildly different arms of the zoological record. Depending on whether your monster is supposed to be 'realistic' (i.e. plausible) or not, you may wish to limit its strangeness to the boundaries of extreme possibility, or you may want to go with a fantastical mix of feathers and claws, manes and fur.

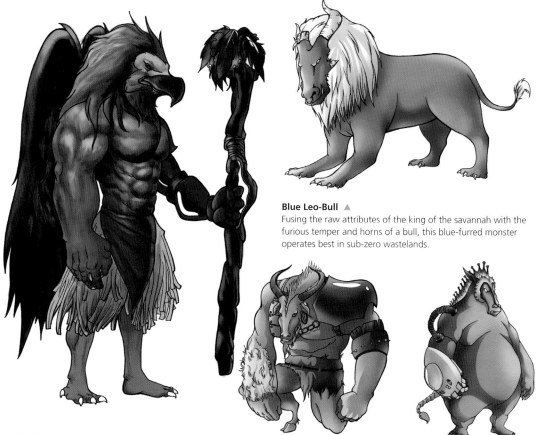

**Blue Leo-Bull** ▲
Fusing the raw attributes of the king of the savannah with the furious temper and horns of a bull, this blue-furred monster operates best in sub-zero wastelands.

**Eagleman scout** ▲
Living in vertiginous city-states clinging to the tips of mountains, Eaglemen eke out a primitive existence, stealing from those who dare cross their territories and bringing what they take as offerings before their twin-beaked god.

**Taurean chieftain** ▲
One of the leaders of a race of humanoid bull-men, vicious defenders of nature.

**Hippohorse warrior** ▲
This gene-splicing has sacrificed fleetness of foot for thick muscle and girth.

## Practice exercise: Hellhound

In this exercise, an ordinary dog is made monstrous. The key is in how you alter its build. This dog does not have an athletic physique, with its fat body and sinewy legs. It is an ugly beast with some surprising features. It will also need far less hair – a few tufts on its back and behind the front legs, perhaps a few straggly bits on the tail if you choose, but no more.

**Materials**
- *soft lead pencil*
- *pen and ink*
- *colouring method of your choice*

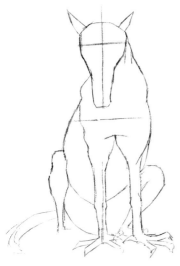

**1** Using the proportions of the realistic dog as a template, form the body shape using the same guide lines and joints for the legs, as well as the circle for the head and the rectangular muzzle. Elongate all of the proportions, from the spine to the yawning lower jaw, keeping your lines tight to the bone to show how the muscle has all but wasted away. The paws are now more like hideous claws.

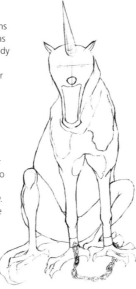

**2** Hang the jaw open and ready to reveal racks of prominent teeth, and position the nose. Bulk up the muscles of the neck by making the back arch farther away from the upper body. This will give the creature a hunched or razor-backed look. Add bony protrusions, such as the horn-like spar protruding from the forehead, to suggest hellish mutations and deranged cross-breeding experiments. Add manacles to the front claws, restraining the hellhound's aggression, but not completely denying the beast its freedom.

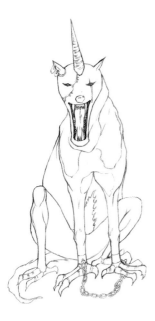

**3** Draw in the details of the hellhound implying a deranged, possessive owner. Add piercings to the ears. Draw the eyes as demonic slits, burning with hatred. The hellhound can take all the damage you throw at it and still be aggressive so make the creature's skin look patchy and flayed, even slashed open in parts to show organs or muscle tissue, such as in the stomach. Fill in the deadly maw of jagged teeth and the hot, panting tongue. Add striations to the horn and claws and jagged fur to the whiplike tail. Ink the image when done, and erase the pencil lines.

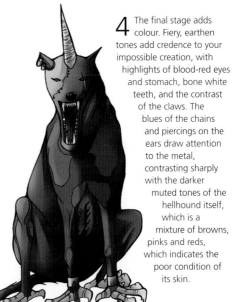

**4** The final stage adds colour. Fiery, earthen tones add credence to your impossible creation, with highlights of blood-red eyes and stomach, bone white teeth, and the contrast of the claws. The blues of the chains and piercings on the ears draw attention to the metal, contrasting sharply with the darker muted tones of the hellhound itself, which is a mixture of browns, pinks and reds, which indicates the poor condition of its skin.

# Alien life forms

Aliens can be a lot of fun, as you can populate entire worlds with stunning new species. Aliens don't have to be a life form you'd ordinarily recognize. Even if humanoid, their characteristics may be based on completely different organisms. Alternatively, your aliens may look completely bizarre – take the creature from *The Blob*, for example: a roaming gelatinous mass. Once you've decided your aliens' physiology, you can develop interesting traits for them, which may similarly challenge convention. If you make your aliens drooling, snarling and generally threatening in appearance, that doesn't mean they have to be warmongering megalomaniacs. They could be peace-loving, with external features that make other races too afraid to have any sort of contact with them. Alternatively, you could develop an alien that appears serene, but which uses its calm exterior to lure others into a false sense of security.

## Insects and reptiles

Here are some ideas for alien characters based on various existing Earth species. The first is a melding of ant, lion and dragonfly. The second is a fusion of earthworm, scorpion and octopus. The third is a blending of bat, dog and horse. All share an upright, humanoid gait. These alien forms have been inspired by insects, mammals and reptiles. Because the physiology of animals is so different from our own, combining their attributes always provides fertile ground for interesting ideas. Species such as ants and termites, for instance, live in hive-like colonies of workers dominated by a single queen, so creating alien societies based on these creatures could extend into their social practices within your story, sparking off potential ideas for thrilling interspecies conflicts.

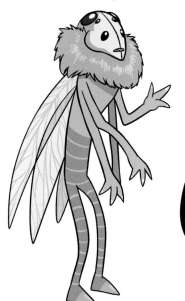

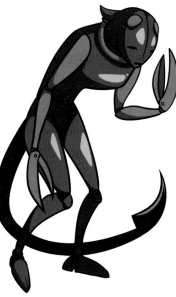

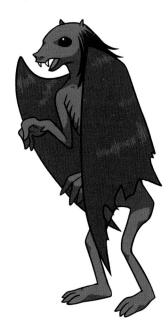

**Dragantflion** ▲
No more than 15cm (6in) tall, dragantflions are the most brutal hunters in their food chain, swarming on victims with the use of pheromonal hive signals. Don't just cut and paste your animal attributes, think of how you can convincingly meld together elements that would never arise in nature.

**Wormoction** ▲
Caught between claws and squirting ink, a wormoction's prey never has a chance. Sometimes adding in pseudo-mechanical elements can add an extra element of the alien to your created species. Here, visible joints suggest an exoskeleton, or perhaps even naturally occurring hinges.

**Bathorschien** ▲
These monstrous-looking beings are simply misunderstood. On their holy days, thousands fill the skies with song. Think of surface textures for different alien skins. Applying fur instead of scales, or changing the colour of an Earth-based dermal covering can be enough to convince.

## Practice exercise: Mantoid

The armoured mantoid, a soldier of a man/ant race, is naturally well-suited to battle. Its segmented limbs and anthead make it look sufficiently alien, while its humanoid body could allow it to blend in on Earth – just.

### Materials
- *blue pencil 10*
- *soft lead pencil*
- *pen and ink*
- *colouring method of your choice*

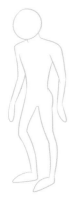
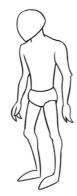
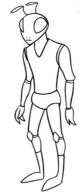
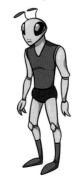

**1** Start with a rough outline with the blue pencil, building on what you have learned of human proportions. Use guidelines if you wish. The head will be large and fairly triangular compared to the norm, while the other proportions fall well within standard deviation for a human. Give the mantoid a warrior's broad shoulders.

**2** Start to flesh out the line work of the body, using your guide. The hands taper to two claw-like fingers and a sharp thumb, while the feet are toeless triangles. The head is plectrum-shaped, with a thick neck to support it. Begin to clothe the mantoid in the protective garment he wears around the body, creating a bottom and a top garment.

**3** Start with the head, adding in large, light-absorbing eyes. Note how the eyes reflect the shape of the head. Add two pinpricks for nostrils and a straight line for a mouth. The antennae are thin loops, like golf clubs, protruding from the top of the head. Segment the limbs at every joint, as shown. Complete with knee pads and boots.

**4** Add shading to the eyes, ink and erase the pencil lines and proceed to colour. Light flesh tones contrast well against cool blues, with purple eyes as an accent.

> **Tip:** When creating a species, start with a 'benchmark' character that you can exaggerate and mutate to make individualized aliens.

## Extended family

We know that ants are ruled by a queen, which is much larger than any other member of the species. Would you have a king or queen for this race, and would they be larger and very different from the rest? What kind of social structure would the mantoids possess? Worker mantoids, for example, could be adapted primarily for labour. You could assign a special role to the flying mants, making them the planet's police force. From here, it's a fairly straightforward process to develop ideas for the buildings and vehicles of your mantoid world, keeping the man/ant theme throughout.

### Snapshot of a society ▶
You may find it helpful to create an image showcasing many different elements of your alien society in operation, trying to capture the 'essence' of what makes them tick. This picture shows a cross-section of mantoids engaged in the frantic act of hive construction, under the watchful and commanding eye of the queen.

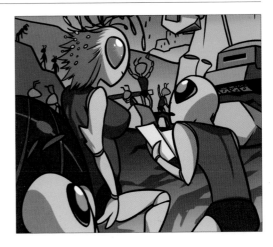

# Mecha giant robots

One of the most popular strands of science-fiction manga is that featuring mecha (short for mechanoid). Mecha are giant robots, at least one to two storeys tall (sometimes as large as several city blocks) and capable of insane amounts of damage. The difference between mecha and true robots is that mecha tend to be piloted by a human operative – often one specially chosen, born or bred for the purpose. Mecha proved very popular when they appeared in anime series such as *Gundam* in the late 1970s and early 80s. Mecha are often portrayed as Earth's – and humanity's – last, best hope against a similarly titanic alien menace: so why not pit your mecha designs against city-sized monsters and aliens?

## Designing a robot

Using the human form as a basis is a good way to start dabbling with robot design, particularly if you haven't drawn any before. It also conforms neatly to the idea of a robot with a human pilot – when the pilot moves their arm or leg, the mecha duplicates their action on a far grander scale. Start with a basic human shape, but make variations in the outline, incorporating armoured segments and visible joints at every opportunity. If you've managed to design a few different human characters, it is only a few short steps from here into the mechanical world.

**Rapid-fire machine** ▷
Test your imagination. With each deadly weapon the size of two stretch-limousines, how will your mecha be resupplied in combat?

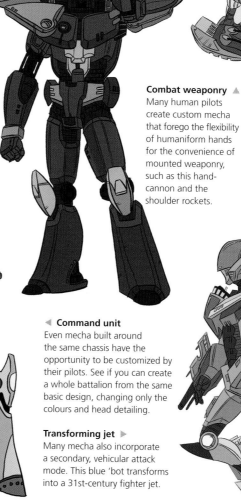

**Combat weaponry** ▲
Many human pilots create custom mecha that forego the flexibility of humaniform hands for the convenience of mounted weaponry, such as this hand-cannon and the shoulder rockets.

◀ **Command unit**
Even mecha built around the same chassis have the opportunity to be customized by their pilots. See if you can create a whole battalion from the same basic design, changing only the colours and head detailing.

**Transforming jet** ▷
Many mecha also incorporate a secondary, vehicular attack mode. This blue 'bot transforms into a 31st-century fighter jet.

## Developing your mecha character

To make your mecha stand out, experiment with ways of
arranging its features in order to make them unique.
You don't have to obey any previous norms of mecha design.

### Head ▶

Multiple lights or lenses, or a slit around the head that lights
up, often represent visual senses. A single eye could also flash
when the mecha 'speaks', transmitting the commands of its
pilot. As mecha generally magnify their pilot's body language
a hundredfold, an expressionless face may be the only
opportunity to maintain some reserve.

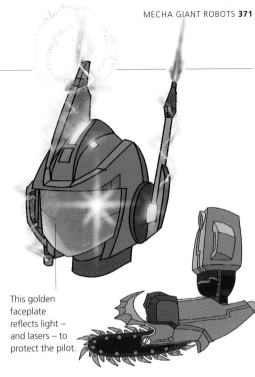

Shoulder-
mounted
sensors
transmit a
3-D view of
the battlefield
to the
cockpit.

This golden
faceplate
reflects light –
and lasers – to
protect the pilot.

This mecha's
digits can
retract in
favour of
twin pulse
cannons.

Sturdy feet keep
the weight of the
mecha anchored,
and house
projectiles and
flight capabilities.

### Arms ▲

The arms need to look convincing, although they don't
necessarily have to be physically possible. For interesting
shape ideas, look to a mechanic's toolbox. You could choose
something like a hammer, upturn it, and use it as the upper
part of the arm that connects to the shoulder, with the head
of the hammer acting as the elbow. For the forearm, construct
a cylinder, add a few bumps for implied muscle, and rather
than end with a hand, choose a weapon, such as a miniature
cannon or a chainsaw blade.

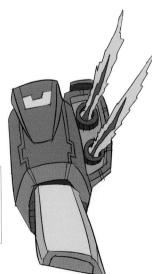

### ◀ Legs

Instead of a cylinder, why
not choose a square-edged
shape for the thigh?
For the knee, draw a small,
turned-in block. Beneath
that, draw a giant foot-
shaped block that bends
off the knee by being
attached to either side of
it. Add enormous shin pads
that extend to the floor,
housing the heel but
leaving the foot/toe area
sticking out at the front.

**Tip:** It can be difficult to suggest the scale of humanoid robots.
When drawing them, be sure to surround them with visual clues,
whether in the shape of skyscrapers for them to tower over, standard
vehicles to crush, or human pilots climbing on board. Give the
reader's eye something to estimate height with.

# Sidekicks and friends

You'll have noticed that it is extremely rare for a manga hero to walk around unaccompanied. In manga, the protagonists always have at least one or two companions who follow them on their journey. These are the supporting cast, the sidekicks, who come in many forms. They're not always people – a friend might be a creature, such as a pet or even an alien. This section, however, provides examples of some human sidekicks, who may help your lead in their quest.

## The importance of a sidekick

When you create a sidekick, you add a further dimension to your story. Giving your protagonist a constant companion helps show the depths of his or her personality and, most importantly, gives them someone to have a dialogue with and explain the story to. Use yourself as an example and think about how your interaction with your friends, parents, teachers and bosses defines you as a person, in relation to others. Sidekicks are often a double-edged sword. Some are incredibly helpful, and may be more skilful than the lead character. Others, despite a wealth of technical skills or fighting prowess, are a constant hindrance to the main character. You could have a sidekick who is the lead character's best friend and always shows an unparalleled level of support. It could be that the this companion is over-confident and arrogant, leaping in, fists whirling whenever the lead character pleads for diplomacy or stealth. This would leave the protagonist frustrated at having to keep his companion's pugnacious nature under control.

## Practice exercise: Genius

This sidekick is petite and slender, but makes up for what she lacks in muscles with the depth and breadth of her knowledge base. Fluent in dozens of languages, with a photographic memory, she's an irreplaceable asset to the main character.

### Materials
- *soft lead pencil*
- *pen and ink*
- *colouring method of your choice*

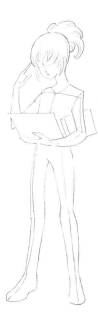

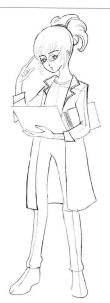

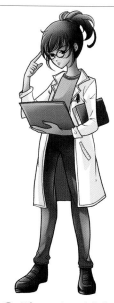

1 Rough out the proportions of a standard female in her teens with a soft pencil, fleshing out your simple guidelines into a sketchy pose. To emphasize her IQ or her photographic memory, this genius points to her temple. She is examining some important documents clasped in her other hand and holds some papers under her arm. Keep the outline of your character minimal and the body slim. Sketch in some long hair, tied up at the back, with a ragged fringe (bangs) falling around to frame her face.

**Tip:** Glasses on a brainy character may be stereotypical, but in manga, common denominators are a way to establish characters quickly. You may decide to turn a stereotype on its head during the course of a story, subverting the expectations of your audience.

2 Give your character more definition with your pencil lines. Give the character narrowed, concentrating eyes and glasses over the top. Aim for a scientific-casual look with a lab coat, as if a PhD student has gone into the lab on her day off. Note the subtle sixth digit, giving her the appearance of being slightly unusual.

3 When you're satisfied with your pencil lines, ink them and erase the guidelines, and proceed to colour. Use a strong hair colour to direct attention to the character's head (and mammoth brain), and use colourful accents on the trousers and T-shirt to complement the stark white of the lab coat.

## Practice exercise: Arrogant fighter

This guy is always in the mood for a fight, and while his physical presence may help the protagonist intimidate his opponents when they face enemies, thinking is not one of his special skills. He benefits from being around the cleverer lead, who does his best to keep him on a (metaphorical) leash.

### Materials
• *soft lead pencil*
• *pen and ink*
• *colouring method of your choice*

1 Start with a rough set of guidelines, using a soft lead pencil. Unlike our protagonist, who might be around three heads wide from shoulder to shoulder, this character is around four to five heads wide and about six heads tall. Keep the head small, not much bigger than a normal head, to emphasize this character's limbs.

2 When defining the body, keep the neck wide to suit his muscular build. Arms and legs need to be broader than in a standard adult male, so that his physique emphasizes his strength. Define the main muscle groups to a greater degree than you usually would, particularly in the biceps, chest muscles and calves.

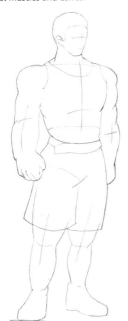

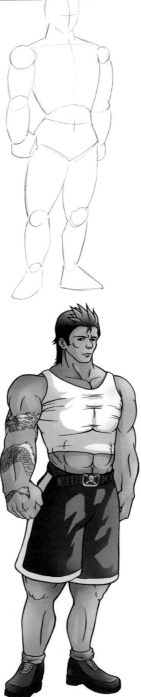

3 When detailing his face, give more definition to the nose and mouth. Keep his hair short with small spikes. Draw a tight, sleeveless T-shirt, keeping the arms exposed. Baggy shorts will give him freedom to kick. Add a heavy belt over the top. To show his past as a fighter, add a colourful tattoo around one arm.

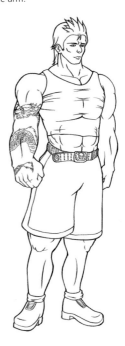

4 When you're satisfied with your pencil lines, ink them and erase the guidelines, and proceed to colour. On this figure note that the skin is deeply tanned and his clothes plain, making the tattoo stand out in sharp relief.

**Tip:** It helps to get acquainted with your characters. Practise their proportions, and the most relevant poses likely to be used in a manga story. Keep a lasting record of all the characters you create to help maintain continuity and make sure that figures are not drawn incorrectly as your work progresses.

# Elderly characters

Inevitably, since manga is a product of youth culture, elderly characters are not as prominent as their younger counterparts. When it comes to older sidekicks, manga tends to deal in two stock characters. The less common is the elderly martial arts sensei, who maintains an impressive physique even after several generations of fighting and teaching classes of young and boisterous students. The other is a mischievous character, often possessing special abilities. An elderly trickster will both lend the story some comic relief (inverting the 'respect your elders' paradigm) while, at the same time, constantly throwing complications into the path of the lead character as they try to get them out of trouble.

## Practice exercise: Martial arts expert

This is a large character, almost imposing, but still in proportion, unlike the 'arrogant fighter' of the previous exercise. His strength and experience should be half-implied from his build, and half from the way he carries himself. Any up-and-coming student wouldn't dream of getting cocky. The martial arts expert is at his peak of fitness and keeps his moves disciplined, but his uniform has suffered over the years – think about whether you want to stick in rips and tears, or frayed edges. From a story perspective, consider why he'd want to carry on wearing this old uniform. Perhaps he wore it when he finally beat his own master in single combat.

### Materials
• soft lead pencil
• pen and ink
• colouring method of your choice

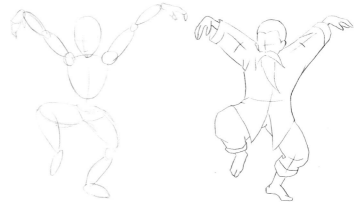

1 Make the frame broad in the shoulders, and wider than the waist. This character's pose is inspired by many styles – this could be the beginning of a Mantis or Drunken Master move.

2 Dress your character, paying attention to the way the loose trousers and thick coat hang over his frame. The hair is close-cropped and the beard and moustache relatively long and thick around the lower part of his face.

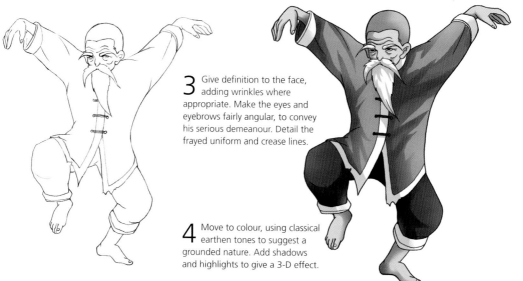

3 Give definition to the face, adding wrinkles where appropriate. Make the eyes and eyebrows fairly angular, to convey his serious demeanour. Detail the frayed uniform and crease lines.

4 Move to colour, using classical earthen tones to suggest a grounded nature. Add shadows and highlights to give a 3-D effect.

## Practice exercise: Crafty old wizard

This is an example of one of the more comical old characters, reminiscent of a chibi-style character, particularly as he's only going to be three heads high. His head will look quite large for his shoulders. If you decide to use a similar character in one of your stories, he could get his robes caught continually in doorways or be trodden underfoot to humorous effect.

### Materials
- *blue pencil*
- *soft lead pencil*
- *pen and ink*
- *colouring method of your choice*

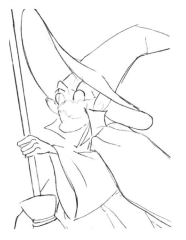

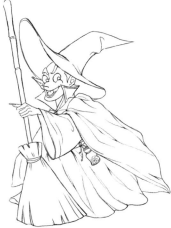

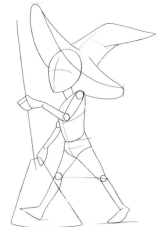

1 For the frame, make the shoulders and hips narrow. Keep the outline of his body thin but draw fully developed, rather than chibi-style, fingers. He will hold a long thin staff or broomstick that's over twice his height, so sketch a line into one clasped hand.

2 Sketch in large eyes, with an equally large grin and lines around the mouth. Draw pronounced cheekbones (when we age, features like the cheeks sink into the face, and the skin thins, so the bone structure of the skull becomes more obvious). Make a small, downward-pointing nose. Outline thick eyebrows and make the ears larger than normal, to divert attention to the head. Cover the wizard's receding hairline under an enormous pointed hat.

3 Finalize the features to give the face an impish expression and dress your character in a long robe that looks over-large, particularly at the sleeves. A high-collared cape flows out behind him. Draw a thin sash round his waist to draw his robes together, and add a small, hanging potions flask. Add texture lines to the broom and crease lines to the garments.

**Tip:** Remember, it's not only your hero who will be changed by the outcome of your narrative – his or her travelling companions may also undergo a metamorphosis, changing from good to bad, dying, changing forms or betraying the lead character and then sacrificing themselves to save them: all are possibilities along the way.

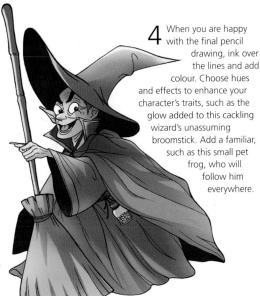

4 When you are happy with the final pencil drawing, ink over the lines and add colour. Choose hues and effects to enhance your character's traits, such as the glow added to this cackling wizard's unassuming broomstick. Add a familiar, such as this small pet frog, who will follow him everywhere.

# Villains

Now you can move on to the bad guys. And let's face it, designing the villains is as much fun as designing your protagonist. This is your chance to create characters who will stop at nothing to defeat your protagonist. Often, a villain will have another motive as well, such as world domination, or a raging desire to destroy an entire city. Or your villain may be more subtle: a character who merely mirrors the protagonist, with similar abilities, like a rival in a sport which both characters play. Of course, the rival/villain resorts to cheating, while the protagonist always plays by the book.

## Planning villains

When planning your villains, start with the main antagonist. Decide how you want them to look, and also the reasons why he or she and your main character are at odds. If you have a well-motivated, powerful antagonist, your protagonist's journey to his or her final confrontation will be tough and satisfying. It's crucial that your story of the protagonist's trials and tribulations is convincing. To this end, you should create a series of villains, escalating in toughness and evil, all guided by the near-omniscient hand of the master manipulator. Many shonen manga function like video games, with the protagonist defeating a series of 'bosses' in order to 'level up'. Ensure each 'boss' is engrossing and unique in order to maintain interest.

> **Tip:** Ensure the villain has all the latest equipment, gadgets and outfits at their disposal, putting them on a pedestal that the lowly protagonist can topple them from. Arrange for the hero and villain to meet, so you can highlight the extent of the differences between them.

**Alien princess**
With thousands of ships at her disposal, this beautiful yet evil Martian princess is bent on domination of planet Earth. She has conquered a hundred worlds, and keeps all neighbouring planets under the yoke of her tyranny. But Earth will not bow, and she is constantly frustrated by its scuppering of her plans.

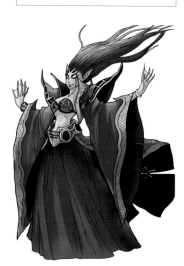

**◄ High-school rival**
Your protagonist seems somewhat average in comparison to this guy, who is a youthful, charismatic all-rounder. However, he hates to lose, and his arrogance is often his undoing. Then again, with so many people thinking that he's the greatest, he rarely fails. It will take a particularly brave student to challenge him at what he does best, especially when others have been completely humiliated as a result of their failure.

**Vampire count** ▲
This character has the feel of a classic manga villain. He is well dressed, powerful and good-looking. However, his glossy exterior hides less-reputable traits. Imagine him sitting high in his castle, holding the nearby town in his vice-like grip of terror. The moon is full, and the lord has sent his minions out for a fresh young bride to sate his bloodlust. Many strange creatures are at this villain's command, primed to stop any would-be hero from entering his domain.

# Villain characteristics

As a general rule, keep your villains' features and clothing dark and dramatic. A protagonist dressed in lighter colours will provide contrast. Villains in manga are typically tall, and physically more impressive than the protagonist. Keep their eyes and eyebrows angular, so that they always look threatening. At the beginning of your story, your protagonist shouldn't have a hope of defeating your villain.

The idea is that he or she has to learn and train along the way. To make things more interesting, you might want to make your villain short on patience, so that anyone who dares to interfere with his plans will quickly fall victim to his temper – this can also include their various underlings.

Just as the hero or heroine has sidekicks, a villain always has aides: trusted henchmen, monsters of untold strength or manipulative strategists to advise them on their evil plans. But for every villain, there must be a flaw, a weakness, which will eventually be their downfall. Is it physical – an allergy to a potion or poison? Is it mental – a hubristic oversight to be exploited? With every villain you create, consider how your protagonist will discover their weaknesses and then make use of them to emerge victorious.

> **Tip:** Many great stories begin with the heroes or heroines having already lost – a land pillaged, a city destroyed or subjugated to a common enemy. Rallying your characters to unite against this defeat can be very satisfying.

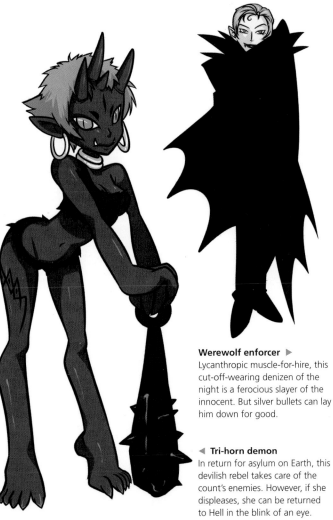

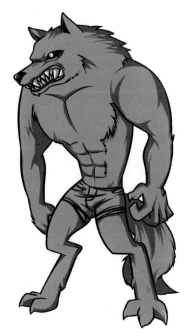

◀ **Freshly made vampire**
The recently sired 'son' of the vampire count, his bloodlust and vigour are stronger than his father's. However, he still retains many of his human memories, which can cause conflict.

**Werewolf enforcer** ▶
Lycanthropic muscle-for-hire, this cut-off-wearing denizen of the night is a ferocious slayer of the innocent. But silver bullets can lay him down for good.

◀ **Tri-horn demon**
In return for asylum on Earth, this devilish rebel takes care of the count's enemies. However, if she displeases, she can be returned to Hell in the blink of an eye.

# Supporting cast gallery

With a world of boundless possibilities ahead of you, it can often be difficult to find a place to start. With that in mind, this spread showcases some of the more esoteric combinations of attributes you can put together to create your supporting cast and their villainous antagonists. Remember to subvert expectations wherever you can – most, if not all, of these possibilities could work equally well for strange allies as for terrible adversaries, given a compelling backstory and reason to work alongside your heroic characters, rather than competing with them or devouring them.

## Backup and adversaries

What makes a good character? An easily identifiable visual 'hook' always helps – many of the characters on this page are simple twists on the standard human physique, with alterations in colour and silhouette, and an inhuman feature such as horns or a tail.

**The zombie** ▶
This creation is a creepy twist on a 'normal' zombie character. The recognizable basics of human physiology are re-imagined as the 'living dead'. This shirtless zombie is emaciated and lacks coordination, his limbs stiffened and near-useless from rigor mortis. His clothing may be ripped or missing, and because of his emaciated state, will look several sizes too big. His face is a mess, with staring eyes and a gaping, dislocated jaw. For further fright, shade the eyes to shadows so they look almost hollow. The zombie communicates in moans; wind whistling over a grave.

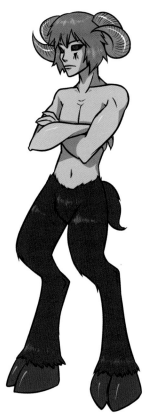

**Demonic faun** ▲
Impish and mischievous, but not truly evil, this creature of the underworld enjoys nothing more than meddling in the plots and affairs of state.

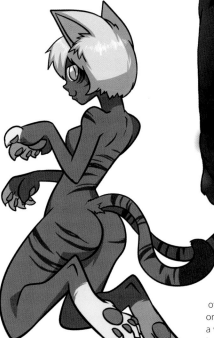

◀ **Catgirl**
A hyper-evolved form of the common housecat, this sprightly, twin-tailed humanoid could be from the future, the result of a gene-blending experiment, or the magically uplifted form of a wizard's familiar. Perhaps she is indentured to her evil master, but longs to be free.

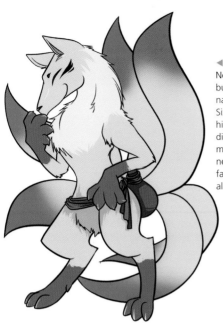

**◀ Six-tailed fox**
Neither good nor evil,
but serving the capricious
nature of the Universe,
Six-Tailed Fox roams the
highways of his fantasy
dimension, directing and
misdirecting travellers to
new paths – and new
fates. His magical tails
allow him to fly.

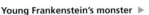

**Young Frankenstein's monster ▶**
Stitched together from the corpses
of a high school rock and roll band,
this poor unfortunate wants
nothing more than to rock out on
the guitar, bass, drums and vocals,
all at the same time. However,
while he attempts to get his new
life together, the scientist who
resurrected him wants him to rob
more corpses to create the ultimate
girl band in one monstrous,
immortal body.

**Hydragon ▼**
Cut one head off and two more will
grow in its place, until eventually
the hydragon will be so top-heavy
that you can probably walk around
it and steal
whatever
you like.
In the
meantime,
though, it is a
deadly, reptilian
predator.

**Mersorceress ▶**
Born from a breed of
humans who decided
to follow the evolving
dolphins back into the
water, this mercreature
practises an esoteric blend
of water magic, one that
requires the feeding of
sacrificial victims to the
Great Behemoth of
the Deep.

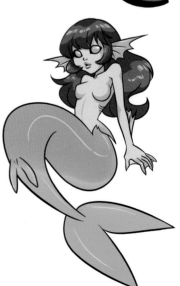

# Battle scene project

Every now and then it's great – and necessary – to draw good and evil into a massive conflict. It makes for a very satisfying payoff for your readers, and can be equally satisfying to draw. The main drawback is that it takes time, and can easily become confusing. Sometimes you can have two dozen characters on a single spread all involved in the fight, all performing a different action. As cool as it is to draw these entanglements, you should not make a habit of it. Manga – and stories in general – thrive on repeated waves of build-up and pay-off, so each great battle must be accompanied by a

similarly weighty section of plot development, a character-based 'fallow period' in between the waging of war. One way to keep track of your characters in these battles is to give each one a list of aims, goals and actions to undertake throughout, so that in each panel you know what all of your cast are doing.

▶ Good meets evil in a battle against a mecha warlord and his following.

### Materials
- *soft lead pencil*
- *pen and ink*
- *colouring method of your choice*

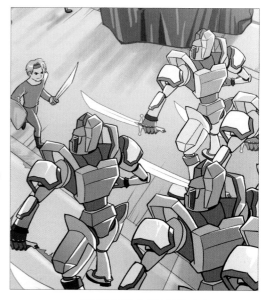

**1** List the characters involved in the fight, and their objectives within it; for example: 'Baron Von Struckmeer, a mecha-piloting local warlord wants to take

the head off the rebellious upstart Rainer Darksturm, so will ignore all lesser foes on the battlefield in order to engage him in hand-to-hand combat.'

**2** Draw an overhead map of the battleground 'arena'. Wherever you are, making a map and tracing the positions of your combatants on it will allow you to keep a continuity of action from

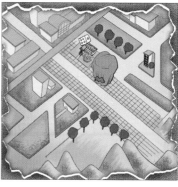

any angle. When in doubt, create a couple of key 'landmarks' to anchor your action no matter which direction you view the fight from. Using your character objectives and overhead map, plot out your battle, panel by panel. Remember that your notes can be very brief: a note that 'X engages Y near to Z' is all you need. The map is there so that you can pick a spot on the map, choose a direction from which to view the action, and know at a glance what landmarks you will see from that direction. Try to rotate your 'camera' around the battlefield throughout your scene, alighting on the important struggles of each pair or group of main characters, even as you seek to capture the chaos of the larger, pitched battle raging around, in front and behind them.

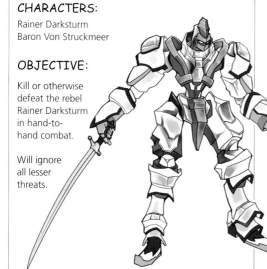

## CHARACTERS:

Rainer Darksturm
Baron Von Struckmeer

## OBJECTIVE:

Kill or otherwise defeat the rebel Rainer Darksturm in hand-to-hand combat.

Will ignore all lesser threats.

3 When you have your plot of how the battle will flow, sketch out some thumbnails of your first spread. Keep the thumbnails small, and use stick figures or loose shapes to indicate where each of your characters will be placed. You may want to start with a large overview panel of the entire battle, before zooming in to focus on individual fights – or you might want to start small, and zoom back to show the enormity of what is going on.

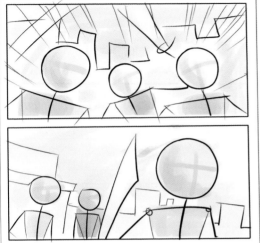
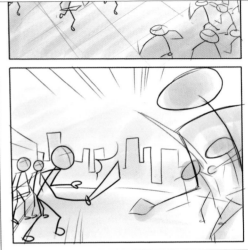

4 When you are happy that your thumbnails 'read' well, and that your battle, while chaotic, still flows from panel to panel, it's time to transfer your sketches to full-size pages and pencil, ink and render in colour your characters and backgrounds. Remember, too, that visuals and sound effects alone can often be enough to 'sell' a battle – the time for descriptive speech is long past, save for snarls and growls as long-time enemies lunge for each other's throats.

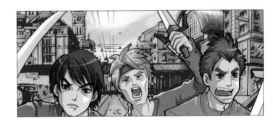

5 With larger-scale battles filled with complex elements and dozens of characters, you may find it easier to draw all of the panels individually, at a larger scale, before scanning them in, colouring them, and compositing them into your chosen layout. The beauty of creating thumbnails first is that it allows you to compose each panel as part of the final page so that each one flows correctly across the entire spread, regardless of whether you drew them all on the same scale or piece of paper.

**Tip:** If you are featuring characters in a number of different scales – humans and giants, for example, or humans and mecha – remember to show how each of these scales relate to one another, and how they interact within the fight. This can be as simple as showing two humans battling in the shadow of an enormous foot, or as complex as two people scaling the artificial mountain of a striding mecha in order to pull out its control cords.

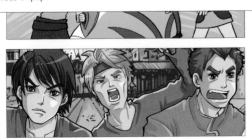
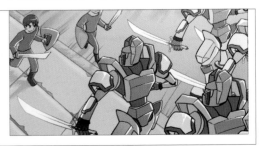

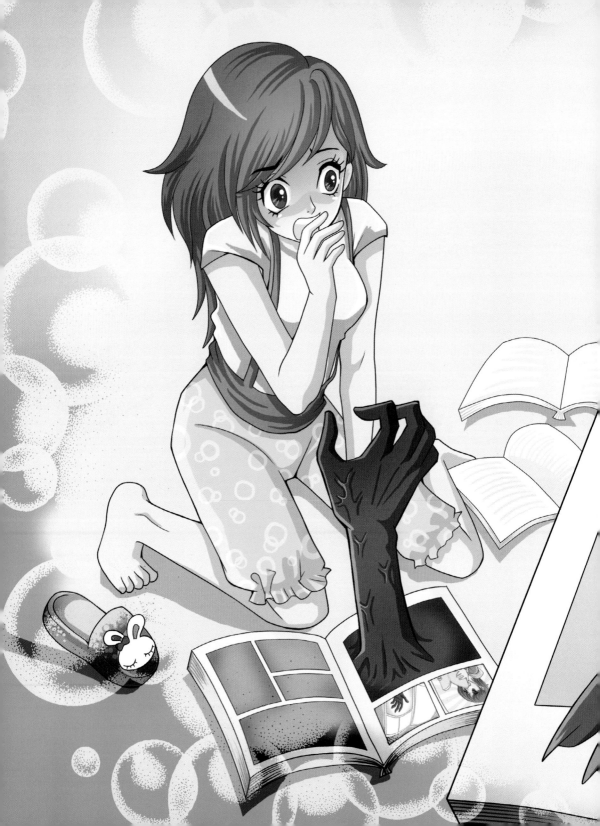

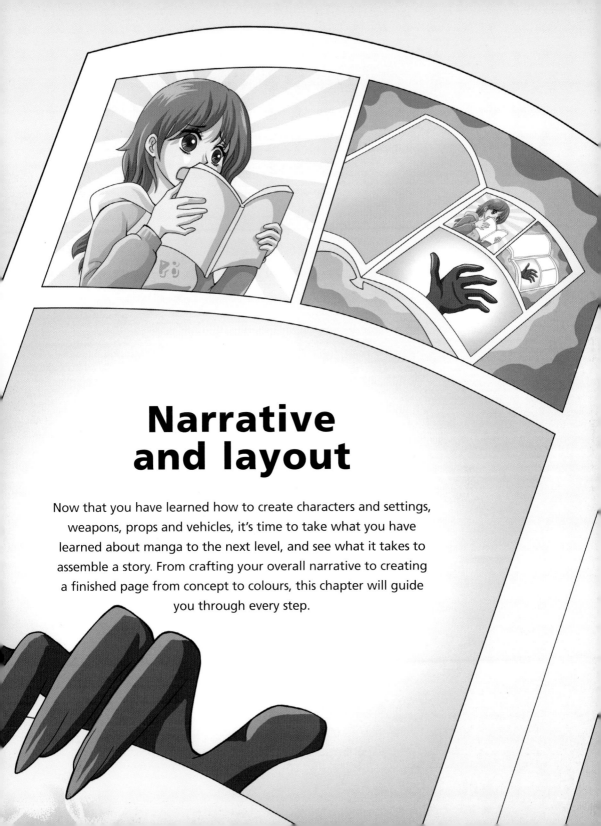

# Narrative
# and layout

Now that you have learned how to create characters and settings,
weapons, props and vehicles, it's time to take what you have
learned about manga to the next level, and see what it takes to
assemble a story. From crafting your overall narrative to creating
a finished page from concept to colours, this chapter will guide
you through every step.

# What's in a story?

Your story is the most important element of your manga. Artwork and dialogue, no matter how polished, are all created in service of your narrative. Manga is a medium of narrative told through sequential art – each panel building on the one that went before it, melding words and pictures to create a sequence that accurately communicates the intent of the writer and artist. The story must keep your reader engrossed throughout, leading gradually to a climactic ending. In this section, you'll learn the basic tools of page-to-page storytelling: using images in sequence, building suspense and releasing tension, framing images in panels, and arranging your panels to control pace and flow.

## Narrative rhythm

Within every story, you need to convey meaning and sustain interest, but you must also reveal your story effectively, in a logical order. Arrange the events of your story so that your audience can follow the action easily, and try to make the drawings and dialogue flow together to create a good narrative rhythm. Such rhythms are controlled by your choice of shots: long, wide panels will slow the eye down, as will large sections of dialogue, while small, choppy, silent panels will prove exceedingly quick to read. A mixture of both – and every step in between – will allow you to pace each scene as appropriate to its content. Different genres may have different rhythms: a shonen action manga will be relatively faster and choppier than a more contemplative shojo romance.

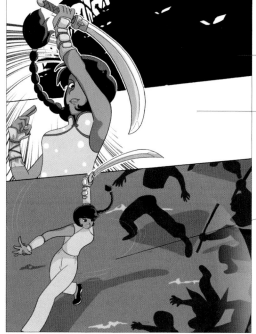

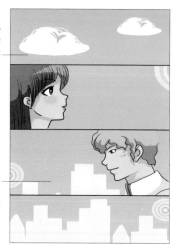

Preoccupation with surroundings punctuates the romantic moment

Shadowed panel builds suspense and mystery

White space creates expectation of action to follow

'Widescreen' panels create langorous pacing

Wide shot slows down the moment so we appreciate the scale of battle and the length of the sword swing

Close-ups make us focus on eyes and characters' interior lives

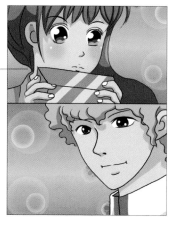

**Shonen** ▲
This page literally bursts with action, with its warrior protagonist extending out of the boundaries of every panel, her sword providing the focus that draws us down the page. Note the use of negative space to create mystery and expectation of the action to come.

**Shojo** ▶
This romantic story, on the other hand, provides plenty of opportunity to focus on what the characters are saying or thinking, as everything but their faces has dropped out of the frame. The wide panels replicate awkward or thoughtful pauses in conversation.

## Narrative movement

The way the reader's eye moves across the page is called the narrative movement. Keeping control of this keeps readers interested. It's important to think in terms of character and camera movement – a dialogue scene of 'talking heads' that repeats the same heads for pages on end will kill momentum and reader sympathy dead. Keep your 'camera' moving around static cameras, or keep your characters moving even as they talk. It is crucial to keep this movement in order to maintain the energy of each scene. Change between close-ups, mid-shots and long shots depending on the tenor of the dialogue: focusing on the surroundings as a character's attention wanders; cutting to an extreme close-up when a character reveals shocking information.

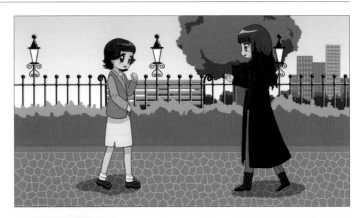

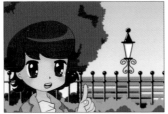

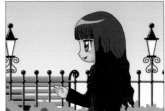

**Conversation on the move** ▶
The two characters meet in a long-shot, before cutting to a close-up of the first character to speak.

## Drama, action and tension

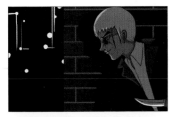

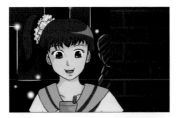

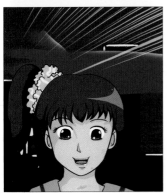

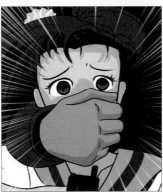

Your stories will need tension. If, for example, your story is designed to be split into instalments, you will need your audience to want to come back for more at the end of each chapter. In a murder mystery, for instance, the detectives will start with the body alone, but as the story progresses, they will collect evidence and clues to lead them to the perpetrator – with plenty of twists and turns along the way. It's up to you to reveal your clues and moments of shock and suspense at the optimum points in the story.

Storytelling doesn't depend solely on dialogue. In some instances, you may wish to let the action speak for itself.

◀ **Kidnap, mugging or murder?**
Tension builds because the reader is aware of the danger the girl faces from the first panel, while the girl is oblivious – until her attacker vaults from the shadows! What happens next? We can't help but turn the page.

## Moving around the setting

Sequences tend to spread over more than one panel – whether they are fights or conversations. How do you create the flow of a sequence? Here we have two characters in conversation. One is asking for directions from the other. The first panel is a shot of the characters from the waist up, facing one another. The dialogue is: 'Do you know the way to the police station?' Instead of giving the answer as to where it is located in this shot, the reply is illustrated in the next panel, which also

changes the angle, a 'camera move' to maintain interest. The conversation flows across the panels, the reader's eye is drawn from one panel to the next, and their interest is piqued, maintained and satisfied within the space of two frames. The second panel is a close-up of the character answering.

Practise keeping conversations interesting. Take a similar pair of characters and create an extended dialogue between them. Focus on how the listener and the speaker react to

each other. Start with a view over the shoulders of the first speaker, perhaps, so that we can't see the expression on their face, only how the listener is reacting, then swap the view in the second panel. Practise mixing long shots, mid-shots and close-ups.

**Getting directions** ▼
How would you continue this exchange? Would you add dialogue, or segue into the young character's journey to the police station?

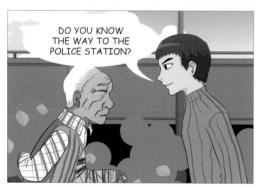

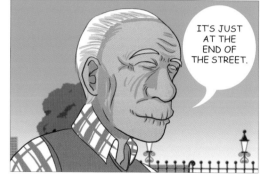

## Change of location

This device is often used to change scenes and locations in a more fluid and natural manner than with a narrative caption (e.g. 'Four Hours Later...', 'In a Warehouse Downtown...'). The first panel of the new scene shows either an exterior shot of a building with a speech balloon directed towards it, or the exterior of a room, with a speech balloon similarly placed.

In the example to the right, a female investigator is eavesdropping at a locked office door. The following panel cuts to a view of the person who is speaking, and the new scene proceeds from there.

Be careful to only shift back to an exterior view when beginning a new sequence, or when adding emphasis that require a long shot of the characters' location, as hopping back and forth between interiors and exteriors will only confuse your reader.

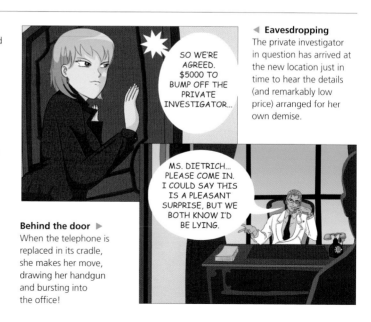

**Behind the door** ▶
When the telephone is replaced in its cradle, she makes her move, drawing her handgun and bursting into the office!

◀ **Eavesdropping**
The private investigator in question has arrived at the new location just in time to hear the details (and remarkably low price) arranged for her own demise.

## Length of dialogue

Dialogue delivers crucial details concerning the characters and their motives, but too much slows the pace and ruins the timing you're trying to establish. You match your dialogue to the artwork and the narrative rhythm. In fast-paced sequences especially, don't let dialogue dictate the speed. If you have a sequence showing a character running towards a building – they're late for school, say, as shown here – don't *state* the reasons why they're late; they don't have time. Keep the dialogue succinct to emphasize their speed – and breathlessness. Explanations can come later.

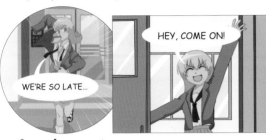

**Sense of urgency** ▲
As the two students bolt out of their apartment block, the emphasis in the dialogue is on reinforcing the main reason why they're running – they're late – without going into any further detail.

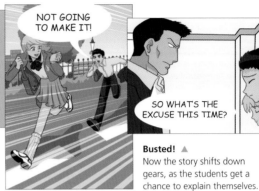

**Busted!** ▲
Now the story shifts down gears, as the students get a chance to explain themselves.

## No need for dialogue

Sometimes you don't need dialogue at all, as the action itself will reveal the drama. Your characters shouldn't describe through dialogue what is shown – it's repetitive, slows the pace, and implies your audience needs assistance. In this example, the destruction of one jet fighter by another is clearly depicted without the need for commentary.

**Deadly dogfight** ▶
The black jet fighter swoops in (1); achieves a target lock on the blue jet (2); fires a homing missile (3) that targets blue's engines (4); the missile detonates (5), and the blue jet plummets out of the sky on fire (6). Note the use (or lack) of borders on the panels, and the use of spot sky blue in the bottom two panels.

**Tip:** When pacing scenes, choose moments that actually drive your story along – don't string out brushing teeth or making coffee over six pages in an effort to 'build tension', unless your story involves possessed toothpaste or a poisoned espresso.

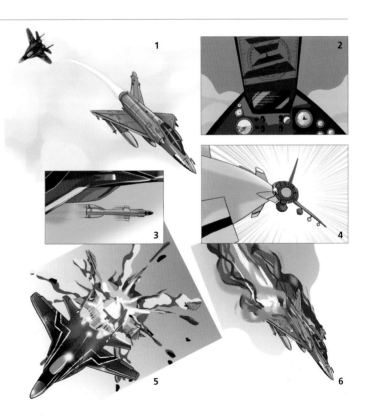

# Composing the panel contents

Knowing what to place within a panel, and how to build and release narrative tension, is extremely important in manga. As with composing a frame of film, the contents of a panel must direct the reader's eye to what is most important about this snapshot of the scene. Unlike film, manga panels can disregard extraneous background information – there's usually no need to draw anything that isn't essential to the ongoing story, and this can often involve backgrounds dropping out at moments of high tension, or detailed facial work on background characters being kept to a minimum. Each panel should show the reader exactly what they need to know, and work as part of a sequence. In quick-paced manga, the storyteller often only has a few panels to build tension – especially when working to a weekly schedule.

## Provide a focus

Each panel must have a focus, and the art should guide the audience to that centre. Keep the contents of each panel varied, to add interest. Don't draw your characters from the same angles all the time, or with the same facial expressions. You need to vary the appearance and perspectives of the characters to reflect their mood, situation, or what they are saying.

**A lesson in contrasts ▶**
The strips shown here communicate the same information in very different ways. The first repeats the same art, in the same way as comic strips found in many newspapers, while the second mixes angles, expressions and colour backgrounds to far more vibrant effect.

The strips begin the same way, with a two-shot of the talking characters.

The first strip re-uses the first panel all the way through, with only minor variations, relying on the dialogue to drive the story.

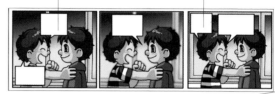
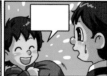

The mixture of panel widths and colours in the second strip creates art bursting with energy.

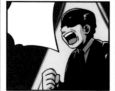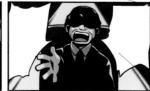

Abstract backgrounds illustrate character's emotions.

## Composition

It is very important that your audience is shown exactly what they need to see. For example, if you are showing a company boss giving a speech to a boardroom full of directors or employees, the boss should be the focus of the majority of your panels, because he is the central speaker. By all means start with a long shot to establish the boss's location and placement with regards to the rest of his employees, but assist the flow of the story and the focal point of the scene by locking your 'camera' on to the speaker. If the boss singles out a particular employee in his speech, by all means insert a panel to show that employee's reaction, but then cut back to the boss as he continues his diatribe. If he opens the meeting up to questions, you could create a new panel establishing how the employees feel, before they respond.

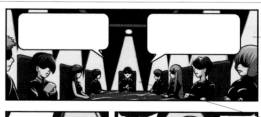

Long shot establishes scale of boardroom and relation of characters to one another.

Perspective directs eye to far end of table, and the boss sitting there.

Backgrounds drop out, save for chair and downlight, to emphasize the boss character.

**Shadowy boardroom ▲**
Although the body language of the board is tense, it's clear that there is only one chairman in this room – and he has a lot of angry things to say.

## Laying out the page

The best way to plan out a sequence is to sketch out the panels in relation to the whole page. Remember that manga compositions rely on whole pages, and sequences, for their effect, and designing and illustrating panels in isolation will never give you the best results.

**Symmetrical layout and panels** ▶
Pages that are symmetrically composed like this have no centre of attention, nothing to draw the eye to any significant part of the page. The eye flits from left to right, left to right, which can make for dull reading. Symmetrical layouts are mostly used for conversations, in which characters are imparting information to one another. If you use a grid like this throughout your story, it has the benefit of becoming 'invisible', like a picture frame or a TV screen through which the action is viewed. This is also the format for Japanese four-panel gag strips, which, unlike those in the West, are arranged vertically and reprinted two to a page.

**Asymmetrical layout** ▶
For a more showy, graphical approach, you can create designed, asymmetrical pages, which use the size and shape of each panel to showcase their relative importance, control pacing and drive the reader's eye around the page. This is a style of composition that draws a lot more attention to itself, making the act of layout a part of the story itself and keeps the reader on a rollercoaster ride across the page. Using different angles and rotated, unconventional panels maintains drama and interest in what is happening on the page – sustain this across a sequence, and your audience will be hooked for the journey.

> **Tip:** Panel size matters. The larger the panel, the more emphasis you place on it. Smaller panels increase pace. The smaller the panel, the less detail you can render, and the faster the reader takes it in and moves on.

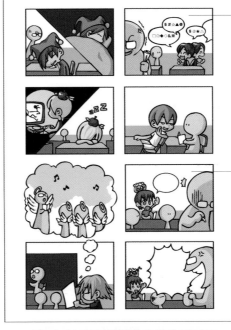

Using the same size panel for every image creates a conformity of importance across the strip, where every image carries equal weight.

The repetition of the same frame across the pages causes the reader to focus on its contents, rather than the method of delivery (the shape of the panel).

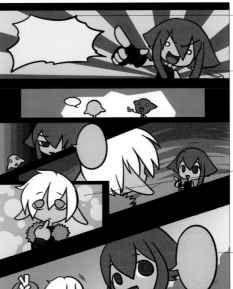

Irregularly shaped bubble for dramatic effect.

Large panel with plenty of emphasis.

Pace is slowed. Background dictates a thoughtful pose.

Unconventional panels give the cartoon a fresh feel and look.

# Narrative dramatization in panels

The use of perspective in your panel frames will not only help the look of the page, but can also set the pace or increase the drama of your story. There are a wide, even infinite, variety of perspectives from which to view your art (close-up, medium view, wide-angle to name just a few) which you can use in your art. For the time being, use a selection of the examples shown here: they are all you need to tell a compelling story and create good-looking pages.

## Common types of panels

Some panel shapes are termed 'neutral' and allow the art to dictate the pace of the story. Others speed up the pace, encouraging the reader's eye to race around the page.

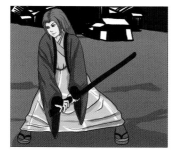

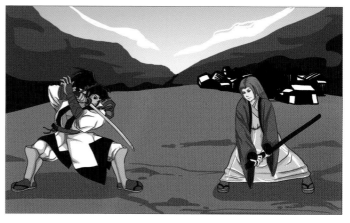

**Standard view** ▲
This panel reveals a lot of information at a character level, demonstrating a character's visual identity, through their clothing and accessories, as well as their stance, motivation and expression. It also encompasses detail of the character's immediate environment, allowing a reader to keep track of them as they move through a location.

**Wide-angle view** ▲
Panels that provide a wide-angle view are often used to introduce new locations or cut to a new scene. They are often half a page high, but can be extended to single or double-page spreads to increase their impact. They can effectively establish a new story or add dramatic impact to an event. If you have two mythical warriors facing one another with their swords drawn, for instance, a wide-angle panel gives you space to set the scene, showing the characters in relation to their environment.

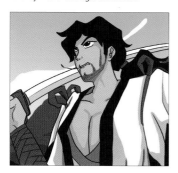

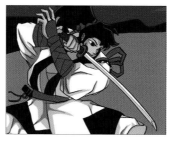

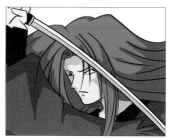

**Medium view** ▲
A waist-up shot allows the reader to focus on the character's expression while also including more visual cues about their clothing, weaponry and stance than a pure head shot.

**Western comic panel** ▲
Heavily influenced by the grammar of film, this type of panel shows the character mainly from the waist up, but may go down as far as the knees. It is used to emphasize a character's stance and emotional state. The legs aren't necessarily included, as they are the least expressive part of the body. Such panels also provide a detailed view of the character's environment.

**Close-up view** ▲
This dramatic view concentrates the reader's focus purely on the character's expression, tightly cropping the shot around the character's head. Shading or colour giving an impression of the character's emotional state may be used in the background, or it may be left blank, as in this example, to emphasize the facial features.

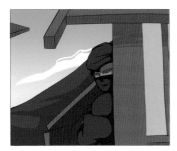

**Plot shot** ▲
Another type of close-up panel, this time focused on something that is intrinsic to the development of the story, with relevance to the narrative: here, a figure well disguised against the background lurks in the shadows.

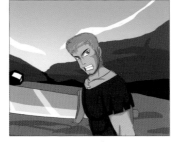

**Horizon** ▲
A natural-looking panel shape that resembles the perception we have of our surroundings in real life. There is typically a character in the foreground, and the horizon of the story's environment in the background.

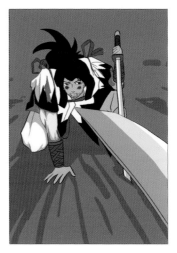

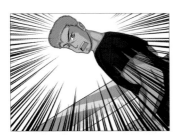

◀ **Tilt**
This panel conveys everything on a slant, offering an unbalanced view that adds tension and uncertainty. The background may consist simply of speed lines in a circular zoom formation, pointed at the character's head, which is a good way of freezing time for an instant to emphasize the character's tension or alarm.

**Bird's-eye view** ▲
A dramatic device, looking down on a character. It can establish the character in their environment at the start of a story, or highlight a dangerous situation by making the character smaller in relation to the dangerous object or entity in the foreground, demonstrating a character's vulnerability and the struggle they face.

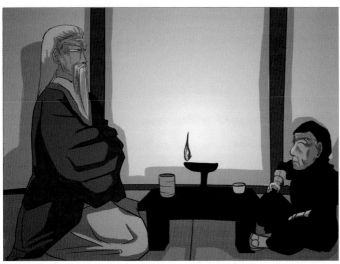

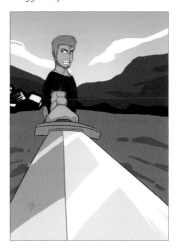

**Tatami view** ▲
This view is derived from the Japanese tradition of sitting on tatami mats on the floor while eating. The horizontal view is used to show two characters, usually in a historical setting, having a discussion across a meal or in a hut. *Blade of the Immortal* and *Lone Wolf and Cub*, both set in feudal Japan, often use this view.

**Mouse's-eye view** ▲
The opposite of the bird's-eye view, this panel conveys a character's strength and superiority, making a character dominant within the panel. It can also make the reader feel threatened and insignificant by proxy.

# Panel shapes and sizes

The panels are the individual pieces of artwork in the sequence of your story, and each is defined by the frame (or lack thereof) that surrounds it. Frames can be anything from a simple black line that divides each panel from one another (leaving the 'gutter' or white space between) to intricately rendered pieces of baroque architecture that, by calling attention to themselves, reveal as much about the setting and period of the story as their contents. See for yourself how altering the frame can change the intent and effect of your artwork by copying the same piece of action on to a single sheet of paper several times. Render some panel borders around the pictures using the examples shown here.

## Main panel and frame types

Some panel shapes are only used for specific occasions, while others will crop up constantly throughout a story. You may develop your own shapes with time, but the six panel shapes illustrated here provide a good foundation.

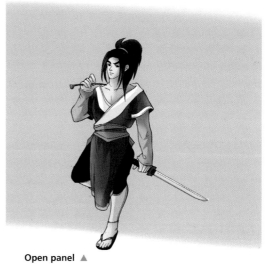

**Open panel** ▲
This is a boundless panel that is used during a scene where the character is lost in thought or taking stock of their surroundings. The pace is definitely slowed by using this technique, and not putting a boundary around the art allows it to stop and take a breather. It is the comic-book equivalent of a dramatic pause in a film as it throws all of the focus on to the character.

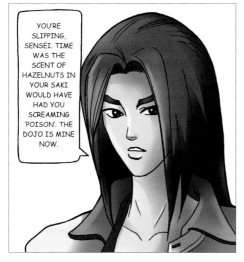

YOU'RE SLIPPING, SENSEI. TIME WAS THE SCENT OF HAZELNUTS IN YOUR SAKI WOULD HAVE HAD YOU SCREAMING 'POISON'. THE DOJO IS MINE NOW.

**Standard frame** ▲
Square or rectangular, and drawn in a regular fashion, the standard frame's main use is to call as little attention to itself as possible, merely dividing two pieces of action from one another.

**Tip:** Any shape can be used to create a panel, but be warned that a story full of star shapes, dodecahedrons and similar shapes may drive away more readers than it impresses. Panels are there to contain your artwork, not overshadow it.

**Parallelogram frame** ▶
Essentially a standard frame with the left and right 'walls' tilted to one side, this panel is used to add pace and verve to action sequences. Its shape psychologically influences the reader to flip through the pages at a faster pace. The panel should slant in the direction the audience is reading.

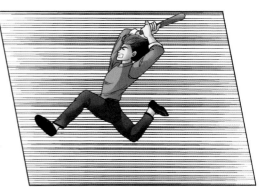

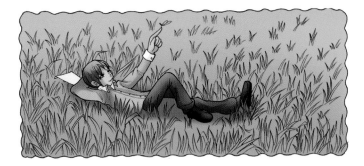

**◄ Cloud panel**
The cloud panel has a specific use in manga, usually indicating a sequence of daydreams, nightmares, flashbacks or similar. The softer, rippled edges of these panels are the standard method of establishing that reality has taken a back seat, and the character's imagination and subconscious have been thrown to the fore.

**Trapezium pairs ▶**
Used for fast, focused scenes, these frames normally involve extreme close-ups on the point of action. They are generally drawn as a pair within the space of a single standard panel. Because they are small and angular, they help propel the action forward. In this example of a sword fight, one panel shows a rapid parry between the swords, the second shows the protagonists circling for another swing. Both focus purely on the motion of the blades. The second example shows the two swordsmen, each reacting to the way the fight is going. Placing both trapezium pairs on the same page fulfils the same function as rapid cuts between cinematic close-ups in a chaotic action sequence.

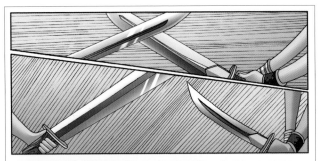
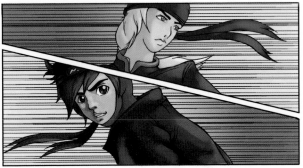

**Tip:** These panels work best for simultaneous moments: the panels show a moment of time literally sliced in half and apportioned to each of two points-of-view.

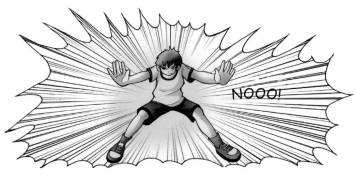
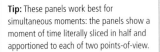

**◄ Panel with 'jaggies' (jagged edge)**
The jagged edges of this panel help convey a dangerous situation, or illustrate a violent act as it is committed by a character. These tend to be used singularly, with never more than one per page, or the rhythm of the piece would be jeopardized. Think of this as the exclamation mark of sequential framing, and use it sparingly. The reader only needs to be told once that the coming sequence is rife with danger. Then they want to see the action you've just brought to their attention.

# Laying out an entire page

To lay out a page, you use a variety of panels of differing shapes, each appropriate to their content and importance, to present one sequence out of your larger story. Creating a sequential narrative is not something to undertake in a haphazard fashion. Each panel must flow into the next, with links according to shape, content and dialogue, so that the sequence follows a logical progression in the eye and mind

of the reader. When laying out a page, consider yourself a one-person film unit. Your actions alone decide how fast or slow the story moves, based on the panels' size, content, shape and frame (or lack of). Why not try reworking an existing page of your favourite manga, deliberately altering the pacing? Bear in mind that, in the West, we read from left to right – this will affect how you design your page.

## Panel sequence

Each panel is a point in time in your story. The page is a collection of these points, each following on from the previous panel, while also simultaneously existing as a coherent whole. It's the artist's job to make the page work in unison, carrying the

reader through the story in a natural and fluent manner. When laying out a page, you need to make sure your panels follow each other in a way that the reader understands. Arranging the panels obscurely as an artistic flourish will only serve to hamper your

storytelling, as readers will spend more time working out what comes next than focusing on the panel they are reading. Take a look at the examples. One is simple, running left to right in a zigzag down the page, the other is based on a single, dominant image.

Note how the speech balloons also guide the eye down the page from top left to bottom right.

Predominance of background in first panel subtly draws attention to the windows – and what is outside them.

Cutting off the character's eyes focuses us on his mouth – and his dialogue.

**Tip:** Traditional manga is read from right to left. Because of the increasing popularity of 'real' manga (and the cost of 'flopping' the artwork) many books are now being reprinted in their original direction. Try laying out pages from right to left as well as left to right.

Reversed direction of glare on glass is subtle continuity clue tying in to the first panel.

Highlighted character guides the reader's attention across the panel towards the speaker under surveillance.

**Tip:** You don't have to use panels that are a regular shape throughout an entire page – the reader's interest may flag. Instead, think about how you can vary your shapes to increase the interest and appeal of your layout.

**Make it interesting** ▶
Note the extreme differences in shading between the deep blacks of the character in the bushes and the brightly lit, almost sterile quality of the room it is observing.

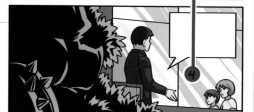

The page as a whole presents a switch in viewpoint, from the children in the room to the skulker in the bushes.

**Call-outs on a
splash page** ▶
This design is useful for
a slower, dialogue-based
sequence, or a shocking
moment that needs time
to sink in. The panels with
extreme close-ups of the
characters' faces could almost
be occuring at the same time
as the large image, which
forms the backdrop and sets
the timing for the whole page.

One of the strengths
of manga over film is
that it allows you to
present and view
both the close-up and
the long shot at the
same time.

These narrative
captions offer us
the girl's thoughts
during the dominant,
backlit panel.

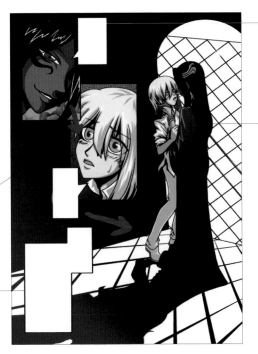

Again, note how
much good balloon
placement has to do
with controlling the
direction of flow on
a page.

The reader is invited
to linger over these
full figures – like the
blonde-haired
character, the reader
is caught like a rabbit
in the headlights.

**Tip:** Only move on to double-
page spreads when you are
confident you can control the
flow of story across two
linked pages. Bear in mind
that people are used to
reading a single page at a
time, and may read them out
of sequence.

## Web comic panel layout

Web comics follow slightly different
rules. While it's true that many are laid
out in the same manner as traditional
printed comics with a number of panels
on each page, in practice you can flout
the rules of page and panel layout. In an
electronic format, you are not restricted
by a page count, or by the number of
panels you can fit on the page.

If you work electronically, you could
just as easily lay out a single panel at a
time, creating what is essentially an
electronic storyboard, whereby the
importance of keeping your audience
no longer depends upon planning the
page along with everything else, but
instead concentrates far more on each
panel being well composed by the
artist. The need for each panel to
communicate its action well becomes
paramount, because the reader will
move from one to the next a lot faster
than if they had an entire page of
panels to get through. In fact, your
narrative rhythm is driven purely by how
much information you give the reader
in each panel.

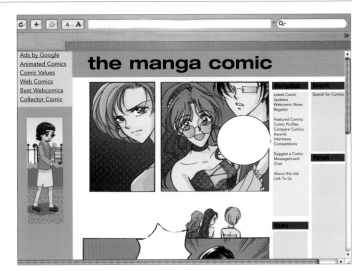

**Traditional web comic layout** ▲
This web comic uses a traditional manga page layout, allowing the viewer to
scroll through the page from top to bottom (the page is sized so that it fits the
width of the screen). Each new page can be reached through a link that 'turns' the
virtual page. Surprises in the story can be hidden at the bottom of the page so that
they aren't seen at the same instant the page loads.

# Dialogue and speech balloons

Once your page layout is decided, you can add dialogue and captions. Character dialogue emphasizes and adds a secondary (potentially antagonistic) layer to the actions depicted. It also demonstrates your characters' verbalized motivation and carries the majority of their interactions with one another. Dialogue is housed within speech balloons, or speech bubbles as they're sometimes called. Thought balloons

are the equivalent for the unspoken, though fashions sometimes dictate that thoughts are written in caption boxes. Remember to leave space for your balloons when drawing your panels or you will end up obscuring your artwork when it comes to adding them later. Most readers tend to read the balloons first and focus on the artwork second, so use your balloons to guide your reader's eyes.

## Placing balloons

Placing balloons is as much a science as an art, but bear in mind that a balloon larger than a third of the panel space available is excessive, and that balloons, like panels, are read from top left to bottom right, and must be placed accordingly if more than one character is talking. Nowadays, most speech balloons are placed by computer, but there are still artists who prefer the traditional method of using templates to draw balloons on to the page. If this includes you, pencil in your balloon and text first, and ink afterwards.

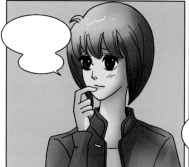
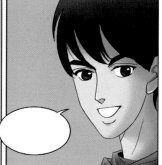

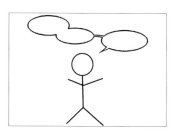

**Balloon placement in panel** ▲
The above example shows how you can replicate pauses in dialogue within a single panel. Short pauses can be shown by 'budding' balloons off of other balloons, while longer pauses require a complete break – perhaps joined by a thin 'tail' between two balloons.

**Balloon flow** ▶
This example shows how dialogue has been placed to guide the eye across and down the page, in a manner that also takes pains not to cover up any important areas of the artwork.

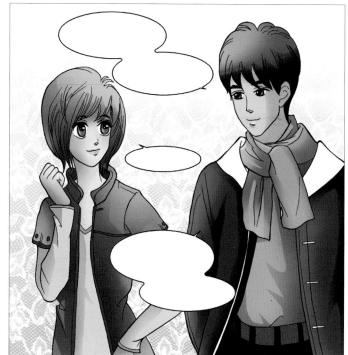

## Balloon shapes

Although the dialogue within a balloon will help reveal a character's emotional state, the shape of the balloon itself can further emphasize it.

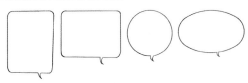

**The four most common shapes** ▲
Dialogue delivered in a normal way (without extreme emphasis) is contained in the standard, rounded-edged, rectangular or ovular shapes. All finish in a small point, or 'tail' that indicates who is speaking. Japanese bubbles are tall not wide, as the dialogue is written in vertical columns.

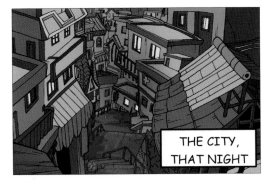

**Captions describing a place or a scene** ▲
Although rare in manga, captions describing a place, or setting a scene, are sometimes included. Essentially, this is the neutral voice of a narrator, allowing you to cut to a different point in time, or to move between characters in different locations, with phrases such as 'meanwhile, across town' or 'later that day'. Captions are most commonly delivered in a rectangle in an establishing panel.

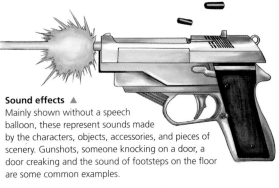

**Sound effects** ▲
Mainly shown without a speech balloon, these represent sounds made by the characters, objects, accessories, and pieces of scenery. Gunshots, someone knocking on a door, a door creaking and the sound of footsteps on the floor are some common examples.

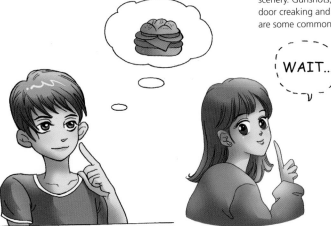

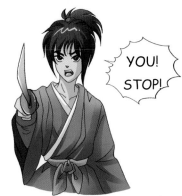

**Inner feelings and thoughts** ▲
Use cloud balloons for thoughts. Instead of a tail, a series of smaller clouds or bubbles lead to the balloon. In humorous stories, a simple illustration to show the character's thoughts can be used instead, as in this example.

**Dotted-line balloons** ▲
Used to convey a quiet voice or a whisper, these balloons are not used much in manga. A more common method is to use a standard bubble with the text written smaller than it would be for a normal speaking voice.

**Jagged-edge balloons** ▲
These balloons are used to convey a character's extreme emotion or a loud 'outside' voice, such as a character who is screaming in pain, shouting with anger and aggression, or yelling a warning to someone.

# Panel shapes gallery

This spread contains a veritable cornucopia of further examples of panel shapes, page layouts and balloon placements. Take note of how the colour of your gutters influences the mood of the page – try adding in blues, reds and greens and seeing what effect they cast over your stories. Examine, too, how the use of different colours – and different fonts – in your speech balloons can imply different voices, strange languages and unfamiliar tongues.

## More panels, page layouts and speech bubbles

The purpose of each panel is to show the reader the elements, characters and situations that will take him or her through the story keeping their interest throughout. It is the managa-ka who selects the most appropriate panel for each scene to show the reader the essential elements to understand the plot. Each panel is part of thinking about a whole page.

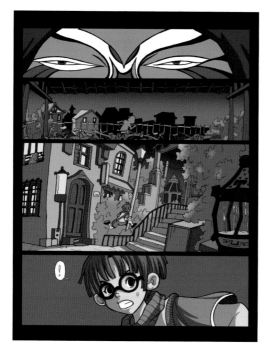

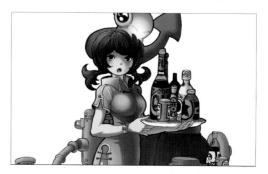

**Sharp focus** ▲
The background of this panel drops out to focus on the girl and the paraphernalia surrounding her.

**Oval-shaped panel** ▲
The shape focuses the eye on the shining wand, and carries through the soft and cute shape of the characters.

**Cinematic horror** ▲
The 'widescreen' panels and black borders create a cinematic feel and give plenty of scope for background detail.

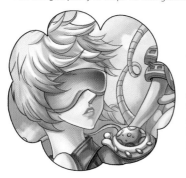

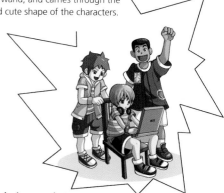

◀ **Cloud dreams**
Hooked up to a dream-influencing terminal, this character's lucid dreams take her into various fantastic scenarios – with the cloud borders delineating the boundaries of the real and dreamed.

**Explosive panel** ▲
The explosive shape of the panel adds visual interest to an activity that is, in reality, rather dull. Hacking firewalls sounds a lot more exciting in theory than in practice.

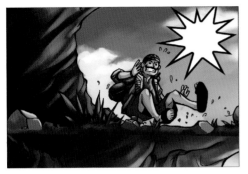

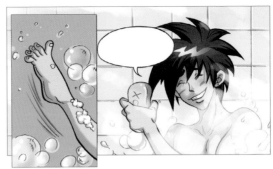

**Jagged balloon** ▲
A character slips and begins to curse – the perfect opportunity for a jagged balloon and a loud exclamation.

**New balloon colouring** ▼
This illustration, featuring non-standard balloon colouring, has a creative, but highly readable, layout.

**Superimposed panels** ▲
Inset panels are close-ups superimposed over wider shots. This is a 'teaser' panel, not showing the bath straight away.

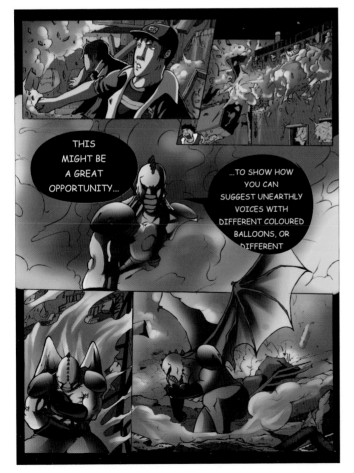

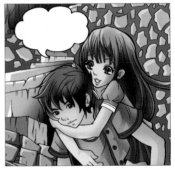

**Thought-speech bubble** ▲
Although the boy would never complain out loud, he can say whatever he wants in the privacy of his own head.

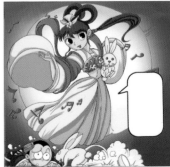

**Colour border** ▲
When it gets too much for the sorcerer, his assistant gets a chance to shine in this panel bordered only by colour.

# Sketching thumbnails

Most manga creators, even those both writing and drawing their story, prefer to write a script as a guide before starting to illustrate their tale. Scripts contain brief descriptions of the characters and action in each panel, along with any dialogue and captions. The first step in transferring your script to the page as illustrations is to 'thumbnail' your script as a series of small sketches, showing the position of characters, the angles you have selected to best show the action, and the size of each panel in relation to the others. This way, you can spot any compositional problems before you start drawing for real.

## Why thumbnail?

Once you have completed your script, you need to plan the look of your pages, making some panels more dominant than others, choosing your close-ups and long shots and spotting any areas where an obtuse passage in the script may need to be made more clear through an additional panel or some expositional dialogue. Thumbnails are named for their relative size – while not literally the size of a thumb, you should be able to sketch an entire page on half a sheet of A4, or half that again. The small size makes you focus on what is truly important in each panel, and to view each panel as an element of the whole page. You may find it useful to spot areas of light and shade at this scale as well, colouring areas of shadow in a way that makes the page easier, rather than harder, to read.

Thumbnailing may seem like an extra stage, and it's natural to want to get stuck into putting your art on to the page as soon as possible, but the more problems you solve during thumbnailing, the less chopping and changing you'll have to do later. It's also worth thinking about pacing – would a page work better if the final panel was moved to the next page and given more space, for instance? Does a reveal need a full page all of its own? Are some sections moving sluggishly, others cramming too much in?

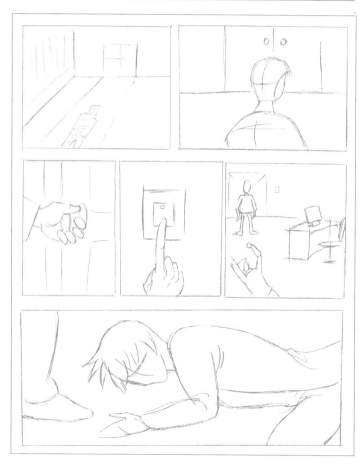

**Tip:** Thumbnails are the first stage in drawing a finished page – not the point at which you begin to design your characters and costumes. However, they can also be useful for a writer/artist in a hurry: rather than spending time in a script describing characters, locations and actions with which they are familiar, they can leapfrog straight to the thumbnail script stage, playing around with layouts and dialogue on the same page.

**Keeping it simple** ▲

Thumbnails are illustrations stripped to the absolute basics. Choose only the data that allows you to see whether a panel's composition is working, and enough to remind you of what you need to draw. Leave everything else out, keeping anatomy to stick-men or rough sketches, if you prefer (adding an eyeline to show where a character is looking can often be a useful addition), and backgrounds to symbolic shapes and squiggles.

## Planning the details

The thumbnail stage is the point at which to make sure the art you have planned for is going to fit, particularly considering speech balloons. Focus your problem-solving attention on text-heavy panels: there is no point trying to fit in lots of detail if it will be covered up. Make sure the panels you have laid out give you sufficient space for the characters you want to appear, any background that is necessary to suggest location, and all of the required dialogue. This is also an excellent opportunity to edit your script. Writing your dialogue and stage directions in isolation is one thing, but you may change your mind when you see the art laid out on the page. Take the time to trim balloons that are too long, or add in extra ones to help smooth any awkward panel transitions.

### Balloon placement ▼
Thumbnails are also great opportunities to test ways of controlling the flow of the reader's eye across the page, as with the sketched balloons below.

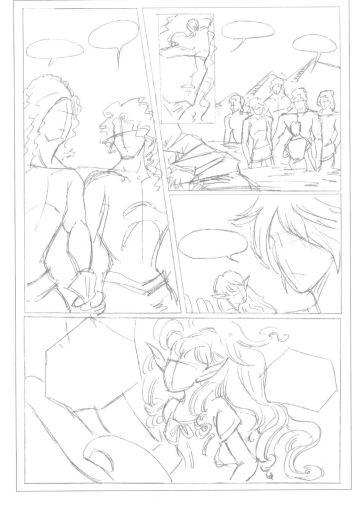

## Thumbnail practice

To practise thumbnails, here's a relatively simple exercise. Choose a favourite or familiar manga and draft a script based on five to ten pages, writing down the descriptions of the setting, character, action and dialogue in each panel. Now close the manga, and, using your script, create your own thumbnailed versions of the pages, choosing the size and shape of the panels and presenting the action as you see fit. When you have finished, compare your versions of the pages to the final result – how close are they? Which version do you prefer? You may find that the thumbnails are close, as you are familiar with the existing pages, or you may find you have improved on the layout and panel flow! If you have a friend or fellow artist who is also learning to create manga, why not transcribe a script each and then swap? That way, you'll be approaching the script completely fresh, and may be even more pleasantly surprised by the results.

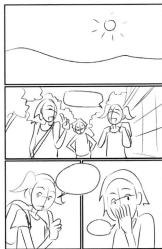

**Same script, different story** ▲
The aim of thumbnails is to save you time later by allowing you to experiment at a much smaller scale. Focus on bold shapes and whole-page compositions: worrying about the details is for later.

# Creating roughs

The roughs are the next stage in refining your manga strip, offering a halfway house between the near-abstract planning of the thumbnails and the ready-for-print detail of the pencilling and inking stages. Roughs are all about experimentation and artistic problem-solving, refining the stick-men and blobby backgrounds of your thumbnails on the same scale as your actual art. While some artists produce roughs on a separate sheet and then transfer the line work to a fresh sheet of paper using a lightbox, other artists produce their roughs and finished pencils on the same page, refining one into the other. For those working in digital colour, on pages that will be scanned, many artists use blue-line pencils for their rough stage, followed by HB pencils for their finished line work. Whether scanned in as pencils or inked and then scanned, the blue lines are not picked up by the scanner, producing cleaner reproductions with less messy erasing.

## Roughing it

Unlike thumbnails, your roughs should be done to the scale of the finished art, and should contain a lot more detail. One way to start laying out roughs is to blow up your completed thumbnails to actual size and either transfer them to a fresh sheet on the lightbox or redraw them by eye, using the originals as reference. You will hopefully find that your redrawn versions are better than your originals in many ways.

Thumbnails are all about speed and generalized compositional problem-solving, in that most artists use very simple shorthands for their figures, from stick-people to circles with lines indicating the direction of view. Backgrounds are usually absent or consist of boxes and lines. Roughs, on the other hand, are about expanding these simple notes and directions into something approximating the finished page. You need to flesh out anatomy ensure that it's in proportion, and make sure that perspectives mesh with any items and characters they share panels with. Don't be afraid to redraw challenging aspects of your page until you are satisfied with them – roughs are about saving you time later on.

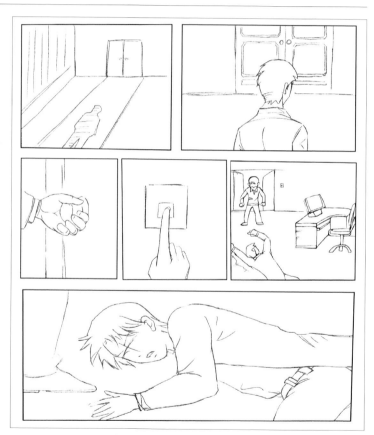

**Tip:** While each of these stages is designed to give you and your drawing ability more thinking and problem-solving time, you may find as you develop – and as the deadlines come knocking – that you begin to combine different stages to make the whole process quicker. Don't be ashamed about taking shortcuts to deliver timely art – it's what the manga industry is based on, after all – but be sure you aren't doing your talents a disservice at any stage.

**Tightening the layout** ▲
A confident artist would have no trouble inking a final page from these lines, at 1:1 scale, block in accurate proportions and indicate all areas of background. Take particular note of the lack of shading or line width differentiation, however.

## Rough backgrounds

Roughs allow you to sketch out a more established view of the scenery in your story, working from the details included in your initial script. As well as working on the anatomy of your characters, you should fill out and block in the proportions of your backgrounds, using photo reference, collated sketches, or your own imagination. If working from reference, block in backgrounds in the rough stage, but try not to refer back to your reference when drawing your finished pencils, so keeping a looser and more imaginative line. The main thing to think about at the roughs stage is integration: do your characters convincingly exist within their environment? Does the background overwhelm the character work, or detract from an important emotional moment? If so, now is the time to scale back your detail, or drop a background from a panel altogether. If your roughs show too little background information, now is the time to scout for suitable reference or inspiration.

If you're drawing your roughs on a separate sheet of paper, you can always refer back to them if and when you get stuck. Treat them as a 'first draft'. If you've drawn them on the same sheet as your roughs, your artwork will evolve as you incorporate each new stage of detail into the drawing. The more confident you can be when you put your final lines on the page the less likely you'll be to need an eraser.

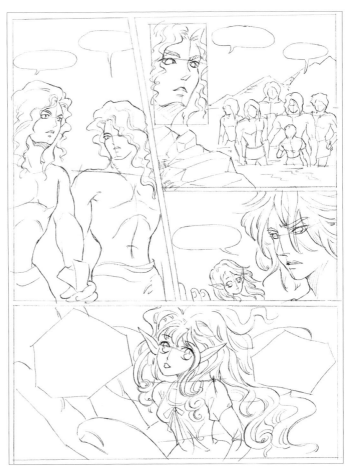

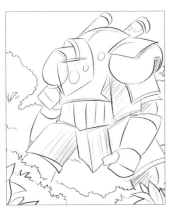

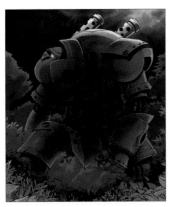

**Complete composition** ▲
This is another example of a rough page in which all of the basic character information is present. All that remains is to add a further stage of detail, shading, line weight and visual flair.

◀ **Figure-drawing roughs**
This image, with its intricate foreground detail and involved figurework, requires some thought in the rough composition before you start to draw the thousands of leaves. Here's the rough with the completed artwork.

# Inking and finishing off the page

So you're finally ready to bring everything together. Now you can pencil your first page for real. You've designed your characters, your setting, and the story that brings it all together. You've laid out the pages and checked that each set of panels flows well and is easy to understand. You may have worked ahead and thumbnailed your entire story before you begin to draw the first page to a finished standard, so check that your story builds to a satisfying conclusion. Give everything a final check before you set to work. Do your layouts work on each page? Have you illustrated what you need to show from your script, or have you been distracted by 'cool' but unimportant things to draw along the way (and have you shied away from aspects necessary but tricky to draw?). When you're ready, take a deep breath and dive in.

## Finishing touches

Keep final pencil lines clean and tight so they are ready for inking.

**Background** ▶ Note the use of very sparse backgrounds, only showcasing elements absolutely essential to the storytelling, such as the door and the staircase.

**Detail** ▶ This is the stage to check whether everything is correct: lines, balloons and detail.

▼ **Inking** The finished pencils are inked for easier scanning, and because the lines will hold colour better.

◀ **Palette** The colour palette is very limited: a rich range of reds and browns, save for the 'shocking' elements of the blue door and the boy's blond hair that serve to contrast against the main character and her world.

◀ **Digital method** The page is coloured digitally, using a narrow palette. Digital colours are bright and excellent for reproduction.

Make sure that your roughs have brought you to the point where you are happy with the look of each page. Check the panels are in order, that each page is composed well and that your story flows well from panel to panel and from page to page. Is there still enough space for your dialogue, and are there areas of art that will be covered by balloons? Is your figurework believable, and, most of all, loose enough? At this stage one thing to keep in mind – and your drawing hand – is to try to keep some of the looseness of line work that was present in the early planning.

Technical proficiency isn't everything: readers will often respond better to an imperfect image that hums with energy than a pristine, highly accurate drawing that is rendered sterile by reworking. The most important part of pencilling is knowing when to put down pencil and eraser and declare a page finished. If in doubt, leave a page, go on to the next, and come back to it after a couple of days. You'll be able to spot any problems far more easily after getting some distance. When you are happy with your pencils, ink and colour them using your favoured methods.

**Final piece** ▲ Line work is finalized, inked and shaded, paying attention to line weight. The page is scanned and coloured on the computer, picking out a mood with the use of pale brown shades.

> **Tip:** Before you declare a page finished, compare it with your original thumbnail. Hold your larger artwork at arm's length if need be. Has the energy and information contained in the thumbnail translated across? If not, is there anything you can do to fix it at the inking stage?

Whether you end up giving your pencils to another person to ink, as is the norm in larger 'creative teams' where time is of the essence, or you're going to do it yourself, get into the habit of marking the areas that will be completely filled with black with an 'X'. This saves you shading time at the pencilling stage and helps the inker, as most inks adhere better to the page when applied directly to bare paper.

Some artists who have become comfortable with tablet pens prefer to do their inking directly on to a computer, which, while fiddly, allows for much greater control over the line work and the ability to erase and redraw lines without having to use white-out or patch in new panels. However, inking via a software package such as Photoshop tends to produce rather stiff lines for artists beginning to explore the technique. If you want to give it a go, scan your pencils in at about 600 dpi for print resolution.

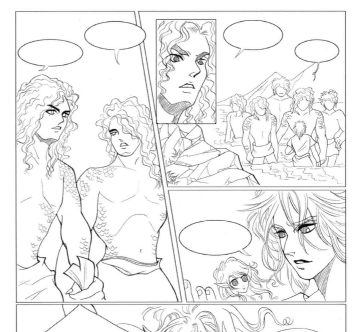

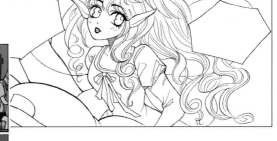

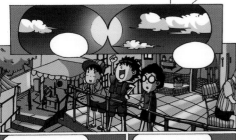

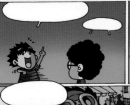

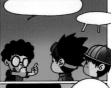

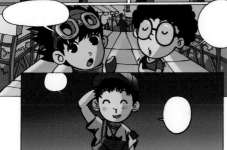

◀ **Inks and colour**
Inks tighten up the art for clearer reproduction, and add visual interest by differentiating foreground and background elements through different line widths. Colours influence mood, make changing time, scene and setting easier, and generate final artwork that is easier to read.

**Roughs** ▲
This page lays out all of the storytelling information and detail work in a clear, consistent manner. Balloon placements have been made, figures have been fully rendered, and the page is ready for inking. Your pencilwork may not be as tidy as this, but don't worry: that's what the inking stage is for!

**Tip:** Inks and colours should always be building on the clear storytelling you establish at the pencilling stage. It is possible to polish up your weaknesses, and it's equally true that bad inks and colours can ruin great pencils but clarity at the pencil stage pays dividends later.

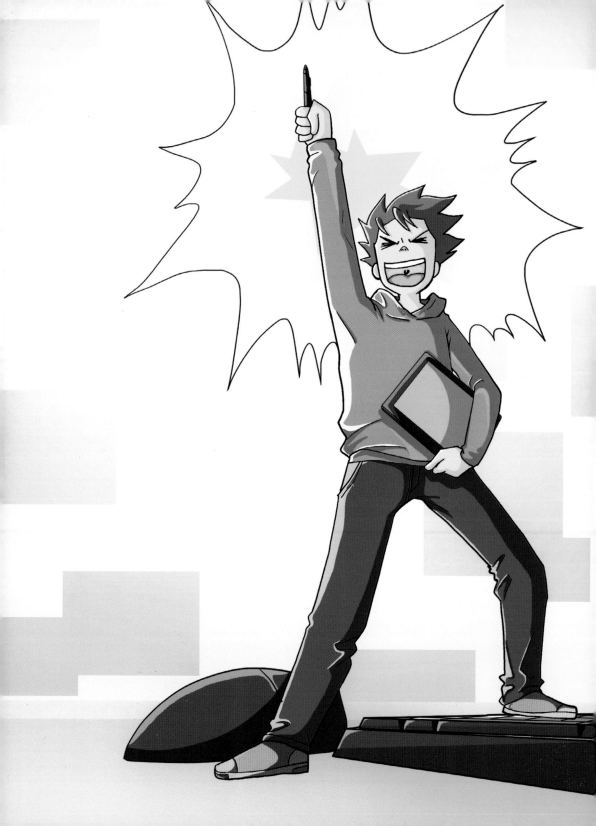

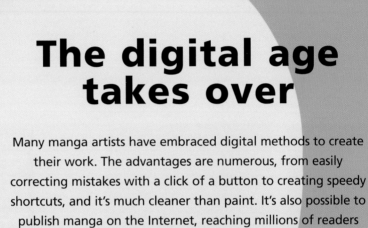

# The digital age takes over

Many manga artists have embraced digital methods to create their work. The advantages are numerous, from easily correcting mistakes with a click of a button to creating speedy shortcuts, and it's much cleaner than paint. It's also possible to publish manga on the Internet, reaching millions of readers and saving on expensive printing costs.

# Tools of the digital trade

Most modern manga artists use computers to help them create artwork, to greater or lesser extents. Some draw and tone everything on paper, using the computer to clean up the pages and publish them online. Others draw directly into the computer, using a mouse or stylus and graphics tablet, and publish the results as a traditional paper-based graphic novel.

Digital methods can be used whenever and wherever the artist finds them convenient and comfortable. It is possible to work with just pen and paper, but in this digital era, it is hard to avoid computers completely. Once a few simple techniques are mastered, they usually prove faster and more convenient than traditional methods.

## Hardware – PC or Mac?

The most important and expensive piece of equipment a digital manga artist will have to invest in will be a computer and monitor. However, provided it has a large enough memory, and fast enough processor, a good computer should last about 4–5 years before it needs replacing. Most computers have dual processor chips of at least 500MHz, which is powerful enough to deliver 7 billion calculations per second. The monitor should be a high-definition screen with a viewing area of at least 15 inches. Most monitors are flat-screen LCD display panels with 1600 x 1024 resolution. A storage device, such as an external hard drive, is extremely handy as well, as it will save large files that would slow down the computer, and will backup important documents, should the main hard drive break down.

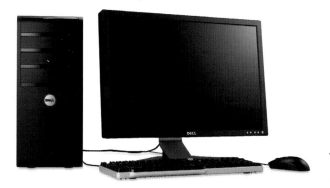

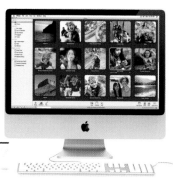

**Computer** ▲
A home computer is no longer a rare device in households; most families have at least one to store music and photos, watch movies and surf the Internet on. But not all home computers are suitable for drawing manga. Some will be too slow to run graphics packages, such as Photoshop or Corel Painter. In order to make sure the computer is powerful enough, check the software's minimum system requirements, normally printed on the box. The computer must match these. Of course, this is only the minimum requirement for dealing with relatively small pictures. Working with larger, high-resolution files requires a more powerful machine. A good starting point is 4GB of RAM memory and a dual-core 2.4GHz processor.

**Monitor** ▲
It is important that the monitor displays images correctly. This is vital for colour work, and in order to ensure precise image quality the monitor needs to be calibrated with professional software or devices, such as ColorEyes Display Pro. If the monitor is not calibrated correctly then the colour of images when they are printed on pages may not match exactly what is on the screen.

> **Tip:** When drawing with a computer, most technical choices are made with a mouse or stylus pen. However, it is important to use the keyboard for shortcuts, which save significant time and effort. A smaller keyboard is helpful if used alongside a graphics tablet.

**Apple Mac versus PC** ▲
Many manga artists tend to work on an Apple Macintosh, rather than a standard PC. The reason for this is that, until recently, the best painting and creative software was only available on the Mac. The Mac's operating system is more intuitive and better suited to how creative people think and work. Also, Macs were the preferred computer of publishers and printers, and traditionally preparing for print would have been done on a Mac. However, PCs now have all the same software available as the Mac, and the latest operating systems (Mac OSX and Windows Vista) 'talk' to each other without any major technical issues. The choice of one system over another is now more of a personal preference.

### Printer ▶

Printing out work at home requires a good printer. There are two types of printer to choose from: inkjet or laser. Inkjet printers are initially cheaper and therefore more popular for home users, although ink runs out quickly and replacement cartridges can

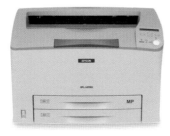

be expensive. However, as long as photographic paper is used to print on, the quality of modern inkjet printers is quite sufficient. Laser printers, especially colour ones, are initially expensive by comparison, but the advantages are higher-quality pages, lower running costs and a water-resistant printed picture.

### Scanner ▼

If a drawing on paper requires more processing, or colouring, on a computer, a scanner will be needed to import the image. All-in-one A4 scanner/copier/ printers can be bought quite cheaply and save a lot of desk space.

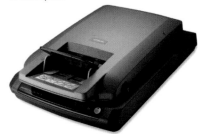

### Mouse ▶

An optical cordless mouse is the best option for digital illustration, as they are more precise than a traditional ball-based mouse and won't clog or jam. Remember to change their batteries regularly.

### Graphics tablet ▶

A graphics tablet is a far better choice for digital illustration than a mouse. Tablets are usually small boards that plug into the computer via a USB lead. Users draw on the pressure-sensitive board with a stylus, creating an image on screen instead of on paper. But quality isn't cheap: some graphics tablets are too simple for serious graphics work, so choose carefully and test your chosen model in-store if at all possible.

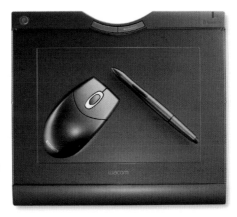

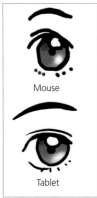

Mouse

Tablet

## Conventional versus digital imagery

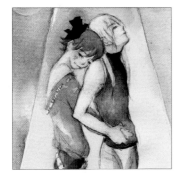

**Hand-drawn ▲**
This traditional watercolour painting shows the paper texture beneath the washes. With a little practice this effect can be recreated digitally.

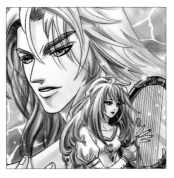

**Corel Painter ▲**
Different colour schemes can be tested and blended on the same line art, allowing you to experiment with variations until you are content.

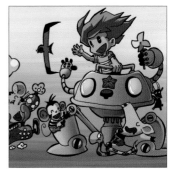

**Photoshop ▲**
The advantages of digital art include the easy mixing of techniques. Here, a graduated background contrasts with figures in a crisp animation style.

# Introduction to Adobe Photoshop

Photoshop is one of the most comprehensive and powerful image-processing software packages available, and it is popular with home users and art professionals alike. This makes it the perfect program for manga artists to use.

Photoshop comes in many different versions. For the beginner, investing in the fully functional latest version can be expensive. There is a cheaper, reduced version called Photoshop Elements which is sufficient for a manga novice.

While Photoshop can appear complicated and seem nerve-racking at first, it isn't necessary to learn everything in advance to be able to use it productively. Here is a guide to the basics that will get you started on the more common drawing and painting tools and techniques. Knowledge builds with increased usage and simply playing around with different buttons can reveal exciting new art effects. The key is to get involved and to experiment.

## Getting started

Depending on the computer's available memory and processor, Photoshop may take a while to open, as it is a large program. When first opening Photoshop, it will default to showing the Menu and Options bars running along the top of the screen, just like other applications. To the left of the screen is a vertical toolbox and to the right, the four palette groups: Navigator, Info and Histogram; Color, Swatches and Styles; History, Actions; and Layers, Channels and Paths. These are the key tools and components in Photoshop required to make digital manga artwork or any other artwork you choose to create. Without mastering these it will be impossible to work in the application successfully.

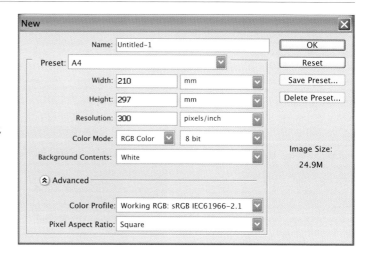

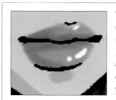

**Tip:** Resolution refers to the number of dots of ink per inch (for print) or pixels per inch (on screen). The higher the resolution, the better the quality. Most print images are 300 dpi, while online images tend to be 72 dpi. Print-quality comics are most often coloured at 600 dpi and printed at 300 dpi. Always scan and colour your imagery at a larger size than your final page to avoid unsightly pixellation or blurring.

**The Title Bar** ▼
This includes the current filename (in this example Untitled-1) and current zoom percentage (25%), as well as the colour mode and bits per channel (RGB/8).

**Opening a blank canvas** ▲
Go to File > New and a pop-up window will ask the size, resolution and mode of a new canvas. Set the image as an A4 page in the Preset box, the Resolution at 300 pixels/inch (or dpi) and the Color Mode to RGB Color. In Background Contents select White. Click OK and an active window with a white canvas will appear. It is possible to have several canvas windows open simultaneously, but only one is active at any given time.

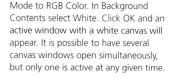

**The Menu Bar** ▲
This is directly below the Title Bar, and includes options such as File, Edit, Image, Layer, Select, Filter, View, Window and Help, just like other standard applications. The Photoshop menu also uses the same keyboard shortcuts, for example, the [Alt]+F will select the File menu, or click on a menu name to see its drop-down menu.

**The Options Bar** ▲
This appears below the Menu Bar and displays the options for the currently selected tool. The above example shows the Rectangular Marquee Tool options.

## The toolbox ▶

Normally the toolbox is on the left of the window, but if it is not visible, go to Window > Tools to display it. The toolbox is a convenient way to choose tools for working on images in Photoshop. To select a tool, click on its icon in the toolbox. Only one tool can be selected at a time, and only the primary tools are readily visible. When a tool is clicked on, the button will 'stick' to show it is selected. In the example on the right, the Zoom Tool (indicated by the magnifying glass) is currently in use. The cursor's pointer will also change shape to reflect which tool is currently in use.

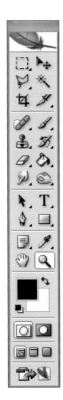

## Palettes ▶

These are indispensable components of the tool set. They supplement the toolbox with additional options. On first opening Photoshop, the palettes are stacked along the right side of the screen in palette groups. By default, there are four palette groups:

The first group is the Navigator, Info and Histogram. The second is Color, Swatches and Styles. The third is History and Actions. At the bottom are the Layers, Channels and Paths palettes.

The default settings can be modified by clicking on Window on the Menu Bar and selecting the palettes that you wish to display. Dragging the Title Bar of each palette window allows you to place it anywhere within the Photoshop window.

Each palette has a Palette Menu Button (a small arrow) in the upper right corner, which, when clicked, displays a drop-down menu with options for that specific palette.

The most commonly used palettes are History and Layers. The History palette is an 'Undo' list of every step taken in the current Photoshop session. Selecting a step in the sequence restores the image to that stage and steps can be deleted as required. Layers are useful for organization and editing and are explained later in this chapter.

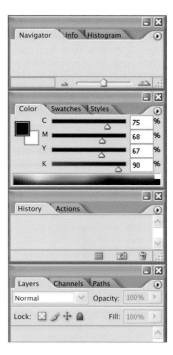

## A digitized illustration

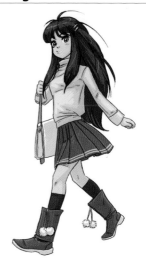

Digital colour grants you a near-infinite palette of colours that remain bright and unmuddied, even when mixed. Colouring can be bold or finely detailed, results can be exported to the page or web, and custom palettes can be saved and reused for multiple illustrations.

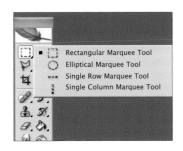

Rectangular Marquee Tool
Elliptical Marquee Tool
Single Row Marquee Tool
Single Column Marquee Tool

## Toolbox options ▲

A small triangle in the lower right corner of a tool icon means it has more options. To see these options simply click and hold the tool icon for a few seconds, and the alternatives will appear in a pop-up menu. Once a tool is chosen from the pop-up menu it becomes the default tool for this group, until you select another.

## Foreground and background colours ▶

These two overlapping squares, near the bottom of the toolbox, are used to select the foreground colour (front square) and the background colour (back square). Click on the foreground colour square and a colour palette window will pop up and the colour required can be chosen from the slider. The process is repeated to select a background colour. The arrow in the upper right corner swaps the foreground and background colours over, and the small black and white icon in the lower left corner resets the colours to the black and white default.

# View and selection tools

The view and selection tools are used to choose particular areas of the art to work on or manipulate. They can be switched from one to the other by pressing the shortcut Function [fn] key on a Mac, and then pressing the relevant letter in the text below. Pressing [fn]+T selects the Hand Tool. On a PC, press the appropriate letter.

**Hand Tool** (Mac = T) [PC = H]
This time-saving tool is used to drag the image around when zoomed into a picture that is larger than the viewing window. Pressing down [spacebar] while dragging with the mouse has the same effect.

**Zoom Tool** (Z)
The Zoom Tool allows zooming in and out of images. Click the image where you want it to centre and then zoom in, or hold the [Alt] key while clicking to zoom out. You can perform the same function by using the Navigator Palette.

**Move Tool** (V)
This tool moves an area selected by the Marquee or Lasso tools, or an entire layer when nothing else is selected. Hold the [Shift] key to limit the movements to vertical or horizontal.

**Eyedropper Tool** (I)
This tool selects whatever colour the pipette icon is clicked on and makes it the foreground colour. Holding the [Alt] key when clicking will make it the background colour. When using the Brush Tool, press down the [Alt] key while clicking on a colour for the same result.

**Rectangular Marquee Tool** (M) ▶
Use this tool to make rectangular or square selections on images. While this tool is active only the areas within the selection can be affected by other tools or actions. To make a perfect square hold down the [Shift] key while dragging the selection. Clicking the little triangle in the corner offers up different tools in the group: Elliptical Marquee, Single Row Marquee and Single Column Marquee. Each of these will make different regular-shaped selections.

**Polygonal Lasso Tool** (L) ▶
The Lasso tools are used to select an irregular area. In the drop-down menu you can find another two types of Lasso tools: Lasso and Magnetic Lasso. A lot of people find the Polygonal Lasso Tool, with its straight-edged selection, easier to control than the freehand Lasso Tool. To close the selection made by the Polygonal Lasso Tool, click on the beginning point or simply double-click. If your image has high-contrast edges, then you can use the Magnetic Lasso Tool, which automatically snaps to these edges.

**Magic Wand Tool** (W) ▶
The Magic Wand Tool is used to select a colour range, either as a block of colour or as a transparency. The settings for this tool can be changed in the Options Bar at the top. Adjusting the Tolerance value (0 to 255) allows selections to be more, or less, precise. A low number will select only colours that are very similar to the pixel clicked on; a high number will select a wider range of colours. Check 'Anti-alias' to create a smooth edge to the selection (at other times keep it switched off),

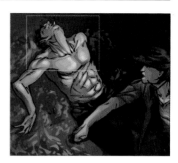

**Tip:** The Lasso Tool creates freehand selections, but by holding down the [Alt] key, straight lines can be drawn. Conversely, while the Polygonal Lasso Tool normally produces straight-edged selections, you can draw freehand selections by holding down the [Alt] key.

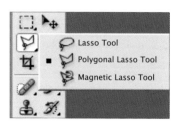

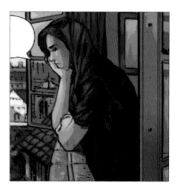

'Contiguous' to select only adjacent areas, and 'Use All Layers' to select areas from all layers. Uncheck them when necessary. Add to or subtract from the selection by pressing down the [Shift] or [Alt] keys.

# Select and transform

This example shows how to select a character's eyes and make them bigger using Free Transform. This allows the area selected to be transformed in any way. Instead of choosing different commands (move, rotate, scale, skew, distort, perspective and wrap), a key on the keyboard is held down to switch between transformation types.

### Opening the image ▶
First, open the scanned line art and convert it to a colour file. The eyes are not big enough for a manga character, so they will be enlarged.

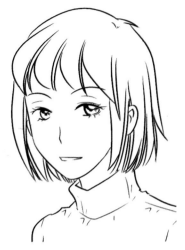

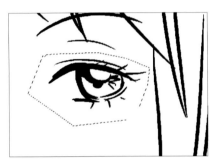

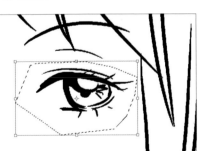

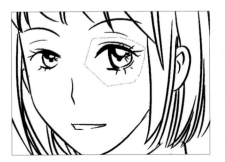

**Tip:** When Free Transforming a selected area of an image, if a middle point is clicked, the area can only be scaled up or down. If a corner is clicked and dragged the image can be distorted in any direction. Holding down the [Shift] key and clicking and dragging a corner keeps the selected area in proportion.

◀ **Selecting the area**
The Polygonal Lasso Tool selects an area around one eye. For line art, you may wish to use the Magic Wand Tool to erase selected areas of white (leaving only the black selected) so that your enlargement does not erase its surroundings.

◀ **Transforming the eye**
Click [Ctrl]+T to select the 'Free Transform' command (or go to Edit > Free Transform). A rectangle will enclose the shape made by the Polygonal Lasso Tool.

◀ **Enlarging the eye**
Drag the bottom of the rectangular frame to scale the selection vertically (making the eye bigger) until the size is correct, then double-click the area to confirm the transformation. Deselect the eye by clicking [Ctrl]+D. Select the other eye and transform it, making sure that both eyes match.

### Finished eyes ▼
When colouring from line art, it is best to reconvert your Free Transformed image back into a black and white bitmap, then to a colour image again, before attempting to shade it. This keeps all of the black lines crisp and unblurred.

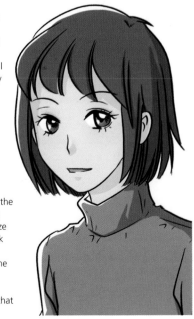

# The paint tools

In Photoshop, Paint Tools are used to draw in freehand. There are a wide variety, including Paint Brush, Pencil, Airbrush, Paint Bucket and Eraser. These tools can be used to create manga digitally or to enhance and colour black and white artwork that has been scanned in. These are the most important tools required to create comic pages on a computer. Each one has an important function and can be altered to an individual artist's preferences. However, a good manga artist will need to learn how to use all of the Paint Tools in order to create exceptional artwork.

## The Brush Tool

This tool shares the same button with the Pencil Tool. The Brush Tool is the most commonly used tool when creating a digital manga page. The edge of Brush Tool is softer and slightly more transparent when compared to the harsher line of the Pencil Tool. There are also quite a few different options in the Brush toolbar. Instead of the auto erase of the Pencil Tool, there is Flow and Airbrush, which are explained in the section that follows.

**Mode** ▼
This is the blending mode of the brush. For most brush work, 'Normal' is the best setting. Experimenting with various mode settings can create unusual effects, often replicating natural media.

**Brush variety** ▶
Using a mixture of sizes, opacities, shapes and textures helps render different materials more naturally, as shown here. Softer brushes on the faces contrast with sharper shading on the boy's jacket.

**Opacity** ▼
The Opacity defines how transparent the brushstrokes will be. An Opacity of 100% is completely opaque, while an opacity of 0% is no paint at all. Your brush will paint with the same level of Opacity as long as the mouse/graphics pen is not released, in which case drawing over a previously brushed area will build up the Opacity and colour. This can provide you with a useful way to vary tones.

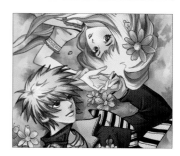

**Flow** ▼
The Flow determines how quickly the paint is applied at your chosen Opacity. When the mouse button/graphics pen is held down on an area, the Opacity of the colour will build up, based on the Flow rate, until it reaches the set Opacity level.

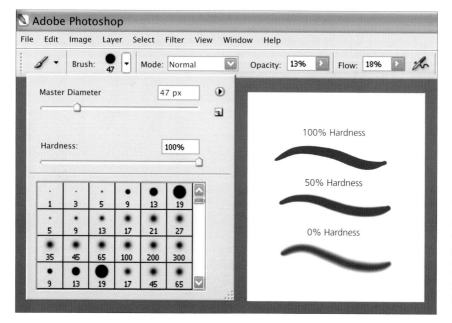

◀ **Brush**
The size, hardness and shape of the brush can all be altered to taste. The Hardness slider defines how sharp the edges will be. When you are drawing black line work on a manga page, it is best to use 100% Hardness, but a dreamy atmospheric painting in colour would require a very low Hardness setting. The Master Diameter sets how wide the brushstroke will be in pixels.

# Brush settings

The Brushes Palette is revealed by either clicking on the Options Bar icon, or selecting Window > Brushes. This palette provides greater control over the brush settings. There are two columns of settings: On the left are the brush stroke options and on the right are the specific settings for each brush option. The right column changes according to the option clicked in the left column. At the bottom is a preview window that reveals what the chosen brushstroke will look like.

> **Tip:** Once a brush has been created it can be locked by clicking on the padlock icon to prevent accidental changes.

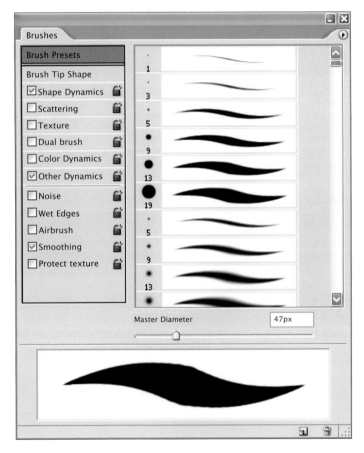

**Selecting brush settings** ▲
There are numerous ways in which brushes can be set up to create effects. For instance, choosing 'Wet Edges' with 10% Hardness and a 30px Master Diameter will create a watercolour-effect brushstroke. For the best results when drawing manga line work, select 'Smoothing' and 'Shape Dynamics', with Size Jitter set to Pen Pressure 0%. This brush setting produces very clean lines that respond well to a graphics pen's pressure. For more stylized line work, or colour art, try out a variety of different options in this palette. The trick is to experiment and to have fun.

# The Airbrush Tool

As the Brush Tool is so adaptable, the Airbrush is no longer such a unique tool, and now appears in the Options Bar. The main difference between the Airbrush and Paintbrush is that when the mouse button is held down on the former, a constant flow of paint appears, just like holding down the nozzle of a can of spray paint. This paint builds up gradually and is good for creating softer, lighter images.

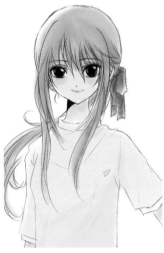

**Soft strokes** ▲
This soft-focus image was created using a variety of brush shapes and sizes, building up layers of colour, each with a maximum Opacity of 50%.

> **Tip:** The Pencil Tool draws sharp-edged lines. Unlike the Paintbrush Tool, the Pencil has neither subtle tones nor soft edges; it is either 100% colour or not at all. When painting manga pages it is best to avoid using the Pencil as the edged lines look stiff and jagged, especially at lower resolutions. Nevertheless, the Pencil Tool is still useful for clean unfuzzy lines, particularly when creating digital animation and pixel art, such as small icons and mobile games.

## The Paint Bucket Tool

This tool is used for filling in selected areas, or areas based on colour similarity to the pixel that is clicked. The Paint Bucket Tool will use the foreground colour as the default, but this can be altered to a pattern selected in the Options Bar. Mode, Opacity and Tolerance can also all be tweaked and tinkered with there.

**Tolerance** ▼
The Paint Bucket Tool's Tolerance ranges from 0 to 255. A low tolerance means only very similar colours will be affected while a high tolerance means more pixels are selected. A tolerance of 0 selects only the exact same colour as the clicked pixel. If the level is 255, then all colours will be selected.

**Anti-alias** ▼
Use sparingly, but checking this makes edges of colour smoother by blending with adjoining pixels.

**All layers** ▼
Checking this fills all layers with your current option, otherwise only the current layer will be filled.

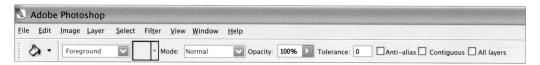

After checking or unchecking the Anti-alias and Contiguous, and All layers options, choose a foreground colour and click on the area required. When filling solid black or colours in manga linework, the lines must be perfectly enclosed; otherwise paint will escape through the gaps of the area being filled. If this happens, using [Ctrl]+Z will undo the mistake. Check where the gap is and seal it using the Pencil Tool. Alternatively, fill using a selection.

**Contiguous** ▲
When selected, only pixels connected to the clicked pixel are affected. Otherwise, all pixels in the image within the tolerance range are filled. Useful for replacing one colour with another.

## The Gradient Tool

This tool shares the same button with the Paint Bucket Tool, but it doesn't fill with solid colour. Instead, it creates a gradual blend between colours. It is useful when you want to create things such as metal or sky, and works on a selected area or layer. To create a gradient, a style needs to be selected in the Options Bar. There are five basic styles to choose from: Linear, Radial, Angle, Reflected and Diamond.

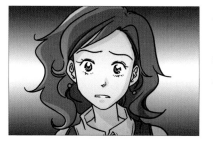

◄ **The eyes have it**
The use of a Reflected gradient in the background focuses the reader's attention on the girl's surprised eyes, emphasizing her emotional state and the tense mood.

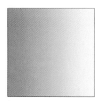

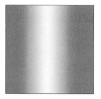

**Linear gradient** ▲
Create vertical, horizontal or diagonal gradients in this style. Click, hold and drag the cursor, and release it when you have covered the area required.

**Radial gradient** ▲
This style of gradient creates a circular pattern. Click and start dragging from where the centre of the radial is required. A longer line creates a whiter circle.

**Angle gradient** ▲
This gradient creates a 360-degree sweep of colour, back around to the starting point. It may not often be useful for colouring manga characters and backgrounds.

**Reflected gradient** ▲
This is a symmetrical Linear gradient. It is sometimes used in manga to show a character's shock or surprise (as in the example above).

**Diamond gradient** ▲
This style creates a star-shaped pattern, formed in the same way as the Radial gradient. You are able to control each colour in the mix.

## Colouring the gradient

Once the Gradient style has been chosen, the colours must be selected. The Options Bar holds numerous combinations, including the default, which uses the current foreground and background colours. Changing these will define any two colour gradients. For a more complex combination – perhaps a rainbow-like gradient, for example – double-clicking the colour bar reveals the Gradient Editor window. Double-clicking the colour stops along the colour belt allows the colours to be customized; dragging their positions alters where they blend. Clicking anywhere under the belt adds another colour stop.

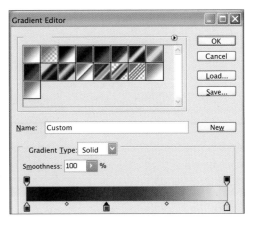

◀ **Paint a rainbow**
It is possible to make gradients up of as many colours as desired, by adding or removing colour stops and dragging them up and down the colour bar. These customized gradients can be saved and used at a later date.

## The Eraser Tool

This tool is the opposite of the Pencil/Brush tools. The Eraser's Modes can be set in the Options Bar to soft-edged brush or airbrush, hard-edged pencil or square block. Pixels are erased to transparency, or to the background colour on a locked layer.

In the Eraser Tool's Options Bar there is an option called Erase to History. When this option is checked, instead of painting to a transparency level or the background colour, the Eraser paints from a History state or from a snapshot set in the History Palette, allowing you to repaint erased areas.

The Opacity and Flow of the Eraser Tool can be defined in the same way as the Brush Tool.

**Magic Eraser Tool and Background Eraser Tool** ▶
There are two other tools sharing the same button with the Eraser Tool: the Magic Eraser and the Background Eraser.

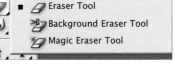

**Magic Eraser Tool** ▼
This tool is useful when removing colour from line work, if they have been merged by mistake. It works in a similar way to the Magic Wand Tool, but instead of making a selection, it makes clicked pixels transparent. Options such as Tolerance and Contiguous are just like the ones in the Magic Wand Tool.

**Background Eraser Tool** ▼
You can also erase more complicated (gradated) backgrounds to transparency using this tool, by sampling the colour in the centre of the brush continuously. Make sure the Cross Hair remains outside the edge of the areas that need protecting, so it won't sample that colour and erase it.

**Tip:** To create a snapshot in the History Palette, just check the little box on the left of the stage you want.

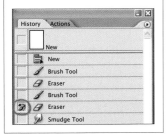

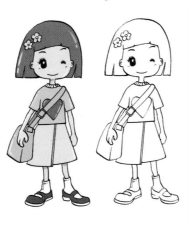

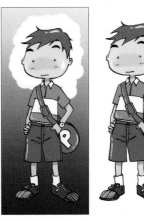

# Other useful tools

Apart from the previously mentioned Paint Tools there are many other tools that will aid the creation of excellent manga art. Most of these, like Clone Stamp, Blur, Sharpen, Smudge, Dodge, Burn and Sponge, affect existing drawings, rather than originate them, and can be used for a wide variety of effects. Dodge, Burn and Sponge can be used to create highlights and shadows, while the Smudge Tool allows the artist to hand-blend colours like digital pastels.

## The Clone Stamp Tool

This tool copies a section of an image on to another part of the picture or on to a completely different image. Using the Clone Stamp Tool in manga drawing allows the artist to paint tones or patterns on to a manga page underneath or on top of existing artwork. Once mastered, it is a fantastic time-saving device for making duplicates.

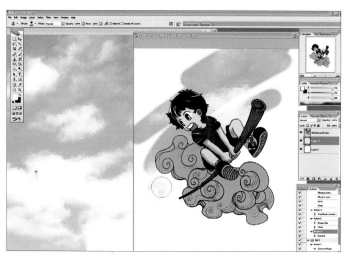

◀ **Using the Clone Stamp Tool**
After [Alt]+clicking the part of the image that needs be cloned from, creating a sampling point, it is simply a matter of painting directly on to the area that needs to be cloned to. Normally the 'Aligned' option in the Options Bar is checked, so the sampling point moves simultaneously with the painting cursor's movement and the new cloned image is drawn continuously. If this is not required, uncheck the 'Aligned' option. This will make the clone brush begin drawing again from the original sampling point each time the mouse button/pen is released. If the 'Use All Layers' option is selected, then all the image's layers will be cloned from the source. Otherwise, only the currently active layer is used.

## The Blur and Sharpen tools

**Different uses for Blur and Sharpen**
These two easily controllable tools can be used in various ways, from sharpening up out-of-focus scanned-in line art, to deliberately blurring a figure in order to push the figure into the background, creating an impressive 'photographic' effect.

**Blur Tool** ▶
The Blur Tool blurs image areas by reducing the colour contrast between pixels. In the Options Bar the 'strength' can be altered. The 'Sample All Layers' option affects all layers; otherwise, only the current active layer will be blurred. The Blur Tool is usually used to soften the edges of colours so that they merge together smoothly.

Sharpen

Blur

Original

◀ **Sharpen Tool**
The Sharpen Tool is the opposite of the Blur Tool. It increases the contrast between pixels, thus sharpening the focus.

**Tip:** Pressing the [Alt] key while dragging in Blur mode, will sharpen the image, while [Alt] key and dragging within Sharpen mode will blur it.

**Sharpening line work** ▶
Sometimes scanned-in line work can be a bit blurred. The Sharpen Tool can gradually sharpen the line art, but rescan if necessary.

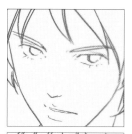

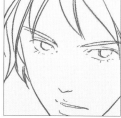

## The Smudge Tool

Using the Smudge Tool is like smudging a wet painting with a finger, just as the icon of this tool indicates. This tool uses the colour where the stroke begins and spreads it in the direction in which the tool is dragged. This is very useful for drawing natural-looking hair. Try different strength settings to see what's best for your drawing.

**Smudged hair** ▶
Individual smudged strands of hair produce a wilder, more natural look.

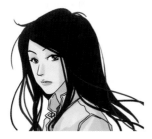

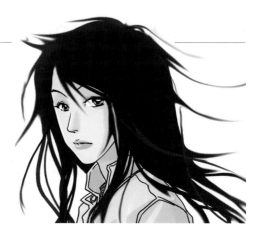

## The Dodge, Burn and Sponge tools

These three toning tools get their names from traditional photography methods and share the same button. These tools all use customizable brushes, just like the Brush Tool. Often they are used on fully painted manga, rather than black and white line art, and create a softer, three-dimensional look. The Dodge Tool lightens up areas of an image. It is very useful for adding a light source quickly to a flat-colour manga character. The result will not be as good as the normal Brush Tool, because the Dodge Tool washes out colour and details.

The Burn Tool is the opposite of the Dodge Tool: it darkens the area it is dragged over. Normally it is used for adding shadows quickly. Again, the result is not as good as using the Brush Tool. The Options Bar is the same as that for the Dodge Tool.

The Sponge Tool has two modes: Desaturate and Saturate. While in the Saturate mode, the Sponge Tool adds colour saturation to the areas dragged over. In Desaturate mode it does the opposite. In a greyscale picture, it increases or decreases the contrast.

**Dodging and burning manga art** ▶
These examples show how the Dodge and Burn tools can be used on a flat-colour character (left) to create shadows and highlights (right). The colour on the girl's right arm has been washed away by the Dodge Tool, to create the highlight.

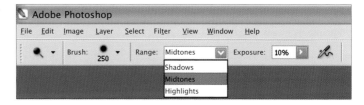

**Selecting a range** ▲
In the Options Bar, there are three ranges to choose from: 'Highlights', 'Midtones' and 'Shadows'. If 'Highlights' is selected, only the lightest areas will be affected, and so on. The 'Exposure' level decides how intense the effect is; this is usually set at a low level: between 10 and 50%.

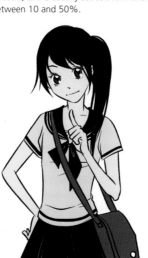

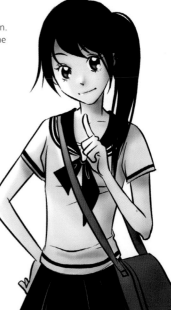

# Photoshop layers

One of the most powerful features of Photoshop is layers. Traditional manga would occasionally use semi-transparent acetate paper laid on top of the artwork to draw and letter the speech balloons on. This allowed for the lettering to be moved around and the language and style to be changed without affecting the original art. This is now done digitally, using layers; but layers are also perfect for adding colour, gradients, tones and more. Because of layers, each layer can be changed independently without affecting the others, allowing complex images to be created. Imagine each layer as a clear plastic sheet with part of the image printed on it, all of which are stacked to make the complete picture.

## The layered image

After creating a new canvas, or opening any image, there is already at least one layer in the Layer Palette. The image portrayed below shows how layers work; each individual element on its own separate layer, allowing them to be edited independently.

**Tip:** Always add new elements on a new layer. This way the original image can be preserved. Doing this allows for easier editing of mistakes. The layers can always be merged at a later stage, if the end results are satisfactory.

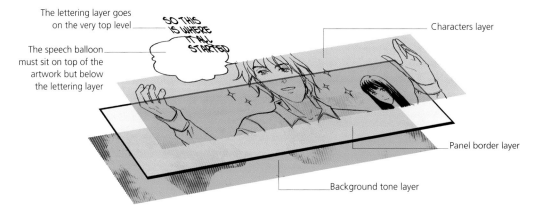

The lettering layer goes on the very top level

The speech balloon must sit on top of the artwork but below the lettering layer

Characters layer

Panel border layer

Background tone layer

**Shuffle the deck** ▲
The layers can be arranged in any order, allowing a character to be pushed into the background or an object to be brought into the foreground at the click of a button.

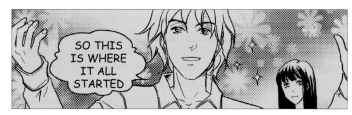

**Invisible layers** ▶
When the final artwork is seen, the layers are invisible, or flattened into a single layer, so although the characters, the background tone, the dialogue bubble, the text and the panel border are all on separate layers, the reader sees the image as a unified whole. Always save the files as layered .psd files for future editing.

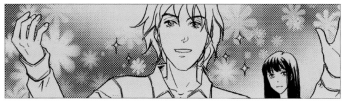

**Removing lettering**
After this panel was lettered it was decided that it would be better with no dialogue. In the past, this would have been a huge problem. The speech balloon would have had to be covered up or cut out, and then the background tone would have been added to match the art exactly where the balloon was. Using Photoshop's layers, the balloon and text are created on separate layers and are thus easily deleted.

## The Layers Palette

Layers are controlled through the Layers Palette (Window > Layers). On the palette, each layer is displayed as a small thumbnail, with the name of the layer next to it. The final appearance of a layered Photoshop image is the view from the top, down through all the layers. The order of the layers in the Layers palette represents their order in the image.

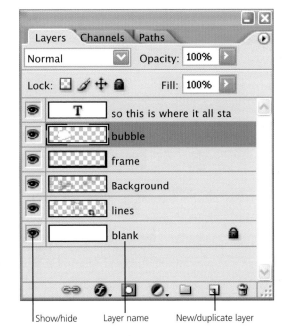

Show/hide    Layer name    New/duplicate layer

**New/duplicate layer**
Clicking this icon creates a new layer above the current active layer. Duplicate a layer by dragging it on to the icon. The new (duplicated) layer appears on top of the previous one.

**Layer via copy, cut or drag**
To copy or cut part of a layer to make a new layer, simply select the area required and the option 'Layer via copy' or 'Layer via cut'. The new layer with the selected area will appear on top of the original layer. Dragging and dropping a layer on to an open image is also possible.

**Naming layers** ▲
Double-click on the default layer name to rename the layer as something more memorable.

**Changing the layer order** ▲
To change the layer stacking order in the Layer Palette,

just click and drag it up or down the stack and place it where it is needed.

**Deleting a layer** ▲
To delete a layer, simply drag the layer to the Bin icon at the bottom right of the palette. Don't do it unless the layer is never needed again.

◀ **Hiding layers**
Sometimes it is useful to hide a layer in order to be able to concentrate more easily on the layers underneath. Clicking (and removing) the eye icon makes the layer temporarily invisible. Clicking the eye again makes the layer visible once more.

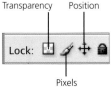

Transparency    Position

Lock:    Pixels

To avoid working on the wrong layer they can be locked as follows:

**Transparency:** Once checked, it is impossible to paint on transparent areas.

**Pixels:** Once checked, cannot be drawn on.

**Position:** Prevents the image on the layer being moved, but all other functions work.

**All:** Stops all editing.

## Layer-blending modes

Each layer has its own blending mode, which allows one layer to blend with the layers underneath. Under the Layer Palette's default setting, 'Normal', is a list of blending modes in the drop-down menu. Along with 'Normal', the other most commonly used blending modes in digital manga creation are 'Multiply' and 'Screen'. The examples here reveal their effects. The red heart is the upper layer, the purple heart the lower. Don't forget that the Opacity and Fill of a layer can also be changed using the sliders on the Layer Palette.

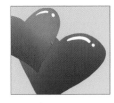

**Normal** ▲
The upper layer displays the full colour value and the image on the layer underneath is covered.

**Multiply** ▼
This multiplies the upper layer's colour intensity, so the lower layer gets darker. The upper layer's white becomes clear.

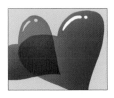

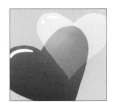

**Screen** ▲
Darker colours in the lower layer appear lighter when this is applied to the upper layer.

# Scanning and retouching an image

Hand-drawn pictures can be processed digitally by importing the image into the computer using a scanner. This is extremely convenient for artists who prefer the feel of working with pen and paper, but still want the advantages working digitally can offer. Large areas of black shadows can be added quickly using the Fill Bucket Tool, saving hours of laborious inking,

and any smudges or mistakes can be easily removed and cleaned up. The other advantages are obvious. The drawing can be coloured digitally without affecting the original artwork; and it can be emailed or posted on the Internet and shared with millions of people: all impossible without first being able to scan in a paper drawing.

## Practice exercise: Scanning, adjusting and cleaning an image

Here is a quick guide to scanning in simple line work, the most common requirement for a manga artist. The higher the dpi, the bigger the file will be when scanned in; but the quality of the picture will also improve, thus you can get into more details of the image and can print out bigger pictures later.

1 Place the drawn image face down on the glass in the scanner, aligned with its edges.

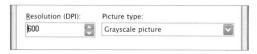

In Photoshop, choose File > Import to open the scanning software. Choose 'Grayscale picture' (if scanning in a colour image, choose 'Color') and set the resolution to 600 dpi.

2 Click 'Preview' and wait for the scanner to show a preview version of the image. Select the area in the preview image required to scan, then click 'Scan'. The picture will be scanned in and appear in a new Photoshop window.

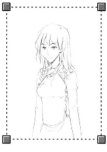

3 Go to Image > Mode, and change the image to Grayscale (if grey tones are needed), or RGB, if working in colour later. Click File > Save as... to save the file as a .psd file and give it a new name. The image is ready for further adjustments. The lines in this example are too grey and not black enough. To adjust this, go to Image > Adjustments > Levels to open the Levels window. Sliding the three pointers controls the image's amount of black, white and grey.

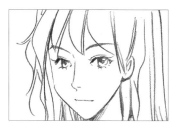

**Tip:** A shortcut to balancing the black and white is to go to Image > Adjustments > Levels and in the window check the black Eyedropper Tool. Then click on the blackest part of the line art. Repeat, using the white Eyedropper Tool, clicking on the whitest part of the image. This will remove most of the mid-tones.

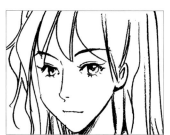

4 Watch the changes on the original image and when the lines become solid black and are still delicate. Click OK.

**Tip:** Sometimes part of the line work might be very light, and adjusting the Levels may cause these light, fine lines to disappear. Use the Burn Tool to darken them before using the Levels adjustment.

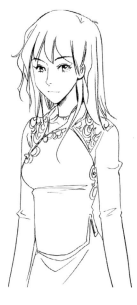

5 Now use the Eraser Tool to clean up the remaining dirty dots and anything else that needs removing from the image. Using a fine point, you can sharpen lines to details that would be impossible with an actual pen, if you so wish. Details can also now be added to the image, using a tablet pen or mouse. This is the perfect time to tweak and hone the picture until the line work is just right.

## Practice exercise: Separating the line art from the white background

It is good practice to separate the black line art from the white background so that the line work can be manipulated at a later stage, such as changing the colour of the lines or even altering the lines after feedback from friends or colleagues. It also allows for additional colour layers to be added underneath, ensuring the black line art is always on top, like an acetate sheet over a painting. Here is the quick and simple method of separating the line art from the background.

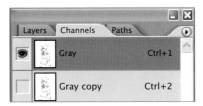

**Tip:** Channels visibility can be turned on and off, like the Layers. In RGB and CMYK mode this allows different colours to be switched on and off, giving interesting alternate hues.

**1** On the Layers Palette, click the 'Channels' tab to activate the Channels Palette. Initially, there is one layer called 'Gray'. Duplicate this layer by dragging it to the 'Create new channel' icon at the bottom of the window. Go back to the Layers Palette and create a new layer. Next, delete the original layer with line art on.

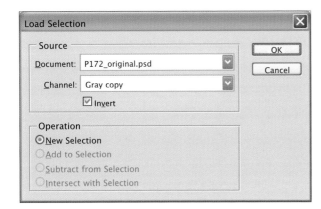

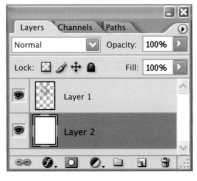

**2** Go to Select > Load Selection. Check 'Invert' and in the 'Channel' drop-down box choose 'Gray copy'. Click OK and the selected line artwork will appear.

**3** Use the Paint Bucket Tool to fill the selection with black. Underneath this layer, create a new layer and fill it with white using the Paint Bucket Tool. A separate layer for the line work has just been created.

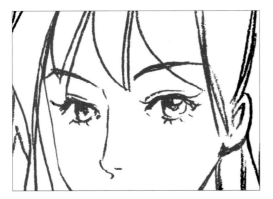

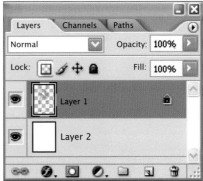

**4** Because the line art is on its own layer, with a transparent background, the Lock Transparency icon can be clicked. If this is checked, the Brush Tool can only draw on areas that are not transparent, meaning only the actual line work itself. Switching to RGB mode will allow the lines to be changed into any colour.

# Digital inking

It is becoming increasingly popular among manga artists to use digital inking. This method allows manga artists to draw perfectly smooth and crisp lines without worrying about making mistakes. There are several ways to digitally ink a pencil sketch. Traditionally the manga artist creates a new layer on top of the sketch and effectively 'traces' the sketch, adding subtle changes, shading and nuances. A cruder method is to simply convert the image to a grayscale and in Image >

Adjustments > Levels open up the Levels window. Here, adjust the black and white levels by sliding the pointers up and down until the background is pure white and the lines are no longer grey, but solid black. However, if there is too much white, delicate lines will be lost. Conversely, too much black will make the artwork look thick and blobby, with no variation in the thickness of the line. It is always recommended to ink the page in the first manner to add vitality to the art.

## Practice exercise: Inking a scanned image

It is a good idea to have practised inking on paper, as shown earlier in the book, in order to get a feel for drawing smooth lines with a real pen. Inking in Photoshop with a graphics tablet pen can be done in several ways. A pencilled image can be scanned in or you can sketch directly into Photoshop. Because the 'ink' is usually 100% black, it is best to have your pencilled image as a lighter shade, so you can see what you have already inked.

**Tip:** Practise a variety of brushstrokes on smaller pencilled studies with either a mouse or a graphics tablet pen before attempting to ink an entire image.

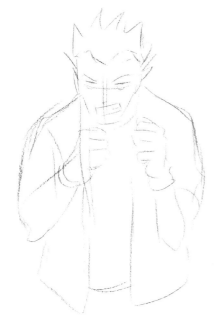

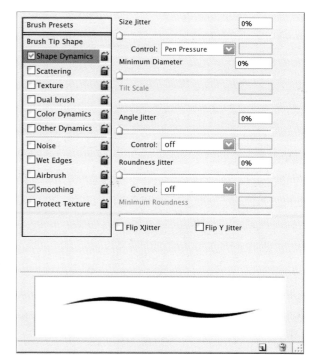

1 Before inking, a sketch is required to work on. This example is a scanned-in greyscale image at 600 dpi. Alternatively, a sketch can be created straight on the screen using the graphics tablet. Switch the image's Mode to Grayscale, rather than RGB, as the files are smaller, thus making the computer run faster. If colour is needed later, the image's mode can be changed back to RGB once the inks are complete. Create a new layer and call it 'inks'. This is the layer that will be digitally inked on. Set the Mode to 'Normal'.

2 Choose the Brush Tool. Open the Brush Palette, check 'Shape Dynamics' and 'Smoothing', and in the setting for Shape Dynamics, set the Size Jitter to Pen Pressure 0%. Choose a round brush and set the Hardness to 100%. Vary the line width while working.

**Tip:** Pressing D will reset the default foreground colour back to black, and the background colour back to white.

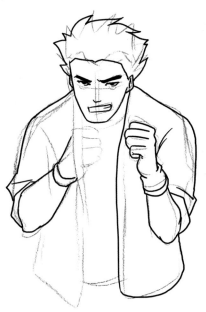

3 On the 'inks' layer, begin drawing over the pencil lines. Use thinner lines and vary the brush sizes for small details and relatively thicker lines for longer strokes. Occasionally, the pencil design may be weaker than you originally thought: this is a good time to make any alterations on the 'sketch' layer. In this example, the details of the man's hands and face were tightened and the anatomy strengthened.

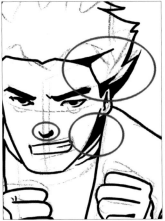

4 Finish the basic inking, making sure nothing is missing. Go back and ensure there are ample details to enrich the picture. Here, thicker shadows have been added in the hair and on the face in order to indicate depth. If the 'sketch' layer has become too messy and it is difficult to see where to ink, create a new layer between the 'inks' and 'sketch' layers and fill it with white, in 'Normal' mode. Turn this middle layer on and off and your inking progress can be checked easily. Varying the thickness of your lines and shadows enhances the depth of the image. The thicker the lines, the heavier and more solid the object will look; the thinner the lines, the more delicate the object will look.

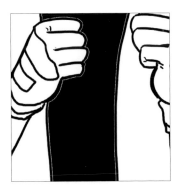

5 Use the Paint Bucket Tool to fill in solid black areas. The Brush Tool's stokes have soft edges, and they appear slightly grey. Because of this, when using the Magic Wand or Paint Bucket tools, they may not be able to select the whole area (experiment with Tolerance first). Instead, there may be a tiny belt of white between the selection and the surrounding brushstroke line. To correct this, select the area that needs filling, then go to Select > Modify > Expand and expand the selection by one or two pixels. After this expansion, the selection will cover the white belt area and the area can now be filled in with the black colour.

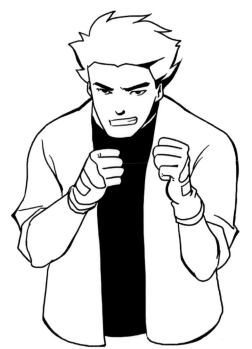

**Tip:** Remain stable when using the graphics tablet pen, and don't shake too much. It can be difficult, especially drawing longer lines, but with practice, your stability will improve considerably. Some lines will need a few attempts to get them right. If a mistake is made, use [Ctrl]+Z to undo it. The Eraser Tool can also be used to remove mistakes or sharpen blunt lines.

6 Once satisfied with the inking, delete the 'sketch' layer. There will be two remaining layers left; the line art layer and the layer filled with white as background. The image is now ready for further developments.

# Toning techniques

The majority of manga books are in black and white, and consequently grey tones are a manga artist's essential tool. Grey tones add shadow, lighting, texture and depth to black and white line work, essentially forming the 'colour' of black and white manga. The traditional way of adding grey tone, still practised by many modern Japanese manga artists,

is to use rubdown Letratone sheets. This involves selecting the appropriate-size grey-tone sheet, pasting it to the original artwork, then using a blade to cut carefully around the artwork. It is expensive, time-consuming and requires a lot of practice. Thanks to Photoshop, the digital alternative is much quicker, cheaper and easier.

## Practice exercise: Adding tone

Adding tone to a line image is very simple, but can be incredibly effective in enlivening a basic manga line drawing. Essentially, it is the same as adding colour using the Paint Bucket Tool, with the blues, greens and yellows being replaced by various shades of grey.

1 Open the image. This should have two layers: one white background and one for line art. Ensure the image is in Grayscale mode. Create a new layer between these two layers and set the mode to 'Normal'. Call this layer 'tones'. Go to Window > Color to reveal the Color Palette. The Color Palette contains only one slider scale; from white to black. It is better to pick a grey tone in the Color Palette, rather than the Color Picker on the Toolbox, because it is possible to define the exact percentage of grey required. The grey tones are defined as 0% being pure white and 100% being solid black, therefore 50% is an exact grey. The lower the percentage, the lighter the grey tone.

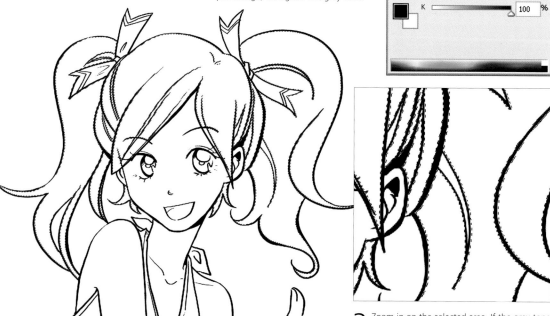

2 Use the Magic Wand Tool to select the girl's hair. Check 'Contiguous' and 'Sample all Layers' in the Options Bar. If there is a gap in the line art, then the Magic Wand Tool will select more than required, in which case, the area needs to be deselected ([Ctrl]+D) and the gap joined using the Brush Tool. Alternatively, you can trim areas from the selection using the Lasso tools and the [Alt] key. To select multiple areas, press down the [Shift] key while selecting the area. To deselect an area from the current selection, press down [Alt]+click.

3 Zoom in on the selected area. If the grey tone is filled in now, when the selection does not exactly butt up with the line art, there will be a terrible white gap between the grey and line. To solve this, go to Select > Modify > Expand and expand the selection by one or two pixels. It is important to make sure the edge of the selection is actually just underneath the line art, so if the first pixel expansion is not enough, increase it by another one or two pixels.

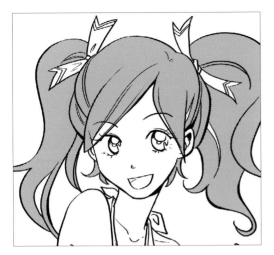

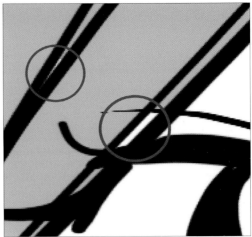

**4** Ensuring that the 'tones' layer is selected, choose a grey tone required for the hair (as per step 1) and select the Paint Bucket Tool. Uncheck all the options in the Options Bar, ignoring the Tolerance levels at this stage, and fill the area.

**5** After the grey has been filled in, zooming in may reveal some areas in the hair that have been missed in the selection. Use [Ctrl]+D to deselect the current selection and then use the same selecting method to select the missed areas and fill them in. Zoom in again to confirm all the areas have been filled.

**Tip:** Always remember that the layered manner of working in Photoshop means that it's possible to 'fix' areas of missing colour quickly and simply, by drawing directly on to the 'tones' layer beneath the line art, which remains untouched. Use the Pencil or Brush tools for exceptionally fiddly areas that may be missed by the Magic Wand Tool's selection process.

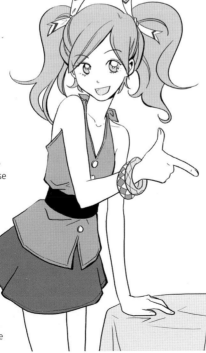

**6** Repeat the process with the other parts of the image. Use the Pencil Tool to apply the grey tones carefully to tight areas where the Magic Wand and Paint Bucket method doesn't work so well, or where it would prove time consuming. Choose complementary shades of grey to give your image the illusion of colour and depth. Push the extremes more than you would in a full-colour drawing, as you only have 256 shades to work with.

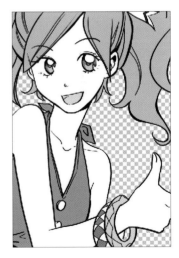

**7** When filling in the areas of the image, don't forget to fill in all the transparent areas within the character, with solid white, including the skin. Turning off the white background layer will give you a clear view of where to fill. The solid white needs to be filled in, otherwise when you come to fill in the background layer, it will show through the uncoloured skin.

## Practice exercise: Adding shadow, highlights and pattern

After the toning in the last two pages, you will now have a plainly toned image. Depending on personal taste, for some people this is a finished work.

For a more professional look, you still need to add further details to the image, building up areas of shadows, highlights and patterns.

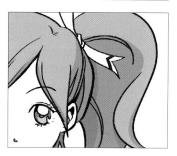

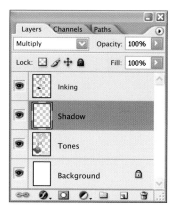

1 Add a new layer on top of the 'tones' layer and name it 'shadow'. Set the Layers mode to 'Multiply'.

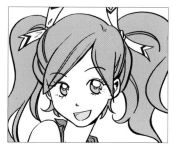

2 To add shadow to the hair, go to the 'Tones' layer and use the Magic Wand Tool to select the hair colour. Uncheck 'Contiguous' and set the Tolerance to 0. This will make the Magic Wand select only the hair colour. If you have used the same shade of grey anywhere else on the image, it will select those areas as well, but in this instance, the hair is the only part of the image so shaded.

3 Flip to the 'Shadow' layer. Choose a light grey tone and, within the selection, paint shadows on to the hair. Here the light comes from the top left corner. Use the Eraser Tool to clear up mistakes. Use a darker shade of grey to draw heavier shadows at the darkest points; for example, where an object casts a shadow on another one.

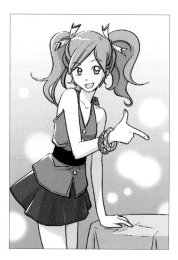

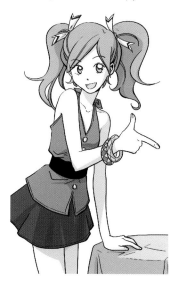

4 Selecting the areas as before, add shadows to the rest of the image in the same way, paying attention to the way shadows may fall differently on fabrics and skin. Turn off the 'Tones' layer periodically to spot areas you have missed.

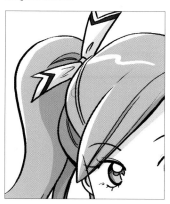

5 Next, add highlights to the image. Create a new layer called 'Highlight' on top of the 'Tones' and 'Shadow' layers and set the mode to 'Normal'. Consider your light source, and at the point where the light is strongest, add pure white highlights. You will still need to use the Magic Wand Tool to select each area individually to ensure your highlights don't go outside of the lines.

6 The image could do with a background. Create a new layer underneath the 'Tones' layer, setting the mode to Normal. Select the Gradient Tool and drag a Linear gradient from white to mid-grey over the whole picture. Create another 'Normal' layer on top of this one and choose a soft-edged, big brush with Opacity of around 50. Paint big white dots to create a dreamy atmosphere. Merge your tone layers together and rename them 'Gray'.

## Practice exercise: Converting grey tone to black dots

If you want to publish the previous image online, then we have finished the toning procedure. If, however, you want to publish your image professionally, it is not finished yet. In many printed manga, the grey tones are not grey, but made up of countless black dots. The bigger the dots and the closer they are printed, the darker the grey appears.

Many manga/comic printers don't print colour (mainly for cost reasons), so we need to convert our grey layer to black dots.

**Halftone shading** ▶
While many printers use halftone screens for their regular output, manga makes an art out of necessity.

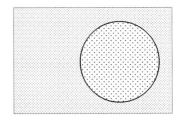

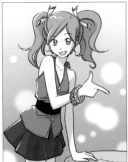

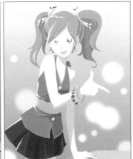

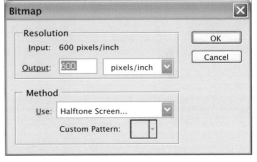

**1** Create a new document the same size and resolution as the current one. The current document ('Cutie.psd', above left) is a Grayscale A4 page at 600 dpi. Go to File > New. Choose the appropriate settings in the pop-up window, then click OK. Drag the flattened 'Gray' layer from the layer palette of 'Cutie.psd' (as shown above right) and drop it into the new document. Make sure it fits within the canvas.

**2** In the new document, click Image > Mode > Bitmap to reduce it to pure black and white. In the first pop-up window, click OK to Flatten Layer, and in the second pop-up window, choose to output the image at 600 (the current resolution, often used interchangeably as dots per inch and pixels per inch) and select Halftone Screen as your method. Click OK to go ahead.

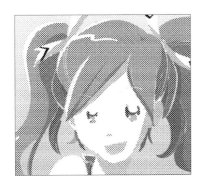

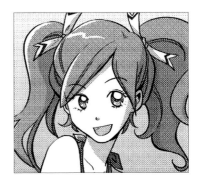

**3** In the third pop-up window, change the Frequency to 32, make the Angle 45 degrees and select Round as the shape. If you want to try out different values or shapes, experiment with a number of different options in case an alternative method takes your fancy. When you have entered the values, click OK. All of the grey tones are converted into black dots.

**Tip:** If you have the hard drive storage space, it is well worth hanging on to layered .psd files, as you never know when you may need an editable version of your illustration. For instance, if you wanted to create a colour version of this picture, you will regret only saving a merged tiff or jpg file. Layered files are large, so backup your archives to CD or DVD periodically. Don't forget, you can save a flattened jpg to display online by using the File > Save as... command. If saving a large .psd file for the web, you will probably want to reduce the width to between 600 and 9000 pixels so it can be viewed on a monitor without horizontal scrolling.

**4** Now go to Image > Mode > Grayscale to change the image to Grayscale. Set the size ratio to 1 in the pop-up window. Drag the layer back to 'Cutie.psd' and move the shading so that it matches the lines, ensuring it is on top of the 'Gray' layer and beneath the 'Inking' layer. You can now either merge all layers or just save this image as a layered .psd file.

# Speedlines and focus lines

The method of creating speedlines and focus lines is often discussed together, as both are used to create an impact on the reader by communicating shock, surprise, tension and movement. Speedlines are a group of parallel (or nearly parallel) lines that show movement, while focus lines are a group of lines radiating out from one central focal point. They add impetus and interest to a single-colour background especially when something is moving quickly towards the reader's point of view. The effects themselves are easily created in Photoshop, and this tutorial will show you how.

## Practice exercise: Creating speedlines

Drawing speedlines the traditional way requires huge amounts of concentration and patience – or a crack team of assistants blessed with the same. Hundreds of lines must be drawn on paper with exacting care, using pen and ruler, with no respite but white-out if a mistake is made. Now, there is Photoshop, which can produce excellent results in a fraction of the time. There are many speedlines available online, ready to paste into an image. If you can't find them online, here is an easy way to make some yourself.

1 Create a new file at the same resolution as the image you will be dragging the speedlines into later (300-600 dpi). Don't make the image too big, just a little bigger than the manga panel you want to cover. Set the file Mode to Grayscale. Use the Single Column Marquee Tool to select a single column on the image, then fill it with the grey tone of your choice.

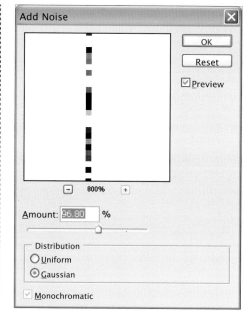

2 With the grey-toned area still selected, go to Filter > Noise > Add Noise. The higher the number you choose, the more intense the speedlines will be.

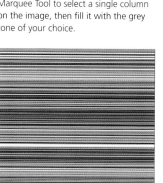

3 Go to Edit > Transform > Scale to transform the selection. Drag the selection from both sides, stretching out the single vertical column of pixels to fill the whole page from left to right. Double-click the image when you are finished to confirm the transformation.

4 Zooming in on the image will reveal that most of the lines are grey rather than black. To correct this, go to Image > Adjustments > Brightness/Contrast. Increase the brightness, and turn the contrast level up to maximum. Now the speedlines are ready to use. Paste them into your manga panel and use the 'Free Transform' function to fit the angle you require.

**Tip:** There are other ways in which you can integrate your speed and focus effects with your colour pages. Try varying the colour of the line, for instance, so that you use a dark purple shade on a light purple background. Alternatively, use the Magic Wand Tool with 'Contiguous' unchecked on your speedlines layer to select all the black lines, then apply a gradient from light to dark in the direction of travel. Finally, try playing around with the layer blend and layer fill Opacity settings: how do your speedlines and focus lines look when blended in 'Multiply' or 'Screen' modes, for example?

## Speedlines in action

Compare these four pictures of a running boy. The first lacks impact without speedlines. The second is 'naturalistic', with a speedline shadow and blurring. The third ups the strength (and speed) of the lines, while the fourth creates a background from them, freezing a moment in time and generating an intense atmosphere.

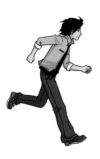 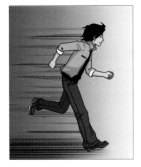 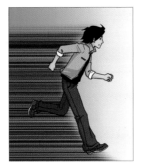 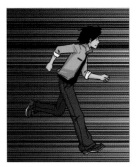

## Practice exercise: Creating focus lines

Focus lines are normally used to express tension or surprise. Their near-interchangeability with speedlines visually also means they sometimes function as 'speedlines in perspective'. In either case, they isolate a character or vehicle in the centre of a panel, drawing the reader's attention to it and its current condition.

1 Use the speedlines you have just created. We need to turn the canvas 90 degrees to make the lines vertical. Go to Image > Rotate Canvas > 90' CW.

2 Now go to Filter > Distort > Polar Coordinates and bring up the option window. Choose 'Rectangular to Polar' and click OK. Your image is converted to a page of focus lines converging on a central point.

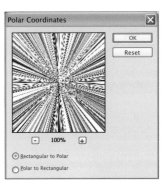

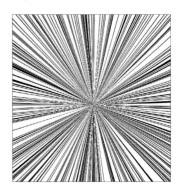

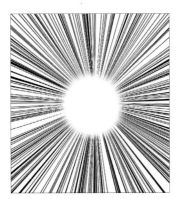

3 The lines don't usually go all the way to the centre of the image. Use a big, soft-edged Eraser Tool to clear the middle. If you think the focus lines are too crowded, use a hard-edged Eraser Tool to clean up some of the lines.

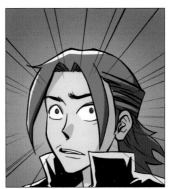

◄ **Polarized image**
This is an example of an image with vertical speedlines after they have been passed through the Polar Coordinates filter.

# Style of lettering

Lettering is an essential part of manga, forming half of the interplay between words and pictures that makes manga unique. While the action of your story may be clear from the illustrations, dialogue, captions, speech balloons and sound effects all allow you to dive deeper into your world and the motivations of your characters, as well as adding 'verbal' wit, humour and tension to your tale. Lettering also serves as a guide to the reader through the page: skilfully deployed balloon placements move the eye from panel to panel and control the pace at which a reader consumes the story.

Snappy dialogue and well-placed balloons can often cover up deficiencies in artwork or panel-to-panel storytelling, so never underestimate the importance of lettering. The most common devices to show spoken dialogue are speech balloons: the ellipses containing lettering, with 'tails' that point towards the relevant speaker. Remember to integrate your balloons and digital lettering with your art style – conventional word processor fonts look bland and out of place, so find a font that meshes with your art. Visit www.blambot.com for a selection that are free for personal use.

## Placing speech balloons

Dialogue and balloons cannot be simply dumped on to the page; they must be added with the same care and attention to the overall composition that characterized your panel layouts. Remember that balloons should not cover up vital parts of the artwork, and should direct the eye from the top left to bottom right of the page.

**Speech balloons in action** ▼ ▶
These two panels both show successful balloon placement. Below, an unusual font suggests a non-human character, while the balloon is offset so it doesn't cover up any of the art. The balloon to the right overlaps with non-essential art (the character's hair) in order to fit within the panel bounds.

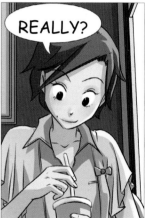

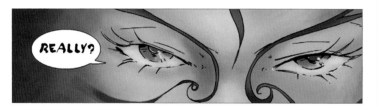

## Practice exercise: Adding lettering

Professionals digitally letter manga in a number of different and esoteric ways. This method, which stays within Photoshop, is the most straight-forward, and is suitable for all skill levels and complexities of projects.

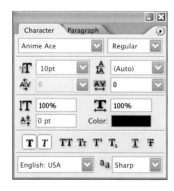

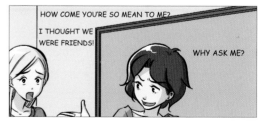

**1** Open the page you wish to letter in Photoshop and bring up the Character Palette (Window > Character). Choose a font from the drop-down menu at the top left and select a size appropriate to your page from the menu underneath. Make sure your lettering is legible at your final print size.

**2** Set your colour to black, select the text tool ([Ctrl]+T) and click where you want to place the text, creating a 'Text' layer where you can type. If you are working from a script, you can copy and paste dialogue on to your page.

**Tip:** Manga tends to use capital letters for all its dialogue, with bolds and italics for emphasis. If your script is in sentence case, select your text once you have pasted it across, click the small arrow at the top of the Character Palette, and select 'All Caps'.

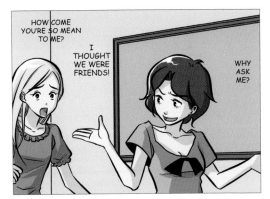

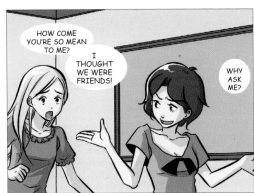

**3** Each balloon forms a new 'Text' Layer; select each one as required. Centre the text ([Ctrl]+[Shift]+C) and use the Return key to arrange the text into a relatively elliptical shape. Arrange your dialogue blocks so that they don't cover important elements of the image, and they flow from top left to bottom right. Add emphasis to dialogue by making stressed words bold and/or italic. Finally, check that all your important text is well within the boundaries of the page – in case the page is trimmed too close at the printing stage.

**4** Add a new layer beneath all of the 'Text' Layers for balloons. Set the mode to 'Normal'. Select the Ellipse Tool, checking 'Fill Pixels' in the Options Bar. Set the foreground colour to white. Click and drag the mouse/tablet pen to make white filled ellipses beneath all of your blocks of text, making the balloons just a little bit bigger than the text they encompass. Even if your ellipses are not placed exactly, the layer capabilities of Photoshop mean that you can move the text or the balloons around to your satisfaction at a later stage.

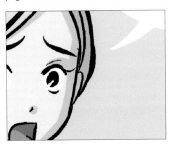

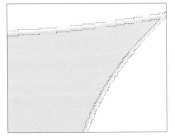

**Tip:** You can also squash more text into less space by attaching balloons to the top of panels, so that your ellipse is cut off to some degree, forming a large, straight edge at the panel border. Arrange your text with a long first line, slightly shorter second line, shorter again third line, and so on.

**5** Using the Brush Tool or Pencil Tool, add tails to the balloons. Ensure that the tail points towards the character who is speaking. Finish the tail a little distance away from their head.

**6** Select the balloons and tails on your balloon layer using the Magic Wand. Then go to Select > Modify > Border. In the pop-up window, select how thick you wish the border of the

balloons to be (along with font size, this will change depending on the size and resolution of your page). Two to four pixels should be enough. Click OK to create a two to four pixel selection.

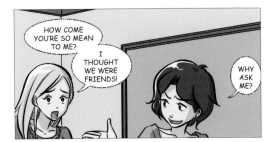

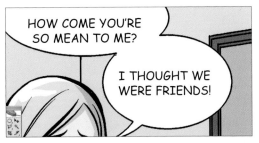

**7** Choose the Paint Bucket Tool (with Tolerance set to 255, 'Contiguous' and 'All Layers' unchecked) and use black to fill the current selection, creating black borders.

**8** The final stage is to troubleshoot your balloons. If some words are still too long for their position, you can make them narrower using the Character Palette (<-T->).

# SFX lettering

SFX (sound effects) is a special, individualistic type of lettering that communicates an impression of sound. SFX are lettered directly on to the page, at a generally much larger size than dialogue. The louder the sound, the larger the type. Just as the onomatopaeic content of the SFX reflects the noise the sound makes, so the font should try to replicate the sound in visual form – from jagged type for explosions to soft and sinuous replications of running water.

## Creating sound effects

Manga artists have created thousands of SFX words across the years, some relatively common and some unique to individual artists. Rarely, however, is the same SFX word deployed in the same way: each appearance will look different, or be incorporated into the art in a new and exciting way. Don't feel limited by existing SFX: try to create your own onomatopaeic words. The current trend is away from literal words like 'BEEP' and 'CRASH' and towards more abstract coinages like 'CZZZTT' (live electrical cable) and 'FWUTHOOOOM' (an explosion). Experiment: if the sound reads right to you on the page, it works.

Your choice of font, and its size, is very important. A small 'BEEP' in an electrical font is appropriate for a mobile phone, while an enormous 'BANG' should feature letters of suitable girth. Don't forget to 'scuff up' your lettering to make it look more natural and less digitally perfect.

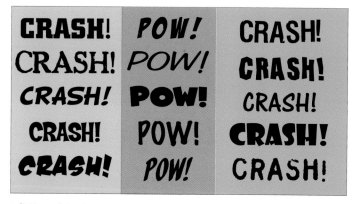

**Infinite variety ▲**
While there are timeless 'classics' among the SFX canon, from 'CRASH' to 'POW', every new sound effect is an opportunity to generate a new sound-alike, or to visually interpret an old cliché in a new and exciting manner.

**Deafening impact ▼**
The armoured robot collides with the ground with a resounding 'BANG' of mangled metal and compressed earth.

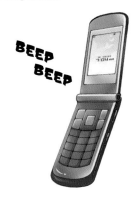

**Incoming call ▲**
'BEEP BEEP' can represent an actual generic ringtone; it also lets the reader interpret it as any tone they know.

**Tip:** Switch things up by scanning in a hand-drawn sound effect, manipulating its colours and angles in Photoshop and compositing it into your digital page.

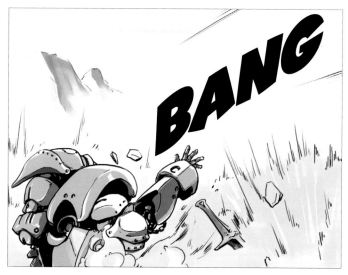

## Practice exercise: Adding SFX to a panel

Just as with lettering balloons, adding SFX to a finished manga panel is a relatively straightforward process. The example here transforms an 'off-the-peg' font to create its special effect, but you could achieve even more impressive results with a freehand rendering of your SFX, either direct to the screen with a tablet pen, or by scanning in hand-drawn lettering and digitally manipulating it.

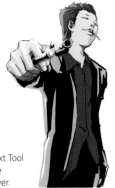

1 Open your chosen image. Choose the Text Tool and open the Character Palette. Click the image with the tool to create a new 'Text' layer.

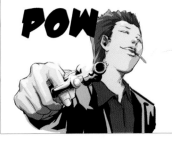

2 Select your font ('Damn Noisy Kids' in this instance) and choose a suitably big size. It doesn't really matter where you place the effect at this stage, as you will move it later. Type your lettering.

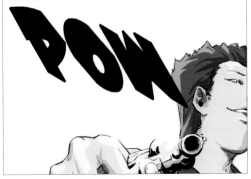

3 Press [Ctrl]+T to Free Transform the text, making it less 'factory fresh' and more visually interesting. Here the letters are tilted to show the trajectory of the fired bullet.

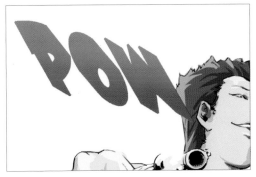

4 Rasterize the text, then select it with the Magic Wand Tool (with Contiguous off). Use the Paint Bucket Tool or the Gradient Tool to fill the selected area with the colour or colours of your choice. Here, the image has been filled with a subtle gradient of orange to red.

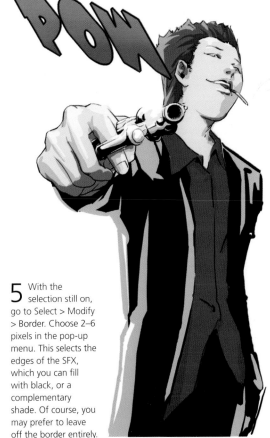

5 With the selection still on, go to Select > Modify > Border. Choose 2–6 pixels in the pop-up menu. This selects the edges of the SFX, which you can fill with black, or a complementary shade. Of course, you may prefer to leave off the border entirely.

# Using filters

You have already used a small selection of Photoshop filters as earlier in the chapter to create speedlines and focus lines. However, we have yet to explain what exactly a Photoshop filter is. Photoshop, as the name suggests, developed out of a digital photography toolkit: a way to improve and digitally alter photos. That it doubles as a superb pure-graphics package is an added bonus. In photography, filters are placed over camera lenses to alter how a picture looks, once taken, from adding burnt umber to skies to adding a soft-focus sheen

to a portrait shoot. Photoshop filters do much the same thing but with a much greater variety of filters and the capability of applying these filters to everything from photographs to illustrations long after they have been imported or drawn. Photoshop comes with some filters built in already. If you find them useful, or want to pursue a particular effect they can be helpful. For further filters investigate on the web where there are thousands of freeware and commercial filters available – but a great many of them may not be useful to you at all.

## Photoshop filters

For manga, the native filters in Photoshop are more than enough for most users to choose from. Some do little more than make your drawings look weird; others, when applied to the right picture, can create amazing effects you could never produce on your own. Have fun experimenting and combining multiple filters.

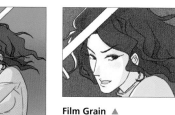

**Original picture** ▲

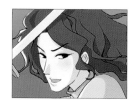

**Film Grain** ▲

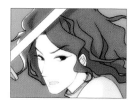

**Diffused Light** ▲

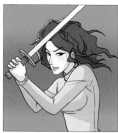

**Accented Edges** ▲

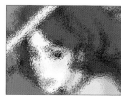

**Ocean Ripples** ▲

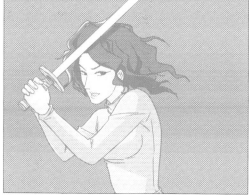

**Halftone Pattern** ▲

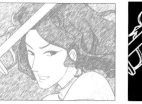

**Graphic Pen** ▲

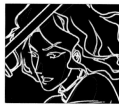

**Glowing Edges** ▲

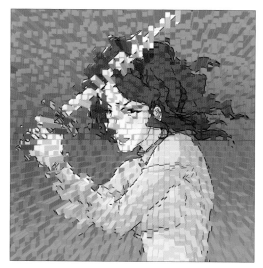

**Extrude** ▲

## Practice exercise: Using the Liquify filter

The Liquify filter is quite similar to the Smudge Tool, but the advantage of the Liquify filter is that it is far more accurate and can transform your images without losing any sharpness or detail. Here, the expression of the sad girl in this image can be transformed by the magic of the Liquify filter into a happy face.

**Tip:** Liquify is most useful when applied to black and white line work, but it can also be used on finished colour pieces and photographs. There may be more visible blur and distortion in these instances, so it is best to apply your changes before colouring.

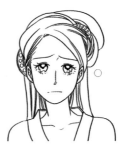

**1** Start with an image of a sad girl. Go to Filter > Liquify and a new, separate window will pop up, allowing you to apply the filter manually.

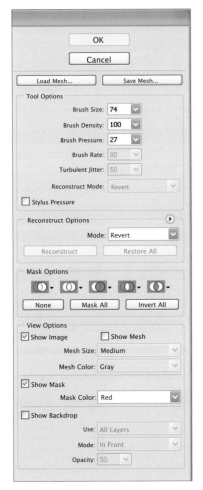

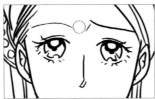

**2** Using the finger tool in the top left corner, choose a large brush size. Click to touch the left eyebrow of the girl, and you will see the lines 'pushed away' by the cursor. Keep pushing until you are happy. Use the reconstruction tool, second at the top left, to undo any mistakes.

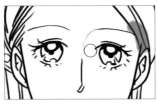

**3** Move to the right eyebrow. There is hair at the end of the line that should remain untouched. To protect it, press F to activate the Freeze Mask tool. Carefully paint the area you don't want to Liquify: this will turn red. Now you can safely change the right eyebrow.

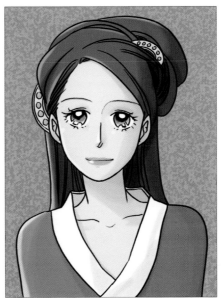

**4** Using the same mixture of tools as before, lift the corners of the mouth upwards to make the sad girl smile, and then click OK. You will be left with your amended image in the standard Photoshop window.

**Tip:** The act of Liquifying a line tends to thin it, so be prepared for subsequent touch-up work on thick-lined images. Go slowly and gently with fragile line work so that the lines remain uncompressed.

**The Liquify toolbar** ▲
The main elements to concern yourself with are the Brush Size and Brush Density drop-down menus, and the toolbar along the left-hand side of the Liquify window.

# Inked background project

For most of us, designing and drawing original manga characters is difficult enough. Drawing detailed backgrounds in perspective can be a real headache. But don't worry: thanks to Photoshop and digital inking, there is an easy way to produce backgrounds as perfect as those from professional manga artists. As long as you have a suitable photo for the background you want to draw into your panel, all you need is time and a little patience. You learned how to ink digitally earlier in the chapter. This project applies those same skills to ink directly over a photo. You cannot always rely on tracing photos for backgrounds, of course, especially for fantasy stories, but tracing and inking will give you a good grounding in perspective, line weight and appropriate levels of detail.

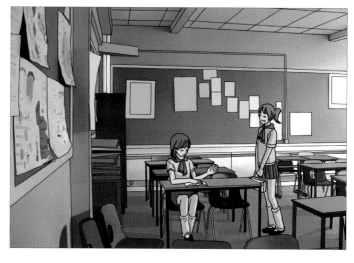

**Photographic colour/Digital line art fusion** ▲
The image above shows another time- and labour-saving shortcut. Once the line art has been finished, a blurring filter is passed over the photograph and the colours are tweaked in line with the rest of the manga, then the layers are flattened. This saves time that would have been spent colouring the background, allowing the artist to spend that time on the characters instead. Note how the posters at the back have been changed to white to make the image more coherent.

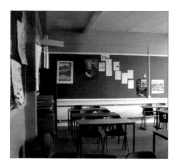

1 If you took your reference photo with a digital camera, then just open it in Photoshop. If you took it with a traditional camera, you will need to develop the photo first and scan it in. The photo above is of a typical classroom, and will form the reference for this project. Create a new, RGB Photoshop document of at least 300 dpi and drag the classroom photo into it. If the photo appears small on the new canvas, scale it up using Transform.

**Tip:** Creating your backgrounds on a separate document, rather than tracing them directly into your manga pages, allows you to reuse them in the future.

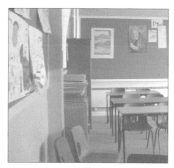

2 Create a new 'Normal' layer above the photo. Fill it with white using the Paint Bucket Tool and turn the Layer Fill Opacity setting to 50%. This lightens the photo making it easier to pick out details and see existing lines when inking.

3 Create another new 'Normal' layer on top of the other two and call it 'Line art'. This is where the inking takes place. Pick the Pencil Tool and set the foreground colour to black.

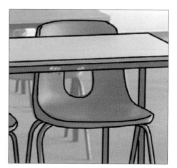

4 Start inking by tracing the edges of objects. To draw straight lines, first ensure the 'Shape Dynamic' option is turned off in the Brushes Palette. Then, when drawing the line, hold down [Shift], click the start point, then click the end point. A line will be drawn between the two points. Curved lines can either be drawn freehand, or by the method above, clicking between points that are very close together. Use the Eraser Tool to clean up mistakes.

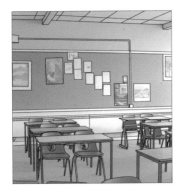

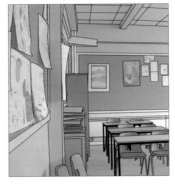

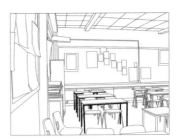

**5** Ink all the main edges. Be patient, and take your time with the details. If parts of the picture remain obscure, increase the layer fill opacity percentage on the white layer to throw the darker lines into greater relief.

**6** After you have traced all of the main edges, fill in any areas of solid black on the 'Line art' layer using the Paint Bucket Tool. Use the original photo to guide your placement of these shadowed areas.

**7** When finished, delete the two layers beneath the 'Line art' layer. The image is now ready for colouring, combining with your characters, and integration into a panel or page.

> **Tip:** It's always a good idea to bear copyright in mind when tracing from photographs. Ideally, you will have taken the photos you use for reference yourself, but if this isn't practical, then do your best to disguise the origins of your chosen image, either by combining elements of two or more different pictures, or adding in elements from your imagination. Furthermore, be sure to colour such digitally inked photos yourself, so that the final product is, technically at least, all your own work. Lightboxing, 'swiping' or digital plagiarism is a touchy issue in the manga and comics industries.

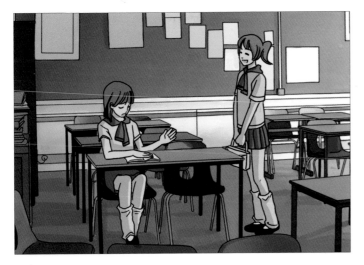

**8** Here is a completed version of the image. Simple, cel-shaded characters work surprisingly well in photo-realistic contexts. Remember, too, that with judicious cropping and by changing character poses, you will be able to use this one background across many different panels.

## Outside the classroom

### Into the wild ▶
While the natural world provides fewer straight edges and flat surfaces than the classroom scene, what it lacks in easily inked lines it makes up for in endless variety and intriguing organic shapes. The principles behind inking the classroom photo are just as applicable here, but when inking trees and foliage, you may wish to ink just an abstract outline, filling in detail and shading at the colour stage.

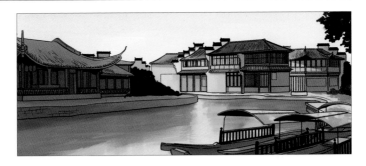

# Robot in space project

This project brings together a wide range of the toning techniques you have previously studied, showing how hard-edged and soft-edged brushes can be used to create different textures and patterns of shading, and how an image can be toned using a very limited palette of greys. It also shows how the judicious use of filters (in this case, the 'Add Noise' feature) can spruce up your artwork with simple textures, saving time while also increasing the rewarding complexity of your image. Note, too, the restricted palette used for the flat colours: the first stage of the robot uses only four or five shades of grey. The addition of highlights and shadows increases this, but the initially limited palette holds the image together. Although the example here features the blunt, hard lines of a giant robot, the shading techniques are just as applicable to more fleshy subjects, although their skins will, of course, be far less reflective.

**Halftone robot in space** ▶
The final image blends together a number of techniques to produce a professional result. Flat greys, metallic highlights and filter-applied textures are all unified by transferring them into halftone patterns.

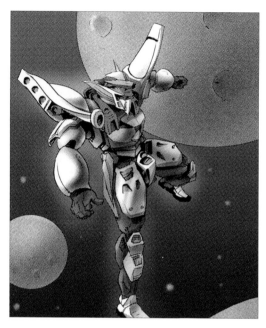

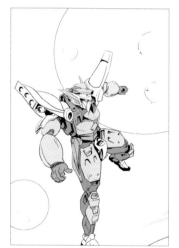

1 Open the line art: here, a giant robot with planets and stars in the background. Separate the line art from the white background as before. Using grey tones, add flat colour on a new 'Flats' layer. If you have difficulty selecting areas with the Magic Wand Tool, use the Pencil Tool to apply greys.

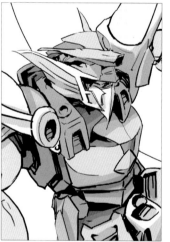

2 Create a new 'Multiply' layer and call it 'Shading'. Select areas on 'Flats' using the Magic Wand Tool, then brush shading on to the 'Shading' layer. Overpaint your first pass with darker shadows. When finished, duplicate 'Flats' and merge it with 'Shading'. Turn off the original layer.

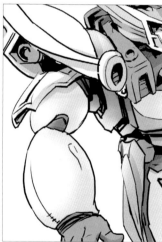

3 To apply metallic light-reflective effects to curved areas, select the Dodge Tool and set Range to 'Midtones' and Exposure to 10%. Choose a soft brush tip and gradually brighten up any areas facing the light. Here, our light source is positioned at the top left of the image.

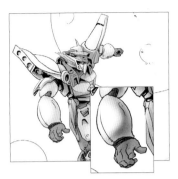

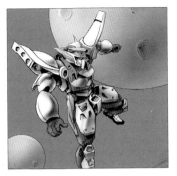

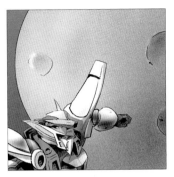

4 On the same layer, switch to the Burn Tool. Set Range to 'Midtones' and Exposure to 8%. Use the tool to create shadows on the areas where little light is being cast. Remember, metal not only reflects the light from the main light source, it will also reflect light bouncing off surfaces nearby. In the close-up example, above, you can see how the arm reflects a little of the light bouncing off the main robot body. If the shiny metallic effect is not strong enough, use Image > Adjustments > Brightness/Contrast to up the distinction between light and dark.

5 Underneath the 'Flats' layer, make a new 'Background' layer. Use the Paint Bucket Tool to fill in the flat colours. Select the planets and use the Dodge and Burn tools to apply light and shade to the spheres, as well as creating details, such as the shadowed craters, using Burn to pick out highlighted rims.

**Tip:** Reserve your strongest highlights and shadows for foreground elements, such as the robot shown here. Background elements should never stray too far from neutral mid-tones.

6 Select the planets and add a new layer, set to 'Soft Light'. Fill the selections on this new layer with a dark grey, then go to Filter > Noise > Add Noise. Give the amount a high value and make the Distribution 'Uniform'. Click OK. The texture of the planet is now more convincing. Merge this layer with 'Background'. Use the Magic Wand to select the space backdrop, and apply a gradation with the Gradient Tool. As the light source strikes your robot from the top left, it makes sense to have your gradient lighter towards the top left of the image as well.

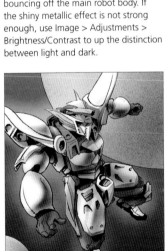

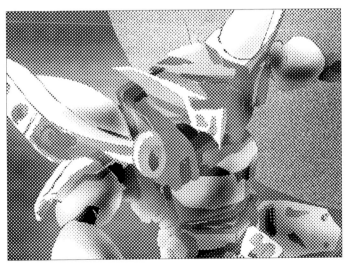

7 On top of the merged 'Background' layer, create a new layer to add some atmosphere. Choose a soft brush with Opacity and Flow set to 20. Paint a white light around the robot to separate it from the background. Using a variety of brush sizes and opacities, draw some stars in the infinite night.

8 For printing, you need to convert greyscale into black dots. Merge the tone layers into a single layer. Create a new file with the same resolution and size as this image and drag the tone layer into the new file. Ensure it fits. Go to Image > Mode > Bitmap and change this image to a bitmap file, choosing the Halftoning options as before. Next, use Image > Mode > Grayscale to change it back to greyscale. Drag the layer back to your original file and remerge it with the line art.

# Fight scene project

Fight scenes form the backbone of many manga adventures. Though the imagery itself is often strong enough to 'sell' the furious interchange of blows, you'll find that the addition of powerful sound effects ups the ante of your combats, making them weightier and more impressive.

To the right is a typical impact, with one fighter punched hard enough to throw him out of the panel. Without SFX, the action is readable enough, but their addition gives focus to the punch's force, punctuating the action for the reader. This project shows how to incorporate SFX into an image.

**Brutal beatdown** ▷
The final image shows, with the SFX, the exact point where the puncher's fist connects with his opponent's face, as well as indicating the magnitude of the blow by the size of the typeface.

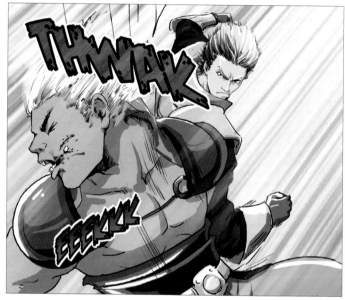

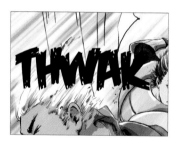

**1** First, select the Text tool, and choose a suitably chunky font in a large, even bolded, typeface. Type in your chosen SFX word for the sound of a connecting punch. Here, we've used 'THWAK', but 'WUNNCH', 'THUDD' or any other word you believe captures the spirit of the action are equally applicable.

**Tip:** The first font you choose will not always be the best for your chosen sound effect, so keep the Character Palette open as you work, and try a few alternatives before you settle on one. You may want to print out a selection of your favourite SFX fonts for speedy reference.

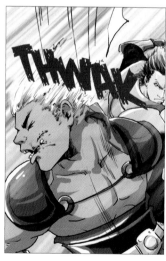

**2** Using [Ctrl]+T to Transform the text, angle your SFX to the direction of the impact. Rasterize the text, then use the Magic Wand to select it. Colour your selection with an appropriate colour or gradient. Don't worry too much about the colour at this stage – you can easily change it later.

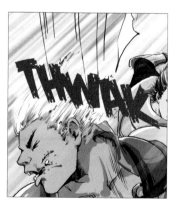

**3** To integrate the SFX with the background action more, you can add some speedlines. With the text still selected, duplicate your SFX layer. On this new layer, go to Filter > Noise > Add Noise and set the noise amount to a high value. Next, go to Filter > Blur > Motion Blur. Set the angle so that it matches the angle of the speedlines in the background, and choose a medium blur radius. Change the layer blend mode of the duplicate layer to 'Linear Light'. It will blend with your red layer.

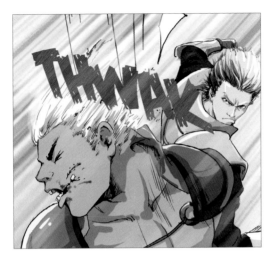

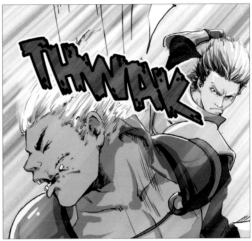

4 Merge the duplicated layer with the original one. You can now adjust the colour further by using Image > Adjustments > Hue/Saturation. In order to make the speedlines on the SFX more visible, you can use the Brightness/Contrast settings. If you still feel that your sound effect needs further personalization, you can make it more individual and interesting by attacking it with the Burn or Dodge tools, lightening and darkening various areas.

5 Your SFX should still be selected. At this point, you can add a border around your selection. First, go to Select > Modify > Border, setting the value at around 4 or 6, to fill in the selected area with the colour of your choice. Use standard black. Then, with the border selection still on, go to Select > Modify > Expand and put in a value of 8 or so (for this image). Add a new layer underneath the SFX layer and fill the selection with white. Merge this layer with the SFX layer.

6 We have concentrated solely on the SFX point of impact so far, but you can also increase the drama by including a sound effect from the victim. Grunts upon impact may be shown in speech balloons, as SFX, or even as SFX within speech balloons. Typical shouts include 'UNFF!', 'ARRGH!', 'ERGGH!' and so on. This is accomplished in the same way as the punch, but in a smaller font, and with a dimmer colour. This is because the 'THWAK' forms the focus of the panel, with the 'EEEKKK' the secondary and less important element. The image at right shows what happens when you reverse this: the screaming fighter looks like he is hamming up the result of the impact.

**Tip:** Sound effects, like dialogue, should guide the reader's eye down the page, from top left to bottom right. Remember that size is a great indicator to a reader of importance, as well as amplitude: while an earthquake and an alarm clock may not emit the same decibels, the latter might seem just as loud to a light sleeper.

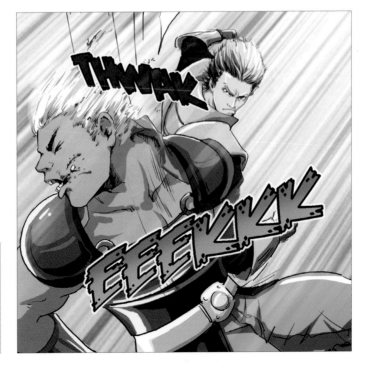

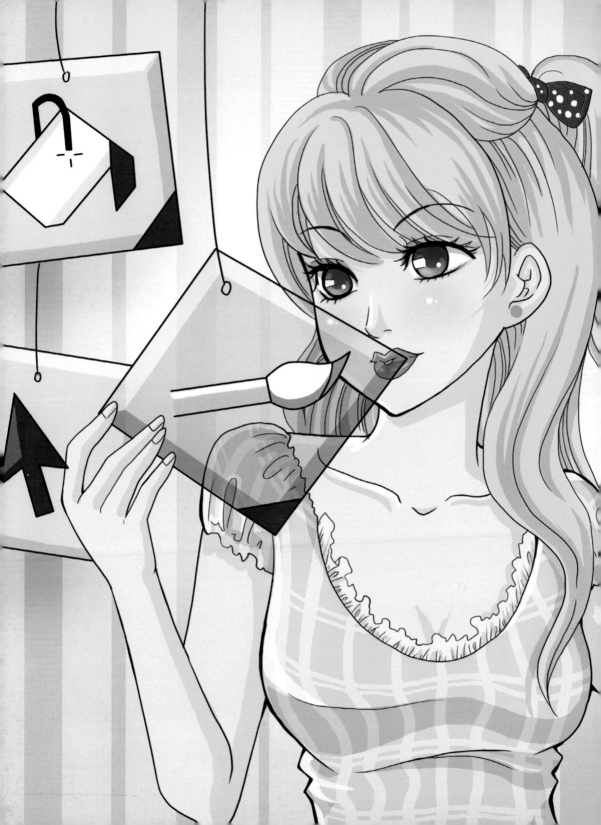

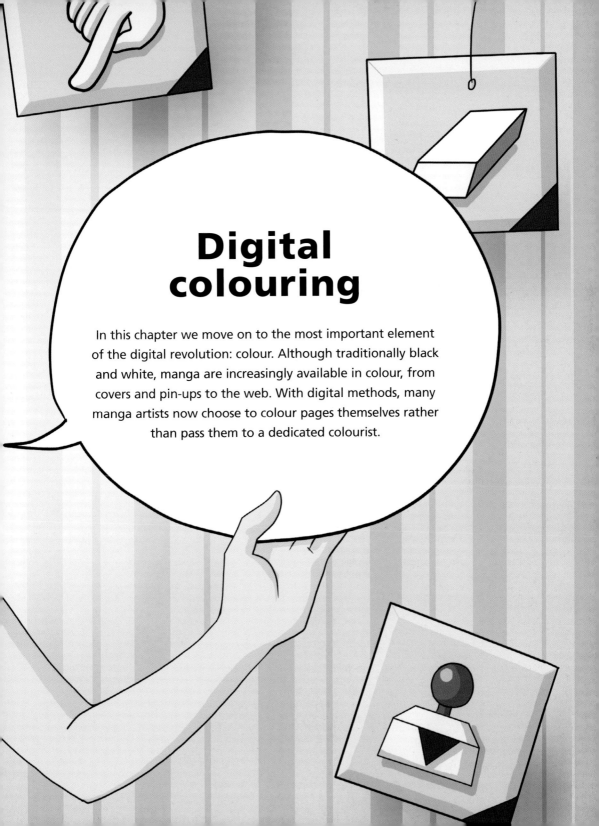

# Digital colouring

In this chapter we move on to the most important element of the digital revolution: colour. Although traditionally black and white, manga are increasingly available in colour, from covers and pin-ups to the web. With digital methods, many manga artists now choose to colour pages themselves rather than pass them to a dedicated colourist.

# Colouring basics

The basic Photoshop tools used to apply grey tones and shading in the previous chapter are much the same tools you will use to colour your illustrations. However, using colour means that, along with a palette running into millions of possible colours, you will need to explore the more advanced settings of each of these tools in order to get the best out of them. Knowing the basics of light and shade from your grey toning exercises will stand you in good stead.

## Settings

As we have already seen the Hardness, Opacity and Flow settings of the Brush and Eraser tools can be altered in the Options Bar. These settings become stylistically important when applying colour.

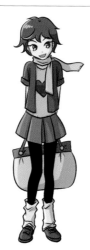

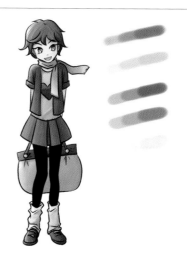

**Hard edge** ▶
A cel-shaded, animation look can be achieved with layered flat colours, a hard-edged brush and 100% Opacity.

**Soft edge** ▶
A more natural look can be created by blending soft-edged brushstrokes together with colours at 50% Opacity.

## Adjusting colours the easy way

Whether you are first creating colour schemes for your characters and wish to amend them before you roll out a palette across an extended sequence, or you want to tweak your final pages after they have been coloured, you may find some useful tools in the Image > Adjustments menu. The Levels tool has already proved useful for controlling light and dark while inking, but three further options – Color Balance, Brightness/Contrast and Hue/Saturation – should be explored.

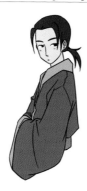

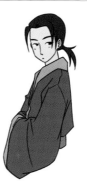

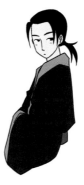

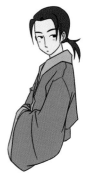

**Original** ▲
Apply Adjustments on a layer separate to (beneath) your line art. If you have enough RAM, use an Adjustment Layer instead, which allows you to re-alter the changes indefinitely.

**Color Balance** ▲
This makes changes within the highlights, midtones or shadows. Its sliders represent the six colour polarities. Use the Color Balance to adjust the whole atmosphere of a piece.

**Brightness/ Contrast** ▲
One slider controls brightness, the other contrast. Exaggerate extremes to punch up 'flat' colour on a piece. Brighten dull shades or dampen startling ones.

**Hue/Saturation** ▲
Hue is used to change the colour of objects, such as this robe. Saturation makes the colour more intense or muter. Brightness works in much the same way as in Brightness/Contrast.

# Colour modes

RGB and CMYK are the colour modes that will be used most often when digitally colouring. RGB is the standard used in televisions and computer monitors. It stands for red, green and blue, the primary colours that can be blended together to create every visible colour. White is the combination of these colours; black, their absence.

CMYK is the standard of print media. It stands for cyan, magenta, yellow and black, the secondary colours on the colour wheel. Printing presses use differing percentages of the three colours, plus black, to produce a wide colour spectrum. In colour theory, the combination of cyan, magenta and yellow produces black; however, on real presses this tends to result in brown, so black is added as a fourth 'colour'. The vast majority of commercially printed books and magazines are produced on CMYK presses. If you want to release your manga on the web, it is better to use RGB. If you want to print your colour manga professionally in books and magazines, you'll need CMYK.

◀ **The colour wheels**
The primary colours of red, green and blue blend together to produce the whole spectrum of visible colours. The secondary colours produced by a 50/50 blending of two of the primaries are cyan, magenta and yellow. Appropriately, when these colours are used as the starting point, the result of a 50/50 intersection between the CMY colours are the RGB hues, as shown in the second diagram. The RGB spectrum is one of addition, blending to white, the CMY spectrum one of subtraction, blending to black.

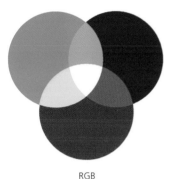

RGB

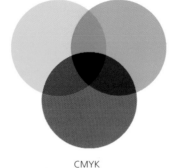

CMYK

## RGB versus CMYK

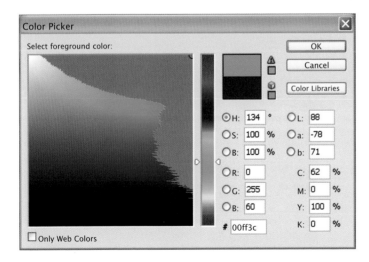

#### Color Picker ▲
If you are having your manga printed, it is essential to work with colours that definitely exist in the CYMK mode. When the Color Picker is open, press [Ctrl]+[Shift]+Y. This changes the colours that are not available in CMYK mode to grey, while the ones that are printable appear as usual. Pick your colours from the 'safe' area. Use the same command to return the Color Picker to normal.

If creating artwork for print, you may think it best to work in CMYK mode to save the trouble of converting, and ensure that you only use the colours on screen that will show up in print. However, CMYK files take up 25% more space on your hard drive than their RGB equivalents, and many Photoshop filters will only work in RGB mode. For those with lower-specification computers, it is best to work in RGB and convert to CMYK just before sending the file to the printer. Don't flip between RGB and CMYK mode while working, as each switch loses a little clarity in the image. If you want to see your RGB image in CMYK without having to convert it, select View > Proof Colors.

As computer screens use RGB and printers use CMYK, the image on your monitor will not be exactly the same as the one printed on paper. Some RGB colours don't exist in CMYK, particularly the yellow/greens and bright reds. This isn't a problem when publishing online, but may cause changes when outputting to CMYK for paper publication.

# Colouring techniques

Colouring a manga page is more complicated than toning it, although the principles are much the same. For most, the experience and results of colouring are more satisfying. Using colour is more forgiving than grayscale on one level, as the more expansive palette allows you to use different hues that share similar luminosities – different shades of the same grey on a non-colour image. This spread shows how to set up a line art image for every colouring style.

## Practice exercise: Applying flat colours

Flat colours are the basic colours you add to your initial line art to divide areas from one another to make more advanced colouring easier and quicker down the line. Although it is not necessary to choose the same colours you will be using in your final image – many colourists use near-random, conflicting hues just to quickly subdivide characters from backgrounds and skintones from clothes, leaving colour decisions for later – it often helps to use colours close to those you will be using later, to get an idea of your page's colour composition. The most important function of the flat colour layer is that it allows you to easily select areas with the Magic Wand Tool without worrying about the line work. You can select individual areas (with 'Contiguous' checked) or all areas sharing the same colour (unchecked), which can shave hours off the time it would otherwise take to complete it.

**Tip:** If you are using non-bitmapped line art (art you have scanned in grayscale and altered with the Levels function), you need to be careful when selecting an area to expand your selection so that it goes fully underneath the lines. Otherwise, a white edge may be left between the lines and colour. In most cases, it should be enough to increase the tolerance on the Magic Wand Tool, but be aware of high-detail areas or tight spots on your illustration.

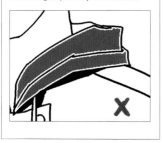

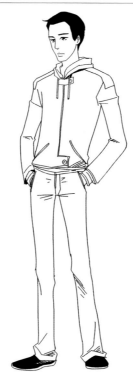

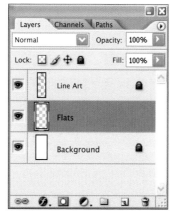

1 Open your line art and set it to RGB mode (Image > Mode > RGB). If you have separated your line art from the white background, create a new 'Normal' layer called 'Flats' between the background and line art layers. If the line art and white background are on the same layer, duplicate it, set the mode to 'Multiply', then create a new 'Normal' layer called 'Flats' in between the two identical layers.

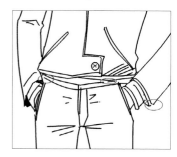

2 If your lines do not perfectly join up, create a new layer and use a 1-pixel black Pencil Tool to seal them. If you prefer 'gappy' line work, you can delete this layer after completing the flats.

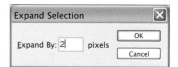

3 On the 'Flats' layer, use the Magic Wand Tool to highlight and select areas to colour. For non-bitmapped line work (some grey in the lines), select a Tolerance of 50. Check 'Contiguous' and 'Sample All Layers' and leave 'Anti-alias' unchecked. Press down [Shift] to select multiple areas, or [Alt] to unselect areas. Next, choose Select > Modify > Expand, set the value to 1 or 2 and click OK.

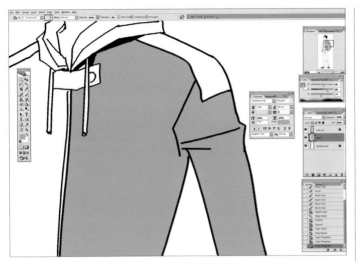

**4** On the 'Flats' layer, use the Paint Bucket Tool (with 'Anti-alias', 'Contiguous' and 'All Layers' unchecked) to block in the desired colour for the selected area. Alternatively, place the colour you want as the Background Color in the palette and press [Delete]. Use [Ctrl]+D to deselect the area.

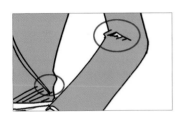

**5** Some parts of the image may be missed by the Magic Wand Tool and will not be coloured. Use the Pencil Tool to fill these areas. The Pencil Tool is used to ensure the colour has a sharp edge, for easier future selection. For the same reason, if you use the Eraser Tool, ensure the mode is set to 'Pencil'.

**6** Repeat the above steps to fill in all of the flat colours. If you created one, delete the layer you used to seal the black lines. If you wish to adjust the colours to make them more complementary to one another, use the Magic Wand Tool, with 'Contiguous' and 'Sample All Layers' unchecked, to select all areas of green on the 'Flats' layer, for example. Next, use Image > Adjustment > Hue/Saturation or Color Balance to adjust until you are happy.

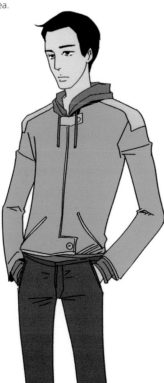

## Colouring styles

There are two main styles of colouring. The first is called 'Cel Shading', which is similar to the colour schemes seen in cartoons and anime, while the other is 'Soft Shading', which provides a more natural look with greater gradations between colours. Both modes begin with the flattening process.

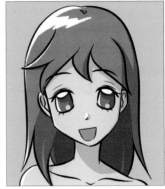

**Cel shading** ▲
Uses pure, unblended colours; sharp distinctions between bold highlights and strong shadows. While it requires no less skill, the limited palette can prove quicker to implement.

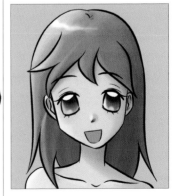

**Soft shading** ▲
A more natural, painterly style, blending a range of colours in each area, from light to dark, while paying greater attention to light reflection and the layering of shadows.

## Practice exercise: Cel shading (shadows)

Cel shading is the most basic and common way to colour manga. Drawn from animation cels, where budget and time constraints rewarded bold, hard-edged shadows, cel shading is now a popular style in its own right. In real life, the complexity of lighting means that objects rarely cast a lone, clear shadow, but manga can simplify and exaggerate colour, shadows and highlights just as it simplifies the characters themselves. This exercise shows you an easy method of adding cel-shaded shadows to your flats while leaving the original colours intact.

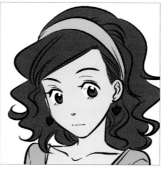

**1** First, lock your 'Flats' and 'Line Art' layers, and create a new layer, set to 'Multiply', on top of your 'Flats' layer. Call it 'Shading'. This is where you will apply your shades as grey tones.

**2** Use the Magic Wand on the 'Flats' layer to select the area you want to colour, with the Tolerance set to 0 and 'Contiguous' and 'Sample All Layers' unchecked. Here, the hair is selected. Now switch to the 'Shading' layer. Pick a grey shade from the Color Picker and select the Paint Brush. You can always adjust the grey with Color Balance at a later stage.

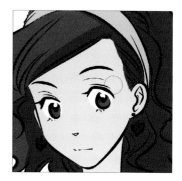

**3** Choose a hard-edged brush with Opacity and Flow both set to 100%. Select your light source (here, the top left again) and paint the areas not facing it with the grey. Remember to keep your light source consistent.

**4** Here is the image with the 'Flats' layer hidden. Emphasize the depth of your shadows with a darker grey, painted over the first. Turn the 'Flats' layer on and off periodically in order to check your progress. Use an Eraser Tool at 100% Flow and Opacity to correct any mistakes.

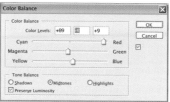

**5** Use the same method to add shadows to the other parts of the image. Once you have finished, you can use Color Balance to adjust the shading, or leave them as simple grey.

> **Tip:** If you have used a limited palette on your image, you will find that using the Magic Wand Tool with 'Contiguous' unchecked will select all like-coloured areas (here, the hair and the eyes). Use the Lasso Tool and the [Alt] key to deselect unwanted areas.

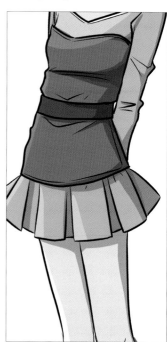

## Practice exercise: Cel shading (highlights)

Highlights are just as important as shadows when colouring in a cel shaded style, and they are created in much the same fashion as shadows – on a separate layer. This time, however, the highlights are painted in using brightened shades of the colour of the material in question. This exercise shows you how to get the most out of your highlights. As before, we start with our character's hair.

> **Tip:** Remember that not all materials reflect and refract light in the same way. Hair, eyes and metals are usually the most reflective elements of a character, with skin, leather and so on coming a near second. Fabrics and matt objects absorb light, so dresses, wool coats, jeans and the like should not have highlights applied to them as shinier textured elements.

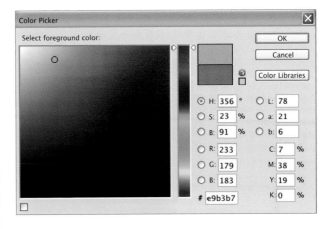

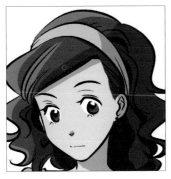

**2** Use the Magic Wand Tool to select the hair, then go to the 'Highlights' layer. Paint areas facing the light source with the colour selected in Step 1. Keep the light source consistent.

> **Tip:** Adding some soft-edged shading to your cel art is an easy way to humanize your characters and stop them looking too much like dolls.

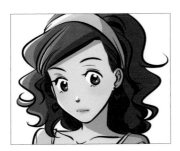

**1** Create a new 'Normal' layer called 'Highlights' between the 'Flats' and 'Shading' layers. Select the Brush Tool and double-click on the Color Picker to bring up the colour selection window. Use the Eyedropper Tool to sample the

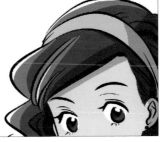

**3** When this is done, add an extra, white highlight on the shiniest areas. Keep this effect subtle, limiting it to a few areas, ensuring the shine is consistent with the type of object.

**5** For the final touches, create a new layer between the 'Flats' and 'Highlights' layers to add small but necessary details to the image. Set the mode to 'Normal'. To the left, colour is softly added to the cheeks and lips. Rather than a hard-edged brush, this stage uses a brush with Opacity set to roughly 20%. Choose a soft pink colour and gradually build up the peachy cheeks and lips of the girl.

hair colour from your image. A small circle indicates that colour on the colour spectrum. Move the sensor up and to the left a bit (above) to pick a colour lighter than the current shade of hair, but within the same colour family.

**4** Continue to add appropriate highlights to the other parts of the image. In this example, highlights have been applied to the headband, leg and sock, shoes and dress.

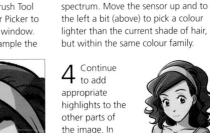

## Practice exercise: Soft shading

Soft shading produces a finished look that is closer to natural media than cel shading. It replicates the spirit, if not the exact materials, of a freehand painting, as opposed to the pixel-perfect, highlight-midtone-shadow images produced by the method outlined on the previous spread. Soft shading grants you the intricacy and layering of colour in a traditional painting alongside the accuracy, flexibility and, best of all, the multiple levels of Undo found in your graphics software. As the name suggests, soft shading is built up out of gentle brushstrokes, using multiple shades of the same colour and overpainting of areas in order to increase the depth of shadows or the brightness of highlights. As a result, it requires more skill and patience than cel shading. This exercise will teach you the basics of applying soft shading to an already flattened image, and the way to blend colours together.

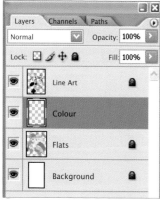

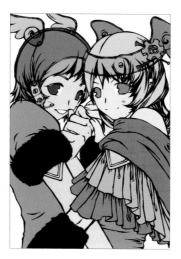

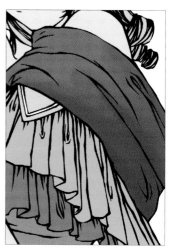

1 We begin with an already flattened image. Duplicate the 'Flats' layer and name it 'Colour'. Set its mode to 'Normal', making sure the 'Colour' layer is above the 'Flats' layer. Keep the 'Flats' layer, as it will make Magic Wand Tool selections easier if you later decide to reselect areas you have already soft-shaded ('flat' areas are simpler to select than those that mix a number of similar colours, especially if using soft brushes).

2 This time, we will start our shading with the shawl, as its folds make colouring interesting. At this point, the colours on the 'Colour' layer are still untouched, so it's fine to use the Magic Wand Tool to select the shawl directly on this layer. Leave 'Contiguous' and 'Sample All Layers' unchecked.

3 Choose a soft-edged brush and pick a colour a few shades darker than the flat shawl colour. Set Opacity and Flow to 40%. Increase the brush size with [Shift]+] ([Shift]+[ decreases the size) until you get a big brush (or right-click and drag the slider). Paint shadowed areas.

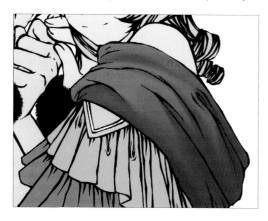

4 As with cel shading, the next step is to pick an even darker colour for the darkest areas of the shawl and paint these with a smaller brush. Having the Opacity and Flow at 40% allows you to build up colour gradually. Paint plenty of strokes in the places where the shadows are darkest. If you make a mistake, don't use the Eraser because this will reveal the layer underneath. Use the Paint Brush to paint over the mistake – or the Undo function, of course.

**Tip:** Remember again that fabric, skin and metal all reflect light in different ways, so you may find some elements of your image need less rendering than others. Conversely, the brightest, shiniest elements (for example, eyes and hair) may need additional layers of highlights to be added, or even the use of brushes at a higher Opacity and Flow.

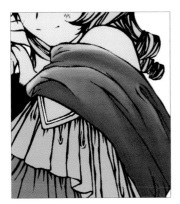

**Tip:** If you change your mind about a particular colour area, you can switch to the 'Flats' layer, use the Magic Wand Tool to select a whole section, then flip back to the 'Colours' layer, using the Hue/Saturation sliders to alter the colours to your satisfaction.

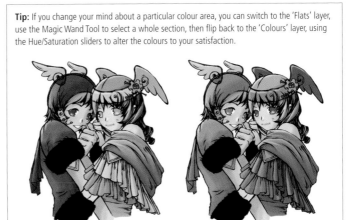

5 Now pick a colour a few shades lighter than the original shawl mid-tone, and paint those areas or folds facing the light source.

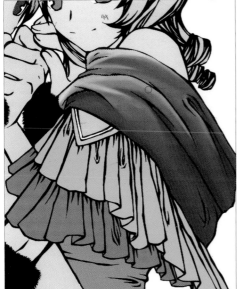

6 The lighter and darker colours of the shawl have now been implemented, but the transitions between them aren't very smooth, and some of the folds are lacking detail. To build up the transitions, you will need to select colours inbetween the existing ones and blend using a smaller brush. Many of the in-between colours may already exist in the image at the edges of your brushstrokes, so use the [Alt] button and Brush to grab them with the Eyedropper Tool. Patience is the key: you may need to paint certain areas over and over again to create a convincing effect.

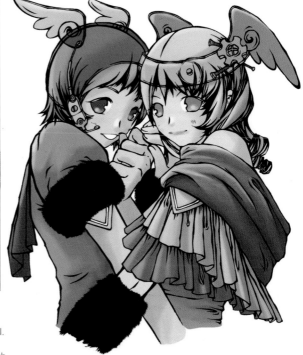

7 Use the same methods to colour the rest of the picture. Remember to zoom out periodically to check that you aren't over-working some smaller elements to the detriment of the whole: knowing when to stop colouring is often the hardest part of the soft-shading process.

# Colouring a page

The two methods you have learned to colour characters are flexible, and can even be intermingled within a panel or page. Colouring a full panel follows exactly the same steps, but the number of characters may be higher, and there will usually be background elements to think about at the same time. Colouring an entire page takes a few more steps, and requires a little more thought. The first thing you should consider is how to make your pages cohesive and coherent, rather than a rag-tag collection of disparate panels. Think about limited colour palettes and background colours, and how a single dominant colour on each page can influence atmosphere and mood, as well as indicate scene changes.

## Practice exercise: Mixing shading techniques

Using Photoshop allows you to be very flexible with the methods you use to colour each page, mixing and matching the techniques you know so that they fit the content, rather than being beholden to one style or another. The examples below are mostly cel shaded, with soft-shaded details on the characters and gradients to add depth and texture to the single-colour backdrops. This exercise allows you to put what you've learned into action.

**Tip:** The background of each panel sets the atmosphere for the page. Using similar tones across panels maintains integrity: though an out-of-place flash of a conflicting colour can create surprise.

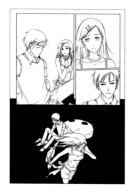

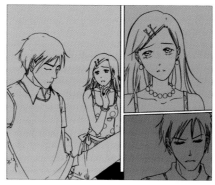

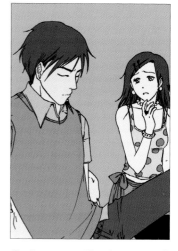

**1** Open your line art in Photoshop and clean the page. Separate the lines from the white background if they are not yet on an individual layer. Lock your 'Background' and 'Line Art' layers so that you won't mistakenly draw on them.

**2** Create a new layer between 'Background' and 'Line Art' called 'Panels'. Fill a background colour for each panel. By using a different colour for each one, you'll be able to use the Magic Wand Tool to select the whole panel later. The colours here represent natural daylight. Each panel is selected with the Polygonal Lasso Tool (use the Magic Wand Tool and [Alt] on 'Line Art' to delete overspill). Fill using the Paint Bucket Tool.

**3** Create a new 'Flats' layer on top of 'Panels'. Colour in the flats using the Paint Bucket and Pencil tools, as in previous exercises.

**4** On top of the 'Flats' layer, create a new 'Multiply' layer called 'Shadows'. Use a hard-edged brush at maximum Opacity to shade in areas of darkness using a grey colour. Return with a darker grey colour to areas of deeper shadow. These shadows use the cel shading method. Remember, if you want to get a clearer view of the shadows you are painting at any point, switch off the 'Flats' and 'Panels' layers to view the shadows against a white background.

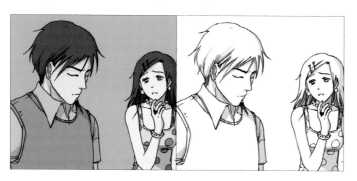

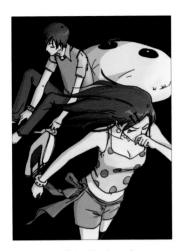

**6** Create a new layer on top named 'Detail'. Here, you will colour the elements you haven't added detail to

yet, such as the eyes, hair clips and rosiness in the cheeks. Be flexible in your Brush settings: you may wish to use a soft, low-Opacity brush for the cheeks, and a hard-edged brush for the hair clip. Pay attention to the reflections in the eyes.

**7** When you are happy with the page, duplicate the 'Flats' layer, and merge the copy with the 'Shadows',

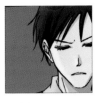

'Highlights' and 'Detail' layers, renaming the merged layer 'Colour'. If you want to make adjustments to any areas of colour, you can now select areas on the 'Flats' layer and make changes on the 'Colour' layer using the tools in Image > Adjustments.

**5** On top of the 'Shadows' layer, create a new 'Normal' layer called 'Highlights'. Here, the highlights are applied as soft shading. Use a soft-edged brush in a lighter version of the appropriate colour, with Opacity set to 40%, to paint over areas facing the light source. Overpaint several times to create the brightest highlights.

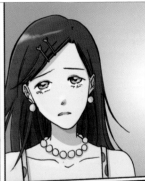

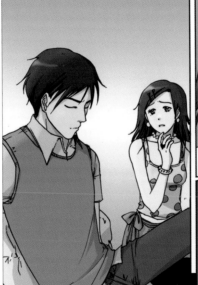

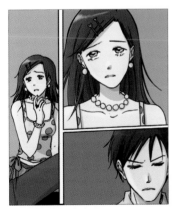

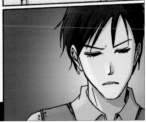

**8** If you want to adjust the colours or atmosphere of an entire panel, use the 'Panels' layer to select a panel with the Magic Wand, and adjust from there. As an example, the bottom-right panel above has been desaturated to make it more dramatic. The panel is selected in the 'Panels' layer; the adjustment are made on the 'Colour' layer using Hue/Saturation.

**9** You may want to add some gradients to the flat background colours in order to enrich them. Create a new 'Gradients' layer above the 'Panels' layer, and select the panel you want in 'Panels'. On the 'Gradients' layer, with the appropriate panel selected, choose the Gradient Tool. Set the foreground colour to the current background of the panel using the Eyedropper Tool, set the background colour to a dark shade of the same colour, select the kind of gradient you want to use and drag the Gradient Tool across the panel. The gradient will be created. The three panels above use Radial gradients.

**Tip:** If you decide that you want to add in fully rendered backgrounds or Photoshop-altered photographs after you have already coloured your page, remember that you can copy them in on a new layer underneath the colours of your characters. You can even place them beneath a semi-transparent Gradient layer if you still wish to communicate the atmosphere of each panel in this way. A page isn't finished until you are satisfied with it, so experiment with every new technique you learn to develop your style.

# Night image project

Over the previous few pages, you have learned how to colour an image in two different styles, and how to compose and coordinate panels in order to create a pleasing and atmospheric page. With these techniques, you should be able to cope with any of the colouring projects you may encounter in your manga career.

However, one of the more difficult scenes for a colourist who is just starting out is one set at night. Everything changes colour in the darkness, not only becoming paler, bluer and more desaturated, but also being influenced and transformed in shade by the light sources acting upon them. Moonlight transmutes reds to purples, fades flesh to bone-white and strips warmth away. Neon tones its subjects in sickly greens, pinks and yellows. Streetlights cast unnatural 'fires' across those that walk beneath them. In short, at night everything you know about colour changes. This project will give you an excellent grounding in working by moonlight, with an image of a partygoer stepping out for some air.

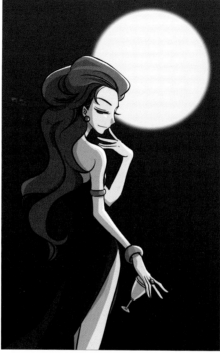

◀ **Met by moonlight**
This image shows a very simple technique for creating nocturnal images: a carefully chosen, blue-tinged palette to begin with, followed by shading as usual and, as a final step, a wash of colour over the whole image to further transmute the shades. Try using the same wash technique with yellows or reds to add atmosphere to daytime scenes. Where this image is concerned, as a final step, you may wish to develop the background with a gradient effect (on the 'Blue' layer) and tighten the palette yet further by compressing the colour layers and using the tools in Image > Adjustment.

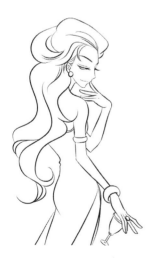

1 First, open your 'Line Art' layer and prepare it for colouring by cleaning up the lines and separating the line work from the white background.

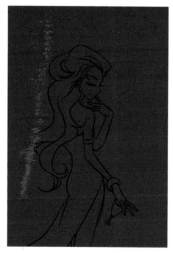

2 Create a new layer named 'Blue' beneath the 'Line Art' layer, and fill it with a dark blue colour. This will form the background for your night scene.

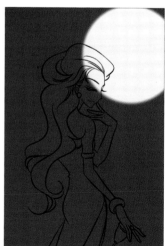

3 Create another layer on top of the 'Blue' layer and name it 'Moon'. Pick a large, soft round brush, and use a pale yellow to draw the moon.

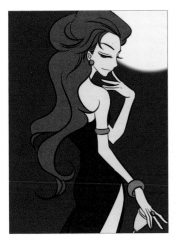

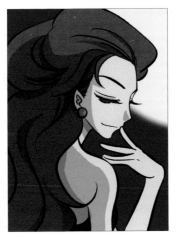

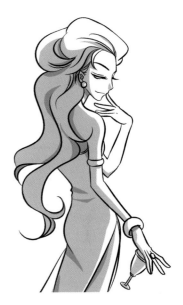

4 Fill in the flat colours of the character on another new layer, above 'Moon', using the techniques you have already learned.

5 On a new 'Multiply' layer named 'Shadows', draw shading with a purple-grey colour. Turn off the other layers to get a better view (right).

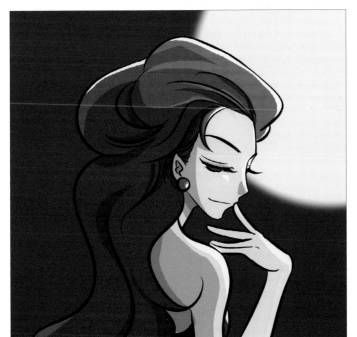

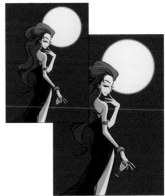

6 Create a new 'Normal' layer called 'Pale Highlights' and paint some of the lighter areas facing the moonlight. On the extreme edges facing the moon, add some of the pale yellow colour to the hair, skin and dress, reflecting some of the full moon's bright light back to the source.

7 Create a new layer on top of the other colour layers, naming it 'Blueish'. Set this layer's mode to 'Color'. Now go to the 'Flats' layer, and select the entire character with the Magic Wand Tool, using the [Shift] key to select multiple areas. When the whole character is selected, go back to 'Blueish' and fill your selection with the blue from your background. The character's colour changes to blue. Don't panic: change the Layer Fill Opacity to about 40% (on the Layers Palette) and your character's colours will show through.

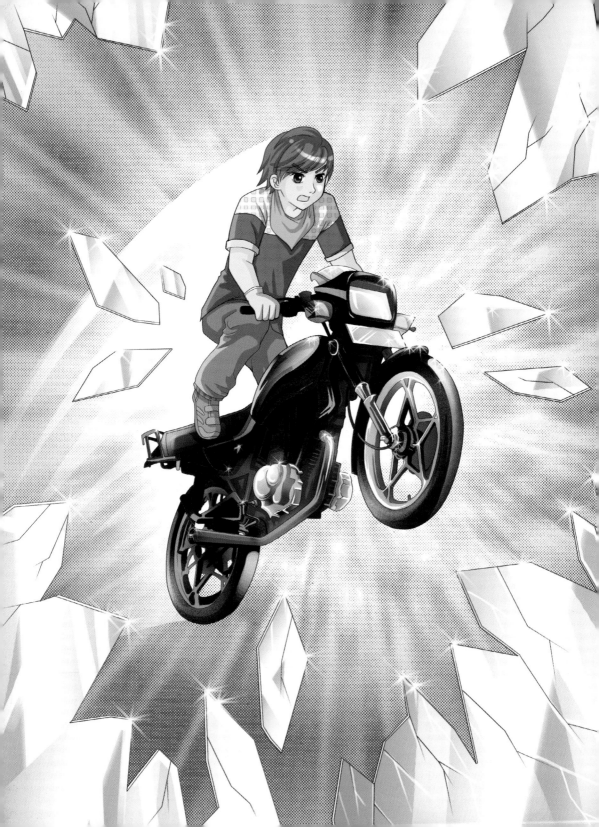

# Improvements and beyond

Photoshop is an incredibly versatile graphics package, filled with possibilities for you and your manga creations. The more you create or colour your manga digitally, the more useful you will find Photoshop and the greater the number of options, techniques and effects you will discover. This chapter will introduce you to a selection of them.

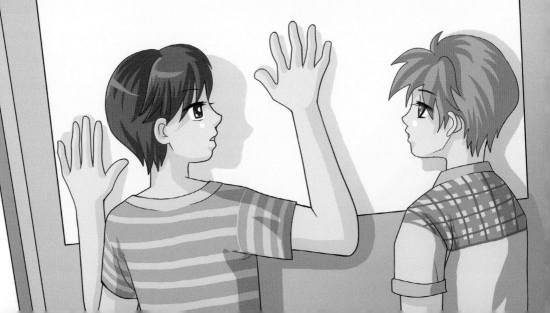

# Customizing colour palettes

Sometimes, choosing colour schemes can be exceptionally difficult: it can be easy to stay with what you know and are comfortable with, and hard to stray out of the 'blue for sky, green for grass' mindset. That's why 'borrowing' the colour palettes of images that creatively inspire you can be a useful shortcut. The process is simple: find an image the colours of which you admire and think are appropriate for your own uncoloured piece, import the picture into Photoshop, and convert the image into a custom colour palette, which you can then use to digitally paint your own creation. This exercise will show you how to convert a scanned or downloaded picture into just such a customized palette.

### Practice exercise: Converting an image to your Color Palette

1 First, find a colour image that you like from a book, photograph, manga or the Internet. Scan it in or save it to your computer, and open the image in Photoshop.

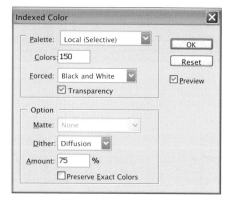

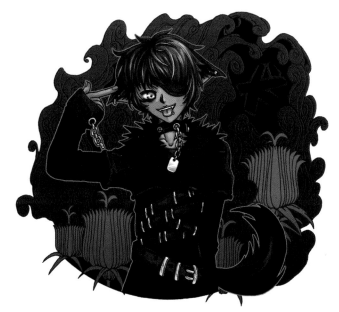

2 Now, convert the image to Indexed Color mode by going to Image > Mode > Indexed Color. Indexed Color specifies a limited, 'indexed' palette for your file, rather than the millions of colours that are available to you in RGB or CMYK modes. Go to 'Color' and enter the number of colours that you want to extract from the image. A good number is in the range from 150 to 250: you want enough colours to be able to accurately capture any blends or gradients, but not so many that any shades you want specifically get lost among thousands.

3 To view the colour palette you've created based on this image, go to Image > Mode > Color Table. If you want to add more colours to the palette, click the last empty slot and pick the colour up using the Eyedropper Tool in this options window. Click 'Save' to save the colour palette as a *.act file and OK to exit. Remember where you save the file so that you can load the palette later.

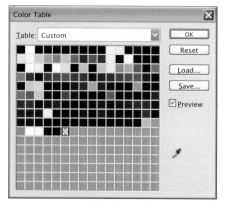

**Tip:** Choose a memorable filename for the palette, not just 'Palette 1'. Name it after the colour range it contains ('Deep Reds') or the image you pulled the palette from.

**Tip:** The tighter and more limited your colour palette (i.e., the fewer colours you choose to import), the more useful it will prove to you, as you can create shades and highlights yourself from imported median tones. For the same reason, you will get better results from illustrations with limited palettes than from more naturalistic photographs.

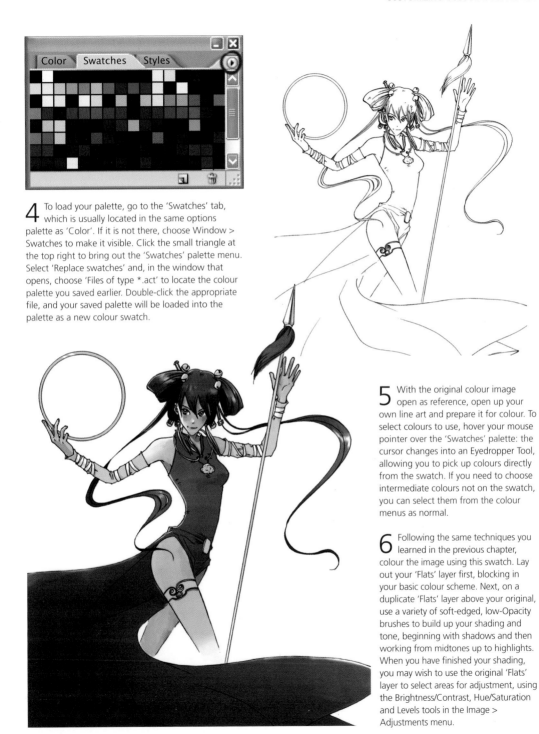

4 To load your palette, go to the 'Swatches' tab, which is usually located in the same options palette as 'Color'. If it is not there, choose Window > Swatches to make it visible. Click the small triangle at the top right to bring out the 'Swatches' palette menu. Select 'Replace swatches' and, in the window that opens, choose 'Files of type *.act' to locate the colour palette you saved earlier. Double-click the appropriate file, and your saved palette will be loaded into the palette as a new colour swatch.

5 With the original colour image open as reference, open up your own line art and prepare it for colour. To select colours to use, hover your mouse pointer over the 'Swatches' palette: the cursor changes into an Eyedropper Tool, allowing you to pick up colours directly from the swatch. If you need to choose intermediate colours not on the swatch, you can select them from the colour menus as normal.

6 Following the same techniques you learned in the previous chapter, colour the image using this swatch. Lay out your 'Flats' layer first, blocking in your basic colour scheme. Next, on a duplicate 'Flats' layer above your original, use a variety of soft-edged, low-Opacity brushes to build up your shading and tone, beginning with shadows and then working from midtones up to highlights. When you have finished your shading, you may wish to use the original 'Flats' layer to select areas for adjustment, using the Brightness/Contrast, Hue/Saturation and Levels tools in the Image > Adjustments menu.

# Creating motion

In previous chapters, you have learned how to represent extremes of movement using black and white speedlines and focus lines. However, these options can often cause a colour page to look cramped or over-rendered by the sheer amount of line work, limiting their efficiency at replicating speed. While the simplest option is to 'knock back' these black lines

to a lighter colour, there are a number of more advanced techniques using blurs, smudging and changes of focus that create more cinematic effects in glorious colour. The following pages will walk you through some of the options available, many of which will suit some styles of panel or forms of motion better than others.

## Practice exercise: Motion in colour 1

This method is the equivalent of drawing black and white speedlines. Rather than just drawing different kinds of lines, we can create a similar effect, better suited to colour, using the Motion Blur filter and the Smudge Tool.

**1** Open a colour image in Photoshop. Merge your line art and character colour (leave the background). Save as a new .psd file. Duplicate the character layer, place it behind the original and set its mode to 'Normal'.

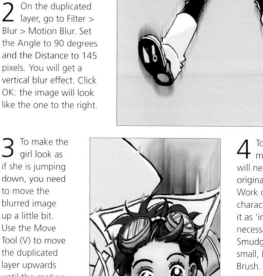

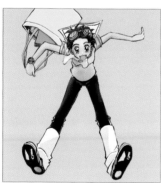

**2** On the duplicated layer, go to Filter > Blur > Motion Blur. Set the Angle to 90 degrees and the Distance to 145 pixels. You will get a vertical blur effect. Click OK: the image will look like the one to the right.

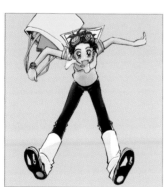

**3** To make the girl look as if she is jumping down, you need to move the blurred image up a little bit. Use the Move Tool (V) to move the duplicated layer upwards until the motion effect comes from the upper side of the character only.

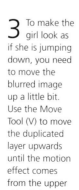

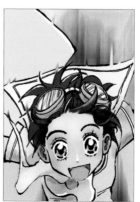

**4** To further sell the motion effect, you will need to alter the original character work. Work on the original character layer (duplicate it as 'insurance' if necessary). Select the Smudge Tool, with a small, high-strength Brush. Smudge the upper edges of the character in the direction of movement. Subtlety is key here: a few smudges are enough.

## Practice exercise: Motion in colour 2

This example introduces you to the colour equivalent of focus lines, perfect for images containing one- or two-point perspectives. This is a one-point perspective shot of a character running towards the reader. The background will blur in a radial point around him, focusing the reader's attention.

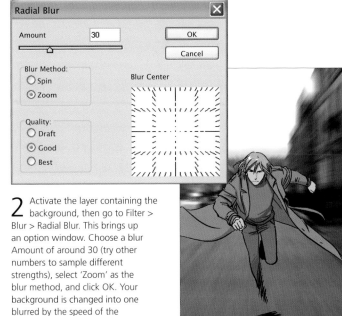

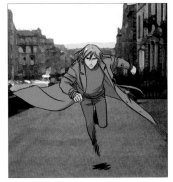

1 Open the colour image in Photoshop. Keep the background and character on separate layers.

2 Activate the layer containing the background, then go to Filter > Blur > Radial Blur. This brings up an option window. Choose a blur Amount of around 30 (try other numbers to sample different strengths), select 'Zoom' as the blur method, and click OK. Your background is changed into one blurred by the speed of the focal character.

3 Now you need to add the same speed effect on the character's layer. However, you do not want the whole character to be blurred, as this will obscure the face and your line work and detract from the focal point of the image. To avoid this, you need to enter the Quick Mask mode to 'mask' the areas you don't want to apply the filter to. To do this, click the Quick Mask button below the Color Picker on the toolbox (or press Q). Use a black brush to paint over the areas you want to leave unaffected. The areas you paint over turn red, but don't worry, you are not applying paint to the image itself. If you make a mistake, use a white brush to correct it. Once you have finished painting over the relevant areas (in this case, those at the very centre of the image), click the small icon next to the 'Enter Quick Mask' icon, and everything but the areas painted in red will be converted into a selection.

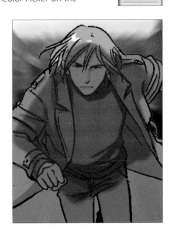

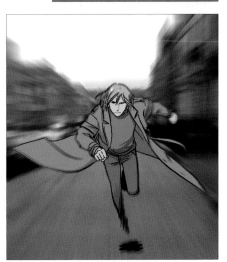

4 With the selection on, use the Radial Blur filter again, this time using a smaller blur amount. Use [Ctrl]+D to deselect the area around your character to see the result: a character in sharp focus while the background recedes at speed.

# Creating a metallic look

In black and white manga, the texture of metal is always expressed through a mixture of toned shades and strong, contrasting highlights. While it usually looks convincing on a printed page, such approximations are the best you can get in black and white. In digital colour, however, you have far greater opportunity for photo-realism, or at least for a higher-quality approach to texturization. While there are laborious processes that are highly rewarding, it is easy to create a realistic metal effect by applying filters to your coloured line work. The examples below will show you how.

## Practice exercise: Metal armour

There are many ways to create metallic effects: from sampling photographic metallic textures and blending them on a 'Multiply' layer with coloured artwork, to painstakingly building up layers of shade and reflection piece by piece using a soft-edged brush, often using photo-reference. This method is much more straightforward, offering an easily created metallic texture with the individuality of hand-applied reflections and light 'blooms' on the metalwork. Use of textures in this way ensures that the objects on your page don't just look like different-coloured versions of the same substance: gold, bronze, silver and iron all respond differently to light. This exercise will take you step by step through the process of applying a metallic texture to the body armour of a futuristic warrior, from line art to finished composite.

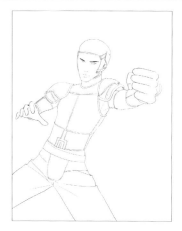

1 Open your line art in Photoshop, and prepare it for colour, fixing errors or dirt marks and separating lines from the white background.

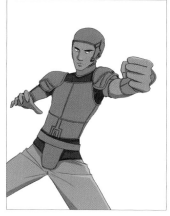

2 As practised in previous chapters, fill in the flat colours. Colour in shadows using the cel-shading method, everywhere but the armour.

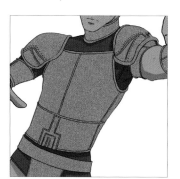

3 Use the Magic Wand Tool to select all of the armour areas and then go to Filter > Noise > Add Noise. Choose 'Uniform' and check 'Monochromatic' and set a medium value for the amount of noise to be added, then view the effect in the preview window. When you are happy with the amount, click OK to apply the noise to the armour.

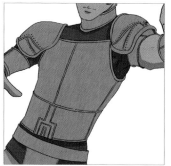

4 Keep the selection on and go to Filter > Blur > Motion Blur. Set the angle to ensure it blurs in the same direction as the incline of the body. In our example, the character's body is leaning to the left, so we set the angle to -63 degrees. Clicking OK applies the effect: you can already see the texture of steel in the armour plate.

**Tip:** Not all metals are the same, so it can help to build up a reference library of photographs and panels from your favourite manga of metallic effects, as such a resource may prove useful. Some metals, particularly those with elements of iron in their makeup, will also be subject to rust, which can prove to be an interesting effect for aged or weathered weapons, armour or vehicles. Use a separate layer and a textured brush to apply different shades of brown and gold to joints, wheel trims, handles and edges, or anywhere likely to have suffered from water damage. Rust can add a great deal of character, suggesting great age, or implying a lack of care on the part of an item's owner.

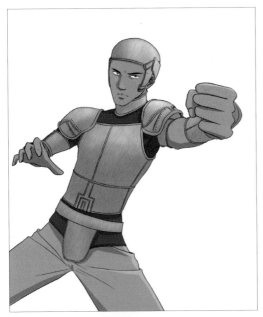

**5** Now you can add the first layer of highlights and reflections to the armour. Duplicate the layer first so you can return to the original if you are unhappy with your modifications. Hide the original and work on the duplicate. For the highlights, use the Dodge Tool. Pick a brush with a soft edge, set its range to 'Highlights' and its Exposure to roughly 7%. Use a large brush to paint over areas that face the light source. In this case, the light source is from above and to the right. Be gentle with your brushstrokes, and don't obscure too much texture at this stage.

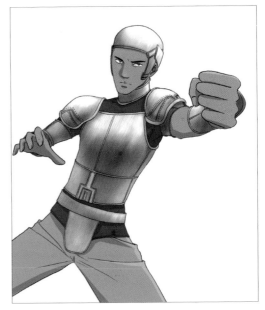

**6** Still using the Dodge Tool, apply the more extreme, shiny highlights to the metal – an important step in your presentation of the material. Apply the Dodge Tool most heavily in the areas that should be shiniest, reducing the colour almost to white as necessary. When this is complete, add some shading and darker areas to the armour by switching to the Burn Tool. Use the same settings: a range set to 'Highlights' and an Exposure of around 7%. Gently paint over the areas facing away from the light with a soft brush, in this case the centre of the chest and the undersides of the helmet, throat and shoulder pads. Use the Dodge Tool to add further elements of reflection if needed.

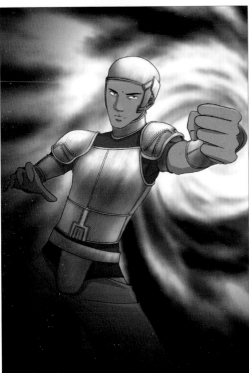

**7** As a final step, alter the colour balance to your satisfaction with Image > Adjustments > Color Balance. Set Tone Balance to 'Highlights' and uncheck 'Preserve Luminosity'. Don't oversaturate the armour; keep it tinted a silverish hue. Cyan and yellow were added to make the metal more realistic, and a background taken from an altered photo was inserted to make the shot more dramatic.

# Creating reflections

Drawing precise reflections freehand usually involves many hours of painstaking labour, the judicious use of mirrors and the occasional bout of advanced mathematics. The majority of reflections found in manga drawn with traditional media tend to be rough approximations: a character looking in a mirror isn't too much of a stretch, but the same character looking into a pool of water may see his or her reflection as a series of wiggly lines, or some splotches of tone or colour.

Photoshop, however, with its array of layers and tools and filters to copy, flip, rotate, mirror and blur, proves to be the perfect vehicle for creating such reflective moments. The example on this spread shows how to create a reflection in a pool of water, but you could just as easily extend this technique to a mirror viewed side-on, the reflective gateway to another dimension, or an angry biker reflected in the windscreen of the car he is about to demolish. Experiment.

## Practice exercise: Dreamy reflection

As mentioned above, traditionally drawing reflective water requires a lot of skill and the investment of a great deal of time on the part of the artist. Thanks

to Photoshop, we can now do it in a few steps. Remember that Photoshop is not so advanced that it can reflect elements you have not drawn: this

technique works best for reflections viewed from a side-on perspective, not the back of head/front of head examples mentioned earlier.

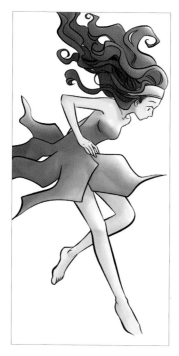

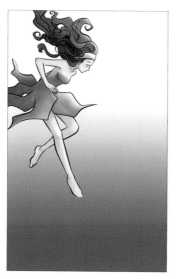

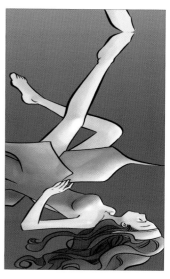

1 Open your line art in Photoshop: here, a fairy lightly touching some water with her foot. Of course, the 'touching the water' part is yet to be added. First, prepare the line art for colour, tidying it and separating the lines from the white canvas. Colour the fairy as you have learned previously: soft shading adds a dreamlike quality to the fantasy character.

2 Underneath the character colour layers, create a new layer named 'Water'. Pick an aquatic blue and fill this layer with a gradient of white to blue, from dark blue at the bottom of the image to white at the top.

**Tip:** If you are feeling adventurous, you could try to blend a photograph you have taken of a body of water with the blue/white gradient, in order to give it texture and realism. Place the photo beneath the gradient and set the Gradient blend mode to 'Color', altering the fill Opacity of the layer as appropriate.

3 Duplicate the line art and the character colours layer and merge these duplicated layers together. Rename this merged layer 'Reflection' and move it underneath the original character colour layer. This, as the name suggests, is where you will create your reflection. First, the reflection must be correctly oriented. Use Edit > Transform > Flip Vertical to flip 'Reflection' upside down. Scale the image down vertically using the Transform controls so the reflection is smaller than the original version, then move the reflection up the canvas to meet the original's extended foot.

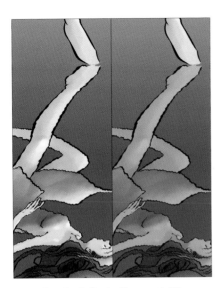

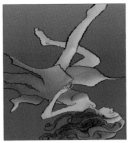

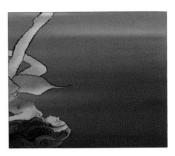

**4** Still on the 'Reflection' layer, go to Filter > Distort > Ripple. Here, you can choose the amount and size of the ripple's distortion; you can also preview what the revised image will look like in the preview window. Click OK when you find a result you are happy with. Your 'Reflection' layer is now wrinkled up to simulate the effect of flowing water.

**5** The reflection is too bright and saturated. Turn down the Layer Fill Opacity to 80%. The reflection in the water should also be blueish. To achieve this, duplicate the 'Water' layer and move the duplicate on top of 'Reflection'. Set the duplicate's blending mode to Hue and set the layer fill Opacity to around 50%.

**6** Now merge the 'Water', 'Water Copy' and 'Reflection' layers together. You can draw some water effects on this new merged layer to simulate a water texture. Use the Dodge and Burn tools with a soft brush to make horizontal strokes on the surface of the water. You can also use the Desaturate Tool (located on the same button as the Dodge and Burn tools) to tone down some areas of the water, creating a spread of different hues.

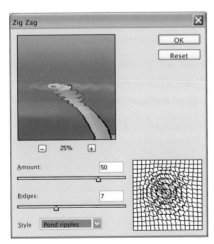

**7** At the point on the merged 'Water' layer where the foot of the fairy meets the surface, make an elliptical selection with the Elliptical Marquee Tool. Then go to Filter > Distort > Zig Zag. Choose 'Rough Ripples'. Set the Amount and Ridges while looking at the effect in the preview window. Click OK when you are satisfied.

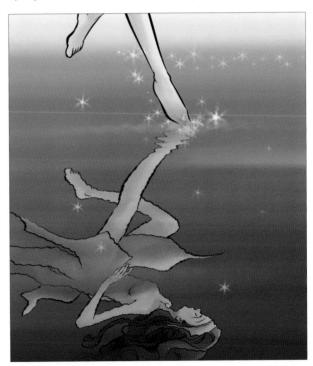

**8** On top of all the colour layers, create a new layer for your finishing touches. In this example, an array of sparkling reflections were added to lend the water a more magical, romantic feel.

# Converting a photo

Backgrounds are often the most difficult and time-consuming element of a manga page, and even the most successful manga professionals are often resistant to illustrating them from scratch. While you have learned how to ink a background from your own photograph in the previous chapter, there is an even 'lazier' method of background creation for those in a deadline-bind or inspiration furrow. If you use this method too often where it is stylistically inappropriate, your talent will be called into question, so keep your actual background illustration skills up to scratch.

## Practice exercise: Turning a photo into lines

The process behind this exercise is basically that of reducing a full-colour photograph to a two-tone bitmap, and then building it back up into a greytoned or coloured image.

The method may sound long-winded, but it is, in reality, anything but. Remember to use your own photos, rather than copyrighted imagery.

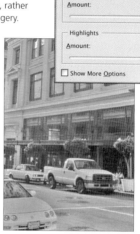

1 Open the photo you want to use. For best results, the image needs to be at a large size (a minimum of 300 dpi is recommended), with sharp detail, taken in clear (though not overpowering) daylight. First, convert the photo to Grayscale using Image > Mode > Grayscale. Duplicate the layer and work on that, saving the original image for later use.

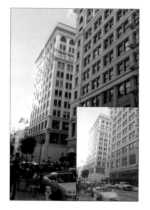

2 At the moment, the highlights and shadows in our example photo are too extreme. To fix this, use Image > Adjustments > Shadow/Highlight. In the options window, move both sliders to the highest value. The results are shown at left.

3 Now go to Image > Adjustments > Threshold and bring up the options window. Check 'Preview' and move the Threshold Level slider. Watch the changes in your image: your 'sweet spot' is when there is still detail in your black lines, but not too many areas of solid black. Click OK to apply the adjustment, creating a black and white image.

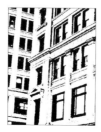

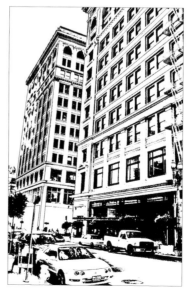

4 It is likely that your picture will still look messy thanks to some extraneous patches of black. Use the Eraser Tool to clear these, if necessary. Some areas in extreme highlight may have vanished, so use the Pencil Tool to fix these. If you want to add more details to the converted image, turn on the original layer and set the current layer to 'Multiply' and trace the appropriate lines. Eventually you will have a line art representation of your original photo. Drag this to your manga page and cut or Transform to fit.

## Practice exercise: Tone the converted image

The photo is already converted to a black and white background. If you wish, you can either add tones manually, as before, or use the original photo to do the job, as below.

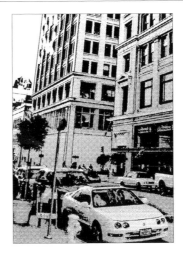

**1** Use the same file as in the previous exercise. Drag the original photo layer to a new canvas at the same resolution. Use Brightness/Contrast to brighten the image and reduce the contrast a little. Now go to Image > Mode > Bitmap. Select 'Halftone Screen' as your conversion Method. The image changes to a dotted bitmap picture, as shown above. If the conversion looks successful, switch back to 'Grayscale' mode.

**2** Re-import your grey tone layer into your original document, behind your black and white background layer. Match the tones with the lines. The line art layer must be in 'Multiply' mode in order for you to see the tones beneath.

## Practice exercise: Colour the converted image

Colouring the photo yourself will help soften the blow of 'cheating' by using the previous steps, but if time is really tight, you can colour the image using the actual photo.

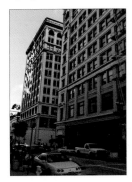

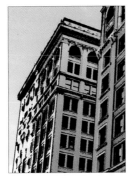

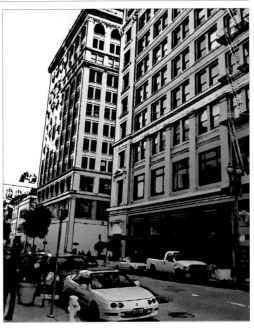

**1** Change the mode of your line art background file to RGB, and set the line art layer to 'Multiply' mode. Open your original colour photo and drag it into your black and white document, underneath the converted line art. The points should match up. Duplicate the colour photo layer, make the original invisible, and only work on the duplicated layer from now on.

**2** Go to Filter > Artistic > Dry Brush and apply the filter. Use the preview window to try out all of the options. Click OK when you find the best effect.

**Tip:** Try layering a colour or gradient 'wash' (a layer set to 'Color' or 'Hue' blending modes) in between the colour photograph and the line art to create atmosphere.

**3** Adjust the Brightness/Contrast of the colour to ensure the line art stands out enough. You may need to adjust the Hue/Saturation or Color Balance of the colouring if you need it to fit into the rest of your manga page. Remember that there are other filters you can use to get the hand-coloured effect, so sample those if you need to.

# Creating lighting

Although shadows and highlights are applied during the colouring process to indicate the presence or otherwise of light, it is useful to know that these simple methods can be improved or jazzed up with a Photoshop filter effect. This is not to say that there is a shortcut to the rendering of light and shade with colour and brush: there is no quick fix. However, using a lighting filter in tandem with other methods can bring an extra dimension to your artwork, capturing, say, the bloom of candles in ways difficult to accomplish by hand. The following exercise shows one such method.

## Practice exercise: Add digital lighting

As previously mentioned, digital lighting is a way of adding a final touch to an image, not a colouring shortcut. However, rather than an element you bolt on at the last minute, it helps you to bear in mind your lighting effects from the very first pencil stroke. Digital, single-source lighting is often most effective when unbounded by line work, which is why there is no candle flame illustrated in the example, just a wick and candlestick. Your shadows and highlights, likewise, are reacting to a light source you are yet to add. Follow the steps to light the candle.

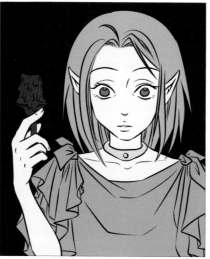

1 Open the line art as usual: our example here is of a scared-looking elven girl holding a candle. For the most dramatic lighting effects, the image will be in darkness, the candle the only light source. Add the flat colours, using a purple-blue as the background to indicate a deep darkness. Keep the colours desaturated as darkness trends colours towards grey.

**Tip:** This type of image works best when there are clear extremes between light and dark, illuminated by a single, dominant light source that can provide a focal point in the image for the reader. To gather reference on how a single light source casts shadows on a face, use a desk lamp and a digital camera to take photos of yourself from different angles.

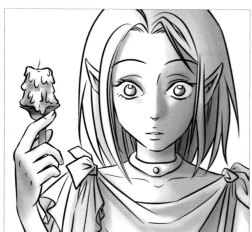

2 On another 'Multiply' layer, add shadows. Pay particular attention to the light source, the candle, as everything not facing it should be in shadow. Grey-purple is used for shading, another element to represent the dark of night. Add highlights on a separate layer.

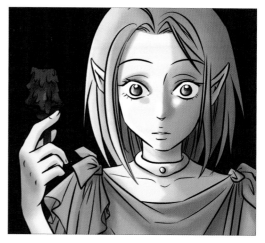

3 When you are happy with your highlights and shadows, make a copy of all three colour layers and merge the copies together into a single layer. Place the merged layer on top of the original colours. Next, we will apply the filters on this merged layer.

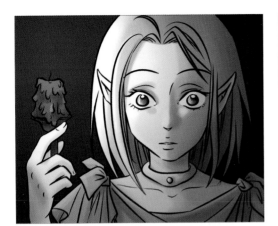

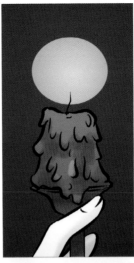

4 Go to Filter > Render > Lighting Effects. In the option window, choose the Light Type as 'Omni', sliding the option bars and keeping an eye on the preview in the preview window. You should not make the intensity of the lighting too high, as that will make any areas affected by the light lose their colours. Clicking OK applies the lighting effect.

5 With the nimbus of the light applied, you next need to add in the candle flame. Create a new layer on top of the other colour layers first. Use the Elliptical Marquee Tool to make a small, rough selection on top of the candlewick: don't worry about being precise, an approximate area will do. Use the Gradient Tool to apply a Radial gradient to the selection: set the foreground colour to bright orange and the background colour to a bright yellow.

6 When this is done, deselect the area and go to Filter > Blur > Gaussian Blur to blur the candlelight, allowing it to merge convincingly with the background.

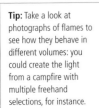

**Tip:** Take a look at photographs of flames to see how they behave in different volumes: you could create the light from a campfire with multiple freehand selections, for instance.

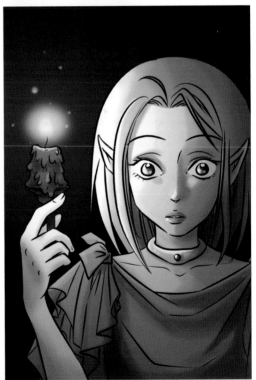

7 If the light doesn't look bright enough, use the Dodge Tool with the range set to 'Highlights', to dodge the middle of the flame. Add flame and spark details and adjust the overall colours using Color Balance and Brightness/Contrast.

# Combining software

For those with the budget to experiment and the time to get to know new software, the best part about the latest home computers is the range of graphics packages available. While Photoshop is incredibly flexible, many manga artists use Adobe Illustrator for its infinite scalability and editability of lines (an Illustrator document can be printed, without loss of resolution, at the size of a postage stamp or an office block), or Corel Painter for its wide range of well-simulated natural media. Often, images will be transferred between multiple packages, the better to take advantage of the strengths of

each: line work drawn in Illustrator can be transferred to Photoshop for colouring, as Illustrator is best for bold, graphic images and type, while images can pass between Photoshop and Painter to take full advantage of the digital replications of chalks, paints, pastels and oils to be found within. The examples below combine Photoshop and Painter. It is simple to lay in flat colours with Photoshop and then switch to Painter for a more naturally painted look. For cel shading or unfussy soft shading, Photoshop is easily sufficient, but the examples below give you an extra option.

## Photoshop and Painter

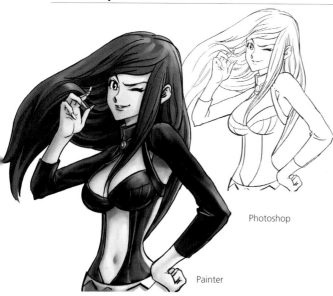

Photoshop

Painter

It is easy to show the differences between Photoshop and Painter. While Photoshop can do its best to simulate natural media with a range of brushes, textures and opacities, the results are still just combinations of various levels of colour: a 20% white over a 50% green, for example. Painter, on the other hand, has swathes of algorithms dedicated to reproducing the feel of natural media. Painter can simulate different styles of painting, from watercolours to pastels and oils, each of which allows the colours to act like 'real' pigments: blending, blurring, seeping naturally into one another, sitting in lumps on the canvas, picking up the texture of the page, and so on – all with the full levels of Undo provided by the digital realm. It can often be hard to tell the image has been created digitally at all.

◀ **Different strokes**
The image on the right, from Photoshop, clearly shows the digital crispness in the line art that is the package's strong point, while the example from Painter displays the effortless blending and natural textures for which it is famous. Either image can now be imported into the other package for further tinkering.

## Switching between programs

It is easy to move files back and forth between Painter and Photoshop, but there are a few places where the translation is not exact (mainly for patent reasons).
- Use the .psd format to save files. The layers and quality will be best preserved when the file is moved.
- RGB is Painter's native colour mode. Although Painter *can* open files in CMYK, for best results it is better to stick to RGB if exporting to Painter.
- A Photoshop document without a Background layer will open in Painter as layers over a white background.

- Painter and Photoshop recognize most of the other's layer modes (Photoshop calls them blending modes, Painter compositing modes), but they have different names. For example, 'Magic Combine' in Painter is 'Lighten' in Photoshop, while 'Shadow Map' is Photoshop's 'Multiply'. There are some layer modes they cannot recognize: they will default to the basic layer mode.
- Photoshop type layers will be rasterized when imported to Painter. Don't letter pages before you have finished with Painter.

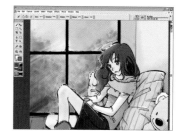

**Painter interface** ▲
Many of the Painter tools have clear Photoshop equivalents; the interface and menus are just as intuitive.

## Practice exercise: Combined image

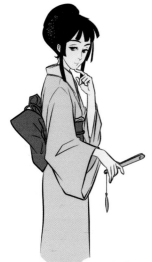

**1** Open the line art in Photoshop. Fill in the flat colours and save the file as a .psd with layers. Close Photoshop and open Corel Painter (don't close Photoshop if your computer is powerful enough). Go to File > Open to open the .psd file.

**2** Make a new layer, clicking the icon at the bottom of the Layers Palette. You will use mainly Digital Watercolor to paint this image. Select the skin areas using the Magic Wand first. Click on the Brushes, choose Digital Watercolor and pick the Simple Water Brush in the drop-down list. Choose a skin colour in the color palette or pick it from the flats using the Eyedropper Tool (J).

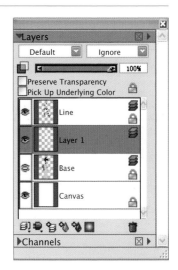

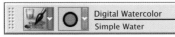

Digital Watercolor
Simple Water

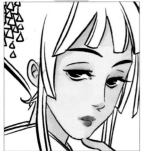

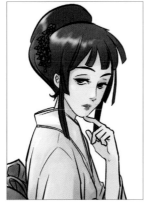

**3** Using a large brush, paint the basic skin colour. Dry the colour with Layers > Dry Digital Watercolor. Pick up darker shades of the skintone, using a smaller brush to build up shadow and detail. Dry the watercolour when finished. (Please note: only skin tones show on this layer.)

**4** Select the Oils Brush and use a Thick Oil Bristle Brush to paint highlights in white. Use a mix of these two techniques to colour the rest of the image.

**5** To add interest to the illustration, you could add a pattern to the kimono. Add a new layer above the colouring layers. In the Brush drop-down list, choose Image Hose, then Spray-Size-P, Angle-R. In the toolbox, click the icon at the bottom right to choose a pattern: here, the pattern is 'Bay Leaves'. Spray areas where you want the pattern, clearing excess areas with the Eraser Tool. At the moment the pattern doesn't look quite right: it is too bright and the wrong colour, but you will fix this in Photoshop.

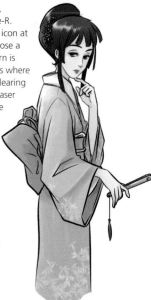

**6** Save the image as a .psd file and open it back in Photoshop. First, blur the pattern layer using Filter > Blur > Gaussian Blur, with the blur set to a low radius. Next, change the layer blending mode to 'Screen'. The pattern now looks elegant and delicate, almost etched into the fabric.

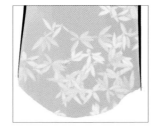

**7** Merge this pattern layer with your colours. If you want to change the hue of any area, now is the time to do so. Photoshop has a stronger post-colouring editing ability than Painter, which finds the process awkward.

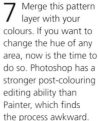

# Digital shojo project

Shojo manga is largely aimed at young and teenage girls, and the artwork tends to be feminine and romantic. Shojo stories revolve around a female protagonist, and though they can take place in any genre, the focus of the story tends to be on the protagonist's search for love. Typically, there are many more panels depicting subtle changes of facial expression and a greater emphasis on feelings than in other manga, as well as specific visual cues that are rarely seen outside of shojo. As an example, flowers, bubbles or hearts surrounding a figure will give clues to her emotional state: romantic scenes of a similar ilk would be played for laughs in a shonen manga.

This project will show you how to create a typical shojo page, with an airy, panel-light layout, ornamental flowers, and tight focus on the central figures.

**Leave-taking ▶**

A warrior goes off to battle, his lover bids him goodbye ... before he offers her the chance to adventure at his side. The ornamental flowers speak of our heroine's love, but also press in around her claustrophobically, presaging the sadness she would feel in her lover's absence.

**1** Sketch out a very rough thumbnail of your page, focusing on facial expressions and character poses above all else: the scene is about the connection between two characters. When you are satisfied, pencil a more detailed layout to give you a clearer idea of how to ink it in Photoshop.

**2** Import the pencilled image into Photoshop using a scanner, at a resolution of at least 300 dpi. Convert the file to Grayscale and ink it digitally using the Brush Tool as you learned earlier, cleaning with the Eraser Tool and sharpening lines with the Pencil Tool as appropriate. Once you have finished, delete the rough image layer and add a new layer of white underneath the inks. Convert the image to RGB.

Create a new 'Normal' layer between the existing two and name it 'Flats'. On this layer, use the Paint Bucket Tool to fill the basic colours, using the Pencil Tool to seal improperly sealed areas if necessary, or to fill awkward nooks and crannies. Adjust the colours with the Hue/Saturation options (Image > Adjustments > Hue/Saturation) until you are content with the final result.

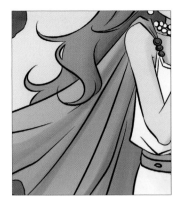

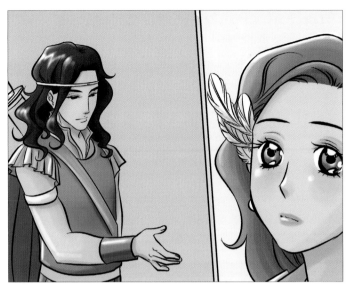

**3** The soft shading colouring method is best suited to creating a romantic atmosphere. Duplicate 'Flats', rename the duplicated layer 'Colour' and set the mode to 'Normal'. Lock the 'Flats' layer, and use it to make selections of areas with the Magic Wand. On the 'Colours' layer, choose slightly darker colours than your original flats and use a soft brush with Opacity and Flow of around 30% to gradually build up the shading. Use still darker versions of the same hues to give the image depth by painting in darker shadows using a smaller brush.

**4** You can either add your highlights on the currently active layer, or create a new 'Normal' layer and work on that. The second method is usually preferred, as it is easier to correct mistakes and will not interfere with your previously applied shading. Select lighter colours than your original flats and build up your layers of highlights with a brush as in the previous step. Add a bright white highlight, sparingly, on shiny areas that face the light. Add shine, shadow and detail to small areas you may have missed, such as the cheeks, lips, eyes and accessories.

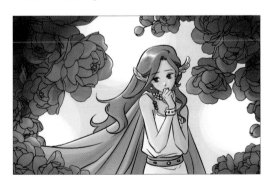

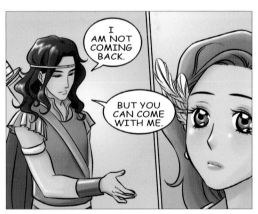

**5** At present, the backgrounds are still very flat, and lacking in ambience. It is a very simple matter to select the flat areas on the 'Flats' layer and use the Dodge Tool to add flares of light to the areas of flat blue. The roses can be toned using the same soft-shading method used to colour the characters.

**Tip:** Experiment further with the use of abstract backgrounds: why not select all of the black lines making up the roses with a Lasso Tool and use the Paint Bucket Tool to colour the black a deep shade of pink? This 'knocks back' the line work even further and brings your characters to the fore.

**6** The colours are complete: you just need to add your speech balloons. Use the Text Tool to type in dialogue in your chosen font, centring the text and arranging the content of each balloon in a roughly elliptical shape. Create a new layer underneath the text. Use the Filled Ellipse Tool with white as the foreground colour to draw balloons, moving the text to fit as necessary. Draw tails. Select the balloons using the Magic Wand Tool, and use Select > Modify > Border to add a 4–5 pixel empty selection around them. Fill this with black.

# Digital shonen project

Compared to shojo, shonen manga is traditionally aimed at young and teenage boys. However, with the unisex success stories of manga like *Naruto*, today you are just as likely to find girls reading them too. Shonen manga is usually packed with fast-moving action and often focuses on a male protagonist.

This project will guide you in the creation of an action-packed shonen page: a pulse-pounding fight scene between our teen heroes and some angry, ambulatory trees.

### Arboreal action ▶

There's no time to pause for breath in this thrilling, fantasy action scene. Impacts are heightened to a physically impossible level to sell the extreme power involved.

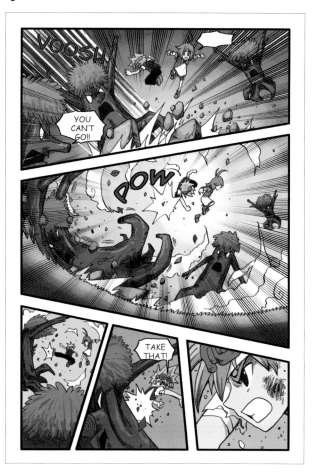

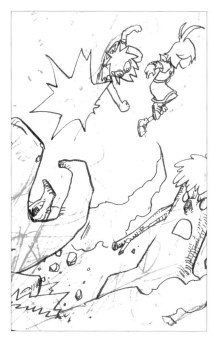

1 Begin by sketching out a rough thumbnail of the whole page. Here, the first two panels take up most of the page to show the scale and impact of the fight. At a larger scale, and still in pencil, create a more detailed, rough layout. The example above shows only a portion of the full page at this stage. Remember that you are creating a guide to make digitally inking your page easier in the next step.

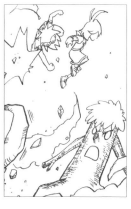

2 Before scanning your page, add some more textural details in pencil, such as the bark of the trees or the exploding rock. When you are happy, import the detailed rough into Photoshop, scanning the page at a minimum resolution of 300 dpi. Convert the page to Grayscale mode and digitally ink the lines on a separate layer. Build up line weights by using different-sized brushes or going over existing lines. After you have finished inking, add a white background layer underneath the inking layer and delete your original rough pencils.

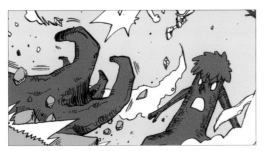

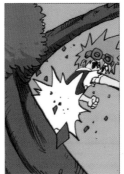

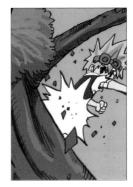

3 To begin colouring, change the mode to RGB. Add a new 'Normal' layer between the inks and white background: call it 'Flats'. Fill in your flat colours using the Paint Bucket Tool, sealing areas with the Pencil Tool as required, or using the Pencil Tool to colour in awkward areas in the line work.

4 The cel-shaded method works best for this project. Create a new 'Multiply' layer on top of 'Flats': call it 'Shading'. Using a light grey brush, paint areas of shadow. Use the 'Flats' layer to select colour areas using the Magic Wand Tool. Add another 'Multiply' layer above 'Shading' and call it 'Shadows': brush areas with a darker grey. Finally, create a new 'Normal' layer above the shadows called 'Highlights'. Add highlights in lighter colours facing the light source.

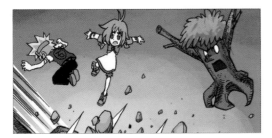

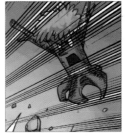

5 Backgrounds of solid colour leave the page looking flat. Add variations to make it look more vibrant. Duplicate 'Flats' and hide the original. Use the duplicate to select the backgrounds of panels 1 and 2, and the Dodge Tool to lighten the areas around the focal points: in panel 1, where the ground is breaking; in panel 2, the main characters.

6 To make the page more dramatic, add some speedlines. Use a stock image you have prepared earlier. Drag the speedlines to your image, Transform them to fit, and Erase unwanted lines. Add colour gradients to the lines and use layer blend and Opacity settings to integrate them.

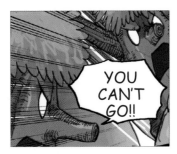

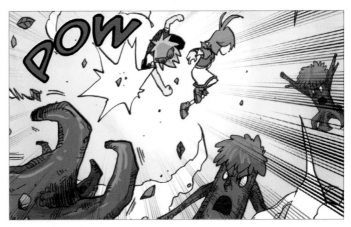

7 Now, add dialogue and balloons. Add the dialogue using the Text Tool, and draw balloons on a layer underneath. Jagged balloons amp up the drama: draw them freehand with a Pencil Tool or Lasso Tool, fill them with black, then select them with the Magic Wand Tool, Contract the selection by 4–5 pixels, and fill with white.

8 Sound effects are very important to shonen manga, especially in the high-stakes environment of a fight scene. Accompany every jarring impact with a tooth-rattling piece of SFX, adding coloured borders to manipulate text.

# Digital kodomo project

Kodomo manga is aimed at younger children. It is often educational, based around the acquisition of vocabulary in a fun, adventurous context. Few kodomo manga have been exported to the West, aside from famous brands such as *Hello Kitty* and *Doraemon*. Kodomo can accommodate many genres, so long as they are child-friendly and use relatively simple dialogue.

This project will show you how to create a typical kodomo page. The key is to keep everything simple and the characters cute.

**Rampaging robot** ▶
Note how the giant robot manages to look threatening and safe at the same time: the bulbous body and rounded edge make him a cute antagonist. Note, too, the bright colours, simple dialogue and reasonable font size.

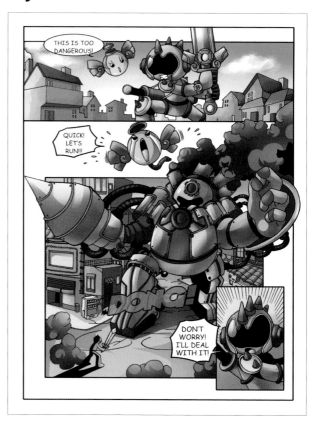

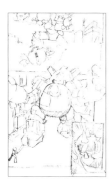

**1** Draw a thumbnail version of your page in pencil, sketching in your characters and the layout of the entire page. The dominant entity on this page is the giant robot, so make that the focus.

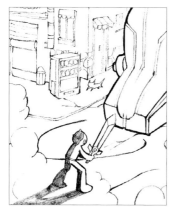

**2** Create a scaled-up, more detailed version of your rough illustration with enough information to ink over.

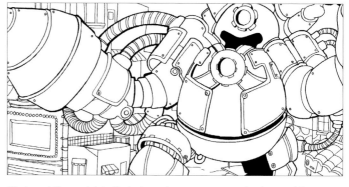

**3** Import the rough into Photoshop using a scanner, scanning it at a minimum resolution of 300 dpi. Convert the file to Grayscale and digitally ink it on a layer above your rough pencils. Keep the lines clean, bold, simple and open for colour, using bold outlines around your characters to separate them from the background. When the inks are finished, delete the roughs and add a white layer underneath.

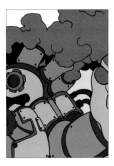
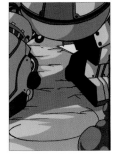
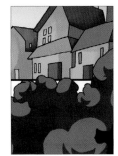
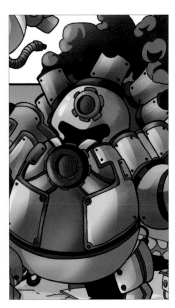

4 Add a new layer between the inks and the white background layers, setting the mode to 'Normal' and naming it 'Flats'. Fill in the flat colours on this layer, choosing bright and attractive colours, erring on the side of visual interest rather than fidelity to real life. For example, the robot's smoke is here a bright orange, rather than a dull grey.

5 On a new 'Multiply' layer named 'Shading', use a light grey brush to add shadows, using the 'Flats' layer to make selections. Adjust the greys with Hue/ Saturation to make individual parts of the image more colourful.

6 Create another new 'Multiply' layer, name it 'Shadows' and add darker shadows again. Use a soft brush with Opacity set to 30% to give the dark shadows a more realistic, blended look, especially on the belching smoke and the blue sky in panel 1.

**Tip:** Use bold and contrasting colours that leap out at the eye – note the interplay between the blue and the orange in this example. Pick up children's picture books for the very young and take inspiration from their heightened, almost primary palettes.

7 Add a 'Normal' layer named 'Highlights' above the colour layers. Use a soft brush with Opacity set to 30% to lighten areas facing the light source, especially on the robot and the armoured boy. Use solid white to pick out extreme highlights.

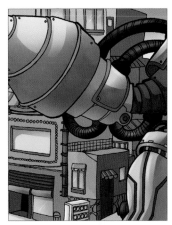
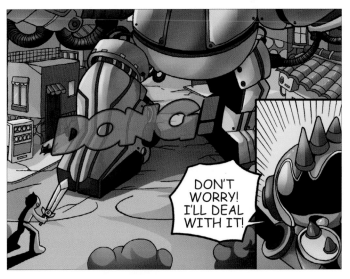

8 Make a new 'Normal' layer for details on top of 'Highlights'. Use the same soft brush as in previous steps to paint some reflected colours on to your metallic, armoured elements, and add some wispy clouds to the sky in the first panel.

9 Use the Text tool to add dialogue, keeping the point size large and the vocabulary age-appropriate. Draw speech balloons on a layer beneath the dialogue and fill them with white as before; and then, as a final step, add some SFX.

# Digital seinen project

Like shonen, seinen is aimed at males, but its target demographic is several years older – teens and twenty-somethings – and it also has a following among an older audience of people up to about forty years old. It normally attracts young people who are moving away from shonen and shojo. Seinen has a lot of overlaps with shonen, but will accommodate more mature themes, whether that be the 'maturity' of graphic violence, sex and nudity, or more adult approaches to inner feelings and emotional states. Seinen protagonists will also be older than shonen stars.

This project shows how to illustrate a typical seinen page in a relatively realistic style.

### First date ▶

At a surface level, this page from a romantic comedy could be mistaken for a shojo tale, but note that although the woman is shown in close-up panels, the focal point of our attention is the man: it is his thoughts to which we are granted access.

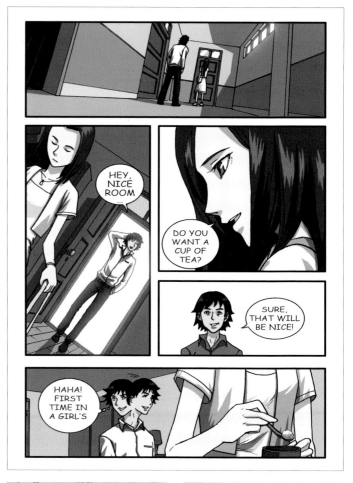

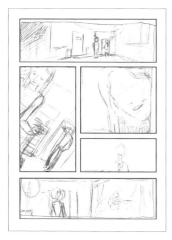

**1** Sketch out a very rough thumbnail in pencil to plan your page. As the scene is very 'talky' and not very dynamic, here each panel has been given a different perspective in order to add visual excitement.

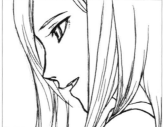

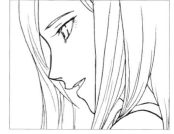

**2** Detail the rough in pencil to your satisfaction, and import it into Photoshop by scanner at a minimum of 300 dpi. Digitally ink the Grayscale roughs on a separate layer, then delete the rough when you have finished. Add a layer filled with white underneath the inks as a plain background.

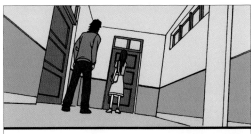

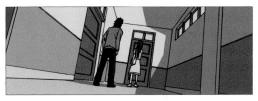

4 This page best suits the cel-shading method. Add a new 'Multiply' layer called 'Shading' on top of the 'Flats', painting your shadows on this layer using a hard brush. Change the shaded colour from grey to a darker version of the area you are shading if it looks better. Use the 'Flats' layer to make your selections using the Magic Wand Tool.

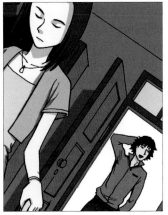

5 On a new 'Multiply' layer named 'Shadows', added on top of the 'Shading' layer, deepen your shadowed areas by using a darker grey. Use this on areas such as the woman's hair (in the detailed close-up), the man's collar and behind the door.

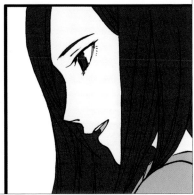

3 Create a 'Flats' layer between the background and inks, and block in flat colours. Keep the colours muted to suit the realistic tone: browns, greys, greens and pale blues. The purples and pinks of the woman make her stand out.

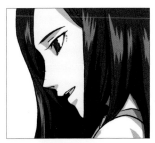

6 Create a 'Normal' layer called 'Highlights'. Select the area you want to add highlights to using 'Flats'. Pick the appropriate colour from the 'Flats' layer, make it lighter in the Colour Palette, then paint the area using a brush.

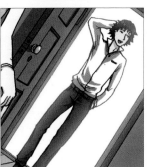

7 Finally, add some effects to the page using another layer. To add the effect of light coming from the windows and door, use an 'Overlay' layer on top of all layers (including inks) and paint over the image using a light yellow.

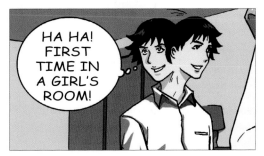

8 Now add your dialogue to the page, using the Text Tool to input and layout the conversation between your characters, as well as detailing the thoughts of your male lead. Create a 'Normal' layer for balloons beneath the text layer. Draw the balloons with the Ellipse Tool. Set the foreground colour to white and check 'Fill Pixels' in the Options Bar. Draw tails pointing towards the right characters (thought balloons need a trail of dots). Select all the white balloons using the Magic Wand Tool and use Select > Modify > Border to add an empty selection of 4–5 pixels to each balloon. Fill this selection with black to create your finished balloons. Move the text or Transform your balloons to fit.

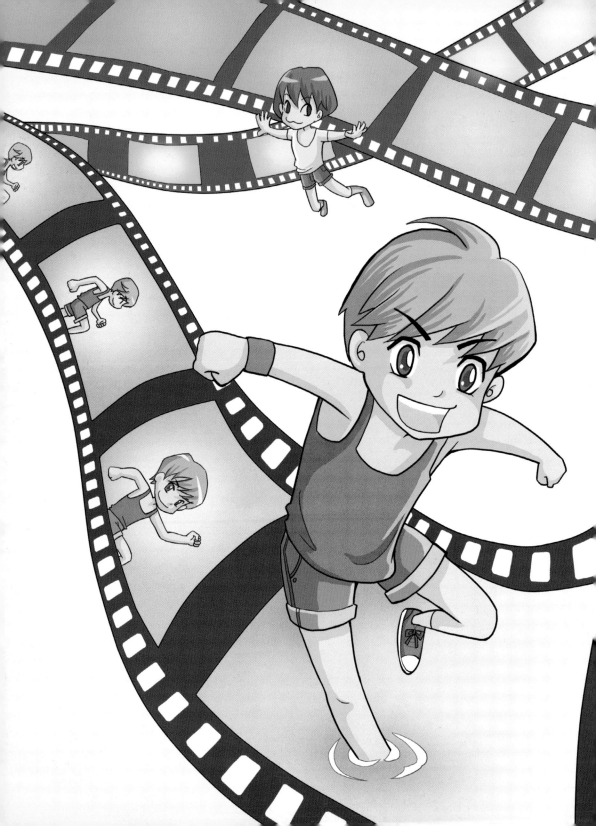

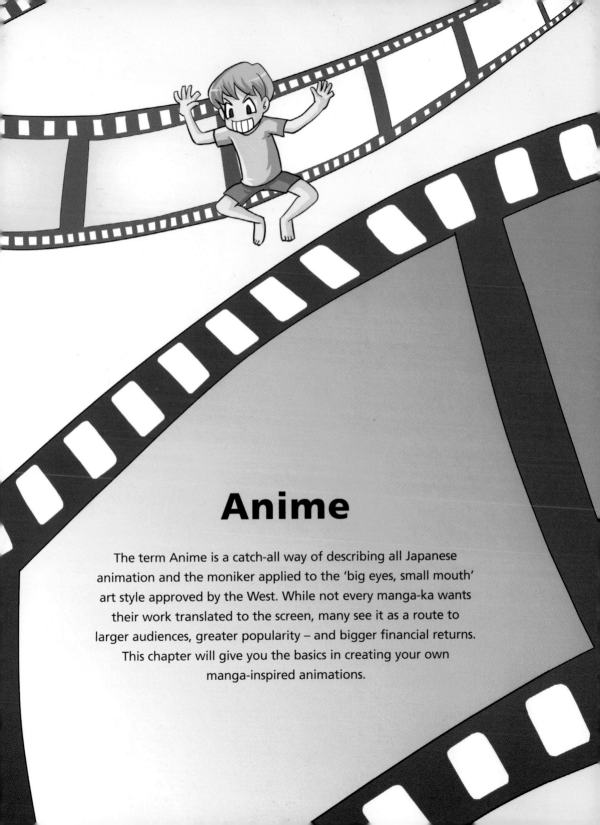

# Anime

The term Anime is a catch-all way of describing all Japanese
animation and the moniker applied to the 'big eyes, small mouth'
art style approved by the West. While not every manga-ka wants
their work translated to the screen, many see it as a route to
larger audiences, greater popularity – and bigger financial returns.
This chapter will give you the basics in creating your own
manga-inspired animations.

# The history of anime

'Anime' is coined from half of animation – literally 'anima', pronounced 'a-nee-may' – and is the common description for Japanese animated films and television shows. A large proportion of anime is based on popular manga. This means many, if not all, of the titles that have blazed to print popularity are also available as TV series or films. Long-running anime will often hit between 200 and 600 episodes before coming to a close. It is often said that the reason the Japanese took so strongly to anime is that their own live-action industry was so small compared to the mass-production factories found, for instance, in Los Angeles. Anime offered limitless possibilities for the filmmaker – in scenery, cast of characters and storytelling. The only barrier to the imagination was the time it took to transfer an idea from brain to transparent cel.

## Format

Anime is released either through TV syndication – often as half-hour, 26-episode series – or as Original Video Animations (OVAs). For years, 'anime' was synonymous with low-quality animation. While the drawings and storylines would be of a high standard, the number of frames per second was low, for fiscal expediency. These cost-cutting measures often led to the stylistic tics we associate with anime: frames where little but the mouth and eyes move; lengthy pans across still, painted backdrops; and 'money shots', where an important sequence is animated with more frames than the surrounding animation.

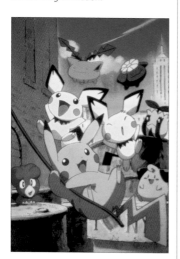

**Pokémon** ▲
One of the most popular exports of children's anime in recent years has been the *Pokémon* series of films and TV shows, all based on the Nintendo Game Boy series of games.

## First steps

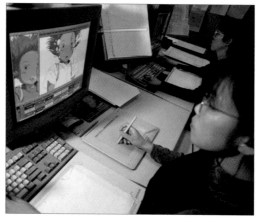

◀ **Studio work**
A woman works in digital animation at Studio Ghibli in Tokyo. Colour is now often applied on the computer, which, along with the ability to add more frames, leads to a newfound digital smoothness in many anime.

The first true 'anime' is considered to be *Hakujaden,* or *The Tale of the White Serpent,* released by Toei Animation in 1958. Like the new wave of manga, it wore its Disney influences on its sleeve, and was a great success. Toei continued to release such films throughout the 1960s and 70s, eventually becoming a lynchpin of television with *Dragon Ball Z* and *Sailor Moon.*

Osamu Tezuka, the 'father of manga', was also heavily involved in the development of anime. He started a rival company to Toei, Mushi Productions, and released *Tetsuwan ATOM,* or *Astro Boy,* in 1963. Its success led to the creation of innumerable competing series, including similar success stories like *Tesujiin 28-go (Gigantor), Mach Go Go Go (Speed Racer)* and *Jungle Emperor (Kimba The White Lion).*

The anime form, like manga, encompasses every genre and type of narrative, from the straightforward to the more esoteric.

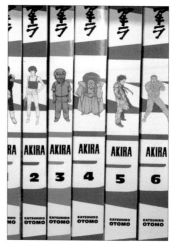

**Print inspiration** ▲
Manga-ka Katsuhiro Otomo began the screen adaptation of his magnum opus *Akira* years before the print story would be completed, leading the film to adapt only the first half of the epic.

## Western breakthrough

The breakthrough in the Western awareness of anime was twofold: the cinematic release of *Akira* in 1989, and the rise of VHS. The expense of localizing a dub for each country meant such videos were expensive, but fans lapped them up. Ironically, at the point that anime films began their breakthrough, many Japanese studios were facing bankruptcy. With the death of Tezuka from cancer in 1989, a golden era of Japanese animation ended – but not before international curiosity had been piqued.

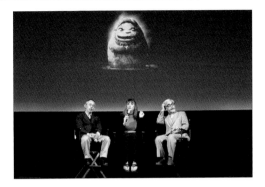

◀ *Spirited Away*
This 2002 Hollywood press conference at the El Capitan Theater marked another high for the international popularity of Hayao Miyazaki's films, and the penetration of anime culture into the mainstream.

## 1990s and 2000s

The 1990s and 2000s saw many exciting developments in anime, including the the advent of multi-tracked DVDs (allowing multiple dubs and subtitles to be placed on a single disc), and increasing use of digital techniques to bring lush and impressive imagery to OVAs, films and anime series. Where films and television are concerned, highlights include the release of *Ghost in the Shell* in 1994, which captured the same adult-oriented market as *Akira*; Hideaki Anno's *Neon Genesis Evangelion* in 1995, which revolutionized and scandalized in equal measure; the runaway international success of *Dragon Ball Z*, *Pokémon* and *Sailor Moon*; and the release of Hayao Miyazaki's *Princess Mononoke* in 1997,

which was the most expensive animated film at that point. Miyazaki, and his Studio Ghibli, is one of the leading anime *auteurs*. The studio, created with the proceeds from *Nausicaä of the Valley of the Wind*, continues to capture critical and popular acclaim with titles such as *Laputa: Castle in the Sky*, *Mononoke* and *Spirited Away*.

After the millennium, big-budget, adult anime spectaculars in the form of *Appleseed* (2001) and *Steamboy* (2004),

### Princess Mononoke ▼
The film was released to US and UK cinemas in both dubbed and subtitled versions, the dub version receiving a sympathetic translation from famed novelist Neil Gaiman.

among others, returned to the cinema screen. Television anime productions continue to push the envelopes of creativity, style and provocative content, while the popular manga *Death Note* and *Fullmetal Alchemist* have swiftly made the transition from page to screen. Last, but by no means least, 2008 saw the creation of the position of Anime Ambassador by the Japanese government: a post filled by Doraemon, a (fictional) time-travelling robotic cat.

### Ashitaka, prince of the Emishi ▼
Miyazaki's films fuse environmental awareness and lush cinematography with more contemplative and spiritual layers – as the unusual, cursed hero of *Princess Mononoke* illustrates.

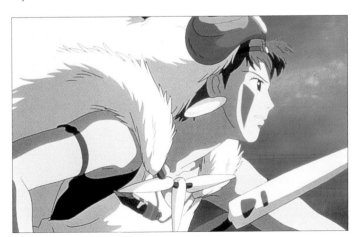

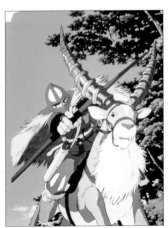

# Software

The first step in creating an animation is assembling all the tools you will need. There are certainly plenty of options to choose from. Fear not, however, as this section will introduce you to the most common digital animation software (and some hidden gems) so you'll have a good idea of what will suit you. It's worth investing a little time researching your tools, and most will offer trial periods so you can give them a test-drive. All of these programs are updated with new versions on a regular (often annual) basis, but if it helps you save money, there's often little need to be on the bleeding-edge of technology, as older versions will often be just as powerful as the latest iterations.

## Flash

Adobe Flash is an extremely popular vector-based animation program with a powerful scripting language. The current version is CS4, which incorporates advanced features such as 'bone-rigging' and 3-D object manipulation. Flash can import images from other programs to use as backgrounds or as sketches to work over, but also contains all the tools you need to create an animation from scratch. Being the most popular, Flash has many websites dedicated to tutorials, tips and free SFX which can be very welcoming for beginners.

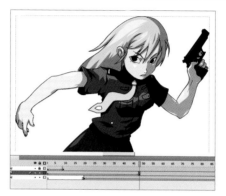

◀ **Flash animation**
Flash can save your finished animations as video files which can be burnt to DVD, uploaded to YouTube or saved to its web-ready format (.SWF). Flash is more than just an animation package, which means you can even add interactive elements to your animation. While Flash is rather expensive, a free trial version can be downloaded from Adobe's website.

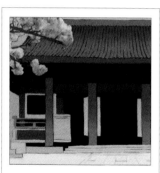

**Tip:** Corel Painter is ideal for creating stunning backgrounds as it emulates natural media. This is because they look as if they have been traditionally painted. The latest version is Painter X, though Painter Essentials is a cheaper edition aimed at the casual user. While Painter has no animation features, it is included here as cel-style animation stands out better atop beautifully painted backgrounds. Find a couple of brushes and a blender you like and put them in a tool palette before you start painting, as too much choice can prove overwhelming.

## Toon Boom

Unlike Flash, the Toon Boom range of products focus solely on creating animation, so while not as versatile, they can feel less overwhelming. Toon Boom has software for every level of animator, catering for kids, home users and professional studios. Toon Boom Studio features everything you need to create great animations and remains competitively priced, though the top of the range costs significantly more. Toon Boom is great at importing and manipulating existing artwork and has all the tools animators need, like 'onion skinning', automatic gap-closing and a full-screen rotary light table so you can always draw at the most comfortable angle. Toon Boom Studio can export your animations to a massive variety of formats including .SWF and video to suit devices from iPods to HDTVs.

### Ready for his close-up ▶
Here we see a zoomed-in element of the Toon Boom window: a painted cel against the light table grid that makes compositing and scaling so simple.

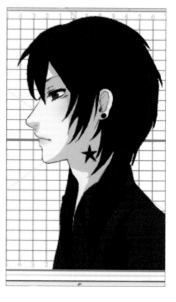

# Photoshop

Adobe Photoshop is a very powerful image-editing program which can be used for backgrounds, pixel/sprite animation or cel animation, although this versatility and power (and the fact it is universal image-editing software rather than a dedicated animation program) mean it's expensive. It can be tricky to use the animation window unless you're already familiar with Photoshop's layout and approach to layers, but as with all popular applications, you'll find dozens of tutorials online. Photoshop has had integrated animation capabilities since CS1, but in really old versions, the animation window can be found in the bundled software ImageReady (File > 'Edit in ImageReady').

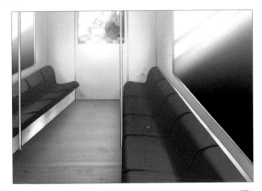

**Fully painted background** ▲
Photoshop is just as versatile as Painter when it comes to creating painted backdrops, although it doesn't attempt to simulate natural media.

**Drawing cels** ▼
Using Photoshop's powerful layer tools can make it very simple to draw traditional cel animations one frame at a time.

# EasyToon

EasyToon is mysterious little Japanese program (PC only) for creating preliminary 'pencil test' animations: basic sketched animations which are integral to making smooth and fluid progressions from frame to frame. While its functionality is limited, this makes it extremely effective and very quick to learn. A quick Internet search will find you a translated version, completely free to download.

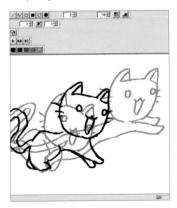

**Frame by frame** ▲
'Onion skinning' effects show previous and next frames in different colours and levels of Opacity.

# AnimeStudio

While AnimeStudio is not a traditional animation tool, it's fantastic for very quickly creating single scenes that you can tweak and perfect. Avoiding frame-by-frame animation, AnimeStudio relies entirely on a bone-rigging system to animate 2-D characters' limbs from pose to pose, thus speeding up the animation process. Working in AnimeStudio is quick and fun – but the animating method is restrictive and only one scene can be produced at a time: multiple scenes need Flash or a video editor to compile them together. Its soundtrack capabilities are also very limited.

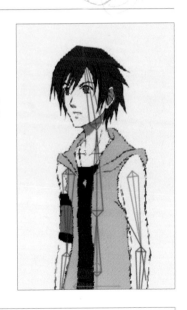

**Bone-rigging** ▶
Each element of the character is a separate 2-D vector graphic, 'mapped' on to a 3-D skeleton that can be animated like a puppet.

**Tip:** If you're thinking of creating 3-D animation, Maya is a popular high-end choice thanks to its modern layout and extreme flexibility. Although Maya can be very expensive, there are options for varying skill levels and even a free Personal Learning Edition to enable beginners to get to grips with its complexities before committing. As with all 3-D animation, creating objects and characters takes a long time, but once created they can be brought to life with stunning results. Maya also includes many shading and lighting effects: you can render your animation with 'Toon Shading' to recreate the anime look of painted cels.

# Pre-production

The first step to a successful animation is planning. Before beginning to animate, it's important to refine your ideas. After all, if you redesign a character's hair halfway through production, you will find yourself tediously reworking all the frames you thought you were done with. Many anime are adapted from manga, which are in turn usually drawn from a written script. This process means the story, locations, characters and even the kind of shots to be used have all already been considered. Even so, some details will need to be changed to suit animation. For example, many manga feature intricately detailed outfits that need simplifying for animation – removing buckles and frills or changing chainmail to plate at the beginning of a project can significantly reduce the man-hours involved. Whether based on your own manga, or on an idea that hasn't left your head yet, it's best to work out your animation in advance.

## Creating your characters

Designing or adapting characters for animation doesn't differ greatly from other forms of character design, but there are a few things to bear in mind. First, the character should be simplified enough to draw efficiently thousands of times. Outfits, hairstyles and number of colours used can be simplified without losing the essence of the character. Patterned cloth can be replaced by flat colours, and soft shading represented by solid shadow.

Another thing to think about is 'secondary motion'. Also known as 'secondary animation', this is the name for reactive movements created from the main 'primary motion'. If a character is running, the secondary animation could be her hair bouncing and flowing behind her. When she stops, her hair will keep travelling (sometimes called

follow-through) before falling back down. Secondary motion creates smoother-looking animation and can be applied not only to hair, but ribbons, a karate headband, or anything light and loose.

**Secondary motion** ▶
This animation is best used to flow two distinct movements into one another: from walking to jumping, for instance, or from sitting to standing.

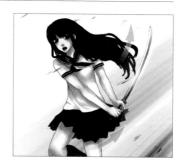

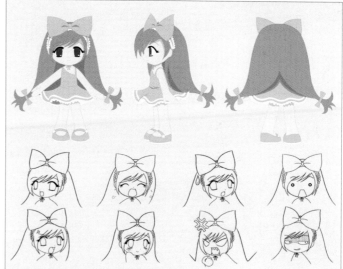

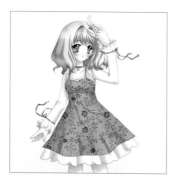

**Original character** ▲
Here we have a manga character whom we wish to adapt for animation. Note the soft shading, the many individual strands of hair, the floral print on the dress, and the numerous, reflective colours in her eyes.

**Revised model sheet for animation** ▲
A model sheet – pinning down your designs in a uniform way – makes it easier to maintain consistency. This is important if you're collaborating with other people, as everyone involved will know how tall the character should be drawn, what colour their eyes are and so on. A good model sheet includes multiple character angles (called a turnaround) and the colour palette. Additional sketches show facial expressions, body language and other subtleties.

## Storyboarding

It's good practice to get action and dialogue down on paper (or screen) in some form before beginning. Not only will this avoid production problems, but the process of recording your ideas will refine your story. You can animate directly from a screenplay or from manga, but storyboards will help you plan every aspect of what appears on screen. Draw a new storyboard for each change of action, angle or scene.

### Planning ▶
A storyboard shows a sketch representing the scene with dialogue, sound effects and camera movements noted nearby.

**Action:** Hand inserts coin.
**Camera:** Zoom in.
**Shot:** Close-up.

**Action:** Flicks through pages, stops and looks up.
**Camera:** Still.
**Shot:** Medium.

**Action:** Side view, walking left to right, yawning.
**Camera:** Still.
**Shot:** Medium.

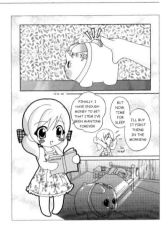

## Different perspectives

Cinematic shots, camera angles and movements will add style to your story, as well as help shape it. The examples to the right show various angles by which you can approach your scenes, each of which can present the same action in a different way.

While storyboarding, it's useful to think how you'll approach the actual animating. If a certain scene would be easier but no less effective from a different perspective, change it and save yourself valuable time later. Watch anime analytically: you will notice instances of time-saving 'limited animation' that can be planned for. Looped animations over a moving background, lower frame rates, extreme close-ups and panned stills are all examples of methods employed to save production time. Being efficient in this way leaves you extra time to perfect the most important sequences.

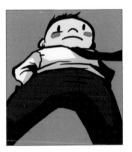

**Low angle** ▲
Looking up at the character from very low down. This grants the character a great deal of power.

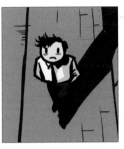

**High angle** ▲
Looking down at a character from high up makes the character look vulnerable, small and isolated.

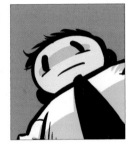

**Dutch angle** ▲
Low-angled shot, but from a tilted angle. This is used to portray tension or create unease in the viewer.

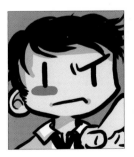

**Close-up** ▲
Tightly framed shot, used to bring attention to an item of significance.

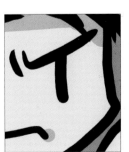

**Extreme close-up** ▲
Zoomed in on one part (the eyes, for example) to emphasize emotion.

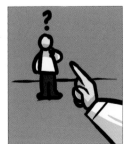

**Point-of-view** ▲
Shows what a character can see, as if we are looking through their eyes.

## Backgrounds

Character animation needs to be placed on top of a background to complete a scene. It is usually better to create the background (or at least a rough version) before beginning the animating process. Background styles vary widely, from the detailed painted backgrounds Studio Ghibli is famed for, to the fun and childish scribbled backgrounds of Digi Charat. No matter the style, remember to make your background at least as large as your animation window. In most cases, the background will be a single image depicting the set or location, but some scenes will need extra layers or effects, or be longer or taller to facilitate pans, zooms or tilted scenes.

> **Tip:** You learned earlier how to create digital backgrounds from photographs, so why not apply the knowledge here? You can create extremely detailed background images with which your cel-shaded, wholly fantastical characters can interact.

### Multi-layered ▶

If part of the foreground will obscure a character (here, a chain-link fence), the top layer can be designed and exported as a separate image. Most animation software will support images with transparency information (commonly using the .png format).

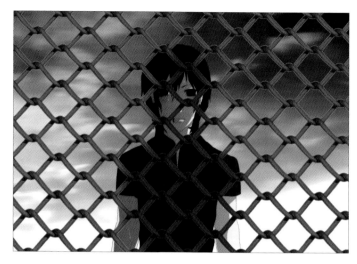

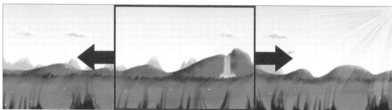

### ◀ Pans

Panned (or scrolling) scenes should be much larger than the screen size, so that the 'camera' can move across the background to the full extent required by the scene.

### Parallax scrolling ▼

This is a method used to add a sense of depth to a background. It is produced with multiple layers, those layers that are closer to the camera moving faster than those farther away. The layers should be saved as separate images, with the layers nearer to the 'camera' being wider than those at the back, as they will scroll for a longer distance.

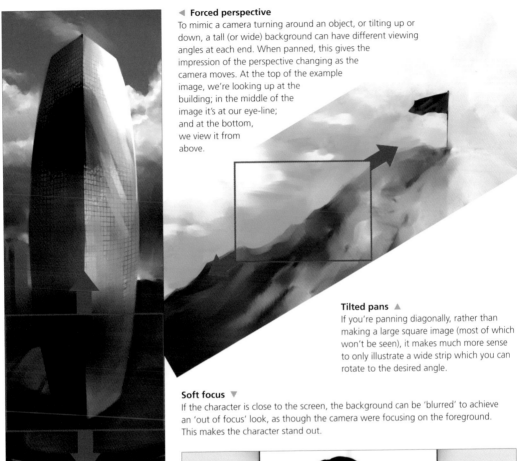

**◄ Forced perspective**

To mimic a camera turning around an object, or tilting up or down, a tall (or wide) background can have different viewing angles at each end. When panned, this gives the impression of the perspective changing as the camera moves. At the top of the example image, we're looking up at the building; in the middle of the image it's at our eye-line; and at the bottom, we view it from above.

**Tilted pans ▲**

If you're panning diagonally, rather than making a large square image (most of which won't be seen), it makes much more sense to only illustrate a wide strip which you can rotate to the desired angle.

**Soft focus ▼**

If the character is close to the screen, the background can be 'blurred' to achieve an 'out of focus' look, as though the camera were focusing on the foreground. This makes the character stand out.

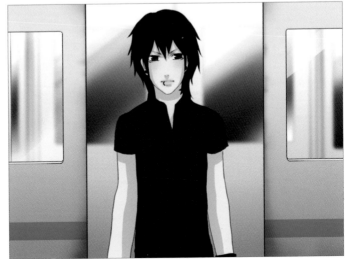

**Tip:** You will soon find that many of the best animation tricks you learn are those that save you time in some manner, often while 'violating' a rule – of perspective, of finished art – that you held in high regard earlier in the book. Because drawing takes so long compared with doing a single image, 'perfection' should be found in an enjoyable finished result, but not in a single frame. There's no point in drawing (or animating) every single blade of grass in a field if the grass will be on screen for less than 20 seconds – the viewer's eye won't appreciate the detail. Apply detail only where it is needed: everywhere else, it is worth cheating.

# Animation

Creating a fully animated character can certainly appear daunting at first. The scenes should be taken one at a time and can be split into a few simple steps. Even working digitally, the most effective method for character animation mimics traditional hand-drawn frames, a process which can be divided into three main steps: rough key-frames, in-betweens and

cleaning-up. Once your character animation is done, you can compile the scene atop your great background, add your sound effects and move on to the next. Remember that you don't need to work on the animation in chronological order – it's best to tackle the simplest scenes first. It can also help to have a group of similarly minded friends to help you.

## Rough key-frames

Once you've chosen a scene to animate, you should think about how the character moves and divide the movement into key poses.

Your key poses should show the start (and end) of each action or motion. For example, a character jumping could be divided into: standing pose; knees bent; apex of jump; knees bent; and back to standing. No matter what software you use, a graphics tablet will make drawing your frames much easier than using a mouse or trackball. These key-frame drawings aren't meant to be final artwork, and should only be sketched out at this stage.

Once you've drawn your rough keys, you can adjust the timing. A two-second jump at 12 frames per second should have the key-frames span 24 frames (2x12=24). Although this sounds

like a lot of frames for a short amount of animation, remember that many frames will be identical and you can hold the first and final pose to add a few seconds to the animation. Now you need to think about in-betweening.

**Beginning and ending frames** ▼
In this example, our character begins shocked by something, and ends by pulling out a rocket launcher and declaring war. The movements are all in the arms and face.

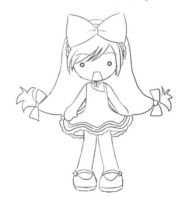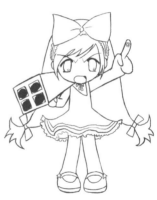

## In-betweening (tweening)

The process of drawing the frames between your rough key-frames to create smooth transitions is called in-betweening or tweening. At animation studios it's common for in-betweens to be drawn by assistant animators, but assuming you can't afford that luxury, let's get to work. Drawing a frame between two others can be tricky at first, but turning on 'onion skinning' will show faint versions of the previous and next frames, emulating a lightbox. To create your first in-between, simply redraw the character's body parts halfway between the two surrounding frames. Repeat the process to add more frames between. In-betweening can take some practice to get right, but there are a few tricks to creating smoother in-betweening.

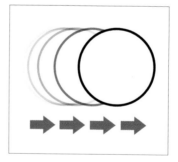

**Ease in** ▲
Equal distances between each frame can make animations look robotic. To 'ease in' to a movement, the first in-betweens should be closer together, the distance increasing with each frame, making the action accelerate.

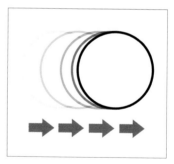

**Ease out** ▲
'Easing out' from an action makes a movement slow down to a stop. The end of the 'tween' should become tighter with the distance gradually decreasing between each frame until the movement reaches a standstill.

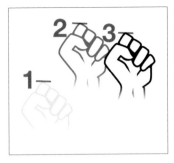

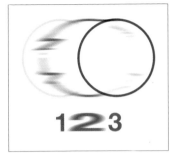

**Overstretch** ▲

Fast-moving limbs coming to an abrupt stop (punching the air, for example) look unnatural. For smoother-looking animations, add an extra frame before coming to rest which continues the momentum farther than the final frame.

**Motion blur** ▲

One frame might have to convey movement over a relatively large distance with a fast-moving object. Stretch or blur it across the full distance to make the animation smoother. Experiment with blur effects.

**Tip:** Before moving on to cleaning up your frames, be sure to play and analyse the animation several times, tweaking and adjusting individual frames as necessary. This is often called a 'line test', as you view the animation in its raw, line art state. Most modern software will provide you with ways of adjusting your in-betweens in much easier ways than by doing it manually on paper, giving you the ability to select and move small areas of each frame. Test and test again – it is important to get the motion of your characters perfect when it is in this state, as it's much harder – not to mention hair-pullingly time-consuming – to fix any problems in the animation when the frames are inked and coloured.

## Cleaning up

Once you're happy with how the rough animation flows, you can start turning your rough frames into final artwork. There are many methods for doing this, but with traditional anime the roughs would be traced on to cels (transparent celluloid sheets). To reproduce this method digitally you can create a new 'layer' above your digital pencil test where you can trace your neat artwork. Alternatively, you can work directly on the sketches to clean them up.

Once clean versions of your rough frames are prepared, you can begin to colour the frames. Once all the pieces are ready, you can put everything together, add sound effects if needed, and finish the scene.

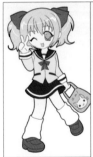

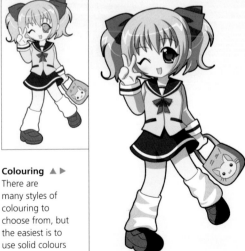

**Colouring** ▲ ▶

There are many styles of colouring to choose from, but the easiest is to use solid colours with no shading. The majority of anime, however, uses the distinctive visual characteristic of shading at a high contrast from the flat colours. To reproduce this look, you should outline and in-between the shapes of the shadows before filling them with colour.

**Filling with colours** ▲

Choosing which colours to use can be difficult. The characters have to stand out from the background, but not look out of place. Consider the lighting of the background. Night scenes might be rendered in shades of blue, summer scenes in bright saturated colours. In Flash you can adjust colours of an object with the colour settings of the properties panel, even changing the colours of characters within a scene: so your characters can meet and interact as the sun is going down, or in a darkened warehouse where fluorescent lights are suddenly turned on.

# Cute dancer project

A cute dancing animation is an ideal first project, as the animation required is relatively simple; and the same frames can easily be repurposed to any kind of soundtrack you desire, whether by changing the timing using key-frames to sync up the dancing with the music, or by quickly recolouring your dancer and swapping in a new background to better suit a different genre. Such addictive and amusing animations – often of no more than 15 individual frames, repeating to crazy, sped-up music – can be found all over the Internet, spliced together by budding animators eager to make their mark on a worldwide craze. While you could seek out one of these animations and directly copy the poses as practice, for this project you will be creating your own completely original dance moves. The instructions for this project apply to Adobe Flash, but if you are using another animation package, the steps and process will likely be very similar.

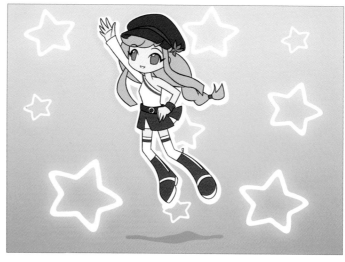

**Dance dance animation revolution** ▲
The animation uses a vibrant, abstract background, and couples it with an extremely simple flat colour scheme for the central character. Only a few frames are needed to capture the dancing movement effectively.

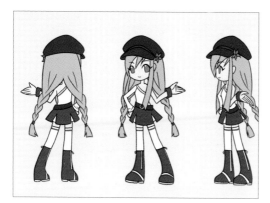

1 The first step in your animation is to create your dancer. You will need to start with a model sheet turnaround of your character. The key here is simplicity: simple anatomy, engagingly cute form, minimalist colours and relatively few extraneous details. Our example, show above, is 'Eclair', a design that takes elements of a cheerleader and knocks them ever so slightly off kilter. The character herself is almost Chibi in proportion, with simplified hands and feet, and a face that is mostly large, shiny eyes. She contains only six colours. She also boasts long flowing hair and a segmented skirt that will react to her jumping around with interesting secondary movements.

Standing key-frame    Contracting key-frame    Apex of jump key-frame

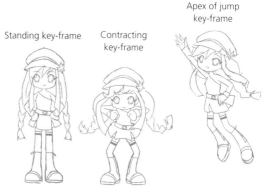

2 As mentioned in the project outline, your dance will not need many frames to be effective, with only three key-frames being unique. The rough keys you will have to draw will therefore be the initial, neutral standing pose, followed by a second pose featuring the character contracting, ready to jump, and the third and final key-frame, the apex (highest point) of her jump. In our example animation, Eclair will jump to the side, rather than straight up, as this means that you can effectively double the length of your animation by having the character jump to each side in turn. The second jump can be, more or less a repeat of the first only with the jumping frames flipped.

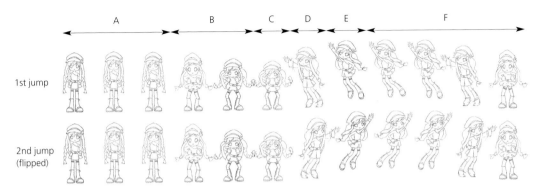

1st jump

2nd jump
(flipped)

**3** With your key-frames complete, it's time to move to in-betweening. As the second jump reuses frames from the first, you only have to in-between one. You can then modify it, rather than having to in-between both jumps. The stages below correspond to the timeline above.

**A** Before contracting, move the character in the opposite direction to her jump, extending her body as she 'inhales'. This keeps the animation 'bouncy' and makes the crouching frame more pronounced. This frame is a modified version of the first, head higher up, body slightly stretched. Her hair swings inwards. You can select portions of the sketch with the Lasso Tool, Transforming them to make slight changes.

**B** After returning to her original position, drop the character to her ducked-down position. The in-between is a halfway frame between standing and crouching. As she's moving very fast, stretch her to produce a motion blur effect. Leave her hat higher up to show it falling more slowly.

**C** After the crouching frame, ease out the movement of the previous two frames. Duplicate the crouching key-frame, moving her head farther down, her legs closer together and continuing her hair's momentum.

**D** Moving between the contracted pose and the jump should be very quick: it's in-betweened in a single frame. The jump key-frame is used as a base, but redraw and blur her limbs and stretch her hair and skirt.

**E** A modified jump frame follows the key-frame as the actual apex of the jump, easing out the motion as gravity catches up with the character. Bend her legs slightly, make her hair bounce and continue the momentum of her hand.

**F** On the character's descent, the frames making up the ascent are reused in reverse order. Modify the blurred frame slightly so that the hair falls slower. Before returning to the default pose, the blurred crouching pose is reused to show the character quickly dipping on impact.

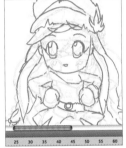

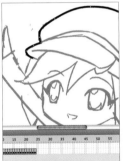

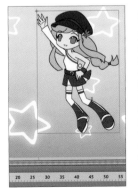

**4** Play the animation and analyse it, tweaking any frames that need adjustments. The frames are then all repeated, with the second jump's frames flipped. Of course, as the design is asymmetrical, some of the details, particularly in the top, will need editing after the frames are flipped.

**5** When you are content with your animation, clean up the frames. Copy the frames into a new graphic symbol called 'Eclair' and add a new layer. Trace unique frames with either the Pen Tool or Brush Tool. Alternatively, prepare your frames in another program and import them into Flash. Don't draw identical frames more than once.

**6** Once all the frames are finished in the top layer, you can remove your roughs, exit the graphic object, and place it into context on the stage. You can then add a simple background in a new layer below the object. Make sure the 'Eclair' graphic symbol is set to Loop mode, then insert enough frames (on both layers) to cover whatever music you want her to dance to.

# Walk-cycle project

The somewhat daunting 'walk-cycle' is essential to the animation of human or bipedal characters. Its complex nature makes it great practice for all the fundamentals of animation. The resulting frames can be reused in a variety of ways and circumstances in your animations. It is slightly more advanced than the previous project, but breaking it down into small steps simplifies the process. Like many artistic endeavours, it is more time-consuming than difficult. Unlike our last project, a walk-cycle will almost certainly be a part of a larger project. If you're planning a project that could use a walk-cycle, this is a great place to test and hone your abilities.

**Walk-cycling the mean streets** ▷
Using a scrolling, repeating background, a similarly repeating walk-cycle and a number of foreground elements that pass in front of the character, you can create a very convincing – and reusable – animation of a character out for a walk.

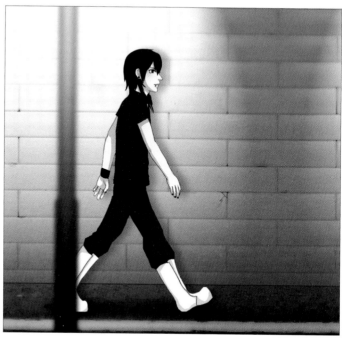

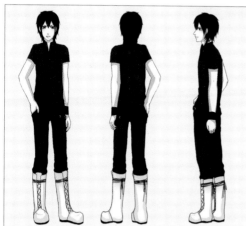

1 Before beginning your animation, you will need to create a model sheet for your walker. Here, we have created a more complex character in a mature style, making use of six base colours and their attendant shades. Anime-style cel-shading significantly increases the amount of colours in use on every frame, but this character's relatively simple clothing keeps the colouring process from becoming too complex.

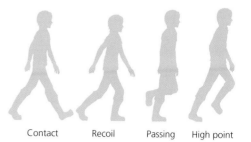

Contact      Recoil      Passing      High point

2 When you are satisfied with your character, start creating your rough key-frames. A walk-cycle typically has four key-frames per stride: 'contact', 'recoil', 'passing' and the 'high point', making eight key-frames for a full cycle (four for each leg). The animation starts with the most important 'contact' pose, where the foot touches the floor. In this frame, the legs and arms are at their farthest apart. The second key-frame is the 'recoil' pose, where the character's weight is transferred on to the grounded foot. This is followed by the 'passing' pose where the character's legs and arms pass each other. The character then pushes himself into the 'high point' pose, bringing his opposite foot forward ready to land into a second 'contact' pose.

**3** Rough in key-frames for both strides, as shown at right. How far the character contracts and expands during the recoil and high point can change the look of the walk. Posture and the swing of arms and legs can also help represent their personality.

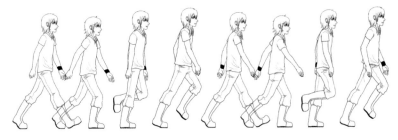

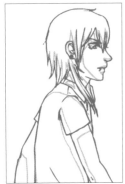

**4** As the walk-cycle has a relatively high number of key-frames, you can play-test and adjust your keys before adding in-betweens, making sure the animation plays nicely. Because this character is rendered with cel-style shading, it can be useful to outline shadows at the key-frame stage.

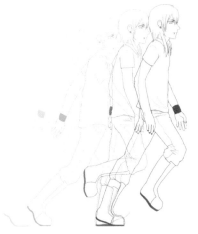

**5** Once the key-frames have been tested and tweaked, add in-betweens. For animation at 12 frames per second, a single in-between for each key will be sufficient for a stroll (totalling 16 frames). The walk-cycle is one continuous motion, so each in-between should be halfway between the surrounding frames, with no easing in or out.

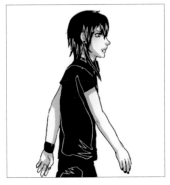

**6** Clean up your frames after tweening. Copy them into a new graphic symbol and add a new layer. Trace each frame with the Pen Tool or Brush Tool. Once the frames are inked and coloured, add shading by selecting each fill and drawing in the shadow. You may need to move your rough layer to the top. You can then delete your roughs, exit the object, and place it on the stage. Set it to loop mode.

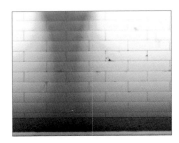

**7** Create a seamless background (the left edge must match perfectly with the right) in Photoshop and then import it into Flash, so that the character can walk across the screen, or have the camera tracking the character with the background scrolling past.

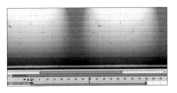

**8** To animate your background, make a graphic symbol called 'looping bg' with two copies of the background. Convert the backgrounds to their own symbols and layers and 'motion tween' (or 'classic tween') them, so that the second ends up in the place of the first. Adjust the number of frames so that the tween moves at the right speed. 'Create Key-frame' on the penultimate frame, then delete the final frame. This removes the duplicate of the first frame.

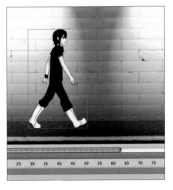

**9** You now have a symbol containing a looping background which you can drop into the stage on a layer beneath your looping character.

# Glossary

**Adobe Photoshop** The market leader for digital art software. Photoshop is a program equally adept with naturalistic shading and bright cel-colours, and comes with a wide range of useful tools, effects and filters.

**Animation/anime** Moving imagery using drawings, stop-motion models or 3-D computer rendering to tell a story. Flash and I-movie are two popular programs used to create simple animation. Many anime – the widely adopted term for Japanese animation – are adapted from manga, and utilize a similar style.

**Anthropomorphism** Taking objects or creatures and offering them human characteristics or mannerisms.

**Archetypes** Characters you would expect to find in a particular genre of story, without whom the story may be unable to progress. Archetypes include a young protagonist who is destined to become a hero, along with the old man who will become his mentor.

**Artboard** Card or heavyweight paper, smooth or surfaced, used for drawing and tinting cartoons.

**Background** The items or characters in the rear of a panel or scene; the scenery created around characters.

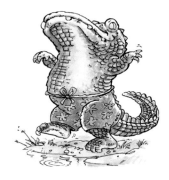

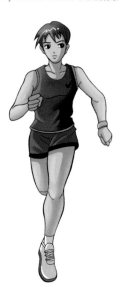

**Balloons (speech)** White oval shapes with a short, directional arrow pointing to the mouth of a cartoon character, containing the conversational speech. Thought balloons are a variation projecting thoughts.

**Bezier curve** A digital line that is a mathematically defined curve linking two points, drawn in a computer program.

**Body language** The body expressing a variety of moods and expressions via posture, movement and positioning of limbs.

**Bitmap** A type of image file, so named because it provides a map of all the bits – or units of digital information – contained within it.

**Bristol board** The most commonly used form of 'paper' among comics professionals – its consistency is perfect for both pencil and ink work.

**Brush tools** Computer program palette tools that convert the function of mouse and its cursor into a number of digital mark-makers, emulating the styles of actual paint brushes.

**Caption** A small block or panel of text running along the top or bottom of a cartoon to title it, or set the scene, ready for the dialogue between characters.

**Caricature** Exaggerating, distorting or twisting the physical attributes of characters to create humour.

**Cartoon** A humorous or satirical style of drawing developed in a gag, strip, animation or comic-book format.

**Cartridge paper** Machine-made paper with a slightly matt surface, which responds well to most wet and dry media.

**Cel shading** A colouring technique made famous by anime utilizing a bright midtone and sharp-edged shadows.

**Character** A single active entity in your story. They can be human, alien, animal, monstrous or other: they count as long as they play a part whether large, small or cameo in a narrative.

**Chibi** Japanese word to describe characters that are shrunk into a small, cute, child-like form. This drawing style is sometimes called 'super-deformed'.

**CMYK** Cyan, Magenta, Yellow and Black. The percentages of those inks create all colours in the four-colour print processes.

**Collage** Forming a picture by physically gluing found materials on to a flat surface such as paper.

**Colour – flat; limited; print** Anything that is not in grayscale. Flat colour is opaque without tonal variation. Limited colour is when a few colours are deliberately used to enhance a mood or effect. Print colour is CMYK – all colours for reproduction are derived from these four saturated colours. In digital terms, this can be anything from two to millions of colours.

**Comic (book)** A sequential narrative that uses a mixture of complimentary words and pictures to tell a story.

**Composition** The organization of elements containing tone, colour and form within a picture.

**Contour** Line defining shape or form in drawing. It is the depiction of solid objects using lines but no shading.

**Corel Painter** A digital art program that accurately reproduces the look and feel of traditional media such as water colours, oils and pastels. It can be used in conjunction with leading programs such as Adobe Photoshop.

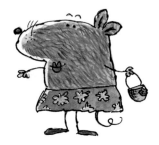

**Cross-hatching** A method of pen or pencil shading by which parallel lines are crossed over one another to form 'hatches'. The closer and more dense the lines, the darker the area.

**Cyberpunk** A genre that confronts the future potentials of technology and increasing prevalence of the internet in the modern world. Often, cyberpunk stories are set in future dystopias where technology has run rampant, but it can just as easily raise philosophical questions of consciousness, humanity and spirituality in a world of artificial intelligence, cyborgs, robots and human augmentation.

**Deformation** The distortion and stress offered to a cartoon character to show a specific movement or mood to the viewer.

**Dialogue** The words spoken by characters during a story, shown on the page as the contents of 'speech balloons'.

**Digital** Produced or viewed on the computer, as opposed to traditional media, where everything is created offline using physical materials. A digital comic can be entirely created, distributed and viewed on the computer, without creating a physical piece of artwork.

**Dip pen** The most commonly used form of inking pen. A plastic handle grips a metal nib, which is then dipped into a pot of ink.

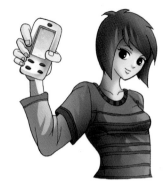

**Distortion** Stretching, squashing or altering a cartoon image significantly to add drama or exaggeration to it, in order to present the message more effectively or quickly. Distortion can be used to change, size, shape, or place an image into perspective.

**Dots** The smallest unit of ink produced by an inkjet or laser print, and thus the unit of measurement for print resolution.

**DPI** Dots Per Inch. *See* Resolution.

**Drawing tablet (graphic)** A computer hardware input device that allows you to draw or write with greater control using a pen-like stylus on to a rectangular plastic tablet.

**Dyes** Chemical or natural mineral pigment-based liquid stainers that have strong, vibrant colours and easy diluant properties. An alternative to coloured inks or watercolour paints .

**Effects** Applying an effect in Adobe Photoshop or similar transforms a basic image with options such as lens flare, colour blends, and many more. *See* Filters.

**Feathering** Marks made with a brush and ink or watercolour, or a pen, which optically blend with the white space between strokes to form the tone.

**Filters** Algorithmic tools in digital art programs that allow you to apply various advanced effects to finished or in-progress artwork. Filters range from adding blurs and textures to creating blooms of light and film stock noise. Programs such as Adobe Photoshop come bundled with a wide selection of filters, and more can be purchased and installed as 'plug ins'.

**Fineliner pen** Disposable, mechanical pen with a fine metal nib in various sizes, and ideal for drawing controlled lines. Available in waterproof and non-waterproof inks.

**Flash** A vector-based program like Illustrator and Freehand but for the creation of simple animations.

**Focus** Main area of visual interest in a picture, drawing the eye of the viewer.

**Font** A lettering style or typeface, used to write dialogue or sound effects.

**Foreground** Items or characters towards the front of a panel or scene.

**Foreshortening** The act of drawing items larger in a panel as they get closer to the 'camera' in order to exaggerate the perspective.

**Focus lines** Tightly spaced lines radiating out from the focal point of a panel to denote emotion, a shocking moment, or to highlight speed.

**Frames** i) the elements that make up an animation: 24 frames per second produces life-like movement, though many anime average closer to 12. ii) another term for panels; the building blocks of the manga page.

**Freehand** Vector-based drawing program, which uses mathematical plotting to draw in an accurate, linear way.

**Graphic novel** Either a book-length collection of existing, previously serialized material (*see* tankubon for the manga equivalent) or an entirely new, book-length sequential narrative.

**Grayscale** A shading technique using 256 shades of grey.

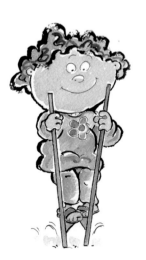

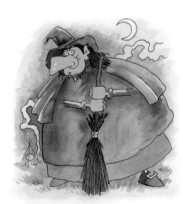

**Halftone** The shading method most widely seen in printed manga, it reduces greyscale shading to a series of moiré dots: a greater concentration of dots, the darker the grey.

**Hero** This can be: i) a brave and noble man distinguished by great ability; ii) the main male character in a piece of fiction.

**Heroine** This can be: i) a brave and noble woman distinguished by great ability; ii) the main female character in a piece of fiction.

**Highlight** Bright areas of colour or grayscale applied on areas facing toward the main light source, in order to add depth to an image.

**Hokusai** A famous artist of ukiyo-e woodcuts, he was the first to use the term 'manga' in connection with illustrated scenes, in the title of one of his portfolios.

**IG/Production IG** An anime company known for its high quality animation. They have been involved in such famous anime as *Ghost in the Shell*, *Blood: The Last Vampire* and *Patlabor*.

**Illustrator** Like Freehand, a vector-based drawing program that uses mathematical plotting to draw in an accurate, linear way.

**Indian ink** The most commonly used form of ink: its consistency is perfect for use in dip pens and with brushes, and it is more resistant to light, heat and water than technical or writing pen inks when dry. Pens and brushes must be thoroughly cleaned after use to avoid clogging.

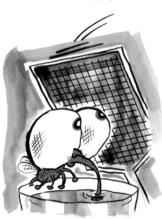

**Ink** The medium used with a dip pen or brush, allowing fluid marks to be made. May be diluted for greater fluidity.

**Inking** The act of drawing over rough or finished pencils in black ink, tightening lines and adding shading, definition and texture in the process, to produce artwork that will scan, colour and reproduce more cleanly. Today, many artists prefer to 'ink' their pages digitally using Photoshop and a stylus – others prefer to colour straight from pencils, missing out the inking stage altogether.

**Jidaimono** Japanese plays that feature historical plots and characters, often based around Samurai. The word is most often translated as 'period plays'.

**Josei** Manga created for late teenage and adult female audiences. They tend to be about the everyday experiences of women living in Japan.

**Jpeg/jpg** A file format created by the Joint Photographic Experts Group, it is the standard file format for full colour images in millions of colours on the web.

**Kodomo** Manga aimed at younger children, often with an educational element, but always using attractive, cute characters, bright colours and uncomplicated dialogue.

**Lady comic** *See* Josei.

**Layers** The building blocks of a digital page. Each element – from line work to colouring – is held on a separate, editable layer, until the final, print-ready file is compressed.

**Layout** This can be: i) the stage of page-creation when one sketches in the placement and size of the panels, and the major characters and features within them; ii) the placement of panels on the page.

**Layout paper** A lightweight paper with a level of transparency to allow an image underneath to be traced over.

**Lettering** The placement of dialogue and sound effects (SFX) on the page, whether by hand or digitally.

**Light and shade** The contrast and balance of tonal and black-and-white values within a cartoon or artwork.

**Line** A mark long in proportion to its breadth, made with a pen, pencil, brush or digital tool. 'Line art' is black ink lines on a white page.

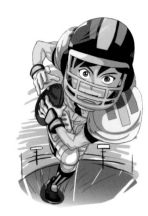

**Line and wash** Black line with watercolour, ink or dye washes.

**Mahokka** 'Magical girls': genre of shojo stories featuring girls with secret identities and special powers, who usually fight monsters and attend school at the same time.

**Manga-ka** The creator – or chief creator, in the case of a manga-ka who runs their own studio – of a manga.

**Materials** A catch-all term for anything used in the process of creating art, from the paper you draw on to the substances used to capture the lines and colours.

**Mecha** Another term for the giant robots that populate many manga (particularly shonen).

**Media** The collective term for materials used to create artwork, and also for the newspaper, magazine and TV industries.

**Meiji Era** The 45-year rule of the Meiji Emperor, from 1868 to 1912, during which Japan began its modernization and ascended to the world stage, ending its isolationist policy.

**Midground** The middle picture plane in a 2-D image, sandwiched between the foreground and background.

**Mixed-media** A collaborative use of various materials for creating an image, such as pen line, watercolour and fabric.

**Montage** Composing an image from miscellaneous drawn, photographic and/or found elements.

**Movement** Use of materials and drawing styles to create the illusion of an object changing from one position to another.

**Narrative** The sequence of events told as a story to link the events. Narratives have a beginning and a conclusion.

**Nib** The tip of a pen, used to hold ink and transfer it to the page. Dip pens use forked prongs to pick up and transfer the ink, the harder the nib is pressed, the wider the line; technical pens use a hard but permeable nib to produce lines of the same thickness and consistency.

**OEL (Original English Language)** Manga produced by artists and writers in either the UK or US, following the stylistic conventions of Japanese manga in an entirely new, untranslated story.

**Opaque** Not transparent; a colour that obscures anything it is placed on top of.

**Outline** This can be: i) the line surrounding a distinct shape or object; ii) the rough form of a story or plot, prior to fleshing it out as either a detailed plot or a full script.

**OVA (Original Video Animations)** Anime productions that are produced to be sold as DVDs (or previously, as VHS) in the first instance, rather than to run on syndicated television. OVAs tend to have higher production values and greater fan reception than many of the TV series they are based on or in competition with. *See* Anime.

**Painter** A bitmap-based paint program allowing the cartoonist to reproduce a variety of different techniques and styles with digital media imitating manual media.

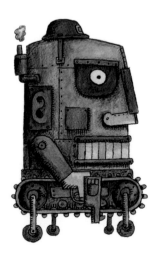

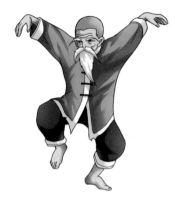

**Palette** This can be: i) the sum total of all the colours used in a particular piece of artwork; ii) the place to select any of the millions of possible colours within a digital art program; iii) the place where your currently used colours are stored.

**Panel** The basic building block of a manga page. Panels can be any size or shape, but each contain a single unit of action. The movement in a manga story happens in the 'gutters', or white areas in between each panel.

**Path (clipping)** Any vector-created line that is constructed as a result of two or more points being placed. A clipping path enables any object to be digitally cut out from its background, as you might do manually with scissors.

**Pattern** An image or series of colours that repeat or can be repeated.

**Perspective** The means by which 3D is simulated on the page, according to one or more vanishing points, to which all of the lines and objects in the panel or page diminish.

**Photoshop** A complex bitmap-based image manipulation program with a vast repertoire of techniques and applications available to create, paint and alter images.

**Pixel** The dot on a computer display. Resolution (image quality) is measured by the number of horizontal dots against the number of vertical scan lines.

**PPI** Pixels Per Inch. *See* Resolution.

**Protagonist** The central character of a story and manga: they may not be a 'hero' in the traditional definition of the term, but the story is told from their viewpoint and readers follow their actions for the bulk of the narrative.

**Quasi-historical** A story set in a roughly historical period, i.e. Samurai-era Japan, without conforming to rigid historical events or personages. Such stories may include anachronistic or contra-historical elements.

**Realism** Term given to any artistic methodology which seeks to reproduce in exact detail, observed life.

**Reference** Source material used by the cartoonist at the early stages of planning and during the various stages of creation.

**Rendering** To cover any surface with paint or collaged material. The action of drawing or painting.

**Resolution** The amount of pixels per inch (on screen) or dots per inch (on paper) that an image is scanned, edited and saved at. The higher the resolution, the sharper the image. 600 dpi is typical for scanning, 300 dpi for print, and 150 dpi for the web.

**Retouch** To clean up artwork, digital imagery or photographs using digital tools to erase dirt marks, mistakes, colour irregularities and continuity errors.

**RGB** The colour mode and spectrum formed from mixtures of the primary colours red, green and blue. It is used to present imagery through monitors and television screens.

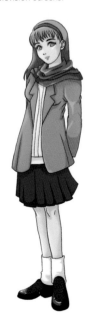

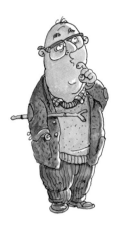

**Roughs** A mocked-up or hastily sketched version of a page, in pencil. This may form the first step in the process of tightening the pencil art for inking, or they may be discarded and kept only for reference.

**Scale** The size of a given piece of art. 'To scale' means to make a piece of digital artwork larger or smaller, a process that can be accomplished with percentages or exact values of pixels, metric or imperial units.

**Scanner** A computer peripheral that inputs physical artwork into the computer using reflected light.

**Scene** A unit of story, denoted by continuity of character or location.

**Script** The last result of the planning phase, when the contents of your panels are written as description and dialogue.

**Seinen** Manga aimed at older males, from late teens and up. Its themes may appear superficially similar to shonen, but it will include more explicit content.

**Sentai** Literally, a military unit, but in manga, anime and Japanese TV, it is often used to denote a squadron of three to seven characters who band together to pilot giant mecha.

**SFX lettering** Lettering designed to mimic a sound effect, in an onomatopaeic fashion. Any sound can receive SFX in this manner, from explosions and gunfire to blinking and breathing.

**Shade** This can be: i) the mixture of a colour with black to reduce lightness; ii) synonym for 'colour'.

**Shading** The method by which objects are made to appear 3-D within a 2-D picture. The simplest practice is to vary the pressure exerted on the pencil or other mark-maker to vary the density of the ensuing marks.

**Shadow** Darker areas of colour or greyscale applied on areas facing away from the main light source, in order to add depth to an image.

**Shojo** Style of manga aimed at young and teen girls, with strong female protagonists. Can cover a multitude of genres, but romance and the emotional interior world are usually paramount.

**Shonen** Style of manga aimed at young and teen boys, with strong male protagonists and an emphasis on action and dominance of a particular field.

**Shortlines** A type of shading that uses very short, overlapping lines to suggest depth and shading. The more lines there are on a given surface, the darker that surface is.

**Sketch** A very rough drawing, done to transfer an idea to paper in the development stage.

**Soft shading** A form of shading using multiple shades of the same colour, blended into one another. Unlike cel shading, soft shading uses multiple intermediate tones to create a more naturalistic effect.

**Speech balloons (bubbles)** Oval or elliptical white balloons that carry the dialogue of characters. A 'tail' points from the main balloon towards the relevant character's mouth.

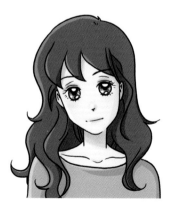

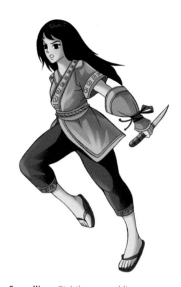

**Speedlines** Tightly grouped lines radiating from or attached to a swiftly moving character in order to denote motion and relative speed. Focus lines can also be used to show a head-on character in motion.

**Spokon** A genre of manga in which the principal characters are athletes, and the majority of the stories revolve around a sport. Usually the 'aim' of the manga is for the team, and the central protagonist, to become the best they can at their chosen sport.

**Steampunk** A genre that takes the superficial trappings of cyberpunk and applies them to a quasi-19th century world, positing that computing and robotics were created in the age of steam and rivets, rather than the silicon age. They tend to be more freewheeling and optimistic stories than their cyberpunk equivalent.

**Stereotype** A preconceived, oversimplified, demeaning and exaggerated assumption about a person or persons based on age, class, ethnicity, occupation, etc. While negative in tone, stereotypes may be used as the basis for characters – either characters who subvert the stereotype, or those who consciously live up to it.

**Stippling** The use of tightly packed individual dots to create shading. The closer the dots are placed, the darker the shade.

**Strip** Any sequence of comic or manga images. In the West, it is most often used to refer to the four panel 'comic strips' found in newspapers, though the terms are largely interchangeable.

**Stylus** A pen-shaped input device used with a drawing tablet to draw imagery directly into a digital art program.

**Super-deformed characters** Characters exaggerated in their cuteness and diminutive stature, often lacking noses, fingers, and anything but the most rudimentary or comical details. They may be characters in their own super-deformed style piece, or represent an extreme emotional state of an otherwise naturalistically-drawn character (*see* Chibi).

**Tankubon** The manga equivalent of graphic novels or trade paperbacks: book-length collections of manga stories previously serialized in a weekly or monthly manga magazine.

**Technical pens** These pens come in a wide variety of styles and nib thicknesses, and usually carry their own ink supply as cartridges. They produce rigid lines, excellent for backgrounds, buildings and mechanical items.

**Theme** Any chief subject for a singular cartoon or strip, around which centre all other stories, gags or plots.

**Thumbnails** Early draft layouts of pages, at diminutive sizes. Most useful for checking page and panel compositions before committing to a larger work.

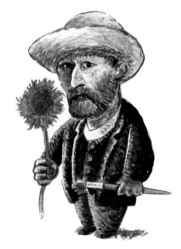

**Tint** This can be: i) the mixture of a colour with white, to produce lightness; ii) synonym for 'colour'.

**Tone** A method of shading using pre-created patterns of moiré dots. In the pre-digital era, tone would be cut with knives and 'rubbed down' on to the page: now tones can be applied as patterns in Adobe Photoshop, or created from greyscale shading.

**Transparent** Allowing light to pass through a medium or be filtered by it.

**Tufts** The bristled ends of paintbrushes, which come in a variety of styles, from pointed round to fan.

**Vector** A computer image made up of plotted points on a curve (Bezier), and created by drawing programs that use Postscript language – for example, Adobe Illustrator.

**Viewpoint** This can be: i) the literal position from which a panel or page is drawn; ii) the perspective through which a given story is filtered or told; iii) a philosophical, ideological or moral perspective.

**Villain** The central antagonist of a story, usually one who is dedicated to tearing down the life of the hero or heroine, or who is endangering the hero's family, city or world with their schemes. Their defeat usually signals the end of a story, though one ongoing manga may feature dozens of minor villains before the final 'big boss' is reached.

**Washes** Diluted watercolours, inks or dyes applied thinly to the paper or support to create a translucent coloured film. A gradated wash is progressively paler or darker.

**Watercolour** Coloured pigment, which when diluted allows wet colour to flow freely across the paper surface using a soft brush to cover large areas with colour.

**Web comic** A comic either presented on the web, or designed specifically for it and its viewable dimensions.

**Weighting (graphic)** The harmonious balancing of separate areas of a composition.

**Working drawing** An alternative to the thumbnail sketch or rough. A developmental drawing vital to the ongoing process of visual problem-solving.

**Year 24 group** A group of female manga-ka born in Showa 24, or 1949. They revolutionized the techniques and content of shojo manga, as well as marking the first time that shojo had been written and drawn, as well as read, by women.

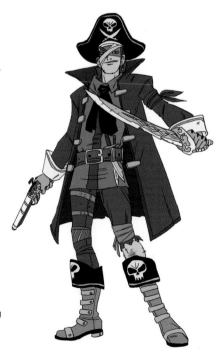

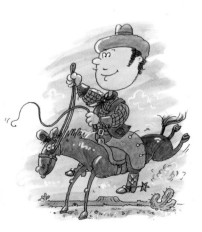

# Index

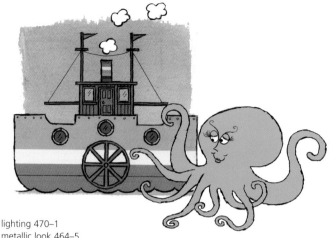

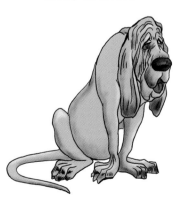

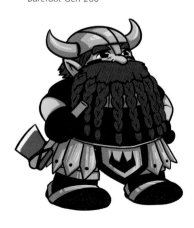

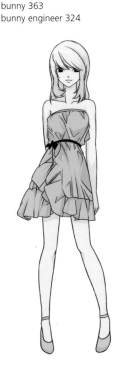

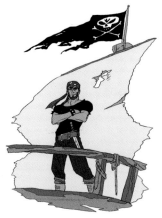

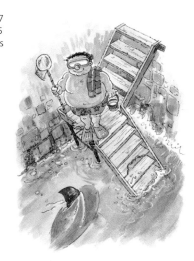

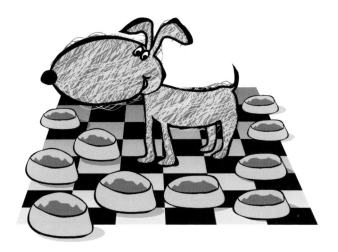

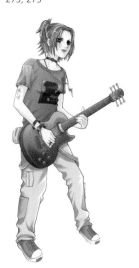

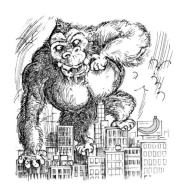

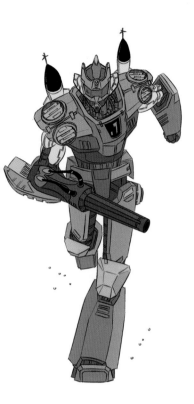

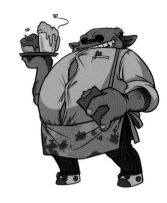

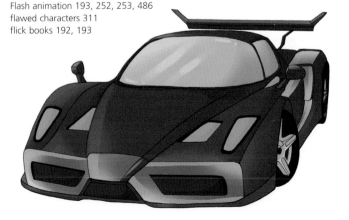

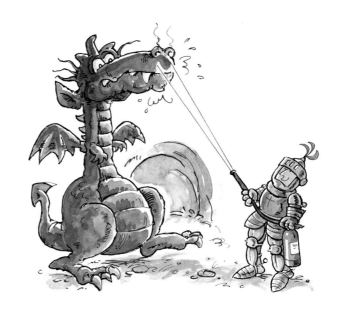

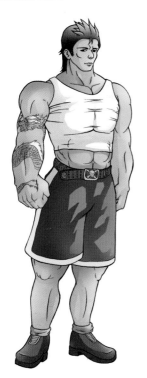

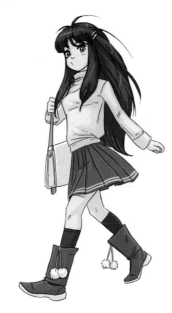

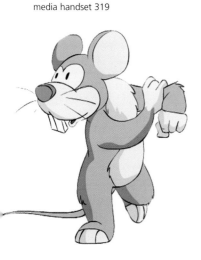

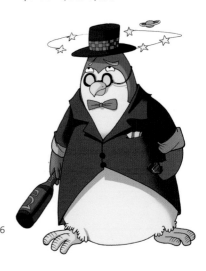

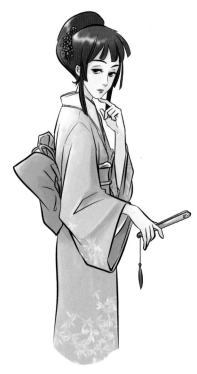
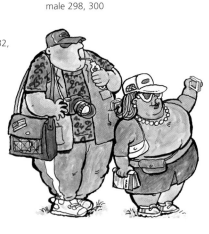
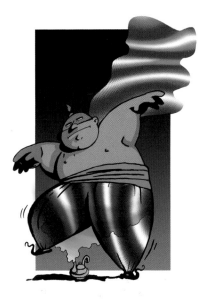

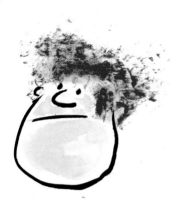

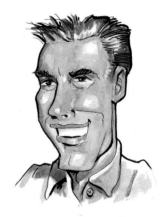
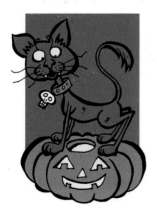

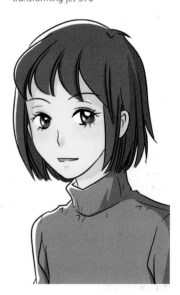

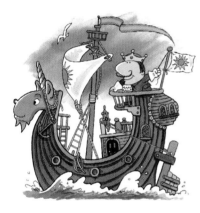

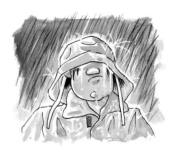

## Acknowledgements

The publisher would like to thank the following for kindly supplying photos for this book: ALAMY: 10*b*, *tl*, 11*bl*; Jeremy Hoare/Alamy 260 (bottom left), Chris Willson/Alamy 261 (top), Digital Vision/Alamy 261 (bottom right), Alamy Photos (12) 485 (bottom left and right); DELL INC: 163*tl*; CANON UK LTD: 163*tr*; CORBIS: John Van Hasselt/Corbis 260 (top), Amet Jean Pierre/Corbis Sygma 259 (bottom left), Annebicque Bernard/ Corbis Sygma, TWPhoto/Corbis 484 (top); EPSON (UK) LTD: 163*tm* and *ml*; GETTY IMAGES: 10*tr*; Getty Images/New Vision Technologies Inc. 261 (bottom left), Getty Images/APF 484 (bottom right), 485; LAST GASP: Keiji Nakazawa 260 (middle); PERRIS, ANDREW: 8*t*, 16*mbr*, *mbl*, *br*, *bl*, 20*br*, 28*tl*, *tml*, *bl*, 29*tl*, *tm* and *tr*; PRACTICAL PICTURES: 20*tl* and 28*tr*; TOKYOPOP INC: 259 (bottom); TOPFOTO: Topham Picturepoint 484 (bottom left); VERTICLE INC: 258 (both), 259 top.WACOM EUROPE GMBH: 163*mr*.

Thanks to Pen to Paper, Lewes for providing the pen nibs and The Art Shop, Wadhurst for supplying artist's materials for photography.

A big thank you to Jane for her enthusiasm and support, and to Curtis for his stamina and constant cheerfulness.
*Ivan Hissey*

Thanks to all who encouraged and supported the making of this book. Firstly to Ivan Hissey who provided outstandingly versatile artwork with true professionalism, making my challenge as author so much easier and very enjoyable. Thanks to Susanne, my wife and manager, for encouraging me throughout and keeping it all on track. To my children, Tilly and Noah, for their enthusiasm and wonderment as the project unfolded – with special thanks to Noah for trying out many of the cartoon exercises! Thanks are also due to all at Bridgewater Books and

Anness Publishing, especially to editors, Polita and Hazel, for toiling so hard with me to guide this product into completion.
*Curtis Tappenden*

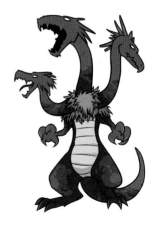

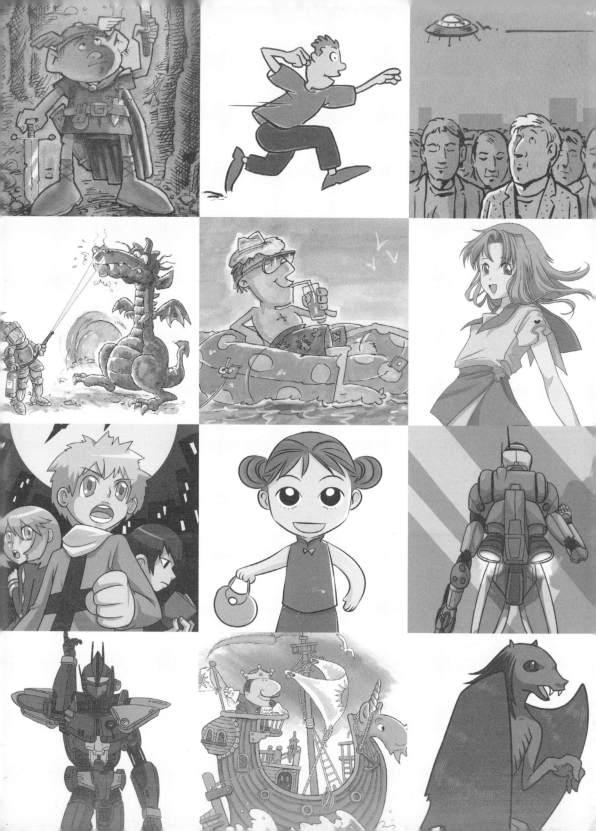